Voyagers
TO THE
West

Voyagers

TO THE

West

A Passage in the Peopling of America

on the Eve of the Revolution

BERNARD BAILYN

with the assistance of

Barbara DeWolfe

VINTAGE BOOKS
A DIVISION OF RANDOM HOUSE
NEW YORK

First Vintage Books Edition, March 1988

Copyright © 1986 by Bernard Bailyn

All rights reserved under International and Pan-American
Copyright Conventions. Published in the United States
by Random House, Inc., New York, and simultaneously
in Canada by Random House of Canada Limited,
Toronto. Originally published, in hardcover,
by Alfred A. Knopf, Inc., in 1986.

Library of Congress Cataloging-in-Publication Data
Bailyn, Bernard.
Voyagers to the West.
Reprint. Originally published: New York: Knopf:
Distributed by Random House, 1986.
Includes index.
1. Great Britain—Emigration and immigration—
History—18th century. 2. North America—Emigration
and immigration—History—18th century.
3. Immigrants—North America—History—
18th century. 4. British—North America—
History—18th century. I. DeWolfe,
Barbara. II.Title.
[JV7618.N7B35 1988]   304.8′73041   87–45917
ISBN 0–394–75778-5 (pbk.)

Manufactured in the United States of America
10 9 8 7 6 5 4 3 2 1

for

John Clive

CONTENTS

V   Peopling the Peripheral Lands: The Great Inland Arc

LIST OF TABLES

LIST OF ILLUSTRATIONS

LIST OF MAPS

LIST OF FIGURES

PREFACE

Ten years ago I started work on "The Peopling of British North America," which I conceived of as a large-scale narrative from the beginning of European colonization to the advent of the industrial revolution. The time was ripe, I thought, for such a synthetic work. The many excellent community studies written over the previous two decades needed to be brought together into a connected account; demographic history had transformed social history and elevated it to a new plane of sophistication; historical geographers had raised a host of new questions about people's relations with their environment; and a rescaling of perspective had made it possible to think of the whole Atlantic world, especially in terms of population movements, as a single historical unit. As a result of these developments the traditional subject of "immigration history" was becoming a new subject, with a new kind of explanatory power.

At the start of the project, which I still hope to complete, I began a number of small exploratory studies, probes of certain topics of particular interest, ranging through the two hundred years and concentrated on various places in the north European and North American world: London, Vermont, southwestern Germany, western Maryland, the Scottish Highlands, Boston, Yorkshire, the east Florida coast, the Mississippi delta. Various sets of documents were tested for density and for the possibility of extensive use. One such probe was of a remarkable listing of every person officially known to have left Britain for America from December 1773 to March 1776, including a range of personal information about the individuals named. This voluminous document, a virtual emigration register, in the Public Record Office, London—no original discovery of mine but never analyzed systematically—seemed to me to be extraordinarily useful, and with the assistance of Barbara DeWolfe I began to study it with great care. As we proceeded I realized that despite its omissions and other weaknesses this register of emigrants was so complete, the range of ancillary sources that could be associated with it so vast, and the geographical scope involved so huge that a kind of cross-sectional analysis of the peopling process, or a significant part of it at least, seemed to be emerging. The work became

xix

engrossing. The listing was computerized, and a great array of tabulations and cross-tabulations came to hand. Files of ships and of passengers, name by name, were created. Places of origin and the circumstances of individual migration and resettlement were identified. The information mounted up into a huge source collection, concentrated on named individuals. My interest in these people grew greater. I wanted to trace every one of them, find out everything about them, probe their origins, the great transition in their lives, and their ultimate destinies. Much, of course, could never be recovered, but from the gathering sources—newspapers, genealogical data, state papers, local histories, town records, and personal manuscript collections on both sides of the Atlantic—a remarkable amount of information could be found. At first a few, then dozens, finally several hundred of these long-forgotten, ordinary people came into focus, and I began to see that from this mass of documentation, all keyed to the emigration listing of 1773–1776, I could present aspects of an entire world in motion—catch on the wing, as it were, one phase of the overall peopling process I had set out to describe, and thereby provide a base line for the story as a whole.

But how could this great mass of information be organized and presented? What mode of historical writing would be appropriate? Not one form, one method, I decided, but several. Part I sets the background; the mode is descriptive exposition. In it I have attempted to explain, in a degree of detail I did not expect to be able to discover when I started the work, how the emigration Register came into being, and its strengths and weaknesses as a source for the story I wanted to tell.

Part II is in a different mode. It is a quantitative analysis, a computer study, of the data contained in the Register; for the dimensions and structure of the migration cannot be inferred impressionistically from literary sources, or deduced by logic, or understood by analogy. The magnitude of the emigrants' recruitment from within the various regions of Britain, their geographical origins, their routes of migration, sex, ages, social and occupational characteristics, family groupings, legal status, stated purposes in emigrating, and specific destinations—all of this can be brought to the surface of history only in the form of numbers; quantities alone convey the necessary sense of dimension. Without these quantitative measures one can only envision the peopling process as vague, impressionistic blurs and blotches, with occasional streaks of vivid color that happen, by some accident of documentation, randomly to penetrate the haze. But beyond these measures, the quantitative study reveals something I had no way of suspecting at the start and that could only have been discovered in the numbers. Cycles of analysis of the computerized data made clear that this was not a singular emigration and resettlement process, but a dual migration. Two processes, quite different from each other, were in motion simultaneously. And that discovery is the key to everything that follows.

To convey those two quite different phenomena, two distinctive modes of expression seemed appropriate. Part III is a structural analysis: its four chapters are organized into functionally related topics that analyze and explain the sources, recruitment, and distribution of a labor force from central and southern England, one of the two migrations under way. But the six chapters of Parts IV and V are different. They are narrative accounts —micro-narratives—of selected strands of the second migration, the transfer of families from northern Britain to an immense spread of settlements ranging from the coastal extremities of North America (Part IV) to an inland arc reaching deep into the unsettled backcountry (Part V). In these chapters the fortunes of selected individuals and families are narrated, traced from their origins to their final destinations. Successive accounts of individual lives and the fortunes of specific families illustrate the range of experiences, the frustrations and successes, and the ways in which newcomers blended into the nascent North American communities. Individuality, concreteness, detail—the stories themselves—are what matter here; the meaning is contained in the narration. These separate small-scale histories form trace lines—a rubbing, as it were, over the incised reality of that distant world—which together constitute a sketch of this aspect of the peopling process.

In all of these ways—through descriptive exposition, quantification, structural analysis, and career-line narration—I have tried to present this passage in the peopling of British North America.

In bringing this first volume of the peopling study to completion I am finally in a position to thank the people who have assisted me along the way. Elsewhere in the book I have expressed my thanks to many of them. But a few individuals have been critically important to the whole project, and I would like to state that here. Elizabeth McCormack saw possibilities in this project from the start; she encouraged me to take the work on, and assisted significantly in finding resources to make it possible. Her early enthusiasm led the way to grants from the Rockefeller Brothers Fund and the National Endowment for the Humanities, for which, and for the continuing interest of William Dietel, I am profoundly grateful. Nothing could have been done without this support.

Barbara DeWolfe has worked with me from the start, first as a research assistant, then as a virtual collaborator. Her research in archives on both sides of the Atlantic has been diligent, imaginative, and profitable beyond any expectation. And in addition she has handled the computer project, supervised the newspaper research, written innumerable reports on separate topics, kept the voluminous documentation in orderly files (in duplicate, at times in triplicate, in case I mislaid anything), and drew my attention to materials, connections, and details that otherwise would have escaped me. I could not have written so full an account of this passage in Anglo-American history without her. And Jane Garrett, an old friend and former collaborator, in her capacity as editor at Knopf, has been a steady supporter of the project. She encouraged me to work the story out as far as the documents allowed; in this and in other ways she manifested the great good will of an excellent publisher, as did Betty Anderson and Melvin Rosenthal, who endured much and were endlessly helpful and skillful. And then there are those faithful, patient, and tireless critics, Lotte Bailyn and John Clive. As on other occasions they have gone with me through all the stages of the work and read the manuscript, section by section, with great care. I am immensely grateful to them for their criticism, their constant prodding, and their generous expectations.

B.B.

LIST OF MANUSCRIPT ABBREVIATIONS

CH	Church of Scotland Records, Scottish Record Office
Cheston-Galloway Papers	Cheston-Galloway Papers, M-1650, Maryland Hall of Records, Annapolis (microfilm copy in Maryland Historical Society)
Cheston Incoming Letters	James Cheston Incoming Letters (1767–1782), boxes 9–15, Cheston-Galloway Papers
Cheston Letterbooks	James Cheston Letterbooks, 1768–1776, box 8, Cheston-Galloway Papers
Chisholm Letters	Letters of John Chisholm, 1751–1764, typescript, Colonial Collection, MS 2018, Maryland Historical Society
CO	Colonial Office Papers, Public Record Office
Coates Genealogy	H. Ward Coates, comp., "Coates Family of Nappan, Nova Scotia," MG 100, vol. 122, no. 42–42(n), Public Archives of Nova Scotia
Cumberland County Deeds	Registry of Deeds for Cumberland County, Amherst, New Brunswick
Dartmouth Papers, Canada	Papers of William Legge, 2d Earl of Dartmouth, MG 23, A1, Public Archives of Canada, Ottawa
Dartmouth Papers, Stafford	Papers of William Legge, 2d Earl of Dartmouth, Staffordshire County Record Office, Stafford, England
DesBarres Papers	Papers of J. F. W. DesBarres, 1762–1894, Public Archives of Canada (microfilm copy in Public Archives of Nova Scotia)
Dixon Papers	Dixon Family Papers, MC 251, Provincial Archives of New Brunswick, Fredericton, New Brunswick
Dundas Papers	Papers of Sir Lawrence Dundas, North Yorkshire Record Office, Northallerton, Yorkshire, England
Egmont Papers	Papers of John Perceval, 2d Earl of Egmont, British Library
Etting Papers	Etting Papers: Ships and Shipping, 1710–1807, Miscellaneous Documents, Historical Society of Pennsylvania
Fordell Muniments	Henderson of Fordell Muniments, GD 172, Scottish Record Office
Freswick Muniments	Sinclair of Freswick Muniments, GD 136, Scottish Record Office
Ganong Collection	Ganong Manuscript Collection, Library and Archives Department, New Brunswick Museum
Glasgow and Greenock Customs Letter Books	Customs and Excise Letter Books, Glasgow and Greenock, CE 60/1/7, Scottish Record Office
Harrison Papers	Harrison Family Papers, MG 1, no. 427, Public Archives of Nova Scotia

Hogg Papers	James Hogg Papers, Southern Historical Collection, University of North Carolina Library, Chapel Hill, North Carolina
Hunt Mss	Benjamin Peter Hunt Manuscripts, Rare Book Room, Boston Public Library
Indentures of Redemptioners	Indentures of Redemptioners: Capt. Peter Osborne, Society Miscellaneous Collection, Box 9C, F13, Historical Society of Pennsylvania
Inglis Letterbook	Shipping Merchant's Letter Book, (James Inglis Letter Book), Court of Sessions Productions, CS 96/2250, 2259, Scottish Record Office
James and Drinker Foreign Letters	Foreign Letters of the Partnership of Abel James and Henry Drinker (1772–1785), Drinker Papers, Historical Society of Pennsylvania, Philadelphia
James and Drinker Letterbook	Letterbook of the Partnership of Abel James and Henry Drinker (1756–1786), Drinker Papers, Historical Society of Pennsylvania
Johnson Letterbooks	Joshua Johnson's Letterbooks (1771–1777), Maryland Hall of Records, Annapolis
Kempe Papers	William and John Tabor Kempe Papers, New-York Historical Society
Kentucky Mss	Draper Manuscript Collection, State Historical Society of Wisconsin, Madison, Wisconsin
Knox Papers	Papers of William Knox, William L. Clements Library, University of Michigan, Ann Arbor
Lansdowne Mss	Papers of William Petty, 2d Earl of Shelburne (Marquess of Lansdowne), William L. Clements Library, University of Michigan (typescript held by St. Augustine Historical Society, St. Augustine, Florida)
Leeds Archives	Leeds City Libraries, Archives Department, Sheepscar Library, Leeds, England
Lochbuie Muniments	Maclaine of Lochbuie Muniments, GD 174, Scottish Record Office
Loyalist Papers	Papers of the Loyalist Claims Commissioners, AO 12 and AO 13, Public Record Office
Loyalist Transcripts	American Loyalists: Transcripts of the Manuscript Books and Papers of the Commission of Enquiry into the Losses and Services of the American Loyalists . . ., 1783–1790, Special Collections, New York Public Library
Lux Letterbook	William Lux Letterbook, 1763–1768, New-York Historical Society
MacAllister Papers	Papers of Colonel Alexander MacAllister of Cumberland County, North Carolina, Southern

	Historical Collection, University of North Carolina Library
MacLeod Mss	MacLeod of MacLeod Manuscripts, NRA(S)/0361, Dunvegan Castle, Isle of Skye, Scotland*
MacPherson-Grant Papers	MacPherson-Grant of Ballindalloch Papers, NRA(S)/0771, Ballindalloch Castle, Banffshire, Scotland*
Monymusk Muniments	Grant of Monymusk Muniments, Scottish Record Office
Neave Account Book	Richard Neave, Jr., Account Book, (1773–1774), AM 9183, Historical Society of Pennsylvania
NS Land Papers	Nova Scotia Land Papers, RG 20, Series A, vols. 13–15, Public Archives of Nova Scotia
Piper Letterbook	Harry Piper Letterbook (1767–1775), MS 2981-A, Alderman Library, University of Virginia, Charlottesville
Ridgely Papers	Ridgely Family Papers, MS 691, Maryland Historical Society
Ridley Letterbook	Matthew Ridley Letterbook (1770–1776), Massachusetts Historical Society, Boston
Russell Account Book	William Russell Account Book (1774–1783), MS 1989, Maryland Historical Society
Russell Papers	James Russell Papers (1767–1806), Coutts and Co., London (microfilm copy in Alderman Library, University of Virginia)
Scottish Customs Minute Book	Scottish Board of Customs, Minute Book, CE 1, Scottish Record Office
Sessions Records	General Sessions of the Peace for the City of London, Miscellaneous MSS 383, Corporation of London Records Office, Guildhall, London
Smith Letterbooks	Letterbooks of John Smith & Sons and William Smith (1774–1821), MS 1152, Maryland Historical Society
SP	State Papers, Public Record Office
Stevens Papers	Stevens Family Papers, box 8, Special Collections, University of Vermont, Burlington
Stornoway Customs Letter Books	Customs and Excise Letter Books, Stornoway, CE 86/2/2, Scottish Record Office
Sutherland Papers	Sutherland Family Estate Papers, Deposits 313 and 314, Department of Manuscripts, National Library of Scotland
T	Treasury Papers, Public Record Office

*Access through National Register of Archives (Scotland).

Webster Collection	J. Clarence Webster Collection, Mt. Allison University Archives, Sackville, New Brunswick
Whitelaw Papers	James Whitelaw Papers, Vermont Historical Society, Montpelier
Woolsey and Salmon Letterbook	Old Letter Book of Baltimore (Letterbook of George Woolsey and George Salmon, 1774–1784), Peter Force Collection, Series 8D, item 189, Manuscripts Division, Library of Congress

NOTE:

In quotations from eighteenth-century writing, the original spelling has been retained throughout, but punctuation and capitalization have been modernized where modern usage would assist in conveying the writer's thought.

I

Background:
The Magnet
of the West

INTRODUCTION

I<small>F, AS SEEMED</small> likely in 1771 and 1772, the struggle between Britain and her American colonies had been peacefully resolved and people had been free to concentrate on other major issues of the day, history would have recorded more clearly than it has the importance of a remarkable development of the 1760s and 1770s that was temporarily cut off by the Revolution. This development of the pre-Revolutionary years was an extraordinary flood of immigration to British mainland North America, and, closely associated with that, a sudden and immense spread of settlement in the backcountry of the coastal colonies and in the trans-Appalachian west. Both the remarkable immigration and the spread of settlement were intensifications of developments that had been in motion before the last of the Anglo-French wars in America, the French and Indian War of 1754–1760, which was the overseas extension of the Seven Years War in Europe. But the magnitudes were so much greater after the war than they had been before, the scale and range of migration and settlement so greatly enlarged, that the essential character of the peopling process seems to have been transformed, and with it some basic elements in American life. For the whole of colonial society had been a product of migration and settlement, renewed and expanded generation after generation, and the sudden intensification of this fundamental process after 1760 affected the entire fabric of American life.

Precisely how it did, what specific effects this swift dilation of the basis of American life had during these years of political turmoil, is difficult to determine. But much can be visualized and depicted: background scenes, of the crowded streets of London—Cheapside, Houndsditch, Spitalfields— from which came a mass of indentured servants; groups of Yorkshire country people walking away from the "over-rented" farms they had lived in, carrying their possessions in carts and bundles across the fields and along

3

the roadways to north-country exit ports; unemployed or embattled Scots fleeing the semi-industrial West Lowlands to join friends and kin in the backcountry of New York and North Carolina; and thousands of disoriented and discontented Scottish Highlanders and offshore islanders, some destitute, some simply adventurous, most threatened with future impoverishment or diminishment, trooping in family groups not only to Greenock, the exit port of Glasgow, but also to local fishing villages where passage to America might occasionally be found—remote maritime corners of northern Britain like Stornoway on the northernmost island of the Outer Hebrides; Thurso, on the northeastern coast of the Scottish mainland; and Lerwick, in the remote Shetland Islands, at the latitude of southern Greenland.

To recapture any of these scenes of a distant reality requires an act of historical imagination. But the counterpart scenes of arrival, relocation, and settlement in the very different world of colonial North America are even more difficult to depict. For though eighteenth-century America's political ideals are familiar to us, as are its material ambitions and expansionist drive, its social life was that of a far different era, scarcely recognizable as the antecedent of the modern world. It is not simply that eighteenth-century America was a pre-industrial and a pre-urban world (the greatest metropolis in British North America numbered only 30,000 to 40,000 souls, and townsmen commonly worked at agricultural pursuits). It was also pre-romantic and pre-humanitarian, little concerned with the problems of social justice or with alleviating human suffering. While Americans of the Revolutionary generation struggled for freedom and equality in public life, they remained remarkably insensitive to the human consequences of deprivation. In such a world—where the blatant humiliation of inferiors by social superiors was a matter of common experience and where degrading physical punishment for civil and criminal offences was routine—the utter debasement of chattel slavery needed little justification, and lesser forms of servitude were regarded as normal.

None of this was unique to America. These were common characteristics of the *ancien régime*, pre-modern in its social concerns and conditions. But while America shared these characteristics of eighteenth-century society, its way of life was unique. The colonists lived in exceptional circumstances and shared a peculiar outlook. Unlike the inhabitants of the British Isles, they were not located at the center of their culture looking outward toward exotic margins. Their experience was the opposite. They lived on the far periphery looking inward toward a distant and superior metropolitan core from which standards and the sanctioned forms of organized life emanated. They lived in the outback, on the far marchlands, where constraints were loosened and where one had to struggle to maintain the forms of civilized existence. This borderland world was a strange mixture, inhabited as it was not only by cultivated gentlepeople and orderly farming villagers indistinguishable from their counterparts "at home," but also by frontiersmen living primitive lives alone in forest clearings; by scatterings of non-British peoples who clung to alien ways; by fierce sectarians, whose bizarre cults mushroomed and died in the unconstrained atmosphere; by an ever-replenished population of convicts whose lives had been spared at the price of banishment from the civilized world; and by half a million enslaved blacks, a fifth of the total population, reduced to the condition of work animals and driven by relays of professional taskmasters. Civil and incivil, cultivated and half-wild, sophisticated and deeply provincial, it was a society of jarring contrasts. And it was a world at constant risk, its gentility preyed upon not only by natives culturally disoriented and dispossessed of their land, but by marauding "crackers" and other "banditti"—creoles gone savage—no better, it was said, than bloodthirsty aborigines.

That this strange world should have attracted thousands of ordinary Britons year after year—people not driven out by plague or famine or war or persecution, people engaged in all the pursuits of a long-familiar way of life—is not something that explains itself. One must search for the reasons. One must discover the attracting forces as well as the propelling. One must probe discontents and ambitions, perceptions and understandings, shifts in circumstance and the opening of new opportunities. One must reconstruct something of the network of communication that spanned the ocean and made contact possible between peoples three thousand miles apart. And one must identify the events that characteristically triggered the movements of these people: the delivery of letters from relatives overseas, the placing of orders for workmen, the issuance of new rental terms, the opening of new lands overseas, the forming of emigration associations, the scheduling of ship departures, the rendering of court judgments.

In the end, the full reality of this segment of the past, like that of every other, will elude us; but like a circling satellite we will have come close enough to this distant world to discern some, at least, of its detailed features and to understand some of its human meaning.

I

An Expanded World, 1760–1776

IN THE years after the cessation of war in North America in 1760, the colonies experienced an extraordinary burst of expansion. By 1775 British North America, for all its remoteness, simplicity, and exotic strangeness, had become a place of interest for Britain, and to a lesser extent for Western Europe generally—talked about, written about, and visited with curiosity, and not merely because of the fame of the growing rebellion. The British North American colonies, still viewed as primitive outlands at the edge of civilization, were now immense in extent, and they were known to be potential gold mines in "futures": futures in land values, in consumer markets, and in supplies of colonial goods. Most important of all, they had acquired a powerfully intensified social role as a magnet and a refuge for the threatened, the discontented, the impoverished, and the ambitious of the western world.

The attractiveness of North America as a refuge and an opportunity was, of course, no new thing. From the beginning of British settlement, North America had been conceived of in those terms by people desperate enough and enterprising enough to consider overseas migration, and the attractiveness had increased in the eighteenth century as the colonies had grown and prospered. But after 1760 the increase in immigration became so great that it constituted a social force in itself, a force that added strain to the established relationship between the colonies and Britain. Even if there had been no political struggle between Britain and America, the relationship between them would have been altered by this growth of America as a powerful magnet and by the greatly increased flow of emigration. For the extraordinary territorial and demographic expansion of the mainland colonies after 1760 presented problems to the British rulers of North America that could not be solved within the limits of the ideas of

7

the time and of the government's administrative capacity, and yet which, unsolved, led to increasingly troubling consequences.

While the world's attention was drawn to the question of the political and constitutional relations between Britain and America, these other problems were developing quickly and dangerously. First was the question of controlling settlement in the great new western land acquisitions. And closely interwoven with that question was the dilemma created by the enlarged emigration to the colonies—its consequences, if unregulated, in both Britain and America, and the apparent impossibility of regulating it.

Conquest and Expansion

The expansion of settlement that took place in North America after 1760 is a dramatic story that can be seen as a whole only from a very high vantage point. It began with the movement to the frontiers of isolated family and community groups moving here and there along a thousand-mile perimeter in search of new locations—a few hundred isolated clusters of people, at first, pulling loaded carts and sledges and driving wagons along Indian paths across the foothills and through the gaps in the first mountain barriers to the west, poling rafts loaded with farm equipment, animals, and household goods, and paddling canoes into the interior. Soon these movements of separate groups, which at first left no visible mark on the settlement maps of British North America, began to multiply, flowed together to form substantial human streams, and ended as a flood of migrants pouring west, north, and south outward from well-settled areas to form new centers of community life. The accelerating momentum of this postwar migration into the interior of America, its geographical range and ultimate numbers, astonished contemporaries, and they remain astonishing to anyone who sees this phase of frontier expansion in its proper historical context.

Hector St. John de Crèvecoeur, the Franco-American traveler, settler, and writer, gathering in the mid-1770s the experiences that would be distilled into his *Letters from an American Farmer,* personally joined the emigrants from Connecticut moving into the disputed Wyoming district of Pennsylvania. He was amazed at what he found: "the prodigious number of houses rearing up, fields cultivating, that great extent of industry open'd to a bold indefatigable enterprising people." It was the boldness of these migrants, the risks they were willing to take, their enterprise and gambling instinct, that most astonished him. He scarcely knew what to make of "the undiffidence with which these new settlers scatter themselves here and there in the bosom of such an extensive country without even a previous path to direct their steps and without being in any number sufficient either to protect or assist one another." So remarkable was this endless scattering

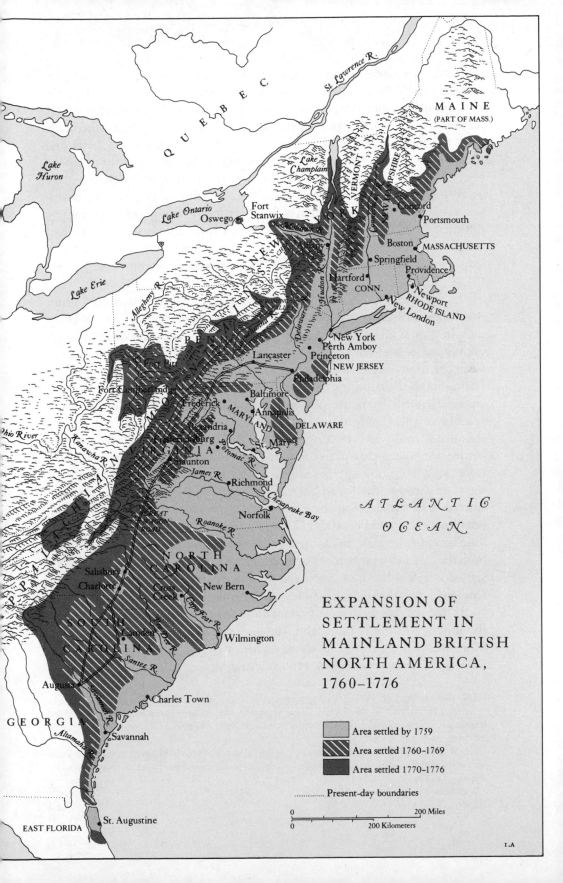

EXPANSION OF
SETTLEMENT IN
MAINLAND BRITISH
NORTH AMERICA,
1760–1776

Area settled by 1759

Area settled 1760–1769

Area settled 1770–1776

.... Present-day boundaries

0   200 Miles

0   200 Kilometers

I.A

of people that he despaired of properly describing even the one small part of it he personally experienced. All he could say was that he had seen, on his trips of 1774 and 1776, an extraordinary diaspora of various "sects and nations" on the western periphery. "Every spring," he recalled, "the roads were full of families travelling towards this new land of Canaan"; they came together as "a strange heterogeneous reunion of people . . . without law or government, without any kind of social bond to unite them all."[1]

What Crèvecoeur witnessed was a small portion of an immense development. In a seemingly boundless proliferation, a new population, utterly different from the original native peoples whose territory this once had been, was spreading over a vast inland arc curving irregularly west and south from Nova Scotia to Florida, far removed from the coastal ports. (Map 1.A.)

In the north the New England borderland was flung outward in an enormous expansion of settlement along three main routes of access. (Map 1.B.) In Maine, the expansion was a bulging out westward from a long-established coastal fringe into the adjacent backcountry; in New Hampshire, in what would become Vermont, and in eastern New York land claims and population moved northward, in a V-shaped pattern reaching 150 miles north from the Massachusetts border, along the fertile upper reaches of the Connecticut and Hudson rivers. The number of towns founded annually in New England tripled, from an average of six per year before 1760 to eighteen per year after 1760—a total of 283 between 1760 and 1776, as some 20,000 migrants moved north across the border of Massachusetts, up through the broad corridor of the Connecticut River, and west from coastal New Hampshire. By 1776 all of New Hampshire save the northeast corner had been staked out and much of it at least thinly settled. The area of cultivation in Maine had doubled, and wide strips of land along both the east and west borders of Vermont—almost none of which had been settled in 1760—had been surveyed for towns and individual grants. New England's population as a whole rose 59% between 1760 and 1780.[2]

In New York the heaviest concentrations of new settlements lay near the juncture of the Hudson and Mohawk rivers. (Map 1.C.) North of the Mohawk, two clusters of wilderness clearings suddenly appeared: in the Saratoga district west of the Hudson, and around the stream known as

[1] H. L. Bourdin and S. T. Williams, eds., "Crèvecoeur on the Susquehanna, 1774–1776," *Yale Review*, 14 (1925), 569, 575–576; John B. Deans, "The Migration of the Connecticut Yankees to the West Branch of the Susquehanna River," Northumberland County Historical Society, *Proceedings and Addresses*, 20 (1954), 34–55.

[2] Jack M. Sosin, *The Revolutionary Frontier, 1763–1783* (Albuquerque, N.M., 1967), pp. 45–49. Averages of the numbers of New England town foundings are worked out in a paper and accompanying maps by Lee Shai Weissbach, Harvard Univ., 1977. For population figures and rates of growth, see Alice Hanson Jones, *American Colonial Wealth: Documents and Methods*, 2d ed. (New York, 1978), III, 1767.

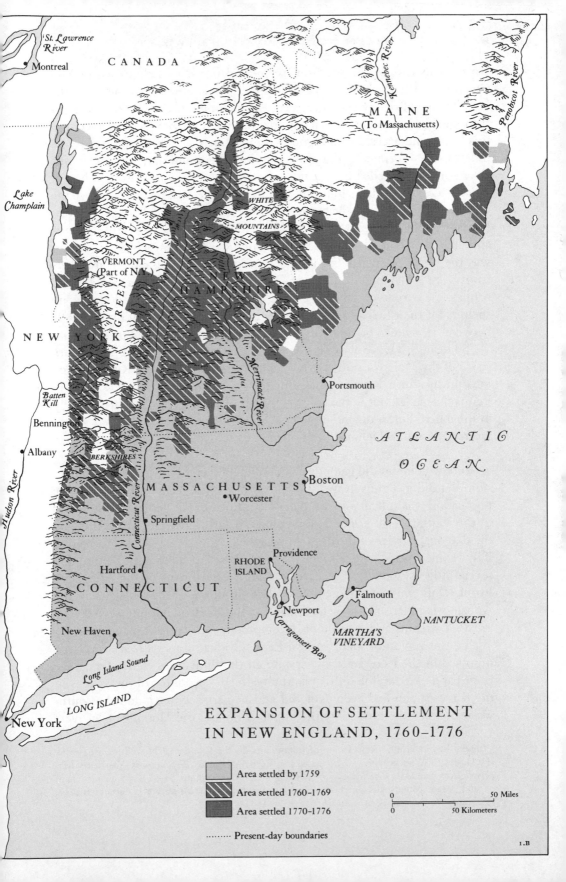

St. Lawrence
River
• Montreal

CANADA

MAINE
(To Massachusetts)

Kennebec River

Penobscot River

Lake Champlain

WHITE

MOUNTAINS

VERMONT
(Part of N.Y.)

NEW
HAMPSHIRE

NEW YORK

GREEN MOUNTAINS

Batten Kill

Bennington •

• Albany

BERKSHIRES

Merrimack River

Portsmouth •

ATLANTIC
OCEAN

Hudson River

Connecticut River

MASSACHUSETTS

Boston •

• Worcester

Springfield •

Hartford •

CONNECTICUT

RHODE
ISLAND

Providence •

Newport •

Narragansett Bay

• New Haven

Falmouth •

NANTUCKET

MARTHA'S
VINEYARD

Long Island Sound

LONG ISLAND

New York •

EXPANSION OF SETTLEMENT
IN NEW ENGLAND, 1760–1776

Area settled by 1759

Area settled 1760–1769

Area settled 1770–1776

.... Present-day boundaries

0   50 Miles
0   50 Kilometers

1.B

Batten Kill east of the Hudson, scattering north to Lakes George and Champlain. But the more powerful magnet was south of the Mohawk—the great wedge of rich, well-watered land stretching more than 100 miles west from the Hudson to the Indian boundary line of 1768. Settlers swarmed into this fertile and accessible polygon of approximately 7,500 square miles (4.8 million acres) formed by the Mohawk, Schoharie, and upper Susquehanna river valleys, preceded by a legion of energetic land speculators, a few of whom, like Sir William Johnson, had lived in the area for years before the war, many of whom had been eyeing the region from afar. By 1776 the great Hudson-Mohawk wedge was a bewildering patchwork of patents, grants, and land claims of all sorts, many of which overlapped each other. And it was the scene of swiftly expanding settlements as thousands of migrants from New England, from lower New York, and from Britain located properties to rent or buy, cleared a few acres hurriedly, and threw up shelters for their first season on the land. New York's population rose 39% between 1760 and 1770 and 29% more in the decade that followed.[3]

Some of this wave of expansion in the rich farming region of New York south of the Mohawk spilled over, through the Susquehanna River system, into northeastern Pennsylvania. But the great expansion of settlement in Pennsylvania lay not in the colony's north, which in 1776 remained largely uninhabited, but in the mountainous Appalachian plateau in the far southwestern corner, which had been opened to settlement by the treaty line of 1768.

In few colonies did geology so completely dictate the pattern of expansion as it did in Pennsylvania. In 1760, after eighty years of settlement, the population was still almost completely confined to the gentle rolling plains in the southeastern corner of the colony, a fertile triangle blocked off by the diagonal barrier of the deep Appalachian ridges and valleys, formed as if by "some cosmic rake" dragged the length of the mountains. Behind that severe ridge system lay the 1,500-foot-high escarpment of the Allegheny Front. Only west of that natural wall could one find the tableland of the Appalachian Plateau, itself a formidable mountain land but intersected with twisting streams and capable of development into useful upland farms.

To this region of southwestern Pennsylvania migrants moved in large numbers in the 1760s and '70s, despite all the difficulties of traversing the ridges and clearing the hilly upland terrain. By 1770 most of the valleys in the ridge system had been explored and in part occupied, and the southwestern rectangle formed by the upper Ohio and the Monongahela rivers

[3]Eugene R. Fingerhut, "Assimilation of Immigrants on the Frontier of New York, 1764–1776" (Ph.D. diss., Columbia Univ., 1962), chaps. 2, 5; Ruth L. Higgins, *Expansion in New York: with Especial Reference to the Eighteenth Century* (Columbus, Ohio, 1931), pp. 90–96, and appended maps of land grants, patents, and purchases; *Historical Statistics of the United States,* bicentennial ed. (Washington, D.C., 1975), pt. 2, 1168.

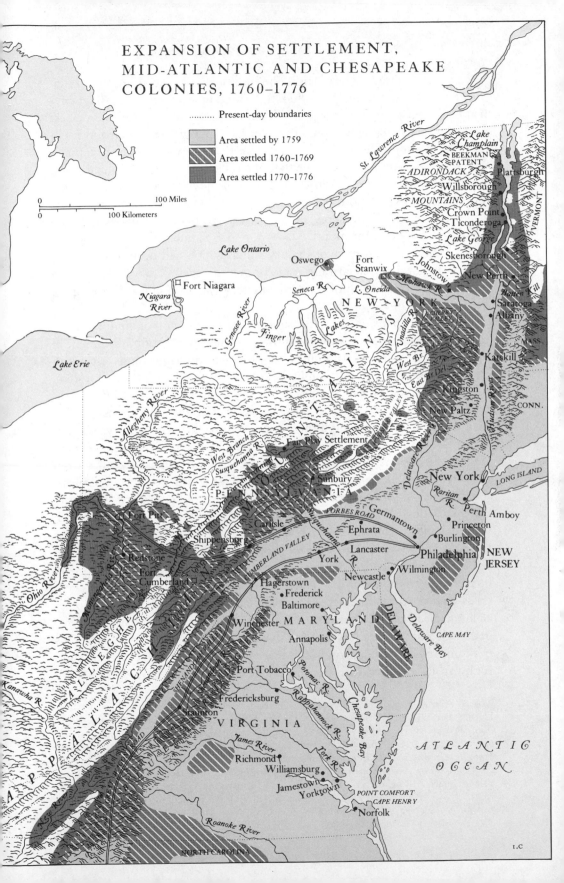

EXPANSION OF SETTLEMENT, MID-ATLANTIC AND CHESAPEAKE COLONIES, 1760–1776

.... Present-day boundaries

Area settled by 1759

Area settled 1760–1769

Area settled 1770–1776

0   100 Miles

0   100 Kilometers

St. Lawrence River

Lake Champlain

BEEKMAN PATENT

ADIRONDACK

Plattsburgh

Willsborough

MOUNTAINS

Crown Point

Ticonderoga

Lake George

Skenesborough

Johnstown

New Perth

VERMONT

Batten Kill

Saratoga

Albany

MASS.

Lake Ontario

Oswego

Fort Stanwix

Seneca R.

L. Oneida

Mohawk R.

NEW YORK

Fort Niagara

Niagara River

Genesee River

Finger Lakes

Unadilla R.

Katskill

West Br.

East Br. Del.

Kingston

New Paltz

CONN.

Lake Erie

Allegheny River

West Branch Susquehanna R.

Fair Play Settlement

APPALACHIAN MOUNTAINS

Delaware River

New York

LONG ISLAND

Raritan R.

Perth Amboy

Sunbury

PENNSYLVANIA

Germantown

Princeton

Burlington

Fort Pitt

Carlisle

Susquehanna R.

FORBES ROAD

Ephrata

Lancaster

Philadelphia

NEW JERSEY

Shippensburg

CUMBERLAND VALLEY

York

Lancaster R.

Newcastle

Wilmington

Redstone

Fort Cumberland

Hagerstown

Frederick

Baltimore

Monongahela R.

Ohio River

Winchester

MARYLAND

DELAWARE

Delaware Bay

CAPE MAY

Annapolis

Kanawha R.

APPALACHIAN

Port Tobacco

Potomac R.

Chesapeake Bay

Fredericksburg

Rappahannock R.

Staunton

VIRGINIA

James River

ATLANTIC OCEAN

Richmond

Williamsburg

York R.

Jamestown

Yorktown

POINT COMFORT

CAPE HENRY

Norfolk

Roanoke River

NORTH CAROLINA

I.C

had been converted to farmland. The hub of the region, Fort Pitt (Pitts-burgh) at the juncture of the Ohio, the Monongahela, and the Allegheny, had become a major transfer point as migrants, bypassing even the newest Pennsylvania settlements, sought fresher land and greater opportunities in the Ohio Valley. The speed of this expansion into southwestern Pennsyl-vania was even more remarkable than the rocketing of settlers north along the Connecticut and Hudson rivers and into the Mohawk salient of New York. The day the land office opened at Fort Pitt in 1769, 2,790 applicants appeared; one million acres of southwestern Pennsylvania land were granted in the first four months. By 1771, 10,000 families were living on this trans-Appalachian frontier of Pennsylvania, which had been a wilderness only a decade before; farming establishments covered the land within a radius of 150 miles south of Fort Pitt. Pennsylvania's population rose 40% between 1760 and 1776.[4]

But this expansion into the southwestern segment of Pennsylvania, remarkable as it was, was not the most important population movement in that colony. A veritable tumult of migrants was pouring southwest out of Pennsylvania, through the Cumberland Valley and its parent valley system, the Great Valley of the Appalachians, into western Virginia, into north-western North Carolina, and into the eastern fringes of Tennessee. The main route of access through these connected backcountry valleys was the Great Wagon Road, a still crude, rock-strewn, occasionally swampy expan-sion of an ancient Indian trail, which by 1770 extended 800 miles from Philadelphia to Augusta, Georgia. It passed first westward through Lancas-ter and York, Pennsylvania, then turned south through western Maryland, the Shenandoah Valley and southern Virginia, then through central North Carolina and upcountry South Carolina, to reach its terminus just across the Savannah River in inland Georgia. Through this corridor passed thou-sands of heavily loaded covered wagons, some pulled by as many as six horses or oxen; homemade "carriages" whose heavy, clumsy wheels were cross-section segments of tree trunks; and, above all, trains of packhorses accompanied by family members on foot and by farm animals roped to-gether or kept in small groups by snapping dogs or flicking whips. This migrant traffic, moving slowly south across the deeply rutted, tree-strewn, rocky road, was met, in the summer and early fall, by herds of livestock

[4]Robert Secor et al., eds., Pennsylvania 1776 (University Park, Pa., 1975), pp. 22–27, 90, 91, 97; John Florin, "The Advance of Frontier Settlement in Pennsylvania, 1638–1850: A Geographic Interpreta-tion," Pennsylvania State Univ., Department of Geography, Papers in Geography, no. 14 (1977), 64–73, 95; Wayland F. Dunaway, "Pennsylvania as an Early Distributing Center of Population," Pennsylvania Magazine of History and Biography, 55 (1931), 159, 160; Alfred P. James, "The First English-Speaking Trans-Appalachian Frontier," Mississippi Valley Historical Review, 17 (1930), 59–66; Homer T. Rosenberger, "Migrations of the Pennsylvania Germans to Western Pennsyl-vania," Western Pennsylvania Historical Magazine, 53 (1970), 329, 332; Ray A. Billington, Westward Expansion: A History of the American Frontier, 4th ed. (New York, 1974), p. 159.

being driven to markets—originally markets in Philadelphia, but by the 1770s also in a number of inland villages like Lancaster, Pennsylvania; Winchester, Virginia; Salisbury, North Carolina; and Camden, South Carolina. Crude "ordinaries" (solitary houses that could provide some food and shelter), taverns, and occasionally inns (drovers' inns, packhorse inns, wagoners' inns) could be found in even some of the most remote stretches of the road; and long, flat-bottomed, high-sided barges, poled or pulled by ropes from either shore, served as ferries across streams that could not be forded.[5]

How many thousands of migrants flocked through this heavily traveled route of expansion in the fifteen years after 1760 is not known. What is known is that by the late 1750s, even before the major migrations of the 1760s, over 2,000 settlers were passing south every year through the Shenandoah Valley—these in excess of the new arrivals who settled permanently in the valley. By 1776 the Shenandoah had a population of 35,000; and Virginia's entire western borderland (the Great Valley together with the southwestern Piedmont) contained more than twice that many settlers. In the 1760s the population of the whole of southwestern Virginia was growing at the rate of 9% a year, hence doubling every eight years, and the expansion of settled land was equally swift.[6]

But while the population of western Virginia grew continuously through this period and more and more unworked land was brought under cultivation, most of that colony had at least been explored before 1763 and thinly settled. That was not true of North Carolina. There the rush into new, altogether unsettled and little-known territory was equivalent to the opening of northern New England and New York and of southwestern Pennsylvania. (Map 1.D.) The inflow of immigrants to North Carolina seeking parcels of fresh land seemed to contemporaries to be a stampede. One observer noted that between January and October 1755, 5,000 migrants crossed the James River in southern Virginia heading for North Carolina, and that the numbers were increasing daily. In 1763 Benjamin Franklin estimated that in the previous three years 10,000 families had migrated to North Carolina from Pennsylvania alone—a guess, to be sure, but roughly substantiated by the overall population figures and by the extent of new land opened to cultivation. In 1766 an observer in Salisbury, North Carolina, which like Fort Pitt was strategically located athwart major westward routes, reported that 1,000 wagons rumbled through the town en route to the west in the autumn and winter months alone. Between 1730 and 1750 the

[5] Parke Rouse, Jr., *The Great Wagon Road* (New York, 1973), bk. 2, esp. chap. 11, p. 266; Robert D. Mitchell, *Commercialism and Frontier: Perspectives on the Early Shenandoah Valley* (Charlottesville, Va., 1977), pp. 16–19, 46.
[6] *Ibid.*, pp. 46, 96; Robert D. Mitchell, "The Shenandoah Valley Frontier," *Annals of the Association of American Geographers*, 62 (1972), 470.

colony's population had doubled, from approximately 35,000 to approximately 70,000; by 1770 it more than doubled once again, reaching a figure between 175,000 and 185,000.[7]

Some of the newcomers to North Carolina moved in through the Wagon Road into the backcountry; others traveled down the east coast and then swung west into the interior; still others moved north from South Carolina along the Catawba River, then overland to Salisbury. But the route most favored by immigrants from abroad, especially the Scots, was inland from the port of Wilmington in the colony's far south, northwestward for approximately a hundred miles along the Cape Fear River to the trading and transfer center of Cross Creek (the modern Fayetteville), from which a network of lesser roads led out into a scattering of swiftly growing settlements close to the South Carolina border. As a result of these population movements the colony's settlements expanded swiftly after 1760 in three main regions: in the far west, from Salisbury and the Wagon Road west to the Appalachian barrier; in the east, inland from the coast toward the still largely unsettled center of the colony; and in the south-central region, in an arc focused on Cross Creek, swinging south to the South Carolina border.[8]

In South Carolina, too, expansion into the west drew heavily on the movements of migrants from the north down the western valley routes that fronted the Appalachian mountain chain, and from the British Isles and western Europe. But the spread of population in that colony was delayed by the Cherokee War of 1760–1761, one of the most savage and brutalizing conflicts in the entire history of Indian-white relations. This border war, the result of scattered but continuous invasions of the grasslands of the backcountry which forced the Cherokee Indians out of their traditional hunting grounds to a small corner against the mountains, left behind a ravaged land and a disoriented white population for whom murder, thievery, and brutality had become commonplace. Most of the decade of the 1760s was consumed in the vigilante efforts of the more respectable frontier settlers to bring the savagery under control and to establish effective public institutions in the west. When this regulator movement and its confused aftermath finally subsided, the broadening expansion into the South Carolina backcountry was resumed, resulting in a more complex, closer intermingling of peoples than had taken place in North Carolina.

The middle-country townships had from the first attracted Scotch-Irish Presbyterians direct from northern Ireland, Welsh Baptists from eastern

---

[7]Harry R. Merrens, *Colonial North Carolina in the Eighteenth Century: A Study in Historical Geography* (Chapel Hill, N.C., 1964), pp. 53, 54; A. Roger Ekirch, *"Poor Carolina": Politics and Society in Colonial North Carolina, 1729–1776* (Chapel Hill, N.C., 1981), pp. 6–8.
[8]Merrens, *Colonial North Carolina*, fig. 23 (p. 68), pp. 74, 116–117, 162.

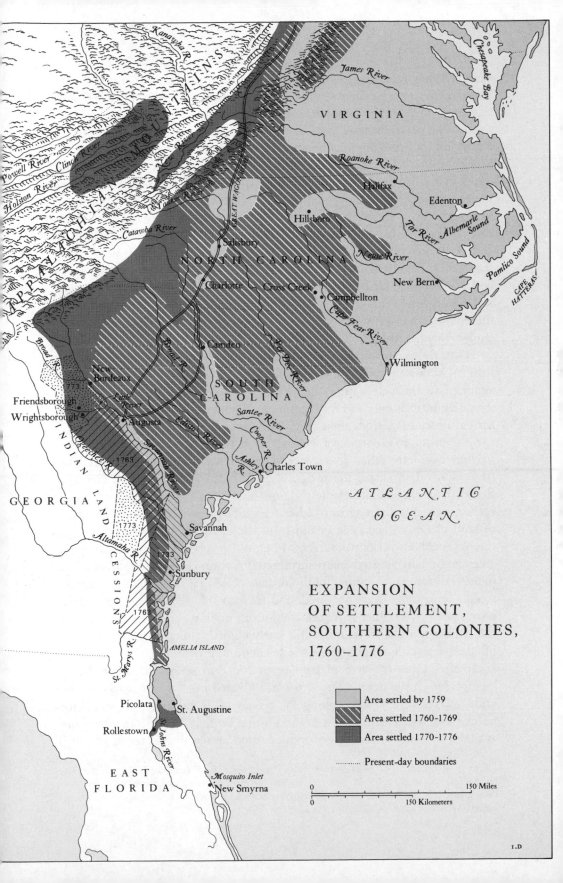

APPALACHIAN MOUNTAINS

Kanawha R.

Powell River
Clinch River
Holston River
Nollichucky River

Catawba River

GREAT WAGON ROAD

Broad R.

Broad R.

Little River

Oconee R.

Savannah River

Edisto River

Cooper R.

Ashley R.

St. Marys R.

St. Johns River

Altamaha R.

VIRGINIA

James River

Chesapeake Bay

Roanoke River

Halifax

Edenton

Hillsboro

Tar River

Albemarle Sound

Salisbury

NORTH CAROLINA

Neuse River

New Bern

Pamlico Sound

CAPE HATTERAS

Charlotte

Cross Creek

Campbellton

Camden

SOUTH CAROLINA

Pee Dee River

Cape Fear River

Wilmington

New Bordeaux

1773

Santee River

Friendsborough
Wrightsborough

Augusta

Charles Town

GEORGIA

1763

1773

ATLANTIC
OCEAN

Savannah

1733

INDIAN LAND CESSIONS

Sunbury

1765

AMELIA ISLAND

Picolata

St. Augustine

Rollestown

EXPANSION
OF SETTLEMENT,
SOUTHERN COLONIES,
1760–1776

EAST
FLORIDA

Mosquito Inlet
New Smyrna

	Area settled by 1759
	Area settled 1760-1769
	Area settled 1770-1776
	Present-day boundaries

0 ————————— 150 Miles

0 ————————— 150 Kilometers

I.D

Pennsylvania, and heavy concentrations of Germans and Swiss, especially in the western region against the Georgia boundary. In addition Virginians migrated south to the same area, and South Carolinians moved west from the tidewater plantations. In time these groups mingled as their farms expanded, and they mingled too with a slave population that grew in these years until it constituted some 20% of the region's inhabitants. Farther west, in the backcountry—where only 4 or 5% of the population were slaves and where settlement boundaries were vaguer—the distribution of new settlers was different. Almost the whole of this new inland population had migrated south down the valley route. They came, chiefly in the 1760s and early '70s, from all of the colonies south of New York, and especially from Virginia and Pennsylvania. Most of the few "South Carolinians" to be found in that far borderland were in fact foreign Protestants on their second or third remove, still hoping to find, in the uncultivated spaces of the colony's westernmost periphery, the prosperity and security that had eluded them in the east.[9]

Thus the expansion of European settlement in South Carolina took the form of both an increase in the density of land occupancy in an area long assumed to lie well within the colony's boundaries, and an ill-defined, irregular infiltration into more remote western territories seized, by no formal procedure, from their original native occupants.

Expansion in Georgia was a much more formal process, and proceeded in quite distinctly articulated stages. Three sets of immense land purchases from the Indians mark the progress of European settlement in Georgia. Before 1763, and mainly at the time of the colony's founding thirty years earlier, over a million acres had been acquired from the Indians—a block of land that stretched back inland from the coast about 30 miles, between the Savannah and Altamaha rivers. Then in 1763 negotiations carried on by an exceptionally shrewd and determined governor, James Wright, resulted in an addition to this initial foothold that totaled 3.4 million acres. In 1766, 20,000 acres more were acquired, and then in 1773 Wright negotiated the purchase of two immense parcels totaling 2.1 million acres, which extended the colony more than 60 miles still farther north along the Savannah and filled in a 72-mile-long strip in the backcountry running north from the Altamaha. Thus the area of land open for European settlement almost quadrupled in the decade after 1763, and formed in all a belt 25 to 50 miles wide, stretching 200 miles along the Savannah River and then south 100 miles along the Atlantic coast to the Florida border. Though this territory available to white settlers in 1776 totaled some 7 million acres (close to a fifth

[9]Julian J. Petty, *The Growth and Distribution of Population in South Carolina* ([1943] Spartanburg, S.C., 1975), pp. 34–48, 57–58; W. Stitt Robinson, *The Southern Colonial Frontier, 1607–1763* (Albuquerque, N.M., 1979), pp. 162–176; Richard M. Brown, *The South Carolina Regulators* (Cambridge, Mass., 1963), chaps. 1, 2.

of the territory that would eventually be included in the state of Georgia), it contained in 1773 only an estimated 33,000 inhabitants, almost half of them slaves—a density of 3 people (1.6 whites) per square mile—and hence was a prime target for new settlement.[10]

Newcomers arrived steadily in the 1760s and '70s—Georgia's population more than tripled between 1760 and 1773—and moved to the fringes of the settlements scattered through the huge strip along the Savannah and the Atlantic coast. They were in part migrants from the northern colonies moving in from the west at the end of the Great Wagon Road; in part too they came from closer by, some of them simply by crossing the Savannah River, which formed the long border with South Carolina. But many were voyagers from abroad—Germans, Swiss, Scots, Italians, Jews, and Irishmen —joining their fellow countrymen in what had become a remarkably poly-ethnic and poly-linguistic community. "To function well in all parts of the colony," a recent historian of colonial Georgia has written, "a person ideally needed what probably no one in Georgia had—fluency in English, French, German, and Gaelic. A knowledge of Spanish would also have been helpful."

When news of Wright's great land purchases of 1763 and 1766 became known, the mixture of peoples in Georgia grew more complex. Besides several thousand blacks (the slave population almost quintupled in the decade and a half after 1760), a variety of other groups arrived. The largest of them was composed of 300 or so Congregationalists, children of New Englanders who had lived in South Carolina for half a century, seeking more fertile land than they had inherited. In the same years six shiploads of Scotch-Irish arrived—perhaps 800 people in all—and more than 600 Pennsylvania Quakers who had resettled in North Carolina and had grown discontented with their lot there. In addition, thousands of other new settlers arrived in these years in smaller contingents—church groups, neighborhood groups, families, and individuals—from most of the colonies in the north, from the West Indies, from the German states, and from Britain.[11]

Like the settlers moving into newly opened territories everywhere along the inland periphery, the new arrivals in Georgia wanted precisely what Governor Wright advertised so shrewdly in a proclamation of 1773 announcing the latest Indian purchase open for settlement: "lands . . . of the most fertile quality." Every detail of this well-publicized advertisement went straight to the hopes and desires of migrants everywhere. The ceded

[10]Harold E. Davis, *The Fledgling Province: Social and Cultural Life in Colonial Georgia, 1733–1776* (Chapel Hill, N.C., 1976), pp. 28–30, 32. For details on the extensions of the boundary lines, see Louis De Vorsey, Jr., *The Indian Boundary in the Southern Colonies, 1763–1775* (Chapel Hill, N.C., 1966), chap. 7.
[11]Davis, *Georgia,* pp. 10, 14, 17, 22–27, 32.

lands, Wright declared, "will be parcelled out in different tracts . . . from 100 to 1,000 acres, the better to accommodate the buyers." The land, he said, relieved of the Crown's quit rents for ten years, was "well watered," close to excellent markets, well protected, within an effective system of law and order, and available to all for inspection. Moreover, the specific where-abouts of its natural resources—timber, cane brakes, sites for wells and of natural springs—had been identified and were marked on a map he had prepared for distribution. The question is not why Georgia's population, after having more than tripled between 1760 and 1773, rose another 70% during the seven years of warfare that followed, but why it did not grow even faster.[12]

The Farther Fringes

So it was that during the decade and a half after 1760 the inland periphery of British settlements in mainland North America was pressed outward, within the boundaries of the established colonies, north, west, and south, as thousands of settlers set out to find land "of the most fertile quality." But this massive *Völkerwanderung*, this surge of innumerable farming families from all over North America and from western Europe, could not be contained within the margins of the existing colonies, or even within the newly extended boundaries of permissible white settlement outside the established provinces. Settlers defied all legal constraints.

While new villages, plantations, and farms were forming outgrowths, spillovers, of older communities, linked to them directly by an elaborating network of roads, other settlements—disconnected fragments flung out beyond the immediate boundaries—suddenly appeared. (Map 1.E.) Such was the transitory Fair Play encampment in north central Pennsylvania— a cluster of about forty frontier families which formed their own unique and independent "fair play system" of law and government, democratic to the core, that lasted until 1784, when it was engulfed by the state and disap-peared into the general population. And such was the extensive Watauga settlement in eastern Tennessee and Kentucky—an illegal invasion of In-dian territory, peopled quickly by several thousand squatters from western Maryland, Virginia, and North Carolina, who organized a crude "Associa-tion" for temporary government, and by 1776 were busy opening roads that

[12]"Georgia. By His Excellency Sir James Wright . . . A Proclamation," Savannah, June 11, 1773, DeRenne Collection, Division of Special Collections, University of Georgia Libraries, Athens, Georgia; Philip Yonge, "A Map of the Lands Ceded to His Majesty . . . at a Congress held in Augusta the 1st June 1773 . . .," MPG 2, Public Record Office, London; Davis, *Georgia*, p. 32; *Historical Statistics*, pt. 2, 1168. Wright's map of his third land purchase, the so-called Ceded Lands, is reproduced below, p. 550.

would connect their cabins and rough farms with the older settlements east of the mountains. More remote—a hundred miles to the northwest of the Watauga Association and accessible mainly by the Ohio River and its tributaries—were the new "Kentucky Stations" in the bluegrass country. These clusters of habitation were located on land that had only been spied out in 1766 and had been opened to settlement, first by Daniel Boone and his "long-hunters," and then by the Virginia militia, which in 1774 defeated the Indian warriors struggling to preserve their ancient hunting grounds. By 1776 several thousand of these Kentucky settlers, recruited from all over the seaboard colonies, claimed title to over half a million acres.[13]

But even these deeper penetrations of the trans-Appalachian Indian territory were mere border forays next to other enterprises of these explosive years, some of which seem scarcely credible when one considers how poorly explored the deep south and trans-Appalachia were in this period, and how primitive transportation was everywhere. New communities suddenly appeared not merely at the bulging frontier line and not merely a hundred or so miles beyond all contiguous settlement, but a thousand or more miles in the interior, at the farthest margins of Britain's half-billion-acre territorial empire, which now stretched west to the Mississippi and south to the Gulf of Mexico and the Florida Keys. Silently, mysteriously, but continuously and in increasing numbers, settlers arrived in these far-distant and isolated marchlands—some sailing down the great arterial flows of the Ohio and the Mississippi rivers and along the Atlantic and Gulf coasts, others seeping, as it were, through the smallest capillaries of creeks, Indian trails, and animal runs, to reach their new frontier homesteads.

They did not do so unaided. Before them, behind them, around them wherever they went were land speculators. Speculation in the American "west"—wherever the west happened to be—was nothing new in American history, but it achieved a new scale in the 1760s and '70s. As thousands of migrants poured into Pennsylvania, settled in clusters west and southwest of the distribution centers on the shores of the Delaware River and Chesapeake Bay, moved farther west into south-central Pennsylvania, joined the extending lines of migration in western Maryland and down into the fertile valleys of Virginia and the uncultivated lands of northern North Carolina—as all of this movement and settlement and resettlement was underway, those with access to large parcels of land or with the means of gaining access rose to exploit the situation. Wherever men gathered to talk about crops, government, and business, and wherever men of property and position met to discuss the trends of the time and the opportunities that lay

[13]George D. Wolf, *The Fair Play Settlers of the West Branch Valley, 1769–1784: A Study of Frontier Ethnography* (Harrisburg, Pa., 1969); Billington, *Westward Expansion*, pp. 160–174, chap. 9. On trans-Appalachia, see below, chap. 14, pp. 536 ff.

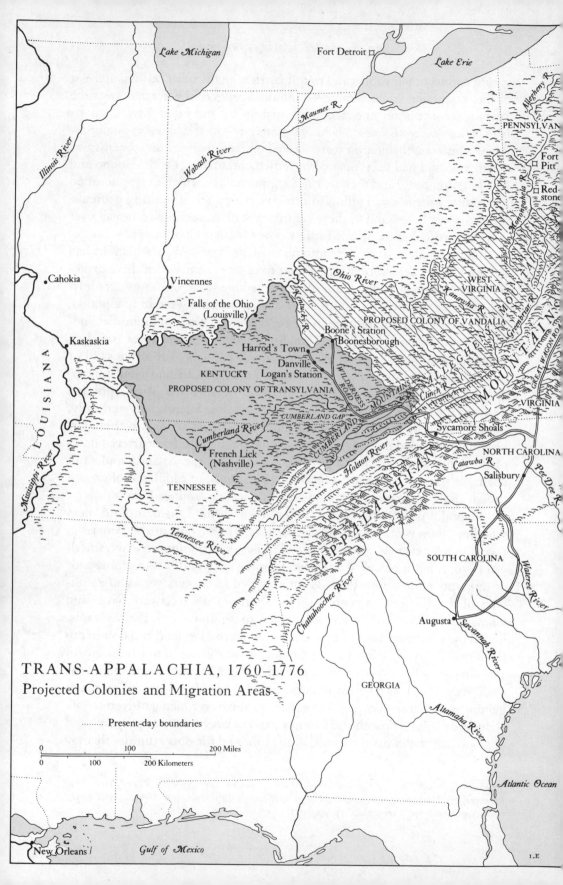

Lake Michigan

Fort Detroit □

Lake Erie

Maumee R.

Illinois River

Wabash River

Allegheny R.

PENNSYLVAN

□ Fort
Pitt

□ Red-
stone

Monongahela R.

• Cahokia

Vincennes

Ohio River

WEST
VIRGINIA

Kanawha R.

Greenbrier R.

ALLEGHE MOUNTAINS

Falls of the Ohio
(Louisville)

Kentucky R.

Boone's Station
Boonesborough

PROPOSED COLONY OF VANDALIA

GREAT WAGON ROAD

• Kaskaskia

Harrod's Town

KENTUCKY

Danville
Logan's Station

PROPOSED COLONY OF TRANSYLVANIA

Clinch R.

VIRGINIA

L O U I S I A N A

Mississippi River

Cumberland River

CUMBERLAND GAP

Holston River

Sycamore Shoals

NORTH CAROLINA

WILDERNESS ROAD

CUMBERLAND MOUNTAINS

• French Lick
(Nashville)

Catawba R.

Salisbury

Pee Dee R.

TENNESSEE

Tennessee River

A P P A L A C H I A N

SOUTH CAROLINA

Wateree River

Chattahoochee River

Augusta
Savannah River

TRANS-APPALACHIA, 1760–1776
Projected Colonies and Migration Areas

GEORGIA

.... Present-day boundaries

| 0 | 100 | 200 Miles |
| 0 | 100 | 200 Kilometers |

Altamaha River

New Orleans

Gulf of Mexico

Atlantic Ocean

I.E

ahead, plans were made, groups formed, and the first steps taken in enterprises whose numbers and scale could not have been seriously considered twenty years before.

Complex, often the product of elaborate, shadowy intrigues, and intricately interrelated, these projects of the 1760s and early 1770s, even now, after generations of assiduous scholarship, can scarcely be sorted out and clearly depicted.[14] Everyone with any ambition and capacity, it seems, on both sides of the Atlantic, sought some profit from what promised to be the greatest land boom in history. Plans were drawn up, revised, expanded, abandoned; companies formed overnight, sometimes quickly disappeared, sometimes grew into syndicates; and connections between American and British groups were universal, conceived of as a requirement for ultimate success.

Everyone, it seems, was involved. The population movement into uncultivated and legally unclaimed lands excited feverish ambitions in land speculators in every corner of the Anglo-American world—speculators as different as George Grenville and Benjamin Franklin, the Reverend John Witherspoon and the Earl of Dartmouth. Among them were most of the officials of colonial America, a large phalanx of British politicians and merchants, and planters and merchants everywhere in America, who were determined to get a substantial piece of the pie.

So Benning Wentworth, governor of New Hampshire and provincial agent of a powerful clique of British merchants and officials, was largely responsible for opening the upper Connecticut River valley and projecting the remarkable number of towns that suddenly appeared north of Massachusetts. Somehow he brought political support in England together with the aspirations of thousands of New Englanders to form the profit-seeking proprietorships of the many new northern New England towns. "By 1765 Wentworth had granted 124 townships, and few men of means and ambition in New Hampshire had failed to increase their estates." His success was notable. Others tried and failed—George Washington, for example, who wrote enthusiastically in 1767 about an "opening prospect in the back country for adventurers, where numbers resort to, and where an enterprising man with very little money may lay the foundation of a noble estate." Anyone, he declared, who neglected the "present opportunity of hunting out good lands and in some measure marking and distinguishing them for his own (in order to keep others from settling them) will never regain it." He wanted a "good deal of land"—2,000 acres on the Ohio, he told his agent at the start; then 15,000, 20,000, or 25,000 acres; finally, as much good land as he could get. And in 1774 he started making plans, which ultimately

---

[14] The bewildering confusion in land speculation is detailed in Thomas P. Abernethy, *Western Lands and the American Revolution* (New York, 1937), chaps. 1, 2, 5, 8, and 10.

failed, to settle these lands with immigrants from the German states, Ireland, or Scotland.[15]

The Surge of Immigration

Others did the same. All of the complex movements into the newly opened far-western periphery of European civilization were interpenetrated with voyagers from abroad. In the years after 1760 transatlantic migration reached levels beyond anything seen before in British America, which is to say, beyond anything seen in the entire history of Europe's and Africa's connections with the Western Hemisphere.

Comparisons are instructive. We do not know exactly how many Spaniards had migrated to Spain's massive American domain, the largest and most populous empire the western world had seen since the fall of Rome. But the most generous estimate we have (undoubtedly inflated: it triples the traditional figure) is an annual average of something like 3,000 persons, from a total population of approximately 8 million, to reach a maximum estimated emigration during the first century and a half (1500–1650) of around 437,000. From Portugal, a reasonable guess is a maximum yearly average of only 500 departures over two centuries of colonial rule. And from France, with a domestic population of around 20 million, the total emigration to Canada from 1608 to 1760 was approximately 27,000—an average of less than 200 a year. At its height in the late seventeenth century, French emigration to *all* of its dependencies in the Western Hemisphere, the Caribbean islands and Canada together, did not exceed 600 a year.[16]

The contrast with the migration to Britain's American colonies is striking. During its first century of American colonization, Britain (that is, England, Scotland, and Wales—but principally England alone) sent nearly 400,000 emigrants to America (more than half of them to the Caribbean), a ratio of emigrants to domestic population almost twice that of Spain's. By 1700 the overall population of Britons or their descendants in the Western Hemisphere was approximately 250,000, which is double the number of

[15]Jere R. Daniell, *Experiment in Republicanism: New Hampshire Politics and the American Revolution, 1741–1794* (Cambridge, Mass., 1970), pp. 15–16; Washington to John Posey, June 24, 1767, to William Crawford, Sept. 21, 1767, to James Wood, March 30, 1773, to Henry Riddell, Feb. 22, 1774, all in *Writings of George Washington*, ed. Worthington C. Ford (New York, 1889–1893), II, 216, 222, 219, 375, 404; cf. Roy B. Cook, *Washington's Western Lands* (Strasburg, Va., 1930).
[16]Magnus Mörner, "Spanish Migration to the New World Prior to 1810: A Report on the State of Research," and Woodrow Borah, "The Mixing of Populations," in *First Images of America*, ed. Fredi Chiappelli (Berkeley, 1976), II, 708, 709, 767; Mario Boleda, "Les Migrations au Canada sous le Régime Français (1608–1760)," Programme de Recherche en Démographie Historique, Univ. of Montreal, *Rapport de l'Année 1982–1983*, App. 7 (reference courtesy of Leslie Choquette); Jean Hamelin, *Économie et Société en Nouvelle-France* (Quebec, 1960), pp. 76–77.

peninsular Spaniards and creoles known to be in Spanish America at the end of Spain's first century of colonization. Indeed, within a single generation—from 1630 to 1660—about 210,000 emigrants had left Britain for America, and this was only a portion of the total number of British who settled overseas in these years.[17]

The extraordinarily heavy British-American migration of the early seventeenth century eased later in the century and subsided in the eighteenth century. But by then the flow of settlers from Britain was supplemented by sizable movements of people from other major sources. The founding of Pennsylvania set in motion the first substantial migrations from the German-speaking world, principally from the Rhineland and Switzerland but also from elsewhere in west-central Europe. Precisely how many came to British America from that region before 1760 we do not yet know, but there are records of close to 60,000 German entries into the port of Philadelphia alone between 1727 and 1760; an overall figure of 75,000 German-speaking arrivals in all the colonies seems reasonable. Then, in addition to the Germans and Swiss, beginning in 1717 and continuing in waves in the decades that followed, the Scotch-Irish joined the emigration to America in large numbers, adding another 100,000 to 150,000 before 1760. And more numerous than either of these flows were the enslaved blacks, whose forced emigration from Africa had begun to contribute significantly to the American population as early as the 1680s. An estimated 175,000 slaves were brought to British North America before 1760, by which time blacks constituted 40% of Virginia's population and 60% of South Carolina's.[18]

How many migrants in all—voluntary and involuntary—had reached the shores of mainland British North America (the thirteen colonies and Nova Scotia) from the beginning of British settlement to 1760 can only be roughly estimated: a total of at least 700,000 seems reasonable. In the context of the time this overall figure, and the yearly average of about 4,500 it implies, are remarkable. But these migration figures to mainland British North America before 1760—far greater than those to any other area of

---

[17]Henry A. Gemery, "Emigration from the British Isles to the New World, 1630–1700: Inferences from Colonial Populations," in Paul Uselding, ed., *Research in Economic History: A Research Annual*, 5 (1980), 197; *Historical Statistics*, pt. 2, 1168.

[18]Marianne Wokeck, "The Flow and Composition of German Immigration to Philadelphia, 1727–1775," *Pennsylvania Magazine of History and Biography*, 105 (1981), 260–261; Oscar Kuhns, *The German and Swiss Settlements of Colonial Pennsylvania* ([1901], Harrisburg, Pa., 1945), p. 55. There is no reliable figure for Scotch-Irish immigration before 1760. James G. Leyburn, *The Scotch-Irish: A Social History* (Chapel Hill, N.C., 1962), pp. 180–181, accepts the traditional estimate of 200,000 between 1717 and 1775, or about 150,000 before 1760. R. J. Dickson, *Ulster Emigration to Colonial America, 1718–1775* ([1966], Antrim, 1976), pp. 32–34, 59, provides estimates of ship departures from Ireland for scattered groups of years that total about 65,000. Other estimates go as high as 300,000. The traditional figure used here seems a reasonable minimum. For slave importations, see Philip D. Curtin, *The Atlantic Slave Trade: A Census* (Madison, Wis., 1969), Table 39 [p. 137]; *Historical Statistics*, pt. 2, 1168.

European colonization—pale next to the figures for the decade and a half that followed.

People flooded into North America between 1760 and 1775, first of all from the British Isles. Between the end of warfare and the disruption of the empire in 1775, over 55,000 Protestant Irish emigrated to America; approximately 40,000 Scots, and over 30,000 Englishmen—a total of at least 125,000 from the British Isles alone. The magnitudes of these figures become clear when they are seen in their local contexts: 40,000 Scots represent 3% of the entire population of Scotland in 1760; 55,000 Irish represent 2.3% of the Irish population. But the British and Irish contributions together constituted only half of the whole number of immigrants. In the same years at least 12,000 German-speaking immigrants entered the port of Philadelphia, and 84,500 enslaved Africans were imported, principally to the southern colonies. The grand total, therefore, is approximately 221,500 arrivals in this fifteen-year period: a conservative figure, but it is equivalent to almost 10% of the entire estimated population of British North America in 1775. An average of about 15,000 people were arriving annually, which is triple the average of the years before 1760 and close to the total estimated population of the town of Boston in this period.[19]

But impressive as these magnitudes are, they do not in themselves express the importance of overseas migration in this period. Immigration was not simply an incremental element in the population growth of the time; it did not simply add a general impetus to the expansion of Anglo-American society. It had a direct and peculiar impact on the leading edge of expansion, the frontier. It is, in fact, as much transatlantic migration as domestic population movements that accounts for the speed and extent of frontier expansion—and it accounts too for much of the social character of the new frontier world.

For unlike the immigration of the nineteenth century, pre-industrial immigration was not, in its main impact, an urban phenomenon. It was not a process by which Old World peasants were suddenly and traumatically translated to tumultuous urban environments. The typical pattern was that of artisans and laborers from European villages, towns, and cities settling on the land in America rather than of peasants suddenly thrust into strange urban worlds.

Wherever one looks in the arc of the expanding frontier, one finds immigrants at the edge of settlement. As thousands of land-hungry native farmers from southern New England moved one hundred or two hundred miles north into the new grants in the upper Connecticut River valley, they were joined by farmers and artisans from Scotland, who arrived, not after

[19]Fingerhut, "Assimilation of Immigrants," Appendix E; Wokeck, "German Immigration," pp. 260–261; Curtin, *Atlantic Slave Trade*, Table 39.

a generation's stay in the coastal region of America, but directly and immediately, in their first remove from the land of their origins. So too in the
far-northern frontier of New York—a largely uninhabited wilderness of
5,000 square miles, organized only in 1772 as Charlotte County—recent
arrivals from Scotland were the first pioneers. By 1775 Scots seemed to be
everywhere along the expanding frontier—in northern New York and in
North Carolina particularly. By 1774, when the famous Flora MacDonald,
who had protected Bonnie Prince Charlie on the Isle of Skye in his flight
during the Jacobite rebellion of '45, arrived there with the flood tide of
emigrants from the Highlands and the western Scottish islands, there were
an estimated 10,000 first- or second-generation Scots living in the sandy
pineland frontier of Cumberland County, west of Campbellton at the head
of navigation.[20]

What was true of the Scots was true of the other immigrant groups,
except the Africans. As many Irish Protestants as Scots moved through the
American ports of entry and found their way quickly to newly opened
borderlands. The swift opening of the southwestern Pennsylvania frontier
after 1768 was largely the work of the Irish—not only Scotch-Irish migrants
from earlier residences in the coastal settlements but native Ulstermen as
well, who flocked to the frontier in particularly large numbers in the years
1771–1773. By the end of the Revolution they had created a distinctive
Scotch-Irish-American culture in that region—and not only there. They
were also on the Georgia and South Carolina frontiers in large numbers,
and in West Florida, in its earliest years as a British colony. Large groups
of Ulstermen can be found throughout the western range of North Carolina, in northern New York, and in the Kentucky settlements south of the
Ohio. Traces of the Irish are everywhere on the frontiers: towns and
counties called Londonderry, Armagh, Derry, and Donegal can be found
throughout the backcountry areas that were opened in the decade before
the Revolution. A map of their main settlements is almost a map of the
pre-Revolutionary frontier.

The thousands of Germans and Swiss who migrated to British America
in these years were less prone to settle on the farthest frontiers, but neither
did they congregate permanently in or close around the main ports of entry.
They moved quickly to join their countrymen dispersed through the countryside, traveling south through the valley routes, to scatter in settlements
in western Pennsylvania, in the valleys of Virginia, and in inland North and
South Carolina. The English emigrants of this period are more difficult to
trace as a distinct group, but their distribution pattern was also widespread;
many of them, individually and in groups, moved directly to the American
frontier. They too added force to the remarkable expansion of settlement

---

[20]See below, 502–506, 592–597, 604–637. Fingerhut, "Assimilation of Immigrants," *passim.*

in the pre-Revolutionary years. And they compounded, at the same time, the difficulties confronting officials in Britain responsible for colonial policy, as well as the perplexities of landlords whose tenants many of these voyagers had been.[21]

For all of this movement—within North America and from Europe to America—involved major problems of public policy, problems that few of Britain's governing aristocracy could grasp let alone solve, and that led with tragic inevitability toward conflicts that threatened to tear the government apart.

[21]Solon J. Buck and Elizabeth H. Buck, *The Planting of Civilization in Western Pennsylvania* (Pittsburgh, 1939), pp. 145–155; E. Estyn Evans, "The Scotch-Irish: Their Cultural Adaptation and Heritage in the American Old West," in *Essays in Scotch-Irish History*, ed. E. R. R. Green (New York, 1969), esp. pp. 74–86, and Figs. 1 and 2, which map the Scotch-Irish settlements in Pennsylvania and trace their routes of expansion out of western Pennsylvania south through the valley system and west into Tennessee and Kentucky; Leyburn, *The Scotch-Irish*, pt. 3. See also maps of German, Scotch, and Irish settlements in 1775 in Lester Cappon *et al.*, eds., *Atlas of Early American History* (Princeton, 1976), p. 24.

2

The Dilemma of British Policy

Hillsborough's Anxieties

THE close relation between these two problems—the settlement of western lands in America and emigration from Britain—was not, at first, perceived by most British officials and did not play a part in the early and failing efforts of the British government to shape a workable western land policy. The Proclamation of 1763, closing off the trans-Appalachian west except to licensed traders and creating the new colonies of Quebec, East Florida, and West Florida, had nothing directly to do with emigration. It was primarily an effort to sanction formally the commitments made to the Indians during the war by which their trans-Appalachian lands were preserved to them, and hence an effort to prevent border violence, which could develop into renewed international warfare. The aim was a slow and controlled expansion of western settlement and the gradual introduction of civil government in the west as legitimate land purchases were made. All of this was a world apart from the myriad enterprises that constitute emigration—the thousands of transatlantic voyages, the painfully disorienting resettlements in a strange land. Yet even in these early postwar years at least one of the leading British officials involved in western land policy understood the implications of expansion in the American west for British emigration, and his influence in this area of policy making was destined to be powerful, at certain points decisive.

The Earl of Hillsborough, who became president of the Board of Trade just before the Proclamation of 1763 was issued, was an Anglo-Irish landowner with properties in Ireland so extensive that they constituted a world in themselves. Concentrated in County Down, near the center of Irish emigration, these holdings were approaching the 100,000-acre mark they would attain by the time of Hillsborough's death in 1793.[1] Ever concerned for the stability and welfare of a large agricultural laboring class, Hillsborough had seen, long before other British landlords, the dangers of mass emigration to America. In 1753 he had entered fervently into a Parliamentary debate on a bill to create a national census, a debate which in large part centered on whether such an enumeration, revealing annual increases and decreases in the population, would "instruct us when to encourage and when to restrain people from going to settle in our American colonies." Why had Spain's population declined? Surely because of the exodus to its colonies. Multitudes of people flock to America, Hillsborough declared, "for no other reason but because they hope to live better, or to earn more money in those countries than they can do at home," and in this they are "encouraged by hearing every day of poor people having in a few years got great estates there." Many eventually regret their decisions, and therefore no sensible person can deny, Hillsborough said, that at times it would be "for the public good to lay a restraint upon poor people leaving the place of their birth without leave from the magistrates of the place." The officials concerned might grant permission, or they might help the would-be emigrants find employment at home. There are always people, he continued, whose delusive hopes are "so sanguine that they are apt to leave a place where they may live very well" despite the fact that the prospects elsewhere, realistically considered, were no better than at home. Surely, he concluded, in a phrase that epitomizes landlord paternalism, "it would be doing them a service to lay them under some restraint." With a census, the magistracy would know

> when we should encourage or restrain the transmigration of people
> from any one part of the British dominions to another, or when we
> should at the public expence encourage foreigners to go and settle
> in our colonies, which we certainly ought to do if it should appear
> that the number of our people is upon the decline at home.

But there were others who saw dangerous implications in the bill—the regimentation implicit in any national register; the possible revelation to Britain's enemies of its demographic strengths and weaknesses; the undue power the scheme might give to local officials; the cost of administering the census; and the likelihood that the act would be opposed "in a riotous manner, and . . . may raise such a popular flame as will endanger the peace if not the existence of our present government."[2]

[1] W. A. Maguire, *The Downshire Estates in Ireland, 1801–1845* (Oxford, 1972), pp. 1–8; *An Archaeological Survey of County Down* (Belfast, 1966), pp. 408–415.
[2] T. C. Hansard, *The Parliamentary History of England . . .* (London, 1806–1820), XIV, cols. 1317–1365 (Hillsborough's speech is at 1360–1365).

The bill, despite the support of George Grenville and the influential Lord Barrington, was defeated, but Hillsborough's commitment to restraining the exodus from Britain and his understanding of the connection between emigration and the extension of settlement in the American west grew firmer. In the years that followed the Proclamation of 1763—as Americans ignored the prohibition on western settlement, as plans to regulate the Indian trade collapsed for want of financing and political support, and as the Proclamation line was amended, violated, and again amended—Hillsborough's views hardened into a rigid and narrow mercantilism, more and more openly hostile to emigration from Britain.

The purpose of the colonies, he argued in the British cabinet, was to benefit "this kingdom"; the North American colonies were to contribute to the benefit of the kingdom through commerce and the production of goods closely related to commerce. The American fisheries should be enlarged, the naval-stores industry encouraged, lumber production increased, and agricultural yields suitable for consumption in the sugar islands should be improved. But as for settling the western lands, he wrote, what sense did it make to encourage the dispersion of the population into inland communities which would not further the primary goals of empire—which would in fact conflict with imperial policy? Not only would it be difficult to keep such remote colonies "in just subordination to and dependence upon this kingdom," but these settlements would inevitably draw settlers both from the productive seaboard colonies and, indirectly if not directly, from Britain and Ireland. "Terribly afraid of dispeopling Ireland," as Franklin reported in 1766, Hillsborough strongly opposed settling the western lands and sought in every way possible to keep the inhabitants of the British Isles from abandoning the lands they traditionally worked and flocking to the colonies.[3]

In 1768 Hillsborough assumed the key post of secretary of state for the colonies, an office he held for four years—years that proved crucial for the interlocked problems of western lands policy and British emigration. In that influential position he stepped up his opposition to western settlements

[3] Hillsborough to Lt. Gen. Thomas Gage, London, July 31, 1770, in *Documents of the American Revolution,* ed. K. G. Davies (Shannon, Ireland, 1976–1981), II, 153–156; Benjamin Franklin to William Franklin [Sept. 12, 1766], in *Papers of Benjamin Franklin,* ed. Leonard Labaree *et al.* (New Haven, 1959–), XIII, 414. Hillsborough's personal view was expanded into the official memorandum of the Board of Trade (of which he was president) advising against establishing inland colonies (a proposition "entirely new," based on principles "different from what has hitherto been the policy of this kingdom," and detrimental to the interests of Great Britain); *Documents of the Revolution,* V, 79–89. The fear of increased emigration, Hillsborough wrote in this comprehensive policy statement, "has for some time past had so great weight with this Board that it has induced us to deny our concurrence to many proposals of grants of land even in those parts of the continent of America where in all other respects we are of opinion that it consists with the true policy of this kingdom to encourage settlements." *Ibid.,* p. 89.

and to emigration from Britain—by reiterating his mercantilist principles to the military leaders in the American west, by dismantling western forts whenever possible, by rejecting or limiting petitions for American land grants by would-be leaders of emigrant groups.[4] But the tide was running strongly against him. The massive array of land speculators and western trading interests, working through an intricate network of lobbyists in London, was overpowering. Not only were these interests powerful in themselves, and not only were they connected with every important agency of government, but they had among their leaders Benjamin Franklin, a figure of international renown, a publicist of genius, and a political manipulator of experience and skill. The conflict that developed between Franklin and Hillsborough was inescapable: it was a direct product of the associated problems of western expansion and emigration; it flowed from deep imperatives on both sides; and it was embittered by intense personal animosity.

Franklin, who was in effect ambassador from America at the Court of St. James's, was the spearhead of the most ambitious plans for western settlement and for the development of American society generally. He had long been fascinated by the remarkable growth and diversity of the American population, and he sensed the potential strength of the American economy. He knew that America's economic and demographic growth meant power—all the power needed, ultimately, to assert the colonies' rights against Britain without bloodshed. For America, therefore, social growth involving territorial expansion was an ultimate political weapon as well as a necessary foundation for progress and individual happiness. The enemy, to him, both symbolically and personally, was Hillsborough. He had disliked the Irish nobleman—whom Washington too disliked for his "malignant disposition towards Americans"—when he first met him in the mid-sixties, and by the early seventies his dislike had turned to hatred. Hillsborough's character, Franklin wrote, was a compound of "conceit, wrong-headedness, obstinacy and passion"; he was "as double and deceitful as any man I ever met with"; "the most unequal in his treatment of people, the most insincere, and the most wrong-headed." Hillsborough had rejected Franklin's credentials as agent for Massachusetts "with something," Franklin wrote, "between a smile and a sneer," and he had first lavished hospitality on him but then had instructed his servants not to let him inside the door. To the American, Hillsborough embodied all the corruption of an aristocratic society and the infuriating arrogance of its privileged leaders. Their obstruction of growth, progress, and the betterment of ordinary

---

[4] Hillsborough to Gage, July 31, 1770, and Dec. 4, 1771, *Documents of the Revolution*, II, 153–156; III, 244–246; V, 132–133; J. P. MacLean, *An Historical Account of the Settlements of Scotch Highlanders in America . . .* (Cleveland, 1900), pp. 450–453.

people was an inescapable consequence, Franklin believed, of their social role.[5]

But Franklin's conflict with Hillsborough had more immediate and less personal roots. Franklin knew of the Irishman's fear of emigration; he knew, as did others, that in discussions in the Privy Council Hillsborough had opposed settlements on the Mississippi on the ground "that the mother country could not, at present, spare any migration." And it was Hillsborough, Franklin knew, who had delayed and was attempting to destroy the proposed Vandalia colony, the greatest effort of the postwar years to colonize the trans-Appalachian west. That plan of a squadron of the most powerful political and commercial operators in Britain and America to turn a twenty-million-acre grant on the Ohio into a huge inland colony fell into the maelstrom of factional fighting among Britain's leading politicians. All of them eyed the project warily, calculating carefully their own possible profit if the proposal went through, some of them scheming to use the issue to force both Hillsborough and North out of office. After a series of Byzantine maneuvers within the cabinet and the Board of Trade, which recommended against the plan, the Privy Council approved the project. To the Irish landlord the issues involved transcended all others. Abandoned by the Privy Council, Lord North, and the King, and refusing to enforce a decision he so strongly opposed, he resigned as secretary of state for the colonies. To have remained in office, his undersecretary, William Knox, observed, would have obliged him to preside over the founding of the Vandalia colony, "recal [sic] all his own orders and contradict himself in a thousand instances." His many enemies, and especially Americans seeking land grants in the west, were greatly relieved. Lord North was amazed. Attempting to hold his fragile ministry together, he viewed the struggle over the petition for the Ohio lands as "a foolish business." Failing to see the profound social implications of the struggle, he could no more understand the Privy Council's approval of the scheme than Hillsborough's resignation. But North's cynical and amused bewilderment ("I am myself

[5]Washington to Thomas Lewis, Feb. 17, 1774, in *Writings of George Washington*, ed. John C. Fitzpatrick (Washington, D.C., 1931–44), III, 184; Franklin to Samuel Cooper, London, Feb. 5, 1771; to William Franklin, London, Aug. 19[–22], 1772; to William Franklin, July 14, 1773; ["Franklin's Account of His Audience with Hillsborough"]; to William Franklin, Jan. 30, 1772, all in *Franklin Papers*, XVIII, 24; XIX, 258; XX, 310; XVIII, 9–16; XIX, 47–49. By 1776 even George III had a poor opinion of Hillsborough, though he had repeatedly appointed him to high office: "I do not know a man of less judgment than Lord Hillsborough." Lewis Namier and John Brooke, *The House of Commons, 1754–1790* (London, 1964), II, 627. Franklin's view of the relation of British emigration to the growth of American power and influence was widely shared, in America as well as in Britain. "The growing population of the colonies," Charles Carroll of Carrollton wrote, "increased by such a considerable annual influx of newcomers, bids fair to render British America in a century or two the most populous and of course the most potent part of the world. I fancy many in England begin to entertain the same opinion." Charles Carroll to William Graves, Sept. 7, 1773, *Maryland Historical Magazine*, 32 (1937), 219.

Benjamin Franklin. Portrait by David Martin, London, 1766. One of Franklin's favorite portraits of himself, it presents him as he wished to appear in his triumphant years in London: thoughtful, analytical (he faces a bust of Isaac Newton), at peace with the world and himself, yet engaged, calmly, in everyday affairs.

The Earl of Hillsborough. Portrait by John Downman. To Franklin the embodiment of aristocratic hauteur and an enemy of American interests, Hillsborough, secretary of state for the American department (1768–1772), refused Franklin's credentials as agent of Massachusetts "with something," Franklin wrote, "between a smile and a sneer."

incapable of reason, for upon the maturest consideration . . . I can not help thinking all the parties in the wrong") did him no credit. Hillsborough on the one side and the Vandalia speculators on the other correctly understood the immensity of the stakes involved. By the time Hillsborough resigned, in August 1772, the problems of emigration and expansion into the American west had become dangerously inflamed, and the connection between them was beginning to be widely understood.[6]

"America That Land of Promise, Is Their Cry"

By 1773 it was commonly believed that emigration was leading to virtual depopulation in certain regions of the British Isles—not everywhere, but in particular territories of the kingdom, and indeed not in the populous and highly urbanized core region of southeastern England from which the largest number of emigrants came. The steady, prolific exodus from that area was seldom complained of: there emigration did not constitute a social problem. Complaints, reflecting fears of radical social disturbance resulting from emigration, centered in the northern regions. Reports from Ireland were particularly ominous. An authoritative summary, which circulated widely, contained startling figures. It stated, first, that between July 1769 and March 1771, 5,870 tons of emigrant shipping had departed from five main Irish ports, which meant, by the traditional calculation, the same number of emigrant departures. Then in the two years that had followed, the report said, the figure had tripled, to 17,400; and in the course of the next fifteen months (March 1773–June 1774) no fewer than 20,450 emigrants had left. The monthly average, therefore, had quintupled in four years. And another report, of 1773, estimated the freight cost of what were believed to be 16,250 departures from northern Ireland to America in 1771 and 1772 at £60,725; it stated too that in the previous five or six years Ulster had "been drained of one fourth of its trading cash and the like proportion of the manufacturing people" by the emigration. Now no longer comprised of "the very meanest of the people" but of industrial workers, farmers, and people "of

---

[6] *Virginia Gazette* (Rind), Oct. 15, 1772; [William Knox], "Lord Hillsborough's Resignation," Historical Manuscripts Commission, *Report on Manuscripts in Various Collections*, VI (Dublin, 1909), pp. 253–255; William Knox to [Gov. James Grant of East Florida], Sept. 4, 1772, Macpherson-Grant Papers, bundle 254; North to Dartmouth, Bushy Park, Aug. 3, 1772, Dartmouth Papers, Canada, V, 5788–5789. Phineas Lyman's jubilation that Hillsborough would now be transferred to "where his ill will will not be so likely to injure me by preventing the emanation of royal goodness" was a typical American reaction. Lyman to Earl of Loudoun, Suffield, Conn., Papers of the Marquess of Bute, NRA(S)/0631, Scottish Record Office, Edinburgh. For a defense of Hillsborough's opposition to distant colonies and to continued emigration, see "Reasons for Lord Hillsborough's Resignation," *Edinburgh Advertiser*, Sept. 4–8, 1772. The entire episode is discussed in Peter Marshall, "Lord Hillsborough, Samuel Wharton and the Ohio Grant, 1769–1775," *English Historical Review*, 80 (1965), 717–739. Cf. *Virginia Gazette* (Rind), Jan. 14, 1773.

some property," the removals were "sensibly felt in this country. . . . Where the evil will end, remains in the womb of time to determine."[7]

At times concern in Ireland seems to have turned to panic. The "incredible" emigration there was said to threaten the future of Ireland's industry as well as its agriculture; in the end it could only lead to a forced reduction of both rents and taxes. Ireland's excise revenues, the secretary to the lord lieutenant of Ireland declared, were as drastically reduced by emigration as by poverty. The Irish poor, who emigrate "in swarms to America," must be allowed at least enough sustenance to be able to pay taxes: "if the cow is to be milked, she must be fed." Belfast newspapers teemed with letters from recent emigrants, many of them instructive, cautionary, warning of the lies and avarice of shipmasters, the swindling advertisements of American land speculators, and the myriad difficulties of resettlement. Some lamented the circumstances that had forced thousands from their homes. "How melancholy is the prospect when poverty at home compels honest and industrious families to expose their lives and quit their established settlements to seek, perhaps in an advanced age, that support amongst strangers in a new world which avarice and corruption have denied them in the land of their nativity."

America was a dream—"a dream of escape," but, to some of these Irish emigrant correspondents, a dark and frightening dream too. Tales were published of savagery on the wild Indian frontiers, and especially of the brutality of "the people called Cracker, who live above Augusta in the province of Georgia." But stories of the dangers posed by savage natives and "associated banditti . . . committing all manner of robberies and violences" could not stay the exodus. "The spirit of emigration hath seized our people," a much-reprinted letter from Dublin stated, "and the several counties hitherto famous for the residence of the linen manufacturers, are now almost dwindled into dreary wastes. The land lies uncultivated; and . . . scarcely a vessel sails from Ireland bound to any of the plantations but what is filled with multitudes of useful artisans, their wives and children. It is to be hoped that some method may be taken to put a stop to so alarming an

---

[7] *Leeds Mercury*, July 19, 1774 (for somewhat different figures, see *Belfast News Letter*, April 16, 1773); *Nova-Scotia Gazette*, July 27, 1773. The relative prosperity of the emigrants, discussed in various contexts below, was a recurrent theme in the newspaper accounts. It reached an apparent climax in a report from London of Oct. 20, 1774, in *Nova-Scotia Gazette*, Feb. 21, 1775: "above one hundred gentlemen, ladies, and families of moderate fortunes intend next May to embark for North America with 5 or 600 families of sober and industrious husbandmen, artificers, and manufactures who cannot get bread in England. Those who have money intend to purchase lands at a very moderate rate, and improve them. . . . Ladies of £2,000 fortune in the funds cannot, in these expensive times, live with tolerabl[e] decency in the cheapest part of England. In America, they can live with all conveniencies and comforts of life upon the produce of that sum carried over there. The plan of this extensive design will be published that more persons may take the advantage of going in company with some gentlemen and ladies of the most respectable characters in this kingdom, who will put themselves at the head of this benevolent design."

evil; for if the numbers of inhabitants constitute the riches of a state, Heaven knows, Ireland will soon be the poorest country under the canopy of Heaven."[8]

The reports from Scotland were even more alarming, and more circumstantial. In 1771 a land agent on the Isle of Skye reported such losses and such elaborate plans for further emigration that if nothing were done major estates would become "wastelands" and land would go begging for buyers. Observers of the exodus from the Western Isles of Scotland noted in 1772 that in the course of the previous four years £10,000 had been taken out of Britain by the emigrants to America, and that "unless some speedy remedy is fallen upon by the government and landholders" Scotland would be fatally depleted, economically as well as demographically. And more than that: "the continual emigrations from Ireland and Scotland will soon render our [American] colonies independent on the mother-country."

The problem was well known; it had become part of popular culture, widely considered and generally regretted. The bard Rob Donn and the poet Donald Matheson bewailed the conditions that drove people from the land: the poverty and disarray of once proud and respectable Highland families "with their heads brought low . . . the land full of distress." The emigrating Scots, said the poet, were like Children of Israel oppressed by "enslaving" landlords. "Oh praise be to Him of highest glory, who opened a way out there and prepared sustenance for them." For from America, it was said in Sutherlandshire, had come "such favourable accounts . . . setting forth the richness of the county [sic], the cheapness of living, and the certain prospects of bettering their fortunes etc. . . . that half the people of this country . . . would emigrate if they were able."[9]

The problem seemed ubiquitous, inescapable. From Bristol came reports that "the spirit of emigration has begun to show itself in the western parts of the kingdom." From Portsmouth came word that the exodus was spreading south and that "captains, carpenters and laborers may then become as scarce as guineas." From the Spitalfields textile center in London it was reported that over two thousand weavers and their families had left for the colonies in the previous two years. Lord Dartmouth, owner of estates throughout England, many of whose inhabitants were troubled and restless, was confronted with the issue directly and personally within a

[8] Joseph Redington et al., eds., Calendar of Home Office Papers of the Reign of George III (London, 1878–1899), IV, #1360; Belfast News Letter, June 8, 1773, Nov. 6, 1767, Feb. 12, 1768; letter from Dublin, Aug. 16, 1773, published in London, Aug. 24, and reprinted in the Virginia Gazette (Rind), Nov. 11.

[9] Alexander MacLeod to [?], Glendale, March 11, 1771, MacLeod MSS, box 62; Scots Magazine, 34 (Sept., 1772), 515–516; Ian Grimble, "Emigration in the Time of Rob Donn, 1714–1778," Scottish Studies, 7 (1963), 140, 141; "Unto the Honourable the Vice Admiral of Zetland, Answers and Defences for James Hogg . . . against the Petitions & Complaints of Alexander Mackay & Others," Nov. 5, 1773, Hogg Papers.

The 2nd Earl of Dartmouth. Portrait by Thomas Gainsborough. Mild-mannered, a religious dissenter sympathetic to American interests, and an investor himself in land in Nova Scotia and Florida, Dartmouth seemed to the colonists a great improvement over Hillsborough as secretary for the American department (1772–1775); but he, too, was concerned about the loss of tenants on his English estates.

month of succeeding Hillsborough as colonial secretary. "I am importuned by two hundred families," one John More of Rothiemurchus, Inverness-shire, wrote Dartmouth, "to intreat of Your Grace to let them have the encouragments given by government (if any) for settling in North America." His people, More wrote, were farmers, "honest, sober, and industrious," who were being forced out of their homes by an excess of population, the impoverishment of the soil, and the oppression of the landlords. Confident of Dartmouth's "principles as a nobleman and a Christian," More begged him to feel for their distress as members of "the human species" and help them to emigrate. He hoped that Dartmouth would direct his clerks to arrange a meeting with them anywhere in Britain within a month or so, so that the people might be delivered from their "present miseries."

Later, in 1775, Dartmouth would receive from the Bishop of Derry in Ireland a summary of the political fears of the consequences of emigration that had been circulating in the early seventies. The bishop attributed much of "the rebellious spirit" in the central colonies in America to the emigration from Ireland "of near thirty three thousand fanatical & hungry republicans in the course of a very few years." A few months earlier the Presbytery of the Isle of Lewis in the Outer Hebrides had set aside a day for public thanksgiving when a favorable harvest and "other concurring causes" seemed to have "cured the people of the epidemical phrenzy which had seized them for migrating to America."[10]

But it was Dr. Johnson, after his famous tour of the Highlands and the Western Isles with Boswell in 1773, who sounded the most eloquent alarms. He was shocked by what he termed the "epidemick disease of wandering" that he found in his travels. The exodus of whole neighborhoods, moving in such numbers that departure scarcely seemed an exile at all, threatened, he wrote, "a total secession" of the Highlanders. And the loss of even one person in such an inhospitable place as the Hebrides "leaves a lasting vacuity, for nobody born in any other parts of the world will choose this country for his residence, and an island once depopulated will remain a desert as long as the present facility of travel gives every one who is discontented and unsettled the choice of his abode." But the tragedy of the emigrations, Johnson believed, lay not simply in the demographic and economic losses. The subtler and deeper catastrophe was cultural; and he evoked a haunting image of people scattered in the wilderness spaces of America where their culture, their spiritual and moral integument, and their familiar, time-sanctioned ways of life simply dissolved, leaving them bereft and primitive, and Britain reduced. The thousands that were leaving for the colonies, he wrote, are forever lost, "for a nation scattered in the boundless regions of America resembles rays diverging from a focus. All the rays remain, but the heat is gone. Their power consisted in their concentration: when they are dispersed, they have no effect."[11]

---

[10]*Lloyd's Evening Post*, Oct. 15, 1773; *Caledonian Mercury*, May 2, 1774; *York Courant*, July 5, 1774; John More to Dartmouth, Rothiemurchus, Sept. 10, 1772, and Bishop of Derry to Dartmouth, Derry, May 23, 1775, Dartmouth Papers, Stafford, D(W) 1778/II/418, 1275; Minutes of the Presbytery of Lewis, Dec. 2, 1774, CH 2/473/1.

[11]Samuel Johnson, *A Journey to the Western Islands of Scotland*, ed. Mary Lascelles (New Haven, 1971), pp. 96, 99, 131.

Later this profound remark would find echoes,[12] but at the time it was the manifest, demographic and economic, losses involved that created the general public concern, a concern that grew wildly as the crisis in Anglo-American political relations swelled to the point of explosion. Between 700 and 800 people were reported to have left the port of Stornoway in the Outer Hebrides on a single day in June 1773, a month in which 800 emigrants on the Isle of Skye completed arrangements for their voyage to North Carolina. On September 1, 425 more were observed leaving Maryburgh in the western Highlands, carrying with them £6,000; a month later, 775 more were known to have left Stromness in the Orkneys. At the end of the year, in the weeks when Johnson and Boswell were completing their journey to Scotland, *The Weekly Magazine, or Edinburgh Amusement* printed four essays and a four-part letter on "the spirit of emigration which seems to be epidemic through Great Britain and Ireland," and then in 1774 continued with sixteen more essays on the subject—an average of two a month between March and October. *The Edinburgh Magazine and Review* published two especially weighty essays on the same theme, and the *Scots Magazine* kept pace. In June 1774 it was said that continued emigration would make the west of Scotland a grass park; in October that the deserted kingdom would come to be the resort of owls and dragons. In November *Lloyd's Evening Post* published a short futuristic drama, dated 1974, in which two visitors "from the empire of America" tour the ruins of London—a scene of utter desolation similar to the famous Piranesi prints of Roman ruins: empty, rubble-strewn streets, a single broken wall remaining of the Parliament buildings, Whitehall a turnip field, Westminster Abbey a stable, the Inns of Court a pile of stones "possessed by hawks and rooks," and St. Paul's, its cupola collapsed, open to the sky. And why all this "stately desolation"? Why had "this antient and once most august city fallen to a similar decay and ruin with Balbec, Persepolis, Palmyra, Athens, and Rome"? Why had its "sun . . . set in the West"? A lonely British survivor scrabbling through the ruins "with a dejected countenance" explains why. The posterity of the city's once great merchants, he tells the American tourists, "are now scattered over the whole world, and more especially have they settled in Imperial America, whither they were followed by most of our artizans and mechanics." This, he says, "was the original cause of our poverty and of your power and grandeur."

The importance of America's benefits from Britain's losses was a constant theme. The colonies, it was reported,

---

[12][Thomas Douglas, 5th] Earl of Selkirk, *Observations on the Present State of the Highlands of Scotland* . . ., 2d ed. (Edinburgh, 1806), p. 3; and Francis Horner's review of the book in *The Economic Writings of Francis Horner* . . ., ed. Frank W. Fetter (London, 1957), p. 116.

are already extended beyond a due proportion to its people at home; and every sensible person must foresee that our fellow subjects in America will, in less than half a century, form a state much more numerous and powerful than their mother-country. At this time, were they inclined to throw off their dependency, it would be very difficult for this kingdom to keep them in subjection. What then will they be in fifty years time when their numbers will be more than trebled by natural propagation only, without the addition of thousands who fly every year to that happy country, where they can live with freedom and get their bread with ease?[13]

The magnitudes involved grew with the telling, and exerted their own fascination. So great was the flow of emigration, a London correspondent wrote, that "was it possible to erect Pont Neuf from hence to the western world, the toll, if any, would exceed that of Black Frairs [sic] [bridge in London], and every one would speak well of the bridge which carried him safe over." The whole of Ayrshire, another wrote, "would in a few days be left very thinly inhabited" if New York and Philadelphia were as close as Belfast and Dublin, for to the ordinary people of the county "America alone is considered as the land of their deliverance." And indeed in Ayrshire, severely hit by the spectacular crash of the Ayr bank and the collapse of ambitious efforts at agricultural reform, merchants were placing bets on the number of emigrants who had left the countryside between October 1763 and October 1773. James Inglis, an Edinburgh shipper engaged in the emigrant trade, volunteered to help his correspondents win their bet by helping them establish the correct numbers: "I'm affraid its difficult but I will write my friends and get you the best account I can as soon as possible." But the most dramatic expression of this universal concern, which like the political crisis was reaching a climax late in 1773, came from a writer in Yorkshire. "The emigration of people from all parts of England," he wrote, "is very amazing indeed, and if no stop is put to it England will really be drained of multitudes of mechanics of all sorts, also people of considerable property; ships are daily taken up for this purpose, and the spirit of emigration daily encreases:—America that land of promise, is their cry."[14]

[13] *London Chronicle*, July 19, 1773 (for slightly higher figures, see *York Courant*, Oct. 5, 1773); *South-Carolina Gazette*, Sept. 13, 1773, quoting a dispatch from Edinburgh, July 2; *Lloyd's Evening Post*, Sept. 22–24, 1773; *Scots Magazine*, 35 (Oct., 1773), 557; *Weekly Magazine, or Edinburgh Amusement*: the four essays—Oct. 12, Nov. 25, and two on Dec. 23, 1773; the letter—Nov. 4, 11, 18, and Dec. 16, 1773; the 1774 pieces—March 24, 31, April 14, 28, May 5, 26, June 30 (two), July 14, 21, Aug. 4, Sept. 1, 8 (two), Oct. 13, 27; *Edinburgh Magazine and Review*, 2 (June and July, 1774); *Scots Magazine*, e.g., 36 (Feb., 1774), 64; *Lloyd's Evening Post*, Nov. 25–28, 1774, and Sept. 24–27, 1773.
[14] *Nova-Scotia Gazette*, Aug. 9, 1774, quoting a dispatch from London, May 12; "Nauta," in *Weekly Magazine, or Edinburgh Amusement*, Sept. 8, 1774; Inglis to James Wilson and Son, Edinburgh,

Explanations

These ominous reports and rumors were not impersonal commentaries by objective observers. They were for the most part communications from concerned people who cared deeply about the outcome. Reporting in alarm the facts they knew, they groped for explanations of what was happening and suggested remedies for the future. A flood of commentary on the causes of emigration appeared amid the news accounts of the early 1770s.

There was no mystery about the causes of the emigration, the lord lieutenant of Ireland wrote in the summer of 1773: rack renting, landlords' absenteeism, and the collapse of the linen industry—all this stimulated, he believed, by the conspiratorial activities of the Hearts of Steel, a band of violent insurrectionists who rioted in protest against their landlords' rent increases, until they themselves joined the emigration to North America. Much evidence was available to support this explanation. The years 1770–1772 were known to have marked the climax of fifty years of increasing rents in Ireland. In Hillsborough's County Down rents in the early seventies were said to be triple what they had been a generation before. In 1770 the absentee Earl of Donegall demanded fees for renewing leases on his estate in County Antrim that were three or four times annual rents, an innovation that touched off a wave of rioting not only in Antrim but also in Counties Down, Londonderry, Tyrone, and Armagh. And in the midst of this sudden escalation of rents—by which, it was said, "the very marrow is screwed out of our bones, and our lives are even become so burdensome to us . . . that we do not care whether we live or die"—the linen industry collapsed as a result of a sudden drop in foreign demand. The cost of bread rose to famine levels, and the laboring population suffered severely.[15]

The absenteeism of landlords was commonly understood to be a major, if indirect, cause of emigration in Ireland. Though the Anglo-Irish land-owners who continued to live in Ireland led lavish and profligate lives and did little to improve the condition of the peasants, they were at least witnesses to the miseries of the laboring population and were susceptible to personal appeals for relief. But many of the largest landlords in Ireland were permanent absentees; their drainage of capital from the island was understood to be crippling the economy. Arthur Young reported in 1779

March 8, 1774, Inglis Letterbook, CS 96/2259; extract of a letter from York, England, June 24, 1774, in *Virginia Gazette or, Norfolk Intelligencer*, Sept. 1, 1774.

[15] *Cal. Home Office Papers*, III, #1525; IV, #235; *York Courant*, April 17, 1772, for an account from Lisbourne of "inhuman landlords" and insurrections by the Hearts of Steel and Hearts of Oak; R. J. Dickson, *Ulster Emigration to Colonial America, 1718–1775* ([1966], Antrim, 1976), pp. 69–81.

that absentee landlords drew off £732,200 a year in rents. He was not far off the mark: a modern scholar's estimate is £600,000 in the 1770s, which was one-eighth of the total rental of Ireland. And a corrupt political establishment completed Ireland's bankruptcy. Young believed the pension list drained another £84,591 from the country each year. And beyond all this, in the distractions of Ireland, was the ancient struggle between religious groups, not so much, in the north, between Catholics and Protestants, as between a brutally intolerant Anglican establishment and the nonconformist Protestant mass, largely Presbyterian, which still suffered from both remembered and actual discrimination.

The whole of Ireland was reported to be pitifully impoverished, hence naturally a source for emigration. Ulster was assumed to be better off than the Catholic south and west of Ireland—a land universally reported to be swarming with beggars, the peasants living so wretchedly in cabins no better than pigsties that the sight of them made the hearts of even the most frivolous travelers ache with pity—but the difference between north and south was believed to be marginal: just enough to make migration possible. The question, witnesses reported, is not why the Protestant Irish turned to emigration as a solution of their miseries but why they did not leave in greater numbers than they did.[16]

Accounts from Scotland, and to a lesser extent from Yorkshire and elsewhere in northern England, stressed some of the same causes of emigration—precipitous raises in rents; collapse of local industries; landlords' absenteeism, though not on the scale of Ireland; the almost universal belief that "North America is the best poor man's country in the world"; and the knowledge that transatlantic transportation was commonly available. But there were special conditions in Scotland, conditions that bore on social organization and cultural disarray, compounded with the evident economic distress. The complex configuration of forces that lay behind the Scottish emigration challenged the analytical powers of some of the keenest minds in Britain.[17]

Most commentators agreed that conversion to commercial agriculture, enclosures, and profiteering in rents were general causes of the Scottish emigration. The Highland chieftains, it was said again and again, were "cruel, hard-hearted and oppressive," having only one object in mind in letting their lands—"raising as much money from them as possible." Some

[16] *Arthur Young's Tour in Ireland (1776–1779)*, ed. Arthur W. Hutton (London, 1892), II, 116–117, 40, 47–49, 56–58; L. M. Cullen, *An Economic History of Ireland since 1660* (London, 1972), pp. 45, 83.
[17] E.g., *A Candid Enquiry into the Causes of the Late and the Intended Migrations from Scotland. In a Letter to J—— R—— Esq.; Lanark-shire* (Glasgow, [1771]), esp. pp. 39, 50, 53. For modern interpretations of conditions in Scotland, see Eric Richards, *A History of the Highland Clearances* (London, 1982), chaps. 1–5; J. M. Bumsted, *The People's Clearance: Highland Emigration to British North America, 1770–1815* (Edinburgh, 1982), chaps. 1, 2. The description of the American colonies as "the best poor man's country" was endlessly repeated: e.g., below, 174, 504.

landlords profited, but whole populations of farm laborers suffered, especially as their numbers increased. For while the Scottish population had grown very slowly in the first half of the eighteenth century—perhaps a total of 20% between 1707 and 1755—thereafter the rate of increase rose rapidly. Between 1755 and 1770 the population probably grew another 10%, and this increased growth rate in itself magnified the pressure on subsistence and increased the number of farm laborers with no reliable means of support. Relatively few of the unemployed or the chronically underemployed could find sufficient work in the growing linen industry, which in any case slumped severely in 1772–1773; in woolen manufactures, struck repeatedly by recessions; or in the processing of kelp, a marketable product of seaweed that was becoming important on the coastal lands. There was overcrowding in the most fertile areas, and everywhere dislocation caused by increases in rent and evictions from properties converted to pasturage.[18]

These perceptions of economic conditions shocked contemporaries, even those familiar with the usual poverty of peasant life, and they found the bearing of these conditions on emigration to be obvious. Thomas Pennant, touring the Highlands in 1772, made the connection automatically. He found in the northern county of Sutherland a destitute and torpid people:

> their hovels most miserable, made of poles, wattled and covered with thin sods. . . . Dispirited and driven to despair by bad management, crowds are now passing, emaciated with hunger, to the eastern coast on the report of a ship being there loaden with meal. Numbers of the miserables of this country were now emigrating: they wandered in a state of desperation; too poor to pay, they madly sell themselves for their passage, preferring a temporary bondage in a strange land to starving for life in their native soil.[19]

But shrewder reporters than Pennant saw deeper causes behind the emigration than simply poverty, which was the common condition of so much of the eighteenth-century world. Dr. Johnson, contemplating deserted lands

---

[18] *Edinburgh Magazine and Review*, 1 (Nov., 1773), 104; *The Present Conduct of the Chieftains and Proprietors of Lands in the Highlands of Scotland*, 2d ed. ([Edinburgh], 1773), esp. pp. 3–5. There are no reliable population statistics for Scotland before the first regular census of 1801 except for the year 1755. The percentages of growth given here are based on Sir John Sinclair's "plausible guess" of 1,048,000 for 1707, Dr. Alexander Webster's "reasonably reliable" figure of 1,265,000 for 1755, and the 1801 census total of 1,608,000. Cf. T. C. Smout, *A History of the Scottish People, 1560–1830*, rev. ed. (Glasgow, 1972), pp. 240–241, chaps. 13, 14. On the severe depression in the linen industry and its relation to unemployment and emigration, see petitions of Scottish manufacturers in *Journals of the House of Commons*, XXXIV (Nov. 26, 1772, to Sept. 15, 1774), 557–632; Alastair J. Durie, *The Scottish Linen Industry in the Eighteenth Century* (Edinburgh, 1979), pp. 22, 64, 76, 80.

[19] [Thomas Pennant], *A Tour in Scotland, and Voyage to the Hebrides; 1772*, 2d ed. (London, 1776), pt. 1, pp. 365–366.

on the Isle of Skye, saw greed everywhere: he cursed the avarice both of the landlords and of the emigration agents who enticed away the desperate Highlanders by false representations of America as the "fortunate islands," luring them into a life of endless toil in the wilderness. But the ultimate cause of the threatening depopulation, he believed, lay not so much in greed and the resulting poverty as in the destruction of the ancient social structure of the clans, the social cohesion that had united lairds and the meanest cottagers in quasi-feudal relationships and which had been systematically destroyed by the punitive laws that had followed the rebellion of '45. For these laws—which abolished private jurisdictions, exiled those rebellious Highland chiefs who had survived the slaughter, handed over their estates to a commission of modernizing Lowland gentry, banned the wearing of the traditional dress, and outlawed all weapons in private hands—had not merely stripped the chiefs of their public functions but had destroyed the social organization of the old clan system. This was the main problem, Johnson said; and somehow it must be solved—somehow the lost social cohesion must be restored if the exodus was to be contained.[20]

Johnson's understanding of the social roots of the Highland emigration was shared by other perceptive observers, though their solution to the problem differed from his. Lord Kames was also concerned with the social costs of emigration, and condemned the land-grabbing tactics of profiteering landlords, "their pride swelling with their riches," and their brutal treatment of their tenants. Not only were they driving out of the country "every man of spirit who has the prospect of more kindly bread elsewhere" but they were destroying all the arts and sciences and even discouraging procreation. But the most elaborate analysis of the roots and costs of the Highland emigration was that of Henry Dundas, the lord advocate of Scotland, member of Parliament, and at age thirty-three well on his way to becoming the most powerful political figure in Scotland and for some years in England as well.

Dundas, a rigorous, unbending imperialist in the Anglo-American political crisis, agreed that "a precipitant and injudicious rise of rents" was a cause of emigration, but only in *certain* parts of Scotland, not everywhere. The "universality of the disease," affecting areas where rents had *not* been raised, required a deeper explanation. The true cause, he explained in an essay-length letter, "is deeper rooted." Like Dr. Johnson, he believed the origins lay in the legislation that followed the rebellion of '45, but he traced a different path from cause to effect. In the old days, the self-respect of the Highland chieftains had rested on their "influence in the country," and the importance of their estates had lain not in the monetary rents they produced but in "what I call a rent in men." "Idle men" on these estates were

[20]Johnson, *Journey to the Western Islands*, pp. 89–96, 99.

*Henry Dundas (later Viscount Melville). Portrait by John Rising. A pow-
erful politician even as a young man, solicitor general of Scotland
1766–1775, lord advocate 1775–1783, he understood his native Scotland thoroughly, and shrewdly analyzed the social forces behind the
emigration of the 1770s.*

considered in the years before the rebellion to be valuable, for "in proportion as his clan was numerous and his estate covered with inhabitants, [the
chieftain] felt himself great and respectable."

This close binding of chieftain and dependent, Dundas believed, was
particularly important because the Highlands had always had a surplus
population. When the new legislation stripped the chieftains of their autonomous authority—their "interest and connection"—and hence their prestige, they lost the veneration and respect of their dependents, whose spirits
in turn became covered with "gloom and damp." More important, the
chieftains, no longer motivated "to have their estates covered with inhabitants" to serve as retainers and personal troops, had begun to think of their
dependents simply as tenants and of themselves as landlords rather than as

chiefs, and had turned to maximizing the commercial value of their lands. In this way, as a result of the perhaps unavoidable "civilizing [of] the Highlands . . . by dissolving the clanships," the "strong cement and bond of union" within the clans had been dissolved, mutual respect and responsibility had been destroyed, and there had developed on the one hand venal profiteering in rents and, on the other, a mass exodus from the land.

But the exodus that had resulted was not a normal, familiar kind of migration, Dundas explained. There had always been emigration from the Highlands. The earlier migrants, however, Dundas said, had not left for America. They had, rather, moved off to the Lowlands, where there was a chronic labor shortage. Traditionally they had supplied "more than half of our [the Lowlands'] day labourers, of our menial servants, our chairmen, porters, of our workmen of every kind." Now, however, the Highlanders, "a set of hardy and brave men," because they were neglected by their natural protectors and leaders, were "induced to look for protection upon the other side of the Atlantic, or, to speak more properly, are induced to wander there for want of that cherishment and protection their fathers had felt in their old habitation." Somehow, and quickly, Dundas concluded, a "radical cure for the emigration" must be devised if the progressive corruption of the Highland society and the devastation of the Lowlands economy were to be controlled.[21]

The theme of corruption ran heavily through the many analyses of the northern emigration that were written in the middle seventies. Some accounts, like Dundas's, were hardheaded. Others were emotive. "When a chieftain left his own hall before 1745 to partake of southern luxury," "A Highlander" wrote in 1774, though he might be inferior in ability and fortune to others, "was he not received with the utmost honour & respect, and was not his company courted by all those who pride themselves in the rank of their associates? . . . Was he not smiled on by his sovereign? Was he not caressed by the great? . . . How alas! are they changed. . . . When one of them comes into company now-a-days he is a very inferior person indeed if a rich nabob or planter happens to be present." Faced with this radical change of fortune and status after the '45, what could the Highland chieftains do? "They had been great, on the old system; they had large tracts of land, & consequently the means of being great in the new way. It remained for them to raise their lands to as high a value as they could." With the result that their followers, gentlemen who themselves had always maintained dependents to work the land, could no longer do so, and having no income-producing skills themselves, went to America as would-be proprietors, taking with them as many dependents for their future support as they

[21]William C. Lehmann, *Henry Home, Lord Kames, and the Scottish Enlightenment* (The Hague, 1971), pp. 329–330; Henry Dundas to William Eden, Melville, Sept. 5, 1775, Add. MSS 34412, 352–357.

could induce to go. And corruption bred corruption. A speculative boom in the commercial world, fueled by the circulation of thousands of pounds of cheap bank currency, "made luxury increase in an astonishing manner" and set off a price inflation. "Thus, as the increased luxury in the manner of living made it necessary for the proprietors to raise their rents so did the advanced price of commodities entitle them to such a rise."[22]

Solutions

Whatever the explanation, almost everyone who commented on the rising tide of emigration in the northern regions of the British Isles recognized that it was a severe problem that required drastic solutions. A few despaired of any remedy. Lord Adam Gordon, back home in Scotland after his extensive tour of the colonies, reiterated the alarm of the landed interests "that so many of their young and usefull hands should migrate to America," but he saw no way of preventing it: "any attempt to that purpose (like persecution in religion) would only incite greater curiosity & render men more obstinate to go." A more positive approach, if quite theoretical, was Arthur Young's rather grandiose scheme to develop, by coordinated private enterprise, the vast wastelands of England and Scotland to counteract the attraction of the American wilderness, especially the trans-Appalachian lands. More practical was the Yorkshireman Sir George Savile, and apparently more successful. When the leases fell due on his estate in County Tyrone, he by-passed his tenants and subtenants—"the overgrown tyrants who grind the faces of the poor"—visited the estate himself, and ascertained personally what the actual inhabitants and workers on the land could afford to pay. He then eliminated the middlemen and set the rents at 50% or more below what they had been. "Since then there is no emigrating from his estate."

Others similarly motivated banded together to extend the range of such private efforts. In July 1773 a group of "landed gentlemen" from both Scotland and Ireland, led by the Earls of Hillsborough and Hertford, met in a London coffeehouse and, considering "the disagreeable consequences" that flowed from "the great emigrations that have been made to America by the artificers and small holders of farms in Ireland and Scotland for a great while past, particularly within these few years," resolved to let out their estates "in small farms and at such easy rents as will enable the holders to pay their landlords, and not only enjoy the necessities but the conveniences of life." But such private solutions were limited in scope and effective-

[22]A Highlander, "An Essay on the Late Emigrations from the Highlands of Scotland" (1774), MacLeod MSS, box 61.

ness. Despite these welcome and well-publicized efforts of the associated landed gentlemen, the London *Daily Advertiser* reported, emigration had reached such a pitch that "many parcels of land cannot be let, even under this encouragement." Hillsborough himself, the *Advertiser* said, deserved his reputation as a good landlord—he had canceled "in full . . . large arrears due to him by several of his tenants"—but it is well known that he had "above 2,000 acres at present unlet."[23]

Increasingly men of position and influence turned to general public solutions—to the possibility of effective action by the government. Since to Dr. Johnson the root of the Scottish emigration lay in the vengeful measures undertaken by the government after the '45, they should all now be repealed. If wearing native costume would "disincline [the Scots] from coalescing with the Pennsylvanians or people of Connecticut," he wrote, let them keep their native dress. If retaining arms would keep them on their ancient lands, let them have arms as before. If rents were too high, force landlords to lower them and compensate them for their loss by pensions. One way or another the cohesion of the old society must be recovered and the depopulation stopped.

Dundas was less impatient, and a better politician. He held out little hope that the Scottish landlords would somehow, by themselves, become inspired with "kind and beneficent" attitudes toward their dependents. "Government must likeways do its part." The legislation that was called for seemed obvious to him. Perhaps, he wrote, the systematic destruction of the Highland clans after the '45 had been necessary, but by the 1770s the clans' threat to the stability of the regime had "totally evanished." "It is to talk like children to talk of any danger from dissafection in the north." Therefore the old punitive legislation should be repealed. By decree of the government, the Highland chiefs should be returned to their estates, restored to something like their "traditional influence," and reinvolved with the lives of their clansmen. Far from being a military threat, these leaders could now provide welcome military strength for the entire nation. In return for the "generous exertion of the beneficence of government," the chiefs should be induced to organize their dependents—who, like all Highlanders, were "born to be soldiers"—into "a millitary establishment," which the British government could certainly use.

[23]Lord Adam Gordon to Sir William Johnson [Peterhead, July 27, 1771], in *Papers of Sir William Johnson*, ed. James Sullivan *et al.* (Albany, 1921–65), VIII, 195; [Arthur Young], *Observations on the Present State of the Waste Lands of Great Britain. Published on the Occasion of the Establishment of a New Colony on the Ohio* (London, 1773); *London Chronicle,* July 27–29, Nov. 9–11, 1773. The long report on Savile's effort to alleviate the situation on his own estates was reprinted in *Scots Magazine,* 35 (1773), 591, and the accounts of the Hillsborough and Hertford reforms appeared in newspapers throughout the English-speaking world: see, e.g., *London Chronicle,* July 27–29, 1773; *Lloyd's Evening Post,* Sept. 15, 22, 1773; *York Courant,* Aug. 3, 31, 1773; *South-Carolina Gazette; And Country Journal,* Oct. 4, 1773; *Nova-Scotia Gazette,* Jan. 11, March 8, May 10, 1774.

[This force] would be the very best mellitia without any of its disadvantages. If the officers were named from the different corners of the Highlands, they would recruit from their own clans, and thereby renew that cement of connection which my opinion leads me to think ought now to be cheerished, not to be checkt. This and this only is the radical cure for emigration.[24]

But Dundas's solution to the emigration problem—amnesty for the rebels of '45 in exchange for their mobilizing the Highlanders into a new military strike force under their own commands—would have required radical government action, as would most of the other solutions proposed in these years. One suggestion, for example, was that the number of passengers emigrant vessels might carry be limited, that they be required to carry more than adequate provisions and adequate crews, and that there be "a surgeon . . . to each vessel conveying 20 passengers or upwards." All of this would raise the cost of passage so high "as to put it wholly out of the power of the greatest part of such people as have hitherto emigrated, to depart." Another proposal was to license emigration: each would-be emigrant to submit in writing an application justifying his intentions to the local magistrates, who might or might not approve it. And still another involved a triple prohibition: a Privy Council resolution to grant no more land in North America for several years; explicit Crown "dissapprobation of these emigrations," coupled with promises of royal favor for those "who shall stay at home"; and, for the next three years, a penalty of imprisonment to any shipmaster who transported a British subject to the colonies without a special license and "forfeiture of the vessel to the owners"—all this coupled with an elaborate plan "for employing & enriching the poor Highlanders." But all such plans assumed that there would be a "seasonable and spirited interposition of our rulers . . . that the *state* [would] interpose by establishing and executing statutes," and this assumption was dubious at best through all of these years. The difficulties that faced anyone contemplating legislative solutions to the problem of emigration, necessarily based on a broad consensus, were great. Some of the difficulties were conceptual, some were legal, some practical.[25]

There was no agreement, to begin with, that retaining a large domestic population was in itself beneficial. Once, in the early years of colonization, it had been argued that an essential purpose of establishing overseas settle-

[24] Johnson, *Journey to the Western Islands,* pp. 96–97; Dundas to Eden, Sept. 5, 1775, Add. MSS 34412, 354–357.
[25] "Thoughts on the Means of Preventing the Emigration of People from This Country to America" [177?], Dartmouth Papers, Stafford, D (W) 1778/II/1940; "Of the Prevailing Spirit of Emigration and Its Remedies," *Weekly Magazine, or Edinburgh Amusement,* 20 (Dec. 16, 1773), 362–363; Highlander, "An Essay," pp. 44 ff.

ments was to draw off the excess population and put to some productive use the swarms of sturdy vagrants who roamed the countryside and infested the city slums, living off the land and contributing nothing to the wealth of the nation. But a century later, opinion had changed. In the eighteenth century it was generally agreed that population in itself was a social and economic good, and should be enlarged for the benefit of the nation. Yet it was also understood that a growing population, discontented, impoverished, and uprooted from the land, could mean social strife and might threaten anarchy, and hence that a divergence overseas would be socially therapeutic as well as humane—an obvious point, except to landlords seeking to maximize rents and to retain a cheap labor force. But even they had no clear view; they too were caught in a cruel dilemma. While they felt justified in raising rents, increasing holdings and dislocating farm laborers, they took alarm when they saw tenants and subtenants drifting from their estates; many were genuinely alarmed at the social consequences of their own quite reasonable actions, and were thoroughly confused. While they shared the belief that economic progress required an increasing population, and while they continued to hanker after "the antient splendour of a numerous train of dependants," they knew the economic facts of life demanded dislocation and probably emigration. As the young Selkirk, with his characteristic acuity, later put it, "Since the removal of the superfluous population is necessary for the advance of [the Highland landlords'] rents, why (it may be asked) do they quarrel with that which is so beneficial to them? But those who reflect how very common it is for men to mistake their own interest will not consider this as a paradox."[26]

The legal and moral questions of government intervention were no simpler. Some, through these years, had no hesitation in recommending that emigration should simply be stopped "by express law." No doubt selfish interests will "cry out that the liberty of the subject is invaded when we can no longer remove from one part of the British dominions to another, & the cruelty of stopping the flight of oppressed tennants from their avaricious landlords will afford an ample field for declamation." But a sufficient reply "to all this noise" is simply the maxim that the interest of the few must give way to the good of the whole, especially when the government will

[26]Mildred Campbell, " 'Of People either too Few or too Many,' " in *Conflict in Stuart England*, ed. William H. Aiken and Basil D. Henning (London, 1960), pp. 171–201; Selkirk, *Observations*, pp. 130–131. The value of people in the calculus of power and wealth was a commonplace of the time. So the *York Chronicle and Weekly Advertiser*, Oct. 8, 1773, stated that "a number of people constitutes the most valuable treasure of a nation, and surely that country must be weakened where the streams of blood are permitted to flow from every vein. Not to know the importance of population argues the most consummate ignorance in a minister and constitutes a crime of omission that calls aloud for punishment."

"set every engine at work" to render the discontented "richer & happier than ever."[27]

But such confident statements were rare and flew in the face of considered opinion. There was in fact no agreement on whether or not the government *could* legally constrain the movements of British subjects from one British territory to another, or whether it *should* do so. Years before, in 1728, the Archbishop of Armagh, primate of all Ireland, viewing with alarm the exodus to North America, had considered whether "by some old laws we can . . . stop all but merchants, that have not a license, from going out of the kingdom," but then had immediately added that "whatever can be done by law, I fear it may be dangerous forcibly to hinder a number of needy people from quitting us"—dangerous, he said, and also "cruel to do it." Such doubts persisted. In 1774 the lord justice clerk (the chief justice) of Scotland, one of the century's most vehement opponents of emigration, admitted that it had always been considered "a difficult matter for government to interpose by any restraint upon the subjects, to remove themselves from one part of His Majesty's dominions to another."

Some were adamant—fierce—on the subject. "Personal liberty," an Edinburgh essayist observed, "and the power of loco-motion, is the undoubted privilege and birthright of every individual. . . . It is not at all clear that the Parliament has a right to hinder the inhabitants of Great Britain from leaving it when they think proper." Nor could such a law be enforced. The whole idea, the writer concluded, was "impossible and absurd." To the extent that it succeeded, "it would make the nation a prison, & the whole members of it prisoners, though not yet guilty of any crime." Is it right, a correspondent wrote the *Scots Magazine,* to prevent people "from flying from a country where they are starved to one where they have the happy prospect of . . . life in abundance?" The idea of confining a British subject to one corner of the realm "where he has the certain prospect of famishing" for the abstract and hypothetical good of the nation as a whole is "detestable" and "unworthy the thought of a British lawgiver." "To hinder free-born subjects," wrote another, "who are really starving, to go wheresoever they can find food & clothes! This would be contrary to all laws, human & divine; but I cannot think it will ever be arrived at by a British parliament." Even Dundas, ever fearful of depopulation, agreed that "coercive measures" to stop emigration were dubious. "In a free country," the lord advocate said, "in a small island, and where there are daily opportunities of getting away, such an idea is impracticable." Only after the King had declared the colonies to be in rebellion (August 23, 1775), and when Dundas had evidence that emigrants were leaving Scotland with money and arms

[27] *Edinburgh Magazine and Review*, 2 (July, 1774), 514; Highlander, "An Essay," pp. 46–47.

that "may afford aid and support to the rebels," did he feel free to prohibit emigration within his Scottish jurisdiction. On September 4, 1775, he arranged to have all Scottish emigration to America declared illegal and all customs officers, sheriffs, and admiralty courts instructed to enforce the prohibition. But he never deluded himself that such measures would be tolerated once the emergency was over. "If there were no such pretence as that of rebellion in America, it would be wild to think of keeping your subjects at home by force." The rebellion in America gave respite only— a pause—he said, which all friends of government should employ as a time to devise methods of permanently regaining the affections of the would-be emigrants which "may operate when pretences for coercion shall be at an end."[28]

But if there was no tradition or legal or moral grounds for the physical restraint of the movement of Britons from one British territory to another, it was nevertheless true that providing for the welfare of the population, mobile or static, was an obligation of the crown, and the causes and consequences of transatlantic migration were matters of evident concern. There were precedents, of sorts, for administrative action, if not for general legislation.

Occasionally and erratically governments at various levels had attempted to assert themselves through administrative action, though with little assurance or general effect. In 1718 the English solicitor general had

---

[28]*Letters Written by His Excellency Hugh Boulter, D.D. . . . from 1724 to 1738* (Oxford, 1769–1770), I, 262, 288; Thomas Miller to the Earl of Suffolk, Edinburgh, July 4, 1774, SP 54/45; *Edinburgh Magazine and Review*, 2 (July, 1774), 513–515; *Scots Magazine*, 36 (Feb., 1774), 64; *Caledonian Mercury*, Jan. 19, 1774; Dundas to Eden, Sept. 5, 1775, Add. MSS 34412, 356. Dundas's justification for prohibiting Scottish emigration and his orders to law-enforcement officers to effect the ban are detailed in the Scottish Customs Minute Book, Sept. 4, 1775, CE 1/14, and in his letter to Lord Suffolk of the same date, *Cal. Home Office Papers*, IV, #1130. In the latter he confessed that it was impossible "to dive into the secret intention of these emigrants; but though they are innocent, yet there is great reason to believe they would, if landed in America, be compelled to assist the rebels." News of Dundas's ban on Scottish emigrant shipping circulated swiftly: e.g., New York's *Constitutional Gazette*, Nov. 25, 1775.

But Dundas had not acted quickly enough to please some of the Scottish landlords. In April, after the Houses of Parliament had informed the King that the colonies were in rebellion, a group led by Sir James Grant, kinsman of the former governor of East Florida, long active in developing his estates in Elginshire, wrote a vehement letter to Dundas asking him to use his police powers immediately to stop the vessels preparing to leave Greenock with emigrants. Only thus could he save "those poor deluded people who in great numbers . . . propose sailing with their wives & families this spring. . . . No time is to be lost, as they sail in May. Government may never have a more proper opportunity of chequing this emigrating disposition without force, and it will show the Highlanders that His Majesty attends to their safety." James Grant to Capt. Forbes, Castle Grant, April 16; Forbes to Grant, Castle Downie, April 18; Grant to Dundas, April 19, 1775: all in Seafield Muniments, GD 248/244/12, 4, 2, Scottish Record Office, Edinburgh. There is no evidence that a similar legal prohibition was ever issued in England. There probably was no need for one, since England was obviously at war with the united colonies. The 26 registered vessels that left England for America with passengers after September 1775 either were destined for the Caribbean colonies or carried Americans returning home or others who were not considered emigrants.

ruled that "the King may prohibit his subject from going out of the realm without license," and in that year and in 1750 Parliament had barred certain skilled mechanics from emigrating to foreign countries; but these laws had never been enforced, and in any case had not extended to British territories overseas. Individual American colonies had imposed restrictions on immigration—attempting to bar convicts and limiting the importation of slaves; and conversely they had actively encouraged the immigration of desired settlers from the British Isles.

The southern colonies were especially effective in offering inducements to prospective immigrants. As early as 1731 South Carolina had embarked on a program of assisted immigration, directing bounties and other benefits specifically to emigrants from Ireland, and the colony maintained that policy for over forty years. Georgia had followed South Carolina in 1766, and in this connection, increasingly, the British government had asserted itself. In 1767 it vetoed Georgia's immigration-assistance act as inadmissible at a time "when so great a number of useful inhabitants of these islands . . . are daily emigrating to the American colonies," and in doing so simply asserted what it took to be self-evident, its superior authority, if not its settled policy, in the area of regulating emigration.[29] And Hillsborough, for the British government, never doubted that he had the administrative authority to act in such matters. He saw to it that a North Carolina act of 1771 providing special benefits for Scottish emigrants was vetoed in England, along with a huge North Carolina land grant for intending emigrants from Skye. And the Board of Trade, under Hillsborough's direction, began writing into new American land grants a clause limiting settlers in newly opened lands to foreign Protestants and Americans.[30]

It was in this area—the policy and procedures for granting land in America—that the British government felt confident it could move, even if only indirectly, to constrain the outflow of people. The motivation behind the Privy Council's order of April 7, 1773, flatly prohibiting all crown governors or other officers from granting land in America until a new policy could be devised, was complex. One element was the desire to increase the crown's income from quit rents, but the major element in that decision was the hope that limiting land grants would limit emigration. Hillsborough's view that the extension of land settlement was a key stimu-

[29] George Chalmers, *Opinions of Eminent Lawyers on Various Points of English Jurisprudence . . .*, American ed. (Burlington, [Vt.], 1858), pp. 548, 333–336, 436–438; 5 Geo. II, c. 27; 23 Geo. II, c. 13; Dickson, *Ulster Emigration*, pp. 34, 47; E. R. R. Green, "Queensborough Township: Scotch-Irish Emigration and the Expansion of Georgia, 1763–1776," *William and Mary Quarterly*, 3d ser., 17 (1960), 185–186; Emberson E. Proper, *Colonial Immigration Laws: A Study of the Regulation of Immigration by the English Colonies in America* (New York, 1900), esp. pp. 17–20.
[30] William L. Saunders, ed., *The Colonial Records of North Carolina . . .*, VIII (Raleigh, 1890), 620–622; *ibid.*, IX, 251–252, 303–304.

lus to the soaring rate of emigration was now given official sanction, nine months after his resignation, though in a way he had not anticipated.

There was great reason to believe, the colonial undersecretary John Pownall wrote in explaining the prohibition of colonial land grants, that "the great emigration of the inhabitants" of Great Britain and Ireland, so prejudicial to the landed interests, the commerce, and the manufactures of the kingdom, "may have been induced . . . by delusive proposals of encouragement . . . held out by persons who have obtained gratuitous grants of lands in His Majesty's colonies in America." The temporary prohibition of such grants, it was hoped, and a revamped policy that would restrain the profligate land grabbing, would help curb the emigration. The revised policy, issued in February 1774, altered the process of land distribution in the royal colonies fundamentally. It prohibited the engrossing of land by the recipients of the governors' favors by ordering all crown land to be surveyed and *sold*—not granted—and sold at public and well-advertised auctions in small lots, of from one hundred to one thousand acres. The fees involved were fixed to keep the governors and their cronies from seeking profits through enlarged land sales, and the whole system, which also aimed to guarantee to the crown the quit rents due on all newly purchased land, was to be kept under the strict scrutiny of the Board of Trade.[31]

But restricting and regulating land grants, clearly within the jurisdiction of the crown, was at best a weak and indirect way of restricting emigration. The basic problem remained: there was no agreement that the British government could legally prohibit or restrict the movement of

---

[31]E. B. O'Callaghan, ed., *Documents Relative to the Colonial History of the State of New York* . . . (Albany, 1856–1887), VIII, 357–358, 410–413; *Lloyd's Evening Post,* Oct. 8–11, 1773 (on quit rents); John Pownall, draft advertisement for the *Gazette,* enclosed in Pownall to Dartmouth, Nov. 6, 1773, Dartmouth Papers, Canada, I, 107–108.

The relation of emigration to the revised policy of land granting was widely recognized. Franklin discussed it explicitly in July 1773 (*Franklin Papers,* XX, 302–303). Charles Williamos, a persistent office seeker, prefaced his proposal for creating an office of inspector of land sales in America, which he hoped to fill, by stating that "the spirit of emigration to North America being now so prevailing in Europe, the immense tracts of lands which the crown possesses in that continent are of course of the greatest importance, and therefore every step ought to be taken to regulate every thing relative to them." [Charles] Williamos to Lord North, Nov. 18, 1773, Dartmouth Papers, Stafford, D (W) 1778/II/743. The newspapers were quite explicit on the connection: "In order to put a stop to the emigration of the subjects of Great Britain and Ireland to America, it is said [that] government has it under consideration to prevent grants of land being made to them in those parts." *Lloyd's Evening Post,* Nov. 12–15, 1773. Later, Burke, in his speech on conciliation (March 1775), abused the government for attempting to check American population growth by stopping land grants, and dilated on the power and inevitability of America's demographic surge (*The Works of the Right Honorable Edmund Burke,* rev. ed. [Boston, 1866], II, 131–132). Later still, the Declaration of Independence accused the crown of attempting "to prevent the population of these states [by] . . . raising the conditions of new appropriations of lands." Cf. St. George L. Sioussat, "The Breakdown of the Royal Management of Lands in the Southern Provinces, 1773–1775," *Agricultural History,* 3 (1929), 67–98, which traces the failure of the new policy in the short period during which attempts were made to implement it.

British subjects from one British territory to another. Even the wartime prohibition of emigration, put into effect after America had been declared to be in rebellion and hence when emigration to America could be construed as supporting treason, touched off violent objections. One justice of the peace and member of Parliament, at a regional meeting of magistrates called to enforce the ban on emigration, spoke "most violently," a witness reported, against any such action—in wartime or otherwise—declaring to his colleagues that "such a stop would be illegal—that we had no power. He said he wished there were more of the Common People there that he might inform them that they were their own masters, and might emigrate if they chose it."[32]

The Crisis of 1773: The Lord Justice Clerk and "The America Madness"

Despite all these confusions and doubts, the pressure on the government to restrain emigration grew stronger in the years just before the American rebellion. The elimination of land grants by colonial officials and the reevaluation of the colonial land-grant policy, while useful, would scarcely stem the tide. A stronger response could not be avoided. In mid-1773, a year that marked the climax of emigration from the British Isles, the leading officers of state at last turned seriously to the possibility of devising legislation or taking other action that would deal directly with the problem.

The immediate instigation came from Scotland, and in particular from the lord justice clerk, Thomas Miller. A member of Parliament, well known and widely respected as a lawyer and jurist in both Scotland and England, Miller had supported the Stamp Act and had opposed its repeal out of an apprehension of the growing independence of the colonies and concern for the magnetism they were exerting on the home islands. The fear he had expressed in the Stamp Act debate grew over the years as he watched the continuing emigration from the Highlands, especially from the Sutherlandshire estates of the young Countess of Sutherland, one of whose "tutors" (custodians and estate managers) Miller was. The lord justice clerk's con-

[32]Thomas Dundas to Sir Lawrence Dundas, Kerse [Stirlingshire], Oct. 5, 1775, Dundas Papers. The speaker, John Johnstone, an immensely rich former East Indian adventurer, fervently pro-American, a supporter of Wilkes and conciliation, was the brother of George Johnstone, first governor of West Florida, who did everything possible during his administration to encourage immigration into the new colony and its neighbors. Namier and Brooke, *House of Commons*, II, 683–687. At the one other such meeting of which a record has been found, the JP's and the sheriffs of Inverness concurred without dissent in every "legal measure" that could be taken to prevent emigration "during the present disturbances in America." Sir James Grant to [?], Sept. 1775, Seafield Muniments, GD 248/52/1, Scottish Record Office.

Sir Thomas Miller, lord justice clerk of Scotland, 1766–1788. Medallion by
James Tassie. A passionate opponent of emigration from Britain and influ-
ential in the highest circles in London, he almost succeeded in banning emi-
gration altogether, and was indirectly responsible for creating
the Register of Emigrants, 1773–1776.

cern, mounting month after month, climaxed in October 1773 when he
presided over the conspiracy trial of twelve journeymen weavers in Paisley.
Not only had these workers struck for higher wages and in "riotous proceedings" forcibly prevented their employers from using scab labor, but
they had rallied thousands of other weavers to their banner and with them
"threatened to goe off in a body to America" if their cause was not vin-

dicated. This was precisely the sort of thing Miller most feared, and he reported the affair in great detail to the secretary of state for the northern department (effectively the home secretary), the Earl of Suffolk.

The conspirators' threat to lead thousands of Paisley's textile workers to America, Miller wrote Suffolk, had made the strike and the subsequent trial "very delicate," and he therefore had handled the matter with extraordinary care. He had appointed a jury consisting of "the most intelligent & disinterested gentlemen" he could find. It was with great relief that he was able to report that in the end the jury had convicted only seven of the strikers, and that in mitigating their punishment to brief imprisonment Miller had convinced them of the "criminality of their conduct and of the lenity with which they had been treated." From all of this, he reported, "I have reason to hope that peace & good order is now restored to that place, and that all thoughts of goeing over to America are for the present laid aside." But the problem of emigration, he told the secretary of state, remained extremely serious: "I pray God, for the sake of this countrey, that such ideas of migration to America may not become epidemical amongst the most usefull of our people." Such a thing might well happen, since the American colonies were becoming dangerously attractive. He had discovered, he said, that the traditional commutation of criminal sentences to "transportation" to the colonies was no longer either a deterrent or a meaningful reprisal: "in this part of the Kingdom transportation to America begins to lose every characteristick of punishment."[33]

But Miller's relief at the conclusion of the Paisley trial was short-lived. Immediately thereafter he attended a meeting of the Ayrshire county magistracy, and it was his attendance at that meeting, on October 26, 1773, and his response to what he learned there, that moved the British government to action. When the regular business of the meeting was done, Miller reported, Sir Adam Fergusson—a prominent Ayrshire landlord, guardian of the Countess of Sutherland, close friend and political ally of the powerful Henry Dundas—"took notice of the dangerous situation this country was in from the various arts used to impose upon our people and entice them to America," and he then produced a broadside advertising in quite specific terms for settlers for St. John (now Prince Edward) Island in the Gulf of St. Lawrence.

The advertisement was the work of a notorious land promoter, the lieutenant governor of St. John, Thomas Desbrisay. This frenetic Irishman had been attempting since 1770 to populate his property on the island, but his elaborate recruitment efforts, which included three published no-

---

[33] George Ormond, *The Lord Advocates of Scotland* (Edinburgh, 1883), II, 68–71; Namier and Brooke, *House of Commons*, III, 139–140; John Ramsay, *Scotland and Scotsmen in the Eighteenth Century*, ed. Alexander Allardyce (Edinburgh, 1888), I, 342–350; Miller to Suffolk, Barskiming.[Ayrshire], Oct. 25, 1773, SP 54/46. For public notice of the trial, *Scots Magazine*, 35 (Oct., 1773), 555–556.

tices each month from February to May 1772, had produced very little. By the end of 1772 his agents were at work on the Irish estates of the Earl of Hertford, privy councillor and lord chamberlain, who was at that very time making every possible effort, along with Hillsborough, to keep the Irish population at home. And then, still frustrated, Desbrisay had extended his range to western Scotland, distributing his enticing ads in Ayrshire, Argyllshire, and the counties to the north. He had also, unknown to Fergusson and Miller, approached Lord Dartmouth with a scheme to populate the St. John lands and had attempted to involve the colonial secretary himself in a deal by which the earl would acquire, through Desbrisay, ten thousand wilderness acres which the Irishman would guarantee would bring in £1,500 a year within six years.

It took no eloquence on Fergusson's part to detonate the lord justice clerk's already overheated concern. The jurist, following the meeting's instructions, immediately transmitted to Lord Suffolk in London an account of the meeting together with a copy of the offending advertisement. Consistent with official policy, Miller informed Suffolk, the terms of Desbrisay's land grant on the island had restricted settlement to foreign Protestants or Americans. Yet despite this restriction, Desbrisay had distributed his broadside, and the other advertisements he had published, widely in Britain and Ireland, and he had had some effect on emigration—how much Miller confessed he did not know. Something had to be done, specifically about Desbrisay and generally about what another concerned Scot called "the America madness" sweeping the land. Surely the problem was ripe for Parliamentary action.[34]

Suffolk had long been plagued with such warnings and requests, but this time he, and through him the British government, responded actively. The secretary of state moved in two directions at once. First, he issued instructions to Miller, and second, he wrote an urgent request to his colleague Lord Dartmouth, the secretary of state for the colonies.

His instructions to the lord justice clerk were to find out what effect Desbrisay's broadside had had in Scotland—that is, "what number of people have emigrated from Scotland since the publication of it." Miller took this to be a request for emigration statistics covering the years 1772 and 1773, and he set to work gathering the information. He wrote first to the Scottish customs commissioners, to whom he passed on Suffolk's request, and they in turn wrote to the chief officers of the emigration ports. But the outports'

---

[34]Miller to Suffolk, Oct. 27, 1773, SP 54/46. On Desbrisay's enterprises, see Dickson, *Ulster Emigration*, pp. 152–164, and Thomas Desbrisay to Dartmouth, Dublin, Aug. 28, 1773, Dartmouth Papers, Canada, III, 3124–3126; on his career generally, George W. Brown *et al.*, eds., *Dictionary of Canadian Biography* (1966–), V, 249–250. For Fergusson's interests and connections, see Namier and Brooke, *House of Commons*, II, 419–421. For "the America madness," see John MacLeod to Mrs. MacLeod, Oct. 9, 1772, MacLeod MSS, Box 62, 194.

returns, Miller discovered, could not be relied on, for vessels were not obliged to clear through customs ports and had in fact "sailed from different bays & creeks of an extensive coast." If the customs officials were not able to furnish the statistics Miller needed for Suffolk, perhaps the local clergy could. So he wrote to the sheriffs of eight Highland counties, asking them to send all the parish ministers in their jurisdictions a circular letter requesting accurate lists of emigrants over the previous two years, "distinguishing men, women, and children." He was careful, he reported to Suffolk, to limit the coverage to the most relevant districts of Scotland so as not to "raise an alarm over the whole countrey, as if this spirit of emigration had allready become general."[35]

The parish returns came in slowly as the messages circulated through the winter of 1773–1774 in a country "divided by many firths and arms of sea and where there are few posts." By the end of April 1774 Miller still had not heard from three of the eight counties, including Inverness-shire, which included the Isle of Skye, though he had independent information about one of them; and many of the returns were incomplete. The totals he was able to report—for 1772–1773, 2,081; for 1769–1773, 3,618—greatly underestimated, he felt, the seriousness of the problem. Despite the scrappy figures, he wrote Suffolk, the spirit of emigration was no longer simply a Highland problem, nor was it only a lower-class phenomenon. It had spread to the Lowlands and to "some of the better sort of farmers & mechanicks who are in good circumstances & can live very comfortably at home." Moreover, he had discovered that land-purchasing associations had been organized. If that practice, which enabled whole communities to move with all their personal associations undisturbed, became popular among affluent Scots "it may in time as effectually depopulate this country as the mines of Peru & Mexico have depopulated the Kingdom of Spain."

But the ultimate danger, he felt, went beyond even this. The present cause of emigration, he believed, was chiefly dire want; and that would sooner or later fade as conditions improved. But if, by the time that happened, a new motivation had become common, namely, the hope simply "of attaining a better situation" in America than could be attained in Scotland, emigration would become entirely uncontrollable. He scarcely knew what to recommend. The most practical idea seemed to be an effort to subsidize the return to Scotland of some of the recent emigrants, which might help dispel some of the glow surrounding America. But neither he nor Suffolk, who apparently tried to implement that idea, believed it would make much difference.[36]

[35] Suffolk to Miller, Nov. 5, 1773, and Miller to Suffolk, April 25, 1774, SP 54/45, 46. Scottish Customs Minute Book, CE 1/13, under date Nov. 24, 1773.
[36] Miller to Suffolk, April 25, May 30, 1774, SP 54/45.

Miller had done his best, though he seemed to have accomplished very little. He continued to warn Suffolk that "the disease may encrease and become epidemicall amongst our people," especially as shipmasters discovered the profits of transporting emigrants; and he forwarded a request that troops be sent to the island of Lewis in the Hebrides to keep American shippers from "ensnaring & seducing" people under obligations—a request Suffolk quickly rejected. The mere suggestion of force, the secretary of state wrote, might be counterproductive, serving "to increase the evil intended to be remedied." But Miller's efforts had borne more fruit, of various kinds, than he realized. By January 1774 the sheriffs' letters to the parish ministers had become general knowledge in Britain, and by April news of them had spread as far as Charleston, South Carolina, and had appeared in German translation in Pennsylvania in the *Wöchentliche Pennsylvanische Staatsbote*. Word that troops had been requested to stop emigration also reached the newspapers and was denounced as the work of "half[-baked] politicians," "silly beyond measure." Furthermore, the Highland clergy had become thoroughly alarmed, "imagining there was some design to make them tools of oppression and tyranny." It was understood that for that reason, among others, they were systematically underreporting the number of emigrants.[37]

This much agitation in Scotland and this much concern elsewhere had been the result of Suffolk's response to Miller's immediate concern and of Miller's zeal in collecting emigration statistics for the previous two years. But at the same time that Suffolk had responded to Miller he had sent a copy of the lord justice clerk's letter, enclosing Desbrisay's advertisement, to the secretary of state for the colonies, Lord Dartmouth, stating it as the King's view that the emigrations referred to were "very detrimental to the general good of the state, and that every proper check, within the power of government, should be given to plans which tend so fatally to depopulate a

---

[37]Miller to Suffolk, May 30, 1774; Memorial for the Earl of Seaforth, n.d.; Suffolk to Seaforth, June 2, 1774; Suffolk to Miller, June 2, 1774: all in *ibid.*; *London Chronicle*, Dec. 7, 1773; *Lloyd's Evening Post*, Dec. 3–6, 1773, and Jan. 24–26, 1774; *York Courant*, Dec. 7, 1773; *York Chronicle and Weekly Advertiser*, Dec. 10, 1773; *Scots Magazine*, 35 (Dec., 1773), 667; *Wöchentliche Pennsylvanische Staatsbote*, April 5, 1774; *South-Carolina and American General Gazette*, April 15–22, 1774, quoting a letter from Argyllshire, Jan. 7; *Virginia Gazette* (Rind), June 9, 1774, quoting a letter from the neighborhood of Glasgow, March 14. Miller proposed distinctive solutions for the problems in the Isle of Lewis. Besides doing something about the underlying causes of the discontent (rent increases, the collapse of local manufactures, and "the enticing accounts of America" published everywhere), he recommended cutting down the profits of the emigrant trade by loading it with encumbrances. The traffic should be legally confined to a few closely supervised exit ports, he advised Suffolk, and generous supplies and shiproom should be required for every passenger. The reduction in the number of exit ports was particularly important: it would lengthen the emigrants' trips from home to shipboard and "give them a little more time to reflect"; their natural doubts and hesitations would overcome their initial, uncertain decisions.

considerable part of his kingdom." Dartmouth's undersecretary, John Pownall, a canny veteran of the bureaucratic wars, opened Suffolk's letter and
read it with astonishment. One secretary of state, he advised Dartmouth
within hours of receiving the letter, is hardly in a position to tell another
what the King thinks and to state peremptorily what the other should do.
"I am at a loss to guess what Lord Suffolk expects from us and what he
means by laying such a business at our door." But Pownall wasted no time
in recriminations. Three days after receiving Suffolk's stiff note he sent
Desbrisay a blistering letter reminding him that he had already been warned
against illegal recruitment and telling him that the landlords in northern
Britain "whose estates have suffered extremely by the emigration of their
tenants" had complained to the King of the Irishman's illegal solicitations.
Furthermore, Pownall noted that Desbrisay had "unwarrantably presumed
to recite, in the preamble of those advertizements, the offices which you
hold under the King's royal commission, evidently with a design to give
the greater colour of authority to your proposals." Pownall ordered him to
suppress all such publications instantly, and informed him that if it turned
out that anyone had in fact emigrated because of his recruitment, Desbrisay
could expect to receive "the strongest marks of His Majesty's displeasure."
Desbrisay was thoroughly squelched, withdrew the ads immediately, and
replied desperately to Pownall that "I never took any tenant out of the
north of Ireland without first asking the consent of either the proprietor or
agent of the lands he lived upon. . . . The Earls of Hillsborough and
Hertford knows [*sic*] this to have been my conduct." And as proof he
enclosed a letter to that effect from Hertford's agent.[38]

But Pownall's chief concern was not to rein in the hustling and annoying Irishman, who thereafter scrambled to regain Dartmouth's favor and to
find other ways of populating his lands, but rather to develop a general and
effective policy for restraining emigration. To that end he sent to Dartmouth for his approval a draft advertisement for the *Gazette* publicizing the
recent ban on "gratuitous" land grants in the colonies, and also, for the
eventual signatures of the Lords of Trade, a much more important document—a document which, when it was approved, finally set the heavy
wheels of the national government in motion.

Recognizing the great complaints about the emigrations that had been
lodged by the landed, commercial, and manufacturing interests of the
realm, the Board of Trade (Pownall wrote) called the matter to the crown's
attention, but confessed itself unable to recommend any remedy "without
knowing with precision the actual extent of the emigration complained of

[38]Pownall to Dartmouth, "Saturday night, November 6," 1773, enclosing Suffolk to Dartmouth,
Nov. 4, 1773, Dartmouth Papers, Canada, I, 90–102; Pownall to Desbrisay, Nov. 9, 1773, and
Desbrisay to Pownall, Nov. 22, 1773, CO 226/5/35–36, 74–75.

and what parts of Your Majesty's kingdoms are principally affected by it."
In order to gain that information

> we most humbly submit to Your Majesty whether it might not be
> adviseable that the officers of Your Majesty's customs in the several
> ports of your said kingdoms should receive directions to take an
> acc[oun]t of all persons that shall embark as passengers on board any
> ships which may clear out from the said ports, and to transmit to
> us monthly, or oftener, a list of all such persons specifying their
> names, ages, sex, and profession, as far as the same can be ascer-
> tained.

In all probability the Treasury, Pownall suggested, had the authority to
order this collection of data through the customs offices, which fell within
its jurisdiction. But if not, a statute of Parliament would be needed, and if
that were the case "we think no time ought to be lost in recommending it
to the consideration of Parliament in the approaching session."[39]

By the end of the month (November 1773) it was clear that direct
administrative procedure, through the Treasury, would suffice. But word
had gone out, not merely that the government was about to take action, but
that Parliament would at the very least discuss the problem at the forthcoming session. Almost every newspaper in Britain and America carried notices
to this effect. Attention was called, suddenly, to the renewal, in August 1772,
of the office of register of indentured servants going to America, a post
created in 1664 that had been held as a sinecure by the same family since
1691, and arguments were mobilized for and against any move actually to
stop emigration.[40] The public furor was further stimulated in mid-Novem-

[39] Desbrisay to Dartmouth, Nov. 22, 1773, Feb. 12, Dec. 10, 1774, Dartmouth Papers, Canada, III,
3133–3135, 3143–3146, 3168–3170; drafts of *Gazette* ad and of recommendation of Board of Trade to
George III, enclosed in Pownall to Dartmouth, Nov. 6, 1773, *ibid*, I, 103–109.

[40] E.g., *Lloyd's Evening Post*, Dec. 3–6, 1773, expressing the hope that "the modes will not be
compulsive, as those would be the means of increasing the people's discontent," and advocating
encouragement of industry and help for rural small holders; *York Courant* (which as early as Aug.
3 had announced that "a bill for limiting the number of emigrants . . . is to be presented early in
the next session"), Dec. 7, 14, 1773; *Caledonian Mercury*, Jan. 19, 1774 ("We are told that Parliament
will make an act to hinder emigrations: a cruel act indeed! To hinder freeborn subjects who are
really starving to go wheresoever they can find food and clothes! This would be contrary to all
laws, human and divine; but I cannot think it will ever be aimed at by a British Parliament");
Virginia Gazette (Rind), Dec. 23, 1773; *South-Carolina Gazette; And Country Journal*, Feb. 22, March
1, 1774. In Ireland word had been circulating since September that the Irish parliament would
restrain emigration in that island, at least temporarily, though there would be "some immunities
to the lower orders of people who have hitherto, in a manner, been forced out of the kingdom from
their necessities." The question was debated at great length and with some bitterness in the Irish
House of Peers, but no action was taken. *Lloyd's Evening Post*, Sept. 27, Nov. 8, 1773. Later in the
fall, the Irish House of Commons instructed the customs commissioners of Ireland to assemble
emigration statistics for the previous two years—a survey equivalent to Miller's preliminary and
incomplete survey of Scotland—though apparently, again, nothing was done. Dickson, *Ulster*

ber when someone in the government sent to the press what purported to be the text of a bill that would be presented to Parliament. It provided for the creation of an office to license, at extremely high fees, the emigration only of agricultural workers and servants, not artisans or manufacturers, who wished to go to America. It imposed severe penalties on shipmasters or others who ignored the licensing system and on artisans or manufacturers who attempted to leave the realm, while exempting from the law all gentlemen and their servants traveling abroad, government employees, and merchants and their factors and servants.

Later the bill, which in fact never reached Parliament, would be savagely lampooned in the American press, but in the excited weeks of mid-November 1773, when every informed person believed that the British government was planning in some way to curb emigration, the bill was taken seriously, at the very least as an attempt by the government to test public opinion. Characteristically Franklin rose to the bait. In a draft essay written in response to the leaked bill, he demolished the proposal systematically, attacking first the necessity for it, then the practicability of it, then the policy of it, and finally the justice of it. The basic issue, he wrote, was simple and clear. There would be no problem, he wrote, if the absentee landlords who grind down the poor to extract the means of living in luxury and dissipation in London and at the court would "return to their family seats, live among their people, and instead of fleecing and skinning, patronize and cherish them, promote their interest, encourage their industry, and make their situation comfortable." "If the poor folks are happier at home than they can be abroad, they will not lightly be prevailed with to cross the ocean. But can their lord blame them for leaving home in search of better living when he first sets them the example?"[41]

Emigration, pp. 199–200. On the office of register of emigrant servants, its history and renewal in 1772, see Charles M. Andrews, ed., *Guide to the Materials for American History, to 1783, in the Public Record Office of Great Britain* (Washington, D.C., 1912–1914), I, 58; *Gentleman's Magazine*, 43 (Jan., 1773), 45; *Nova-Scotia Gazette*, April 13, May 11, 1773. On its origins, see below, chap. 3, n. 2.

[41]The text of the bill that was leaked to the press is printed in *Lloyd's Evening Post*, Nov. 15–17, 1773, and in the *Public Advertiser*, Nov. 16, 1773; Franklin's draft essay opposing the bill is in *Franklin Papers*, XX, 522–528. The lampoon, republished from *Dunlap's Pennsylvania Packet, or the General Advertiser* in the *Nova-Scotia Gazette*, Aug. 16, 1774, and in the *Virginia Gazette or, Norfolk Intelligencer*, July 28, 1774, has eleven points, which include head taxes of £50 sterling on all emigrants; licenses for all colonial marriages at £20 each; fines for all male births in the colonies at £15 each, female births at £10, and bastards at £50; exemption from punishment of all murderers of colonial children; taxing of all exports of wheat and flour; and the use of all the income from the above for building forts and supporting standing armies in America to enforce Parliament's laws. Apparently Franklin, who was still in England, did not write the spoof, but he did publish at about the same time two other lampoons, one advocating the imposition of absolute military rule over the colonies, the other proposing the castration of all American males—which at the very least, he wrote, would "put a stop to the emigrations from this country now grown so very fashionable." *Franklin Papers*, XXI, 183–186, 220–222.

Franklin did not publish this carefully wrought essay. He had no need
to. By the time he had finished writing it, early in December, it was
becoming clear that Parliament would delay consideration of bills curbing
emigration until Pownall's first step, the collection of statistics on who was
leaving, whence and why, was completed. Even that much, it soon developed, would be difficult to accomplish.

3

Searching for the Facts: The Origin and Character of the Register of Emigrants

I T WAS thus John Pownall, the experienced, politically adroit undersecretary of state for the colonies, who at the last moment deflected the growing demand for Parliamentary legislation limiting or banning emigration to the American colonies by proposing as a first step a statistical assessment of "the actual extent of the emigration complained of, and what parts of Your Majesty's kingdoms are principally affected by it." And Pownall sketched the procedure. The customs officials in the nation's ports were to compile information pertaining to "all persons" embarking on voyages overseas: specifically, "their names, ages, sex and profession as far as the same can be ascertained."[1] But this proved to be only the first, rough approach to the problem. By the time the project emerged from the Treasury office, a month later, it had been refined and the terms of the survey elaborated and reduced to a precise formula.

Who it was in the Treasury who gave the questionnaire its specific form is not known, but whoever it was seems to have been familiar with the long-dormant register of servants emigrating to the colonies that had been established in 1664,[2] and in addition had a keen sense of what might be

[1] Draft Representation of Lords of Trade to George III, enclosed in John Pownall to the Earl of Dartmouth, Nov. 6, 1773, Dartmouth Papers, Canada, I, 103–106.

[2] The Register of 1664 had been established by the crown at the request of merchants trading to the colonies, both to overcome the "wicked custome to seduce or spirit away young people to goe as servants to Your Ma^{ts} plantations" and (no doubt more important) to keep servants who had "received mony, cloathes, dyet and other conveniences from your petitioners" from repudiating their contracts on the false ground that they had been coerced. The "office of takeing and registring the consents, agreements and covenants" of voluntary indentured servants was to record "the names, age, quality, place of birth and last residence" of those who chose to provide such information. The commission creating the office located it "within our port and citty of London," but clearly contemplated a national registration system, adding: "and also, if occasion shall so require, in any other our ports within the kingdome of England and dominion of Wales." The creation

learned from such a survey as well as an exaggerated respect for the efficiency of the British customs administration. On December 9, 1773, Britain's Lords of the Treasury, having been informed, they said, "that great numbers of the subjects of this country emigrate to America and foreign parts," ordered the Board of Customs Commissioners in London to instruct its officials in the various ports "to use every proper means in their power" to record not only the name of every person leaving the kingdom but also his or her "age, quality, occupation, employment & former residence," and also "what port or place they propose to go, and on what account, and for what purposes they leave this country, together with such other remarks and information as they may be able to obtain." Port officials were to send all this information weekly (Pownall had suggested "monthly or oftener") to the customs board in London, and the board in turn was to "make a report thereof" to the Treasury "from time to time, as you shall see necessary." The same orders were sent separately to the Board of Customs Commissioners in Scotland, which was administratively independent of the English board and reported directly to the British Treasury.[3]

The work began immediately. Within twenty-four hours of the Treasury's order to the customs board, that body began sending instructions to all the English port officials to collect the required data; six days later, on December 15, the Scottish customs board similarly ordered all the customs officers within its jurisdiction to start compiling the specified information.[4] In the months that followed—while agitated warnings continued to be

of the office was directed to the attention of all port officials in London "and all and every the ports, havens and creeks of this realme of England and dominion of Wales, and port and towne of Berwick." Entry Book on Spiriting, CO 389/2, Public Record Office, London. Earlier, registration offices for the cities of Bristol and London produced important lists of indentured servants emigrating in the seventeenth century, which have been widely studied since the publication of Mildred Campbell's pathbreaking article "Social Origins of Some Early Americans," in *Seventeenth-Century America*, ed. James M. Smith (Chapel Hill, N.C., 1959), 63–89. See particularly David Souden, " 'Rogues, Whores and Vagabonds'? Indentured Servant Emigrants . . . of Mid-seventeenth-century Bristol," *Social History*, 3 (1978), 23–39; James Horn, "Servant Emigration to the Chesapeake in the Seventeenth Century," in *The Chesapeake in the Seventeenth Century*, eds. Thad W. Tate and David L. Ammerman (Chapel Hill, N.C., 1979), 51–95; John Wareing, "Migration to London and Transatlantic Emigration of Indentured Servants, 1683–1775," *Journal of Historical Geography*, 7 (1981), 356–378; and David W. Galenson's quantitative study of the extant English lists, *White Servitude, in Colonial America, an Economic Analysis* (Cambridge, Eng., 1981). For the later history of the office of 1664 and for the records collected under its auspices, see above, chap. 2, n. 40, and Abbot E. Smith, *Colonists in Bondage* (Chapel Hill, N.C., 1947), chap. 4, esp. pp. 78–82.
[3] John Robinson [secretary to the Treasury] to Customs Commissioners "about Ye Subject of this Country Emigrating to America &c.," Dec. 9, 1773, T11/30, 450. The order to the Scottish customs board was dated Dec. 8 (Scottish Customs Minute Book, Aug. 31, 1775, CE 1/14, and the various submissions from the Edinburgh board to the Treasury); the order was received and acknowledged on Dec. 15 (Treasury Minute Books, Jan. 19, 1774, T29/43).
[4] E.g., Board of Customs, London, to Customs Collectors, Hull, Dec. 11, 15, 18, and 31, 1773, and to Customs Collectors, Whitby, Jan. 4, 1774, T92/11, 117, and T90/5; Board of Customs, Edinburgh, to Customs Collectors, Campbeltown, Dec. 15, 1773, Campbeltown Customs Letter Books, CE 82/2/1.

heard of the dangers of excessive emigration, while shipload after shipload of emigrants left the British docks for transatlantic voyages, and while the Anglo-American crisis became explosive after the arrival of news of the Tea Party—customs officials in ports scattered from Devonshire to northern Scotland and from Dover to the Hebrides interviewed hundreds, then thousands, of emigrants as they boarded ship; gathered passenger information from ship captains and port officials; and sent in to the customs headquarters sheet after sheet of detailed compilations. And in the back rooms of the customs headquarters in London and Edinburgh clerks gathered the sheets, in the English case collated the information, and forwarded all of the material to the Treasury.

At first, there was much confusion. The customs collectors at Harwich reported that the only vessels that went overseas from that Channel port were regular packet boats to the Low Countries; if they were to be included, special permission would have to be obtained from the agent of the packet system. From Liverpool came the query whether the usual flow of traffic to Ireland and the Isle of Man was to be included. And the inspectors in Wigtown, in southern Scotland, were politely incredulous of the whole project: did the honorable Board of Customs Commissioners really mean that the ports should "take such a minute account of every individual person as [their] letter would seem to imply," or did they, more reasonably, want only summaries? Answers were given: no, voyagers to the continent, the offshore islands, and Ireland need not be included; but yes, the board meant precisely what its letter implied, "a minute account of every individual person."[5]

The result is a documentary collection that illuminates as does no other source, literary or statistical, essential characteristics of the most mobile elements in British society; the process by which British North America was peopled in the years before the Revolution; and a major segment of the immigrant population in pre-Revolutionary America. There is no other

---

[5] Treasury Minute Books, Jan. 20, 1774, T29/43/273; T47/12/230. Liverpool's explanation of its desire to omit passengers for Ireland and the Isle of Man ("such do not come within the meaning of the emigration") was transmitted with that port's first submission of names and endorsed by Tompkyns on Jan. 20, 1774 (T47/9/5). The Treasury Board, with Lord North in attendance, cleared up all these questions at its Jan. 20 meeting, informing the customs commissioners that if the Harwich officers "shall be satisfied that the persons embarking at that port are going to Holland or the continent of Europe, and their officers at Liverpool that the passengers embarking at that port for Ireland or the Isle of Man are actually going thither, My Lords do not think it necessary that they should take any account of such persons." As a result, the several thousand entries in the Register that document departures for Europe do not represent British voyages to Europe in any comprehensive way. Many passengers on vessels leaving the port of Dover, for example, presumably on cross-Channel voyages, simply "refused further account" of themselves than their names. The entries of voyages to Europe are therefore a random compilation recorded only by those outport officials who did not understand the purpose of the data gathering, did not inquire, and simply sent on whatever information about departures came to hand.

body of immigration data comparable in detail and comprehensiveness for the entire first two centuries of American history. Here, in the sheets received at the Treasury Office—which together comprise what may be called the Register of Emigrants, 1773–1776—well preserved in four large volumes of Treasury papers (T47/9–12), are the answers to the questions that so agitated the Hillsboroughs, Millers, and Suffolks: who were the people leaving Britain—what age, which sex, what occupations were represented and in what proportions? Where did they come from, why did they leave, from what strata of society were they drawn? How did they travel, where were they going? And here are the data from which studies can be made of the fate of individuals and families, from their origins in Britain to their ultimate destinies in North America. From career-line patterns, traced backward and forward through the matrix of the Register one can gain a detailed picture of this movement of people, the crest of a wave that had been sweeping forward for over a decade.

Yet, valuable as it is, this information, collected on the order of the Treasury for the eventual use of Parliament, is by no means ideal as a source for depicting in modern statistical form the immigration of the years preceding the Revolution. For purposes of technical numerical analysis it is incomplete and deficient in many respects. Since it includes only England and Scotland, it illuminates only a small portion of the whole immigration into North America in the years covered; the substantial flows from Africa, from the German and Swiss principalities, and from Ireland are not represented. And even for England and Scotland the record is incomplete, and incomplete in different ways for these two regions of Britain. The gaps and deficiencies are partly a consequence of administrative inadequacies in the central customs offices, partly the result of the difficulties that customs officials in the outports faced in attempting to record the departure of all emigrants, and partly the product of resistance by the Scottish port officials and by the Scottish public at large, made apprehensive by the lord justice clerk's concurrent and independent inquiry.

The Compilation: Procedures

The raw data, compiled by the several English and Scottish port officials, were sent to the two customs boards, in London and Edinburgh. At these headquarters the information was handled differently. The Scottish material, gathered in Edinburgh, went directly to the Treasury in London; it was not collated, refined, or systematically summarized by the Scottish board. The raw data from the English ports, on the other hand, were sent not directly to the London board but to the Treasury's statistical branch, the office of the inspector general of imports and exports. There the many separate English reports were refined and consolidated, and only at that point were they sent to the Treasury. Though the inspector general's office had only to deal with the English data, the labor that fell to this small subdepartment was extremely heavy, especially since in the end the work devolved largely on a single individual.

To John Tompkyns, the veteran assistant inspector general of imports and exports, in effect the head of the office, fell the task of reading the weekly letters from the seventy-two ports, "many of which," he wrote, "require answers," as well as "revising, correcting, and exam[in]ing the said accounts." His procedure was to inspect, and correct where necessary, each incoming report as it arrived and then to have the information copied onto large uniform sheets. Each week's sheets, with a covering letter containing weekly totals for each port separately and for all the ports together, were given a report number. Tompkyns signed and dated each of these amalgamated weekly reports before sending it on to the Treasury. There the reports were checked in and dated when received by John Robinson, the secretary to the Treasury.[6]

It was laborious work, and Tompkyns was soon overwhelmed. Before three months had elapsed he found it necessary to hire an extra clerk full-time, at £40 a year, to help him, but even so he was hard-pressed. In July 1774 he reported that work on the emigration records interfered so much with his normal duties that he was "obliged to carry the letters home and inspect them after office hours"—for which he requested, and received, an extra £50 a year in salary. At first, he worked on the reports promptly, submitting the collated English sheets weekly. By mid-1774, the bundles were being sent to the Treasury only every other week; by mid-1775, only every 6 to 8 weeks. The sheets for the final week of the series, March 31–April 7, 1776, were submitted 10½ weeks after the information had been gathered.[7]

Tompkyns and his assistant worked diligently. They summarized and sent in to the Treasury all of the requested information that came in to them from the English outports pertaining to every person the port officers identified as leaving England as an emigrant for the western hemisphere and also pertaining to many who left for Europe and elsewhere, from early December 1773 to the spring of 1776. In all, Tompkyns submitted reports covering a period of 127 weeks, and in this 2¼-year period only 4 weeks were omitted (or have been lost): 3 weeks in April and May 1774, when the

[6]On the office of inspector general of imports and exports and on Tompkyns's career in it (1759–1785), see G. N. Clark, *Guide to English Commercial Statistics, 1696–1782* (London, 1938), pp. 1–33; on the order to channel the individual reports through the inspector general's office, see Board of Customs, London, to Customs Collectors, Hull, Dec. 31, 1773, T92/117; Memorial of Board of Customs, England, to Treasury, July 28, 1774, T11/30.

[7]*Ibid.*, 482; for the Treasury's compliance with Tompkyns's request, Aug. 4, 1774, Treasury Minute Books, T29/44, and Clark, *Commercial Statistics*, p. 29.

An Account of all Persons who have taken their Passage ... England, with a description of their Age, Quality, Occupation ... & on what Account: & for what purposes they leave the County,

Names	Age	Quality, Occupation or Employment	former Residence
			Embark'd from the
George Webb	—	Planter	Nevis
Mrs Webb, Wife to ditto			D.º
Mrs Howel	40	a Captains Wife	London
William Campbel	9		Kent
Robert Forbes	57	Merchant	London
Mrs Forbes, Wife to d.º	30		D.º
John Bevell	45	Merchant	Barbadoes
William Bennett	20	Farmer	Worcester
George McCaughlin	31	Gentlemans servant	London
Joseph Ikel	20	Planter	Jamaica
Peter Israel	18	D.º	D.º
William Israel	17	D.º	D.º
John Mackay	15	Husbandman	Inverness
Thomas Cannum	17	Weaver	Norfolk
John Bird	16	Sawyer	London
William Cotton	15	Labourer	D.º
John Garrett	15	D.º	D.º
Joseph Clark	18	Baker	Yorkshire
Nath.l Banister	15	Bargeman	Westminster
John Price	18	Weaver	London
Richard Ham	16	Husbandman	Cornwall
Richard Kenny	16	D.º	Kent
John Cook	15	Labourer	Southwark
William Cole	16	D.º	Ipswich
Dan.l Donovan	16	Husbandman	Ireland
John King	17	Weaver	London
Joseph Harvey	18	D.º	D.º
William Bonner	15	Labourer	D.º
James King	21	Husbandman	Greenwich
Edw.d Fawkins	29	Printer	London
Henry Webber	23	Cordwainer	D.º
John Chapple	16	Brickmaker	D.º
Samuel Robinson	16	D.º	D.º
William Page	15	Labourer	Middlesex

A page from the Register (England), showing emigrants leaving London, Jan. 2–9, 1774. Public Record Office, London: T47/9/19.

...ard any Ship or Vessel to go out of this Kingdom, from any Port in
...mployment; former Residence, to what Port or Place they propose to go
...e 2ᵈ to the 9ᵗʰ of January 1774. distinguishing each Port.

...hat Port or Place Bound	by what Ship or Vessel	Masters Name	for what purpose they leave the Country	other remarks
Port of London				
Nivis	Cyrus	J. Clark	to settle there	
Dᵒ	Dᵒ	Dᵒ	Dᵒ	
Geneva	Royᵗ Charlotte	J. Bishop	to see her Husband	
Dunkirk	Loyal Jane	R. Halfnight	for Education	
Dᵒ	Dᵒ	Dᵒ	to Merchandise	
Dᵒ	Dᵒ	Dᵒ		
Barbadoes	Richmond	Wᵐ Singleton	going home	
St Vincents	Britannia	C. Wade	to settle there	
Lisbon	Dutchess of Manchᵗ	J. Casey	going to his Master	
Jamaica	Parnassus	Thoˢ Hall	to his Plantation	
Dᵒ	Dᵒ	Dᵒ	Dᵒ	
Dᵒ	Dᵒ	Dᵒ	Dᵒ	
Philadelphia	Amelia	Jⁿᵈ Villeneuse		
	Dᵒ	Dᵒ		
	Dᵒ	Dᵒ		
Dᵒ	Dᵒ	Dᵒ		
Dᵒ	Dᵒ	Dᵒ		
Dᵒ	Dᵒ	Dᵒ		
Dᵒ	Dᵒ	Dᵒ		
Dᵒ	Dᵒ	Dᵒ		
Dᵒ	Dᵒ	Dᵒ		
Dᵒ	Dᵒ	Dᵒ		
Dᵒ	Dᵒ	Dᵒ		
Dᵒ	Dᵒ	Dᵒ		
Dᵒ	Dᵒ	Dᵒ		
Dᵒ	Dᵒ	Dᵒ		
Dᵒ	Dᵒ	Dᵒ		
Dᵒ	Dᵒ	Dᵒ		
Dᵒ	Dᵒ	Dᵒ		

Indented Servants

Embarked from the

Names	Age	Quality, Occupation or Employment	Former Residence
Robert Jackson	48	Blacksmith, his wife & 3 Children	
William Ellis	24	Farmer, his wife & 1 Child	
Thomas Blackburn	28	Farmer, his wife & 2 Children	
John Robinson	40	Farmer	
John Robinson	41	Farmer, his wife & 6 Children	
Robert Jackson	39	Ploughwright, his wife & 3 D°.	
Francis Wilkinson	23	Blacksmith, his wife & 1 D°.	
Francis Blashell	29	Farmer	
William Johnson	22	Wheelwright &c.	
William Rabishaw	18	Farmer	
John Hilton	22	Farmer	
John Johnson	20	Taylor	
Henry Hutton	21	Taylor	
Thomas Skelton	33	Tallow Chandler	
Alexis Andrew	34	Cooper	
James Douthwaite	34	Farmer	
John Clark	30	D°.	
David Jukes	23	D°.	
Richard Clark	30	D°.	
Thomas Mooring	23	House Carpenter	
William Webster	33	D°.	
John Lamb	21	Farmer	
Mary White	20	Servant	
Thomas Wilson	26	Farmer	
John Duke	25	D°.	
Robert Wilson	49	D°. his wife & 7 Children	
William Webster	33	Joiner	
John Witty	32	D°.	
Matthew Walker	24	Farmer	
John Neel	46	D°. & Son	
John Jaques	26	D°. his wife & 3 Children	
George Sharrow	26	Farmer	
William Wilson	23	D°.	
John Hoppes	23	D°.	
Sam. Brainbridge	24	D°.	
Adam Hawksworth	34	Joiner, his wife & 4 Children	
Richard Garbutt	34	D°. his wife & 6 Children	
Thomas Gray	31	Blacksmith	

A page from the Register (England), showing emigrants leaving Yorkshire for Nova Scotia, April 5–12, 1774. Public Record Office, London: T47/9/121.

what account	by what Ship	Masters Name	for what purposes they leave this Country.

they could not support their Family
on acco.t of the high price of Provisions.

Farm being over Rented could not support
to seek for better Employment   themselves
D.o all Necessaries of Life being so Dear
D.o   D.o
D.o   D.o

going with a view of doing
better for themselves.

*no account sent
from this Port of
the Ship or
Masters Names*

obliged to quit his Farm being too high rented.

to seek for better Employment.

his Rent being raised so high Obliges him to quit

to seek for a better Employment.

all the Small Farms taken into large ones in his Parish could
not get Bread.
to seek for better Employment.

provisions high, could not support their Family

to seek for better Employment

goes as a Hired Servant.

North Riding

work seems to have become exceptionally burdensome, and one week in November 1775. Ultimately, the quality of the documentation was the result of the work done in the individual ports, but the central customs office in London certainly struggled to do its part conscientiously.

The same cannot be said of the Scottish customs officials in Edinburgh, whose jurisdiction was at least as important as that of the English board as far as emigration was concerned. Not only was there no equivalent to Tompkyns in the Edinburgh office and hence no one to collate the incoming records, but the range of information collected and forwarded was more limited. Though the Edinburgh board instructed the Scottish outports to follow the Treasury's order regarding all voyagers to "foreign countries," the Scottish officials understood that information should be collected only for people intending to emigrate to the Western Hemisphere, and it was that more restricted information they forwarded to the Treasury.

During the twenty-one months from December 1773 to early September 1775 the Edinburgh customs office simply sent on to the Treasury what it received from the outports, either the actual pages compiled by the local port officials or certified copies of them. There was no attempt to present the information in standard form, and apparently there was no verification or correction of the raw data similar to the editing Tompkyns performed on the English data. In all, the Edinburgh board forwarded to the Treasury thirty-one bundles of accounts from the outports, each validated by the signatures of three Edinburgh officials; the first group is dated February 15, 1774, the last September 25, 1775. In addition, several lists from Greenock and Glasgow that should have been included in this regular series of dispatches but for some reason were not, should be added to the Register. Further, the bundles that went to the Treasury included quite discursive letters and efforts of the port officials to interpret the causes and local circumstances of the American emigration, something entirely absent from the English reports. In these Scottish letters too are expressions of the difficulties encountered in collecting the information and miscellaneous comments on the people emigrating. While, therefore, the Scottish data are difficult to standardize and to conflate with the parallel English records, they contain valuable flashes of illumination of the human reality of emigration and revelations of the gaps and technical problems in the data that otherwise would not be known. And on one remarkable occasion the flexibility of the Scottish outport officers and their concentration on the substance and real purpose of the whole effort, as opposed to formalized compliance, produced a series of extraordinarily detailed and intimate interviews—richer, more individualized, more circumstantial, and more revealing than the Treasury could ever have hoped to receive.[8]

---

[8]The Greenock and Glasgow reports that were not included in the T47 series (the compilation

Weaknesses and Omissions

Such care and effort in pursuing the objectives of the survey of emigration on the part of the local officials were, however, extraordinary. Most often the outport customs officials made little effort to overcome the many problems they faced in complying with the order of the Treasury.

The major problem, recognized from the start, was that there was no legal requirement for vessels carrying emigrants to register with customs. To be sure, many vessels departing with passengers carried dutiable goods and hence were obliged to exit through official ports and register there. Further, customs officials in the main ports, habituated to struggling with fraud in shipping, commonly had intelligence sources in the countryside through whom they learned of departures, licit and illicit, from minor harbors. But the customs districts were very large and could never be effectively policed. Some included hundreds of miles of coastline containing innumerable small ports and ocean inlets. And vessels carrying emigrants across the Atlantic were often remarkably small and could be accommodated at quite insignificant docks.

One gets a sense of the difficulties the customs officials faced by noting that, while there were 72 official customs ports in England and Wales (either the main centers, officially designated "head-ports," or the secondary locations, called "members"), there were 117 legally recognized minor ports (designated "creeks"), which were lawful ports of exit and entry for nondutiable coastal trade, though not for foreign traffic, and were important enough to justify the presence of minor customs officers to help prevent fraud. And there were undoubtedly many more ocean inlets from which vessels carrying emigrants may have departed. There is no question that the complexity of the coastline of England and Wales and the thinness of staffing of the customs administration made omissions in the emigration Register inevitable. The same was even more true in Scotland, where in 1770 there were 22 official customs ports and in addition no fewer than 169 "creeks." Large areas of the heavily indented Scottish coastline were entirely beyond the range of effective customs surveillance, especially in the far north and west, areas from which a large percentage of the Scottish emigration originated. And there were no customs offices in the three

referred to here as the Register) are in CE 60/1/7. For the detailed interviews (of the survivors of the *Bachelor* [T47/12/29–39]), see below, pp. 508 n.8, 512–519.

In the paragraphs above and at several points in Part II, I have made use of a report by Barbara Nash on the physical characteristics of the sheets of the Register and on the way they were prepared and processed through the government. I am grateful to Ms. Nash for that detailed study, as I am for her expert help in preparing the computer analysis of the Register. See below, p. 639.

groups of outlying islands—the Orkneys, Shetlands, and Hebrides; apparently officers temporarily stationed there to oversee fish exports were pressed into service collecting the data on emigration. The difficulties of assembling the required information, the customs officers at Inverness declared, were overwhelming. Since some of the ships carrying emigrants from the county "had no business at this customhouse," they often left from distant ports "without our knowing anything of them but by report." All they could do was to correspond with "the most intelligent persons we could think of at the places where the emigrations happened" and combine that hearsay evidence with the hard facts they could vouch for.[9]

Beyond these quite obvious difficulties there were technical problems in registrations that account for omissions in the records. Even when vessels did register with the customs officials, they were free to pick up passengers thereafter. As a result, in a number of instances where American arrival figures can be checked against British exit data, the numbers of passengers on vessels registered with British customs are smaller than the numbers known to have arrived in America.[10] Occasionally, vessels seeking to carry a full complement of passengers stopped in at several locations, almost in peddling fashion, as they made their way out. The chatty Scottish officials sometimes recorded such port-hopping departures, sometimes they did not, and there is no way of discovering the numbers of emigrants who boarded ship in the lesser ports after the official registration had been made. Twelve voyages, of all those recorded in the Register, were entered in more than one port's books; one appears five times. Others undoubtedly should have been entered twice or more, but were not. And secondary pick-ups in Irish ports are by definition omitted from the Register and must be established from other sources.

In May 1775, for example, the *Lovely Nelly* stopped for passengers at various places in southern Scotland, along the Solway Firth and on the Isle of Man, before departing for Nova Scotia. It picked up 66 emigrants at Carsethorn, a tiny coastal village near Dumfries, 68 more at Dumfries, 5 at Douglas (Isle of Man), 2 at Whitehaven (Cumberland), and 9 at the port of Kirkcudbright. These stops and pick-ups are registered; how many

---

[9]Elizabeth E. Hoon, *The Organization of the English Customs System, 1696–1786* (New York, 1938), chap. 5. The figure of 72 head-ports and members is Tompkyns's; he should have known (Memorial of Board of Customs, England, to Treasury, July 28, 1774, T11/30). But Samuel Baldwin's *Survey of the British Customs . . .* (London, 1770), pp. 21–22, lists 74, as does Henry Crouch, *A Complete View of the British Customs . . .*, 4th ed. (London, 1745), pp. 371–374; Hoon finds 71 in 1784. The rest of the figures cited above are taken from Baldwin, *Survey*, pp. 21–23. On the situation in the outlying islands, see W. C. Mackensie, *History of the Outer Hebrides* (Paisley, 1903), p. 423; on Inverness: Collector and Comptroller of Customs at Inverness to Board of Customs, Edinburgh, Jan. 3, 1774, T1/500.

[10]E.g., the *Favourite*, registered in June 1775 at Whitehaven with 101 passengers (T47/10/87), arrived in New York with 150 (*New-York Journal; or, the General Advertiser*, Aug. 17, 1775).

others there were we do not know. So too the *Carolina Packet* left Greenock with goods, but no passengers, bound for North Carolina, but stopped at the Isle of Islay in the southern Hebrides on its way out. There it took on 62 emigrants, some from Islay, some who had come over from the nearby island of Mull; but then, buffeted by contrary winds, the vessel was forced to take refuge in the harbor of Campbeltown, to the east of Islay, where its peregrinations, and passengers, were recorded. If the winds had remained favorable, the *Carolina Packet*'s voyage would never have entered the Register. Similarly, only an accidental message from the Isle of Gigha, off the west coast of Kintyre, informed the Campbeltown authorities that the *Lord Dunluce*, which they had just sent off with goods for North Carolina, had in fact gone not directly to America but to Gigha, that obscure speck of land in the maze of islands and jutting headlands in southern Argyllshire, where it picked up over three hundred emigrants. Shippers commonly offered to stop at a series of designated places to pick up emigrants or at any port people favored.[11]

The problem has a peculiar importance for the major Scottish exit area of the River Clyde, to which prospective emigrants from all over central Scotland, especially the region around Glasgow, flocked to find shipping. The head-port and main customs office on the Clyde was at Port Glasgow, 20 miles northwest of the city itself. But 3½ miles west of Port Glasgow (that is, closer to the exit to the sea) was the ancient port of Greenock, which had been a center of British trade to the Western Hemisphere at least since the Treaty of Union in 1707 and was an official "member" port. Vessels commonly stopped both at Port Glasgow and at Greenock in their exits, and could register with customs at either. As a result vessels registered with British customs as departing from Greenock appear from time to time in the American newspapers as arriving from Glasgow, and often it is clear from a comparison of Scottish and American records that vessels whose passengers were listed in Port Glasgow had taken on additional passengers in Greenock or beyond whose identities had not been included in the Register.[12]

Omissions in the emigration Register were not only the result of the incomplete surveillance of the British coastline. Often the local customs officials themselves decided who among the ships' passengers were or were

[11] The *Lovely Nelly:* T47/12/87, 90; the *Carolina Packet:* Customs Collectors, Campbeltown, to Board of Customs, Edinburgh, Dec. 19, 1774, Campbeltown Customs Letter Books, CE 82/1/3; the *Lord Dunluce:* same to same, Sept. 8, 1775, *ibid.*

[12] Thus the *Commerce*, Duncan Ferguson, master, was entered in the records of Greenock in the first week of February 1774 with 212 passengers (T47/12/4–6) and arrived in New York on April 16 "from Glasgow" with 230 passengers (*New-York Gazette: and the Weekly Mercury*, April 18, 1774). Occasionally departures were said to be from both Greenock and Glasgow (e.g., the *Bell* and the *Active* in 1774), but the actual customs listing was only in one of the two Clyde ports: Glasgow and Greenock Customs Letter Book.

not emigrants. They seem to have assumed that all farmers or other agricultural workers, laborers, artisans, or servants by any classification—in short, everyone who could be classified in some sense as of the working class—were emigrants, and so they extracted the required information from them and included them in the official tabulation. But above the level of worker, rural or urban, and particularly in the broad range of "gentle" occupations and statuses, the coverage was erratic. At times professional people and men and women of substance were included in the lists, but we know from ancillary data that often they were not.

Thus, for example, in the most fully documented record that has survived of the organizing, provisioning, and transportation of a shipload of British emigrants during these years, the organizer, James Hogg, a prosperous Scottish tacksman (tenant-in-chief and laird's middleman), and his family were treated by the shipowner as privileged from the start. Hogg, who was partly responsible for the financial success of the undertaking, was consulted on every detail of the planning; he and his party of 16 were provided with the best accommodations in the cabin. The 264 other emigrants were treated by the shipper as so much cargo, their numbers determined by the available cargo space and the desired margin of profit. When Hogg's vessel, the *Bachelor*, was inspected by the customs officials at the final departure port of Lerwick in the Shetlands, they listed the "poor people" (as the shipper always referred to the emigrants in steerage) but not Hogg or his family. From the Register alone one would never know that Hogg and his family had emigrated. Similarly, Thomas Paine recounted in vivid detail his passage from London to America in 1775 aboard the *London Packet*. The ship, he wrote, had 120 "servants" on board, of whom 5 were killed by a "putrid fever" that swept the vessel. These figures agree quite well with those that appeared in the Philadelphia newspapers after the *London Packet* arrived there. But Paine himself is not listed in the Register, and he refers to additional "cabin passengers," who also cannot be found in these records.[13]

Similar omissions are revealed in Janet Schaw's journal "of a lady of quality" in which she recounted her travels from Scotland to America in 1774–1776. She left from Kirkcaldy, a small port facing Edinburgh across the Firth of Forth, in the same month Paine left from London, and she recorded the passengers she traveled with in some detail. In addition to her own party of ten there were the shipowner's "poor devil of a negro man," "emigrants in steerage," and a miscellaneous group of people "voluntarily going to the West Indies to mend or make their fortune," a group consisting of a smith

---

[13]For Hogg and the *Bachelor*, see below, chap. 14 (the Register entry is T47/12/29–39); Thomas Paine to Benjamin Franklin, March 4, 1775, in *The Complete Writings of Thomas Paine*, ed. Philip S. Foner (New York, 1945), p. 1130; *Pennsylvania Journal; and the Weekly Advertiser*, Dec. 14, 1774; Register entry for the *London Packet*, John Cooke, master, is T47/9/252–255.

and his wife, two tailors, and a cooper. But of all these people the Kirkcaldy customs office registered only those Miss Schaw called "emigrants in steerage"—twenty-two men, women, and children, mainly from the Shetland Islands, in occupations ranging from fisherman to spinster and not including the smith, tailors, or cooper "voluntarily going to the West Indies." It is possible that the discrepancy in the passenger list of the *Jamaica Packet* reflects the fact that the vessel was overloaded and the owner kept some of the passengers "shut under the hatches" until the third day at sea. But it is unlikely that any of the "voluntary" emigrants or anyone in Miss Schaw's group were physically confined; the customs people simply decided that they were not emigrants in the meaning of the Treasury's order.[14] How many travelers in all were omitted in this way, and how many others were hidden from view by avaricious shipowners, will never be known. The range of discretion exercised by the customs officials in deciding whom to include and whom not was obviously broad.[15]

Beyond these weaknesses in the information in the Register, there are subtler difficulties as well which affect the accuracy of the social data these lists contain. Some of the personal information collected was the product of rough estimations rather than of careful inquiry, and classifications were often crude and incomplete. The ages of the emigrants, for example, appear at first glance to be recorded quite precisely, but when one examines the complete distribution of ages it becomes clear that either the emigrants themselves or the customs officials frequently lumped the ages in quinquennial groups. Of all the individuals traveling to the mainland colonies whose ages are given, 28% were assigned ages that are multiples of five. Four times as many emigrants were said to be fifteen years old than were listed as being

[14][Janet Schaw], *Journal of a Lady of Quality . . . 1774 to 1776*, ed. Evangeline W. Andrews and Charles M. Andrews (New Haven, 1921), pp. 20 n., 22 n., 27–28, 33–38, 50, 54–55; T47/12/63.

[15]Discrepancies of various kinds show up commonly when eyewitness accounts (themselves often inaccurate) are checked against the official entries. Thomas Curtis, in his vivid account of his crossing on the *Elizabeth* from London to St. John Island (Prince Edward Island) in August-October 1775, mentions 20 passengers in all at the point of departure, but the Register lists only a single emigrant family of 8. Absent from the list are the affluent Curtis and his servant; the agent for a substantial commercial firm, traveling on business; a Mr. Blennerhassett, well connected with the St. John's officials, and his servant; a Mrs. Churchward, her two daughters and a grandchild; and a North American returning home. Curtis also records that when the *Elizabeth* was forced back to London for repairs, two people dropped out, and when it stopped in Ireland on the way west it picked up the newly appointed chief justice of the island and his party of ten. None of these changes are recorded. "A Narrative of the Voyage of Thos. Curtis to the Island of St. John's in . . . 1775 . . . ," in *Journeys to the Island of St. John or Prince Edward Island 1775–1832*, ed. D. C. Harvey (Toronto, 1955), pp. 9–17; the Register entry is T47/10/139. The customs officials did record the departure in 1774 of the rich young William Beckford, nephew of the lord mayor of London, who was leaving England to take up his inherited estates in Jamaica, but only as "W. Beckford and his family." They felt no need to specify the members of his family or to record the presence of the artist George Robertson whom Beckford brought with him and who painted six notable scenes of Beckford's estates, which were later engraved. T47/9/278; Frank Cundall, "William Beckford of Somerly," *Caribbeana*, 1 (1910), 186–187.

eleven, twelve, thirteen, or fourteen. The figures similarly bulge at twenty-five, thirty, and so forth up to fifty, where all the numbers taper off. One emigrant made two voyages a year apart; on the first his age is given as forty, on the second, forty-five. The age of twenty-one had a special importance: the figure for that year is triple the average of the five preceding year groups. And occasionally "children" are simply lumped together without specific ages. While the age distribution is continuous enough to suggest some precision in recording ages, there is also a rough estimation or classification procedure involved.

The specificity of the emigrants' residences and destinations is also complicated. At many customs offices, specific towns and villages in Britain are recorded as the places of origination, but in some ports the officials rarely recorded locations more specific than counties. Only 20% of all those from Yorkshire entered on the sheets, for example, are given residences at the city, town, or village level; all the rest are said to have come simply from Yorkshire. Similarly, while the destinations of many emigrants traveling to South Carolina or North Carolina are recorded quite specifically, the vague designation "Carolina" is also commonly used as a destination. And it is clear in a few cases that the vessels' destinations are not the same as the emigrants': some took ship for Philadelphia, for example, expecting to travel overland to New York. Further, while the occupational listings are most often quite specific, at times they prove to be rough approximations or rather arbitrary choices between reasonable possibilities. Miss Schaw in her journal discussed the case of one of the "emigrants in steerage"—a Mr. Lawson, whom she got to know quite well. She describes his difficulties as a tenant farmer in the Shetlands, the kind of land he farmed, his marriage to the daughter of a neighboring farmer, and his "bold, manly, weather-beaten" farmer's face. But the Register lists Lawson as a fisherman not a farmer, and though, like many Shetlanders, he probably mixed the two occupations, it is likely that his main work was farming and that it was the problems he encountered in farming that led him to emigrate.[16]

Other vital social indicators also prove difficult to specify: family groupings, for example. On most sheets, especially those from the English ports, families are quite clearly indicated, and those designations are of the greatest importance in analyzing the nature of the emigration to America. But in the Scottish records, and some of those from northern England, the family designations are confused; members are scattered randomly through the passenger lists. And the Scottish enumerations have two peculiar complications. First, most Scottish surnames were clan designations, with the result that large clusters of nuclear families are nominally indistinguishable. The Register lists together in batches large groups of Grants and Cummings

[16]Schaw, *Journal*, pp. 37–38.

drawn from their clan territories in Strathspey; Macleans by the dozen from Argyll; MacLeods from Lewis; and MacKays from Caithness and Sutherland. And further to compound the confusion in identifying nuclear families, Scottish wives commonly used their maiden names, so a single Hamilton woman in a list of McDonnells may (or may not) in fact have been the maternal head of the whole group.

Of less importance but even more intriguing is the failing struggle of the customs officials to distinguish, as they were instructed to do, the emigrants' "quality" from their "occupation." *Occupations* could be quite precisely stated; but what were *qualities*? "Quality," Dr. Johnson wrote, means "comparative or relative rank," a sensible enough item of information to include in the Register—if it could be done realistically. While one might list "Irish peer," "gentleman," and "gentlewoman" as a "quality" in the sense of rank, and possibly also "clergyman," or even, more imaginatively, "Negro child," what was the "quality" of a farmer, a merchant, or a bricklayer? Was a tenant farmer's "quality" different from that of an independent landowning yeoman? And did it make sense, as the Greenock officials apparently thought it did, to call a laborer's "quality" that of "common labourer"?[17] No one, certainly not the customs officials at the docksides, could say. The notion that there was such a thing as "quality" in the sense of an established rank, which might simply have been assumed in an earlier era, was still widely accepted in the late eighteenth century, but its precise meanings were impossible to assign in the mobile, growing, changing society of Britain. The bewildered, and short-lived, efforts of the customs officials to use the category in registering the emigrants is in itself an instructive index of the degree to which the traditional society of medieval Europe had been left behind.

Windows into the Past

The British Register of Emigration is thus far from a perfect statistical source. It was produced in a pre-statistical age to provide a general indication of what kinds of people were emigrating from the British Isles, why they were leaving, and where they were going. Though many of the listings can be proved to be generally accurate, the Register as a whole was not compiled according to modern information-gathering methods. The quantities that can be derived from it can only be the product of many decisions of classification and interpretation made by the analyst, some of them inevitably arbitrary, which are buried in the solid-seeming tables that

[17]Customs Commissioners, Greenock, to Board of Customs, Scotland, Jan. 8, 1774, Glasgow and Greenock Customs Letter Books.

result. They provide not rigorously precise information, but windows, insights, into the past, when used in some sensible conjunction with non-quantitative historical sources. The worst blunders in the world are made by attempting to quantify the unquantifiable and by joining high theory with dubious statistics in order to explain, in rigorous-seeming fashion, developments that are in their nature vague and full of the confusion of human affairs.

Still, for all its imperfections, the Register of Emigration remains the most comprehensive, most detailed, and most revealing survey of British emigration and of American immigration that has survived from the pre-Revolutionary era. Used with caution and in close conjunction with literary sources, it can provide deep insights into a major phase of the peopling of America.[18]

[18] A number of historians have used portions of the Register, preserved as volumes 9–12 of Treasury Papers 47, though not the important supplementary material. The first significant study of any of these sheets, however, was made by Mildred Campbell in her important and still resonating article "English Emigration on the Eve of the American Revolution," *American Historical Review*, LXI (Oct. 1955), 1–20. She was the first to attempt to sketch the social characteristics of the emigrants. All later students of the subject, even those who differ with her interpretation of the data, are indebted to her for this pioneering study.

The two main segments of the Register (not the supplementary lists) have been separately transcribed: Gerald Fothergill, comp., *Emigrants from England, 1773–1776* (Baltimore, 1964), and Viola R. Cameron, comp., *Emigrants from Scotland to America, 1774–1775* (Baltimore, 1959). Both transcriptions, however, contain errors far more important than the usual small inaccuracies inevitable in compilations of this kind. Fothergill's list, which includes spelling errors too numerous to count, scrambles residences and destinations (Westminster for Westmorland, for example, London for Whitby, husbandman [the occupation] for Yorkshire, Bedford for Kent); lists purposes that do not appear on the sheets; mixes up other purposes; omits one vessel and merges or misnames others; enters incorrect dates of departure; cites ship departures from the wrong ports; locates passengers on the wrong vessels; and omits all shipmasters' names and in many cases the terms of tenure of indentured servitude. Cameron's list, which contains some similar errors in transcription, in addition omits about half of the passengers on one heavily loaded vessel.

II

Dimensions

INTRODUCTION

THE quantitative analysis of the British emigration to the Western Hemisphere in the three years before American independence, based on the Register of 1773–1776, may be likened to the inspection of a panoramic painting, a scene of huge proportions but crowded with refined details rendered, like the background of a Flemish miniature, with great precision. The overall composition is easily and quickly grasped, and then, slowly, the details begin to come into focus—the origins, gender, ages, occupations, destinations, and purposes of thousands of migrants: their progress to numerous ports of exit, their regrouping on shipboard, their transits, their arrivals, and their ultimate distribution in localities scattered across eastern North America and the British Caribbean islands. Certain patches, certain configurations, seem at first murky, muddled: it is difficult to distinguish the fine lines. But in the end, after careful examination, they too become clear, and one then stands back and once again views the entire scene, now with appreciation for the details that compose it.

At the start there was no way of anticipating the picture that would emerge. Background knowledge of the period suggested certain general notions of who these people might have been, where they might have come from, where they might have gone, and what might have become of them in the end. But these were vague ideas, too vague to be useful in planning the successive computer probes that would be most helpful in analyzing and describing the emigration. One could only proceed experimentally—guessing at the questions to ask and discovering from precise answers to the wrong questions what the right questions were. The analysis had to proceed slowly, therefore, as one extracted the meaning of the information just produced before deciding what the next probe should be. So answers, fresh questions—some useful, some useless—and new patches of information followed in cycles until a particular area became reasonably clear and one could turn to another, still indistinct part of the canvas.

Such was the slow, halting procedure actually followed in analyzing the emigration recorded in the Register. But what is presented in the three chapters that follow is not a step-by-step description of this procedure. Such an account would be endlessly involuted and involve explanations of by-roads that led nowhere and of crude approximations that were later refined into usefulness, and it would focus attention on the historian at work and not on the eighteenth-century emigrants. What follows is, rather, a scanning of the final, completed composition as it eventually emerged. Descriptions of method and discussions of technical problems have been put away in notes, and a few of the more elaborate tables from which certain of the summary figures that appear in the text were derived are referred to and cited rather than reproduced.

4

Magnitudes, Locations, and Flow

O NE's first impression in approaching the scenes of British life in the years immediately preceding the American Revolution is one of infinite complexity—even if one concentrates only on the movements of people that resulted in emigration to the Western Hemisphere. Thousands of people in every region of Britain appear to be moving across the land toward ports of exit. They seem at first to be following a bewildering tangle of routes and to converge randomly in any of the hundreds of British port towns, from Lerwick in the Shetlands to Falmouth in Cornwall. Swarming in all directions along the roadways, dirt paths, and streams of Britain, and traveling by every means available—on foot, on horseback, in wagons, carts, and boats—this mobile population appears to throng port-town wharves of all descriptions along the seacoasts of Britain: the massive, crowded stone wharves of London from which emigrants leave in rowboats, skiffs, and lighters to reach the ocean-sailing vessels anchored in the Thames; the smaller, quieter docks of the major provincial port towns—Bristol, Liverpool, Hull, Greenock, Leith; and the ramshackle wharves of small oceanside villages like Stornoway, on the Isle of Lewis in the Outer Hebrides, whose harbor consisted simply of a crescent beach with a single pier made up, a contemporary wrote, of "a parcel of loose stones not above a yard in height, confusedly thrown together, so that no vessel could ly near it to load or discharge goods."[1]

But this was, in fact, no shapeless, patternless milling about of a randomly restless population swarming across the entire face of Britain. There

---

[1]Customs Collectors, Stornoway, to Board of Customs, Edinburgh, June 18, 1775, Stornoway Customs Letter Books.

The Dock Yard at Deptford, London. Scene of embarkation.

were purpose, shape, and finite dimensions in all of this motion, and there were distinct geographical patterns. As one draws closer one can make out —not at once with perfect clarity but in broad outline—first, the numbers involved in this widespread movement of people toward ports of exit. One can delimit, too, the locations involved—the emigrants' residences, the geographical sources from which they came. And one can depict also the patterns of their movements within Britain, the flow of emigration traffic from residences to ports of exit, the "catchment" areas of the various exit ports, the orbits of recruitment.

Magnitudes

HOW MANY EMIGRANTS TO THE WEST WERE THERE?

From the sheets of the Register come the basic figures from which a reasonable estimate of the overall numbers involved can be made (Table 4.1).

The customs officials, attempting to tabulate every emigrant departure from British shores, recorded the exodus of 9,868 individuals who left for the Western Hemisphere between December 1773 and March 1776—all but 44 of them before late September 1775, when the formal ban on Scottish emigration and the informal restriction of overseas movements from England went into effect (Tables 4.1 and 4.3). But this figure must be adjusted both downward and upward to reach a realistic total of the emigration. First, not all of these travelers were emigrants. A small number—206, or 2%—made clear that they were definitely *not* emigrants. Some were Americans returning home, some were simply traveling for pleasure or health, others were on temporary business or military missions. In addition, 298 were convicts whose sentences had been commuted to transportation to, and labor in, the colonies—a partial list that was included erroneously in the submissions from the port of Bristol.[2] All the rest—9,364—either stated explicitly that they were emigrating permanently or can reasonably be considered to have been emigrants. Since it is likely that anyone *not* intending to migrate permanently would have indicated that fact to the customs officials, one can assume that those who did not state their intentions *were* emigrants, an assumption that accords well with the known occupational and other characteristics of those who failed to make their purposes clear.

Of those who can reasonably be thought to have emigrated voluntarily, 5,196 came from England and 3,872 from Scotland. The other 296 came from a scattering of places: Ireland (132—only a small percentage of the many thousands who left for America from Irish ports and hence were not registered), the German and Swiss principalities (27—again only a trivially small fraction of the whole number entering America, since the Germans passing through Britain were not considered to be British emigrants), Wales (24), the Low Countries (1), and locations unknown (112).

Of the 9,364 emigrants to the Western Hemisphere, the overwhelming majority—8,072, or 86.2%—gave as their destinations locations in the mainland North American colonies south of Nova Scotia, which would soon join to create the United States. The rest divide between the 797 destined for Canada and Nova Scotia and the 495 traveling to the West Indies (491) or to the so-called Mosquito Coast, the eastern shore of modern Nicaragua (4). But these proportions are not uniform throughout Britain; there are significant differences in destinations between the English and the Scottish

[2]Officials in London and in the British outports, which in 1774 and 1775 together dispatched 646 convicts to Maryland and an unknown number to Virginia, did not include them in the lists they submitted to the Treasury, no doubt judging, correctly, that convicts were not the emigrants the Treasury wished to know about. Abbot E. Smith, *Colonists in Bondage* (Chapel Hill, N.C., 1947), pp. 329, 365. So among the emigrants registered on the *Star and Garter*, traveling from Exeter to Maryland in early May 1775 (T47/10/between ff. 72 and 73) was a 29-year-old "wife of one of the convicts who was transported in the said vessel"; but the convict husband himself and the other convicts aboard the vessel were not mentioned in the Register.

TABLE 4.1

DEPARTURES FOR WESTERN HEMISPHERE
RECORDED IN REGISTER OF EMIGRANTS
DECEMBER 1773–MARCH 1776
BY RESIDENCE

(Numbers in Boldface Represent Permanent Emigrants)

DESTINATION	ENGLAND		SCOTLAND		OTHER[1]		TOTAL	
THIRTEEN COLONIES								
Emigrants	4154	} **4215**	2844	} **3589**	251	} **268**	7249	} **8072**
Probable emigrants[2]	61		745		17		823	
Non-emigrants	21		11		37		69	
Convicts[3]	298		0		0		298	
Total	4534		3600		305		8439	
CANADA[4]								
Emigrants	614	} **627**	129	} **164**	2	} **6**	745	} **797**
Probable emigrants[2]	13		35		4		52	
Non-emigrants	6		0		11		17	
Total	633		164		17		814	
WEST INDIES[5]								
Emigrants	335	} **354**	104	} **119**	19	} **22**	458	} **495**
Probable emigrants[2]	19		15		3		37	
Non-emigrants	38		1		81		120	
Total	392		120		103		615	
COMBINED TOTAL								
Emigrants	5103	} **5196**	3077	} **3872**	272	} **296**	8452	} **9364**
Probable emigrants[2]	93		795		24		912	
Non-emigrants	65		12		129		206	
Convicts[3]	298		0		0		298	
Total	5559		3884		425		9868	

SOURCE: T47/9–12, Public Record Office (London).

[1]"Other" includes Wales (24), Ireland (133), Low Countries (1), Germany (27), America (121), and Unknown (119).

[2]Of the total, 8,452 gave clear indication that they intended to emigrate permanently. Of another 87, who were not so clear in stating their intentions, it is reasonable to conclude that they too were undertaking permanent relocation. A much larger group, 825, gave no indication of their intentions; strictly speaking, their purposes in boarding ship for America are "unknown." But the fact that the customs officials themselves excluded from the lists most of those who traveled as high-fare-paying "passengers" and hence may have been on inspection tours and could easily return; the fact that most of the "unknowns" were Scots, who were more likely than the English to be permanent emigrants; and the fact that it was not at all difficult and probably advantageous for voyagers who were making temporary visits to say that to the officials—all this suggests that the "unknowns" were in fact emigrants, and they have been classified as such in these tabulations—hence the figure 9364.

[3]Specific residences are unknown for all but 6 convicts, but all are presumed to be, if not English residents in a normal sense, at least former residents of English jails, since they left from the port of Bristol.

[4]Montreal, Quebec, and Newfoundland: 45, of whom 39 were permanent emigrants. Nova Scotia and the Isle of St. John (now Prince Edward Island): 769, of whom 758 were permanent emigrants.

[5]To Antigua, Barbados, Dominica, Grenada, Montserrat, Nevis, St. Kitts, Tortola, St. Vincent, Tobago, and Mosquito Coast (modern Nicaragua), a total of 303, of whom 238 were permanent emigrants; to Jamaica, 312, of whom 257 were permanent emigrants.

emigrants. The Scots were overwhelmingly (92.7%) migrating to the thirteen mainland colonies; only a bare 3% were traveling to the West Indies and 4.2% to Canada, including Nova Scotia. Of the English, 81.1% were traveling to the thirteen colonies; 12.1% were destined for Nova Scotia and Canada, and 6.8% for the Caribbean.

Such are the overall totals of the emigration to the west in these years as recorded in the Register and summarized in Table 4.1—the totals the Treasury would have discovered if Tompkyns and his assistants had tabulated with care all the surviving lists prepared weekly by the English and Scottish customs officials and if they had included also the additional figures from Scotland that appear not in enumerated passenger lists but in verbal descriptions written in covering letters submitted by the port officials. But these figures do not represent the whole of the western emigration from Britain. Since the law did not require all emigrant ships to register with customs, since the coasts could not be carefully policed, since many passengers in cabin accommodations were omitted from the lists, since certain shipmasters had good reason to wish to evade customs inspection of any kind, and since some vessels picked up unrecorded emigrants after registering with customs—for all of these reasons the Register's figures are minimal. And we know that the records covering three weeks of English registrations in April and May of 1774 are missing from the compilation.

How large the gap is between the Register's totals and the actual number of voyagers from British ports to the west in these years cannot be precisely established. But a reasonable estimate may be made by comparing the Register's figures with the available literary evidence, particularly with the notices of ship arrivals printed in the American newspapers. The figures derived from these sources are undoubtedly rough (occasionally the newspapers provide only rounded totals) and they are clearly low, since they fail to report some of the vessels that appear in the Register and they exclude convicts; but they do provide a basis for estimating at least the lower boundary of the actual totals. Comparison of the Register lists with the notices of ship arrivals in Maryland newspapers and with Maryland customs records shows, for example, an underregistration at the British exit ports of 17% for ships and 12% for people. Therefore the total minimal figure for English and Scottish emigration to Maryland is not 2,328, as recorded in the Register, but 2,645. Similar evidence in New York shows an even higher rate of omission: 33% of all vessels were missed by the British customs officials, and at least 39% of all voyagers (58% of all those from England, 34% of those from Scotland). The lowest percentage of omitted emigrants is that of Virginia: arrival notices indicate that the British customs officials missed only 5% of the emigrants to that colony, and 6% of all ships.[3]

---

[3] Figures compiled from examination of all extant newspapers and, in the case of Maryland, of the

Using the New York percentages as the upper limit, one finds that the Register includes at least three-fifths of the total number of British voyagers to the west who crowded into the small vessels beginning in December 1773, and probably much more than that. The actual number of emigrants from Britain during these months may well have reached 15,300; it was not likely to have been less than 10,000. And the average monthly totals, before the ban of September 1775 went into effect, probably ranged between 475 and somewhat over 725.

The 9,364 permanent emigrants identified in the Register were carried to America in 402 different vessels—an astonishingly large fleet, so large that it naturally invites close examination. Were these vessels emigrant transports regularly crossing the Atlantic, crowded with passengers? This point in the canvas becomes a bit clearer when one notes that few vessels were listed more than once in the Register. Only 28 of these vessels made two voyages and only one made three; the exodus of these years was therefore borne to the Western Hemisphere in 432 separate voyages. In its mode of transportation, then, at the very least, this transatlantic migration was different from the great flows of the nineteenth century, in which millions of people were carried to new homelands by a specialist transportation system organized to profit by their needs.

But this is merely a first crude impression of an intriguingly complex matter. A more detailed view is provided by the figures on passenger loads presented in Table 4.2. What were the average and median passenger loads on these 432 transatlantic crossings? The answers provide a revealing glimpse at the conditions of the voyagers' travel and the organization behind this population movement, topics that will eventually come into much clearer focus and suggest some basic characteristics of the migration as a whole.

While the overall mean passenger load per vessel was 21.7, the median was less than 5. The difference is explained by the columns of Table 4.2 that summarize the detailed distribution of passenger loads. Comparison of the "total" columns of ships and passengers proves that the overwhelming number of vessels could not have been primarily engaged in emigrant transportation: three-fourths of this entire fleet of vessels carried fewer than 20 passengers each; one-half carried fewer than 5 each; indeed, the complete breakdown, not included in the table, shows that in fully one-third (150) of all 432 Atlantic crossings, ships carried only one or two passengers. Obviously most of the 402 vessels were engaged in ordinary commercial voyages

---

Annapolis port records. The Carolina newspapers do not contain enough reliable information on ship arrivals, and migration to New England was too sparse to justify tabulations for that region.

and incidentally accommodated passengers to fill out their cargo and turn an extra profit.[4]

But that is only half of the picture: for while most *ships* carried few people, most *people* went on vessels crowded with fellow emigrants. The great majority of the people who crossed the Atlantic were *not* carried in small numbers as incidental cargo. Only 4.5% of the emigrants went on the vessels that carried four or fewer passengers (half of the entire fleet). The vast majority went in relatively large groups, on board vessels that must have been primarily engaged in passenger traffic, loaded quite heavily with emigrants. Of all the voyages recorded, only 22 (5.1%) carried 100 or more passengers, but those 22 voyages alone accounted for the transportation of 3,649 people, or almost 40% of the total number of voyagers. The vessels that carried between 50 and 100 passengers account for another 2,471 people, or 26.4% of the total. In all, almost two-thirds (6,120) of all the voyagers crossed on vessels bearing 50 or more passengers, despite the fact that it was a very common event for commercial vessels otherwise freighted to pick up a few passengers to supplement their usual cargoes.

These figures are clues to some of the underlying circumstances of the emigration. While they are interesting in themselves, when reanalyzed in terms of the *geography* of the exodus they reveal the outlines of a broad theme in the social history of the emigration. For the transportation patterns of the various regions and ports differ radically.

From Table 4.2 it emerges that the average number of passengers on vessels leaving England was 14.9; but for those leaving Scotland it was 70.3 —almost five times as many; and while the median load from England was only 4.1, the median load of Scottish vessels was a remarkable 30.0. Almost 70% of all vessels leaving England bore fewer than 10 passengers; 78.9% bore fewer than 20; 91.3% fewer than 50. Among the Scottish vessels, only just over 28% bore fewer than 10 passengers and less than 55% fewer than 50. At the other extreme, a bare 2.1% of the English vessels transported 100 or more voyagers, while over a quarter of all Scottish vessels carried such large loads. The differences from the point of view of the passengers are even more striking. Half of all those who left England crossed the Atlantic in groups of less than 50; only one-tenth of those from Scotland did so. Almost one-fourth of those from England traveled in groups of less than 20, almost one-sixth in groups of less than 10. The equivalent figures for Scotland are trivially small (2.6% and 1.3%). On the other hand, almost two-thirds of all the emigrants from Scotland traveled on vessels bearing 150 or more passengers; only one-fifteenth of those from England did so.

---

[4]The total number of registered vessels voyaging to the Western Hemisphere is 471, but only 402 carried those who have been identified as permanent emigrants. Twenty-nine of the 402 made two or more voyages, hence the distinction between ships (402) and ship voyages (432). Cf. below, Table 6.7, n.2.

TABLE 4.2

	LONDON				SOUTHERN ENGLAND				NORTHERN ENGLAND			
	SHIPS		EMIGRANTS		SHIPS		EMIGRANTS		SHIPS		EMIGRANTS	
	N	%	N	%	N	%	N	%	N	%	N	%
PASSENGERS PER SHIP												
1–4	120	48.6	228	5.7	55	66.3	118	21.6	26	53.0	53	4.7
5–9	42	17.0	282	7.1	11	13.3	73	13.4	9	18.4	63	5.6
10–19	24	9.7	337	8.5	10	12.0	135	24.8	2	4.1	32	2.9
20–49	35	14.2	1192	30.0	7	8.4	219	40.2	5	10.2	141	12.6
Total 1–49	221	89.5	2039	51.3	83	100.0	545	100.0	42	85.7	289	25.8
50–99	23	9.3	1604	40.4	0	0	0	0	2	4.1	148	13.2
100–149	3	1.2	330	8.3	0	0	0	0	3	6.1	303	27.1
150–199	0	0	0	0	0	0	0	0	2	4.1	379	33.9
200–249	0	0	0	0	0	0	0	0	0	0	0	0
250–300	0	0	0	0	0	0	0	0	0	0	0	0
Total	247	100.0	3973	100.0	83	100.0	545	100.0	49	100.0	1119	100.0

	LONDON	SOUTHERN ENGLAND	NORTHERN ENGLAND
Median	4.8	3.1	4.0
Mean	16.1	6.6	22.8
Standard deviation	23.8	8.9	44.0

Note: It was originally assumed that each ship's voyage could be assigned a single port of departure. But it was discovered that 12 vessels stopped at more than one port (16 in all) before crossing the Atlantic, picking up emigrants at these additional stops. These "extra" port stops, but not the emigrants picked up on those stops, have been absorbed into the main port of departure—that is, each ship was classified as having departed from a single port so that Table 4.2 would reflect actual vessels as well as actual numbers of passengers on each transatlantic voyage. But this necessary decision created other problems, which were solved in ways that affect Table 4.2 as follows. (1) One ship, departing from 3 Scottish ports with 150 people, stopped at 2 English ports and picked up 7 more English emigrants; the voyage is treated as a single departure from one Scottish port. (2) The *Marlborough* (discussed below, pp. 548–554) made two voyages to America, one in 1774, the other in 1775, and both times picked up passengers first in Whitby, northern England, and then in Kirkwall, Scotland. It crossed the Atlantic with 84 emigrants in 1774, only 29 of whom came from Whitby, and with 71 in 1775, only 18 of

And not a single one of the thousands of people leaving English ports traveled in a group of 200 or over; 1,431 of those departing from Scotland —almost 40% of all who left from Scottish ports—traveled in such crowded vessels.

But these categories are still too crude: "England" was no unified area for these purposes. Table 4.2 also shows that the differences *within* England are almost as great as those between England and Scotland. Three divisions

SIZE OF EMIGRANT SHIPLOADS FOR SHIPS LEAVING ENGLISH AND SCOTTISH PORTS

TOTAL ENGLAND				SCOTLAND				COMBINED TOTAL			
SHIPS		EMIGRANTS		SHIPS		EMIGRANTS		SHIPS		EMIGRANTS	
N	%	N	%	N	%	N	%	N	%	N	%
201	53.0	399	7.1	11	20.8	21	.6	212	49.0	420	4.5
62	16.4	418	7.4	4	7.5	26	.7	66	15.3	444	4.8
36	9.5	504	9.0	4	7.5	49	1.3	40	9.3	553	5.9
47	12.4	1552	27.5	10	18.9	275	7.4	57	13.2	1827	19.5
346	91.3	2873	51.0	29	54.7	371	10.0	375	86.8	3244	34.7
25	6.6	1752	31.1	10	18.9	719	19.3	35	8.1	2471	26.4
6	1.6	633	11.2	3	5.7	373	10.0	9	2.1	1006	10.7
2	.5	379	6.7	5	9.4	833	22.3	7	1.6	1212	12.9
0	0	0	0	4	7.5	880	23.6	4	.9	880	9.4
0	0	0	0	2	3.8	551	14.8	2	.5	551	5.9
379	100.0	5637	100.0	53	100.0	3727	100.0	432	100.0	9364	100.0
		4.1				30.0				4.7	
		14.9				70.3				21.7	
		25.6				80.3				41.1	

whom boarded at Whitby. This ship has been classified, for purposes of Table 4.2, as having departed from Kirkwall, Scotland, and hence the emigration figures for the ports in northern England show 47 fewer emigrants than were actually registered there. (3) A London ship carrying 42 emigrants from London and 1 from Portsmouth was classified as having departed from London; its stop in Portsmouth, southern England, is not recorded as a departure, and the single emigrant who boarded at Portsmouth is included in the London figures. (4) Similarly, 2 ships carrying a total of 5 emigrants from London and 5 from Plymouth were both counted as London departures, hence the emigrants from Plymouth, southern England, were included in the totals of ship departures from London. (5) One ship that left from Plymouth with 4 emigrants, and from London with 1, was classified as having departed from Plymouth; the 1 emigrant leaving from London is therefore recorded as having departed from Plymouth, southern England. Thus while some very small shifts have been made in the exit ports of the emigrants, the sizes of shiploads and the number of actual ships are accurate.

of the English ports are printed in the table: *northern England* (Liverpool, Whitehaven, Newcastle, Stockton, and the three Yorkshire ports of Whitby, Scarborough, and Hull); *southern England* (Bristol, Yarmouth, and the south coast and channel ports of Falmouth, Plymouth, Exeter, Lyme, Poole, Portsmouth, and Deal); and *London*. Of these seventeen ports the northern group is the closest in pattern to the Scottish, and the southern ports are at the opposite extreme. Almost three-fourths (74.2%) of all the emigrants who left from the ports of northern England left on vessels bearing 50 or more passengers; but only 48.7% of those leaving London and none of those leaving from the southern ports had the same experience.

The conclusion is obvious. The incidental traffic in emigrants—commercial vessels picking up a few emigrants to supplement their normal freight—appears to have been common chiefly in the southern English ports; the deliberately organized emigrant traffic as a trade in itself appears to have dominated emigration largely in the north English ports and in Scotland; and there seems to have been some kind of a blending of the two patterns in the case of London.

Some of the finer details, and part of the explanation for these varying patterns, are found in the monthly departure figures in Table 4.3, illustrated by Figure 4.1, which is based on that table. From the last columns it seems clear that, while there was considerable variation from month to month throughout these years, the English figures are relatively stable while the Scottish are more erratic and reach an extraordinary peak in September 1775, just before the ban on emigration went into effect. Significantly, there was no such last-minute explosion in English emigration. Otherwise, in Scotland, May was the month most favored for departures, followed by a steep decline in June; the English figures start high in the early months of the year and then decline. The summer months usually saw little emigration in either region, and in general the bulk of the emigration took place in the first five months of the year.

But these seasonal figures, when taken together with the information in Table 4.2, show much more than simply these monthly or seasonal phasings. The bulges in the monthly emigration figures prove to be reflections not of shifting numbers of registered vessels but of marked changes in the numbers of people per vessel. In May 1774 the total emigration figure was almost 2½ times the average of the other eleven months; vessels departing in May were carrying half again as many emigrants as the average of the previous four months. In 1775, too, May saw the largest number of emigrant departures except for the extraordinary exodus in September, and again the increase is accounted for by the larger sizes of the human cargoes, not by pronounced increases in the number of registered vessels.

These variations in monthly figures illuminate the picture considerably. The increases in the average numbers of passengers per vessel were the result of the occasional departures of a few ships with unusually large numbers of registered passengers. One can picture, therefore, month by month a steady flow of emigrants leaving in small numbers on commercial vessels otherwise engaged in normal transatlantic freight carriage, and then at certain times a few vessels leaving with 50, 100, or even 200 or more passengers, vessels that could not have been ordinary commercial carriers but must have been vessels especially hired and fitted out for emigrant

FIGURE 4.1

DEPARTURES PER MONTH

1774–1775

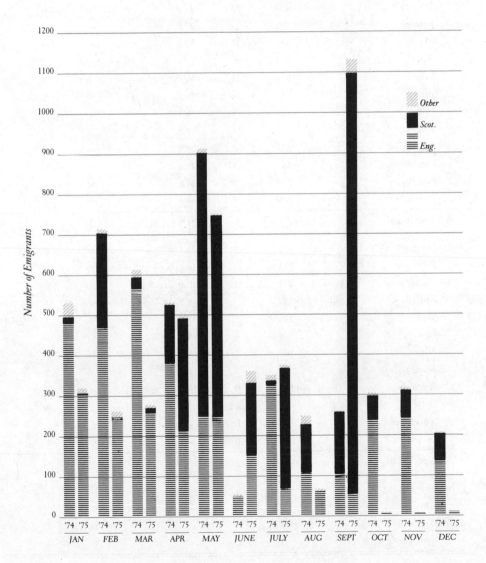

TABLE 4.3

DATE OF DEPARTURE	THIRTEEN COLONIES			CANADA		
	Number of emigrants	Number of ships	Avg. number of emigrants per ship	Number of emigrants	Number of ships	Avg. number of emigrants per ship
1773 December	199	7	28.4	0	0	–
1774 January	473	15	31.5	0	0	–
February	591	23	25.7	104	2	52.0
March	395	33	12.0	190	2	95.0
April	274	10	27.4	227	4	56.8
May	911	22	41.4	0	0	–
June	41	2	20.5	0	0	–
July	329	18	18.3	0	0	–
August	242	14	17.3	6	1	6.0
September	233	8	29.1	0	0	–
October	263	12	21.9	0	0	–
November	279	9	31.0	0	0	–
December	179	4	44.8	0	0	–
Year Total	4210	170	24.8	527	9	58.6
1775 January	302	11	27.5	0	0	–
February	253	13	19.5	0	0	–
March	242	12	20.2	21	4	5.3
April	399	9	44.3	84	3	28.0
May	596	13	45.8	152	2	76.0
June	358	6	59.7	0	0	–
July	340	5	68.0	0	0	–
August	53	3	17.7	13	2	6.5
September	1115	9	123.9	0	0	–
October	5	1	5.0	0	0	–
November	0	0	–	0	0	–
December	0	0	–	0	0	–
Year Total	3663	82	44.7	270	11	24.5
1776 January	0	0	–	0	0	–
February	0	0	–	0	0	–
March	0	0	–	0	0	–
Year Total	0	0	–	0	0	–
Total 1773–1776	8072	259	31.2	797	20	39.9

[1]Includes only vessels that carried permanent emigrants. Each ship-voyage is counted only once, though several vessels stopped at more than one port before crossing the Atlantic.
[2]One vessel carrying passengers to Jamaica went on to New York to deliver one emigrant there. To maintain the relationship between vessels and passengers, this individual was included in the total for the West Indies.

WEST INDIES[2]			TOTAL					ORIGINS OF EMIGRANTS		
Number of emigrants	Number of ships	Avg. number of emigrants per ship	Total emigrants	Ships from English ports[3]	Ships from Scottish ports	Total ships	Avg. number of emigrants per ship	England	Scotland	Other
73	29	2.5	272	34	2	36	7.6	229	30	13
62	24	2.6	535	37	2	39	13.7	481	13	41
17	5	3.4	712	28	2	30	23.7	468	234	10
30	10	3.0	615	39	6	45	13.7	563	29	23
25	5	5.0	526	17	2	19	27.7	378	144	4
0	0	–	911	16	6	22	41.4	248	652	11
11	2	5.5	52	4	0	4	13.0	49	0	3
19	4	4.8	348	22	0	22	15.8	323	8	17
0	0	–	248	13	2	15	16.5	106	120	22
25	3	8.3	258	7	4	11	23.5	105	150	3
40	6	6.7	303	16	2	18	16.8	238	55	10
36	19	1.9	315	27	1	28	11.3	241	67	7
25	8	3.1	204	11	1	12	17.0	135	66	3
290	86	3.4	5027	237	28	265	19.0	3335	1538	154
18	6	3.0	320	17	0	17	18.8	301	3	16
4	1	4.0	257	14	0	14	18.4	242	1	14
13	4	3.3	276	19	1	20	13.8	255	12	9
12	4	3.0	495	12	4	16	30.9	212	277	6
2	2	1.0	750	12	5	17	44.1	247	499	4
0	0	–	358	4	2	6	59.7	151	177	30
31	2	15.5	371	1	6	7	53.0	69	294	8
0	0	–	66	5	0	5	13.2	61	0	5
13	2	6.5	1128	6	5	11	102.5	52	1041	35
4	3	1.3	9	4	0	4	2.3	8	0	1
3	1	3.0	3	1	0	1	3.0	3	0	0
9	5	1.8	9	5	0	5	1.8	9	0	0
109	30	3.6	4042	100	23	123	32.9	1610	2304	128
4	2	2.0	4	2	0	2	2.0	4	0	0
5	1	5.0	5	1	0	1	5.0	5	0	0
14	5	2.8	14	5	0	5	2.8	13	0	1
23	8	2.9	23	8	0	8	2.9	22	0	1
495	153	3.2	9364	379	53	432	21.7	5196	3872	296

[3]The *Marlborough* on two voyages, a year apart (see below, pp. 548–554), picked up passengers in both Whitby, England, and Kirkwall, Scotland. Since most of the passengers boarded at Kirkwall, the vessel was included among those that left from Scottish ports; hence the total of ships leaving English ports is short by 2.

traffic. And the specialist emigrant vessels, loaded with 50–300 passengers each, are found leaving not from all the emigrant ports of Britain but largely from those in the three main areas of emigration: London, northern England, and Scotland. In port after port in southern England a very few passengers were regularly being taken on board transatlantic trading vessels, supplementing the cargoes for which trips were undertaken. But in the north, in London, and in Scotland the situation was different. In Newcastle, for example, three vessels left with emigrants in different months both in 1774 and 1775; five of those six vessels carried a total of only 16 registered passengers, but the sixth vessel carried one hundred voyagers.

The same pattern on a much larger scale holds for the huge emigration from London. Table 4.2 makes clear that half of all the vessels that left from the metropolis with emigrants to the Western Hemisphere carried fewer than 5 passengers each, and that those 120 vessels took only 5.7% of all who left from London. Indeed, the vessels from London that carried fewer than 50 passengers (90% of all registered emigrant carriers leaving that port) account for only half of the emigrant departures from London. On the other hand the relatively few vessels that carried large passenger loads together contributed far more to the emigration than the many small shippers combined. The 26 vessels that transported 50 or more passengers carried almost half of all the emigrants who left from London (1,934 people).

The situation in London is therefore complex. Though it was common practice in the great port, as elsewhere in England, for shippers to pick up a few emigrant passengers to supplement regular freight shipments, there was at the same time a small fleet of vessels that on at least one voyage served primarily as emigrant transports. In the turmoil of dockside London one can discern a constant seepage, as it were, of individuals leaving for America alone or in very small groups, but at the same time merchant shippers were organizing large contingents—entire shiploads—in what must have been a specialist form of mercantile enterprise.

The pattern of specialized emigrant shipping is even clearer—less complicated by a steady flow of small passenger loads—in the northern ports. The three Yorkshire ports—Hull, Scarborough, and Whitby—saw only 13 ship departures in these years, but these few vessels carried 666 passengers —an average load of over 50. It is true that a few vessels, like almost all those leaving the other English outports, carried only small numbers of passengers: 4 of the 10 vessels that left from Hull carried 3 or fewer. But most of the people who left from Yorkshire ports were carried in relatively large vessels filled with emigrants. Three vessels that left Hull carried passenger loads of 80, 103, and 186 passengers; the one departure from the small port of Scarborough sailed with 193 emigrants.

This pattern—of almost the whole emigration borne by heavily loaded vessels employed as transports—holds with even greater consistency in the

Scottish ports. The figures from no other region except Yorkshire are comparable; and those for Yorkshire, like those for the northern English ports generally, show a greater variation in the size of the passenger loads. The contrast with London brings out the distinctiveness of the Scottish pattern especially well. Only 10.5% of the London vessels left with 50 or more passengers; 45.3% of those leaving Scotland carried that number. Over 20% of all the Scottish vessels carried 150 or more emigrants; as has already been noted, not a single vessel from London or elsewhere in southern England did the same.

Thus the spread of differences in shipping patterns: at one extreme, Scotland, there were large, organized groups traveling aboard vessels that must have been hired and fitted for the purpose; at the other extreme, the southern English ports, there were small groups of isolated individuals who found passage on commercial vessels with whatever accommodations luck might provide. Between these two extremes were the exodus from London (a combination of both patterns) and that from the north English ports, where the Scottish pattern is dominant but not consistent.

One can now return to the variations in the calendar of departures (Table 4.3) with greater understanding, and in explaining them catch in a single vision, at a distance from the panorama of the emigration as a whole, the flow and mingling of people from their homes throughout Britain to departure points on the British coasts and then out from these ports to destinations 3,000 miles to the west.

The sudden increases in the monthly figures of emigration from Britain as a whole and their irregular relationship to the average size of the passenger lists can now be seen to reflect the departures of a few heavily loaded vessels in the three main centers, London, Yorkshire, and Scotland. A check through the Register reveals that the high figures for the first five months of 1774 reflect chiefly the departure of eight heavily loaded vessels from Scotland and Yorkshire, which together carried 1,312 emigrants—an average of over 160 passengers each. The extraordinary figures for the single month of May 1774 are largely accounted for by three crowded vessels that left from Scotland, together with one heavier-than-average shipload from London. A year later, in May and in the summer and early fall of 1775, just before emigration was stopped, it was again the sailing of a few crowded vessels from Scotland and northern England that accounts for the exceptionally high figure for the country as a whole. These sudden spurts in emigration from the major centers suggest deliberately concerted movements, planning, and a lack of regularly available transatlantic shipping. The relative stability of the English figures suggests a more constant source of pressure toward emigration, a more direct, less purposefully organized relationship between motivation and accomplishment, and a greater availability of transatlantic shipping.

All of this, however, is based on aggregate figures that relate to large areas of Britain; the picture therefore remains only an outline, its details blurred. The fine lines begin to emerge when the analysis is refined to the level of specific localities in Britain and specific colonies in America, when women are distinguished from men, and when the flows from places of origins to ports of departure are carefully observed. As one moves close enough to the canvas to distinguish these details, a more meaningful picture can be seen.

Locations

WHERE DID THE EMIGRANTS COME FROM?

The general grouping of the voyagers' residences has already been seen (Table 4.1): over half (55.5%) of the emigrants were identified as residents of England; 41.3% were described as residents of Scotland. But these were not "English" and "Scottish" emigrations if these terms are meant to imply an even flow of migrants from the length and breadth of the land. Examination of the emigrants' responses to the customs officials' question of where they had formerly resided not only shows a highly uneven distribution of residences but makes available a new range of information that throws light on the social sources of the British emigration and on its inner character.

How complete and accurate is this information? Completeness is no problem. Of the 9,364 registered emigrants to the Western Hemisphere, 9,068 came from England or Scotland, and of them only 9 from England and 853 from Scotland failed to identify the locality of their residence at least to the county level within the two regions. Thus a total of 8,206, or 90.5% of the total British registration, and no less than 99.8% of the English, recorded former residences in meaningful terms.

Accuracy is a more complicated question. Many emigrants must have found it difficult to identify their residences with precision if only because mobility, especially among the laboring population, was so high throughout Britain. It has been estimated that in the typical English village of the eighteenth century, three out of every four males between the ages of fifteen and nineteen had left home and were in service of some kind; typically two out of every three children of both sexes left their home parishes, to be replaced by children of other parishes.[5] Further, seasonal migration was common, and longer migratory swings were standard in several regions. But these common experiences do not invalidate the residency data. These common movements of people were most often confined to limited areas;

[5] Roger S. Schofield, "Age-Specific Mobility in an Eighteenth Century Rural English Parish," *Annales de Démographie Historique* (1970), 261–274; Peter Spufford, "Population Mobility in Pre-industrial England," *Genealogists' Magazine,* 17 (1973–1974), 420–429, 475–480, 537–543.

they were more a matter of local mobility than of permanent long-distance migration.[6] Since the English responses, except those of "Londoners," are almost always stated in terms of counties rather than of villages or towns, they are identifications that are likely to have bounded the range of such common peregrinations. And if one groups the counties into general *regions* (eleven for England and seven for Scotland), this problem is effectively eliminated. Nor is there any additional problem of deliberate deception. For there was no reason for anyone traveling from their homes to the exit ports and overseas to falsify their geographical origins. No municipality required discharge papers, licenses to leave, or "freedom" certifications, which were commonly demanded of travelers in the continental European states. It seems likely, therefore, that for all but the "Londoners" the identification of former residence at the county, and certainly at the regional, level is reliable. And indeed, in the instances where emigrants' statements of former residence can be checked against other, altogether reliable information, the recorded statements prove to be accurate.

London, however, presents a special problem, because of its extraordinary role in British migration patterns of the eighteenth century. For two centuries it had been the "dominant node in the national migration system." Migrants had flowed to it from all over England, and never in greater numbers than in the eighteenth century. By 1700, when the city comprised approximately 10% of the total population of England and Wales, it was already absorbing newcomers so rapidly that plague deaths of some 15% of its residents could be made up within two years. One estimate puts the number of English migrants to London during the two centuries between 1550 and 1750 at one million, or an average of 5,000 per year. By the early eighteenth century, according to E. A. Wrigley, London's growth, in the light of the city's known excess of deaths over births, can only be accounted for by a *net* immigration from the countryside of some 8,000 persons a year (that is, 8,000 more than the annual loss of immigrants by death or out-migration), and therefore that London must have been absorbing approximately one-half of the entire increase of population in the English countryside. Other calculations suggest that one-third of London's population at any point in the seventeenth century must have been recent arrivals, and the proportion was probably higher in the eighteenth century.[7]

[6] Alan Everitt, "Social Mobility in Early Modern England," *Past and Present*, 33 (1966), 56–73; *idem*, "Farm Labourers," in *The Agrarian History of England and Wales, IV (1500–1640)*, ed. Joan Thirsk (Cambridge, Eng., 1967), chap. 7; John H. C. Patten, "Patterns of Migration and Movement of Labour to Three Pre-industrial East Anglian Towns," *Journal of Historical Geography*, 2 (1976), 111–129; *idem, Rural-Urban Migration in Pre-industrial England*, Oxford Univ., School of Geography, Research Paper no. 6 (Oxford, 1973).
[7] Patten, *Rural-Urban Migration*, pp. 23, 27; Lawrence Stone, "Social Mobility in England, 1500–1700," *Past and Present*, 33 (1966), 30–31; E. A. Wrigley, "A Simple Model of London's Importance in Changing English Society and Economy, 1650–1750," *ibid.*, 37 (1967), 44, 46–47, 49–50; Andrew

It is this high transiency in London's laboring population, its character-istic recency of arrival in the city, that makes the meaning of the stated "former residence" of emigrating "Londoners" difficult to interpret. Were those who stated "London" in response to the customs officials' demand to know their former residence actual residents of the metropolis in a normal meaning of the term, or were they, rather, transients or very recent arrivals, most of whose lives had been spent elsewhere? There is no way of answer-ing these questions with certainty, but the answer in general terms seems clear.

First, scrutiny of the 3,974 registered emigrants who left through the port of London shows that a great many of these emigrants had no hesita-tion in stating residences *other* than London. More than two-fifths (44.5%) of those who emigrated through London identified their residences as other than London, and we know from the difficulties of finding appropriate vessels and arranging departures that many of these 1,768 emigrants must have been residents in the city for weeks or months, some even for a year or more. And these non-Londoners emigrating through London were drawn from all over Britain—from as far away as Northumberland, Dur-ham, Ireland, and Scotland. Indeed, emigrants from the most distant areas of the British Isles—Scotland, Ireland, Wales, Durham, Northumberland, Yorkshire, and Cornwall—comprised almost 10% of those who left from London; those who traveled to London from places more than 150 miles distant comprised 12% of all who emigrated from the port.

These indirect indications of the general reliability of the emigrants' statements of London as their "former residences" are illustrated by direct evidence available in biographical information. We know, for example, from the detailed journal kept by a Scottish emigrant, John Harrower, that he left his home in the Shetlands two months before emigrating through London, that he lived in London for three weeks before finally departing for Virginia, but that it was his native Shetlands and not London or any place in between that he identified as his "former residence" when he responded to the London customs officers' queries.[8] There is direct evi-dence, too, in a number of deeds of indenture that have been located which specify the emigrants' residences down to the village or London parish. In most of these detailed bonds, the residences stated in the Register are confirmed. Such supporting evidence is of course fragmentary, and one can document contrary cases where recent arrivals in the metropolis gave Lon-don as their residence when they might have given an address in the

---

B. Appleby, "Nutrition and Disease: The Case of London, 1550–1750," *Journal of Interdisciplinary History*, 6 (1975), 1–22.

[8] *The Journal of John Harrower: An Indentured Servant in the Colony of Virginia, 1773–1776*, ed. Edward M. Riley (Williamsburg, Va., 1963), pp. 3, 14, 19. The registration of Harrower, "clerk & bookkeeper," aboard the *Planter*, Feb. 7–13, 1774, is in T47/9/56.

countryside from which they had come. But none of the available documentation invalidates the general usefulness of the Register's information on residence, and other sources that parallel the Register and that definitively establish the former residence of similar segments of London's population clearly reinforce it.[9] In the aggregate this information is as reliable as any social indicators of the period save gender, and it makes possible a deeper analysis of the sources and character of the pre-industrial British migration to America than has been made before.

Map 4.A shows the stated residences of the emigrants from Britain at the county level; Map 4.B and Table 4.4 show the distribution of the emigrants' residences among the 18 regions into which England and Scotland have been divided for the purpose of analysis.

From both maps and from the table it becomes clear that the emigration, far from being a universal British phenomenon, was in fact an exodus that was highly concentrated in three areas. The most important—overwhelmingly—was metropolitan London. It was from this urban heart of England that the great majority of the English emigrants came. Greater London was the stated residence of 2,345 emigrants—close to half (45.1%) of the 5,196 English men, women, and children who were registered as voyagers to the west, and approximately a quarter (25.9%) of the 9,068 emigrants whose stated residences were anywhere in Britain. But London's role was even more important than these figures suggest, for its boundaries were vague. There was, in this period, no precise definition of greater London. Its edges faded indistinctly into the surrounding countryside. The great city was the core of a Thames Valley region centered on six "Home" Counties.[10] If one

[9]Indentures of Moses Hains, John Wallis, and Moses Jacobs, March 15, 1775, and Indenture of Alexander Abrahams, Oct. 4, 1774, Indentures of Redemptioners, and Etting Papers. A contrary case is that of John Saunders, a runaway indentured servant in Virginia, who can be traced back to the Register, where he is identified as a resident of London. But his return calls him "a native of Wales"—not, it should be noted, a Welshman, as Harrower was called a Scotsman, but someone *born* in Wales. How long he had been away from Wales and how long he had lived in London, there is no way of knowing. T47/9/2; advertisement in *Virginia Gazette* (Pinkney), March 2, 1775, repeated March 9. Two of Harrower's shipmates may also be contrary cases. But such discrepancies are unusual. For studies of other documents that reinforce the validity of the Londoner's statements of former residence in the Register, see, besides the writing cited in notes 5 and 6, John Wareing, "Migration to London and Transatlantic Emigration of Indentured Servants, 1683–1775," *Journal of Historical Geography*, 7 (1981), 356–378; and David Souden, " 'Rogues, Whores and Vagabonds'? Indentured Servant Emigrants to North America, and the Case of Mid-seventeenth-century Bristol," *Social History*, 3 (1978), 23–40.

[10]Considered here to be the four geographically adjacent counties, Middlesex, Surrey, Essex, and Kent and the near-adjacent Berkshire and Buckinghamshire. The "Home Counties" have been variously defined. As a juridical unit for the circuit of assizes in the eighteenth century, the definition omitted both Berkshire and Buckinghamshire but included Hertfordshire and Sussex. The *Home Counties Magazine*, however, in its first issue of 1899, defined its subject as "the places in which Londoners reside, and the places they often visit," and added Hertfordshire to the six

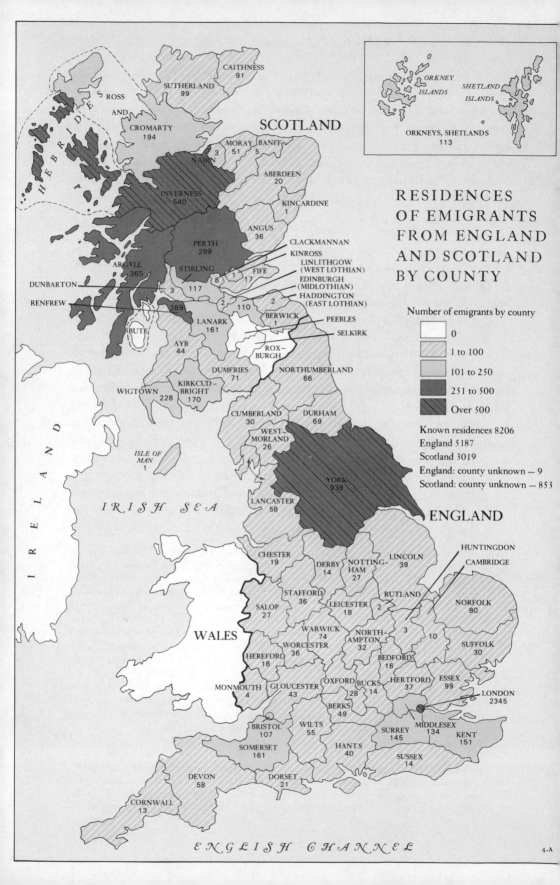

RESIDENCES
OF EMIGRANTS
FROM ENGLAND
AND SCOTLAND
BY COUNTY

Number of emigrants by county

- 0
- 1 to 100
- 101 to 250
- 251 to 500
- Over 500

Known residences 8206
England 5187
Scotland 3019
England: county unknown — 9
Scotland: county unknown — 853

ORKNEY ISLANDS
SHETLAND ISLANDS
ORKNEYS, SHETLANDS 113

SCOTLAND

CAITHNESS 91
SUTHERLAND 99
ROSS AND CROMARTY 194
HEBRIDES
MORAY 51
BANFF 5
NAIRN 3
ABERDEEN 20
INVERNESS 540
KINCARDINE 1
ANGUS 36
PERTH 299
CLACKMANNAN
KINROSS
LINLITHGOW (WEST LOTHIAN)
EDINBURGH (MIDLOTHIAN)
HADDINGTON (EAST LOTHIAN)
STIRLING 117
FIFE 17
6 1
ARGYLL 365
DUNBARTON 3
RENFREW 269
2
110
2
BERWICK 1
PEEBLES
SELKIRK
BUTE
LANARK 161
AYR 44
ROX-BURGH
DUMFRIES 71
NORTHUMBERLAND 66
WIGTOWN 228
KIRKCUD-BRIGHT 170

IRELAND

ISLE OF MAN 1

IRISH SEA

CUMBERLAND 30
WEST-MORLAND 26
DURHAM 69
YORK 938
LANCASTER 58

ENGLAND

CHESTER 19
DERBY 14
NOTTING-HAM 27
LINCOLN 39
HUNTINGDON
CAMBRIDGE
STAFFORD 36
LEICESTER 18
RUTLAND 2
NORFOLK 80
SALOP 27
WARWICK 74
NORTH-AMPTON 32
3
10
SUFFOLK 30
WORCESTER 36
HEREFORD 18
BEDFORD 16
WALES
OXFORD 28
BUCKS 14
HERTFORD 37
ESSEX 99
MONMOUTH 4
GLOUCESTER 43
BERKS 49
LONDON 2345
BRISTOL 107
WILTS 55
SURREY 145
MIDDLESEX 134
KENT 151
SOMERSET 161
HANTS 40
SUSSEX 14
DEVON 58
DORSET 21
CORNWALL 13

ENGLISH CHANNEL

4·A

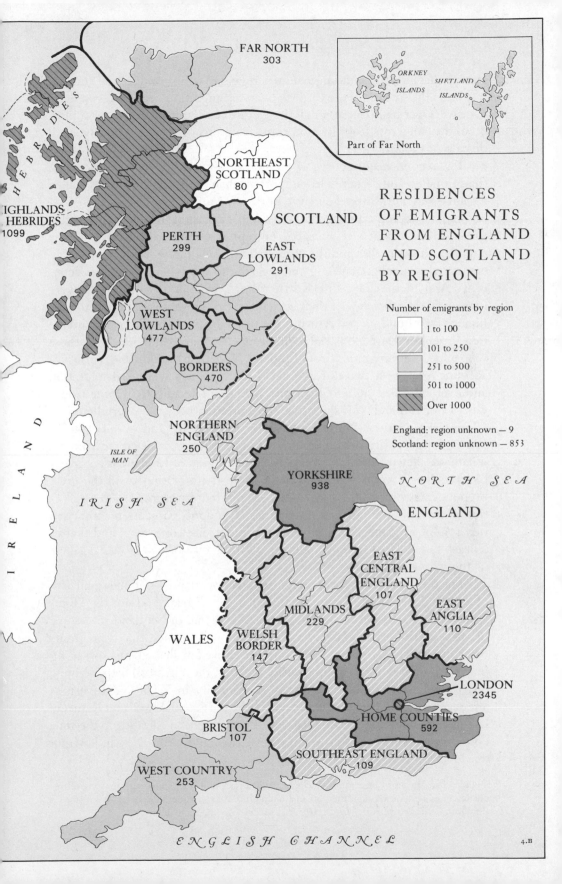

FAR NORTH
303

Part of Far North

ORKNEY
ISLANDS
SHETLAND
ISLANDS

NORTHEAST
SCOTLAND
80

SCOTLAND

HEBRIDES

HIGHLANDS
HEBRIDES
1099

PERTH
299

EAST
LOWLANDS
291

WEST
LOWLANDS
477

BORDERS
470

RESIDENCES
OF EMIGRANTS
FROM ENGLAND
AND SCOTLAND
BY REGION

Number of emigrants by region

	1 to 100
	101 to 250
	251 to 500
	501 to 1000
	Over 1000

England: region unknown — 9
Scotland: region unknown — 853

NORTHERN
ENGLAND
250

ISLE OF
MAN

IRISH SEA

YORKSHIRE
938

NORTH SEA

ENGLAND

EAST
CENTRAL
ENGLAND
107

EAST
ANGLIA
110

WALES

MIDLANDS
229

WELSH
BORDER
147

LONDON
2345

HOME COUNTIES
592

BRISTOL
107

SOUTHEAST ENGLAND
109

WEST COUNTRY
253

IRELAND

ENGLISH CHANNEL

4.B

groups these six surrounding counties together with London, the concentration in the sources of the English overseas migration becomes even more decisive. Over half (56.5%) of all the English emigrants, and almost a third of all the emigrants from Britain, came from this one geographically small district of the kingdom.

The second major source of emigration—considerably less important than London, and certainly less important than the broader Thames Valley region—was Yorkshire. The large northern county, especially in its West Riding, had become the center of a rapid expansion in woolen manufactures, driven forward by energetic entrepreneurs who exploited both the abundant fuel supplies and the cheap labor of smallholders and farm workers forced to combine farming and weaving to survive in the austere economy. And in the East and North ridings, expansive landowners were increasing the efficiency of their agricultural establishments, in part to help finance their building and refurbishing plans. From this still sparsely inhabited agricultural and industrial region came 18.0% (938 individuals) of those who joined the emigration from England. Together London and Yorkshire account for almost two-thirds (63.2%) of England's westward migration and over one-third (36.2%) of Britain's. And, if one adds the Home Counties to London and Yorkshire, the concentration becomes overwhelming. Almost exactly three-fourths (74.6%) of the English and over two-fifths (42.7%) of the entire British emigration of these years came either from the Thames Valley or from Yorkshire. No other region of England is comparable to either of these main centers of English emigration. And the great preponderance of these two regions was not merely a proportional reflection of England's population distribution. London's population comprised not 45% of England's total inhabitants, but at most only 11%, and that of Yorkshire (all three ridings, together with the city of York) was not 18% of the whole but at most 10%.

The third major source of emigration was Scotland—not one small area of Scotland, certainly not any particular urban district, and not the Highlands to the exclusion of the Lowlands. Almost all of Scotland save some of the easternmost counties was involved in the emigration. Emigrants came in relatively large numbers from the entire fan-shaped area spreading out toward the northwest and southwest from the Firth of Forth—a huge district, whose emigrants concentrated primarily in Perth and Inverness and secondarily in Ross and Cromarty in the north and Argyll and Renfrew in the south, and which extended out into the western isles. From the four contiguous counties of Perth, Inverness, Ross and Cromarty, and Argyll

included here. In terms of continuous contact with London in the eighteenth century and frequency of emigration through the port of London, these six counties appear to have formed a significant unit. Patten, *Rural-Urban Migration*, p. 29, uses the same definition.

TABLE 4.4
REGIONAL RESIDENCES FOR ENGLISH AND SCOTTISH EMIGRANTS

ENGLAND	Male	% Male of Males & Females	Female	Sex unknown	Total	% of all English	% of all English & Scottish
Home Counties	525	89.4	62	5	592	11.4	6.5
London	1991	85.9	326	28	2345	45.1	25.9
East Anglia	104	94.5	6	0	110	2.1	1.2
Southeast England	100	94.3	6	3	109	2.1	1.2
West Country	219	87.6	31	3	253	4.9	2.8
Bristol	102	99.0	1	4	107	2.1	1.2
Welsh Border	129	89.0	16	2	147	2.8	1.6
East-Central England	102	95.3	5	0	107	2.1	1.2
Midlands	203	88.6	26	0	229	4.4	2.5
Northern England	171	73.7	61	18	250	4.8	2.8
Yorkshire	525	66.6	263	150	938	18.0	10.3
Region unknown	3	60.0	2	4	9	.2	.1
Total	4174	83.8	805	217	5196	100.0	57.3

SCOTLAND	Male	% Male of Males & Females	Female	Sex unknown	Total	% of all Scottish	% of all English & Scottish
Borders	274	58.8	192	4	470	12.1	5.2
West Lowlands	314	70.9	129	34	477	12.3	5.3
East Lowlands	169	63.8	96	26	291	7.5	3.2
Perthshire	146	62.1	89	64	299	7.7	3.3
Highlands-Hebrides	577	53.4	503	19	1099	28.4	12.1
Northeast Scotland	56	70.0	24	0	80	2.1	.9
Far North	125	56.3	97	81	303	7.8	3.3
Region unknown	345	61.7	214	294	853	22.1	9.4
Total	2006	59.9	1344	522	3872	100.0	42.7
Combined Total	6180	74.2	2149	739	9068		

came 1,398 emigrants—36.1% of the Scottish emigration, 15.4% of the entire British emigration.

Thus the total of 9,068 emigrants whose residences are known to have been British proves to be in large part a combination of three major clusters: those from the Thames Valley (32.4%); from Yorkshire (10.3%); and from Perthshire and the Highlands and Hebrides (15.4%). Almost three-fifths of all the emigrants from Britain came from one or another of these main regional sources. Yet, while recruiting heavily from these three centers, and particularly from greater London, the emigration also drew broadly if thinly from across the land. The Borders area of Scotland (Wigtown, Kirkcudbright, Dumfries, and Berwick) was a secondary center of importance (470 emigrants) as were the hinterlands of Bristol (Devon, Somerset, Wiltshire, and Warwickshire: 348). Small numbers of emigrants came from all over England and Scotland except the easternmost counties of Scotland, the Welsh border area, and east-central counties of England.

The emigration was thus selectively regional in its recruitment. But we have already seen in the geography of the exodus the suggestion of a broad-ranging theme in the history of the emigration. It has already become clear from the figures on the ships' passenger loads and from the monthly calendar of ship departures that the great majority of the vessels that carried emigrants to America took only a very few passengers each; they were vessels engaged not primarily in emigrant transportation but in ordinary commerce and picked up a few emigrants to supplement their normal freight. The vessels that left from Scotland, on the other hand, carried large groups; they were involved principally in transporting emigrants on voyages deliberately organized for this purpose. Table 4.4 adds detail to the motif within this outline by presenting information on a central distinction *within* England and Scotland.

The table shows the sex distribution of the migrants. The English migration, it now appears, consisted overwhelmingly of males: over four-fifths (83.8%) of all English emigrants whose sex is known were males; only three-fifths (59.9%) of the Scots of known sex were males. But equally revealing are the distinctions *within* England—that is, among the separate English regions. In the southern and central regions of England the male predominance is consistently high—in the 80 and 90 percents; but as one moves north and passes the Midlands, the percentage declines below 75% and it falls to the low point of 66.6% in Yorkshire.

To this extent the regional motif—whatever it may ultimately prove to mean—is thus not one dominated by a basic distinction between England and Scotland. The configuration of the north of England is much closer to that of Scotland than it is to the rest of England. Rather than an English and a Scottish there appears to be a southern and a northern pattern, with the former fading out as one moves north beyond the English Midlands and the latter developing clearly in Yorkshire and the northern English counties and holding consistently in Scotland.

Why these differences should have existed we cannot yet tell, but we are beginning to see clusterings of characteristics that seem to be consistent with each other. On the one hand, there was a steady drainage overseas of isolated males picked up alone or in very small groups by normal commercial carriers as additional freight, individuals overwhelmingly from greater London and the Home Counties but also from elsewhere in southern and central England. But from northern England, particularly from Yorkshire, and from all over western, particularly northwestern, Scotland, including the western isles, came a large number of women and girls, traveling in fairly large and probably well-organized groups, on vessels that were undoubtedly hired and fitted for their transportation. So sharp do these differences appear, even from this preliminary information, that one begins to suspect that these voyagers to the west formed, *not a single emigration, but a dual emigration.* There must have been quite different conditions and motivations to account for this highly differentiated pattern.

What these conditions and motivations might have been cannot yet be perceived. But even at this still distant point of observation, where one concentrates on the broad outline and attempts to grasp only the overall magnitudes and general patterns involved, there is more to be seen—particularly the directions of the migrants' movements within Britain, their routes of passage from residences to ports of exit, the direction and distance of this phase of their treks, which would end in a strange half-wilderness land they knew too little about.

Flow

WHAT WERE THE PATTERNS OF THE EMIGRANTS' MOVEMENTS WITHIN BRITAIN, THE ORBITS OF THEIR RECRUITMENT, THE "CATCHMENT" AREAS OF THE VARIOUS PORTS OF EXIT?

Again, at first glance the emigrants' tracks across the face of Britain as they moved to the ports of exit seem almost random in their multiplicity, unclassifiable in their variety. But on closer examination they prove to be far from random. The emigrants did not scatter to the 382 officially recognized ports and "creeks" of Britain, or even to a large number of them, despite the fact that many of the vessels that crossed the Atlantic in this era were small enough to have been berthed in almost any of these exits. As one concentrates on the direction and density of these flows, it becomes clear that they form a few well-traveled corridors, which terminate in a relatively small number of the available ports. Only 37 ports were used by these voyagers; but even this number exaggerates the spread of departure points. Table 4.5 shows that of the 37, only 19 (8 in England and 11 in Scotland) saw the departure of 90 or more permanent emigrants; from these 19 ports 95.2% of all the emigrants left Britain. From the six largest (250 or more voyagers: London, Bristol, Hull, Greenock, Fort William, and Gigha in the Inner Hebrides) came about three-fourths (73.9%) of the voyagers.[11] From the two largest alone, London and Greenock, over half (56.7%) left; from the single port of London, over two-fifths (42.4%).

There was thus not a wild scattering of paths in all directions as emigrants moved from home to shipboard, but convergences from many routes into a relatively small number of ports—nineteen of any consequence, six of particular importance, two of clear preeminence, one that was unique. But what distances were traveled to reach these ports? What were their recruitment fields, the human "catchment" areas that fed them? Which emigrants, from where, passed through these ports?

London's role in Britain's migration system and in the flow of emigrants to the west was altogether distinctive—a phenomenon of extraordinary importance in British and American history—and it must be considered separately. The recruitment patterns of the other ports—the outports—had common characteristics. The emigration from the port of Bristol may be taken as a model. Fig. 4.2 presents the recruitment range of this west-country city, which had been a major center of emigration to the Western Hemisphere for well over a century. Approximately a quarter of the emigrants identified themselves as residents of the city itself, and almost twice that number said they came from localities in the surrounding countryside, within a range of 50 miles (about 80 kilometers).[12]

It is reasonable to think of this segment of Bristol's emigrating population—223, or just over 70% of those of known residence—as "one-stage" emigrants: that is, people who came from places within at most two or three days' walking distance from the port, who were within the city's informal

[11]It should be noted that the departures from Gigha and Fort William were singular affairs—only one or two heavily loaded vessels leaving on single occasions, rather than a series of departures, as in the larger ports.
[12]Except for London, Bristol, and the other exit-port towns, residences in the English section of the Register, as explained above, are mainly stated in terms of counties, not towns or villages. I have therefore followed Wareing, in his "Migration to London and Transatlantic Emigration," p. 376, in calculating the distances of the counties from the various ports as halfway between the counties' nearest and farthest points from the ports in question. I have followed Wareing too (pp. 360 ff.) and the writings he cites in distinguishing between one-stage and two-stage emigrations. Since Wareing's purpose is to use documents like the Register to trace *domestic* migration, not overseas emigration, he is eager to locate as many two-stage emigrants as possible, the first phases of their travels constituting domestic migration. Though approaching some of the same documents with a different interest in mind, I find that his calculations, in the case of London, and mine agree almost perfectly.

TABLE 4.5 115

MAJOR PORTS OF EMBARKATION[1]

| | RESIDENCE | | | | | | TOTAL | |
| PORT OF EXIT | ENGLAND | | SCOTLAND | | OTHER | | | |
	Number	Percent	Number	Percent	Number	Percent	Number	Percent
ENGLAND								
London	3685	70.9	131	3.4	158	53.4	3974	42.4
Bristol	283	5.5	1	0	95	32.1	379	4.1
Plymouth	90	1.7	0	–	0	–	90	1.0
Liverpool	180	3.5	3	.1	8	2.7	191	2.0
Whitehaven	137	2.6	18	.4	6	2.0	161	1.7
Hull	424	8.2	2	.1	0	–	426	4.5
Scarborough	193	3.7	0	–	0	–	193	2.1
Newcastle	63	1.2	55	1.4	0	–	118	1.3
Other Ports[2]	126	2.4	7	.2	26	8.8	159	1.7
Total	5181	99.7	217	5.6	293	99.0	5691	60.8
SCOTLAND								
Dumfries	0	–	137	3.5	0	–	137	1.5
Stranraer	0	–	228	5.9	0	–	228	2.4
Greenock	12	.2	1327	34.3	2	.7	1341	14.3
Kirkwall	0	–	108	2.8	0	–	108	1.2
Leith	3	.1	95	2.5	0	–	98	1.0
Gigha	0	–	547	14.1	0	–	547	5.8
Dunstaffnage Bay	0	–	136	3.5	0	–	136	1.5
Ft. William	0	–	251	6.5	0	–	251	2.7
Lochbroom	0	–	212	5.5	0	–	212	2.3
Stornoway	0	–	189	4.9	0	–	189	2.0
Lerwick	0	–	131	3.4	0	–	131	1.4
Other Ports[3]	0	–	294	7.6	1	.3	295	3.1
Total	15	.3	3655	94.4	3	1.0	3673	39.2
Combined Total	5196	100.0	3872	100.0	296	100.0	9364	100.0

[1]Ports from which 90 or more emigrants departed.
[2]Other ports, ENGLAND: Whitby, 47 emigrants; Portsmouth, 41; Stockton, 31; Exeter, 12; Yarmouth, 8; Poole, 6; Douglas, Isle of Man, 5; Bideford, 4; Falmouth, 4; Deal, 1.
[3]Other ports, SCOTLAND: Lochindale, 62; Water of Fleet, 62; Kirkcaldy, 42; Kirkcudbright, 39; Wigtown, 32; Campbeltown, 25; Glasgow, 22; Ayr, 11.

FIGURE 4.2

RECRUITMENT AREA
FOR EMIGRANTS LEAVING FROM
THE PORT OF BRISTOL

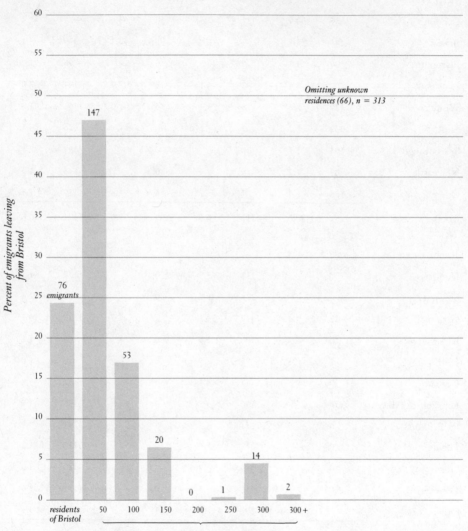

Residence: miles distant from Bristol

communication orbit, and who therefore knew not only the prospects directly before them in their own immediate world but the possibilities reputed to exist overseas. They would have known too when particular vessels were expected to leave and what the procedures were by which one might join the emigration. For them, in all probability, emigration was a deliberate and overriding decision. They seem to have decided on that course, and then to have turned to the nearest port where passenger accommodations for overseas voyages could be found. In their traveling to the exit points there would seem to have been a clear intent: they could have returned home if they had wished to do so. They were purposeful emigrants, not domestic migrants caught up in an overseas voyage they had not initially set out to accomplish.

The same can probably be said of some of the 73 voyagers from the port of Bristol who came from the next two geographical ranges, 50 to 100 and 100 to 150 miles distant from the port. Some of these voyagers too—from Cornwall and nearby Welsh towns and villages—may also have had such clear intentions from the beginning. But others in those geographical categories must have approached emigration differently. Of these 73 individuals, 11 came from London, 2 from Kent, and 1 from Leicestershire. If the former two groups had had emigration in mind to begin with, they surely would have left from London, from which emanated a massive flow of emigrant traffic, and the Leicestershire emigrant would probably have gone north to Hull or southeast to London rather than farther southwest to Bristol to find access to transatlantic shipping.

Even more striking is the presence among the emigrants from the port of Bristol of the remaining 17 voyagers, whose residences were over 200 miles (322 kilometers) from Bristol. None were English: 15 were Irish, 1 was a Scot, and 1 gave his residence as Amsterdam. It seems reasonable to assume that the greater part of the 90 voyagers whose residences were farther than 50 miles from Bristol were "two-stage" migrants—that is, domestic migrants, isolated individuals far from their original residences, who may have been in motion for months or even years, and who did not travel to the ports for the particular purpose of emigrating. One may reasonably assume that they were more rootless than the majority—people who had, perhaps, long been dislodged by poverty or the fear of poverty or by frustrated ambition, had set out to find better employment, security, or fulfillment, had taken on casual work, and had been repelled back into the migratory stream moving through the countryside. Finally lodged in or near the port towns, they had found in emigration a resolution of their problems which they had not originally intended to pursue. For them emigration was not a goal clearly set out in advance, but an opportunity, an occasion, that arose and that promised, if not a radical improvement in their situation, then at least some measure of relief.[13]

This pattern holds, though with significant variations shaped by re-

---

[13] John Harrower, mentioned above, p. 106, and discussed below, pp. 276–278, 343–344, is an exact case in point. His aim in leaving his home in Lerwick was to find employment elsewhere in Scotland or England; at most he planned to travel to the Low Countries in search of work. But ending up completely destitute in London, he took the only avenue open to him, and signed on for four years of indentured servitude in Virginia.

FIGURE 4.3
RECRUITMENT AREA FOR
EMIGRANTS LEAVING FROM THE
PORT OF LIVERPOOL

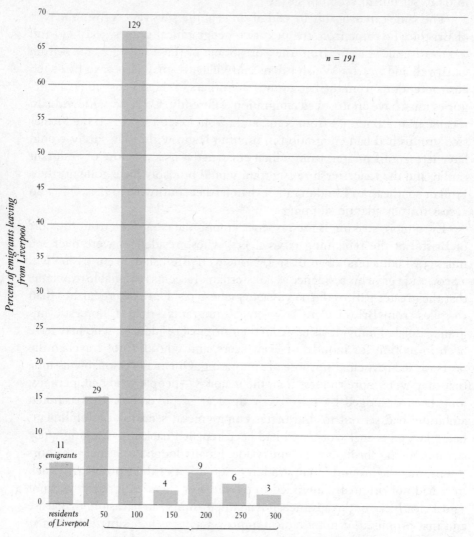

Residence: miles distant from Liverpool

gional circumstances, for the other outports. Bristol, which, with a population estimated at 55,000, was the second-largest urban center of England, was distinctive in the proportion of its emigrants of known origins who were residents of the city itself (24.3%). Newcastle's pattern was similar in that 32 (27.1%) of the 118 emigrants who left from that port claimed to be local residents (5 others came from nearby South Shields). Of the rest, 18 came from localities within a range of 50 miles, but there were also a few who came from remarkably long distances: 6 from London, approximately 250 miles from Newcastle, and 1 each from Berkshire and Warwickshire, almost as far. And undoubtedly some of the 55 whose residences were identified simply as "Scotland" came not from the nearby Scottish border country but from places far to the north.

The recruitment of four of the other English outports—Hull, Scarborough, Whitehaven, and Liverpool—was mainly a function of the large exodus from Yorkshire, which flowed outward in four directions. Almost half of Yorkshire's emigrants moved southeast to the port of Hull; 20.6%, most of them undoubtedly from the East and North ridings, moved north to Scarborough; and the West Riding people divided between Whitehaven (10.8%) and Liverpool (10.4%). Only 15 of Hull's 426 emigrants were residents of the city itself; 407 came from elsewhere in Yorkshire and may be considered "one-stage" migrants who moved to the port for the purpose of emigrating. But even in Hull there were 3 voyagers who came from some distance—1 from Norfolk, 95 miles to the south, and 2 from Scotland. Of the 159 emigrants of known residence who left from Whitehaven, almost two-thirds (63.5%) were from Yorkshire—but 4 were natives of Ireland and 18 were Scots. Liverpool's pattern is similar (Fig. 4.3). Only 11 of the 191 emigrants were residents of that sizable port itself (population 35,000). The largest number came from Yorkshire (98, or 51.3%). But 8 came from greater London and Middlesex County, 6 from Ireland, and 3 from Scotland. Only Scarborough had no long-distance migrants: all 193 of the voyagers from this tiny Yorkshire village on the North Sea coast identified themselves as residents of Yorkshire.

The dominant recruitment center in Scotland was Greenock, the largest Scottish commercial center, the immediate exit port for Glasgow and its environs, and the hub of transportation routes that radiated out across central Scotland and into the lower Highlands (Fig. 4.4). The overwhelming majority of the emigrants from Greenock (95.9%) came from residences within 100 miles of the port, but here too there was a fringe of long-distance migrants. Several came from far northern Scotland—Caithness, Sutherlandshire, Morayshire, Aberdeen. A few came from northern England—Cumberland, Northumberland, and Yorkshire. Some came from Ireland, and one identified his residence as London, approximately 365 miles (587 kilometers) from Greenock. The recruitment range of Leith (Fig. 4.5), the port of Edinburgh, was somewhat narrower, and there was a greater proportion of local residents; but even here there was at least one long-distance migrant—again, a resident of London.

These two Scottish ports—Greenock and Leith, adjuncts of Glasgow and Edinburgh—fit at least loosely the pattern of the English outports; but the other Scottish ports do not. They were not recruitment centers of the

FIGURE 4.4

RECRUITMENT AREA FOR
EMIGRANTS LEAVING
FROM THE PORT OF GREENOCK

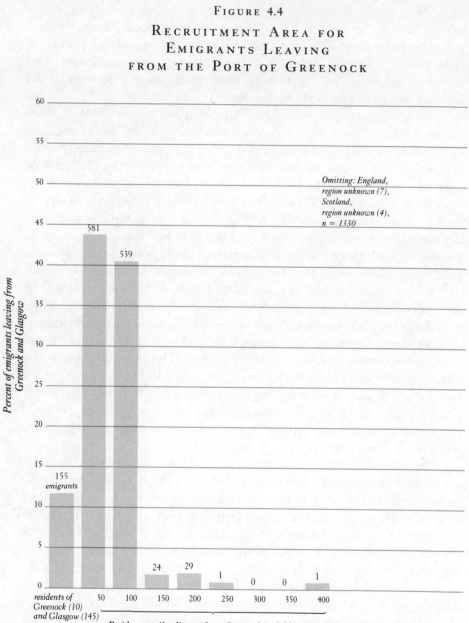

Residence: miles distant from Greenock and Glasgow

same kind. Obscure coastal or riverside villages, they became emigration
ports only on singular occasions and by prearrangement. Groups of emigrants in the countryside decided to emigrate, and organized what shipping
they could in the nearest port, however small and ill-equipped for transatlantic shipping it might be. The catchment areas of these northern exit ports
were therefore extremely limited. Of the 228 who left from Stranraer, at the

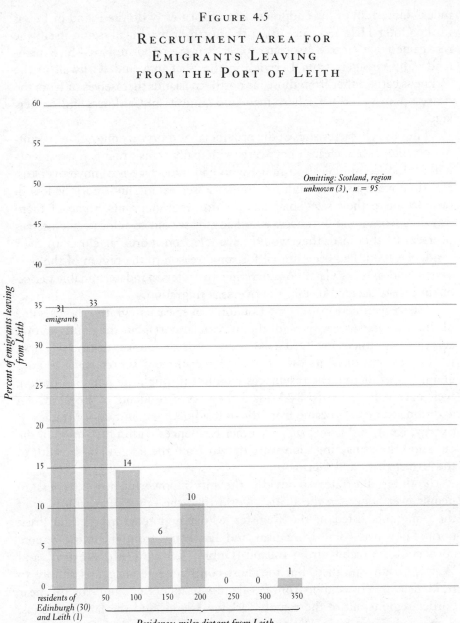

FIGURE 4.5

RECRUITMENT AREA FOR
EMIGRANTS LEAVING
FROM THE PORT OF LEITH

head of the deep Loch Ryan in Wigtownshire, all came from nearby regions of that county and neighboring Ayrshire. All 251 who left from Fort William, 60 miles inland, on upper Loch Linnhe, came from nearby Strathglass, for which Fort William was the nearest Atlantic outlet. All 136 who emigrated from Dunstaffnage Bay, at the mouth of Loch Linnhe, came from adjacent places in that bay region of Argyllshire, within a range of 25 miles. Almost all of the emigrants from Stornoway on the island of Lewis in the Outer Hebrides came from the north of that small island itself; the rest came from closely associated places on the opposite Ross-shire mainland. The voyagers from Lerwick in the Shetlands and Kirkwall in the Orkneys came either from those far northern islands themselves or from the nearest points on the northern mainland counties of Caithness and Sutherland.

Thus the characteristics of the provincial outports as emigration recruitment centers seem clear. They were principally transit points for residents within easy communication range who had undertaken to move overseas. But they were also—though to a much lesser extent, and more or less in proportion to their size—magnets for domestic migrants, some of them travelers from great distances, who had not set out to relocate themselves overseas (if they had, they would have left from ports far closer to their residences), but had been drawn for some reason to the region of the port of exit, and then, as a later consideration and after an indeterminable period of time, had decided to join the overseas migration.

The recruitment pattern of London's overseas emigrants shows some of the same features as those of the provincial ports, but the configuration and the magnitudes involved make it unique. London was distinctive, first, in that it constituted its own principal recruitment source. Of the 3,954 emigrants of identifiable residences who left through the port of London, well over half—2,206 (55.8%)—said they were residents of London. An additional 522 (13.2%) came from the four adjoining counties of Middlesex, Surrey, Kent, and Essex; 126 gave other residences within fifty miles of the city; and the remaining 1,100 were drawn from the length and breadth of the British Isles and Germany.

Nothing illustrates so vividly the city's powerful attractiveness to people everywhere in the British world than the range of recruitment of the emigrants listed in the Register who emigrated through the great port. They had come from near and far, some from the most remote corners of the realm—from Ireland (Dublin, Cork, Meath, Wexford, and Waterford are specified, but the most common reference was simply to residences in "Ireland"); from Scotland—residents not only of the near border regions but of the remote Orkney Islands and the far Highlands. Some had come from Wales; others from Cornwall and Devon; from Durham and Northumberland; from Sussex, and Hampshire, and Dorset; from the Welsh borderland—Cheshire, Shropshire, Herefordshire, and Gloucestershire; and, in larger numbers, from the nearer range of counties just beyond the adjacent territories—Norfolk, Warwickshire, and Wiltshire.

Figure 4.6 describes quantitatively, and articulates more clearly, the range of London's recruitment, and in doing so presents essential aspects

FIGURE 4.6

RECRUITMENT AREA FOR EMIGRANTS LEAVING
FROM THE PORT OF LONDON

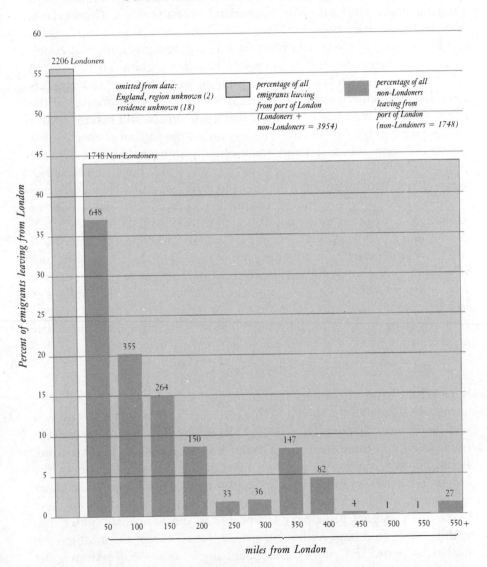

miles from London

of London not merely as an emigration port but also as the primary focus of domestic migration throughout Britain. For it appears that, of the non-Londoners drawn from the British Isles into the emigration flow through London, 1,073 (62.9%) had traveled over 50 miles (80 kilometers) from their homes; 454 (26.0%) had come at least 150 miles (241 kilometers); and 235 were at least 300 miles (483 kilometers) from their origins.[14] All of the last group had come from beyond England's borders: from Scotland and its northern islands (131) and from Ireland (104)—considerably more numerous, these non-English, than the recruits from within the far northern boundaries of England itself: Durham, Northumberland, Westmorland, Cumberland, and the Isle of Man (together, 59).

Thus, many of those who filled the odd corners of commercial vessels and the emigrant quarters of transport vessels weighing anchor in the Thames were "British" only, if at all, in a legal sense. They were wanderers from highly distinctive regions of the British Isles, representatives of the great variety of regional subcultures that made up the still heterogeneous realm governed by British law. There is no simple pattern of recruitment of London's emigrants. Though more came from near than from far, the number of London's emigrants who came from outside the Home Counties was so large that emigration from the metropolis was, in effect, a drainage from Britain as a whole, indeed a funneling, through this single port, of mobile elements of the entire population of the British Isles. Well over half of the non-Londoners who left from London must already have lived through the experience of a melting pot of sorts. For them uprooting and relocation were no new things, and so these voyagers were in some degree free of the parochialism bred by limited experiences within the confines of isolated communities or regions. For these travelers, too, of course, emigration was a long step; but mobility and mingling with strangers in unfamiliar environments could not have been strange experiences.

Such are the basic, elementary facts of the British emigration of these years as they emerge from the thousands of entries in the Treasury's Register. It was a movement that drew from almost all regions of the realm but concentrated heavily in three areas, the Thames Valley, Yorkshire, and Scotland. It did not flow randomly out from most of the available harbors of the kingdom but moved in limited circuits through a relatively small number of ports, of which the most important by far was London. Each of these ports was a magnet principally for people in the immediate hinterland, within two to four days' walking distance. But all except the most remote provincial ports, and above all London, drew some people from great distances—from places hundreds of miles away. There must have been, therefore, a stratum of the British population that was not merely mobile but almost nomadic—a small population of wanderers, for whom emigration was an occasion, an opportunity, that arose after various vicissitudes

[14]Wareing, in "Migration to London and Transatlantic Emigration," p. 370, using the information in the Register, found that in the period 1773–1775, "almost 54% of provincial migrants came from counties over 130 km from London." Our figures, excluding the Germans, agree perfectly: 53.86%.

and that must finally have appeared as a resolution to problems otherwise unsolvable. But the majority of the emigrants left the shores of Britain from ports that were close to their normal residences, and in all probability undertook emigration as a deliberate strategy.

Some of these emigrants left Britain in small groups on commercial vessels that had a few accommodations for passengers. But most were transported on a small number of vessels that carried large groups—vessels that must have been hired and fitted especially for the emigrant trade. It is the irregular departure of these heavily laden transport vessels, chiefly from London, from a few ports of northern England, mainly in Yorkshire, and from Scotland, that accounts for the main fluctuations in the monthly exit figures. The entry of these large cargoes of passengers in the Register drastically increased the monthly departure figures and heightens the appearance of seasonality in the calendar of departures.

All of these, however, are merely the external characteristics, the elemental structure, of the emigration—the general magnitudes, the gross geographical patterns and flows. We see at this distance only the broad outlines, the grand design of the panorama of British mobility and emigration. The detailed questions have only now come into focus. Who were these people, caught up in patterned flows of migration? What were their ages, occupations, and family relationships? What were the conditions of their lives and their motivations in emigrating? Were the long-distance— the two- or three-stage—migrants different in social character from those who left directly from nearby ports? Were they part of a substratum of desperate "subsistence migrants"—itinerant laborers, impoverished craftsmen, petty traders, and wandering entertainers used to camping out in open fields, empty barns, and church porches, and to being buffeted from one local jurisdiction to another?[15]

To answer such questions as these one must draw much closer to the scene, distinguish the fine lines, the shadings and inner designs of the information contained in the Register, and attempt a deeper analysis.

[15] Peter Clark, "Migration in England During the Late Seventeenth and Early Eighteenth Centuries," *Past and Present*, 83 (1979), 81–90. For further discussion of "subsistence" migration, see the Patten and Souden essays cited in notes 6 and 9 above, and Clark's Introduction to *The Transformation of English Provincial Towns, 1600–1800* (London, 1984).

5

Identities and Motivations: The Dual Emigration

MOVING outward to America from residences throughout Britain but chiefly from London and the Thames Valley, from Yorkshire, and from western Scotland, carried to America in a large fleet of vessels, many of them regular commercial freighters, some of them emigrant transport ships, a population of well over 10,000 British subjects removed themselves, in these months, from the world they had known and began the process of transplantation into a new environment and into a new way of life. How radically different this new existence would be from what they had known before, how open, empty, unformed, challenging, frustrating, and exhausting their small corner of America would prove to be, they could not have imagined. Nothing they had personally known or had heard could have prepared them for the experiences they would have, where farms were not so much bought, sold, and lived on as created out of wild land; where the key to success was not so much a matter of inheritance and steady and adroit maneuvering within a structured and known system as shrewd risk-taking in situations in which almost everyone was a speculator in futures and where everything was in motion, beneath a surface approximation to familiar, traditional forms. For these emigrants, it would be a world that called for quick adaptation to the unexpected, that would never be fully settled or permanently adjusted, a world that was ringed about with wildness and savagery and in which the violence and brutality of slavery, usually reserved for work gangs at the outer fringes of civilization, were built into the heart of ordinary domestic existence.

How they would respond to this unfamiliar and uneasy world would largely depend on a complex interaction of subjective characteristics and objective situations. Though the inner experiences of these 10,000 individuals will never be known, and though the precise personal situations of only a few can be reconstructed in detail, there were also group characteristics that helped shape the emigrants' responses and their success or failure in settling into the American environment; and these external attributes can be examined in some detail. The emigrants' ages, sex, family and other groupings, occupations, statuses—and also their professed motivations in emigrating—are recorded, with varying degrees of accuracy, in the Register's pages and in the accompanying information submitted by the customs officials.

These external social characteristics and these stated reasons for emigrating may be seen as responses to six sets of questions.

Age

WERE THE EMIGRANTS OLD OR YOUNG? HOW DO THEIR AGES COMPARE WITH THOSE OF THE HOME POPULATION?

On this question the information in the Register is clear. The ages of the emigrants form nothing like a cross section or representative sample of the age distribution of the populations from which they were drawn. Their ages concentrate at a special point in the age spectrum.

Table 5.1 shows the emigrants' age distribution mainly in five-year groupings and compares it with the distribution of the English and Scottish populations as a whole—the English population as described through "back projection" by modern scholars, the Scottish as described by Alexander Webster in his census of 1755. It is obvious that in the emigrant group the extremes of the age scale were greatly reduced. In the general population of England over a third (34.6%) were children under the age of 15; of the emigrating population from England, of known ages,[1] the figure is 5.6%. Among the Scots of known ages the discrepancy was significantly less: 33.1% in the general population, 24.7% among the emigrants. At the other end of the scale there were fewer than three dozen voyagers of known ages who were 60 years old or older (0.4%); about 8% of the British population as a whole had attained that age. The most populous five-year age group among the emigrants was 20–24: over a third of all those from England fell in that age group, and almost a fifth of the Scots—vastly disproportionate in both cases to the equivalent segments of the general populations. The available figures for the home populations allow a particularly useful com-

---

[1]The ages of about 18% of all emigrants are unknown. Of these "unknowns" on age, all but 133 (1.4%) were referred to—in almost exactly equal numbers—as either "adults" or "children." "Adults," to judge from one ship list that classified passengers both by precise age and as either "children," "men," or "women," were commonly considered to be individuals age 13 and above. (The *Clementina* of Philadelphia, loading 212 passengers in Stornoway, the Isle of Lewis: T47/12/III–115). The age distribution in Table 5.1 may therefore somewhat underrepresent the youngest ages.

TABLE 5.1
AGE DISTRIBUTION OF ENGLISH AND SCOTTISH EMIGRANTS COMPARED WITH THAT OF THE HOME POPULATIONS[1]

AGE	ENGLAND			SCOTLAND			TOTAL	
	REGISTER		% of Eng. Pop. 1776[2]	REGISTER		% of Scottish Pop. 1755[3]	REGISTER	
	Number	Percent		Number	Percent		Number	Percent
1–9 years	175	3.6		423	16.1		598	8.0
10–14	99	2.0		226	8.6		325	4.3
Total 1–14	274	5.6	34.6	649	24.7	33.1	923	12.3
15–19	884	18.1		429	16.4		1,313	17.5
20–24	1,700	34.8		508	19.4		2,208	29.4
Total 15–24	2,584	52.9	17.9	937	35.8	18.0	3,521	46.9
25–29	915	18.7		395	15.1		1,310	17.5
30–34	492	10.1		232	8.9		724	9.6
35–39	298	6.1		158	6.0		456	6.1
40–44	192	3.9		114	4.3		306	4.1
45–49	81	1.7		72	2.7		153	2.0
50–54	33	0.7		25	1.0		58	0.8
55–59	7	0.1		19	0.7		26	0.3
Total 25–59	2,018	41.3	39.1	1,015	38.7	41.1	3,033	40.4
60–64	3	0.05		13	0.5		16	0.2
65–69	3	0.05		5	0.2		8	0.1
70+	6	0.1		2	0.1		8	0.1
Total 60+	12	0.2	8.4	20	0.8	7.8	32	0.4
Total	4,888	100.0	100.0	2,621	100.0	100.0	7,509	100.0

[1]This table excludes emigrants from residences outside England and Scotland, as well as emigrants whose ages are unknown.
[2]Source: E. A. Wrigley and R. S. Schofield, *The Population History of England 1541–1871* (Cambridge, Mass., 1981), p. 529 (Table A3.1).
[3]Source: James G. Kyd, ed., *Scottish Population Statistics, including Webster's Analysis of Population 1755* (Edinburgh, 1952), pp. 80–81.

parison for the ages 15–24: the percentage of the English emigrants in that age span is triple that of the home population; among the Scottish emigrants the percentage is double. The dominant fact that emerges from this table of age distributions is that about two-thirds (64.4%) of all the British emigrants whose ages are known (71.6% of the English) were between the ages of 14 and 30.[2]

An equally striking set of differences emerges from a comparison of the emigrants' ages with those of the settled population of North America. Table 5.2 shows that over half (56.8%) of the free population in the thirteen colonies were below the age of 21. The corresponding figure for the emigration as a whole is 33.2%; the figure for the emigration from England alone is only 26.8%. Table 5.3 shows a more detailed comparison with Connecticut's population. While the percentage of teenagers in the two populations is similar, the rest of the figures are exceedingly dissimilar. Connecticut had four times the percentage of small children as the emigrant population as a whole, but the percentage of adults aged 20 to 69 in the emigrant population was far more than that of Connecticut (70.6% vs. 40.9%).

The first question is therefore answered: the emigration contained no normal distribution of ages. This was a population peculiarly concentrated in the late teens and early twenties, with relatively few young children and adults over the age of thirty-five. But there are significant differences in age distribution between the English and the Scottish voyagers. These differences are so clear that they support, and suggest elaborations to, the notion that has already emerged from the examination of the simple magnitudes of the emigration, that this transplantation of people was not a uniform phenomenon but rather a combination of at least two quite different kinds of social movements. Such social differences must have shaped the ways these thousands of Britons entered into American life and the impact they had upon it. The next question bears directly on this possibility.

Sex

WERE THE EMIGRANTS PREDOMINANTLY MALE OR FEMALE, AND HOW DOES THE SEX DISTRIBUTION RELATE TO THE AGE DISTRIBUTION?

Information on the distribution of the sexes is contained in Table 5.4, which makes clear that, of the 8,613 emigrants whose sex is known (92% of all registered emigrants), about three-fourths were males; but the pattern differs markedly as between England and Scotland. The distinctiveness of the

[2] E. A. Wrigley and R. S. Schofield, *The Population History of England, 1541–1871* (Cambridge, Mass., 1981), p. 529; James G. Kyd, ed., *Scottish Population Statistics including Webster's Analysis of Population 1755 (Publications of the Scottish History Society*, 3d ser., 44, Edinburgh, 1952), pp. 80–81. Cf. Peter Laslett and Richard Wall, eds., *Household and Family in Past Time* (Cambridge, Eng., 1972), pp. 148, 232; Michael Flinn, ed., *Scottish Population History* (Cambridge, Eng., 1977), pp. 250–260.

TABLE 5.2

COMPARISON OF AGES:
EMIGRANTS AND SETTLED POPULATION
OF AMERICA

	AGE			
	Percent under 21	Percent 21–25	Percent 26–44	Percent 45 or older
Thirteen Colonies, Free Population, 1774[1]	56.8	9.7	20.4	13.1
Emigrants from Britain, 1773–1776[2]	33.2	31.2	32.0	3.6
England	26.8	37.1	33.3	2.7
Scotland	45.3	19.9	29.5	5.3

[1]Source: Alice Hanson Jones, *American Colonial Wealth: Documents and Methods,* 2nd ed. (New York, 1978), III, 1787 (Table 4.21). Excludes indentured servants (estimated 2.3% of the population) in transition from emigrants to permanent residents.
[2]Excludes emigrants of unknown age and sex.

Scottish emigration is now further highlighted by the fact that, though the English emigrant population was a third larger than the Scottish, there were two-thirds more females in the Scottish emigration than in the English (1,344 vs. 805). Only 60% of the Scottish voyagers whose sex is known were males; the figure for the English is 83.8%. There were more than 5 times as many males as females among the English, but only 1.5 times as many among the Scots.

Keeping in mind this difference in the numerical balance of the sexes between the English and Scottish emigrants, one may turn back to the age distribution to consider some finer distinctions. Table 5.5 summarizes the relationships between age and sex, of course for a smaller population than

TABLE 5.3

COMPARISON OF AGES:
EMIGRANTS AND THE WHITE POPULATION
OF CONNECTICUT

	AGE			
	Percent under 10	Percent 10–19	Percent 20–69	Percent 70 or older
Connecticut, 1774[1]	32.0	24.5	40.9	2.2
Emigrants from Britain, 1773–1776[2]	7.5	21.9	70.6	0.1
England	3.4	20.1	76.3	0.1
Scotland	15.1	25.2	59.6	0.1

[1]Source: Robert V. Wells, *The Population of the British Colonies in America before 1776* (Princeton, 1975), p. 92 (Table III-9).
[2]Excludes emigrants of unknown age and sex.

TABLE 5.4   131

SEX DISTRIBUTION OF EMIGRANTS
BY RESIDENCE

SEX	ENGLAND		SCOTLAND		OTHER		TOTAL	
	Number	Percent	Number	Percent	Number	Percent	Number	Percent
Known	4979	95.8	3350	86.5	284	95.9	8613	92.0
Male	4174	83.8	2006	59.9	219	77.1	6399	74.3
Female	805	16.2	1344	40.1	65	22.9	2214	25.7
Unknown	217	4.2	522	13.5	12	4.1	751	8.0
Total	5196	100.0	3872	100.0	296	100.0	9364	100.0

we have seen before since there are "unknowns" on both age and sex. The numbers in the "Male" column of the total for all residences show that almost two-fifths (39.3%) of all those for whom there are both age and sex data were men in their twenties. In the most numerous group of all, ages 20–24 (1,901), the proportion of males was just under 83%. Over half (53.2%) of all the emigrants of known ages and sex were males between the ages of 14 and 30. It is only in the youngest age category (children below the age of 10) that there was an even balance between the sexes.

When one goes beyond these overall totals to the main regional distinction, one finds once again a striking difference between the Scottish and English emigrants. We know that in general the balance between the sexes was far closer among the Scots than among the English, but was this the result of high concentrations of women in certain age categories? When the Scottish emigration is segmented by age, it turns out that the relatively large number of females is characteristic of the entire age spectrum and not simply of one or of a few age categories (Table 5.5). In *no* age group among the Scots were there more than 3.5 times more males than females, a ratio that was exceeded among the English in all eight of the age categories between 15 and 55. And the younger the ages of the Scots, the more even the ratio: among Scots over the age of 44 the figure is 2.5; of ages 20–44, 1.9; of ages 1–19, 1.3. Even in the two categories where the sex differences rise to 4.9 and 4.5 for the emigration as a whole (ages 20–24 and 25–29), the ratios for the Scottish contingent remain at 2.2 and 1.9. In only two of the older groups of Scots (45–49 and 55–59) are there more than twice as many males as females.

On the background of this information, one's view of the Scots now comes into sharper focus. Though the movement from Scotland to the Western Hemisphere was concentrated in the pre-40 age group, it was far more evenly balanced with respect to both age and sex than was the English emigration. The shiploads leaving the docks of Greenock and the smaller

T ABLE 5.5

A GE	ENGLAND				SCOTLAND			
	Male	Female	Ratio M/F	Unknown	Male	Female	Ratio M/F	Unknown
1–9	84	83	1.0	8	193	196	1.0	34
10–14	62	34	1.8	3	132	91	1.5	3
15–19	772	112	6.9	0	270	156	1.7	3
20–24	1468	232	6.3	0	345	157	2.2	6
25–29	805	107	7.5	3	259	135	1.9	1
30–34	425	66	6.4	1	149	83	1.8	0
35–39	260	38	6.8	0	99	59	1.7	0
40–44	168	24	7.0	0	69	45	1.5	0
45–49	68	13	5.2	0	56	16	3.5	0
50–54	27	6	4.5	0	16	9	1.8	0
55–59	4	3	1.3	0	13	6	2.2	0
60–64	2	1	2.0	0	8	5	1.6	0
65–70	1	2	0.5	0	2	3	0.7	0
70+	4	2	2.0	0	2	0	0	0
Total	4150	723	5.7	15	1613	961	1.7	47

[1]Excludes emigrants of unknown age.

ports of Leith, Fort William, and Stranraer, down to the village harbors of Stornoway, Gigha, and Lochbroom, consisted not overwhelmingly of men but of women and children as well—almost 2½ times more children below the age of 10 than departed from England and one-third more women and girls, despite the fact that England's overall emigrant population of known age and sex was twice the size of Scotland's. The Scottish males, while their numbers bulge in the early twenties, are distributed fairly evenly among the age groups up to age 35. Among the Scottish females, the numbers remain relatively high up to age 30, with a remarkable number of girls below the age of 10.

The contrast with the English emigration in all these characteristics is striking. Instead of shiploads of men, women, and children fairly evenly distributed up to age 45, the vessels leaving London, Bristol, Hull, Liverpool, Whitehaven, and the lesser English ports, carried principally—in some cases almost exclusively—young men. Almost two of every three English people of known sex who left permanently for the Western Hemi-

| OTHER | | | | TOTAL: ALL RESIDENCES | | | | | | |
Male	Female	Unknown		Male	Female	Male & Female	Ratio M/F	Male % of Male & Female	Unknown	Total
2	0	0		279	279	558	1.0	50.0	42	600
1	0	0		195	125	320	1.6	60.9	6	326
22	1	0		1064	269	1333	4.0	79.8	3	1336
88	2	0		1901	391	2292	4.9	82.9	6	2298
34	3	0		1098	245	1343	4.5	81.8	4	1347
19	1	1		593	150	743	4.0	79.8	2	745
8	1	0		367	98	465	3.7	78.9	0	465
1	0	0		238	69	307	3.4	77.5	0	307
2	0	0		126	29	155	4.3	81.3	0	155
2	0	0		45	15	60	3.0	75.0	0	60
1	0	0		18	9	27	2.0	66.7	0	27
1	0	0		11	6	17	1.8	64.7	0	17
0	0	0		3	5	8	0.6	37.5	0	8
0	0	0		6	2	8	3.0	75.0	0	8
181	8	1		5944	1692	7636	3.5	77.8	63	7699

sphere in these years were young men between the ages of 14 and 30; that group constituted only 1 in 3 of the Scots.

But these relationships between age and sex pertain to "England" and "Scotland" as whole units, as if there were no distinctions within them. Are the figures consistent throughout the two countries? When the totals are subdivided into the eighteen British regions described above, a familiar kind of clustering appears. The eighteen regional tables (not reproduced here) equivalent to Table 5.5 show that the more even age-sex ratios of Scotland as a whole are quite consistent region by region. Where the exodus was the most populous, in the Highlands-Hebrides region, the numerical relationship between the sexes was almost even—1.2—and in no region in the whole of Scotland was the preponderance of males among the emigrants greater than 2.5.

The distinctions within the eleven English regions were altogether different. Everywhere but in the north the male preponderance was far higher. Among the emigrants from London, males outnumbered females

6.2 to 1; in the Home Counties 8.4 to 1; in Southeast England 16.7 to 1, and in the West Country 18.3 to 1. In East Central England the preponderance was no less than 20.4 to 1; and no females at all can be found among the 102 residents of Bristol who were registered as voyagers to America. But as one moves north in England, the situation changes radically. In the Midlands the preponderance levels off to 7.8; in Northern England it is only 2.9 overall and 4.4 in the most numerous age categories; and in Yorkshire the ratio falls to 2.4, with an even balance (1.0) up to age 15 and only 3.5 in the age group 15–29.

These regional subtotals are suggestive of what seems to be emerging as a major fact buried in the thousands of entries in the Register: the dual character of the emigration. The information from the northern areas of England, especially Yorkshire, seems to conform much more closely to the Scottish pattern than it does to that of the rest of England. Different kinds of relationships seem to be involved, different social roots, and different motivations.

What were the patterns of relationships?

Groupings

TO WHAT EXTENT WERE THE EMIGRANTS MEMBERS OF FAMILY GROUPS, TO WHAT EXTENT ISOLATED INDIVIDUALS? IF THEY TRAVELED AS MEMBERS OF FAMILY GROUPS, WHAT KINDS OF FAMILIES WERE THESE—NUCLEAR OR EXTENDED, SMALL OR LARGE? IN ALL OF THIS, WERE THERE SIGNIFICANT VARIATIONS AMONG THE REGIONS OF BRITAIN?

The answers not only fill in details for a large part of the picture but further heighten the impression one has that this was no singular movement of people but two quite distinct movements; and one senses increasingly that these differences are somehow related to the entire broad picture of Anglo-American life, and may in some way help to illuminate it.

Most of the general questions of group associations may be answered from the information contained in Table 5.6, which gives the overall figures for the emigration as a whole. There the two major types of statuses will be seen. By far the largest category—over two-thirds of the entire emigration—is that of emigrants traveling alone, that is, without a determinable personal relationship, however vague, to anyone else in the migration. The second is that of people known to be traveling in family groups (31.1%).[3] All other kinds of groups contributed far fewer emigrants.

[3]In a few cases adult males traveling alone can be shown to be emigrating in advance of their families with the expectation of bringing their wives and children over to join them later. Whether or not their families did follow them, and how many families emigrated in this way, cannot be ascertained. But there is no reason to think the numbers involved are in any way significant.

Among the "other" relationships were 52 people traveling in small groups of nonfamilial companions; and a total of six people traveled in a master-servant relationship outside of family groups. The very few servants who traveled with families were included within families by the customs officials, and are listed within families in the table.

The overall proportions—over two-thirds of the emigrants traveling alone and almost one-third in family groups—were not, however, consistent through the various age groups. Table 5.6 shows that very few young children were sent overseas independent of families. Of the emigrant children known to be less than 10 years of age, 97.5% traveled in family groups; of those below the age of fifteen, 89.4%. But age 15 marks a turning point. Fourteen times more emigrants in the age group 15–19 than in the age group 10–14 traveled alone. Among those of ages 20–24—numerically the most important age group, constituting almost 30% of all the emigrants of known ages—89.3% were traveling independent of families. The percentages of those in families gradually increased again among those 30 years of age and older. Within families too the ages were unevenly distributed. Family members tended to be either very young or relatively old. No less than 68.7% of all family members whose ages are known were either younger than 15 or older than 29.

This age distribution of the family members listed in the Register is not a reflection of some mysterious peculiarities of the migrating population. In the home population it was the common custom to send the young out of the household at around age 15; also, the statute of 1717, regulating the transportation of convicts and related matters, established age 15 as the point at which individuals might legally bind themselves to serve as indentured servants in the colonies, children below the age of 15 presumably being too young for such commitments.[4] But whatever the cause, the families that appear in the Register include far fewer late adolescents and young adults than one would have expected from the proportions of the migration as a whole.

But age is not the only discriminating factor in the group associations and dependency relationships of the emigrants. Gender is equally important, and the combination of age and gender is critical. Of all the males in the emigration, 79.1% were traveling alone, but of the females only 46.2%. These percentages shift in the various age groups. Among the males, the percentage traveling alone increases in almost perfect proportion to the increase in overall numbers in the age groups. Figure 5.1, derived from Table 5.6, shows in the heavy center line the overall percentage, among those

[4] 4 Geo. II, c. 11 (1717), extended to Scotland in 6 Geo. III, c. 32 (1766). Cf. Abbot E. Smith, *Colonists in Bondage* (Chapel Hill, N.C., 1947), p. 80. Indentured servitude is discussed below, esp. pp. 166–185. For instances where children below age 15 *were* indentured, mainly as parts of whole families in that status, see below, pp. 177–182, 185.

TABLE 5.6

| AGE | ALONE | | | | | IN FAMILY | | |
	Male	Female	Unknown	Total	% of Age group	Male	Female	Unknown
1–9	8	2	5	15	2.5	271	277	37
10–14	63	17	0	80	24.5	129	108	6
15–19	949	176	0	1125	84.2	114	89	3
20–24	1767	273	4	2044	88.9	126	117	2
25–29	954	103	4	1061	78.8	138	140	0
30–34	447	36	2	485	65.1	145	114	0
35–39	278	17	0	295	63.4	89	81	0
40–44	139	3	0	142	46.3	98	66	0
45–49	51	4	0	55	35.5	75	25	0
50–54	19	4	0	23	38.3	26	11	0
55–59	8	3	0	11	40.7	10	6	0
60–64	1	1	0	2	11.8	10	5	0
65–69	1	3	0	4	50.0	2	2	0
70 +	2	1	0	3	37.5	4	1	0
Total	4687	643	15	5345	69.4	1237	1042	48
Unknown	374	380	297	1051	63.1	56	137	390
Combined Total	5061	1023	312	6396	68.3	1293	1179	438

[1]This includes all people in all the different family groups (see Table 5.8).
[2]Master-servant relationship (6); independent accompanier (52).

whose ages and sex are both known, of emigrants who traveled outside family groups—its sharp rise to a peak of just under 90% in the age group 20–24 and its subsequent steady decline. In every age group up to age 60 (where the numbers become very small) there is a higher percentage of the male population than of the female population that traveled alone. The gap widens after age 19 and continues to widen until age 40, which is to say that women between the ages of 25 and 40 tended in increasing proportions to migrate as members of families. Yet, while the ratio of males to females among the hundreds of individuals *traveling alone* increases in the ages before 40, the balance of the sexes *within families* remains fairly constant across age groups. Figure 5.2 shows a steady balance in absolute numbers as between males and females within families in the various age groups.

GROUP¹		OTHER GROUP²				TOTAL			
Total	% of Age group	Male	Female	Unknown	Total	Male	Female	Unknown	Total
585	97.5	0	0	0	0	279	279	42	600
243	74.5	3	0	0	3	195	125	6	326
206	15.4	1	4	0	5	1064	269	3	1336
245	10.7	8	1	0	9	1901	391	6	2298
278	20.6	6	2	0	8	1098	245	4	1347
259	34.8	1	0	0	1	593	150	2	745
170	36.6	0	0	0	0	367	98	0	465
164	53.4	1	0	0	1	238	69	0	307
100	64.5	0	0	0	0	126	29	0	155
37	61.7	0	0	0	0	45	15	0	60
16	59.3	0	0	0	0	18	9	0	27
15	88.2	0	0	0	0	11	6	0	17
4	50.0	0	0	0	0	3	5	0	8
5	62.5	0	0	0	0	6	2	0	8
2327	30.2	20	7	0	27	5944	1692	63	7699
583	35.0	25	5	1	31	455	522	688	1665
2910	31.1	45	12	1	58	6399	2214	751	9364

Nowhere is the gap large, and the numbers fall and rise roughly in parallel to each other.

All of this, however, pertains to the entire British migration as if it were an undifferentiated whole. But we know that there were striking differences between the Scottish and English migrations, and it is reasonable to expect now that the two regional groups will have differed in the proportions of individuals versus family migration. Two rather elaborate tables not reproduced here yielded the relevant information: almost half (48.0%) of all the Scottish emigrants but only a fifth of the English traveled as members of family groups. And again, there are significant distinctions by sex. Among the English, of those whose sex is known, nine times as many males as females traveled alone; among the Scots only twice as many. The Scottish

FIGURE 5.1

AGES OF
EMIGRANTS TRAVELING ALONE

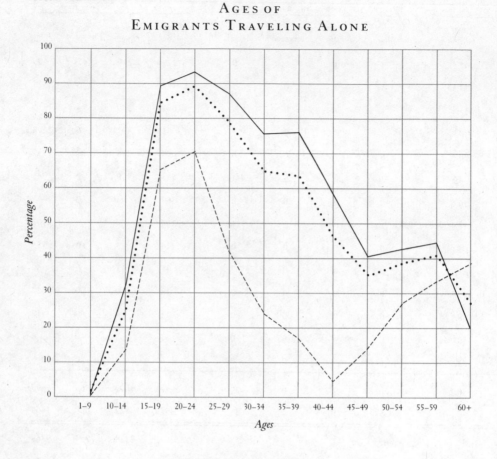

——— percentage of all male emigrants of known ages who traveled alone
- - - - - percentage of all female emigrants of known ages who traveled alone
• • • • • percentage of all emigrants of known ages who traveled alone

migration, in other words, appears to have been fairly well balanced be-tween the sexes whether one looks at family groups or at the throngs of individual migrants. In the English migration the sexes came close to being balanced only *within* families. The emigration from England of individuals not associated with families was overwhelmingly a male phenomenon.

Thus there were significant differences between England and Scotland in these connections. But "England" and "Scotland," we know, are gross terms, in that they obscure what seems to be emerging as a more vital distinction, between southern and central England on the one hand and northern England and Scotland on the other. Table 5.7, which shows the distribution of families among the emigrants from the eighteen regions of England and Scotland, reveals an even clearer outline and an even deeper

FIGURE 5.2

EMIGRANTS TRAVELING IN FAMILIES:
AGE GROUPS

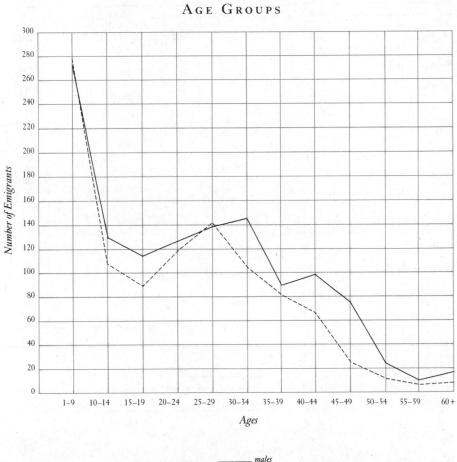

coloration to this increasingly visible distinction. For it now emerges that the overall average of 20.0% of all English emigrants traveling in families is largely a product of extraordinarily high percentages of those from Northern England and Yorkshire (35.6% and 67.2%). Omitting these two regions and also the unclassifiable "Region Unknown" category, one finds the percentage of English people who traveled in families to be only 7.7%; that is, 92.1% of the English emigrants from the regions of central and southern England were traveling alone. In contrast, the incidence of families among the emigrants from every region of Scotland is far higher than from any region of England except the two northern regions; Yorkshire's (67.2%) in fact fits into the upper range of the Scottish percentages. The incidence of families among all the emigrants from the four regions that

TABLE 5.7

REGIONAL RESIDENCES OF EMIGRANTS TRAVELING
ALONE VS. EMIGRANTS TRAVELING IN GROUPS

	ENGLAND				
	IN FAMILY GROUP		ALONE	OTHER GROUP[1]	TOTAL
	Number	% in Region			
Home Counties	43	7.3	549	0	592
London	175	7.5	2165	5	2345
East Anglia	12	10.9	94	4	110
Southeast England	4	3.7	105	0	109
West Country	19	7.5	234	0	253
Bristol	6	5.6	101	0	107
Welsh Border	20	13.6	127	0	147
East-Central England	2	1.9	105	0	107
Midlands	26	11.4	203	0	229
Northern England	89	35.6	161	0	250
Yorkshire	630	67.2	302	6	938
Region unknown	7	77.8	2	0	9
Total	1033	19.9	4148	15	5196

	SCOTLAND				
	IN FAMILY GROUP		ALONE	OTHER GROUP[1]	TOTAL
	Number	% in Region			
Borders	344	73.2	124	2	470
West Lowlands	206	43.2	263	8	477
East Lowlands	129	44.3	158	4	291
Perthshire	234	78.3	65	0	299
Highlands-Hebrides	595	54.1	504	0	1099
Northeast Scotland	31	38.8	49	0	80
Far North	244	80.5	59	0	303
Region unknown	71	8.3	782	0	853
Total	1854	47.9	2004	14	3872
Combined Total	2887	31.8	6152	29	9068

[1]Master-servant relationship, or independent accompanier.

sent the most voyagers (Borders, Perth, Highlands-Hebrides, and Far North) was 65.3%.

The emerging picture of the basic regionalism of the emigration—two great areas of Britain separated not by the Scottish border but by the southern Yorkshire border—is thus deepened and highlighted. Whatever else this distinction may ultimately involve, and however it may in the end be defined, one of its major elements will be the striking difference in the incidence of families. Much else that we have seen—balances between the sexes, distribution of ages—may simply be expressions of the different proportions of families in the emigrating populations.

So much can be said about families simply by examining the numbers of people who traveled in family groups. But equally important are questions concerning the characteristics of families as such—their size and structure and the generational distributions within them. These questions are answered by the information contained in Tables 5.8 and 5.9, which have been assembled from a wide range of information found in the Register.

By using carefully all the information recorded by the customs officials in England and Scotland—both explicit identification of parents, children, and in-laws and also all implications of who was traveling with whom in what relationships, and taking into consideration permutations of name spellings and the fact that Scottish wives were often listed by their maiden names[5]—one can identify 732 families in the migration. Table 5.8 presents the structure of these family groups.

Many of the differences between the English and the Scottish emigration that we have already observed now come into even sharper focus and take on even greater meaning. It is clear, first, that there were far more separate family units among the Scots than among the English—450 vs. 272. This much might have been anticipated from what was earlier seen. But the structure of the 732 family groups could not have been foreseen. These are the simplest, smallest, least-complicated family organizations possible. Not only were 78.2% of all these families nuclear in character, that is, consisting only of conjugal family units (married couples with or without children) but one-fifth of all the families in the migration were composed simply of husband and wife. In this, however, the Scottish and English differed significantly; only 14.7% of the Scottish families consisted merely of husband and wife, but 29.8% of the English were of this elemental form. Children were common (Table 5.9), but any elaboration of family organization beyond the basic conjugal unit was extremely rare. Extended families

[5]D. J. Steel, *Sources for Scottish Genealogy and Family History (National Index of Parish Registers,* XII, London, 1970), 38–39.

FAMILY STRUCTURE[1]		ENGLAND	
		Number of families	Percent
NUCLEAR			
Husband and wife		81	29.8
Husband, wife, and child(ren)		116	42.6
One parent only and child(ren) → F+child(ren)		13 ⎫ 28	4.8 ⎫ 10.3
↘ M+child(ren)		15 ⎭	5.5 ⎭
Total nuclear		225	82.7
EXTENDED			
Lateral [nuclear → H, W, siblings		0 ⎫	0 ⎫
with sibling(s) of ← H, W, chil., sibs.		5 ⎬ 6	1.8 ⎬ 2.2
husband or wife] ↘ H, or W, chil., sibs.		1 ⎭	.4 ⎭
Vertical—upward [nuclear with parent(s) of husband or wife]		3	1.1
Vertical—downward [nuclear with grandchild(ren)]		0	–
Lateral and vertical [husband, wife, sibling(s), parent(s)]		0	–
Total extended		9	3.3
OTHER [Family structure not clear]		38	14.0
Combined Total		272	100.0

[1] In the few cases where customs officers registered an adult(s) and "family", the family was coded as husband, wife and one child. "Children" (unspecified number) were coded as two children, age and sex unknown.

—extended in either way: laterally by the inclusion of the husband's or wife's siblings or other relatives of the same generation, vertically by the presence of one or more of the couple's parents or one or more of the couple's grandchildren—scarcely existed. All told, extended families of any kind constituted only 2.7% of the 732 families, and they were not significantly more numerous among the Scots than among the English. Families containing representatives of three generations are particularly rare.

In the light of recent research on family structure in pre-industrial England, this almost exclusive nuclearity among the emigrating families is not perhaps surprising,[6] but the data in Table 5.8 suggest that these families were even more simple in structure than the British average. It is not surprising to find in Table 5.9, which presents the size of families and the numbers of children and servants within them, that the migrating families were not only simple but, on the average, smaller than the general average of English families.

It has now been established that the average size of English family

[6]Laslett and Wall, *Household and Family*, chaps. 4, 5.

SCOTLAND		OTHER		TOTAL	
Number of families	Percent	Number of families	Percent	Number of families	Percent
66	14.7	2	20.0	149	20.4
235	52.2	0	–	351	48.0
15 } 41	3.3 } 9.1	0 } 3	– } 30.0	28 } 72	3.8 } 9.8
26	5.8	3	30.0	44	6.0
342	76.0	5	50.0	572	78.2
4	.9			4	.5
2 } 7	.4 } 1.6	0	–	7 } 13	1.0 } 1.8
1	.2			2	.3
1	.2	0	–	4	.5
2	.4	0	–	2	.3
1	.2	0	–	1	.1
11	2.4	0	–	20	2.7
97	21.6	5	50.0	140	19.1
450	100.0	10	100.0	732	100.0

households in the period 1750–1821 was 4.75.[7] Table 5.9 shows that the average family size in the migration was 4.4, with the Scottish families larger than the English. In all, 1,402 children were found to be members of families migrating together—15.0% of the entire British migration, with far more, proportionately, among the Scots than among the English (23.6% of the total Scottish migration, 9.3% of the English). The average English family that included children contained 3.1 children (Table 5.10), who, with the very few family servants, brought the average size of emigrating English families to 4.1. The average Scottish family with children had 3.2 children, hence the larger overall size of families. Over one-quarter of all families, however—34.6% of the English families and 20.1% of the Scottish —had no children at all.

Here again, as in so many other aspects of the emigration, there are significant variations among the eighteen regions of Britain. Table 5.10, repeating Table 5.9 in simpler form for each of the regions, shows that the English average of 4.1 people per family is a balance of two very different

[7] Ibid., pp. 126, 139.

TABLE 5.9

		NUMBER	OF			
ORIGIN OF FAMILIES WITH (N) MEMBERS	N = 2	3	4	5	6	7
England	91	30	25	32	21	13
Scotland	81	51	55	59	43	28
Other	2	1	2	0	0	0
Total	174	82	82	91	64	41

		NUMBER	OF			
ORIGIN OF FAMILIES WITH (N) CHILDREN	N = 0	1	2	3	4	5
England	81	39	26	33	24	14
Scotland	71	61	52	61	44	31
Other	2	0	1	2	0	0
Total	154	100	79	96	68	45

		NUMBER	OF			
ORIGIN OF FAMILIES WITH (N) SERVANTS	N = 0	1	2	3	4	5
England	226	3	2	2	0	0
Scotland	340	9	3	1	0	0
Other	5	0	0	0	0	0
Total	571	12	5	3	0	0

[1]Excludes "other" families of Table 5.8.

averages. For London and the Home Counties the average sizes are 2.8 and 2.9 respectively; for Northern England and Yorkshire, 4.6 and 4.7. The Scottish regions conform to, and exaggerate, the tendencies of the northern areas of England. No region of Scotland had an average family size as small as London's or the Home Counties'; the closest was that of the relatively industrialized West Lowlands. The figure for Perthshire is quite extraordinarily high: 6.0. And the two regions of Britain that had the largest numbers of families—Yorkshire (126) and the Highlands-Hebrides (109)—had almost the same high average size (4.7 and 4.5).

PEOPLE IN FAMILY

8	9	10	11	12	13	Total number of families	Total family members	Average size of families
12	4	2	2	1	1	234	948	4.1
18	7	3	4	2	2	353	1615	4.6
0	0	0	0	0	0	5	15	3.0
30	11	5	6	3	3	592	2578	4.4

CHILDREN IN FAMILY

6	7	8	9	10	11	Total number of families with children	Total number of children	Avg. number children in families with children
7	4	2	2	1	1	153	481	3.1
16	7	3	5	2	0	282	913	3.2
0	0	0	0	0	0	3	8	2.7
23	11	5	7	3	1	438	1402	3.2

SERVANTS IN FAMILY

6	7	8	9	10	11	Total number of families with servants	Total number of servants	Avg. number servants in families with servants
1	0	0	0	0	0	8	19	2.4
0	0	0	0	0	0	13	18	1.4
0	0	0	0	0	0	0	0	–
1	0	0	0	0	0	21	37	1.8

From all of this the outline of ascertainable relationships among the emigrants becomes clear. The emigration was largely a movement of isolated individuals, but it included numerous families, especially among the north English migrants and the Scots. Small children almost always, and females far more frequently than men, traveled as members of families, and these family groups were generally small, uncomplicated in structure, and fairly evenly balanced between the sexes. The size of the families rises with their incidence, however, and is especially large in England north of the Midlands, and in Perthshire, the Scottish Highlands, and the Borders

TABLE 5.10
REGIONAL DIFFERENCES IN FAMILY SIZE[1]

ENGLAND					
	Number of families	Average size of families	Avg. number of children in families that had children	Total number of servants in all families	Number of families with servants
Home Counties	15	2.9	2.4	1	1
London	53	2.8	2.7	3	1
Midlands	5	4.0	5.0	0	0
Northern England	19	4.6	3.5	6	1
Yorkshire	126	4.7	3.2	5	3
Region unknown and other regions[2]	16	3.7	3.0	4	2
Total	234	4.1	3.1	19	8

SCOTLAND					
	Number of families	Average size of families	Avg. number of children in families that had children	Total number of servants in all families	Number of families with servants
Borders	56	4.9	3.1	0	0
West Lowlands	49	3.7	2.9	1	1
East Lowlands	25	4.4	3.3	2	2
Perthshire	37	6.0	4.4	2	2
Highlands-Hebrides	109	4.5	3.2	9	5
Northeast Scotland	4	5.8	5.7	0	0
Far North	55	4.4	2.9	4	3
Region unknown	18	3.7	2.5	0	0
Total	353	4.6	3.2	18	13
Combined Total	587	4.4	3.2	37	21

[1]Excludes "other" families of Table 5.8 and families from residences outside England and Scotland.
[2]"Other regions" for this table include East Anglia, Southeast England, West Country, Bristol, Welsh Border, and East-Central England.

and Far North. The impression one has of a dual emigration—two rather different kinds of movements proceeding simultaneously—is heightened by these patches of information, and leads to an even closer examination of the social character of the emigration.

Quality, Occupation, and Class

FROM WHAT STRATA OF BRITISH SOCIETY DID THESE EMIGRANTS COME? CAN THEIR "QUALITY" BE ESTABLISHED, AS THE TREASURY OFFICIALS ASSUMED IT COULD BE? WHAT WERE THEIR OCCUPATIONS? WERE THEY DESTITUTE AND ALIENATED COMMON LABORERS, WITHOUT SKILLS, OR WERE THEY ARTISANS WITH DEFINABLE SKILLS, SUBSTANTIAL YEOMEN, PERHAPS EVEN LANDOWNERS, MEMBERS OF THE GENTRY OR OF THE SECURE MIDDLE CLASS?

First, the intriguing question of the emigrants' "quality."

Whoever it was who inserted this item in the list of questions to be answered by the emigrants was probably repeating the formula of the seventeenth-century registers, but he thereby transmitted to the eighteenth-century customs officials the faint echoes of medieval social orders, of *Stände*, which, except for the nobility, had vanished from British society. Two assumptions underlay the use of this archaic classification: first, that the emigration drew from the entire range of British society, and second, that "quality" and "occupation" formed two kinds of specifications, two degrees of refinement, in the social identification of individuals and hence provided two ways of comprehending the social meaning of the exodus— one in terms of what might be called people's social condition or status, the other in terms of their function in the economy, their occupational activity, the way they earned their livings. Perhaps if the emigration had in fact drawn substantially from all social levels the officials might have been able to extemporize at least a crude approximation of intersecting classifications, though even then there would have been great confusion since there was no formally accepted classification scheme for "quality" or for status ranks more generally, and the reality was full of vague gradations.[8] But, as the emigrants' occupations reveal, the emigration did not draw from all social levels, and it was impossible for the customs officials to devise a useful descriptive scheme for "quality." They groped unsuccessfully for terms to describe people's status or condition, as distinct from their economic roles or functions.

Most of the Scottish officials ignored "quality" altogether in their reports to the Treasury and simply repeated the emigrants' occupations as

---

[8]For an attempt to formulate the status system of pre-industrial England, see Peter Laslett, *The World We Have Lost* (London, 1965), pp. 38–52.

their "qualities." But in registering the emigrants on at least five vessels leaving Scotland an effort was made to use the term "quality" with some care, and the difficulties were dramatized. In the most successful case the passengers were divided into three categories: "gentlemen," "tradesmen," and "common labourers." A surgeon, four merchants, and two students went, sensibly if not entirely smoothly, into the first. Carpenters, shoemakers, tailors, and coopers went easily enough into the second. But the "common labourer" category involved, redundantly, a "labourer" and, anomalously, two "boys." In the other cases the confusion was far worse. Was "servant" a status or a function? No one knew—so pseudo-distinctions were invented. One emigrant was denominated "servant" in "quality" and then classified in occupation as being employed "in different kinds of services." Perhaps that was the solution: one simply *did* what one *was*. Yet not necessarily. What did a woman whose "quality" was that of "farmer's daughter" *do*? The only occupation that could be found for one "farmer's daughter" was "serving her brother." The problem was simpler in the case of a lad whose "quality" was defined as that of a "merchant's son" since his occupation was undeniably that of "schoolboy." Several conscientious Scottish officers forgot about social categories altogether and used "quality" to represent distinctions in shipboard accommodations ("passenger" or "passenger's wife"), the designation "passenger" presumably indicating a certain "quality." Unfortunately, most of the people whose names were recorded were not "passengers" but "emigrants" and it was the social distinctions among the latter that the government was mainly interested in. One official reduced the whole business to marital relationships ("widow," "married"). And a particularly literate official assigned all but one of the passengers on a particular vessel the "quality" of "countryman," the exception being a young man whose occupation was that of "schoolmaster" but whose "quality" was recorded as that of "scholar"—a nice distinction, the latter term vaguely echoing the medieval conception of "clerk."

The English officials were both less conscientious and more decisive than the Scottish. Having struggled through what became nineteen pages of the Register to devise "qualities" for the emigrants and having come up with a short, random list of social categories that in fact applied to very few of the people who boarded the ships (Gentleman, Gentlewoman, Lady, Wife of a Gentleman, Irish Peer, Negro Child, and Clergyman), they gave up completely and thereafter lumped "quality, occupation, and employment" into a single entry which almost always proved to be occupation only.[9] It is obvious that none of the customs officials, either in England or

---

[9] Thus Laslett: "Status amongst the common people, the vast majority, went with occupation in so far as it was marked at all; it was a matter of function, not description." *World We Have Lost*, p. 43.

Scotland, knew how to classify people by their "quality"—that is, by their social rank or status as distinct from their economic function. The attempt to calibrate the emigrants' "qualities" was hopeless from the start, though it reveals, in the resulting confusion, the complexity and mobility of British society in the eighteenth century.

"Occupation or employment" was a different matter. The recorded responses of the emigrants to this question provide some of the most vivid and most clearly articulated patches in the entire panorama of the migration.

Table 5.11 sets out the occupations of the emigrants, which are known for over four-fifths of all those listed in the Register who came from England and for two-fifths of those from Scotland. These are extraordinarily full occupation figures, especially since it can be established that of those leaving England whose occupations were *not* recorded by the customs people, approximately nine-tenths were either children below the age of fifteen or females; of those leaving Scotland an even higher proportion—94.8%—of those of unknown occupations were in the same groups. The occupational listings are therefore remarkably complete for the most numerous and vocationally most important of the voyagers, the males over the age of fourteen.

A glance at the far right column of Table 5.11 reveals the main facts on the occupational characteristics of the emigration. Of the 6,190 emigrants whose occupations are known, only 2.3% claimed occupations that, in the terminology of the time, would have been called "gentle." And that small number was not composed of individuals in the professions (an overall total of only 22) but largely of those who claimed simply to be "gentlemen" or "gentlewomen" and stated no occupation as such. Similarly, only a very small percentage of the emigrants stated that they were engaged in commerce or trade, either wholesale overseas commerce or retail shopkeeping. These two groups (Gentle and Mercantile) at the top of the occupational scale totaled only 473 people, less than 8% of the total of known occupations. Since we know from the literary evidence that the customs officials commonly omitted from the lists cabin passengers and others manifestly more affluent than the mass of migrants, this figure undoubtedly understates the actual proportion of professionals, gentry, and merchants that existed in the emigration. But even a generous estimate of that portion of the emigration based on available cabin space on the vessels shows only a small percentage increase over the figures in the Register. Less expected, and more significant, are the figures under the categories Agriculture and Labor. They are of course larger than those at the upper end of the scale, but they are much smaller than one might reasonably have guessed. The farmers and farmworkers—an imprecise but important distinction, ex-

OCCUPATION	ENGLAND	
	Number	Percent[1]
GENTLE OCCUPATION OR STATUS	107	2.5
Public official	1	0
Gentleman or gentlewoman	89	2.1
Professional	17	.4
Clergyman	5	.1
Lawyer or physician	9	.2
Other	3	.1
MERCHANDISING	226	5.2
Wholesale trade or factorage	63	1.5
Shopkeeping	163	3.7
AGRICULTURE	777	17.8
Independent or semi-independent	671	15.4
Dependent	106	2.4
TRADES OR CRAFTS (ARTISANRY)	2368	54.2
Highly skilled	454	10.4
Ordinary skill level	1914	43.8
Metal trades	235	5.4
Food processing or marketing	209	4.8
Construction[2]	370	8.4
Textile manufacturing or trade	773	17.7
Service trades	196	4.5
Other	131	3.0
LABOR	888	20.3
Servant—domestic	145	3.3
Servant—unspecified	176	4.0
Laborer—maritime	19	.4
Laborer—unspecified	548	12.6
TOTAL KNOWN OCCUPATIONS	4366	100.0
UNKNOWN OCCUPATIONS	830	
Spinster[3]	40	
Other	790	
COMBINED TOTAL (KNOWN & UNKNOWN OCCUPATIONS)	5196	

[1] % of known occupations.   [2] Includes shipbuilding.   [3] For note on spinster, see p. 154, n. 13.

SCOTLAND		OTHER		TOTAL	
Number	Percent[1]	Number	Percent[1]	Number	Percent[1]
20	1.2	18	9.2	145	2.3
1	.1	0	–	2	0
16	.9	16	8.2	121	2.0
3	.2	2	1.0	22	.3
1	.1	1	.5	7	.1
1	.1	0	–	10	.1
1	.1	1	.5	5	.1
84	5.2	18	9.2	328	5.3
40	2.5	6	3.1	109	1.8
44	2.7	12	6.1	219	3.5
391	24.0	41	21.0	1209	19.5
373	22.9	40	20.5	1084	17.5
18	1.1	1	.5	125	2.0
614	37.7	68	34.9	3050	49.3
68	4.2	12	6.2	534	8.6
546	33.5	56	28.7	2516	40.7
50	3.1	6	3.1	291	4.7
18	1.1	7	3.6	234	3.8
106	6.5	13	6.7	489	7.9
333	20.4	23	11.8	1129	18.3
19	1.2	4	2.0	219	3.5
20	1.2	3	1.5	154	2.5
520	31.9	50	25.7	1458	23.6
22	1.3	5	2.6	172	2.8
325	20.0	3	1.5	504	8.1
14	.8	5	2.6	38	.6
159	9.8	37	19.0	744	12.0
1629	100.0	195	100.0	6190	100.0
2243		101		3174	
11		0		51	
2232		101		3123	
3872		296		9364	

pressed here as "independent or semi-independent" versus "dependent" agriculturists[10]—constituted only a fifth of the total known occupations. The unskilled manual laborers, urban and rural, comprised just under a quarter of the total, and they are rarely distinguished by such familiar designations as porters, coal heavers, chimney sweeps, miners, bargemen, and never as the basest laborers: street rakers, peddlers, and, the lowest of the low, nightmen, the laborers who carted away the wagons of human excrement that accumulated in the cellars of urban dwellings. Were such menial laborers not present among the emigrants? Or were there reasons to avoid citing such designations? Later, other records than the Register will suggest the answers.[11]

Simply glancing at this totals column, then, one sees that the exodus, taken as a whole, was not overwhelmingly a movement of farmers and farmworkers displaced from the land, nor was it predominantly the transfer of a portion of the unskilled mass of people living in London's sprawling slums or in the back alleys of the other British cities. Farmers, farmworkers, and laborers of all kinds *did* form a major portion of the migration (43.1%), but even together they were not the largest group.

The largest occupational category among the emigrants whose occupations are known is that of artisans, craftsmen, or workers trained in specific, sometimes highly specialized, skills. Most of these 3,050 artisans, mechanics,

[10]The great majority of those classified as "independent or semi-independent" agriculturists were listed in the Register as "farmers"; but grouped with them are "yeomen," "husbandmen," "planters," and "tenants"—all manifestly of higher socio-economic position than the "dairy maids," "herdsmen," "plowmen," "gardeners," and "wagoners" who are placed in the second subcategory. In the eighteenth century the term "farmer" was generally used to refer to a person of at least some small substance and some degree of security, occasionally a person of affluence. G. E. Mingay, *English Landed Society in the Eighteenth Century* (London, 1963), p. 88, chap. 10. One Yorkshire "farmer," who at his own expense toured Nova Scotia in 1774 to survey the possibilities of making an advantageous "purchase" there, commented on how "English farmers of substance" like himself might improve the uninhabited lands; reported on "six Old England farmers" he found in the colony, "men of substance," one of whom had left "an estate of seventy pounds a year in England . . . and has taken over a house-keeper and men servants"; inspected the "estates" of farmers, one of which consisted of 500 acres, another of 2,500; remarked on the case of one farmer whose property in Nova Scotia was said to have cost him £550; and made repeated distinctions between "farmers" and "labourers." John Robinson and Thomas Rispin, *A Journey through Nova-Scotia . . .* (York, 1774), reprinted in *Report of the . . . Public Archives of Nova Scotia for 1944* (Halifax, 1945), pp. 35, 36, 38, 39, 47. A striking example is Benjamin Franklin's kinsman, Thomas Foulger, described in the Register as a 42-year-old Norfolk "husbandman" and referred to by Franklin as a "farmer." When in November 1774 Foulger left England with his wife and three children "to settle" in America, he took with him £1,315 3d. The Foulgers' friends and neighbors, the Wesleys, also "husbandmen," who accompanied them aboard the *Britannia*, established in London an account of £479 12s 8d to draw on. *Papers of Benjamin Franklin*, ed. Leonard W. Labaree *et al.* (New Haven, 1959–), XXI, 302, 389, 390, 405, 462–463, 504–505. There is undoubtedly a gray area between these two occupational subcategories of "agriculture," but the distinction is so clear that it justifies the separation used in this table and in the others that list occupations.
[11]M. Dorothy George, *London Life in the Eighteenth Century* ([1925], Penguin ed., Harmondsworth, Eng., 1976), pp. 159–162; James Clifford, "Some Aspects of London Life in the Mid-18th Century,"

and craftsmen—almost half (49.3%) of all those whose occupations can be identified—defined their employments with some precision. So varied, so highly articulated are these artisanal designations that one can only conclude that there were people—the emigrants or the customs officials or others somehow involved in the process of emigration—who insisted that the emigrants appear to be, if they were not in fact, workers with well-defined occupational skills. A surprisingly large number—almost a fifth of all the artisans (534 individuals)—were, or claimed to be, highly skilled producers of semi-artistic or high-precision luxury goods. Their skills were defined with care: watchmaker, watch-*movement* maker, engraver, harpsichord maker, goldsmith, gunstock maker, backgammon-table maker, gilder, enameller, mathematical instrument maker, glassblower, lapidary, sword cutter. Over forty such high-skill occupations, whose practitioners could earn up to £4 a week in London, were included in the Register.[12] All the rest of the artisans said they were workers in crafts of ordinary skill levels, which demanded some sort of training, usually in the form of apprenticeship, but not sophisticated education or many years of experience. Just over one hundred such skills or trades appear in the Register, nearly a third of all the trades, professions, and arts listed in the standard handbook, *The London Tradesman* (1747).

Almost 500 of these artisans said they were workers in the construction trades—masons, housewrights, brickmakers, plasterers, ship carpenters, glaziers. Almost 300 said they had been in metal trades—pewterers, tinkers, wire drawers, coppersmiths, locksmiths, brass founders. A somewhat smaller number identified themselves as workers in the food-producing and food-marketing industries—bakers, brewers, butchers, confectioners, grocers, poulterers. Just over 200 said they were employed in the service trades —hairdressers, surgeons and barbers, coachmen, tavern waiters, merchandise clerks. And a large number worked in crafts, trades, and industries that cannot easily be classified: fishhook makers, button makers, ballad sellers, pencil makers, pipe makers, color markers, buckle makers, hoopers. But the largest single category—over a third of all the artisans and craftsmen and fully 18% of all those who stated their occupations—said that they worked

in *City and Society in the Eighteenth Century*, ed. Paul Fritz and David Williams (Toronto, 1973), pp. 25–27. The underrepresentation of unskilled laborers among the emigrants is difficult to measure since classifications differ so greatly among modern analysts. But Gregory King, at the end of the seventeenth century, who included common seamen and soldiers among the unskilled laborers, estimated that they comprised just over half the population of England (Laslett, *World We Have Lost*, p. 32), which was approximately the same proportion that was sustained, in part at least, by charity. See W. A. Speck, *Stability and Strife, England 1714–1760* (London, 1977), p. 34. For discussion of the emigrants' socio-economic condition, see below, chaps. 8 and 9, for the labor force, and throughout Parts IV and V for the settlers on the land.

[12]For an excellent description of the urban trades and crafts, especially the high-precision and luxury crafts, and of the workers in these occupations, see George, *London Life*, chap. 4.

in the manufacture of textile goods or in the distribution of cloth and clothing. In this category (textile manufacturing and the clothing trade) the Register lists at least thirty skills, ranging from weaver and spinner (spinster)[13] through a broad range of more specialized classifications—bleacher, glover, tailor, woolcomber—to fairly sophisticated occupations: mantua maker, calico printer, muff maker, collar maker.

Thus, of the emigrants whose occupations are known, the largest number described themselves as trained artisans and craft workers, most of them specifying occupations that required ordinary skills acquired through apprenticeship, though a surprising number were able to identify themselves with exacting, high-precision arts and crafts. The largest number of the ordinary artisans had worked in the production or distribution of textiles, but a remarkably large number of trades and crafts were represented.

Such are the most general figures, averages cutting across all the distinctions within the emigrant group. Unexpected and revealing details begin to emerge when one subdivides the occupational categories by the emigrants' ages and sex, distinguishing those of English residence from those of Scottish.

In the separate English and Scottish columns of Table 5.11 one can see that, of those whose occupations are known, a much higher percentage of

[13]The designation "spinster" proved to be difficult to classify. In the eighteenth century the word did not mean only an unmarried female. "Silk spinster" is one of the occupations discussed in R. Campbell, *The London Tradesman* ([1747], New York, 1969); "a woman who spins" is the first definition in D. Fenning's *Royal English Dictionary* (London, 1761); and the word appears as an occupation in innumerable lists of specific trades and crafts: "blacksmiths, shoemakers, spinsters of flax and wool, in short every branch of manufactures" (John Campbell to William Sinclair, Bladenburgh, Md., July 26, 1772, Freswick Muniments, GD 136/416/1); "weavers, spinsters, blacksmiths, joiners" (*South-Carolina Gazette; And Country Journal*, May 3, 1774); and in enactments like 7 James I, c.7 (1609): "An Act for the Punishing . . . of . . . Frauds Committed by Sorters, Kembers, and Spinsters of Wool, and Weavers of Woolen Yarns." Legal historians have debated the question: Carol Z. Wiener, "Is a Spinster an Unmarried Woman?" *American Journal of Legal History*, 20 (1976), 27–31, and subsequent discussion, *ibid.*, 21 (1977), 255–265. Since the term occurs frequently in the Register, each use was carefully examined, and a clear pattern emerged. When the term was used for women traveling to the continent of Europe, to the West Indies, and to Canada and Nova Scotia (none of whom was indentured), it invariably meant an unmarried female and not an occupation. With equal regularity, when it was applied to female indentured servants, all of whom were traveling to the mainland colonies south of Nova Scotia, it meant "spinner." The latter usage can be substantiated again and again in newspaper notices of arriving indentured servants; in Register entries like that of the *Mary* (T47/9/59), which explicitly distinguishes a "spinster" from a "singlewoman"; and in the occupations listed for the Ogier family of London traveling on the *Union* to Carolina (T47/9/69), undoubtedly silk workers of Huguenot origin: the father is listed as a "weaver," the two eldest sons as "silk throwsters," and the four daughters, 16, 13, 9, and 6, as "spinsters." In sharp contrast are the "spinsters" who go to Europe "on pleasure," who are "going home" to Jamaica, and who are employed as "servants to a gentleman." The Scottish listings contain more ambiguities, but in the end each of the "spinsters" in these entries could be classified either as "unmarried female" or as "spinner."

the English than of the Scottish were artisans (roughly half vs. a third). Among the Scots there were proportionately more laborers and agriculturists. The textile industry and its marketing branches account for almost the same percentage of all known occupations in the two areas, but relative to the total numbers of artisans and craft workers there were far more textile workers among the Scots than among the English.

Since urban concentrations were more common in England and since Scotland is known to have had a well-developed, and troubled, textile industry, all of this is perhaps not surprising. But the information in the more detailed breakdowns of Tables 5.12 and 5.13, which refine the differences in occupations between the English and Scottish emigrants according to age and sex, could not have been anticipated.

Turning to the English figures first (Table 5.12) one finds that women's occupations concentrate almost entirely in service of some kind or in textile work, in fact all of the latter in "spinning." About half of the 347 English emigrant females whose occupations are known said they were servants— and no doubt many of those who claimed no occupation had also been in service. Two-fifths of the women had been "spinners," a few had been shopkeepers, and only a total of five said they had worked on farms. Not one claimed to have been involved in wholesale trade or factorage. And the women were by no means all young: over a fifth of all the females whose ages are known were 30 or older, and this at a time when the English life expectancy at birth was just over 38.[14]

The ages of the English male emigrants form an especially revealing section of the picture. A surprising number of the few "gentlemen" were young, but almost a third (244) of the farmers and farmworkers were 30 years old or older; 78 were in their forties; 15 were 50 or older. And about 9 out of 10 of these agriculturists age 30 and above gave evidence of being farmers rather than farm hands or field workers. Among the artisans a surprising number were fully mature, even middle-aged. Almost twice as many artisans were in their late twenties as were in their late teens, and a quarter of all male artisans were 30 years old or older. Among the textile workers there were sizable groups in each quinquennium between the ages of 15 and 45. Among the construction workers more than half were over the age of 24 and well over a quarter were 30 years old or older. And the age distribution among the high-skill craftsmen (a fifth of all the artisans) is not significantly different from that of the ordinary artisans. The male laborers —far fewer than the artisans and fewer than the farmers too—were younger, however: more than half were younger than 20; three-quarters were younger than 25.

Thus the breakdown by age and sex among the English emigrants

[14]Wrigley and Schofield, *Population History of England*, p. 529.

TABLE 5.12

OCCUPATION	1–14 Male	1–14 Female	15–19 Male	15–19 Female	20–24 Male	20–24 Female	25–29 Male	25–29 Female	30–34 Male	30–34 Female
GENTLE OCCUPATION OR STATUS	1	0	17	0	25	1	21	1	9	3
Public official	0	0	0	0	0	0	0	0	1	0
Gentleman or gentlewoman	1	0	17	0	19	1	17	1	6	3
Professional	0	0	0	0	6	0	4	0	2	0
Clergyman	0	0	0	0	0	0	1	0	0	0
Lawyer or physician	0	0	0	0	5	0	2	0	2	0
Other	0	0	0	0	1	0	1	0	0	0
MERCHANDISING	0	0	33	1	73	7	55	2	18	0
Wholesale trade or factorage	0	0	2	0	15	0	16	0	6	0
Shopkeeping	0	0	31	1	58	7	39	2	12	0
AGRICULTURE	1	0	93	0	247	3	180	0	99	1
Independent or semi-independent	1	0	81	0	210	0	157	0	91	0
Dependent	0	0	12	0	37	3	23	0	8	1
TRADES OR CRAFTS (ARTISANRY)	5	3	256	36	956	85	457	18	243	6
Highly skilled	0	0	48	0	205	1	89	0	45	1
Ordinary skill level	5	3	208	36	751	84	368	18	198	5
Metal trades	1	0	27	0	110	0	44	0	25	0
Food processing or marketing	1	0	19	0	95	0	48	0	26	0
Construction[2]	1	0	28	0	140	1	95	0	52	0
Textile manufacturing or trade	2	3	93	36	255	83	116	18	58	4
Service trades	0	0	24	0	105	0	40	0	17	0
Other	0	0	17	0	46	0	25	0	20	1
LABOR	22	3	346	38	155	72	89	40	50	12
Servant—domestic	0	0	25	9	18	27	17	14	5	6
Servant—unspecified	5	3	24	29	19	45	6	26	4	6
Laborer—maritime	0	0	4	0	3	0	6	0	4	0
Laborer—unspecified	17	0	293	0	115	0	60	0	37	0
TOTAL KNOWN OCCUPATIONS	29	6	745	75	1456	168	802	61	419	22
UNKNOWN OCCUPATIONS	117	111	27	37	12	64	3	46	6	44
Spinster[3]	0	1	0	12	0	19	0	4	0	3
Other	117	110	27	25	12	45	3	42	6	41
COMBINED TOTAL (KNOWN & UNKNOWN OCCUPATIONS)	146	117	772	112	1468	232	805	107	425	66

[1]Excludes emigrants of unknown age.   [2]Includes shipbuilding.   [3]For note on spinster, see p. 154, n. 13.

35–39		40–44		45–49		50+		ALL AGES			Combined total	% of known occupations
Male	Female	Male	Female	Male	Female	Male	Female	Male	Female	Unknown		
8	0	9	1	2	0	3	0	95	6	0	101	2.3
0	0	0	0	0	0	0	0	1	0	0	1	0
7	0	6	1	2	0	3	0	78	6	0	84	1.9
1	0	3	0	0	0	0	0	16	0	0	16	0.4
0	0	3	0	0	0	0	0	4	0	0	4	0.1
0	0	0	0	0	0	0	0	9	0	0	9	0.2
1	0	0	0	0	0	0	0	3	0	0	3	0.1
12	0	13	0	2	0	4	1	210	11	0	221	5.1
7	0	6	0	2	0	4	0	58	0	0	58	1.3
5	0	7	0	0	0	0	1	152	11	0	163	3.8
52	1	50	0	28	0	15	0	765	5	0	770	17.8
36	1	47	0	26	0	14	0	663	1	0	664	15.3
16	0	3	0	2	0	1	0	102	4	0	106	2.5
165	3	85	0	32	1	14	0	2213	152	0	2365	54.6
39	1	12	0	10	0	2	0	450	3	0	453	10.5
126	2	73	0	22	1	12	0	1763	149	0	1912	44.1
19	0	7	0	2	0	0	0	235	0	0	235	5.4
8	0	5	0	3	0	4	0	209	0	0	209	4.8
31	0	12	0	6	0	4	0	369	1	0	370	8.6
49	2	40	0	10	1	2	0	625	147	0	772	17.8
5	0	4	0	0	0	0	0	195	0	0	195	4.5
14	0	5	0	1	0	2	0	130	1	0	131	3.0
22	6	9	1	4	1	1	0	698	173	4	875	20.2
4	4	1	0	1	1	0	0	71	61	0	132	3.0
1	2	1	1	0	0	0	0	60	112	4	176	4.1
0	0	1	0	0	0	1	0	19	0	0	19	.4
17	0	6	0	3	0	0	0	548	0	0	548	12.7
259	10	166	2	68	2	37	1	3981	347	4	4332	100.0
1	28	2	22	0	11	1	13	169	376	11	556	
0	0	0	0	0	0	0	1	0	40	0	40	
1	28	2	22	0	11	1	12	169	336	11	516	
260	38	168	24	68	13	38	14	4150	723	15	4888	

TABLE 5.13

OCCUPATION	1–14		15–19		20–24		25–29		30–34	
	Male	Female	Male	Female	Male	Female	Male	Female	Male	Female
GENTLE OCCUPATION OR STATUS	0	0	1	0	9	0	3	1	1	0
Public official	0	0	0	0	0	0	0	0	0	0
Gentleman or gentlewoman	0	0	1	0	8	0	2	1	1	0
Professional	0	0	0	0	1	0	1	0	0	0
Clergyman	0	0	0	0	0	0	1	0	0	0
Lawyer or physician	0	0	0	0	1	0	0	0	0	0
Other	0	0	0	0	0	0	0	0	0	0
MERCHANDISING	0	0	30	0	26	1	11	0	5	0
Wholesale trade or factorage	0	0	11	0	13	0	9	0	5	0
Shopkeeping	0	0	19	0	13	1	2	0	0	0
AGRICULTURE	6	1	41	1	72	0	88	1	43	0
Independent or semi-independent	6	1	39	1	64	0	84	1	40	0
Dependent	0	0	2	0	8	0	4	0	3	0
TRADES OR CRAFTS (ARTISANRY)	18	13	97	25	154	18	110	17	67	10
Highly skilled	0	0	11	0	25	0	10	0	6	0
Ordinary skill level	18	13	86	25	129	18	100	17	61	10
Metal trades	0	0	9	0	16	0	12	0	10	0
Food processing or marketing	0	0	4	0	8	0	2	0	3	0
Construction[2]	1	0	8	0	36	0	30	0	20	0
Textile manufacturing or trade	17	13	58	25	53	17	45	17	27	10
Service trades	0	0	5	0	10	0	4	0	0	0
Other	0	0	2	0	6	1	7	0	1	0
LABOR	48	27	81	74	67	61	41	15	31	4
Servant—domestic	2	1	0	3	2	3	1	1	1	0
Servant—unspecified	43	26	53	71	25	58	8	14	8	4
Laborer—maritime	0	0	0	0	4	0	1	0	4	0
Laborer—unspecified	3	0	28	0	36	0	31	0	18	0
TOTAL KNOWN OCCUPATIONS	72	41	250	100	328	80	253	34	147	14
UNKNOWN OCCUPATIONS	253	246	20	56	17	77	6	101	2	69
Spinster[3]	0	1	0	2	0	4	0	4	0	0
Other	253	245	20	54	17	73	6	97	2	69
COMBINED TOTAL (KNOWN & UNKNOWN OCCUPATIONS)	325	287	270	156	345	157	259	135	149	83

[1]Excludes emigrants of unknown age.　　[2]Includes shipbuilding.　　[3]For note on spinster, see p. 154, n. 13.

35–39		40–44		45–49		50+		ALL AGES			Combined total	% of known occupations
Male	Female	Male	Female	Male	Female	Male	Female	Male	Female	Unknown		
0	0	2	0	1	0	0	0	17	1	0	18	1.1
0	0	1	0	0	0	0	0	1	0	0	1	0.1
0	0	0	0	1	0	0	0	13	1	0	14	0.9
0	0	1	0	0	0	0	0	3	0	0	3	0.2
0	0	0	0	0	0	0	0	1	0	0	1	0.1
0	0	0	0	0	0	0	0	1	0	0	1	0.1
0	0	1	0	0	0	0	0	1	0	0	1	0.1
2	0	3	0	1	0	0	0	78	1	0	79	4.9
1	0	1	0	0	0	0	0	40	0	0	40	2.5
1	0	2	0	1	0	0	0	38	1	0	39	2.4
39	2	29	0	34	0	28	0	380	5	1	386	24.1
38	2	29	0	34	0	28	0	362	5	1	368	23.0
1	0	0	0	0	0	0	0	18	0	0	18	1.1
31	6	19	1	13	0	4	2	513	92	0	605	37.8
5	0	6	0	2	0	0	0	65	0	0	65	4.1
26	6	13	1	11	0	4	2	448	92	0	540	33.7
1	0	1	0	0	0	1	0	50	0	0	50	3.1
1	0	0	0	0	0	0	0	18	0	0	18	1.1
4	0	3	0	4	0	0	0	106	0	0	106	6.6
20	6	9	1	6	0	3	2	238	91	0	329	20.5
0	0	0	0	0	0	0	0	19	0	0	19	1.2
0	0	0	0	1	0	0	0	17	1	0	18	1.1
25	3	16	0	7	0	9	0	325	184	4	513	32.1
0	2	1	0	0	0	0	0	7	10	0	17	1.1
7	1	2	0	0	0	1	0	147	174	4	325	20.3
2	0	0	0	2	0	1	0	14	0	0	14	0.9
16	0	13	0	5	0	7	0	157	0	0	157	9.8
97	11	69	1	56	0	41	2	1313	283	5	1601	100.0
2	48	0	44	0	16	0	21	300	678	42	1020	
0	0	0	0	0	0	0	0	0	11	0	11	
2	48	0	44	0	16	0	21	300	667	42	1009	
99	59	69	45	56	16	41	23	1613	961	47	2621	

reveals a surprising inner pattern. The youngest of the male groups were at opposite ends of the occupational span: gentlemen and laborers. The largest groups—artisans and farmers—while they concentrated in the dominant age group, 20–24, include sizable numbers of fully mature and middle-aged men, men in their late thirties and early forties, and a fair number even in their fifties. In the full enumeration, three farmers, a yeoman, a gardener, and an artisan prove to be in their seventies.

From all of this one gains at least a vague impression not of a milling mass of destitute unskilled urban slum dwellers and uprooted peasants, but of certain segments of the lower middle and working classes, artisans and craftsmen with employable skills, for whom emigration would seem to have represented not so much a desperate escape as an opportunity to be reached for. But this is only a vague impression caught from a glance at the average figures for England as a whole. Is the occupational profile of the Scottish emigration different?

Table 5.13 shows that there were certainly differences between the English and the Scottish emigrants. Though the percentages of Scots in the "gentle" occupations and statuses are similar to those of the English, there are proportionately many fewer artisans and more laborers and farmers. A quarter of the Scots who stated their occupations described themselves as farmers of one sort or another, few of them dependent farmworkers; less than a fifth of the English fall in that category. Similarly, a third of the Scots but only a fifth of the English described themselves as laborers. On the other hand only about a third of the Scots of known occupation said they were craftsmen or artisans, as opposed to over half of the English. And within the Scottish artisan group there are differences too. Proportionately more of the Scottish artisans were in textile manufacturing: over half of all artisans as opposed to less than a third among the English.

There are significant differences in the age patterns as well. Among the Scottish men the maturity level is even more striking than among the English. Almost half (45.5%) of all the male farmers and farmworkers (proportionately a larger percentage of the known occupations than among the English emigrants) were 30 years old or older; almost a quarter (23.9%) were 40 years old or older; and 28 (7.4%) were 50 or over. Approximately the same number were in their late thirties as in their late teens. Among the male artisans the spread into the later years is less pronounced but still striking: two-thirds as many male Scottish artisans were in their early thirties as in their late teens.

There are thus differences between the occupational profiles of the English and Scottish males, differences that are consistent with the divergent characteristics of the emigrants that have already been observed. Further, the family orientation, overall youthfulness, and high proportion of females in the Scottish migration are reflected in the relative paucity of stated occupations: only 59 occupations are listed for the Scottish artisans, 135 for the English. And the underdevelopment of the Scottish economy relative to England's is reflected in the increased portion of the emigration engaged in agricultural work.

But these are still only impressions of two masses of people among whom, we know, there were significant regional differences. What is revealed if these general figures for England and Scotland are broken down into the eighteen regions of Britain? Do the general figures mask internal differences that alter the general impression one has of the social character of the emigration? Are the general averages simply balances of opposites, or are the general English and Scottish occupational patterns duplicated in miniature in the various regions?

Table 5.14 provides the summary information for the eleven English regions and the seven Scottish regions. The London and Home Counties columns are particularly noteworthy, since almost exactly half of the English emigrants of known occupation came from London, over three-fifths (63.0%) from London and the Home Counties together. It is immediately apparent that London's contribution to the emigration did *not* concentrate distinctively in the lowest levels of the social scale. London's contingents included slightly *higher* percentages of gentle folk, people in commercial pursuits, and artisans, and a much higher proportion of the most sophisticated craftsmen, than existed in the English emigration as a whole. That the metropolis contributed far fewer farmers is scarcely surprising, but that it contributed somewhat fewer laborers *is* surprising. One would have expected London's pattern to resemble Bristol's. The much smaller emigration from England's second-largest city conforms better to one's image of what an urban exodus would have been: almost no people of "gentle" status, farmers, or highly skilled artisans, but twice the general proportion of common laborers.

The Home Counties bring out the distinctiveness of London's figures, for in these surrounding counties there were very few people with any involvement in trade, fewer artisans than among the Londoners, and especially fewer highly skilled artisans, but over twice London's percentage of farmers. The Midlands conforms well to the national pattern, save for somewhat fewer laborers, but the two northern regions, particularly Yorkshire, are quite distinctive. The proportion of farmers among Yorkshire emigrants of known occupations (47.0%) is more than triple the proportion of the average of the other regions combined (14.4%) and almost every one of Yorkshire's farmers gave some indication of an independent status on the land. On the other hand, the proportion of artisans among the Yorkshiremen was about one-third less than the proportion in the rest of the English regions, and the proportion of its laborers just over half that of the rest of England. Yorkshire's emigration, in other words, while it spread through

TABLE 5.14

	ENGLAND									
OCCUPATION	Home Counties	London	East Anglia	South-east England	West Country	Bristol	Welsh Border	East-Central England	Mid-lands	Northern England
GENTLE										
Male	11	71	0	1	4	1	3	0	2	1
Female	0	6	0	0	0	0	1	0	1	0
Total	11	77	0	1	4	1	4	0	3	1
% of known occupation	2.0	3.5	–	1.0	1.8	1.0	3.0	–	1.4	.6
MERCHANDISING										
Male	14	131	8	2	5	8	3	5	10	13
Female	1	7	0	1	0	0	1	0	0	0
Total	15	138	8	3	5	8	4	5	10	13
% of known occupation	2.7	6.3	7.8	2.9	2.2	7.9	3.0	4.9	4.8	7.9
AGRICULTURE										
Male	134	217	23	17	22	6	23	39	41	32
Female	0	0	0	0	1	0	0	0	1	1
Total	134	217	23	17	23	6	23	39	42	33
% of known occupation	24.1	9.9	22.5	16.3	10.2	5.9	17.3	37.9	20.0	20.1
TRADES OR CRAFTS										
Male	270	1227	53	54	82	46	72	40	117	94
Female	14	116	0	3	2	0	0	1	4	3
Total	284	1343	53	57	84	46	72	41	121	97
% of known occupation	51.1	61.4	52.0	54.8	37.3	45.5	54.1	39.8	57.6	59.1
Highly Skilled										
Male	37	317	7	9	9	8	9	7	19	12
Female	0	3	0	0	0	0	0	0	0	0
Total	37	320	7	9	9	8	9	7	19	12
% of known occupation	6.7	14.6	6.9	8.7	4.0	7.9	6.8	6.8	9.0	7.3
Ordinary Skill										
Male	233	910	46	45	73	38	63	33	98	82
Female	14	113	0	3	2	0	0	1	4	3
Total	247	1023	46	48	75	38	63	34	102	85
% of known occupation	44.4	46.8	45.1	46.2	33.3	37.6	47.4	33.0	48.6	51.8
LABOR										
Male	88	316	17	25	104	40	25	15	28	13
Female	24	95	1	1	5	0	5	3	6	7
Total	112	411	18	26	109	40	30	18	34	20
% of known occupation	20.1	18.8	17.6	25.0	48.4	39.6	22.6	17.5	16.2	12.2
TOTAL KNOWN OCCUPATIONS										
Male	517	1962	101	99	217	101	126	99	198	153
Female	39	224	1	5	8	0	7	4	12	11
Total	556	2186	102	104	225	101	133	103	210	164
UNKNOWN OCCUPATIONS										
Male	8	29	3	1	2	1	3	3	5	18
Female	23	102	5	1	23	1	9	1	14	50
COMBINED TOTAL										
Male	525	1991	104	100	219	102	129	102	203	171
Female	62	326	6	6	31	1	16	5	26	61
Total	587	2317	110	106	250	103	145	107	229	232

[1]Excludes emigrants of unknown sex.

Yorkshire	Region unknown	Total England	SCOTLAND								Total Scotland	Combined Total
			Borders	West Lowlands	East Lowlands	Perthshire	Highlands & Hebrides	North-east Scotland	Far North	Region unknown		
5	0	99	1	2	1	1	5	0	0	9	19	118
0	0	8	0	0	0	0	0	0	0	1	1	9
5	0	107	1	2	1	1	5	0	0	10	20	127
1.1	–	2.5	.6	.5	.5	.7	1.2	–	–	6.5	1.2	2.1
16	0	215	6	23	14	3	8	7	2	20	83	298
1	0	11	0	0	1	0	0	0	0	0	1	12
17	0	226	6	23	15	3	8	7	2	20	84	310
3.6	–	5.2	3.3	6.2	7.9	2.2	1.9	12.5	1.7	12.9	5.2	5.2
216	1	771	48	26	51	52	124	8	38	38	385	1156
3	0	6	0	0	3	1	1	0	0	0	5	11
219	1	777	48	26	54	53	125	8	38	38	390	1167
47.0	33.3	17.8	26.7	7.0	28.3	39.3	29.8	14.3	32.2	24.5	24.0	19.5
159	1	2215	63	202	67	48	35	13	24	68	520	2735
10	0	153	0	73	7	2	8	0	3	1	94	247
169	1	2368	63	275	74	50	43	13	27	69	614	2982
36.3	33.3	54.4	35.0	74.5	38.7	37.0	10.3	23.2	22.9	44.5	37.8	49.9
17	0	451	14	8	17	4	4	3	4	14	68	519
0	0	3	0	0	0	0	0	0	0	0	0	3
17	0	454	14	8	17	4	4	3	4	14	68	522
3.6	–	10.4	7.8	2.2	8.9	3.0	1.0	5.4	3.4	9.0	4.2	8.7
142	1	1764	49	194	50	44	31	10	20	54	452	2216
10	0	150	0	73	7	2	8	0	3	1	94	244
152	1	1914	49	267	57	46	39	10	23	55	546	2460
32.6	33.3	44.0	27.2	72.4	29.8	34.1	9.3	17.9	19.5	35.5	33.6	41.2
27	0	698	62	42	17	6	142	18	31	11	329	1027
29	1	177	0	1	30	22	96	10	20	7	186	363
56	1	875	62	43	47	28	238	28	51	18	515	1390
12.0	33.3	20.1	34.4	11.7	24.6	20.7	56.8	50.0	43.2	11.6	31.7	23.3
423	2	3998	180	295	150	110	314	46	95	146	1336	5334
43	1	355	0	74	41	25	105	10	23	9	287	642
466	3	4353	180	369	191	135	419	56	118	155	1623	5976
102	1	176	94	19	19	36	263	10	30	199	670	846
220	1	450	192	55	55	64	398	14	74	205	1057	1507
525	3	4174	274	314	169	146	577	56	125	345	2006	6180
263	2	805	192	129	96	89	503	24	97	214	1344	2149
788	5	4979	466	443	265	235	1080	80	222	559	3350	8329

all categories except the gentry and merchants, was much more an exodus from the land than was the emigration from elsewhere, and much less a movement of artisans and laborers; but Yorkshire's exodus too included a variety of craft workers, and its preponderant group of farmers does not seem to have been composed of vagrant farm hands wandering across the land. And throughout the English regions the females who listed occupations (44.1% of all females) noted mainly two kinds of employment: they were predominantly servants and secondarily textile workers.

There are, then, variations in the distribution of occupations among the regions of England, but nothing to upset the general impression of the social character of the emigration one gained from the figures for England as a whole. The occupational character of the English emigration was not created by a balance between respectable elements from the provinces and a mass of destitute laborers pouring out from London's slums. The great city and the surrounding counties were contributing more than their share to the upper levels of the social structure of the emigration and somewhat less to the lowest elements. And while there were variations in the occupational profiles of the other regions, ranging from Bristol's urban emphasis to Yorkshire's rural preponderance, nowhere does one find signs of the mass evacuation of a rootless rural proletariat or of an untrained urban slum population. Among the thousands leaving England for America there were undoubtedly vagrants, destitute unemployables, bums, beggars, drunks, and other victims of a society whose welfare institutions were few and inhumane; but such people were exceptional in the English emigration as a whole.[15]

Do the more detailed figures for the seven Scottish regions suggest different conclusions?

There are in fact notable differences between the occupational patterns of the Scottish regions and those of the English, and there are striking variations too within Scotland. The most distinctive occupational profile is that of the West Lowlands, an area that included not only Glasgow and its suburbs and the major port of Greenock, but several centers of textile manufacturing, among them the recently strike-bound town of Paisley.

[15]How many inmates of the poorhouses or workhouses were induced to emigrate is not known, but the practice of attempting to resettle some of the destitute overseas was well known. "It is consistently said," the *York Chronicle and Weekly Advertiser* stated (April 15, 1774), "that the overseers of the poor of the market towns in the seacoast of this county paid freight for as many of the poor in their parish who were, or were likely to become, chargeable and were content to be thus transported in hopes of changing their present poverty for a better prospect in a distant clime." And then the paper added: "How far this method of transporting a working set of poor people by the overseers of any parish is warrantable, may hereafter be inquired into." Similarly, the *Caledonian Mercury* (Feb. 6, 1775), after noting that three women had been sent to the house of correction "for strolling on the streets at unseasonable hours," reported also that two "female streetwalkers, in order to avoid further punishment, indented to go to America."

From this relatively urbanized region came by far the lowest proportion of farmers and farmworkers and of laborers of any district of Scotland. On the other hand, the proportion of artisans among the West Lowlands emigrants of known occupation was almost three times that of the average of the other regions of Scotland combined. Indeed, the West Lowlands emigration had the highest proportion of artisans (74.5%) of any of the 18 regions of Britain; two-thirds of these artisans said they worked in the textile industry.

At the other extreme is the pattern of the Highlands-Hebrides area. From this large district, which included some of the socially most traditional and economically most backward communities in Britain, came a substantial percentage of farmers and agricultural workers, a very low percentage of artisans, and the highest percentage of laborers (56.8%) of all of the 18 British regions; most of these Highlands laborers said they were simply servants of no particular skills. The emigrants from the other two northern regions, the bleak and remote Northeast Scotland and the Far North, also included an exceptionally high proportion of laborers. The occupational profiles of the emigrants from Perthshire and the East Lowlands fall midway between the opposite extremes of the West Lowlands and the Highlands-Hebrides, though relatively more of Perthshire's than of the East Lowlands' emigrants were textile workers. And nowhere did women feature in the Scottish occupational listings. Fewer than 300 women and girls—about one-fifth of all those who can be identified as female in the Scottish records—stated any occupation at all; of those who did, most of them (64.8%) classified themselves as servants or spinsters.

Scotland's emigration, therefore, regionally differentiated, appears to have been composed of two dominant occupational patterns. One might be called semi-industrial, and included an extraordinarily large percentage of artisans, chiefly textile workers, and correspondingly few farmers and laborers. The other might be called Highlands-traditional, and included a large number of farmers, very few artisans of any kind, and an exceptionally large percentage of laborers used to working as general or household servitors. The former pattern prevailed in the more highly developed Lowlands, the latter in the still quite primitive, clan-dominated Highlands.

But do these occupational patterns of the emigrants from the Scottish regions suggest, more than those of the English, a flight of uprooted peasants and farm hands or of desperate urban workers? The emigrants from the semi-industrialized West Lowlands were predominantly textile workers and artisans of ordinary skill (coppersmiths, carpenters, bakers, cordwainers, barbers, coopers, etc.) indistinguishable from artisans found anywhere in Britain; and almost every one of the agriculturists among them was able to indicate at least some small measure of independence. But there *are* signs of a rural proletariat—of helpless, rootless poor leaving the land in large numbers—in the very large contingent of laborers from the Highlands and the north of Scotland. Such groups existed among the English emigrants, but, except for the West Country, not in such concentrations. Most of the Highlands laborers said they had been servants of one sort or another—which, for males, suggests a peculiar kind of rural proletariat: perhaps, considering their origins, a population of displaced or disaffected clansmen; and if that is so they were still closely identified with particular social units, or at least not totally isolated and bereft of support, connections, or community. But precisely who these laborers were, and precisely what their social position was, remain to be seen.

Thus, though some things become clear from these regional figures, some do not. There are hazy patches throughout, and one seeks some further clarification, some more sharply defined details, a different kind of refraction of the emigrants' occupations, in order to see more clearly who these people were and why they were leaving. As one scans the canvas searching for greater clarity, one notices that a remarkable number of emigrants were traveling as indentured servants. Gradually one becomes aware that indentured servitude creates a peculiar and persistent coloration in the occupational picture, which gives a special cast to the entire social character of the emigration.

Indentured Servitude

WHAT IS THE SIGNIFICANCE OF THE STATUS OF "INDENTURED SERVANT," WHICH APPEARS SO COMMONLY IN THE PAGES OF THE REGISTER?

Tables 5.15, 5.16, 5.17, 5.18, 5.19, 5.21, and 5.22 present the Register's information on indentured servants. Table 5.15 shows that no fewer than 4,472 of the 9,364 registered emigrants (47.8%) were indentured servants or redemptioners—3,553 from England and 711 from Scotland.[16] Unable—or unwilling —to pay the cost of migration themselves, they had entered into contracts with entrepreneurs of some sort—ship captains, British merchants, or, through intermediaries, American merchants—who paid the cost of their transportation to America, usually £3 to £4 for an adult, in exchange for full-time service for a period of years, most commonly, for adults, four years. The indentees' labor—which is to say, in effect, the indentees them-

---

[16]Comparison of newspaper notices on both sides of the Atlantic with the Register's listings of indentured servants reveals that for the most part the customs officials in England were quite accurate in identifying indentured servants, but that the Scottish officials were not. The indentured status of 452 Scottish emigrants and 126 English emigrants ignored in the Register can be definitely established by newspaper notices and other sources. They have been included in the total number of indentured servants from Scotland and England.

Redemptioners were emigrants allowed a specified length of time upon their arrival in America to raise the unpaid portion of the cost of their transportation. If they failed, they became ordinary indentees whose length of service was determined in part by the amount owed themselves—was sold upon their arrival in America for whatever the owners of their bonds could get for them. Upon the expiration of these work contracts the newcomers were released, free from all obligation, and in most cases were owed "freedom dues," usually a small sum of money or tools and one or two suits of clothes. But during the term of his or her indenture the indentee was totally committed to the master, with only such relief as the master chose to bestow. Such servants could be employed in any work their purchasers wished to assign them to. Anyone could enter into such an arrangement—man, woman, or child—the terms varying somewhat according to the expected yield of service.

Commonly these contracts were entered into out of sheer necessity, but absolute poverty was not always the reason the emigrants agreed to these near-penal arrangements. Some of the indentures prove to be contingent contracts, a kind of insurance for the shipper, worded so as to become effective only if it turned out upon arrival in America that the emigrant was not able to pay for his transportation. So the customs officials recorded of one group of people that they had "shipped themselves on board the Jane . . . to settle abroad, and by an agreement with the Captain are to pay him so much for their passage to Maryland on their arrival, but if they cannot, then the Captain is to dispose of them for a number of years to defray the expense of their passage." Of another group it was said that "on their arrival . . . [they] are to be disposed of for a number of years provided they are not found capable to pay the Captain for their passage as per agreement."[17]

[17] These examples, taken from entries in the Register, are found in T47/10/15–17, 52; on "freedom dues," see Smith, *Colonists in Bondage,* pp. 238–241.

Indentured servitude, in its most common form, as described here, was one of several kinds of contract labor, the lowest in terms of prestige and independence. The highest status was that of apprenticeship, which though it was a contractual commitment of labor, was most often paid for by the indentee's family, to provide for vocational training. Apprentices, though legally indentured, usually received favorable working conditions and could not be sold by their masters. Indentures for this standard form of apprenticeship do not occur among the servants listed in the Register, though there is other evidence that transatlantic apprenticeship arrangements were occasionally made. But between the apprentices and the ordinary bondsmen was a third kind of contract laborer, which does occur occasionally in the records used here. These indentees, experienced workmen, were able to negotiate contracts for specific employment before shipping out; their indentures provided for salaries or cash payments in addition to maintenance, despite the fact that they were bound to serve their masters for a stipulated length of time. Such salaried indentees were recruited by colonists who needed special skills and who were willing to commit wages as well as shipping costs and upkeep to unknown workers said to qualify, rather than take the chance of finding the skills they wanted in the shipments of ordinary indentees offered for sale upon arrival. Thus, to take an extreme example, the London merchant Joshua Johnson wrote the Baltimore firm of Lux & Bowly, Oct. 4, 1773, that he had located just the foreman for their rope walk they were looking for. Age 40, with 24 years of experience in managing rope walks in London, he would agree to the following terms: transatlantic passage, a subsidy of 500 pounds of beef and pork and 500 pounds of flour, a house for himself and his wife, and £40 a year, in exchange for what Johnson called "the finishing stroak," an indenture of only two years. Johnson Letterbooks, I. Employers sought to avoid wage contracts with unknown workers no matter how well qualified they were said to be, and entered into such arrangements reluctantly. E.g., below, chap. 9, pp. 305–306. They

TABLE 5.15

OCCUPATION	ENGLAND	
	Indentured	*Not indentured*
GENTLE OCCUPATION OR STATUS	1	106
Public official	0	1
Gentleman or gentlewoman	0	89
Professional	1	16
Clergyman	0	5
Lawyer or physician	0	9
Other	1	2
MERCHANDISING	102	124
Wholesale trade or factorage	1	62
Shopkeeping	101	62
AGRICULTURE	488	289
Independent or semi-independent	392	279
Dependent	96	10
TRADES OR CRAFTS (ARTISANRY)	2067	301
Highly skilled	399	55
Ordinary skill level	1668	246
Metal trades	208	27
Food processing or marketing	173	36
Construction[1]	322	48
Textile manufacturing or trade	676	97
Service trades	176	20
Other	113	18
LABOR	779	109
Servant—domestic	109	36
Servant—unspecified	123	53
Laborer—maritime	11	8
Laborer—unspecified	536	12
TOTAL KNOWN OCCUPATIONS	3437	929
UNKNOWN OCCUPATIONS	116	714
Spinster[2]	11	29
Other	105	685
COMBINED TOTAL (KNOWN & UNKNOWN OCCUPATIONS)	3553	1643

[1]Includes shipbuilding.   [2]For note on spinster, see p. 154, n. 13.

SCOTLAND		OTHER		TOTAL	
Indentured	Not indentured	Indentured	Not indentured	Indentured	Not indentured
0	20	0	18	1	144
0	1	0	0	0	2
0	16	0	16	0	121
0	3	0	2	1	21
0	1	0	1	0	7
0	1	0	0	0	10
0	1	0	1	1	4
6	78	11	7	119	209
0	40	0	6	1	108
6	38	11	1	118	101
48	343	37	4	573	636
39	334	36	4	467	617
9	9	1	0	106	19
232	382	61	7	2360	690
18	50	10	2	427	107
214	332	51	5	1933	583
14	36	6	0	228	63
9	9	6	1	188	46
15	91	12	1	349	140
166	167	21	2	863	266
7	12	4	0	187	32
3	17	2	1	118	36
332	188	47	3	1158	300
1	21	4	1	114	58
302	23	2	1	427	77
3	11	4	1	18	20
26	133	37	0	599	145
618	1011	156	39	4211	1979
93	2150	52	49	261	2913
2	9	0	0	13	38
91	2141	52	49	248	2875
711	3161	208	88	4472	4892

TABLE 5.16

Occupation	ENGLAND									
	Home Counties	London	East Anglia	Southeast England	West Country	Bristol	Welsh Border	East-Central England	Mid-lands	Northern England
GENTLE	11	77	0	1	4	1	4	0	3	1
Indentured	1	0	0	0	0	0	0	0	0	0
Not indentured	10	77	0	1	4	1	4	0	3	1
MERCHANDISING	15	138	8	3	5	8	4	5	10	13
Indentured	11	66	4	3	3	0	3	4	2	5
Not indentured	4	72	4	0	2	8	1	1	8	8
AGRICULTURE	134	217	23	17	23	6	23	39	42	33
Indentured	131	170	16	16	23	6	18	39	41	16
Not indentured	3	47	7	1	0	0	5	0	1	17
ALL ARTISANS	284	1343	53	57	84	46	72	41	121	97
Indentured	275	1250	49	57	83	39	62	36	103	59
Not indentured	9	93	4	0	1	7	10	5	18	38
Highly Skilled	37	320	7	9	9	8	9	7	19	12
Indentured	37	297	6	9	9	5	9	6	13	5
Not indentured	0	23	1	0	0	3	0	1	6	7
Ordinary Skill	247	1023	46	48	75	38	63	34	102	85
Indentured	238	953	43	48	74	34	53	30	90	54
Not indentured	9	70	3	0	1	4	10	4	12	31
LABOR	113	417	18	26	109	40	30	18	34	26
Indentured	110	380	17	25	106	38	27	18	32	14
Not indentured	3	37	1	1	3	2	3	0	2	12
TOTAL KNOWN OCCUPATIONS	557	2192	102	104	225	101	133	103	210	170
Indentured	528	1866	86	101	215	83	110	97	178	94
Not indentured	29	326	16	3	10	18	23	6	32	76
UNKNOWN OCCUPATIONS	35	153	8	5	28	6	14	4	19	80
Indentured	14	29	0	0	15	1	2	1	2	30
Not indentured	21	124	8	5	13	5	12	3	17	50
COMBINED TOTAL	592	2345	110	109	253	107	147	107	229	250
Indentured	542	1895	86	101	230	84	112	98	180	124
Percent of all indentured	12.7	44.4	2.0	2.4	5.4	2.0	2.6	2.3	4.2	2.9
Not indentured	50	450	24	8	23	23	35	9	49	126
Percent of all not indentured	1.0	9.4	.5	.2	.5	.5	.7	.2	1.0	2.6

			SCOTLAND									
Yorkshire	Region unknown	Total England	Borders	West Lowlands	East Lowlands	Perthshire	Highlands & Hebrides	North-east Scotland	Far North	Region unknown	Total Scotland	Combined total
5	0	107	1	2	1	1	5	0	0	10	20	127
0	0	1	0	0	0	0	0	0	0	0	0	1
5	0	106	1	2	1	1	5	0	0	10	20	126
17	0	226	6	23	15	3	8	7	2	20	84	310
1	0	102	0	1	1	0	0	0	1	3	6	108
16	0	124	6	22	14	3	8	7	1	17	78	202
219	1	777	49	26	54	53	125	8	38	38	391	1168
11	1	488	0	6	3	0	1	2	9	27	48	536
208	0	289	49	20	51	53	124	6	29	11	343	632
169	1	2368	63	275	74	50	43	13	27	69	614	2982
53	1	2067	0	154	17	0	0	0	13	48	232	2299
116	0	301	63	121	57	50	43	13	14	21	382	683
17	0	454	14	8	17	4	4	3	4	14	68	522
3	0	399	0	1	9	0	0	0	2	6	18	417
14	0	55	14	7	8	4	4	3	2	8	50	105
152	1	1914	49	267	57	46	39	10	23	55	546	2460
50	1	1668	0	153	8	0	0	0	11	42	214	1882
102	0	246	49	114	49	46	39	10	12	13	332	578
56	1	888	62	43	51	29	238	28	51	18	520	1408
12	0	779	2	12	40	6	192	27	36	17	332	1111
44	1	109	60	31	11	23	46	1	15	1	188	297
466	3	4366	181	369	195	136	419	56	118	155	1629	5995
77	2	3437	2	173	61	6	193	29	59	95	618	4055
389	1	929	179	196	134	130	226	27	59	60	1011	1940
472	6	830	289	108	96	163	680	24	185	698	2243	3073
22	0	116	2	8	8	0	0	0	50	25	93	209
450	6	714	287	100	88	163	680	24	135	673	2150	2864
938	9	5196	470	477	291	299	1099	80	303	853	3872	9068
99	2	3553	4	181	69	6	193	29	109	120	711	4264
2.3	.1	83.3	.1	4.3	1.6	.1	4.5	.7	2.6	2.8	16.7	100.0
839	7	1643	466	296	222	293	906	51	194	733	3161	4804
17.5	.1	34.2	9.7	6.2	4.6	6.1	18.8	1.1	4.0	15.3	65.8	100.0

Most indentures were not contingent, however; but even so, such arrangements were sometimes undertaken as a calculated financial strategy. A revealing document, of an earlier era but still directly applicable to the period of the Register, shows the logic of this strategy clearly. In 1701 George Haworth, who had recently arrived in Pennsylvania, wrote back to his relatives in England who were planning to join him in America advising them *not* to indenture themselves but rather, as he put it, to "come free." If you come as indentured servants, he wrote, you will be sold for four or five years of hard work simply to pay for the passage money, but if you come free, as he did, you can earn £19 on a year-long work contract or work without a contract, as he had done, for at least 2s. 6d. a day and victuals. In 1704 he wrote again: for free workers "it is a great deal better living here than in England"—but *only* for free workers. "So if any of my relations have a mind to come to this country, I think it is a very good country and that they may do well, but be sure to come free."[18]

"Come free": for Haworth an important calculation was involved. He assumed that he had had, and his relatives still had, an active option, either to exhaust their last resources in transportation costs and "come free," or to save something to help establish themselves in the new situation by pledging four or more years of bonded service. Haworth argued that the opportunities available in America for a quick establishment in the economy were such that one would do better to maintain one's freedom from the start, at whatever cost, than to save a modicum gained, perhaps, from the sale of household goods and work equipment, at the price of forfeiting freedom. If one had to choose between four years of working time and one's last penny, he was saying, spend the penny and save the time available to work free. Sell everything, Haworth argued, and borrow if necessary, in order to "come free" and start an independent life quickly in the colonies.

This was not, clearly, a common view for those in such marginal circumstances, hence the need to argue for it. Most people near the edge of destitution tried to retain their last slim resources, and were willing to

also broke their commitments whenever possible, as two carpenters in Florida discovered when they were released from their indentures three months early "to get rid of their claim for twenty pounds apiece when their time was elapsed." James Grant to the Earl of Casillis, St. Augustine, July 22, 1769, Ailsa Muniments, GD 25/9, box 27, Scottish Record Office, Edinburgh. Indentees who had little to bargain with occasionally falsified their skills in order to extract salaries or cash payments. For Virginia's effort to reduce fraudulence in claims of special skills, see below, pp. 268–269. The most common point of negotiation open to ordinary indentees was not salary or cash payments but length of service, which was, within narrow limits, adjustable according to age, skills, and demand. The variations in length of term and their determinants are discussed at length in David W. Galenson, *White Servitude in Colonial America: An Economic Analysis* (Cambridge, Eng., 1981).

[18]"Early Letters from Pennsylvania, 1699–1722," *Pennsylvania Magazine of History and Biography*, 37 (1913), 332, 334.

purchase their passages with a commitment to future labor in order to do so. What was said of the German immigrants of the mid-century was true of many British, that they "bring money enough with them to pay their passage, but rather suffer themselves to be sold, with a view that during their servitude they may get some knowledge of the language and quality of the country . . . that they may the better be able to consider what they shall do when they have got their liberty." However evil the condition of indentured servitude may have been in earlier years, a correspondent to Edinburgh's *Weekly Magazine* wrote in 1774, it had become in recent years a benign form of apprenticeship. An indentee was treated with "the greatest humanity and discretion," was well provided for, and was allowed free time to earn money "to begin business for himself." In contrast, those who go over free, with a little money to start with, and are not immediately successful are soon "taken with distress, their little stock being exhausted and none to take care of them. They are in a far worse situation than those who are indented."

A more complicated version of the same positive view appears in a wonderfully detailed and thoughtful letter of 1772 written by one John Campbell, recently emigrated from Scotland to Maryland, in which he described life in that colony and the conditions of emigration and resettlement. He assessed a poor man's life chances in America very favorably. Those who emigrate to the colonies "certainly act for the best" even, he wrote, "at the expense of a few years in servitude"—*provided they are young enough.* For indentured servants of advanced years, the change of climate, the hardship of the work, and "the pressure upon their minds on being rank'd and deemed as slaves are such that they seldom surmount." Younger people, on the other hand, Campbell wrote, bear the work and the ignominy easily, and in fact find in the temporary bondage a kind of apprenticeship into the customs of the country and the system of production that proves to be invaluable.[19]

So Campbell wrote. But others disagreed—the issue was arguable. A Scottish pamphleteer who claimed to have lived for years in America and was much in favor of emigration, advised those unable to pay for their passage to avoid at all costs indenting themselves to "a mercenary shipmaster, who may sell them like cattle in a market." Instead, he hoped more affluent emigrants would purchase land in common for whole communities, pay the expenses of the poor, employ them for a limited time in developing the land, and then pay them off for their services in land or money. Another Scot, with more recent experience, was even more negative, and his tale was more circumstantial. He had arrived in America under

[19] Peter Kalm, *Travels into North America . . .*, trans. J. R. Forster (Warrington, Eng., 1770), I, 389; *Weekly Magazine, or Edinburgh Amusement,* March 24, 1774; Campbell to Sinclair, July 26, 1772, Freswick Muniments (note 13, above).

bond of servitude, had been treated cruelly by his master, and had run away. After various adventures he managed to get his contract bought by a kindly merchant, but even under his new master he felt his situation to be intolerable. In a letter home to his godfather, he asked for every penny that could be spared "that I may be enabled to buy my time & put myself to some tradesman to learn his calling, for a tradesman has good wages in this country. I beg that none of my relations may come to this country except they are able to pay their passage thir selves, and then they may come as soon as they like. This is a good poor mans country when a man once getts into a way of [earning a] liveing."[20]

A few years in servitude . . . come free . . . into a way of earning a living —the data in Tables 5.15, 5.16, 5.17, and 5.18, detailing the incidence of indentures found in the Register, suggest that such considerations played an active role in shaping the migration. Table 5.15 totals the numbers of indentees in each occupational category and contrasts them to the numbers of free men, women, and children in these categories, separately for England and Scotland. It is apparent from the totals column that indentured servitude was by no means the condition only of those in the meanest occupations. It is true that only one indentured servant shows up among the "gentle" occupations—a twenty-two-year-old architect;[21] it is true also that approximately four-fifths of all laborers and dependent farmworkers left Britain under bond of indenture. But there were also many indentured

---

[20]*A Present for an Emigrant . . .* (Edinburgh, 1774), p. 41; Baikia Harvey to Thomas Baikia, Esq[r], "Snowhill, near Augusta in Georgia," Dec. 30, 1775, Breckness MSS, D 3/385. Some of the published denunciations of indentured servitude, usually of dubious provenance, were fierce. *Etherington's York Chronicle*, Jan. 27, 1775, printed a letter purportedly from North America that compared indentured servitude unfavorably to slavery. Sold at public auction, bartered for country produce, indentured servants "might as well fall into the hands of the Turks. They are subject nearly to the same laws as the Negroes and have the same coarse food and clothing, but often in other respects, worse usage, their masters generally endeavouring to work them to death by the time their term of slavery is to expire. This infamous traffic has been carried on so long a time and has been so notorious that many are surprised government has used no effectual means to stop a trade so scandalous to their country and disgraceful to humanity." Only the "art and falsehood" practiced by scheming merchants and shippers, the *Chronicle* said, could explain how people would voluntarily submit themselves to such treatment. For the reality of the sale of indentured servants, see below, chap. 10.

[21]Peter Mathew, 22, a resident of Middlesex leaving London for Maryland aboard the *Elizabeth* in early July, 1774 (T47/9/178), was not the first architect to begin his work in the colonies as an indentured servant. In 1755 William Buckland, a 22-year-old apprentice in the building trade in London, indented himself to the Mason family of Virginia and became one of the most renowned and successful architects and builders in the Chesapeake region. His indenture, printed in full in Rosamond R. Beirne and John H. Scarff, *William Buckland, 1734–1774: Architect of Virginia and Maryland* (Baltimore, 1958), app. B, is typical of salaried labor contracts referred to above, n. 17. It provides for Buckland working for the Masons in Virginia for four years "in the employment of a carpenter & joiner" in exchange for transportation, "all necessary meat, drink, washing, lodging, fit and convenient for him, as covenant servants in such cases are usually provided for," and in addition a salary of £20 a year. There is no indication that Mathew had negotiated so favorable a contract.

servants in occupations in which one would not have expected to find them: one can well imagine decisions of economic strategy on their part by which a modicum was retained at the cost of temporary bondage. It is a remarkable fact that four-fifths of the artisans in the most refined, most highly skilled crafts—producers of the highest-quality consumer goods and luxury products—went to America as indentured servants. Among the English emigrants, the percentage of indentees in these most highly skilled crafts was 87.9%. Among the less highly skilled trades too, in the British migration as a whole, the incidence of indentured servitude is high, ranging from 80.3% of those in food manufacture and distribution to 76.4% of those in textile manufacture and cloth distribution. And further, over two-fifths (467 in all) of the farmers who gave some indication of an independent or semi-independent stake in the land also traveled as indentured servants.

The decisions of four out of five ordinary laborers traveling to America to sell themselves for four years in exchange for transportation are not very difficult to understand. Four or five pounds sterling was a sizable amount of money to produce all at once. But why goldsmiths, cabinetmakers, watch-movement makers, enamelers, and mathematical-instrument makers —together with yeomen, weavers, and bakers—should have been under similar constraints is not clear, except perhaps in terms of economic strategies such as those opposed by Haworth, and the unexpected assumption that there was a better market for such skills in the colonies than at home.[22] And the complexity is compounded when one compares the England and Scotland columns of Table 5.15.

There are huge differences between the incidences of indenture among the English and Scottish emigrants. The overall difference in itself is remarkable: 68.4% of all the English emigrants were indentured, but only 18.4% of the Scots—and that great difference is reflected in every occupa-

[22]The authors of the two standard general works on indentured servitude covering the colonial period both recognize, in different ways, a fundamental shift in the character of the imported white labor force which helps explain the numbers of highly skilled artisans found in the tables presented here. Galenson, in *White Servitude in Colonial America*, notes repeatedly (pp. 63, 117, 127–128, 135–139, 156–168) that white indentees shifted from unskilled to skilled workers in the course of the colonial period as more and more slaves took over the unskilled work and in the eighteenth century were trained too in some of the skilled jobs. A. E. Smith, writing more generally in *Colonists in Bondage*, p. 288, stresses that "towards the end of the colonial period better servants came, and the large migrations of 1773 did not bring nearly as much riff-raff, proportionately, as did the smaller movements of a century before . . . the colonies had settled down into a stable existence; men could go there not as on a wild gamble, but with a fair certainty of making a decent and even a comfortable living." Galenson, who uses portions of the Register in the course of his economic analysis of servitude through the two centuries, concentrates on statistical correlations among such elements as age, occupation, literacy, seasonality, and length of service. Besides its central themes focused on the correlates of length of service, the book contains new and valuable descriptive statistics on servitude in the seventeenth and eighteenth centuries brought together from the fragmentary quantifiable documentation that has survived. On significant points the conclusions in *White Servitude in Colonial America* are supported by the findings presented here.

tional category. Almost 90% of the English artisans were indentured servants, but of the Scots only 37.8%—or, to put it differently, 9 out of every
10 English artisans traveled under bond of servitude; only about 4 out of
10 of the Scottish did so. Of the farming population, 62.8% of the English
were indentured but only 12.3% of the Scots. Similarly, 45.1% of the English
shopkeepers and tradesmen were indentured, but only 7.1% of the Scottish.
The difference was less, reasonably enough, among the laborers: 87.7% of
the English and 63.8% of the Scottish.

But "England" and "Scotland" are broad categories. Table 5.16 specifies
the regional origins of the emigrating indentees, again classified by occupation. The largest number by far—over two-fifths of the total—came from
London itself; over half came from London and the adjoining Home Counties together; two-thirds came from southern England, including a sizable
concentration from Bristol and the West Country (7.4%). The rest were
drawn in fairly even numbers (2 to 4% of the total) from the other regions
of England and, with less regularity, from the Scottish regions, with the
highest incidence there in the Highlands-Hebrides area (4.5%).

An even more striking indication of the concentration of sources of
indentured servants lies in a separate tabulation of the ports through which
the bondsmen left Britain. While just over two-fifths claimed London as
their residence, over three-fourths (77.5%) left for America through the
port of London, and hence that large number (3,306), drawn from all
regions of Britain, must have been residents of London for some period of
time before their departure. London, therefore, to an even greater degree
than the residence figures indicate, was the major source of indentured
labor—and without respect to the occupations claimed by these bonded
laborers. For though the indentees of known occupation from London
were predominantly artisans (67.0%), there were among them also farmers
and farm workers (9.1%), shopkeepers and merchants (3.5%), and of course
unskilled laborers (20.4%). A similar spread of occupations can be found
among the indentees from the other regions of southern England, but as
one approaches the Midlands and northern regions the balance shifts, away
from indentures and away from artisanry, toward a greater emphasis on
agriculture—a trend that on both points becomes magnified in the Scottish
regions and climaxes in the Highlands-Hebrides area, where the predominant categories are non-indentured agriculturists and indentured unskilled
laborers.

No doubt these stark contrasts exaggerate the reality. There may have
been recording errors of some consequence. The occasional scrawls at the
top of some of the Scottish registration sheets declaring everyone on board
to be indentured servants seem at times to have been afterthoughts, and as
such may well have been omitted for certain vessels. In other cases bonded-
ness was simply ignored by the customs people and has to be established,

to the extent that it can be, from the notices of arrivals in America.

Yet, even if the differences in the incidence of indenture as between the English and the Scottish emigrants were exaggerated by the inefficiency of the Scottish officials, such differences—and very large differences—undoubtedly existed, and they are important. They demonstrate at the very least that there were no intrinsic or inescapable imperatives in certain occupations that led workers to enter into these stringent work contracts. Even allowing for omissions in registering indentures by the Scottish customs officers, it is clear that the Scottish emigrants in almost every occupation rarely bound themselves, while the English commonly did so. Why the difference? Can it be explained by significant sex and age differences? How do the disproportions of children and females, already shown in general terms, relate to the incidences of indentures?

Tables 5.17, 5.18, and 5.19 contain the answers to these questions. Tables 5.17 and 5.18 in effect take the first and third columns of Table 5.15 (totals of indentured servants from England and Scotland by occupational categories) and enlarge them in two dimensions—by subdividing the group by age differences and by separating the sexes within each age-occupation cell. Now the details submerged in the totals of Table 5.15 stand out clearly. First, it is clear that indentured servitude was largely a male condition among both the English and Scottish emigrants, but far more so, proportionately, among the English. No less than nine-tenths of all English indentees of known age and sex were males, but only six-tenths of all the Scottish emigrants. The age patterns are equally revealing. Table 5.19 compares the average and median ages of indentees as opposed to free emigrants separately for England and Scotland. It is clear, first, that the average ages of indentured servants in both regions were markedly lower than those of free emigrants, except among English women. And further, not only were the gaps greater among the Scots than among the English, but the mean and median ages of the Scottish indentees were considerably lower than those of the English.

From all of this it is obvious that there is no peculiar dependency pattern, with respect to either sex or age, among the English to account for the high incidence of indenture. Whatever explains this striking phenomenon lies not on the surface of the picture but deep in the social background, and will be revealed not in the numbers compiled in the Register but in other evidence altogether. Yet, though the information in Tables 5.17, 5.18, and 5.19 cannot explain the difference in the incidence of indenture as between the English and the Scottish emigrants, it does draw attention to two still unexamined patches in the occupational and social description of the emigration.

The first derives from the remarkable youthfulness of the indentees among the Scottish emigrants (Table 5.18). No fewer than 42 Scottish

Occupation	1–14 Male	Female	15–19 Male	Female	20–24 Male	Female	25–29 Male	Female	30–34 Male	Female
GENTLE OCCUPATION OR STATUS	0	0	0	0	1	0	0	0	0	0
MERCHANDISING	0	0	9	1	43	6	25	2	8	0
Wholesale trade or factorage	0	0	0	0	0	0	0	0	0	0
Shopkeeping	0	0	9	1	43	6	25	2	8	0
AGRICULTURE	0	0	70	0	193	1	112	0	50	0
Independent or semi-independent	0	0	59	0	157	0	93	0	42	0
Dependent	0	0	11	0	36	1	19	0	8	0
TRADES OR CRAFTS (ARTISANRY)	2	0	235	34	873	85	389	18	190	5
Highly skilled	0	0	39	0	192	1	74	0	32	1
Ordinary skill level	2	0	196	34	681	84	315	18	158	4
Metal trades	1	0	27	0	102	0	36	0	17	0
Food processing or marketing	0	0	18	0	84	0	39	0	21	0
Construction[2]	0	0	25	0	127	1	84	0	44	0
Textile manufacturing or trade	1	0	85	34	229	83	98	18	49	3
Service trades	0	0	24	0	97	0	35	0	13	0
Other	0	0	17	0	42	0	23	0	14	1
LABOR	18	0	338	29	146	54	75	29	46	7
Servant—domestic	0	0	23	4	17	20	14	13	5	3
Servant—unspecified	1	0	19	25	15	34	2	16	3	4
Laborer—maritime	0	0	4	0	1	0	3	0	2	0
Laborer—unspecified	17	0	292	0	113	0	56	0	36	0
TOTAL KNOWN OCCUPATIONS	20	0	652	64	1256	146	601	49	294	12
UNKNOWN OCCUPATIONS	5	7	0	7	1	27	0	15	0	11
Spinster[3]	0	0	0	4	0	5	0	1	0	1
Other	5	7	0	3	1	22	0	14	0	10
COMBINED TOTAL (KNOWN & UNKNOWN OCCUPATIONS)	25	7	652	71	1257	173	601	64	294	23

[1]Excludes emigrants of either unknown age or unknown sex.
[2]Includes shipbuilding.
[3]For note on spinster, see p. 154, n. 13.

35–39 Male	Female	40–44 Male	Female	45–49 Male	Female	50+ Male	Female	TOTAL Male	Female	Combined total	% of known occupations
0	0	0	0	0	0	0	0	1	0	1	0
6	0	2	0	0	0	0	0	93	9	102	3.0
1	0	0	0	0	0	0	0	1	0	1	0
5	0	2	0	0	0	0	0	92	9	101	3.0
42	0	15	0	4	0	1	0	487	1	488	14.2
26	0	12	0	2	0	1	0	392	0	392	11.4
16	0	3	0	2	0	0	0	95	1	96	2.8
144	0	64	0	25	0	3	0	1925	142	2067	60.1
39	0	10	0	10	0	1	0	397	2	399	11.6
105	0	54	0	15	0	2	0	1528	140	1668	48.5
19	0	5	0	1	0	0	0	208	0	208	6.0
5	0	4	0	2	0	0	0	173	0	173	5.0
27	0	9	0	5	0	0	0	321	1	322	9.4
39	0	29	0	6	0	2	0	538	138	676	19.7
4	0	3	0	0	0	0	0	176	0	176	5.1
11	0	4	0	1	0	0	0	112	1	113	3.3
21	6	6	1	3	0	0	0	653	126	779	22.7
4	4	1	0	1	0	0	0	65	44	109	3.2
0	2	1	1	0	0	0	0	41	82	123	3.6
0	0	1	0	0	0	0	0	11	0	11	0.3
17	0	3	0	2	0	0	0	536	0	536	15.6
213	6	87	1	32	0	4	0	3159	278	3437	100.0
1	7	0	1	0	0	0	0	7	75	82	
0	0	0	0	0	0	0	0	0	11	11	
1	7	0	1	0	0	0	0	7	64	71	
214	13	87	2	32	0	4	0	3166	353	3519	

OCCUPATION	1–9		10–14		15–19		20–24		25–29		30–34	
	Male	Female	Male	Female	Male	Female	Male	Female	Male	Female	Male	Female
GENTLE OCCUPATION OR STATUS	0	0	0	0	0	0	0	0	0	0	0	0
MERCHANDISING	0	0	0	0	0	0	4	0	0	0	0	0
Wholesale trade or factorage	0	0	0	0	0	0	0	0	0	0	0	0
Shopkeeping	0	0	0	0	0	0	4	0	0	0	0	0
AGRICULTURE	0	0	0	0	7	0	8	0	16	0	9	0
Independent or semi-independent	0	0	0	0	7	0	4	0	13	0	8	0
Dependent	0	0	0	0	0	0	4	0	3	0	1	0
TRADES OR CRAFTS (ARTISANRY)	0	0	3	1	50	21	56	15	21	14	17	8
Highly skilled	0	0	0	0	1	0	12	0	2	0	2	0
Ordinary skill level	0	0	3	1	49	21	44	15	19	14	15	8
Metal trades	0	0	0	0	5	0	4	0	4	0	0	0
Food processing or marketing	0	0	0	0	2	0	5	0	0	0	2	0
Construction[2]	0	0	0	0	1	0	7	0	2	0	2	0
Textile manufacturing or trade	0	0	3	1	39	21	23	15	11	14	10	8
Service trades	0	0	0	0	1	0	5	0	1	0	0	0
Other	0	0	0	0	1	0	0	0	1	0	1	0
LABOR	11	5	32	21	59	63	30	49	17	13	10	4
Servant—domestic	0	0	0	0	0	0	0	1	0	0	0	0
Servant—unspecified	11	5	31	21	51	63	25	48	8	13	8	4
Laborer—maritime	0	0	0	0	0	0	1	0	0	0	0	0
Laborer—unspecified	0	0	1	0	8	0	4	0	9	0	2	0
TOTAL KNOWN OCCUPATIONS	11	5	35	22	116	84	98	64	54	27	36	12
UNKNOWN OCCUPATIONS	11	15	14	6	0	9	0	8	1	9	0	5
Spinster[3]	0	0	0	0	0	0	0	2	0	0	0	0
Other	11	15	14	6	0	9	0	6	1	9	0	5
COMBINED TOTAL	22	20	49	28	116	93	98	72	55	36	36	17

[1]Excludes emigrants of either unknown age or unknown sex.   [3]For note on spinster, see p. 154, n. 13.
[2]Includes shipbuilding.

35–39		40–44		45–49		50+		TOTAL		Combined total	% of known occupations
Male	Female	Male	Female	Male	Female	Male	Female	Male	Female		
0	0	0	0	0	0	0	0	0	0	0	0
0	0	2	0	0	0	0	0	6	0	6	1.0
0	0	0	0	0	0	0	0	0	0	0	0
0	0	2	0	0	0	0	0	6	0	6	1.0
6	0	2	0	0	0	0	0	48	0	48	7.8
5	0	2	0	0	0	0	0	39	0	39	6.3
1	0	0	0	0	0	0	0	9	0	9	1.5
14	3	5	1	3	0	0	0	169	63	232	37.7
0	0	1	0	0	0	0	0	18	0	18	2.9
14	3	4	1	3	0	0	0	151	63	214	34.8
1	0	0	0	0	0	0	0	14	0	14	2.3
0	0	0	0	0	0	0	0	9	0	9	1.5
0	0	1	0	2	0	0	0	15	0	15	2.4
13	3	3	1	1	0	0	0	103	63	166	27.0
0	0	0	0	0	0	0	0	7	0	7	1.1
0	0	0	0	0	0	0	0	3	0	3	.5
10	1	2	0	1	0	1	0	173	156	329	53.5
0	0	0	0	0	0	0	0	0	1	1	0.2
7	1	2	0	0	0	1	0	144	155	299	48.6
1	0	0	0	1	0	0	0	3	0	3	.5
2	0	0	0	0	0	0	0	26	0	26	4.2
30	4	11	1	4	0	1	0	396	219	615	100.0
0	7	0	2	0	0	0	0	26	61	87	
0	0	0	0	0	0	0	0	0	2	2	
0	7	0	2	0	0	0	0	26	59	85	
30	11	11	3	4	0	1	0	422	280	702	

TABLE 5.19

AGES OF INDENTURED SERVANTS AND
FREE EMIGRANTS: AVERAGES AND MEDIANS
BY RESIDENCE

		ENGLAND		SCOTLAND	
SEX	STATUS	*Average age*	*Median age*	*Average age*	*Median age*
Male	Indentured	24.4	23.0	21.8	20.0
	Not indentured	26.1	25.0	23.8	23.0
Female	Indentured	22.7	22.0	20.0	19.0
	Not indentured	22.8	22.0	21.6	21.0

children below the age of 10, and 119 below the age of 15, were bonded for future service; 48 of these 119 indentured children were girls. The largest number of Scottish indentees were in their late teens, but by far the largest number of English were in their early twenties. Why were so many very young Scottish children going overseas as bonded servants? It was sometimes claimed that shipping agents were kidnapping small children in the isolated fishing villages of the western islands, and that families reduced to penury were selling their children into bondage, in this way assuring the children's survival and providing them with the opportunity to start out in a new life. There is some evidence that in a few cases this may have been true. But there is a different, and a more benign and convincing, explanation.

The high incidence of children among the indentees suggests that whole families were traveling together under indentures—that the high proportion of families among the Scots is reflected in this category of bonded servants as it is in the Scottish emigration in general. The plausibility of this explanation is strengthened by the remarkably high proportion of women 15 years of age and older among the indentured servants (33.0% among the Scots vs. 9.8% among the English). And in fact this explanation, when the relevant data are separately analyzed, proves to be correct: just over one-third of the Scottish indentees but only 3.8% of the English traveled as members of families. Of the 119 Scottish children below age 15 who were indentured, 69 were members of families.

But what kinds of families were these? What arrangements were there for families that included bonded servants? Were families divided between bond and free members? Did heads of households indenture themselves in order to emigrate, allowing other members of their families to travel free?

The key to the answers lies in the occupational distribution of all heads of households, free and indentured (Tables 5.20 and 5.21), hence in the social character of the migrating families. We have already seen (Table 5.11) that

O C C U P A T I O N S   O F   H E A D S   O F   H O U S E H O L D S [1]
B Y   R E S I D E N C E

OCCUPATION	ENGLAND		SCOTLAND		TOTAL [2]	
	Number	Percent of known	Number	Percent of known	Number	Percent of known
Gentle occupation or status	9	4.3	3	.9	12	2.2
Merchandising	8	3.8	4	1.2	12	2.2
Wholesale trade or factorage	6	2.8	4	1.2	10	1.8
Shopkeeping	2	1.0	0	–	2	.4
Agriculture	98	46.7	168	51.4	267	49.6
Independent or semi-independent	97	46.2	166	50.8	264	49.0
Dependent	1	.5	2	6	3	6
Trades or crafts (artisanry)	87	41.4	99	30.3	187	34.7
Highly skilled	12	5.7	12	3.7	24	4.5
Ordinary skill level	75	35.7	87	26.6	163	30.2
Labor	8	3.8	53	16.2	61	11.3
Total known occupations	210	100.0	327	100.0	539	100.0
Unknown occupations	24		26		53	
Combined Total	234		353		592	

[1]Excludes "other" families of Table 5.8.
[2]Includes "other" residences (n = 5).

about half of all emigrants who gave occupations identified their work with some kind of craft or trade that can be classified as *non-* agricultural, and that only approximately a fifth claimed to be farmers or farm laborers. But the occupational pattern of family heads among the emigrants is quite different. They are drawn far more from the countryside. Half (49.6%) of the family heads whose occupations are known were either farmers or farm workers and only a third claimed to be craftsmen, artisans, or tradesmen. Though this difference is slightly more pronounced among the Scottish heads of families than among the English, even among the latter, 46.7% were agriculturists as opposed to 17.8% among the English emigrants as a whole.

Thus the emigration of families was peculiarly a product of the countryside. But not the countryside in general. When one separates out the independent or semi-independent or substantial farmers from those who were probably farm laborers, the disproportion grows. In the migration as a whole these more substantial agriculturists constituted 17.5% of all those whose occupations were stated. Among the heads of families that were emigrating, that percentage more than doubles, rising to 49.0%, and the

TABLE 5.21

OCCUPATIONS OF
INDENTURED HEADS OF HOUSEHOLDS
BY RESIDENCE[1]

OCCUPATION	ENGLAND		SCOTLAND		TOTAL	
	Male	*Female*	*Male*	*Female*	*Male*	*Female*
Gentle occupation or status	0	0	0	0	0	0
Merchandising	1	0	0	0	1	0
Agriculture	6	0	12	0	18	0
Trades or crafts (artisanry)	34	0	27	1	61	1
Labor	5	0	12	1	17	1
Total known occupations	46	0	51	2	97	2
Unknown occupations	1	1	3	0	4	1
Combined Total	47	1	54	2	101	3

[1]Excludes "other" families of Table 5.8 and emigrants of unknown sex.

otherwise persistent differences between the English and Scottish migrations almost disappear. Whereas only 15.4% of *all* English emigrants whose occupations are known can be classified as independent or semi-independent agriculturists, no less than 46.2% of all *heads of families* emigrating from England fall into that category; the equivalent figures for Scotland are 22.9% and 50.8%. In other words, whole families or significant parts of families that migrate are far more likely to be drawn from among the better-established farming families than from any other sector of the economy or occupational structure. And this is true whether one looks at England or at Scotland.

It follows logically from this picture of emigrating families that few of the family heads were likely to be indentured servants, and indeed Table 5.21 shows that that is in fact the case. Only 17.6% of all heads of households were indentured servants, and more of them Scottish than English. Of the 4,264 Scottish and English indentured servants only a very small number—104, or 2.4%—were heads of households, and over half of the "households" over which they presided consisted simply of husband and wife.

Thus very few family heads left Britain under bond of indenture. But when they did, were they the only ones in their families constrained by such bondage? Were the members of families, in other words, divided in legal status and hence divided in the condition of their lives during the settling years?

At times, we know, they were. Janet Schaw, on the *Jamaica Packet*, reported that John Lawson "bound himself double, to save his wife and daughter." But most often they were not separated in legal status. Commonly the legal situation of the head of household is found to be shared by all the accompanying members of the family: children were not commonly distinguished from parents in this way, nor brothers from sisters. The records of two voyages to Georgia of the *Marlborough* from Whitby, Yorkshire, with a stopover in Kirkwall, the Orkneys—one in 1774, the other in 1775—are complete in the Register, and the legal status of the passengers is independently confirmed by muster rolls of the indentees compiled by the shipper for his own use. The two sets of records show that entire family groups traveled together on the *Marlborough* as indentured servants. Some were simply husband and wife, some were parents with 1 child, but some were large and complete families of indentees—families with 4, 5, or 6 children, in one of which the youngest were 8, 6, and 2 years old.[23]

Thus in the migration as a whole, indentures were contracted overwhelmingly by individuals traveling alone. When that status is held by members of families it most often pertains to all members, even, though uncommonly, very young children.

All of the questions we have asked and, in part at least, answered from the data of the Register—questions concerning the emigrants' ages and sex; the groupings in which they traveled; the character of their families; their social situations and occupations; and the incidence of bonded servitude among them—help clarify blurred patches in a panorama that becomes increasingly vivid and ever more sharply articulated. But one important detail in the social composition of the emigration is still vague, still unexamined and lost in the complex design.

In tracing the migration flows in chapter 4 it became clear that though

[23][Janet Schaw], *Journal of a Lady of Quality . . . 1774 to 1776*, ed. Evangeline W. Andrews and Charles M. Andrews (New Haven, 1921), p. 55. The voyages of the *Marlborough*, discussed at length in chap. 15, below, are recorded in T47/9/207 and T47/12/124; the muster rolls of indentured servants are in AO 13/34/122–123. The disposal of very small children of indebted and indentured parents was a problem. Among the Germans they were frequently given away by their parents "for nothing, to be brought up by strangers; and in return these children must stay in service until they are twenty-one years old." Gottlieb Mittelberger, *Journey to Pennsylvania*, ed. and trans. Oscar Handlin and John Clive (Cambridge, Mass., 1960), p. 18. As explained in chap. 10 below, merchants could get a good price for vigorous teen-aged boys, but they had little use for those under 13. So Harry Piper, an American commission merchant specializing in the sale of indentured servants sent him by his principals in England, was disgusted with certain of the people he was expected to dispose of. Convict women found to be pregnant were bad enough, but he discovered in one shipload "a boy of about 9 years old, bound for four years, another around 12 years, for the same time, also an idiot, bound for four years—these are no servants." Harry Piper to Dixon & Littledale, Alexandria, Va., Oct. 24, 1767, Piper Letterbook.

TABLE 5.22

OCCUPATION	TOTAL LONDON²	
	N = 3,698	
	Percent	*Average age*
Gentle	1.8	25.4
Merchandising	5.2	25.0
Wholesale	0.8	30.6
Shopkeeping	4.5	24.1
Agriculture	15.5	25.7
Trades or crafts (artisanry)	59.2	25.2
Highly skilled	11.8	25.6
Ordinary skill	47.3	25.1
Textile	18.8	24.7
Labor	18.3	21.6
Total	100.0	24.6

Numbers in parentheses represent indentured servants.
[1]Table omits those of age unknown and/or occupation unknown.

the exodus to the Western Hemisphere was largely a one-stage migration —a deliberated movement of people moving directly to ports of exit—it also included significant numbers of two- or even three-stage migrants, for whom emigration was not the original purpose of their departures from home, but an occasion that arose later, after earlier moves. Some of these emigrants were hundreds of miles from their stated residences when they left Britain. Were they "subsistence migrants"—destitute wanderers, itinerants, victims of several ejections as vagrants, hence likely to be older than the average migrant and less likely to be able to claim a marketable skill or trade? Were these long-distance migrants, in other words, a peculiar proletariat within the migration as a whole?

The question can now be answered. Of the emigrants who left through the port of London, 454 had come from places in the British Isles 150 miles (242 kilometers) or more distant from the point of their embarkation (Fig. 4.6); all but 25 of them stated their occupations. Table 5.22 shows the occupational and age characteristics of this group of 429 as compared with those of the emigration through London as a whole. In terms of occupational distribution this was no concealed proletariat. In proportion to their numbers, at least as many of these long-distance migrants claimed "gentle" occupations as did the London emigrants as a whole, and, surprisingly,

OCCUPATIONS AND AVERAGE AGES
OF EMIGRANTS LEAVING FROM LONDON,
COMPARING TOTAL EMIGRANTS WITH
LONG-DISTANCE MIGRANTS:[1] 150 miles+

LONG DISTANCE MIGRANTS[3]					
BRITISH ISLES		SCOTLAND		IRELAND	
N = 429 (371)		N = 116 (74)		N = 104 (102)	
Percent	Average age	Percent	Average age	Percent	Average age
1.9	21.4	6.9	21.4	–	–
8.8 (5.8)	25.3 (25.9)	12.9 (4.3)	23.6 (25.8)	9.6 (8.7)	26.6 (26.8)
0.9	33.5	1.7	35.0	–	–
7.9	24.4	11.2	21.9	9.6	26.6
24.0 (21.2)	24.9 (24.2)	19.8 (16.4)	25.4 (25.2)	32.7 (31.7)	24.5 (24.1)
52.2 (46.6)	25.2 (25.0)	55.2 (38.8)	24.5 (24.0)	39.4 (39.4)	23.2 (23.2)
8.2	24.1	14.7	23.3	5.8	22.7
44.0	25.3	40.5	24.9	33.6	23.3
14.0	26.4	8.6	27.3	14.4	24.6
13.1 (12.8)	23.9 (23.8)	5.2 (4.3)	25.2 (24.2)	18.3 (18.3)	22.4 (22.4)
100.0 (86.4)	24.9 (24.7)	100.0 (63.8)	24.4 (24.4)	100.0 (98.1)	23.8 (23.7)

[2] All emigrants who left through port of London.
[3] Emigrants who traveled more than 150 miles to exit from port of London.

more were in commerce, though mainly in shopkeeping rather than whole-sale merchandising. Less surprising is the higher percentage in agriculture, but that figure (24.0%) is not wholly at the expense of the numbers of artisans: 52.2% of the long-distance migrants were artisans; the percentage among all the emigrants who came through London was 59.2. The higher proportions in agriculture and commerce are also in large part balanced in the least-expected category: labor. There were relatively *fewer* laborers among the long-distance migrants than among the entire population of emigrants through London Nor were the long-distance migrants older: the second columns in each group give the average ages. The ages of the smaller group are almost identical to those of the London emigrants as a whole, the only interesting difference appearing in the greater youth of the few long-distance migrants who claimed "gentle" occupations.

To test all of this further, the Scots and Irish were distinguished from the others (last four columns) on the chance that among these, who came the farthest distance, a significantly older and humbler group might be concealed. Nothing of the sort can be said of the Scots. Quite the contrary: the occupational profile shows a higher concentration in "gentle" and commercial occupations and a smaller proportion of laborers. Only among the 104 Irish is there an interesting contrast to the whole population of

London's emigrants: none are "gentle," far more worked in agriculture, fewer were artisans—but even here the percentage of laborers is the same as that of the whole population emigrating through London.

Other tabulations, not reproduced here, reinforce this general conclusion. As one might expect, there were far fewer children and old people among the long-distance migrants (none of specified age under 15 or over 54), but the spread of ages is otherwise almost identical to the overall pattern except for a compensating increase in the most populous age group, 20–24. There were very few females among these long-distance migrants—only 26 (5.8%) of the 446 whose sex is known: more among the Scots (10.2%) and less among the Irish (one woman in a total of 104). And approximately the same small proportion of these long-distance migrants traveled as members of families—5.5% overall; 11.5% of the Scots, 10.0% of those from Yorkshire, and none of the Irish or Welsh.

But there is one remaining question—and it is fundamental: the incidence of indentured servitude. Were these long-distance emigrants through London more likely to be indentured servants than others who left from that port? Separate tabulations show that they *were*—overwhelmingly. In the entire emigration from Britain, 47.8% were indentees; among the English, 68.4%; among the Scots, 18.4%; and among the non-British, 70.3%. The percentages among the long-distance emigrants through the port of London are the following: residents of the British Isles, 82.6%; English residents, 90.0%; Scots, 57.3%; Welsh, 100.0%; Irish, 98.1%. Thus, except for the Scottish emigrants, who retain something of the balance of the sexes and the family involvement that appears in their emigration as a whole, practically all of these emigrants from distant parts—two- or three-stage emigrants—traveled to America as indentured servants.

Some conclusions may now be reached. The recent suggestion of studies that the long-distance "subsistence migration" of the sixteenth and seventeenth centuries had largely disappeared, and that those who migrated long distances in Britain in the eighteenth century were from "upper social groups—gentlemen and merchants, as well as professional men"—is not reflected in the London Register. Which is not surprising: emigrants, after all, are not likely to be "better off members of society . . . in pursuit of leisure and the fashionable 'high life.' "[24] But neither does the Register identify in

[24]Peter Clark, "Migration in England During the Late Seventeenth and Early Eighteenth Centuries," *Past and Present*, 83 (May, 1979), 81–90: "Many ordinary poor people thus found it increasingly difficult, if not dangerous, to move extended distances. . . . By 1700 long-distance movement was progressively confined to a rump of three or four groups of itinerant poor"—Scots or Irish, gypsies, and petty chapmen and traveling entertainers. See also, John Wareing, "Migration to London and Transatlantic Emigration of Indentured Servants, 1683–1775," *Journal of Historical Geography*, 7 (1981), 375–377; Peter Clark, in his edited volume, *The Transformation of English Provincial Towns, 1600–1800* (London, 1984), pp. 17–18. For incisive comments on the validity of distinguishing "subsistence" from "betterment" migration, see John Patten, *Rural-Urban Migration in Pre-industrial England* (Oxford Univ., School of Geography, *Research Papers*, No. 6, 1973), 10–11, 23–25.

these long-distance migrants a distinctive proletarian subgroup. In terms of occupation and age they were typical of the emigration from London— except that as a group they were probably poorer than most. Unattached young men—artisans and farmworkers, for the most part—hundreds of miles from home, they had moved from their places of origin some months or even years before they registered their departures from Britain, but had failed to reestablish themselves as planned. Then, drained of the resources that had sustained them in their travels, they had moved on to the capital, and there, failing once again to find the security they sought, they took the final plunge and committed themselves to a period of bonded servitude in the colonies. Their deviance, in this population emigrating through London, lay in their exaggeration of standard trends. They were extreme cases, dilations of the norm, for whom emigration was the final resolution of difficulties long endured, an unplanned occasion that promised relief from immediate exigencies and at least vague prospects of future advantage.

But to suggest this is to touch on the ultimate, most elusive, issue of all: the question of motivation.

Purpose and Motivation

WHY WERE THESE THOUSANDS OF PEOPLE EMIGRATING? WHAT HAD DRIVEN THEM OUT? WHAT ATTRACTED THEM TO AMERICA? WHAT BEARING DID THE EMIGRANTS' SOCIAL CHARACTERISTICS HAVE ON THEIR MOTIVATIONS AND GOALS?

The complete answers to these questions will never be known, but we have indications of what at least some of the answers probably were in the recorded responses that emigrants gave to the query set by the Treasury, "for what purposes they leave the country." This body of data, though important and revealing, is incomplete and difficult to interpret. To begin with, there were at least two levels of perception and transmission involved that undoubtedly created distortions: the emigrants' understanding of their own motives, diminished no doubt by their ability to express them, and the customs officials' understanding of, and accuracy in recording, what was told them. Often the emigrants spoke in very general terms, at times in formulas which certainly oversimplified their feelings; and the officials further simplified the responses in transcribing them. In addition, the dockside investigators frequently used the "purposes" column in ways that had not been intended.

Thus, when indentured servants were encountered, the officials, faced with the fact that these emigrants had specific occupations that had to be recorded and finding nowhere else to record their status as indentured

TABLE 5.23

REASON FOR LEAVING	RESIDENTS OF ENGLAND									
	Home Counties	London	East Anglia	South-east England	West Country	Bristol	Welsh Border	East-Central England	Mid-lands	Northern England
Positive										
To settle	13	241	15	1	8	2	8	2	18	24
To better self	4	12	0	0	3	0	0	0	5	55
To follow occupation	13	100	4	1	5	13	9	4	13	22
Total	30	353	19	2	16	15	17	6	36	101
Negative										
Unemployment	0	5	0	1	0	2	5	0	3	1
Poverty	0	0	0	0	0	0	0	0	0	0
High rents	0	0	0	0	0	0	0	0	0	0
Bad economic conditions	0	0	0	0	0	0	0	0	0	0
Total	0	5	0	1	0	2	5	0	3	1
Combined Total	30	358	19	3	16	17	22	6	39	102

servants, wrote "indentured servants" in the purposes column, often against a large brace enclosing a whole page of names. The implication was that this legal designation in itself was an explanation of the emigrants' purposes in leaving, which in a very loose way perhaps it was. This practice makes possible the identification of the status of the great majority of indentured servants, and of their occupations as well; but at the same time it precludes our ever knowing how this large group would have described their purposes in emigrating. These omissions obviously bias any broad interpretation of the emigrants' purposes.

And there are other limitations in the entries in the purposes column. For a few ships the customs officials failed to record individual statements and simply assigned a single purpose to all the emigrants aboard. In over 800 cases the "purpose" space was simply left blank. Further, 251 responses were ancillary to the question of motivation (e.g., to join spouse), or indeterminate (e.g., do not choose to stay at home); 13 people were recorded as refusing to explain their motives; 298 "emigrants" were in fact convicts being shipped involuntarily; and over 1,900 emigrants were dependents or people who otherwise did not have determining roles in the decisions to emigrate but accompanied those who did. In all, only approximately one-quarter of all the entries of purposes prove useful in analyzing this portion of the Register, but this quarter of the whole includes 2,532 people from England and Scotland, and this group spoke for, and determined the fate of 1,924 other emigrants, their dependents, hence the total number of Brit-

			RESIDENTS OF SCOTLAND									
York-shire	Region unknown	Total England	Borders	West Low-lands	East Low-lands	Perth-shire	Highlands & Hebrides	North-east Scotland	Far north	Region unknown	Total Scotland	Combined total
70	1	403	3	5	7	1	4	2	1	35	58	461
173	0	252	42	11	55	15	134	36	45	45	383	635
49	0	233	5	38	23	7	3	7	2	24	109	342
292	1	888	50	54	85	23	141	45	48	104	550	1438
0	0	17	95	71	50	38	20	2	3	1	280	297
0	0	0	19	141	0	15	114	2	14	2	307	307
63	0	63	4	52	45	57	196	7	30	2	393	456
22	0	22	2	0	0	0	0	0	10	0	12	34
85	0	102	120	264	95	110	330	11	57	5	992	1094
377	1	990	170	318	180	133	471	56	105	109	1542	2532

ons involved in these valid responses is 4,456 individuals, or about half of all the emigrants.

There are, then, significant omissions, which undoubtedly create biases in the conclusions that are reached. And there are other, subtler problems as well. To discern patterns among these responses one must arrange the information in categories. But groupings of such information will inevitably be arbitrary to some extent, for the lines of demarcation between one group of stated motives or purposes and another are inevitably blurred. No matter how the boundaries are defined, some responses will span several categories. As a result of these problems, a great many individual decisions must be made in the process of analyzing the responses, and the overall pattern one discerns—the trend and meaning one extracts from these thousands of recorded remarks—is to some extent shaped by this complex classification process itself. Finally, beyond all of this, one knows from the start that what are involved are the most elusive aspects of life—hopes, fears, and the kinds of ultimate aspirations that one does not always understand oneself or admit to oneself.

So one scans these traces left behind by thousands of emigrants giving offhand explanations of their purposes—scans them with the utmost care and caution, responding as sensitively as possible to every shading of phrase, and attempting to group like with like and to distinguish the unique from the typical. The unique—the responses that cannot, even with the greatest care, be grouped in any meaningful category—include some of the most intrigu-

TABLE 5.24

| OCCUPATION | POSITIVE REASON FOR LEAVING | | | | | | | |
| | TO SETTLE | | TO BETTER SELF | | TO FOLLOW OCCUPATION | | TOTAL | |
	England	Scotland	England	Scotland	England	Scotland	England	Scotland
GENTLE OCCUPATION OR STATUS	68	6	7	0	22	5	97	11
Public official	1	0	0	0	0	0	1	0
Gentleman or gentlewoman	59	4	6	0	18	5	83	9
Professional	8	2	1	0	4	0	13	2
MERCHANDISING	49	11	3	2	67	35	119	48
Wholesale trade or factorage	23	7	0	1	37	20	60	28
Shopkeeping	26	4	3	1	30	15	59	20
AGRICULTURE	105	11	88	49	19	6	212	66
Independent or semi-independent	102	11	86	42	16	5	204	58
Dependent	3	0	2	7	3	1	8	8
TRADES OR CRAFTS (ARTISANRY)	98	17	92	69	84	57	274	143
Highly skilled	16	6	17	16	20	8	53	30
Ordinary skill level	82	11	75	53	64	49	221	113
LABOR	30	1	39	237	16	4	85	242
TOTAL KNOWN OCCUPATIONS	350	46	229	357	208	107	787	510
UNKNOWN OCCUPATIONS	53	12	23	26	25	2	101	40
COMBINED TOTAL	403	58	252	383	233	109	888	550

ing responses, simply in terms of the human drama involved. One finds here and there among such responses brief anecdotal vignettes that suddenly illuminate individual scenes of eighteenth-century life otherwise lost in the dark background. One emigrant, the customs recorders stated, was "shamed to appear" before them for the understandable reason that he was eloping "with a young widow, to avoid a wicked wife"—though how they managed to extract this information from him if he never appeared before them is not explained. One boy confessed he was running away; his master, he explained, was a brute. Five people expected to improve their health. A schoolmaster said he was driven by "fervent zeal to propagate Christian knowledge." A dozen or so said they were simply curious; people all around them were leaving for America: why should they be left behind? They would see what they could see in the colonies and then decide whether they would stay. Three of the Scottish women shipping out to the mainland colonies knew exactly what they were after: "to get a husband."

NEGATIVE REASON FOR LEAVING											
UNEMPLOYMENT		POVERTY		HIGH RENTS		BAD ECONOMIC CONDITIONS		TOTAL		COMBINED TOTAL	
England	Scotland	England	Scotland	England	Scotland	England	Scotland	England	Scotland	England	Scotland
1	0	0	1	0	3	0	0	1	4	98	15
0	0	0	1	0	0	0	0	0	1	1	1
1	0	0	0	0	2	0	0	1	2	84	11
0	0	0	0	0	1	0	0	0	1	13	3
2	9	0	3	1	13	1	0	4	25	123	73
0	6	0	1	0	2	1	0	1	9	61	37
2	3	0	2	1	11	0	0	3	16	62	36
1	28	0	16	52	215	13	11	66	270	278	336
1	25	0	15	52	215	12	11	65	266	269	324
0	3	0	1	0	0	1	0	1	4	9	12
11	127	0	145	7	50	6	0	24	322	298	465
2	11	0	5	0	1	0	0	2	17	55	47
9	116	0	140	7	49	6	0	22	305	243	418
1	81	0	125	3	10	0	1	4	217	89	459
16	245	0	290	63	291	20	12	99	838	886	1348
1	35	0	17	0	102	2	0	3	154	104	194
17	280	0	307	63	393	22	12	102	992	990	1542

The overwhelming number of emigrants whose purposes were recorded, however, made clear that economic circumstances lay behind their
emigration—but economic circumstances of various kinds, at various levels
of poverty and relative affluence. These circumstances, and the emigrants'
responses to them, fall into several large categories, which are subdivided
by region in Table 5.23 and by occupation in Table 5.24.

Of these large groupings of explanations offered by the emigrants—
groupings, it must be repeated, that admittedly overlap and whose boundaries are admittedly indistinct—four are mainly negative: variations on the
theme of flight, impelled by conditions of economic pressure. The first of
these is unambiguous. It includes those who stated that unemployment had
driven them out, either outright unemployment or gross underemployment. A second category merges with this first grouping. It consists of
those who described their purpose in emigrating as the want of "bread"—
they were leaving to "get bread" or "for poverty and to get bread" or

because they "could not earn bread sufficient to support [their] family"—
phrases commonly used to mean the search, not narrowly for food but more
broadly for security and a substantial level of subsistence, and that expressed
the fear of encroaching poverty.[25] A third group of negative statements
includes those who stated in one way or another that their goal was escape
from—as it was most commonly put—"the tyranny of landlords." The
phrasing is flexible, and takes many forms: the tyranny of landlords, racking
rents, high rents and oppression, distress by landlord, or oppression of
landlord. All versions of this theme accuse the landlords or land managers
of driving up rents, hence farmers' costs, beyond endurance and threatening tenants with severe impoverishment if relief were not obtained. Some
entries of this sort are specific in their accusations. One group was emigrating "on account of their rents being raised by William Weddell, Esq., their
landlord," another because of the rack renting of "Mr. Chapman." A Yorkshireman said he was faced with poverty because "all the small farms [were]
taken into large ones in his parish." Still another explained that he had been
"turned off his farm, it being taken into a large one." But most such
statements were more general: "their rents being raised so high they cannot
live"; "high rents and oppression"; "farm being over rented, could not
support themselves"; "obliged to quit his farm, being too high rented."

The fourth negative category is a miscellany of complaints about miserable economic conditions: crop disasters, extreme dearness of provisions,
collapse of the cattle markets, and destruction of cattle by disease.

The positive statements—of people who said nothing about fleeing
impoverishment or high rents or about any other expulsive force, but who
stated, rather, that they were emigrating to improve their condition or to
develop quite specific opportunities—fall into fewer categories. Two en-
close most such statements; each includes a wide range of expressions
surrounding a broad central theme. The first theme centers on plans to
develop property in America or to establish oneself as a property owner.
It includes statements of intentions "to settle as an estate owner," or "to take
up property in America" (property to which, presumably, one had some
claim or of which one had at least some prior knowledge), or "to be a
planter" there, or "to settle as a planter," or "to plant" in America, or,

[25]Thus, typical of a series of petitions submitted to the Commissioners of the Forfeited Estates in
Scotland, the representation of 176 tenants on the annexed estate of Lovat, Jan. 27, 1773, listed a series
of problems—high rents and interest rates, enclosures, insecurity of tenure—which, they said, had
brought them "to this fatal issue, that unless we are relieved, we are apprehensive we must follow
the same steps which our unhappy neighbours have pointed out to us, of quitting our farms,
transporting ourselves and family's to new & distant lands to find that bread which our native
country denies us." Forfeited Estates Papers, E 769/91/315, Scottish Record Office, Edinburgh.
Similarly, R. Campbell's *The London Tradesman* ([1747], New York, 1969), p. 261: "Spinning the
hard silk and winding it employs a great number of female hands, who may make good bread of
it, if they refrain from the common vice of drinking and sotting away their time and senses."

minimally, "to farm," which is different from laboring on someone else's farm.[26] These phrases obviously convey different degrees of confidence, affluence, optimism, and concrete planning, but they have in common the expectation of substantial settlement on the land. These respondents were not people who were fleeing in desperation and taking blind chances on a vaguely promising future. Many apparently had claims of some sort to actual pieces of property; others intended, in the ancient term, to "plant" themselves, that is, to establish a stake in the land; still others viewed themselves as making "a settlement." These phrases are not the language of destitute wage earners or of displaced farm laborers; they convey the expectation of autonomous agricultural enterprise.

The other comprehensive positive grouping includes statements of people who, the customs officials reported, mentioning nothing about fleeing impoverishment or about high rents or about other expulsive forces, stated that their aim was to better themselves. They believed they "would do better in America"; they were "in hopes of a better support"; they expected "to improve in business"; they felt able to "push [their] fortune." They were choosing the option of a more promising future, and choosing often on the basis of recent information they considered reliable. In addition to these two major categories of positive statements, a third group stressed the desire to pursue one's occupation, to follow one's business, to seek a more positive work situation—not to escape and not to change one's way of life but to fulfill one's occupational possibilities under improved conditions.

These seven groupings include the great majority of the emigrants' responses to the question "for what purposes they leave the country?" The boundaries are not precise: close decisions are involved in classifying many of these statements—though perhaps fewer than one might expect. Positive notes are here and there intermingled with those of frustration. Complaints about high rents are sometimes coupled with "hopes of bettering their fortune." And it is now and then clear that some of these tenants had been considering the advantages of America before the rent increases had occurred, hence the immediate disaster they cited was merely a precipitant of plans for betterment that had long been under way. William MacKay, thirty-seven, a farmer on the Bighouse estate in Caithness, northern Scotland, said that he had long had assurances "from a brother and sister already in Carolina, that a sober industrious man could not fail of living comfortably, lands could be rented cheap, and grounds not cleared purchased for 6d an acre; that the soil was fertile, and if a man could bring a small sum of money with him he might make rich very fast." But what finally drove him out was the sudden collapse of the cattle market and the severe rise in

[26]On the distinction between farmers and farm workers, and on the affluence of some farmers and others who came "to plant" in America or "make a settlement," see above, note 10.

rents.[27] Similarly, Nathaniel Smith, a fifty-two-year-old Yorkshire farmer who emigrated with his wife and six children because of the rent hikes of "his landlord Mr Chapman," had in fact "made a purchase of some land in North America" before he left Britain. And occasionally the poverty complained of proves to be cushioned. A group of farmers and fishermen emigrating from the Shetlands explained that they were leaving because rents had been raised so high "that they could not live without sinking the little matter they had left." They were not destitute; their "little matter" was still intact, and they intended to carry it with them.

Their *little matter*: the two words illuminate the social landscape like a flare. Even some of the very poorest of those who seemed to be driven from the land were able to "make shift," it was reported, for their passage. It is the generality of these carefully preserved "little matters," even on the part of people fleeing the land, that accounts for the belief that an estimated £10,000 in specie had left western Scotland with the emigrants from 1768 to 1772, and that £6,000 "in ready cash" was carried out of the Highlands by the emigrants leaving on a single day.[28]

But though these categories are here and there vague at the boundaries, they represent real distinctions at least in emphasis. The thousands of notations of individual purposes and motivations that survive in the customs records, grouped in these categories and analyzed by region and occupation, reveal aspects of the emigration that are not otherwise perceptible.

They reveal, first (Table 5.23), that 888 English respondents—nine-tenths of all the English emigrants whose purposes were recorded, representing with their dependents a total of 1,211 individuals—were migrating for largely positive reasons. They were being lured, not driven overseas, by their own ambitions, plans, and expectations. The largest number came, as one would expect, from London and Yorkshire, and the number of Londoners who emigrated with the expectation of settling on the land is surprisingly large. Only very few—a tenth—of the English people whose purposes are recorded indicated that they were driven out, that they were fleeing desperate situations; and almost all of those who did say that were Yorkshiremen faced with increases in rent.

These English emigrants who looked forward to positive prospects in America and were leaving with hopeful expectations included a disproportionate number of those in upper-occupational or upper-status categories

[27]MacKay's testimony is among the extensive interviews of the survivors of the wrecked *Bachelor*, discussed at length below, pp. 508, 512–519. The interviews (T47/12/29–39) have been published: see below, p. 508 n.8.
[28]For Nathaniel Smith see T47/9/84; for the Shetlands farmers, "Port Kirkcaldy, An Account of Emigration," June 5–11, 1775, T47/12/100; for the £10,000, *Scots Magazine*, 34 (Sept., 1772), 515–516; for the £6,000, *Lloyd's Evening Post*, Sept. 22–24, 1773.

(Table 5.24). Forty-six percent of those whose occupations are known were gentlemen, merchants, and independent farmers—which is more than double the proportion of those groups in the English emigration as a whole. But positive anticipations and enterprising plans were not confined to those from these upper socio-occupational levels. Over a third of those whose purposes were positive and whose occupations are known were artisans (as opposed to over half in the emigration generally) and approximately 10% were laborers.

Thus the purposes stated by the English emigrants are to a significant degree positive. These appear to be people who are largely being drawn, not propelled; who have plans to develop, not catastrophes to escape. But they are not, of course, the whole of the English emigration. With their dependents they represent approximately one-quarter of the 5,196 emigrants from England; almost all of the rest were indentured servants. How the 3,553 indentured servants from England (Table 5.15) would have expressed their purposes can only be guessed, but it is reasonable to assume that most of them, if their phrases had been recorded, would have spoken of chronic unemployment or poverty. For the indentured servants—who concentrate in just the lower socio-economic levels at which the expulsive forces were strongest (they include almost nine-tenths of the laborers and artisans)—are likely to have been impoverished. Though some undoubtedly accepted indentured servitude as a strategy by which to retain a modicum of resources, most had probably experienced unemployment and pressing or threatening poverty.

Yet few of the indentured servants bore responsibility for anyone besides themselves, and even if every one of them had been driven out by poverty and was attempting to escape from misery, the incidence of confidence, optimism, and hopeful risk taking among the English emigration as a whole is surprisingly high—surprisingly, since people who have a margin of stability and confidence in their futures do not commonly uproot themselves in large numbers and emigrate to a new land. Of the 990 English emigrants who explained their purposes in leaving only 17 said they were driven out by lack of employment, and none indicated that they were impoverished.

There is thus evidence of a large proportion of English emigrants who were leaving hopefully, expectantly, seeking betterment; but because of the high incidence of indentured servants among the English, the balance of motivations must remain to some extent conjectural. The situation among the Scots is more certain because of the low incidence of indenture and the high incidence of recorded and usable statements.

As Table 5.15 made clear, only 18.4% of the 3,872 Scottish emigrants were indentured, and we know that the Scottish emigrants included an unusually large number of families and hence of dependents. As a result, the 1,542 recorded statements prove to represent the purposes of 75% of all the Scottish emigrants.

A glance at the totals columns for Scotland of Table 5.23 reveals that there were almost twice as many negative as positive statements. The negative statements are highly concentrated in a few regions, chiefly the Highlands-Hebrides and the West Lowlands, though with sizable numbers in three other regions: the Borders, Perthshire, and the East Lowlands. A third of all those who were fleeing Scotland because of severe economic difficulties (all four negative columns) came from the Highlands-Hebrides, most of them reacting to the problems of sharp rent increases, or land clearances, or "tyrannical" landlordism in general; three-fifths of all those attempting to escape hardship came from the Highlands-Hebrides and the West Lowlands combined. The proportion of negative statements from those leaving the West Lowlands is particularly striking. For the Highlands responses are mixed: while 330 respondents from that region gave negative responses, 141 gave optimistic, positive answers to the officials' query, a more than two-to-one balance between negative and positive that was similar to that of the Scottish emigrants generally. There was no such balance among the West Lowlands emigrants. The voyagers from that region, leaving such highly disturbed textile districts as Paisley—sunk in a depression, it was said, that reduced thousands "to the utmost distress for want of employ" and forced hundreds to emigrate "to prevent them from starving"—included almost five times as many negative as positive responses.[29]

The Scots' explanations of their negative responses are distributed fairly evenly among the problems of land rentals, poverty generally, and unemployment, but there are regional emphases. The problem of land rents was far more highly concentrated in the Highlands than elsewhere, and the combination of poverty and unemployment was disproportionately high in the West Lowlands. A further refraction of the same underlying reality is found in the occupational distribution of the emigrants' statements in Table 5.24. The largest single incidence of negative statements is found among two groups: first, artisans, overwhelmingly those of ordinary skills, chiefly workers in the textile industry,[30] and second, farmers, with some degree of independence in the land. About a third (266 out of 838) of the Scottish emigrants of known occupation who gave negative statements of purpose were people who had been farmers, not farm laborers, hence at least semi-independent in relation to the land. The only other significant category is that of laborers.

Most, though not all, of this follows one's expectations; the numbers

[29] *Caledonian Mercury*, March 23, 1774.
[30] Of the Scottish textile workers whose purposes were recorded, 44 gave positive reasons, 158 negative.

both regionally and occupationally for the most part conform to what one otherwise knows of the conditions that prevailed. It is the more striking, therefore, that almost two out of every five Scots voyaging overseas who stated their intentions and motivations indicated that they were *not* fleeing the country, were *not* attempting to escape intolerable conditions. They appear to have been ambitiously enterprising people, attempting to exploit opportunities they knew about and which they thought they could plan for; they were looking forward to a more expansive future. These enterprising emigrants came from all regions, for the most part in the same proportion that each region represents in the Scottish migration generally. Only the depressed West Lowlands shows a sizable discrepancy.[31]

With this information in mind one can attempt to characterize generally the motives of the British emigrants of these years—those, at least, whose explanations were recorded. Seen through the imperfect medium of the responses to the customs officials' query "for what purposes they leave this country," these motivations appear far from uniform. They vary greatly according to the regions of the emigrants' origins, their occupations, and their economic positions. But overall they convey a sense, not of the utter desperation that would later drive 3 to 4 million Irish peasants to North America as an alternative to death by starvation, but a sense, rather, of threatening but not annihilating difficulties, of dislocations that both demanded and allowed redeeming decisions, and of more or less reasoned choices. No doubt the 4,264 indentured servants and redemptioners from England and Scotland, whose purposes were not recorded, were different —though how desperate even they were, how close to the destitution level, we will never know; many undoubtedly calculated that the preservation of a small fund for ultimate settlement in America might well be worth the

[31]This view coincides almost exactly with that of R. D. Lobban, in his study, "The Migration of Highlanders into Lowland Scotland (c. 1750–1890) with Particular Reference to Greenock" (Ph.D. diss., Univ. of Edinburgh, 1969). Using different sources from those used here and concentrating particularly on the Highlanders' migration to the Lowlands, Lobban concludes (pp. 343–345) that the forces behind the exodus of the Highlanders in the eighteenth century were complex; partly expulsive, but partly attractive too. "The traditional archetype has been the pathetic figure of the migrant looking back sadly from the emigrant ship towards the distant Highland hills, but to do full justice to the movement, this figure should perhaps be accompanied by another of a keen, eager Highlander hurrying towards the bright lights of Glasgow and Greenock, his eyes fixed unblinkingly on some bright rosy dream of the future. . . . They were not at all a pathetic host of poor, underprivileged characters driven forth by the winds of change and modern improvements, but men who as individuals could take advantage of these changes, could help to shape and forge them, could find a profitable and comfortable niche in new environments, and could help to mold the future of their reception areas. . . . The Lowlands and the overseas countries thus provided a solution to the problems of landlords and people, and a means of satisfying the aspirations of countless numbers of individual Highlanders, but for Highland society it was a disastrous if not fatal remedy."

price of four years of bondage, and that, as John Campbell wrote, indentured service could be a useful introduction to American society and a protected entry into its economy.

Yet even if the mass of indentured servants had been altogether despairing, they formed less than half of the total emigration. The 2,532 people who were *not* indentured servants and whose purposes in emigrating *were* recorded, constituted, together with their 1,926 dependents, a larger group, and these were people of hope, not despair; they were enterprising, not defeated. Considerably less than half (1,094) of the recorded responses of these free voyagers are negative in that they refer to a background of unemployment or poverty or crippling difficulties in maintaining security on tenanted estates; but many even of these statements allude confidently to joining relatives already well settled in America or to following up promising reports. The rest of the responses were unambiguously positive. The respondents were seeking to better themselves, or planning to "plant" themselves on American soil, or hoping to establish a "settlement" for their families there, or expecting to join relatives there with whom they had been in communication, or assuming that they would be able to engage abroad in crafts or trades for which they had been trained. Emigrants from Bristol, it was said in 1774, "carry their arts and manufactures with them." Some even of those who found "it next to impossible," the *Leeds Mercury* reported, "in the lamentable state of trade and dearness of provisions, to provide in any sort for themselves & their families . . . are persons of considerable property."[32] Almost all, searching rationally for personal betterment or greater security, were, or hoped to be, family-scale entrepreneurs.[33] Though in the aggregate, viewed from afar, they seem to form part of a movement to the west as instinctive as the seasonal flights of birds, examined individually in the lists of the Register they can be seen to be autonomous, calculating, hopefully aspiring people well suited to life in the loosely organized society of the colonies and prepared to struggle for security, if not for comfort, by exploiting some small corner of the vast American world. Little wonder that a perceptive Scotsman resident in America, when asked to comment on emigration to the colonies, began with a forth-

[32] *South-Carolina Gazette,* June 3, 1774; *Leeds Mercury,* May 17, 1774.
[33] The reasonable choice seemed obvious to one group of Highlands emigrants in 1773, according to a writer in Inverness. They calculated that, "1. The price of land is so low in some of the British colonies that forty or fifty pounds will purchase as much ground there as one thousand in this country. 2. There are few or no taxes at present in the colonies, most of their public debt being paid off since the last peace. 3. The climate in general is very healthy, and provisions of all kinds are extraordinary good and so cheap that a shilling will go as far in America as four shillings in Scotland. 4. The price of labour . . . is high in the colonies: a day labourer can gain there thrice the wages he can in this country. [5]. There are no beggars in North-America, the poor, when they appear, are amply provided for. Lastly, there are no titled, proud lords to tyrannize over the lower sort of people, men there being upon a level and more valued, in proportion to their abilities, than they are in Scotland." *South-Carolina Gazette,* April 11, 1774.

right definition: "I imagine," he wrote, that "by emigrants you mean people possessed of some property at home, but rather discontented with their situation who would work to convert what little they have into some of the fruitful acres of the West." And little wonder too that Dean Tucker, arguing that Britain would be better off without the colonies, claimed that

> the emigrants who lately sailed in such multitudes from the north of Scotland and more especially from the north of Ireland were far from being the most indigent or the least capable of subsisting in their own country. No, it was not poverty or necessity which compelled, but ambition which enticed them to forsake their native soil. For after they began to taste the sweets of industry and to partake of the comforts of life, then they became a valuable prey for these harpies [emigration agents]. In short, such were the persons to whom these seducers principally applied, because they found that they had got some little substance together worth devouring.[34]

Such are the details of the emigrants' identities as far as they can be derived from the data of the Register—details concerning the ages, sex, family, and other groupings, occupations, and statuses—and such, less fully and less clearly, are their professed motivations in emigrating. These group characteristics were powerful determinants of the emigrants' responses to the new environment they would encounter in America, of their success and failure in settling into an alien world which no amount of anticipation could have prepared them for. But there is more in this body of information than a mass of discrete details arranged in response to six sets of questions. Wound in among all the detailed local and regional information is the outline of an inner structure within this movement of people that is a key to their settlement overseas.

For it has become clear repeatedly that this was no unified or singular migration. It appears from the answers to the six sets of questions above that, far from being a singular phenomenon, the British exodus was a dual migration. There are two patterns, not one. The emigrants who traveled outward to America from the metropolitan center of Britain in the Thames Valley were different in essential respects from those drawn from the northern British provinces. The differences form a spectrum stretching from the urban concentration of London out to the remote northern provinces, and they are so great at the extremities—London on the one hand, Yorkshire and the Scottish Highlands on the other—that at those two poles

---

[34]Campbell to Sinclair, July 26, 1772, Freswick Muniments (note 13, above); *Universal Magazine of Knowledge and Pleasure*, 54 (Feb. 1774), 87.

they form two quite different kinds of emigration, which may now be designated "metropolitan" on the one hand and "provincial" on the other. And these differences profoundly shaped the way these emigrants would enter into American life and the impact they would have in the new land.

The metropolitan pattern, which characterizes the central migration from the Thames Valley, is typified by a young man, in his early twenties, who appears to be acting individually and who decides as an individual to migrate to America. He is not drawn from London's desperate, totally unskilled laborers sunk in absolute destitution; nor is he drawn from the more affluent segments of the population. He is, rather, an impecunious young artisan or craftsman who has probably served an apprenticeship or otherwise learned something of a trade, found employment irregular or nonexistent, and, without prospects, still unmarried and without other family encumbrances, is heading out to the colonies alone. In doing so, whether to preserve "a small matter" of savings for later settlement in the new land or out of sheer necessity, he assumes a burden of debt for his transportation, to be paid off by four or more years of bonded labor. There are few children of either sex in this migration, and few women. When women appear in these groups, they conform to the male pattern with respect to age and legal status. And not only are there few families in this migration but those that can be found are of the simplest possible structure —almost all of them simply husband and wife, or siblings traveling together.

In economic terms the typical metropolitan migrant, though unbound by family ties or responsibilities, was not autonomous. He was committed to years of bonded servitude and therefore highly responsive to the needs of the labor market—indeed, he had no choice but to be absolutely responsive to the market in the particular corner of the colonial economy to which he was directed. Vigorous and most often in some minor way skilled in the productive work of the pre-industrial economy, these emigrants were bound to contribute to its productivity yet were prevented for some years from drawing personal gain from it, hence limited in their consumption for that period. And their natural contribution to population growth was also delayed for the period of their servitude, hence significantly diminished.

Such is the "ideal type" of the metropolitan emigrant. But ideal types are of course only abstractions; in reality there were many variations even among the Londoners. The variations increase significantly as one shifts one's view away from the London center of the metropolitan region out into the countryside, particularly as one looks northward into the Midlands, the northern counties of England, and Scotland. At the outer margin the variations have multiplied so greatly and the metropolitan model has attenuated so far that a new pattern altogether has taken shape. In this provincial pattern (Yorkshire, Northern England, and Scotland) the predominant unit is not, as in the metropolitan migration, an isolated male artisan in his early twenties, a bondsman for several years of unlimited servitude. It is not even a person. It is, rather, a family, and a family that contains not only mature women but also small children, including a remarkable number of young girls. The size of these families emigrating from northern England and Scotland is surprising. The average was almost as large as the average English family in the non-emigrating population, and hence it would appear that these family units of the English population were moving essentially intact. Consistent with this fact is the likely economic background of these families. If indenture is a sign of poverty, the provincial migration does not seem to have been totally impoverished. For there were very few indentured servants among these provincial emigrants, even among those who were traveling alone and were in their early twenties. There would appear to have been a sufficient mobilization of small resources among these families and individuals—or sufficient financial sponsorship—to permit freedom of movement without the severe encumbrance of bonded servitude. In one way or another they had raised sufficient funds to retain their freedom, or had somehow been subsidized by others.

The provincial emigration was predominantly the transfer of farming families, whose heads were men of some small substance, or at least to some extent economically autonomous. These were families, therefore, likely to contribute quickly to the growth of the American population. And they would contribute quickly too to the growth of the American economy, not only by their constructive enterprise but by the demand they created, the markets they enlarged, as consumers. Above all, they were eager from the start to take advantage of opportunities created by the opening up of new land in America. They could, and did, seek out new settlements and move quickly into the most attractive areas available in the backcountry. They, and not the great mass of isolated artisans bound to serve any master who could buy their services, seemed destined to be the frontiersmen of this new segment of the American population.

6

Arrivals and Destinations

T HE picture of the emigration has now clarified. Initially this movement of people could only be seen as a large, distant blur without discernible dimensions, arising, apparently, from everywhere in Britain, moving vaguely in all directions, flowing out of Britain perhaps through many ports, perhaps through only one or two. Now it has become finite, measurable, palpable. We know the approximate numbers of these emigrants, their ages, sex, occupations, residential origins, family and other groupings, routes of migration, and something of their purposes and motivations. And within the migration as a whole we have found two distinctive patterns, two separate submigrations significant in fundamental ways. But we know nothing, so far, about where these migrants went. What were the patterns of their arrival in the Western Hemisphere and their distribution among the thirteen colonies, Nova Scotia, Canada, and the Caribbean islands? Which parts of Britain, geographically and socially, were supplying which colonies with which groups of emigrants? How did the distinctive social patterns of the emigration distribute among the colonies? Can anything be surmised of the impact they might have had? Above all, can one find in the arrival information clues to the fortunes of these thousands of individuals in America and the manner in which their destinies flowed into the developing streams of American life?

That is the ultimate view one hopes to glimpse, however fleetingly—the blending of these lives, removed from altogether different worlds into American society, and the coloration, however faint and diffused, that these lives gave to the emerging scene. The complete panorama, stretching far beyond the areas we have so far seen, carries the viewer's eye away from Britain, across the sea and into the American port towns, and beyond these arrival points into the communities and farms of a huge territory extending from the islands at the mouth of the St. Lawrence down fifteen hundred miles of coastal North America to Florida and extending west to the Mississippi and south through the Caribbean islands, from Jamaica to Antigua and from Barbados west to Nicaragua. Viewing the emigration in the perspective of its destinations one finds new dimensions in this process of transplantation and new implications for American history.

Where Did the Emigrants Go?

They did not travel to all the colonies in anything like equal numbers. They concentrated in only a few colonies, in proportions indicated in Table 6.1. The great majority (86.2%) went to the mainland colonies that would soon comprise the United States, but they distributed unevenly among them. They largely ignored New England and the deep south and congregated overwhelmingly (93.6% of those who went to the thirteen colonies) in five contiguous middle-Atlantic and upper-south colonies (New York, Pennsylvania, Maryland, Virginia, and North Carolina)—and not equally in all of them. Three-quarters of those who went to this band of adjacent colonies were in fact destined for only three colonies: Maryland, Pennsylvania, and New York. Maryland was the single most powerful magnet for the emigrants. A quarter of the entire emigration went to this one colony; a fifth went to New York. To view the concentrations somewhat differently: three-fifths (60.8%) of all the emigrants listed in the Register went to only three colonies—Maryland, New York, and Pennsylvania; four-fifths (80.7%) went to that area plus the upper south (Virginia and North Carolina).

Such is the general distribution pattern, illustrated in Map 6.A. But this is only a crude first approximation to the complex reality of the emigrants' distribution in America. For when one separates out the English from the Scottish emigrants and analyzes them apart from each other, two very different destination patterns emerge. The subtotals by destination for England and Scotland in Table 6.1 show vividly that the emigrants from the two areas concentrated in altogether different *sets* of destinations. The *English*, but not the Scots, chiefly populated what might be called a central core of colonies, Pennsylvania, Maryland, and Virginia, and overwhelmingly Maryland alone: over two-fifths of all the *English* emigrants (2,146 of 5,196) were in passage to that one colony. Of all the immigrants to Maryland recorded in the Register, 92.2% were English. The *Scots*, on the other hand, ignored Maryland and Virginia almost completely and Pennsylvania largely; 70.8% of their entire number went to two colonies, New York and North Carolina, north and south of the main English destinations.

These are remarkably distinctive—almost mutually exclusive—pat-

TABLE 6.1

DESTINATION	ENGLAND				SCOTLAND			
	Male	Female	Total[1]	% of English emigrants	Male	Female	Total[1]	% of Scottish emigrants
New England	31	13	45	.9	22	10	32	.8
New York	154	67	277	5.3	869	615	1664	43.0
Pennsylvania	689	111	819	15.8	269	210	518	13.4
Maryland	1890	240	2146	41.3	34	3	37	1.0
Virginia	645	62	707	13.6	40	0	40	1.0
North Carolina	8	1	9	.2	441	364	1076	27.8
South Carolina[2]	51	21	75	1.4	20	2	22	.6
Georgia	74	37	131	2.5	126	72	198	5.1
Florida	1	1	2	0	2	0	2	0
Total	3543	553	4211	81.0	1823	1276	3589	92.7
Canada	7	9	19	.4	10	3	16	.4
Nova Scotia	340	187	608	11.7	84	56	148	3.8
West Indies	280	56	354	6.8	89	9	119	3.1
Destination unspecified	4	0	4	.1	0	0	0	–
Combined Total	4174	805	5196	100.0	2006	1344	3872	100.0

[1]Includes those of sex unknown.
[2]Includes "Carolina."

terns. Few English (a mere 5.5% of their total) went either to New York or North Carolina; not many Scots (15.4% of their total) went to the three colonies of heaviest English immigration, and those who did went almost entirely to Pennsylvania. Differences also appear to persist outside the boundaries of the future United States. A sizable number of English emigrants, but many fewer Scots (981 vs. 283), were voyaging to Canada (mainly Nova Scotia) and the West Indies.

The Multiple Immigration

The English and Scottish migrations, then, moved for the most part toward separate destinations. This fact is important if only because it suggests somewhat different cultural influences within particular areas of the American population. But its importance goes beyond that. For the two streams

| | OTHER | | | | TOTAL | | |
Male	Female	Total[1]	% of other emigrants	Male	Female	Total[1]	% of all emigrants
0	0	0	–	53	23	77	.8
10	3	13	4.4	1033	685	1954	20.9
34	32	77	26.0	992	353	1414	15.1
119	25	145	49.0	2043	268	2328	24.9
27	0	27	9.1	712	62	774	8.3
0	0	0	–	449	365	1085	11.6
5	1	6	2.0	76	24	103	1.1
0	0	0	–	200	109	329	3.5
0	0	0	–	3	1	4	0
195	61	268	90.5	5561	1890	8068	86.2
3	1	4	1.4	20	13	39	.4
2	0	2	.7	426	243	758	8.1
19	3	22	7.4	388	68	495	5.3
0	0	0	–	4	0	4	0
219	65	296	100.0	6399	2214	9364	100.0

of people, drawn from different regions of Britain and diverging so clearly in their destinations, differed in those social characteristics that distinguish the metropolitan from the northern, provincial emigrations—a distinction that has already been seen to be a dominant social fact of the exodus from Britain.

A full analysis of the destination patterns as they relate to the social duality of the emigration requires a breakdown of figures into the eighteen British regions of origin. But even the crude division of Table 6.1 into English and Scottish subtotals reflects the familiar social clusters of the two kinds of migrations. The groups, as they channeled off into different colonies, retained their original profiles—indeed, the distinctive elements became even more pronounced as the groups distributed in America than they had been as they had assembled in Britain. Thus Table 6.1 shows the numbers of males and females by destination. Among the English, the overall high male preponderance (5.2 to 1) is even higher in the three colonies in which the English particularly congregated; it is 6.2 in Pennsylvania, 7.9 in Maryland, 10.4 in Virginia. Among the Scots, the very low male preponderance, approaching equality of the sexes (1.5 to 1 overall), is even lower among those moving to the two colonies favored by the Scots, New York and North Carolina (1.4 and 1.2). The higher the concentration of English, it seems, the greater the numerical preponderance of males; the higher the concentration of Scots, the lower the preponderance of males and the more even the numerical balance between the sexes.

What of families? Table 6.2 shows that the pre-migration patterns are even bolder in their outline when viewed in terms of destinations. The immigrations to New York, North Carolina, and Nova Scotia include the largest number of families of any of the streams of voyagers. Over a third of the 592 families identified in the migration went to New York; one-half went to either New York or North Carolina. Maryland, Pennsylvania, and Virginia together attracted a total of only 106 families, 17.9% of the total number of families recorded. Predictably, the same emphases result if one examines the number of people within families. While half of all the people who went to New York and well over a third of all those who went to North Carolina traveled as members of families, only 2.8% of those who went to Maryland, 5.6% of those to Virginia, and 16.8% of those to Pennsylvania were members of families.

From this information, it appears that the related characteristics of the *metropolitan* migration, which emerged so clearly from the departure data, are emerging again, in similarly related clusters, among the immigrants to the central area of Maryland, Pennsylvania, and Virginia; and it is equally clear that aspects of the northern *provincial* pattern can be found again among those voyaging to New York and North Carolina. The Caribbean islands seem close to the metropolitan pattern. And Nova Scotia drew a relatively large number of families and a high percentage of people within families (68.1%), but they were attracting far more people from England than from Scotland. Some uniquely "provincial" part of the English emigration, yet to be determined, must have had a special relationship with Nova Scotia.

Assuming now that all of the more detailed elements that compose these departure patterns cohere in the arrival patterns, one can expect to find the various colonies differently affected by the migration. Indentured servitude, for example, a major characteristic of the "metropolitan" migration, was overwhelmingly dominant in the flows to Maryland, Pennsylvania, and Virginia. Table 6.3 shows that more than 4 out of 5 of the emigrants to these three colonies were indentured servants, and in the case of Maryland, the chief magnet of the emigration of these years, the figure rises to no less than 97.2%. In vivid contrast are the figures for the other colonies. Less than 9% of the combined migration to New York and North Carolina were inden-

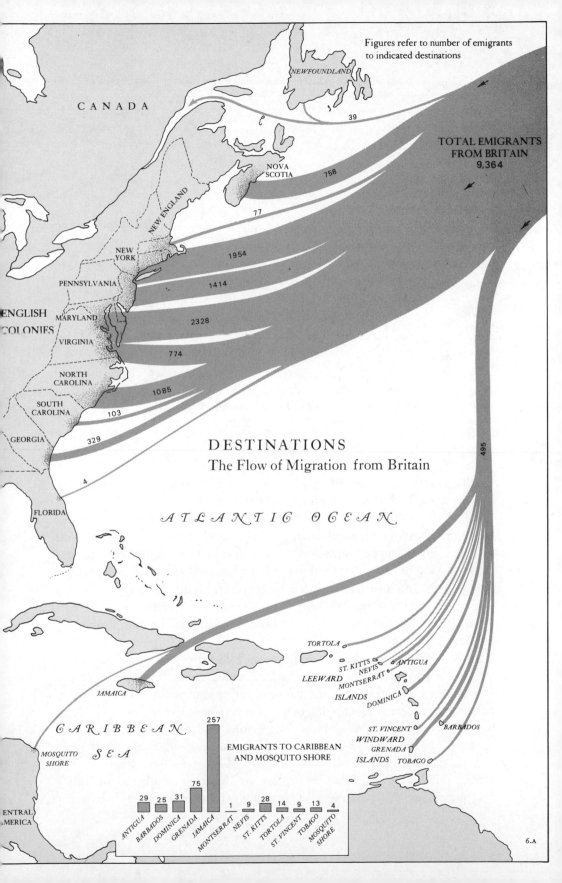

Figures refer to number of emigrants
to indicated destinations

CANADA

NEWFOUNDLAND

39

TOTAL EMIGRANTS
FROM BRITAIN
9,364

NOVA
SCOTIA   758

NEW ENGLAND   77

NEW
YORK   1954

PENNSYLVANIA   1414

ENGLISH
COLONIES   MARYLAND

VIRGINIA   2328

774

NORTH
CAROLINA   1085

SOUTH
CAROLINA   103

GEORGIA   329

4

495

FLORIDA

ATLANTIC OCEAN

DESTINATIONS
The Flow of Migration from Britain

TORTOLA

ST. KITTS
NEVIS   ANTIGUA
LEEWARD   MONTSERRAT
ISLANDS   DOMINICA

JAMAICA

ST. VINCENT   BARBADOS

CARIBBEAN   257   WINDWARD
GRENADA
ISLANDS   TOBAGO

MOSQUITO   SEA   EMIGRANTS TO CARIBBEAN
SHORE   AND MOSQUITO SHORE

75

CENTRAL
AMERICA   29   25   31   1   9   28   14   9   13   4

ANTIGUA BARBADOS DOMINICA GRENADA JAMAICA MONTSERRAT NEVIS ST. KITTS TORTOLA ST. VINCENT TOBAGO MOSQUITO SHORE

6.A

TABLE 6.2

DESTINATION	ENGLAND			SCOT[LAND]	
	Number of families	Number of people in families	Percent of people in families	Number of families	Number of people in families
New England	4	22	48.9	2	10
New York	38	169	61.0	163	809
Pennsylvania	26	79	9.6	39	147
Maryland	25	66	3.1	0	0
Virginia	13	43	6.1	0	0
North Carolina	0	0	–	94	405
South Carolina[2]	6	26	34.7	1	2
Georgia	16	64	48.9	28	110
Canada	3	13	68.4	1	5
Nova Scotia	83	410	67.4	20	106
West Indies	19	53	15.0	5	21
Destination unspecified	1	3	75.0	0	0
Total	234	948	18.2	353	1615

[1]Excludes "other" families of Table 5.8.   [2]Includes "Carolina."

tured servants—less than 1% in the case of North Carolina. And elsewhere too, with the exception of Georgia, whose total numbers were very small, there were few indentees. Not a single indentured servant can be found among those who emigrated either to New England or to Nova Scotia and Canada; only 16 can be found among those destined for South Carolina, and only 8 among the 495 who went to the Caribbean islands. In all, no less than 87.8% of the indentured servants among the emigrants—3,925 out of 4,472 —went to the three central colonies of Maryland, Pennsylvania, and Virginia; fully half (50.6%) of all the indentured servants in the migration went to Maryland alone.

What of the indentees' occupations? These percentages apply quite uniformly across the spectrum of stated occupations. There is no great bunching of indentees in particular occupations according to destination. In colonies where the percentages of indentees among the immigrants are high, they are high for all or most occupations, even the least likely. Where they are low, they are low for most occupations. *Every one* of the 258 artisans in high-skill occupations who emigrated to Maryland was indentured, and among them were 12 goldsmiths or silversmiths, 7 gunsmiths, 4 bookbinders, 20 clockmakers, 3 engravers, 2 glassblowers, 2 mathematical-instrument

LAND	OTHER			TOTAL		
Percent of people in families	Number of families	Number of people in families	Percent of people in families	Number of families	Number of people in families	Percent of people in families
31.3	0	0	–	6	32	41.6
48.6	1	2	15.4	202	980	50.2
28.4	3	11	14.3	68	237	16.8
–	0	0	–	25	66	2.8
–	0	0	–	13	43	5.6
37.6	0	0	–	94	405	37.3
9.1	1	2	33.3	8	30	29.1
55.6	0	0	–	44	174	52.9
31.3	0	0	–	4	18	46.2
71.6	0	0	–	103	516	68.1
17.6	0	0	–	24	74	14.9
0	0	0	–	1	3	75.0
41.7	5	15	5.1	592	2578	27.5

makers, and 3 gilders. Of 303 immigrants to Maryland who were registered as workers in agriculture, both as independent or semi-independent farmers and as farmworkers, all but 1 were indentured; of 1,342 artisans, all but 6 were bonded servants. And so it goes through the entire list of occupations. All but 2 of 433 in the textile industry traveling to Maryland were indentured; all but 1 of 119 in the service trades, and all but 3 of the 532 in the metal, food, construction, and miscellaneous trades.

In sharp contrast are the immigrants in the same occupations who went to New York and North Carolina. Of 267 farmers and farmworkers who went to New York, 257 (96.3%) were *not* indentured; of 424 artisans, only two-fifths were indentured; of 274 textile workers, just over half were indentured; and among the laborers, just under a third. And the pattern is similar in the case of North Carolina; there, *none* of the 42 laborers was indentured and only 8 of 53 artisans. The most extreme case, already referred to, is that of the voyagers to Canada, Nova Scotia, and New England: not one of them—in any occupational category whatever—was indentured.

These clusters of characteristics—balance between the sexes, incidence of families, and indentured servitude—make clear beyond any question that the distinctiveness of the metropolitan and the northern provincial migra-

TABLE 6.3

DESTINATION	GENTLE	MERCHANDISING	AGRICULTURE		
			Independent	Dependent	Total
CENTRAL CORE OF IMMIGRATION: THE "ENGLISH" COLONIES					
Maryland					
All emigrants	3	77	241	62	303
Indentured servants	1	72	240	62	302
Pennsylvania					
All emigrants	20	40	111	21	132
Indentured servants	0	16	69	14	83
Virginia					
All emigrants	4	40	131	25	156
Indentured servants	0	28	113	24	137
Total					
All emigrants	27	157	483	108	591
Indentured servants	1	116	422	100	522
THE "SCOTTISH" COLONIES					
New York					
All emigrants	10	22	261	6	267
Indentured servants	0	2	8	2	10
North Carolina					
All emigrants	4	5	65	1	66
Indentured servants	0	0	0	0	0
Total					
All emigrants	14	27	326	7	333
Indentured servants	0	2	8	2	10
NEW ENGLAND					
All emigrants	6	2	13	0	13
Indentured servants	0	0	0	0	0
DEEP SOUTH (S.C., Ga., Fla.)					
All emigrants	10	19	57	4	61
Indentured servants	0	0	35	4	39
CANADA					
All emigrants	2	2	1	0	1
Indentured servants	0	0	0	0	0
NOVA SCOTIA					
All emigrants	2	7	156	4	160
Indentured servants	0	0	0	0	0
WEST INDIES					
All emigrants	83	114	48	2	50
Indentured servants	0	1	2	0	2
COMBINED TOTAL					
All emigrants	144	328	1084	125	1209
Indentured servants	1	119	467	106	573

[1]Excludes destination unspecified.

| Highly skilled | TRADES OR CRAFTS | | | | LABOR | TOTAL | | COMBINED TOTAL |
	Textile	Service	Other	Total		Known	Unknown	
258	433	119	532	1342	496	2221	107	2328
258	431	118	529	1336	494	2205	57	2262
75	166	33	160	434	533	1159	255	1414
60	120	27	117	324	499	922	49	971
94	138	33	196	461	77	738	36	774
85	134	32	188	439	75	679	13	692
427	737	185	888	2237	1106	4118	398	4516
403	685	177	834	2099	1068	3806	119	3925
29	274	8	113	424	150	873	1081	1954
3	147	3	13	166	48	226	24	250
10	34	2	7	53	42	170	915	1085
3	2	1	2	8	0	8	1	9
39	308	10	120	477	192	1043	1996	3039
6	149	4	15	174	48	234	25	259
1	6	1	10	18	5	44	33	77
0	0	0	0	0	0	0	0	0
31	41	8	40	120	52	262	174	436
18	29	6	29	82	42	163	117	280
1	0	0	11	12	0	17	22	39
0	0	0	0	0	0	0	0	0
14	23	1	49	87	68	324	434	758
0	0	0	0	0	0	0	0	0
21	14	14	47	96	35	378	117	495
0	0	0	5	5	0	8	0	8
534	1129	219	1165	3047	1458	6186	3174	9360
427	863	187	883	2360	1158	4211	261	4472

tions was carried over into the arrivals in America. The two patterns of emigrating types formed in Britain seem to have moved out of Britain intact and to have been distributed intact among the American colonies. And there follows, logically and actually, a further consideration. The dual emigration was first identified and defined in terms of the detailed geography of the emigrants' residences in Britain—those from Scotland and the north of England forming most of one group and those from central and southern England forming most of another. Table 6.4, illustrated in Map 6.A, shows that the arrival patterns reflect the voyagers' geographical origins. The immigrant flow to the central colonies of Maryland, Pennsylvania, and Virginia came predominantly—in a ratio of over 4 to 1—from the central and southern areas of England (the Midlands and south), and overwhelmingly from London alone. All of Scotland contributed only 13.9% of the flow to these colonies, London and the Home Counties together almost 60%. The proportions for Maryland alone are even more extreme. Of the recruits to Maryland, the preponderance of those from metropolitan as opposed to provincial Britain was more than 15 to 1 (2,052 vs. 131). Over half (55.1%) of all the immigrants to Maryland came from London; 70.4% came from London and the Home Counties combined, while all those from the north of England, together with all those from Scotland, contributed only 6.0%. The figures for Pennsylvania and Virginia are less extreme but they have the same emphasis.

Conversely, the whole of the metropolitan area contributed only 1.9% of the migration to New York and North Carolina, London and the Home Counties even less. Of the emigrants to North Carolina, 99.3% came from the provincial areas of northern England and Scotland; of those to New York, 97.5%. Yorkshire is a particularly sensitive index to the distribution of the provincial emigrants, just as London is for the metropolitan. Yorkshire's contribution to the emigration to New York and North Carolina was half again as large as its contribution to the emigration to Maryland, Pennsylvania, and Virginia. And the figures for Nova Scotia now explain the anomaly, noted above, that though that province's immigrants included relatively few Scots, they nevertheless fitted the provincial pattern closely. The explanation is simply that a very high proportion (74.3%) of the voyagers to Nova Scotia came from Yorkshire, whose emigrants had characteristics closer to those of the Scots than to those of the English south of the Midlands. Three-fifths of all those who left Yorkshire for America went to Nova Scotia. The only other destination to which Yorkshiremen went in sizable numbers was New York: 21.0% of all the emigrants from Yorkshire went to that colony. No other location attracted more than 5%.

Thus the immigrations into the two distinctive clusters of colonies—the "central core" (Maryland, Pennsylvania, and Virginia) and New York and

North Carolina—are distinguishable not only by the proportions of the sexes among the migrants, by different incidences of families among them, and by the numbers traveling as indentured servants, but also by the immigrants' specific geographical origins in Britain as well. But there remains among these now increasingly predictable elements in the distribution patterns the fundamental question of occupations.

Table 6.3 shows that there was, to begin with, a basic difference between the two groups of colonies in the percentage of people who claimed any occupation at all. Nine-tenths of all those emigrating to the central core colonies—overwhelmingly young male indentured servants—stated specific occupations. But among those going to New York and North Carolina —a great many of whom were women and children traveling in families —only a third did so. Elsewhere between two-fifths and three-fifths claimed occupations—except for the voyagers to the West Indies. Over three-quarters of those emigrants—largely men who were *not* bound servants—stated their occupations, and an extraordinarily high percentage—52.1%—claimed either to be gentlemen or to be engaged in commerce. This is unique. In no other colony or group of colonies was there anything like this percentage of gentlemen, officials, professionals, and merchants. The percentage in those classifications among all 6,186 emigrants whose occupations are known is only 7.6%; for the central group, only 4.5%; for New York and North Carolina, only 3.9%, and there were very small percentages also among the voyagers to all other destinations. Thus the emigration to the West Indies is obviously distinctive in that it consisted largely of what must have been more or less well-placed or well-connected young men, almost none of whom were indentured servants, heading for the islands to make their fortunes. One can conjecture that many of them contemplated an eventual return to Britain and therefore may not have been "emigrants" in the full sense that the voyagers to the mainland were.

Far different is the occupational profile of those voyaging to the central colonies of Maryland, Pennsylvania, and Virginia. More than half (54.3%) of all those emigrating to those colonies were artisans, almost a third of whom (737) were textile workers, and a fifth (427) workers in high-skill crafts. There were considerably fewer agricultural workers or general laborers: only half as many laborers as artisans. Even if every one of the emigrants to those colonies who stated no occupation (including all the women and children among them) is considered to have been a general laborer, there would still be many fewer laborers than artisans.

The occupational profiles of these three central colonies are not, of course, identical. The proportion of artisans is considerably higher in Maryland and Virginia than in Pennsylvania; the farmers and farmworkers are relatively numerous in Virginia, the laborers in Pennsylvania. But despite the differences among them, the profiles of the three central colo-

TABLE 6.4

DESTINATION CENTRAL CORE OF IMMIGRATION: THE "ENGLISH" COLONIES	Home Counties	London	Bristol	England: Other Southern and central residences	Midlands	TOTAL "METROPOLITAN"
Maryland	333	1203	43	369	104	2052
Pennsylvania	76	384	37	207	49	753
Virginia	132	367	6	96	34	635
Total	541	1954	86	672	187	3440
THE "SCOTTISH" COLONIES						
New York	5	19	8	7	10	49
North Carolina	2	3	0	1	2	8
Total	7	22	8	8	12	57
NEW ENGLAND	2	25	0	0	8	35
DEEP SOUTH (S.C., Ga., Fla.)	12	74	0	22	9	117
CANADA	2	8	0	2	6	18
NOVA SCOTIA	9	5	0	0	0	14
WEST INDIES	19	256	13	31	7	326
COMBINED TOTAL	592	2344	107	735	229	4007

[1]Excludes destination unspecified.

nies have common characteristics distinct from those of the other colonies. A far greater percentage of those going to New York and North Carolina were farmers and farmworkers; far fewer, proportionately, were artisans or laborers. Nova Scotia is particularly interesting. Almost all of its immigrants came from provincial England and from Scotland in family groups that were almost evenly balanced between the sexes, and there was an unusually small percentage of artisans among them. The largest single occupational group was farmers, and almost every one of them can be considered to have had some degree of independence as farmers and were not simply farm laborers of one sort or another. So distinctive do these occupational profiles appear to be that one is inclined to probe the logical connections among elements even more deeply. How do the occupational patterns of the various destinations relate to the immigrants' geographical origins? The answers—derived from separate tables, not reproduced here—contribute vivid patches of color to the developing picture.

Maryland's many immigrant artisans, almost all of them indentured

Northern England	Yorkshire	West Lowlands	Perth-shire	Highlands-Hebrides	Scotland: Other residences	TOTAL "PROVINCIAL"	COMBINED TOTAL
47	47	2	0	0	35	131	2183
29	37	44	13	269	192	584	1337
29	43	3	2	0	35	112	747
105	127	49	15	269	262	827	4267
31	197	365	269	491	539	1892	1941
0	1	9	0	327	740	1077	1085
31	198	374	269	818	1279	2969	3026
10	0	17	4	0	11	42	77
47	44	7	7	3	205	313	430
1	0	8	0	0	8	17	35
32	562	1	0	0	147	742	756
21	7	21	4	9	85	147	473
247	938	477	299	1099	1997	5057	9064

servants, though drawn in small numbers from all over England (not Scotland), came principally from London (57.7%), as did its laborers (50.6%); Maryland's skilled artisans too came overwhelmingly from London (71.3%). Only the West Country and the Midlands, among all the regions besides London and the Home Counties, contributed contingents of any size to Maryland's newcomers (a total of about 9%). And in certain crafts London's preponderance among the immigrants to Maryland was especially high: three-fifths of the textile workers came from London; *none* of them came from the Scottish semi-industrial West Lowlands. Virginia's pattern conforms closely to Maryland's; Pennsylvania's somewhat less closely. Though almost half of Pennsylvania's artisans too came from London, another fifth of them came from the northern provincial areas of Britain; and half of Pennsylvania's immigrant laborers were Scots, chiefly from the Highlands and the western islands. But even in the case of Pennsylvania, two-thirds of the highly skilled artisans came from London.

As is now easily predictable, the occupation/residence relationship of the emigrants to New York and North Carolina is altogether different.

Almost none of New York's artisans came from the Thames Valley; they were primarily (85.4%) Scots, mainly from the West Lowlands, the center of the Scottish textile industry: over half of New York's artisans came from that one small region of Britain. The farmers among New York's immigrants came overwhelmingly (96.6%) from provincial Britain—Yorkshire and all of Scotland except the northeastern districts. Most of the laborers among New York's immigrants were also Scots, as were the mass of those, chiefly women and children, who gave no occupation at all. North Carolina's pattern was almost the same as New York's: its artisans, laborers, and farmers, among those whose occupations are known, were predominantly Scots, as were almost all the future Carolinians who gave no occupation at all. Of the other colonies, it is notable that Nova Scotia drew almost exclusively from Yorkshire in every occupational category; the few exceptions were almost all Scots. And the voyagers to the Caribbean drew from still a different configuration of regions. Three-fifths of its remarkable number of gentlemen and professionals came from London, and most of its sizable group of merchants came either from London (39.0%) or from Scotland (33.9%) and within Scotland mainly from the West Lowlands industrial area. London was the chief source of the future West Indian artisans too (47.9%) and of the laborers who emigrated there as well (54.3%).

Age as an Indicator: Work Force and Society

Thus the complex reality of the emigration becomes more clearly visible as one examines the patterns that emerge from the data pertaining to destinations. But one searches for a still more revealing refraction, a more advantageous viewpoint or perspective by which to examine the emigration's inner character. What of the migrants' ages? Do the groups that went to different destinations differ in age patterns? And if so, what do such differences indicate about the character of this movement of people from Britain to America?

Table 6.5 shows the emigrants' average ages by occupation as well as by colony or region of destination. The seven-year discrepancy in average age between those emigrants who stated occupations and those who did not, shown in the "Total" column, is not surprising, since the latter figure includes the dependent population—predominantly children—and hence would naturally be lower than the average figure for the nondependent part of the population—heads of households or otherwise self-directing people. And it follows logically that the discrepancy is higher where the incidence of families is greater. But the age levels of the various occupational groups are what matter particularly, and there are differences according to destination. Not, however, among those of "gentle" occupations: the average ages in this category are high, ranging in the continental colonies from a low of 27.8 (New York) to a high of 40.5 (Canada, though there the numbers are extremely small). The only anomaly in average ages in this occupational category appears among those who went to the West Indies: their average age of 25.4 is uniquely low; they, as opposed to their equivalents voyaging to other destinations, were *youthful* men of relatively high status or position. Nor are there important differences in age level among the artisans. The average ages of the artisans in the two main groups of colonies are almost identical (25.2 vs. 25.3) except for those of high skill (25.6 vs. 28.1).

The difference in the average ages of the voyagers to the two groups of colonies is the result of the discrepant ages primarily of the agricultural population, and secondarily of the laborers and merchants. To be sure, Table 6.5 shows that the farmers who went to almost all of the American colonies were more advanced in years than the migrants in other occupations (an average age of 28.7 vs. 25.1 for all other occupations combined). But the average age of the farmers going to New York and North Carolina is exceptionally high (32.4), and it is over 6 years higher than the average of the farmers who went to the three central colonies.

Given the low life expectancy at birth (in England approximately 38, in Scotland a year or so longer),[1] and the normal reluctance of people of middle age (as people of 30 were in the eighteenth century) to uproot themselves, an average age of over 32 years in any emigrant group is extraordinary. The spread of ages telescoped into this average is large (standard deviation 11.95), but the average figure is nevertheless remarkably high, and it is the chief reason for the high overall average age of all those of known occupations voyaging to these two colonies.

The second source of the higher age level among the voyagers to New York and North Carolina lies in the ages of the general laborers. They were relatively young throughout the migration (21.8); but they were significantly older (25.9) among those traveling to these colonies. And the third source of the difference lies among those who called themselves merchants or merchants' factors or agents. In this "commercial" category, again, the average age of those voyaging to New York and North Carolina is high (28.2 vs. 25.4 for the central colonies)—an age level of merchants exceeded only by the very few who migrated to Nova Scotia (39.1) and New England (33.5).

The differences in ages between the two main groups of colonies are notable in another way too. A glance across the "Total" row of the central colonies, and particularly the Maryland row, shows a general consistency

---

[1] E. A. Wrigley and R. S. Schofield, *The Population History of England, 1541–1871* (Cambridge, Mass., 1981), p. 529; Michael Flinn, ed., *Scottish Population History* (Cambridge, Eng., 1977), p. 270.

Table 6.5

DESTINATION	GENTLE	MERCHANDISING	AGRICULTURE		
			Independent	Dependent	Total
CENTRAL CORE OF IMMIGRATION: **THE ''ENGLISH'' COLONIES**					
Maryland					
Mean age	29.0	25.0	25.3	25.8	25.4
Number	3	77	241	62	303
Pennsylvania					
Mean age	29.6	26.9	26.4	26.1	26.3
Number	19	40	110	21	131
Virginia					
Mean age	33.0	24.9	26.6	27.6	26.7
Number	4	36	131	25	156
Total					
Mean age	30.1	25.4	25.9	26.3	26.0
Number	26	153	482	108	590
THE ''SCOTTISH'' COLONIES					
New York					
Mean age	27.8	28.8	31.1	27.5	31.0
Number	8	22	260	6	266
North Carolina					
Mean age	29.8	25.6	38.6	20.0	38.3
Number	4	5	61	1	62
Total					
Mean age	28.4	28.2	32.5	26.4	32.4
Number	12	27	321	7	328
NEW ENGLAND					
Mean age	32.0	33.5	30.3	–	30.3
Number	6	2	13	0	13
DEEP SOUTH (S.C., Ga., Fla.)					
Mean age	30.1	25.7	27.8	27.0	27.8
Number	10	19	57	4	61
CANADA					
Mean age	40.5	25.0	36.0	–	36.0
Number	2	1	1	0	1
NOVA SCOTIA					
Mean age	29.0	39.1	31.7	36.8	31.8
Number	2	7	154	4	158
WEST INDIES					
Mean age	25.4	23.5	26.5	27.0	26.5
Number	64	108	44	2	46
TOTAL					
Mean age	27.7	25.4	28.9	26.7	28.7
Number	122	317	1072	125	1197

[1]Excludes emigrants of unknown age, and those who gave no specific destination.

Highly skilled	Textile	Service	Other	Total	Labor	Known	Unknown	Combined Total
25.7	24.8	23.3	25.9	25.3	22.2	24.6	26.5	24.6
258	433	119	532	1342	496	2221	43	2264
25.2	25.1	23.1	25.1	25.0	19.2	22.6	19.1	22.2
75	164	33	160	432	531	1153	142	1295
25.7	24.4	23.5	25.7	25.1	22.4	25.2	21.4	25.0
93	138	33	196	460	77	733	36	769
25.6	24.8	23.3	25.7	25.2	20.8	24.1	20.9	24.0
426	735	185	888	2234	1104	4107	221	4328
28.5	23.7	23.0	26.5	24.7	24.7	26.8	17.6	23.3
29	273	8	113	423	150	869	539	1408
26.8	32.2	21.0	26.8	30.2	31.1	33.5	16.9	23.5
8	32	2	5	47	36	154	235	389
28.1	24.6	22.6	26.5	25.3	25.9	27.8	17.4	23.3
37	305	10	118	470	186	1023	774	1797
28.0	29.5	23.0	26.9	27.6	26.2	29.1	18.0	24.3
1	6	1	10	18	5	44	33	77
26.1	23.9	22.4	27.2	25.5	23.1	25.8	17.5	22.8
31	41	8	40	120	49	259	141	400
–	–	–	31.3	31.3	–	32.4	23.0	27.6
0	0	0	11	11	0	15	16	31
30.4	28.4	–	31.1	30.3	24.5	30.0	15.8	23.0
14	23	0	49	86	68	321	316	637
24.0	23.8	26.1	25.4	25.0	24.5	24.8	21.5	24.1
20	14	14	47	95	26	339	86	425
25.9	24.8	23.4	26.1	25.4	21.8	25.2	17.9	23.7
529	1124	218	1163	3034	1438	6108	1587	7695

TABLE 6.5A

DESTINATION	GENTLE	MERCHANDISING	AGRICULTURE		
			Indepen-dent	Dependent	Total
CENTRAL CORE OF IMMIGRATION: THE "ENGLISH" COLONIES					
Maryland					
Mean age	40.0	36.0	38.0	21.0	33.8
Number	1	1	3	1	4
Pennsylvania					
Mean age	30.0	–	36.7	33.0	36.6
Number	2	0	19	1	20
Virginia					
Mean age	–	–	37.0	–	37.0
Number	0	0	5	0	5
Total					
Mean age	33.3	36.0	36.9	27.0	36.2
Number	3	1	27	2	29
THE "SCOTTISH" COLONIES					
New York					
Mean age	40.0	33.8	35.2	–	35.2
Number	1	4	126	0	126
North Carolina					
Mean age	37.0	27.0	39.3	–	39.3
Number	2	1	57	0	57
Total					
Mean age	38.0	32.4	36.5	–	36.5
Number	3	5	183	0	183
NEW ENGLAND					
Mean age	43.0	–	38.0	–	38.0
Number	1	0	4	0	4
DEEP SOUTH (S.C., Ga., Fla.)					
Mean age	24.5	32.0	34.4	–	34.4
Number	2	2	17	0	17
CANADA					
Mean age	21.0	–	36.0	–	36.0
Number	1	0	1	0	1
NOVA SCOTIA					
Mean age	–	41.5	37.2	30.0	37.1
Number	0	2	56	1	57
WEST INDIES					
Mean age	27.6	24.0	33.7	–	33.7
Number	5	1	6	0	6
TOTAL					
Mean age	31.0	33.6	36.5	28.0	36.4
Number	15	11	294	3	297

[1]Excludes emigrants of unknown age, those who gave no specific destination, and those whose family relationship was unclear.

Highly skilled	Textile	Service	Other	Total	LABOR	Known	Unknown	COMBINED TOTAL
25.0	30.0	–	32.0	29.3	33.7	31.4	27.9	29.6
4	5	0	5	14	3	23	26	49
25.3	36.3	–	36.0	34.3	17.5	28.3	18.8	22.5
4	7	0	13	24	29	75	117	192
–	21.8	28.0	22.8	22.8	34.0	27.7	19.0	22.4
0	5	1	5	11	1	17	26	43
25.1	30.2	28.0	32.3	30.3	19.4	28.8	20.2	23.7
8	17	1	23	49	33	115	169	284
38.5	25.0	–	28.7	26.4	27.5	30.2	17.4	22.9
8	113	0	26	147	38	316	417	733
40.0	36.2	–	25.0	35.8	34.5	37.5	16.6	23.0
1	18	0	1	20	21	101	229	330
38.7	26.6	–	28.5	27.5	30.0	31.9	17.1	22.9
9	131	0	27	167	59	417	646	1063
–	37.0	–	33.0	35.7	–	37.8	14.3	20.1
0	2	0	1	3	0	8	24	32
43.0	25.5	24.0	34.7	29.1	34.2	31.3	16.0	21.1
2	17	1	7	27	6	54	110	164
–	–	–	44.0	44.0	–	36.3	24.4	28.1
0	0	0	2	2	0	4	9	13
33.2	34.0	–	35.6	34.8	33.6	36.0	14.6	20.1
6	7	0	19	32	12	103	297	400
–	–	–	28.3	28.3	33.3	30.5	21.5	24.9
0	0	0	3	3	3	18	30	48
33.4	27.2	26.0	32.2	29.2	27.6	32.0	16.9	22.3
25	174	2	82	283	113	719	1285	2004

in age averages. Except for the very few "gentle" people and laborers, the ages were quite consistent throughout all the occupational groups, and the spread of ages brought within these averages quite narrow. The only other row where the figures are similarly consistent is that of the West Indies; these figures are the most consistent of all: even the gentlemen and laborers, among the future West Indians, fall in the same small range of ages in the mid-twenties. The figures for Canada and Nova Scotia are also more or less consistent—consistently high. In contrast, the averages for the various occupations among the voyagers to New York and North Carolina are *not* consistent. They are quite high for commerce, remarkably high for agriculture, average for artisans, and relatively high for laborers—and of course exceptionally low for all those without stated occupations.

Behind these figures lies a reality one seeks to grasp. Why these variations? What do the figures reflect or suggest?

They reflect, first, the migration not merely of family groups, including children, from provincial Britain to New York, North Carolina, and Nova Scotia but of *mature* family groups—that is, families headed by men of advanced years and containing, if not all the children they were likely to have, at least a large percentage of them. And these were families sufficiently prosperous or well connected to have managed their transportation and resettlement without resorting to bonded servitude.

The issues can be focused more sharply by running the same tests for average ages seen in Table 6.5 for only those who were traveling as members of families. The results of isolating family members' ages (Table 6.5a) are striking. The average ages of family members who did not state occupations remain approximately the same as the emigrants' ages in Table 6.5, since in both tables they largely pertain to the same group of children and other family dependents. But the ages of those who did state occupations, largely heads of households, are higher in almost every occupational category, and especially in New York, North Carolina, and Nova Scotia. The average age of the 57 family farmers migrating to North Carolina is almost 40, of the 126 traveling to New York over 35, of the 57 traveling to Nova Scotia over 37. Even the many fewer family farmers migrating to the central colonies averaged over 36 years of age. The artisans within families, though fewer in number, are mature too: an average of 27.5 in North Carolina and New York taken together, and approximately 35 years in North Carolina and in Nova Scotia. And even the laborers traveling in families from provincial Britain were far from youthful: an average age of 30.0 among the migrants to North Carolina and New York (34.5 among those traveling to North Carolina alone) and 33.6 among the migrants to Nova Scotia.

Thus, by eliminating the non-family men and women and hence to a large extent isolating the non-indentured heads of families, one sees far more clearly the maturity, perhaps the substantiality, of the family units migrating to New York, North Carolina, and Nova Scotia. An inverse test is to isolate the indentured servants, very few of whom were heads of families or even traveling in families. The results (Table 6.5b) show that, as expected, the weight of numbers falls heavily on the central colonies of Pennsylvania, Maryland, and Virginia. But they show too that the uniformity of indentured servants' ages, clustered heavily in the early and mid-twenties, is an average not of great differences among the separate destinations but rather of similar age characteristics. Barely a year separates the average ages of the indentured artisans traveling to Pennsylvania, Maryland, and Virginia. And when there are differences from the overall norm, they are consistent across the region. The average age of indentured servants in service trades, for example, is almost identical in the three colonies, consistently a year or so younger than the average ages of the highly skilled artisans.

If we use age as an indicator, therefore, the picture of the migration to the various destinations becomes clearer. The flow of people from provincial Britain into New York and North Carolina that seems to emerge is that of substantial segments of a society in process of transplantation. The voyagers to these regions appear to form rudimentary communities composed largely of families who worked the land but including elements of the lower gentry, merchants, artisans, and laborers. And they are *mature* families, led by men at or near the crest of their careers, not newly formed couples of young adventurers. The migration to Pennsylvania, Maryland, and Virginia is altogether different. It is the transfer of a specific kind of *work force*, drawn, not from the provincial areas of Britain, but largely from the metropolis of London and its immediate environs. Predominantly men in their early or mid-twenties, almost all of whom could claim some experience, however small, in an art or craft or mode of industrial production, the immigrants to these colonies were almost all poor enough—even those in the most sophisticated high-skill crafts—to agree to submit in advance to four years or more of unpaid servitude in exchange for their passage to America. The farmers and farmworkers among them do not differ from these norms: they too were largely unmarried male indentured servants in their early twenties and they came from the same geographical centers; they too appear to have been caught in the same labor-market network. The general laborers, drawn from the metropolis into this network, were not venerable work hands, veterans of many labor fairs and of years of constant perambulation, but youngsters—teenagers, most of them—assembled by some means or other from the milling thousands of untrained workers available in metropolitan England. And the few who stated no occupation at all were not children or women predominantly; they too were recruits

TABLE 6.5B

DESTINATION	GENTLE	MERCHANDISING	AGRICULTURE		
			Independent	Dependent	Total
CENTRAL CORE OF IMMIGRATION: THE "ENGLISH" COLONIES					
Maryland					
Mean age	22.0	24.8	25.2	25.8	25.3
Number	1	72	240	62	302
Pennsylvania					
Mean age	–	25.1	22.6	28.0	23.5
Number	0	16	69	14	83
Virginia					
Mean age	–	25.7	25.9	27.8	26.3
Number	0	28	113	24	137
Total					
Mean age	22.0	25.0	25.0	26.6	25.3
Number	1	116	422	100	522
THE "SCOTTISH" COLONIES					
New York					
Mean age	–	35.5	27.1	31.5	28.0
Number	0	2	8	2	10
North Carolina					
Mean age	–	–	–	–	–
Number	0	0	0	0	0
Total					
Mean age	–	35.5	27.1	31.5	28.0
Number	0	2	8	2	10
NEW ENGLAND					
Mean age	–	–	–	–	–
Number	0	0	0	0	0
DEEP SOUTH (S.C., Ga., Fla.)					
Mean age	–	–	27.6	27.0	27.5
Number	0	0	35	4	39
CANADA					
Mean age	–	–	–	–	–
Number	0	0	0	0	0
NOVA SCOTIA					
Mean age	–	–	–	–	–
Number	0	0	0	0	0
WEST INDIES					
Mean age	–	23.0	21.0	–	21.0
Number	0	1	2	0	2
TOTAL					
Mean age	22.0	25.2	25.2	26.7	25.5
Number	1	119	467	106	573

[1]Excludes emigrants of unknown age, and those who gave no specific destination.

TRADES OR CRAFTS					LABOR	TOTAL		COMBINED TOTAL
Highly skilled	Textile	Service	Other	Total		Known	Unknown	
25.7	24.7	23.3	25.8	25.2	22.2	24.5	25.6	24.5
258	431	118	529	1336	494	2205	33	2238
25.5	24.0	23.9	23.9	24.3	18.7	21.2	26.3	21.2
60	120	27	117	324	499	922	8	930
26.0	24.5	23.7	25.6	25.2	22.4	25.1	25.1	25.1
85	134	32	188	439	75	679	13	692
25.7	24.6	23.5	25.5	25.1	20.6	23.8	25.5	23.9
403	685	177	834	2099	1068	3806	54	3860
23.7	23.2	19.7	22.7	23.1	21.0	23.0	22.4	23.0
3	147	3	13	166	48	226	18	244
23.7	21.5	21.0	35.5	25.8	–	25.8	35.0	26.8
3	2	1	2	8	0	8	1	9
23.7	23.2	20.0	24.4	23.3	21.0	23.1	23.1	23.1
6	149	4	15	174	48	234	19	253
–	–	–	–	–	–	–	–	–
0	0	0	0	0	0	0	0	0
26.5	24.7	19.8	26.5	25.3	23.8	25.5	16.1	22.0
18	29	6	29	82	42	163	97	260
–	–	–	–	–	–	–	–	–
0	0	0	0	0	0	0	0	0
–	–	–	–	–	–	–	–	–
0	0	0	0	0	0	0	0	0
–	–	–	22.6	22.6	–	22.3	–	22.3
0	0	0	5	5	0	8	0	8
25.7	24.3	23.3	25.5	24.9	20.7	23.8	19.9	23.7
427	863	187	883	2360	1158	4211	170	4381

to the same Anglo-American labor markets who for some reason did not record their occupations.

The minor flows may be pictured against these major currents. Those who voyaged to Nova Scotia bore characteristics similar to—that are even exaggerations of—those of the families migrating to New York and North Carolina. But the voyagers to the West Indies, though in some ways similar to the immigrants to the central colonies, were unique: there is something remarkable in the almost perfect uniformity of the average ages. Even the gentlemen among them were close in average age to the 25+-year average of those of known occupation. This is strange: there must have been quite peculiar characteristics in this group that have not, so far, emerged.

The evidence could hardly be stronger that the migration was not a general milling and thronging of people from Britain to America but discrete and patterned movements of people: a work force to the central colonies; a social movement of substantial families to New York, North Carolina, and Nova Scotia; and something different, but not yet clear, in the migration to the West Indies. Sensitive now to these distinctive currents, one can turn back to the panorama of the migration with a more perceptive eye and attempt to detect relationships hitherto obscure, seeking always to draw closer to the individual human experience involved.

Patterns in Transportation

What *kinds* of flows were these distinctive currents of migration? Did the emigrants to these areas come together in large groups or in small? In many frequent voyages or in a few? Did they go through a few British ports or through many? And did they differ significantly with respect to these questions?

The information in Tables 6.6 and 6.7 reveals that the management and organization of the emigration involved three distinguishable though overlapping patterns, aspects of which have been noted in other connections. It shows, first, an underlying and continuous series of small transactions involving many vessels but few people. As we have already seen, ships carrying only a handful of passengers were voyaging out from Britain constantly. Almost all of the emigrants to the West Indies can be accounted for in this way. Less than 500 voyagers (only 5.3% of all the emigrants in the Register) were destined for the islands, but they were transported in no fewer than 153 vessels, in average groups of only 3.2 persons per vessel. These ships left from English rather than Scottish ports, and undoubtedly were part of the normal heavy shipping that traveled between England and its West Indian possessions. The flow was continuous (Table 4.3), and the number of passengers consistently small. In December 1773 the average number of emigrants per vessel was 2.5; in all of 1774, 3.4; in all of 1775, 3.6. Not one of the emigrants to the West Indies arrived in a vessel bearing 50 or more voyagers; almost half arrived in vessels bearing fewer than 5 voyagers; almost three-quarters (72.3%) arrived with fewer than 10 emigrants. The port of London was naturally the main exit point: 79 vessels left London for the West Indies carrying on the average 2.7 emigrants each.

This pattern of small numbers of people on many vessels voyaging out continuously over the years is not confined to emigration to the Caribbean, however. It accounts for *some* of the emigration to almost all of the North American colonies. While the Yorkshire port of Hull sent out a few heavily loaded vessels, it also sent 1 vessel with 9 passengers to Maryland, 1 with 2 to Pennsylvania, 2 with 18 to New York, and 2 with 4 to the islands. London's ships bore similarly small contingents to almost all locations outside the central core colonies: ships averaged 5.7 passengers to New York, 7.5 to North Carolina, and 6.5 to Nova Scotia. So too Bristol sent out 16 vessels bearing a total of only 37 people to New York and the Caribbean; Portsmouth, one of the "southern English ports," sent 18 vessels bearing a total of 40 to Virginia and the Caribbean; and other "southern English ports" sent 9 vessels bearing 27 people to a number of American colonies.

This casual traffic in emigrants, an incidental part of the extensive maritime communication between England (but not Scotland) and America penetrated almost everywhere in the colonies. Almost every colony— from Canada through to the southernmost Caribbean islands—acquired newcomers through such small shipments. This pattern is likely to have been a constant feature of Anglo-American life from the colonies' earliest days.

But this constant trickle of emigration accounts for only a modest part of the total number of emigrants. Only a third of all the 9,364 registered newcomers arrived in vessels bearing fewer than 50 permanent emigrants; only 9.2% on vessels bearing fewer than 10. Far more important in terms of numbers—numerically the dominant part of the emigration—is a second kind of flow: the departure, almost exclusively from London and Bristol, of vessels carrying between 20 and 100 emigrants to the central core colonies of Maryland, Pennsylvania, and Virginia. These were shiploads almost entirely of indentured servants: tradesmen, artisans, farmworkers, and laborers from all over the metropolitan area but predominantly from London and the Home Counties, assembled and contracted for by shippers and merchants for disposition in the three central colonies.

The third pattern differs in all respects from the first two. The data used to compile Table 6.6 show that 89.6% of the emigrants to New York and North Carolina, who constituted a third of the entire emigration, left on 26 vessels from Scottish ports. The main port of exit was the commercial metropolis of Greenock and Glasgow, but they left also from the tiny island

TABLE 6.6

DESTINATION	ENGLISH			PORTS			
CENTRAL CORE OF IMMIGRATION: THE "ENGLISH" COLONIES	London	Bristol	Other southern English ports	Hull	Scarborough	Newcastle	Northwestern English ports[4]
Maryland							
Ships	67	9	1	1	0	0	0
Emigrants	2167	148	4	9	0	0	0
Average shipload	32.3	16.4	4.0	9.0	–	–	–
Pennsylvania							
Ships	22	11	1	1	0	0	7
Emigrants	634	194	4	2	0	0	64
Average shipload	28.8	17.6	4.0	2.0	–	–	9.1
Virginia							
Ships	28	0	1	1	0	0	9
Emigrants	710	0	1	24	0	0	28
Average shipload	25.4	–	1.0	24.0	–	–	3.1
Total							
Ships	117	20	3	3	0	0	16
Emigrants	3511	342	9	35	0	0	92
Average shipload	30.0	17.1	3.0	11.7	–	–	5.8
THE "SCOTTISH" COLONIES							
New York							
Ships	7	2	0	2	0	1	4
Emigrants	40	12	0	18	0	2	229
Average shipload	5.7	6.0	–	9.0	–	2.0	57.3
North Carolina							
Ships	2	0	0	0	0	1	0
Emigrants	15	0	0	0	0	1	0
Average shipload	7.5	–	–	–	–	1.0	–
Total							
Ships	9	2	0	2	0	2	4
Emigrants	55	12	0	18	0	3	229
Average shipload	6.1	6.0	–	9.0	–	1.5	57.3
DEEP SOUTH[2]							
Ships	21	0	2	0	0	1	2
Emigrants	121	0	9	0	0	100	7
Average shipload	5.8	–	4.5	–	–	100.0	3.5
CANADA							
Ships	7	0	2	0	0	0	0
Emigrants	25	0	6	0	0	0	0
Average shipload	3.6	–	3.0	–	–	–	–
NOVA SCOTIA							
Ships	2	0	1	3	1	1	0
Emigrants	13	0	1	369	193	1	0
Average shipload	6.5	–	1.0	123.0	193.0	1.0	–
WEST INDIES							
Ships	79	14	37	2	0	3	6
Emigrants	210	25	133	4	0	5	20
Average shipload	2.7	1.8	3.6	2.0	–	1.7	3.3
TOTAL[3]							
Ships	248	36	45	10	1	8	28
Emigrants	3973	379	158	426	193	118	348
Average shipload	16.0	10.5	3.5	42.6	193.0	14.8	12.4

[1]Excludes emigrants with destination unspecified. For the relationship between ship voyages and ports of departure, see footnote to Table 4.2. See also Table 6.7, n. 2 and n. 3.

[2]South Carolina, Georgia, Florida.
[3]Includes New England (15 ships, 77 people).
[4]Liverpool and Whitehaven.

Other English ports[5]	Total English ports	SCOTTISH PORTS							Combined total
		The Clyde[6]	The Firth of Forth[7]	West Highland ports[8]	Lowland ports[9]	Northern Island ports[10]	Other Scottish ports	Total Scottish ports	
0	78	0	0	0	0	0	0	0	78
0	2328	0	0	0	0	0	0	0	2328
-	29.9	-	-	-	-	-	-	-	29.9
0	42	2	1	2	0	0	1	6	48
0	898	76	98	318	0	0	25	517	1415
-	21.4	38.0	98.0	159.0	-	-	25.0	86.2	29.5
0	39	5	0	0	0	0	0	5	44
0	763	11	0	0	0	0	0	11	774
-	19.6	2.2	-	-	-	-	-	2.2	17.6
0	159	7	1	2	0	0	1	11	170
0	3989	87	98	318	0	0	25	528	4517
-	25.1	12.4	98.0	159.0	-	-	25.0	48.0	26.6
0	16	7	0	3	3	0	0	13	29
0	301	993	0	334	326	0	0	1653	1954
-	18.8	141.9	-	111.3	108.7	-	-	127.2	67.4
0	3	6	1	3	1	1	1	13	16
0	16	144	20	683	29	131	62	1069	1085
-	5.3	24.0	20.0	227.7	29.0	131.0	62.0	82.2	67.8
0	19	13	1	6	4	1	1	26	45
0	317	1137	20	1017	355	131	62	2722	3039
-	16.7	87.5	20.0	169.5	88.8	131.0	62.0	104.7	67.5
0	26	3	0	0	0	2	0	5	31
0	237	44	0	0	0	155	0	199	436
-	9.1	14.7	-	-	-	77.5	-	39.8	14.1
0	9	1	0	0	0	0	0	1	10
0	31	8	0	0	0	0	0	8	39
-	3.4	8.0	-	-	-	-	-	8.0	3.9
1	9	0	0	0	1	0	0	1	10
31	608	0	0	0	150	0	0	150	758
31.0	67.6	-	-	-	150.0	-	-	150.0	75.8
3	144	7	1	0	0	0	1	9	153
8	405	57	22	0	0	0	11	90	495
2.7	2.8	8.1	22.0	-	-	-	11.0	10.0	3.2
4	380	32	3	8	5	3	3	54	434
39	5634	1363	140	1335	505	286	98	3727	9361
9.8	14.8	42.6	46.7	166.9	101.0	95.3	32.7	69.0	21.6

[5]Stockton, Yarmouth, and Isle of Man.
[6]Greenock and Glasgow.
[7]Leith and Kirkcaldy.
[8]Gigha, Ft. William, Dunstaffnage Bay, Lochbroom, and Stornoway.
[9]Stranraer, Dumfries, Kirkcudbright, and Wigtown.
[10]Kirkwall and Lerwick.

of Gigha; from Fort William; from Dunstaffnage Bay; from Stranraer in Wigtonshire; from Stornoway on the Hebridean Isle of Lewis; from Lerwick in the Shetlands; and from a few other minor ports in southern and central Scotland.

These shipments from Scotland to New York and North Carolina are altogether distinctive. The information gathered for Tables 6.6 and 6.7 indicates that approximately three-quarters of all emigrants to New York and North Carolina arrived in shiploads of between 100 and 300 passengers. The *average* size of the shiploads of emigrants from Scotland to New York and North Carolina is 104.7, which is twice the size of the average shipments to the central colonies of Pennsylvania, Maryland, and Virginia, and anywhere from 3 to 50 times as large as the casual shipments that can be found arriving almost anywhere at any time in the American colonies from the various ports south of Yorkshire.

There was, then, an overlay, as it were, of three distinct patterns in transportation: first, a constant trickle of very small groups of emigrants throughout the period going from many English ports to almost all the colonies in America; second, a separate, heavy flow of young, unattached male indentured servants transported in groups of between 20 and 100 mainly from London and Bristol to the three central colonies of Pennsylvania, Maryland, and Virginia; and third, a sizable flow of free (nonindentured) men, women, and children traveling as families in very large shipments from Scottish ports to New York and North Carolina. The traffic to Nova Scotia—8.1% of all the emigrants—is similar to that to New York and North Carolina, except that more of the emigrants originated in Yorkshire than in Scotland, and they left Britain through the ports of Hull and Scarborough.

Purposes, Motives, Plans, and Expectations

As we have seen, the only direct clues to the emigrants' motives, plans, and expectations that exist in the Register are the responses they gave to the customs officials' inquiry, "for what purposes they leave the country?" These responses, we know, are incomplete; they resulted from filtration through two levels of possible misinterpretation; often they are formulaic; and they cannot be classified in entirely discrete categories. Nevertheless, in the aggregate these responses are useful indicators of attitudes and expectations, and they contain some rather unexpected information when arranged according to the migrants' destinations.

It will be recalled from the earlier discussion of these stated purposes

that the recorded responses of the *free English* emigrants were preponder-
antly positive—they appear to be optimistic, calculating, hopefully risk-
taking—though against them must be placed the 3,553 English indentured
servants whose purposes were not recorded but who were undoubtedly
motivated by the desire to escape from poverty or the threat of poverty,
from unemployment or the lack of prospects. It has been seen also that the
free Scots (and few Scots were indented) expressed predominantly negative
views (about 2 to 1). The exodus from the Highlands, it appeared from these
responses, was impelled chiefly by sharp rent increases and other imposi-
tions of "tyrannical" landlords; the emigration from the West Lowlands
appeared from these notations to have been motivated by the fact or threat
of poverty and unemployment. But despite all the negative statements, over
a third of all the Scots whose purposes were recorded and nine-tenths of
the English were affirmative in their attitude to their departures. The
majority of these British respondents appeared to have been enterprising
people, attempting to exploit opportunities they knew at least something
about and which they thought they could to some extent plan for. It seems
reasonable to characterize this part of the emigration as a movement of
expectant people, seeking betterment and not simply a refuge from desperation; these emigrants seemed to convey a sense of threatening but not
annihilating difficulties, of dislocations that both demanded and allowed
redeeming decisions, and of more or less reasoned choices.

Now, in Table 6.8, the uneven distribution of these attitudes and expectations among the various destinations can be seen. It is clear from the
"Total" column that the positive and negative responses are evenly distributed for this area as a whole. But the subtotals for the two distinctive
areas—the central colonies of Pennsylvania, Maryland, and Virginia and
New York and North Carolina—reveal not merely different but opposite
emphases. Those who went *as freemen* to the former group of colonies were
overwhelmingly (over 4 to 1) positive in their attitudes and expectations.
The largest number of them left Britain with expectations of personal
betterment and with few recorded expressions of distress or harassment. In
contrast, the free immigrants to New York and North Carolina, predominantly from Scotland and the north of England, gave negative responses
in about the same proportion, 4 to 1, citing primarily distress caused by the
escalation of rents and other "tyrannies" of landlords, and secondarily
unemployment and poverty in almost equal proportions.

Taken together with the very different incidences of indentured servitude, these differences in attitude suggest the outline of two quite different
processes of migration. The central colonies appear to have constituted a
large labor market that favored young workmen, artisans for the most part,
unencumbered by families or other obligations, whose services could be
purchased in advance and maintained at minimal cost for a number of years.

234

TABLE 6.7

| DESTINATION | NUMBER OF | | | | |
	1–4	5–9	10–19	20–49	Total 1–49
CENTRAL CORE OF IMMIGRATION: THE "ENGLISH" COLONIES					
Maryland					
Ships	10	11	13	26	60
Emigrants	23	72	204	786	1085
Pennsylvania					
Ships	10	11	9	11	41
Emigrants	25	78	127	385	615
Virginia					
Ships	21	7	4	7	39
Emigrants	39	47	57	270	413
Total					
Ships	41	29	26	44	140
Emigrants	87	197	388	1441	2113
THE "SCOTTISH" COLONIES					
New York					
Ships	8	1	2	5	16
Emigrants	12	5	26	160	203
North Carolina					
Ships	4	2	1	3	10
Emigrants	5	15	11	85	116
Total					
Ships	12	3	3	8	26
Emigrants	17	20	37	245	319
NEW ENGLAND					
Ships	11	3	0	1	15
Emigrants	22	25	0	30	77
DEEP SOUTH (S.C., Ga., Fla.)					
Ships	17	6	3	2	28
Emigrants	43	40	40	58	181
CANADA					
Ships	6	4	0	0	10
Emigrants	13	26	0	0	39
NOVA SCOTIA					
Ships	2	2	0	1	5
Emigrants	2	13	0	31	46
WEST INDIES					
Ships	124	19	8	2	153
Emigrants	235	123	88	49	495
TOTAL					
Ships	213	66	40	58	377
Emigrants	419	444	553	1854	3270

[1]Excludes destination unspecified.

[2]The total 434 represents what might be called "ship destinations" rather than ship voyages, of which there were only 431 (omitting the one vessel, with three passengers, whose destination was "America"). Three of the vessels went to two destinations and left passengers off at both: one to Maryland and Virginia, one to New York and North Carolina, and one

PASSENGERS-PER-SHIP
ACCORDING TO DESTINATION[1]

	PASSENGERS	PER	SHIP			
50–99	100–149	150–199	200–249	250–300	Combined Total	Mean number of passengers
18	0	0	0	0	78	29.8
1243	0	0	0	0	2328	
2	4	0	1	0	48	29.5
152	436	0	212	0	1415[3]	
5	0	0	0	0	44	17.6
361	0	0	0	0	774	
25	4	0	1	0	170	26.6
1756	436	0	212	0	4517	
5	1	4	2	1	29	67.4
296	100	683	421	251	1954	
2	2	0	1	1	16	67.8
155	267	0	247	300	1085	
7	3	4	3	2	45	67.5
451	367	683	668	551	3039	
0	0	0	0	0	15	5.1
0	0	0	0	0	77	
2	1	0	0	0	31	14.1
155	100	0	0	0	436	
0	0	0	0	0	10	3.9
0	0	0	0	0	39	
1	1	3	0	0	10	75.8
80	103	529	0	0	758	
0	0	0	0	0	153	3.2
0	0	0	0	0	495	
35	9	7	4	2	434[2]	21.6
2442	1006	1212	880	551	9361	

to Jamaica and New York. There were therefore three more destinations than vessels. To clear up the anomaly, each of the three vessels was listed separately for both of its destinations, hence the total number of "ship destinations" is 434. [3]One voyager who said he was going to "America" was among 16 passengers on a ship bound for Philadelphia: he was included with the other 15 as destined for Pennsylvania since it was assumed he was traveling there too.

TABLE 6.8

| | THE "ENGLISH" COLONIES | | | | THE "SCOTTISH" COLONIES | | |
	Maryland	Pennsyl-vania	Virginia	Total	New York	North Carolina	Total
REASON FOR LEAVING							
Positive							
To settle as a planter, an estate owner; to buy land, property; to "plant," to farm	31	72	16	119	83	4	87
To better self	3	246	13	262	49	15	64
To follow occupation	5	81	28	114	39	12	51
Total	39	399	57	495	171	31	202
Negative							
Unemployment	0	41	0	41	209	14	223
Poverty: "to get bread"	0	68	0	68	187	23	210
High rents, tyranny of landlords	0	2	2	4	293	71	364
Miscellaneous economic distress	0	0	0	0	2	4	6
Total	0	111	2	113	691	112	803
All reasons for leaving	39	510	59	608	862	143	1005
Indentured servants	2262	971	692	3925	250	9	259
Combined Total	2301	1481	751	4533	1112	152	1264

[1]Excludes destination unspecified.

The combination of artisanal skills, some of them quite sophisticated, and indentures indicates specific labor needs quite above the level of brute manpower, and an effective mechanism for recruiting this needed labor. But the same labor market was also open enough and attractive enough to draw about 500 unbound, completely free immigrants of high expectation, willing freely to take their chances in this long-settled area of the colonial world. Taken together, the large number of young male indentured artisans and the incidence of positive expectations on the part of the free immigrants suggest a high degree of economic specialization and both the fact and the general awareness of an expanding economy. The eagerness to acquire a white labor force of youthful, semiskilled or skilled artisans on the part of employers in these colonies and the expectation of economic opportunities on the part of the free immigrants reinforce the picture of a rapidly growing and sophisticated economy, with expanding opportunities.

STATED REASONS FOR EMIGRATING AND DESTINATIONS OF "DECISION MAKERS"[1]

NEW ENGLAND	DEEP SOUTH	TOTAL	CANADA	NOVA SCOTIA	WEST INDIES	COMBINED TOTAL
24	40	270	8	16	212	506
6	106	438	0	179	18	635
5	22	192	4	9	147	352
35	168	900	12	204	377	1493
10	18	292	0	0	6	298
0	10	288	0	19	0	307
10	8	386	0	60	10	456
0	6	12	0	22	0	34
20	42	978	0	101	16	1095
55	210	1878	12	305	393	2588
0	280	4464	0	0	8	4472
55	490	6342	12	305	401	7060

The contrast with the recruitment pattern in New York and North Carolina is striking. These colonies seem to have been magnets not primarily for an artisan labor force but for farming families from northern Britain escaping poverty and social change, families led by men of mature years, dislodged or threatened with displacement from their established situations, seeking resettlement on the land in America. While their attitudes were of course mixed, they appear to have been responding more to distress than to positive attractions, seeking to recover a lost security.

All of this pertains to the colonies that would constitute the United States. The other regions of British America are distinctive too and emphasize by contrast the peculiar characteristics of the immigrant flows to the seaboard colonies. The immigrants to Nova Scotia—drawn, we know, from farming families in the north of Britain and with no indentured servants among them—were positive in their attitude to resettlement in a ratio of more than 2 to 1. They were socially and occupationally similar to the immigrants to New York and North Carolina, but they were more positive in their expectations than were the free voyagers to those communities to the south. Over four-fifths of the respondents in the Nova Scotia group were Yorkshiremen or emigrants from northern England, and though many of them cited the desire simply to escape high rents and economic distress as the purpose of their emigration, two-thirds of them were positive in their statements. To a striking degree their responses reflect the attitudes of informed and enterprising people, planning ahead to a profitable reestablishment on the land. They had reason to expect betterment in their lives, which in any case appear not to have been sunk in deep distress. So William Johnson, a 49-year-old Yorkshire farmer bound for Nova Scotia in a party of seven, informed the customs officials that he had already "purchased an estate" in that colony and was "going over with his family & servants to reside." Among his shipmates was William Black, a Yorkshire linen draper and grocer, who was also leading a party of seven and had similarly "made a purchase [and] is going with his family to reside there."[2]

Distinctive too is the pattern of the 393 free respondents traveling to the Caribbean. Unencumbered young men, in age almost identical to those traveling to the central mainland colonies but of higher social condition and free of servitude, they carried with them positive plans and expectations. Over half of those whose purposes were recorded stated that they intended "to be a planter" or "to plant" or to take up property or to occupy a position in trade or commerce. Over half (56%) of these enterprising voyagers, setting out to make their fortunes in the sugar colonies, were Londoners. Ten of the sixteen who said they were escaping poor conditions were Scots faced with high rents or unemployment.

Looking, now, across the whole of Table 6.8, one finds an unmistakable channeling of emigrants among the various colonies of Britain's western empire. Nova Scotia and the West Indies were target areas for the better established and more confidently outward-reaching. The thirteen mainland colonies attracted, into two distinctly different regions, first, a large labor force recruited in London and metropolitan England generally for employment in the central colonies of Pennsylvania, Maryland, and Virginia; and second, hard-pressed families seeking, principally in New York and North Carolina, relief from the social and economic dislocations of the Scottish

---

[2] Johnson and Black left Hull on the *Jenny* in the first week of April 1775 (T 47/10/59). For Black's later career, see below, pp. 425–426.

Highlands, the economic disturbances of the West Lowlands, and the difficulties of life in the northern agricultural areas of England.

How distressed these provincial families in fact were; how desperate the thousands of emigrating artisans who committed themselves to years of servitude; and how enterprising the Yorkshire farmers, what plans they had on foot, what led them to the northern region and not elsewhere—in general, what explains this patterning of the emigrants' distribution among Britain's American colonies: none of this is revealed in the figures compiled from the Register. What is revealed is something that can be conveyed only by numbers—magnitudes, dimensions, internal structure, and composition. But now having established this information from the tables derived from the Register, one may turn back to the mass of scattered literary sources to discover the circumstantial reality of this multiple movement of people, its meaning as human experience, which quantities alone can never convey.

III

Mobilizing a Labor Force

INTRODUCTION

IN THE preceding chapters it has become clear that a large part of the British migration to America was the movement of a labor force, working people seeking some kind of economic security and a more promising way of life. Almost half settled in America as indentured servants: two out of three of the emigrants from England arrived in the colonies committed to that peculiar form of temporary bondage, and they were demographically excellent as a labor force. Most of them, drawn from metropolitan England, were unmarried males in their early twenties, and the majority claimed to be artisans with specified and useful skills. Less than a quarter of these English indentured servants said they were merely laborers, and less than a sixth said they were farmers or farm workers. Very few were burdened with families, and the families occasionally found among them consisted for the most part simply of husband and wife. The Scots and the northern English were different. Only about one out of five of the emigrating Scots was an indentured servant, and of these bonded workers approximately three out of five were males. Nor were they, like the English, chiefly artisans; almost half of the Scottish indentured servants called themselves laborers.

The destinations of this unfree labor force among the emigrants were found to be highly selective. The indentured servants were not migrating to all, or even to most, of the British colonies in America. About 90% of the entire group went to only three colonies: Pennsylvania, Maryland, and Virginia. More striking still, over half of them went to only one colony, Maryland, where no less than 97.2% of all the registered immigrants were unfree. Maryland, to judge by these figures alone, must have had some special role as a labor market, must have been some special kind of production center with a peculiar demand for labor, or must have been a major distribution center for workers of all kinds. On the other hand, not one of the 4,264 indentured servants from England and Scotland went either to the New England colonies or to Canada, including Nova Scotia, and only a very few went to the Caribbean colonies, to New York or North Carolina, or to anywhere in the deep south except Georgia.

But not all recruits to the work force were indentured—unfree—servants, with or without wages. There were many fully free workers too among the 9,364 registered emigrants from Britain—workers like the thirty-one-year-old blacksmith, the twenty-eight-year-old butcher, and the nineteen-year-old gardener who left Yorkshire together in 1774, having been "hired," they said—presumably by employers in Nova Scotia.[1] They were unbound wage workers, who, unmarried and otherwise unencumbered, were in every way as free as any wage worker in England. But most free workers came without prior arrangements of any kind and simply expected to make their way in America as wage earners and to establish themselves as craftsmen, laborers, or farm hands.

Thus a labor force—part free, part bound—flowed west to the colonies. Why? What were the propelling or attracting forces? What drew or forced these thousands of people from their homes, led them to undertake transatlantic voyages that were both deeply disorienting and dangerous, and deposited them on the far margins of the British world? Why were these workers available for overseas migration? Who arranged their transfer from one continent to another, and why were they distributed so unevenly among the colonies?

---

[1] John Robinson, Thomas Gray, and George Cass, leaving Scarborough in the first week of April 1774, each testified that he was emigrating "as a hired servant." T47/9/121, 122. There is no indication that they were contract workers as described above, chap. 5, n. 17.

7

The Demand

THE forces of attraction were powerful, generated by the magnet of a labor-short American economy, which grew swiftly in certain regions and in certain kinds of activities. The demand, arising from the small-scale labor needs of hundreds of obscure American employers, impressed itself on an elaborate communication mechanism linking entrepreneurs on both sides of the Atlantic, and elicited responses in towns, villages, and farms throughout Britain, particularly in the population center of greater London. No one person or group of people could have been aware of the overall magnitude of these innumerable small-scale needs. For they developed in isolation, were never summarized, and did not feed into or draw from a centralized labor market.

How decentralized and yet how powerful the American labor demand was, how multifarious its sources, is seen most vividly in what was probably the largest labor-consuming industry in America, the manufacture of iron and the products of iron. The labor history of this remarkably well-developed industry illustrates in dilated form the way in which a powerful aggregate labor demand was generated in the American economy—a demand that could be satisfied only by drawing in workers from overseas.

Iron

The colonial American iron industry created no dark satanic mills, no giant infernos, no skylines of smokestacks. There were no Ruhrs or Birminghams in eighteenth-century America. Pittsburgh was a palisaded frontier fort where, in an atmosphere of chronic disorder and violence, Indian traders mingled with hunters of both races, and pioneering families, preparing to move off to wilderness farms, came and went. Yet on the eve of the Revolution the mainland colonies of British North America were producing about one-seventh of the world's iron supply—30,000 tons annually—a proportion the independent United States would not match until after the Civil War. This tonnage was the product of more units of production than existed in Britain, operating under peculiarly difficult conditions.[1]

During the months when the customs officials in Britain were entering the emigrants in the Register, over 250 ironworks were functioning in America—blast furnaces, forges, and slitting and plating mills. They were scattered through the colonies but concentrated in three areas: the highlands region of southwestern New York and northern New Jersey, eastern Pennsylvania (there were 73 ironworks in that colony alone), and northern Maryland along the western shore of Chesapeake Bay. Maryland, developing rapidly in wealth and population, was a major center of iron production. In the early 1750s, 45 percent of all the iron that left America for Britain came from that one colony, and the colony's productive capacity doubled by the outbreak of the Revolution. But an indeterminable portion of the iron exported from Maryland's ports was produced in Pennsylvania, and it seems likely that on the eve of the Revolution Pennsylvania had overtaken Maryland as the leading exporter and probably the leading producer of American iron: in 1773, two-fifths of all American iron exports left from that colony.[2]

The iron-producing centers seem, on Map 7.A, to be clustered and adjacent. One can include more than half of all the American ironworks in an arc swinging in a southwesterly direction from the New Jersey–New York boundary through eastern Pennsylvania to Maryland, with a particularly heavy concentration in the eastern parts of Maryland and Pennsylvania. Yet there was, in fact, no contiguous concentration of ironworks. These plants were built in isolation, adjacent to, often surrounded by, heavily wooded land. For the furnaces and forges were fueled by wood—trees chopped into four-foot lengths and smoldered into charcoal. Just as transportation costs and the need for energy to work the huge bellows and forge hammers made location near running streams necessary, so the fuel needs of the smelting process required immediate access to immense supplies of timber. Each ton of pig iron, it was estimated at the Mount Hope, New Jersey, ironworks just before the Revolution, required fourteen cords

[1] Arthur C. Bining, *British Regulation of the Colonial Iron Industry* (Philadelphia, 1933), pp. 26–30, 122–123, 134.

[2] *Ibid.*, pp. 26, 29, 16; Lester Cappon *et al.*, eds., *Atlas of Early American History* (Princeton, 1976), p. 105; Paul H. Giddens, "Trade and Industry in Colonial Maryland, 1753–1769," *Journal of Economic and Business History*, 4 (1932), 522–524, 538; Arthur C. Bining, *Pennsylvania Iron Manufacture in the Eighteenth Century* (Harrisburg, Pa., 1973), p. 162.

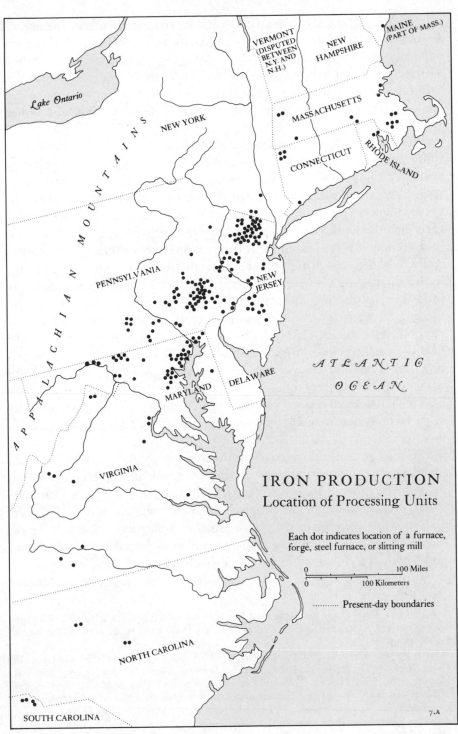

VERMONT
(DISPUTED
BETWEEN
N.Y. AND
N.H.)

MAINE
(PART OF MASS.)

NEW
HAMPSHIRE

Lake Ontario

NEW YORK

MASSACHUSETTS

A P P A L A C H I A N   M O U N T A I N S

CONNECTICUT

RHODE ISLAND

PENNSYLVANIA

NEW
JERSEY

ATLANTIC

OCEAN

DELAWARE

MARYLAND

VIRGINIA

IRON PRODUCTION
Location of Processing Units

Each dot indicates location of a furnace,
forge, steel furnace, or slitting mill

0   100 Miles
0   100 Kilometers

·········· Present-day boundaries

NORTH CAROLINA

7.A

SOUTH CAROLINA

of wood turned into charcoal. If this figure can be generalized, the annual timber consumption by all the late colonial ironworks combined must have approximated half a million cords, which meant the annual deforestation of 15,000 to 20,000 acres of wooded land. A single New Jersey furnace, it was reported just after the Revolution, had exhausted a forest of nearly 20,000 acres in less than fifteen years, "and the works had to be abandoned for lack of wood."[3]

Timber was essential, and available in abundance; but turning timber into charcoal fuel required a large labor force, and that was not abundantly available. Though all aspects of the iron industry were labor intensive— wages accounted for 70 percent of the cost of producing pig iron—the greatest consumption of labor took place in the preparation of charcoal. Over half the work force at any eighteenth-century furnace or forge was in some way involved in charcoal production. Every ironworks employed teams of laborers to fell and trim the trees and haul timber by cart and sledge to the charcoal pits. There colliers stacked the logs in cones and carefully fired them, protecting the smoldering flames against shifting winds and nursing the fires to just the right charring effect. In the most productive season, May through October, the colliers camped out in primitive huts near the smoking cones "to maintain a round-the-clock watch on the operation." In the end carters were needed to haul the nearly pure carbon lumps of charcoal to the tops of the twenty- to thirty-foot-high stone furnaces, into which they were dumped, together with the iron ore dug and blasted by other laborers out of nearby open-face mines, and with limestone used for flux.[4]

So miners, colliers, quarriers, and carters were needed, together with woodcutters, simply to extract the raw material, produce the fuel, and prepare the mixture for smelting. Once in blast, the furnaces had to be closely tended to assure the proper balance of materials. Skilled founders and assistants were needed to draw off the impurities and cast the molten metal into open molds to form large lumps of crude iron—sows and pigs—and into closed molds to make cast-iron ware. At the forges, finers were needed to operate the huge power-driven forge hammers that beat

[3]Theodore W. Kury, "Iron and Settlement: The New York-New Jersey Highlands in the Eighteenth Century," in *Man and Cultural Heritage*, ed. H. J. Walker and W. G. Haag (Baton Rouge, La., 1974), pp. 15, 21.

[4]Paul F. Paskoff, "Labor Productivity and Managerial Efficiency against a Static Technology: The Pennsylvania Iron Industry, 1750–1800," *Journal of Economic History*, 40 (1980), 132–134; James M. Ransom, *Vanishing Ironworks of the Ramapos* (New Brunswick, N.J., 1966), pp. 11–12. For an excellent illustrated description of charcoal manufacture, see Robert J. Sim and Harvey B. Weiss, *Charcoal-Burning in New Jersey* . . . (Trenton, N.J., 1955), pp. 20 ff. On timber consumption, confirming the Mount Hope estimate above, *ibid.*, p. 50. Cf. Joseph E. Walker, *Hopewell Village* (Philadelphia, 1966), pp. 238–249.

the reheated pigs into bars. These semi-finished products were at certain works further refined and made into wire, nails, and wrought-iron goods.

Thus iron was produced—but then the pigs and bars and finished iron goods had to be transported to markets. In a few areas such as northern Maryland the furnaces and forges were located within a mile or two of major water routes like Chesapeake Bay or were adjacent to streams leading directly into such passageways, and there transportation presented few problems. But most of the 250 works were more remote, some completely isolated in the forests, and carters were needed to drive ox teams pulling carts and sledges loaded with as much as 3,000 pounds of iron goods. Where the trails were particularly long, ox farms were established at relay points to provide replacements for exhausted animals. And here and there trains of horses and mules, each bearing a 200-pound pig of iron shaped into a U to fit over its back, could be found moving slowly, single file, through the woods and over the mountains to transfer points along the rivers. So numerous were these carters and packers and shippers of iron goods and so constant their tramping with packhorses, mules, oxen, and carts through "ungraded, stump-filled tracks" that they gradually created, by their everyday routines, permanent networks of roads. And besides the carters there were others, ancillary to the production process, also employed at the ironworks: carpenters, blacksmiths, and cooks. The larger establishments, like those of the Principio Company of northern Maryland, had all the facilities of self-sufficient communities—stores, farms, gristmills and sawmills—manned by shopkeepers, millers, and enough farm hands to produce food sufficient for town-sized populations.[5]

The ironworks had long been semi-autonomous villages. In 1732 William Byrd had toured Virginia's first ironworks—four furnaces built by former Governor Spotswood deep in the Piedmont wilderness—and had discovered that each producing unit required a labor force of approximately 120, many of whom lived on the site with their families. The figure remained more or less constant throughout the century. Only Peter Hasenclever's disastrously overblown venture of 1764—an effort to build a coordinated industrial center of five furnaces and seven forges deep in the Ramapo Mountains of northern New Jersey—required many more: he began by mobilizing a work force of over 500 men and their families. In all, the combined labor force of the 250 ironworks operating in the colonies during the months when the Register was being compiled must have accounted for at least 30,000 workers, a labor force larger by about a third than the combined adult male populations of the five colonial cities. George Wash-

[5]Kury, "Iron and Settlement," p. 21; Bining, *British Regulation*, p. 19; Bining, *Pennsylvania Iron Manufacture*, chap. 2; for the trains of pack animals, *ibid.*, p. 31.

ington, surveying local manpower sources on his retreat through New Jersey to the Delaware, believed, reasonably, that ironworkers formed "a great majority of the people" in the northern and central parts of the colony.[6]

Slaves, especially in the South but not only there, provided much of the unskilled labor. Bought by the iron companies or rented seasonally from their owners, occasionally even given bonuses that approximated wages, they could be found everywhere in the colonial ironworks, chopping wood, hauling logs and iron goods, and working at odd jobs around the furnaces and forges. In some works they took over some of the skilled jobs: foundry-man, forgeman, gutterman, and collier. There was constant recruitment too of freemen, blacks as well as whites, from the local populations. By 1776 certain native families had provided skilled ironworkers for two or three generations. But recruitment from the local, native white populations was always limited. Work in the mines and quarries, in the charcoal pits, furnaces, and forges, was repellent—hot, filthy, at times dangerous. Mining was the worst: "the most laborious employment allotted to worthless ser-vants," William Eddis wrote from Maryland in 1770.

There were very few satisfactions for any of the workers. Isolated in forest encampments dominated by smoldering wood, hot, smoky furnaces, and clanging forge hammers, the work gangs found relief, commonly, in drunken brawls and brutal disorder. As early as 1726 and then again in 1736 Pennsylvania had prohibited the sale of liquor at or near the furnaces, and in 1773 the colony tried to ban fairs in towns that the ironworkers frequented because of the "debauchery, idleness, and drunkenness" that resulted from their visits. While some local farmers and unemployed laborers could at times be drawn into the nonspecialist work at the furnaces—particularly farmers willing to rent out their idle draft animals for winter hauling—and while some specialists could be found in the local populations, workers in every aspect of the industry, from preparing the charcoal fuel and mining the ore to forging the finished products, were in short supply and had to be recruited from abroad.[7]

[6]William Byrd, "A Progress to the Mines in the Year 1732," in *The Prose Works of William Byrd of Westover*, ed. Louis B. Wright (Cambridge, Mass., 1966), p. 348; Ransom, *Vanishing Ironworks*, pp. 17–27; Bining, *British Regulation*, p. 18; Washington to R. H. Lee, April 24, 1777, *Writings of George Washington*, ed. John C. Fitzpatrick (Washington, D.C., 1931–1944), VII, 464. For a shrewd analysis of the labor problem in iron production by the Philadelphia merchant Henry Drinker, who had invested successfully in an ironworks in southern New Jersey, see Thomas M. Doerflinger, ed., "How to Run an Ironworks," *Pennsylvania Magazine of History and Biography*, 108 (1984), 363–366.

[7]Michael W. Robbins, "The Principio Company: Ironmaking in Colonial Maryland, 1720–1781" (Ph.D. diss., George Washington Univ., 1972), pp. 110–111; Bining, *Pennsylvania Iron Manufacture*, pp. 100–102, 28–29, 30; Kury, "Iron and Settlement," p. 15; William Eddis, *Letters from America*, ed. Aubrey C. Land (Cambridge, Mass., 1969), p. 43. For details on the contracting of iron-ore carting during the winter months, see *Archives of the State of New Jersey*, 1st ser., 28 (1916), 259. Advertise-

This had been so from the industry's earliest years. In 1714 Spotswood had initiated the importation of skilled German ironworkers. With the help of Baron von Graffenried, who had founded a settlement of Swiss and Germans in North Carolina, he rescued a group of about 42 German ironworkers and their families stranded in London, contracted with them for three years of labor in the ironworks he planned, and established them in a tiny palisaded log-cabin settlement he called Germanna, at the edge of Virginia's northern frontier. These Germans, part of the first sizable exodus from the upper Rhine through Rotterdam and England to America, had been recruited for other purposes by the "chief miner" to Queen Anne; they came, as many other such workers would come, from the ancient ironworking district of Nassau-Siegen, forty-five miles east of the Rhine. What these Siegenlanders, living "very miserably . . . thirty miles from any inhabitants," made of life in the primitive world of frontier Virginia—so different from the populous, elaborately institutionalized Rhineland communities they had lived in before—we will never know. But before they left Germanna for land of their own even deeper in the Virginia frontier, they established the ironworks Spotswood wanted; and they were soon followed by others. Alsatians and then a variety of other Rhinelanders took over at Germanna in 1717, and the tradition was established.[8]

In the decades that followed, workers were imported from all over central and southwestern Germany, and especially from Nassau-Siegen, to help run the ironworks that sprang up in the forests between New England and North Carolina. Preferred over other available ironworkers for their experience, diligence, and skill, they could be found at every new ironworking center in the expanding frontier—in the Shenandoah Valley in the thirties and forties, in the foothills of the Alleghenies in the fifties, in the New Jersey Highlands in the sixties. In 1764 Hasenclever, who himself had worked in a steel mill in Westphalia as a boy, sent his "535 persons . . . miners, founders, forgemen, colliers, carpenters, masons, and labourers, with their wives and children" direct from Germany to the unsettled New Jersey Highlands, where at the outbreak of the Revolution they could still be found, speaking very little English, working at the furnaces and forges that remained, and farming in areas where the ironworks, having devastated the forests, had given way to marginal agriculture. Germans provided

ments for ironworkers, skilled and semiskilled, are commonly found in the colonial newspapers: e.g., citations in Richard B. Morris, *Government and Labor in Early America* (New York, 1946), p. 40 n. The miners' violence and debauchery were famous from the earliest years (Byrd, "Progress to the Mines," p. 354) and generated fearful legends. One, "The Legend of the Hounds," tells of a drunken, sadistic ironmaster who drove his hounds, after a frustrating day of hunting, one by one into the blazing mouth of his furnace, and shortly thereafter died of fright in his sleep. Bining, *Pennsylvania Iron Manufacture*, pp. 34–35.
[8] Elizabeth C. D. Vann and Margaret C. D. Dixon, *Virginia's First German Colony* (Richmond, Va., 1961), pp. 9–29; John W. Wayland, *Germanna . . . 1714–1956* (Staunton, Va., 1956), pp. 10–21.

unskilled labor elsewhere too. In 1770 Mark Bird, a hustling second-generation Pennsylvania ironmaster, in order to man his ambitious Hopewell
Furnace in Berks County, bought five whole families of Germans—5 men,
5 women, and 6 children—and settled them in log cabins on company land
where they were to work off the purchase price of their 7-year indentures
(worth from £22 to £50 each) by chopping cordwood at the rate of 22 pence
a cord. Occasionally individual faces emerge from the crowd. In April 1774
a "German servant man named Gottlieb Fuhrman," a migrant miner from
Eisleben, Saxony, ran away from his master in southern Pennsylvania; he
was described as "5 feet 7 or 8 inches high, well set, and one of his little
fingers is rendered useless by a shot, wherefore he hides it as much as he
can . . . a great lover of strong liquor and a great smoker of tobacco and
snufftaker."[9]

The Germans were prominent in the work force at the many ironworks, but workers from elsewhere were recruited too—Welsh miners,
Scotch-Irish workers of all kinds, who followed the Germans in Pennsylvania and Virginia, and above all English. Hasenclever imported English
ironworkers as well as German, and Thomas Penn in 1764 sent over to his
province a contingent of experienced English colliers to teach the colonists
economical ways of producing charcoal. The labor force at many of the
iron-producing communities was consequently multi-ethnic and polyglot,
and they worked in a variety of statuses. There were slaves almost everywhere; there were transported convicts working off their commuted death
sentences by seven or fourteen years of servitude; there were indentured
servants; and there were free workers hired by the year or month or day,
or paid at a piece rate for the work they accomplished in the furnaces,
forges, and pits. Most numerous were the unfree: the slaves, convicts, and
indentured servants, all of whom could be bought, most of whom were
drawn from overseas.[10] Their purchase, in an industry in which labor was
the most expensive and most problematic element and could be acquired
in a confusing variety of forms, was the subject of the most careful calculations by the owners and managers. They weighed the advantages of free

[9]Kathleen Bruce, *Virginia Iron Manufacture in the Slave Era* (New York, 1930), p. 21; Ransom,
Vanishing Ironworks, pp. 17–27; Charles S. Boyer, *Early Forges and Furnaces in New Jersey* (Philadelphia, 1931), pp. 12–15; Samuel McKee, Jr., "Indentured Servitude in Colonial New York," New York
State Historical Association, *Quarterly Journal*, 12 (1931), 156; Cheesman A. Herrick, *White Servitude
in Pennsylvania* (Philadelphia, 1926), pp. 212–213. The advertisement to recover the runaway Fuhrman appeared on Sept. 25, 1774, in *Dunlap's Pennsylvania Packet, or, the General Advertiser* and the
next day in German in the *Wöchentliche Pennsylvanische Staatsbote*. For Hasenclever's own account
of his efforts to establish the ironworks complex, his controversy with the company's trustees, and
his recruitment of a labor force (which proved to be "refractory"), see his pamphlet, *The Remarkable
Case of Peter Hasenclever, Merchant* (London, 1773).
[10]Kury, "Iron and Settlement," p. 18; Bining, *Pennsylvania Iron Manufacture*, p. 95, chap. 6;
Frederick H. Schmidt, "British Convict Servant Labor in Colonial Virginia" (Ph.D. diss., College
of William and Mary, 1976), pp. 115, 160, 186–193.

workers vs. bond, slaves vs. indentured servants, contract laborers vs. piece workers. The factors involved were complicated, the balance of judgment often delicate, and an error could be disastrous.

So Charles Carroll of Carrollton, a part owner of the important Baltimore Company ironworks, wrote his partners in early December 1773 that the only solution to the labor problem was to get rid of most of the free wage laborers ("hirelings") and substitute for them "35 or 40 young, healthy and stout country born negroes." By his reckoning the lost annual income from the capital required to buy these slaves would be about two-thirds of the annual cost of the free workers' wages. And there would be other good results: "The business would be carried on with more alacrity and fewer disappointments," the equity invested in the slaves would be redeemable if the partners decided to sell out, and they would have eliminated the annoying problem of the company's clerks fobbing off on them as wage laborers their own personal servants. In the end the decision was a compromise: "to purchase five negroes and five white servants for the current year, and . . . as many more for the next year." But when the company's manager, Clement Brooks, heard of this decision he raised serious questions. Ten new white servants acquired from overseas over a two-year period was reasonable enough, he wrote the owners; ten indentees were "as many of that sort as will be necessary or proper to have at a time." But together with only ten new slaves, they would not be able to handle all the work, and in the end the company would have to turn again to local wage laborers. He recommended that a total of thirty slaves be acquired over a six-year period and all dependence on free wage labor be eliminated. But he acknowledged that his calculations were unreliable; he was not certain he was right. Perhaps "it would be more advisable to go on slow than to run any risk with so many green hands at a time—I have already bought five convicts for laborers and [for] a shoemaker." The bill for these convicts had come to £129 10s local currency, a sum he felt he could cover from current funds.[11]

A tiny episode, this transaction, in a multitude of small-scale labor acquisitions which together account for a significant, but indeterminable, part of the flow of emigrants from Britain to America. Wherever one turns there are signs of migrations from overseas to this one industry. They are found in runaway ads (to recover, for example, an Irishman, McGork, late of England, a talkative drunken furnaceman last seen in November 1774 fleeing north from Pennsylvania); in account books and business letters that record the efforts to provide for the labor needs of individual enterprises; in visitors' accounts of the works.[12] The emigration Register of 1773–1776

[11]Charles Carroll to [Company], Dec. 8, 1773, and Clement Brooks to [Company], Feb. 4, 1774, Carroll-Maccubbin Papers, box 7.

[12]*Pennsylvania Gazette,* Nov. 23, 1774; see also, for runaway ironworkers, *Virginia Gazette* (Pinkney), Jan. 6, 1776; *Maryland Journal, and the Baltimore Advertiser,* May 28, 1774; *Pennsylvania*

lists 57 emigrants whose occupations qualified them for specialized work in the iron industry: 35 were foundrymen, 10 were nailers and wire drawers, 5 were miners, 4 forgemen. Drawn not only from London and the Home Counties (18 out of 57) but from all over Britain, including the Midlands, Scotland, and Wales, they traveled mainly to the colonies with the highest concentration of ironworks: 33 went to Maryland, 10 to Pennsylvania, 8 to Virginia. These are minimal figures. Undoubtedly many more of the registered emigrants—how many more it is impossible to tell—ended up working in some capacity in the iron industry.

Construction

The labor demand of the scattered iron industry was remarkable in its overall magnitude and in the distinctiveness of some of the skills it sought to recruit. The only other industry comparable in size was shipbuilding. In the late colonial period the mainland colonies were producing approximately four hundred ocean-going vessels a year, a quarter of which, worth close to £100,000 exclusive of fittings, were sold to Britain. Almost a third of all British-owned vessels were built in the colonies.[13] But it is impossible to estimate the number of workers employed in shipbuilding or the degree to which it specifically functioned as a magnet to overseas labor. Master shipwrights, to be sure, like other master craftsmen, imported both skilled and unskilled workers from overseas, even in Charleston, where slaves probably comprised over half the labor force in shipbuilding. But shipbuilding was even more decentralized than iron production. While the major centers were in Massachusetts and New Hampshire, and, to the south of New England, in Pennsylvania, Maryland, and Virginia, there was scarcely a port town from the Penobscot to the Savannah in which shipbuilding of some sort was not under way at some time of the year. And further, most of the skills involved in shipbuilding were easily transferable to other kinds of work. Ship carpenters easily became house builders, and the many specialist craftsmen whose skills were also needed

---

Gazette, Jan. 5, 1774, Jan. 25, 1775; *Dunlap's Pennsylvania Packet, or, the General Advertiser,* Feb. 14, 1774. For typical runs of business records that involve labor recruitment for individuals and firms of many needs, including manning ironworks, see Ridgely Papers and Carroll-Maccubbin Papers.
[13]James F. Shepherd and Gary M. Walton, *Shipping, Maritime Trade, and the Economic Development of Colonial North America* (Cambridge, Eng., 1972), pp. 242, 244 n. There was of course a far larger number of ships built for local use. Shipyards in Virginia, for example, located in seventeen places along the river and coastlines from Alexandria to Norfolk, were building at least thirty vessels a year between 1763 and 1774, a total of 360 in all, with a total tonnage of 25,627. How many workmen of all kinds were employed in this ship production is not known. William M. Kelso, "Shipbuilding in Virginia, 1763–1774," *Records of the Columbia Historical Society of Washington, D.C.* [48] (1971–1972), 1–13.

—joiners, carvers, cabinetmakers, painters, smiths, braziers, coopers, turners—were artisans generally employed in the colonies' booming construction industry.[14]

It is that most inclusive industry, building—ubiquitous and elemental —that accounts for much of the impetus behind the recruitment of artisans from abroad. Wherever new lands were being opened to settlement and labor was in short supply and wherever established communities and individual properties were being multiplied, enlarged, and embellished, construction workers of all kinds were needed—carpenters, joiners, masons, bricklayers, glaziers, housewrights, millwrights, blacksmiths—and they were needed in numbers that far exceeded the local labor supplies. Unskilled laborers too were in short supply, especially those young enough and intelligent enough to adapt easily to a variety of demands, and experienced farmers and farm hands were also sought. But in the labor-short areas of most rapid land settlement the most urgent demand was for skilled and semiskilled artisans, including those useful in construction work—the building of houses, barns, mills, churches, bridges, fences, furniture, wagons. It is that demand that is most clearly reflected in the shiploads of indentured servants that landed week after week and month after month in the port towns of the mainland colonies.

The connections can clearly be made between the escalating need for artisans and the inflow of indentured servants. In some regions the demand was weak. New England, the most mature region demographically and the least buoyant economically, was generating its own "surplus" population and had little attraction for workers in Britain. New York's growth was unusually slow.[15] And in the far north and far south—Canada, Nova Scotia, the Carolinas, Georgia, and the Floridas—the needs were less sophisticated, mainly for settlers to stake out the land and establish themselves on it. It was in the region between the Hudson and the Carolinas—where settlement was expanding most rapidly into the open backcountry and where established communities were growing quickly and private properties were being rapidly improved—that the need for artisans skilled in any kind of construction work was greatest, and it was there, consequently, that indentured servitude was most common.

Governor Sharpe of Maryland was probably correct when he reported in 1756 that there were more indentured servants in Maryland and Pennsylvania than in all the other colonies combined; there were in fact almost 9,000 in Maryland when Sharpe wrote, approximately 6 percent of the colony's total population. And both demand and supply seemed to rise constantly, espe-

[14]Joseph A. Goldenberg, *Shipbuilding in Colonial America* (Charlottesville, Va., 1976), pp. 99, 67, and chaps. 4 and 6 generally; Carl Bridenbaugh, *The Colonial Craftsman* (New York, 1950), p. 94.
[15]Charles M. Haar, "White Indentured Servants in Colonial New York," *Americana*, 34 (1940), 378–379. See above, Table 5.11.

cially after 1765 and particularly in Maryland, where there was a building boom in the early 1770s.[16] Various estimates of the numbers of incoming indentees were made in the 1770s: one well-informed merchant guessed that 6,000 were sold in Baltimore alone in 1773–1774; according to another, there were more servant arrivals in Philadelphia in 1772–1773 than in any one year since the founding of the colony; still another said that in the first four months of 1774 between 1,000 and 1,100 arrived in Baltimore alone. No one in fact knew precisely how many servants were arriving, being sold, and being absorbed into the colonial communities. But everyone knew that, in this central area of mainland North America, as Governor Sharpe put it, "the people cannot well manage their business without their assistance."[17]

The bulk of the demand arose, not principally in the few major towns, but in the innumerable country villages of Pennsylvania, Maryland, and Virginia, in the crossroads hamlets, ferry stations, and farming centers that were multiplying in the rapidly growing central and backcountry territories. Overnight, it seemed, as settlement spread westward from the tidewater, cattle and Indian trails—lonely pathways across the fields and through the woods—became well-traveled roads. And the few arterial routes, leading west from the tidewater and south down the valleys of western Pennsylvania and Maryland into the Virginia Piedmont and the Shenandoah Valley, became highways over whose rock-strewn, ungraded surfaces increasing numbers of wagons and carts rumbled and clattered and from which ancillary networks of trails and by-roads radiated out into the countryside. In Pennsylvania, 2 new counties and 25 new towns, all in the central and western areas, were founded between 1761 and 1775. In western Maryland, which was a single county, Frederick, four north-south river valleys served as convenient passageways for the migrating Pennsylvanians, and at the same time the region proved a magnet to tidewater families moving west from Maryland's well-settled east in search of fresh land. Frederick County's population rose from 13,800 to 30,000 in the decade before the Revolution; 4 substantial towns were added to the 1 that had existed before, and 11 new religious communities appeared—5 Lutheran, 3 Reformed, 2 Methodist, and 1 Moravian. And in Virginia between 1760 and 1776, 12 new counties were added, not in the Tidewater but in the Piedmont (5), in the Shenandoah Valley (3), and in the near trans-Allegheny west (4).[18]

[16]Gov. Horatio Sharpe to Cecilius Calvert, Annapolis, Aug. 21, 1756, *Archives of Maryland*, [VI] (1888), 467; Charles A. Barker, *The Background of the Revolution in Maryland* (New Haven, 1940), p. 3; David C. Skaggs, *Roots of Maryland Democracy, 1753–1776* (Westport, Conn., 1973), p. 59.
[17]George Woolsey to James Ford, n.d. [probably Dec. 1774], Woolsey and Salmon Letterbook; Grace H. Larsen, "Profile of a Colonial Merchant: Thomas Clifford of Pre-Revolutionary Philadelphia" (Ph.D. diss., Columbia Univ., 1955), p. 120; James Cheston to Stevenson, Randolph, & Cheston, Baltimore, April 30, 1774, Cheston Letterbooks; Sharpe to Calvert, Aug. 21, 1756.
[18]James T. Lemon, *The Best Poor Man's Country* (Baltimore, 1972), pp. 123, 124; Lee Shai Weissbach,

Throughout this huge expanse between New York and North Carolina, isolated frontier homesteads became well-cultivated farms and small plantations; established plantations and surplus-producing farms grew prosperous, expanded, and were embellished; shops and church buildings multiplied at settlement clusters; and remote ferry landings—makeshift docks so isolated that boatmen had to be summoned by smoke signals—were enlarged first into serviceable shelters and then into taverns and inns around which riverside villages formed. And as all this growth mounted, the need became acute to build more of everything—houses, barns, mills, churches, field shelters, slave quarters, wagons, furniture—and somehow to locate and engage the artisans necessary for all this work.

The correspondence of the established inhabitants of this mid-region of North America is full of references to the search for labor and the importation of servants from overseas. John Augustine Washington, George's brother, wrote the London merchant James Russell in August 1774 that he had been waiting for two years "for a couple of tradesmen," but when one of Russell's shiploads of indentured servants finally arrived, Washington found that his neighbors, the Turbervilles, were given priority in the choice of the available servants and took precisely the "compleat joiner" that Washington himself needed most. He was left, as a consequence, with a Swiss who "called himself a carpenter" and "a man that called himself a tailor." He hoped he would be charged only rock-bottom prices for such workmen as these, and urged Russell to send him, by the next ship if possible, "a compleat cabinet joiner." But George Turberville had his troubles too. He was delighted with his new artisan-servant—"an exceeding orderly man and a good workman"; unfortunately, however, the new employee, who obviously knew his value in the situation, decided that he could not work with the poor tools available. Turberville was obliged to write posthaste to London to get the special equipment the workman said he needed.[19]

"The Peopling of Western Maryland" (unpublished survey report, Harvard Univ., 1977); Barker, *Background . . . in Maryland*, pp. 5–10; Morgan P. Robinson, *Virginia Counties . . .*, Virginia State Library, *Bulletin*, no. 9 (Richmond, Va., 1916), pp. 135, 140, 144–145.

[19] John Augustine Washington to James Russell, Bushville, Va., Aug. 16, 1774, and George Turberville to Russell, March 21, 1774, Russell Papers. The Turbervilles' troubles with their prize joiner were minor next to other difficulties they had with their servants. Five of them, in the first or second years of their indentures—a farmer, a carpenter, a gardener, a blacksmith (convict), and a joiner —ran away on July 9, 1775. The four nonconvicts among them had arrived on two voyages of the *Carolina* from London, both entered in the Register. John Turberville's elaborate advertisements to recover the runaways describe the five in great detail ("a swarthy complexion, 37 years of age, 5 feet 8 inches high, wears his own dark hair tied behind in a club, is a little pitted with the smallpox, has lost two of his fore teeth, and is a very proud fellow"; "slim made, dark hair, near-sighted, and his eyes generally inflamed," etc.). The information in the advertisements agrees almost perfectly with the shipboard identifications of the four and gives a vivid reality to the abstract listing in the Register. Turberville wanted the runaways returned either to himself or to his neighbor, John A. Washington. *Virginia Gazette* (Purdie), July 28, 1775, repeated Aug. 11 and 18.

Specific skills, some of them quite refined, were of vital importance in the expanding economy—a miner could not build a sideboard nor a tailor construct a bridge—and they were mentioned again and again by would-be purchasers. "There is a shoemaker on board," James Cheston, an importer of servants, wrote from Baltimore to one customer, "but on looking over my memorandums I find I have promised one to Mr. Gittings here, who spoke to me for one several months ago. There was not a carpenter among them; if any should come in [the] next ship, I believe you are the first now that has bespoke any, and I think it probable that you will not be disappointed." Another of Cheston's customers sought to buy "a joiner," or a "cart wheel wright . . . but a joyner would sute best." Still another wrote Cheston, after hearing of a ship arrival, that he was sending an agent "to see if you have any coopers." And yet another requested not merely a weaver but "a man who can weave both woolen and linnen, but certainly can weave woolen well, especially the coarser sorts of kerseys or serge, as the weaving [of] linnen is much easier acquired than the other." The Ridgelys of "Northampton" in Baltimore County, Maryland, recorded their servants' official trades and real capacities with meticulous care. The nuances in their occupational descriptions are subtle. They described one worker as both "a carpenter & sawier"; another, they recorded, could "work at black or white smiths business but not compleat at either"; another was both a [horse] "coller and harness maker." And there were others at "Northampton" with rather esoteric crafts and trades, all carefully recorded: a "papper maker," a "horse jockey & keeper of rase horses," a tinman, and a workman who was both a "stoneclour [cutter, breaker] and nailer."[20]

Everywhere the building craftsmen and clothing makers were in great demand. Philip Fendell, on the upper Potomac, told Russell in London that "the more weavers, shoemakers, tailors, joiners, carpenters, bricklayers and farmers, and the fewer women," he sent, "the better." Harry Piper, a merchant's agent in Alexandria, Virginia, wrote his principals in Whitehaven, Cumberland, who were in touch with labor markets throughout northern Britain and eastern Ireland, that more carpenters were needed. He did not need to place special orders for them; they could always be sold, or if free, placed, in the colonies. His letters reflect the aggregate of such individual needs as that of Joseph Mullan, of Patuxent, Maryland, who ordered, for immediate delivery (he was naïvely optimistic), "a good

[20]Cheston to Thomas Smyth, Baltimore, April 3, 1773, Cheston Letterbooks; Richard Gresham to Cheston, May 8, 1771, William Ringgold to Cheston, Chestertown, June 16, 1773, John Chapple to Cheston, Queen Anne County, Nov. 28, 1774, all in Cheston Incoming Letters. For the Ridgelys' servants at "Northampton," see "Description of White Servants taken January 1772" (includes 1773 and 1774), Ridgely Papers, box 14. For a general account of this listing, see William D. Hoyt, Jr., "The White Servants at 'Northampton,' 1772–74," *Maryland Historical Magazine*, 33 (1938), 126–33.

house carpenter . . . indented for four years," but only if he was "a sober orderly fellow"—"such a one," he assured Russell, "will be very happy with me."

Many employers had to provide special inducements to get what they wanted and often had to accept compromises. Thomas Reeder declared himself willing to tip anyone a guinea who could help him find "a servant woman this fall" to assist in "cooking, washing, etc"; he preferred "a middle aged person and under indenture for four years." Earlier, John Chisholm, in Anne Arundel County, Maryland, had asked his brother in Scotland to get him a number of workmen, including a shoemaker and a blacksmith, but when a year went by with no response, he had to satisfy himself with "two seven-years servants, one of them as he says a good weaver, the other a countryman and understands farming." John Lucas, of Queentree, Patuxent, Maryland, did manage to get the maidservant he ordered, but then discovered that she came with a husband. After some consideration Lucas decided "it would be cruel to part them," and so bought the husband too; he could always find use for another hand.[21]

In the mid-colonial region the overall need to recruit workers of all kinds from overseas, particularly skilled and semiskilled craftsmen purchasable as indentured servants, was continuous, though in local areas, as the economy dipped and rose and supply and demand fluctuated, there were slack periods and even stoppages. The peopling of the Shenandoah Valley, for example, had been remarkably swift. Beginning in significant numbers only in the 1730s, migrants moving south from western Pennsylvania and Maryland and west from the Virginia Piedmont had flooded into the valley to create a population of approximately forty thousand by 1775, 5 percent of whom were slaves, the rest divided in almost equal parts among English, Scotch-Irish, and Germans. In the most intense period of immigration and settlement, 1764–1770, as the valley emerged from its frontier phase, there was an acute shortage of skilled and semiskilled artisans as well as of farm hands. But suppliers had responded so efficiently that by 1774 demand had ceased. By then servants were abundant, and many of the farmers were in debt for the purchases of servants they had already made.[22]

---

[21]Philip Fendell to Russell, Potomack, Md., Aug. 26, 1774, Russell Papers (cf. Aug. 13: "Tradesmen and farmers will answer best, next to them common laborers, the fewer women the better"); Harry Piper to Dixon and Littledale, Alexandria, Va., Sept. 23, 1769, Piper Letterbook; Joseph Mullan to Russell, June 25, 1774, and Thomas A. Reeder to Russell, St. Mary's County, Maryland, Aug. 5, 1774, Russell Papers; John Chisholm to James Chisholm, Elk-Ridge Furnace, Anne Arundel Co., Md., Aug. 16, 1759, Chisholm Letters; John Lucas to Russell, Queentree, Patuxent, Md., April 4, June 14, Aug. 17, 1775, Russell Papers.

[22]Robert D. Mitchell, *Commercialism and Frontier: Perspectives on the Early Shenandoah Valley* (Charlottesville, Va., 1977), pp. 95, 96, 100, 125; John R. Commons *et al.*, eds., *A Documentary History of American Industrial Society* ([1910–1911], New York, 1958), II, 287.

Qualities and Deficiencies

The qualities the colonists sought in the servants they hired were clearly stated; so too were the deficiencies they sought to avoid. Though occasionally women servants were specifically asked for, to work as household help, spinners, or weavers, in general they were not desired, and in fact were so commonly avoided by purchasers of indentured labor that at times the price of their indentures fell to the point where sellers could not recover the cost of transportation. Redemptioners too were avoided where possible, since they had the legal option of searching for relatives, friends, or patrons who would pay off their transportation debts and thus free them from all obligation to work as bonded servants—and they had to be allowed time to carry on such negotiations. In general, men over 35 were considered too old for most kinds of work, and agents were told not to send over "broken" tradesmen—that is, bankrupts or obvious incompetents.[23]

The most sought-after indentured servants were first of all skilled artisans, especially those trained in construction trades; then adaptable and "likely" (that is, promising or manifestly competent) teenage boys, even if untrained; then experienced farmers and farm hands; and finally energetic and physically capable laborers—more or less in that order. The length of indenture counted too: five-year contracts were preferred to four-year and seven-year to both, provided the servants involved were tractable, respectable, and decent—which was a continuing problem, since most of the adult seven-year indentees were convicts.[24]

It is a measure of the colonists' need for extended labor commitments that they were generally willing to take on as servants convicted felons whose sentences, many of them death sentences, had been commuted to banishment in the colonies. Where labor needs were greatest, the distinction between "free" indentees and transported criminals tended to fade. They had much in common. Both were committed to total service during the time of their bondage; convicts too had usable skills; and many of the convicts were respectable poor who had fallen afoul of eighteenth-century criminal laws.[25] Few of the transportees, in fact, were professional or habit-

---

[23]". . . with the freedom dues, the women are dearer than they can be hired for in the country" —Piper to Dixon and Littledale, Sept. 10, 1768, Piper Letterbook; ". . . never take any redemptioners again"—Woolsey to Thomas McCabe, April 10, 1775, Woolsey and Salmon Letterbook; Herrick, *White Servitude*, p. 199. For a study of the low demand for women servants in Pennsylvania, see Sharon V. Salinger, " 'Send No More Women': Female Servants in Eighteenth-Century Philadelphia," *Pennsylvania Magazine of History and Biography*, 107 (1983), 29–48.

[24]David W. Galenson, *White Servitude in Colonial America: An Economic Analysis* (Cambridge, Eng., 1981), pp. 102–113.

[25]"Transportation" was banishment, exile, for at least seven years, and not in itself a commitment

ual criminals, however much they may have been debased by squalor and prison life—which did not mean that they had ever been desired in the colonies. Despite the length of their obligatory servitude, they had never been preferred to ordinary indentured servants. In 1670 the Virginia Assembly had prohibited the importation of *"jaile birds* or such others who for notorious offences have deserved to dye in England" because of "the danger which apparently threatens us from the barbarous designs and felonious practices of such wicked villains," and in 1676 and repeatedly thereafter Maryland had passed similar laws. A survey of 1697 revealed that only the Leeward Islands, of all the British colonies in America, would willingly receive convicts, but they continued to arrive despite some colonists' resistance, which increased as the gentility of life in the seaboard communities rose. For the interest of merchants who saw profits in the convict trade was growing, as was the market for this kind of labor.

By 1700 the home government was disallowing colonial laws prohibiting the importation of convicts, and then in 1717 Parliament, in a comprehensive enactment, put the entire business on a statutory basis. Existing punishments for felony, the statute explained, had failed to deter criminals, and furthermore "in many of His Majesty's colonies and plantations in America there is a great want of servants, who by their labour and industry might be the means of improving and making the said colonies and plantations more useful to this nation." The courts were therefore authorized to use seven-year terms of transportation to the colonies for purposes of labor as a punishment for the whole range of noncapital felonious offenses and, with the royal consent, to commute capital punishment to the same sen-

---

to labor. "Many convicts who had money," the last of the convict contractors testified, "bought off their servitude, and their punishment was only banishment for the term prescribed." *Journals of the House of Commons,* XXXVII (Nov. 26, 1778, to Aug. 24, 1780), 310. In most cases, however, penal servitude naturally followed, since the convicts were destitute and hence were sold for their transportation costs, to the considerable profit of the merchants who contracted to dispose of them. Occasionally, though, a convict appeared with some property or cash and sought to buy out all or part of his labor contract—and so remain free, as long as he did not return to Britain during his term of banishment. (If he did return prematurely, he could be executed forthwith.) Such negotiations often failed, since the jailers and ship captains systematically fleeced the convicts, who were quite helpless. Thus Stevenson and Randolph in Bristol, in dispatching a group of convicts to James Cheston in Chestertown, Md., wrote (Sept. 25, 1773): "John Hellery had a silver watch, which we now send you and think you had best sell it and take off a proportion of his time of servitude, as also from William Pinton, as they ought to reap ye benefit of their money, which we have reason to think ye captains have sometimes appropriated to their own use, or even, should they carry it into ye country, it becomes ye property of those who buy them; all therefore we mean by it is to serve these ignorant people, as we wish to prevent their being imposed on." And again two days later: "The bearer, William Stone, having paid us in part for his passage (and freedom) in our ship Isabella, we beg you will take off a proportionable part of his time for which he was sentenced to serve, £7 being the money we received, for which deduct 8/ [shillings] being so much deficient in weight." Cheston Incoming Letters. For the main characteristics of the convict trade between 1718 and 1775, see A. Roger Ekirch, "Bound for America: A Profile of British Convicts Transported to the Colonies, 1718–1775," *William and Mary Quarterly,* 3d ser., 42 (1985), 185–200.

tence for fourteen years or in some cases for life. Colonial assemblies were forbidden to obstruct the importation of criminals, and the system was actively promoted by government subsidies to merchants who contracted to receive the felons from the jails, transport them, and sell them in the colonies.[26]

Energetic merchants seized this enhanced opportunity for profit, and the flow of transported felons rose rapidly. The contractors, led by a London merchant with rather dubious connections, Jonathan Forward, quickly involved themselves in defeating all attempts by the colonists to prohibit, or inhibit, the dumping of convicts.[27] Virginia and Maryland, the colonies most affected, continued to struggle against the trade despite the fact that their own planters supported it by buying the convicts when they were offered for sale. In 1722 and 1723, as the magnitude of the problem became clear, both of the Chesapeake colonies passed laws to reduce the dangers the felons represented. They legislated that the felons be kept in bondage as long as possible and not be freed prematurely to prey upon the community; that they be kept on board ship until sold; and that their owners at each stage become legally responsible for their good behavior. But these enactments were disallowed in England as constituting "a prohibition of any convicts being imported," and local regulations of similar intent also came under fire. The colonists, eager for labor but fearful of the social consequences of continued importation of convicts, were caught in a dilemma. In the early 1720s the Virginia legislature debated a plan that would reconcile Britain's policy and Virginia's social welfare by accepting the convicts but then segregating them all in a single county—a county that would become, in effect, a penal camp.[28]

For thoughtful Americans concerned with the character of American society, the banishment of convicts to America was an abomination,[29] and for those with an eye for macabre humor it was ludicrous. The most famous

[26]William W. Hening, ed., *The Statutes at Large . . . of Virginia . . .* (New York, 1823), II, 510; Basil Sollers, "Transported Convict Laborers in Maryland during the Colonial Period," *Maryland Historical Magazine,* 2 (1907), 22–25; Abbot E. Smith, *Colonists in Bondage* (Chapel Hill, N.C., 1947), pp. 111–112, and chap. 6 generally; 4 Geo. II, c. 11; Leonard W. Labaree, ed., *Royal Instructions to British Colonial Governors, 1670–1776* (New York, 1935), II, 673–675.
[27]For Forward's connection with the celebrated master criminal Jonathan Wild and their joint racketeering in the convict trade to America, see Gerald Howson, *Thief-Taker General: The Rise and Fall of Jonathan Wild* (London, 1970), pp. 168–169.
[28]Sollers, "Transported Convict Laborers," pp. 28–29; Smith, *Colonists in Bondage,* pp. 119–122; Fairfax Harrison, "When the Convicts Came," *Virginia Magazine of History and Biography,* 30 (1922), 250–260; Hugh Jones, *The Present State of Virginia . . .* [1724], ed. Richard L. Morton (Chapel Hill, N.C., 1956), p. 135 (cf. pp. 87–88). The government's reasoning in barring restrictions on the convict trade was explained by the counsel to the Board of Trade, Richard West: George Chalmers, *Opinions of Eminent Lawyers on Various Points of English Jurisprudence . . .,* American ed. (Burlington [Vt.], 1858), pp. 436–438.
[29]William Livingston, *The Independent Reflector . . .* [1752–53], ed. Milton M. Klein (Cambridge, Mass., 1963), No. 16.

comment on the problem was Franklin's proposal—published after a crime wave, perpetrated in Virginia, Maryland, and Pennsylvania chiefly by convict servants, was luridly reported in the press—that the colonies should be authorized to "transport" their rattlesnakes to Britain in exchange for "the human *serpents* sent us by the mother country." Later, in 1766, when Parliament authorized transportation from Scotland as well as from England, Franklin drafted a petition to Parliament to grant the colonists an "equitable" arrangement, by allowing them to transport *their* felons to Scotland in exchange for the Scotch convicts sent out to the colonies.[30] But neither Franklin's lampoons nor the more prosaic, and indignant, objections that other Americans expressed succeeded in reversing the government's policy. Though regulation and taxing of the trade by the colonies were permitted, and though Pennsylvania, in defiance of Parliament, managed to block the trade entirely for a time by legislation that was not submitted to England for confirmation, the system of sending to America what Cecilius Calvert in 1755 called "the scum and dregs" of the English people survived legally and succeeded economically—indeed flourished, so great was the need for cheap labor. In the year Calvert wrote, convicts constituted 3.6 percent of the total adult white population of Maryland; the colony contained a third as many convicts as indentured and free servants. The system was so successful, in fact, that in 1772 the British government ended the subsidy to the contractors as unnecessary; the merchants seldom lacked buyers and could profit well enough without government subventions.[31]

The drawbacks of these workers were obvious. The felons were more likely than ordinary servants to be disease-ridden, intractable, and determined to escape from their bondage, and their "felonious practices" continued to threaten the peace and security of law-abiding Americans. But the controlling fact was simply that transported convicts too had skills, or if not

[30] *Papers of Benjamin Franklin*, ed. Leonard W. Labaree *et al.* (New Haven, 1959–   ), IV, 131–133; XIII, 240–242.

[31] *Ibid.*, IV, 132 n.; Chalmers, *Opinions of Eminent Lawyers*, pp. 333–336; Sollers, "Transported Convict Laborers," pp. 35, 45; Smith, *Colonists in Bondage*, p. 115. There were constant rumors in the late colonial period, referred to repeatedly in merchants' correspondences and in the British newspapers, that the colonies chiefly involved had succeeded in blocking the importation of convicts. The Stevenson, Randolph, & Cheston firm went to great lengths to protest and evade Maryland's law (1769) requiring the local registration of the criminals' convictions, thus making it more difficult for them to be absorbed into the general population of indentured servants and perhaps weakening sales (Cheston to [Stevenson, Randolph and Cheston], Jan. 1, [1771], Cheston Letterbooks; Notarized Protest against the Act, Legal Papers, boxes 8 and 18, Cheston-Galloway Papers). Piper believed convicts were prohibited in Philadelphia (to Dixon and Littledale, Feb. 9, 1768, Piper Letterbook). In England the *York Courant* first reported (Aug. 17, 1773) that Virginia had prohibited the trade and that Maryland and Pennsylvania would follow, and then (Nov. 7) that, since all three colonies had taken this action, the next shiploads would have to be sent to East Florida. The same appears in *Lloyd's Evening Post*, Oct. 28, 1773, and in the *Newcastle Journal*, Oct. 30–Nov. 6, 1773.

skills, then at least muscle power. So where labor needs were great the distinction between voluntary indentees and transported convicts tended to fade. A Maryland planter in great need of help in developing his property put the point precisely: "[I] would chuse," he wrote the Baltimore servant importer James Cheston, "an indented servant in preference to a convict, but rather than not have one some [time] this summer or next autumn, would consent to take a convict. I shall therefore be much obliged if you'll reserve one for me out of your next cargo and send him down by the first boat coming this way and let me know his price which shall be remitted you immediately."[32]

Ordering and Skills

Again and again individual householders, planters, and farmers expressed to local merchants their needs for indentured servants, rarely distinguishing between transported convicts and voluntary indentees, and the local merchants turned these needs into orders to their ship captains, supercargoes, and suppliers overseas. James and Drinker, a prominent Philadelphia merchant firm, regularly instructed their ship captains to bring back from Bristol as many "likely sound young men & boys" as they could, "avoiding elderly persons or even younger that have been broken tradesmen, or such as are not qualified for laborious work, yet remembering that hearty likely boys are generally the readiest sale." Another Philadelphia Quaker merchant, Thomas Clifford, also stressed youth, ordering from England "healthy, clever boys, single and at liberty to migrate," while specifying the need for craftsmen such as nailers, who could help produce commodities critical to the developing economy. But, unlike most dealers in servants, Clifford was something of a social philosopher, conceiving of his work in buying and selling servants as serving general community betterment and as opening up unique opportunities for the self-improvement of the ambitious poor. In America, he pointed out, wages were high, work plentiful, and provisions cheap—the opposite on all three points to the situation in England. "Youth," he wrote, "have a two-fold advantage by coming over, as they are early instructed in the ways of the country, well supplied with all necessarys, & when their service is ended they are qualified not only to procure themselves a comfortable living but stand candidates to be valuable members of community & usefully to fill the various stations of life." Again and again he ordered his ship captains and agents to "acquaint the poor labouring people with the genuine state of this country, & the opportunitie industrious honest poor men have of supporting themselves by their labour

[32] Turbutt Wright to Cheston, Love Point, April 11, 1773, Cheston Incoming Letters.

here." And he told them particularly to choose, if a choice were available, "young healthy people, tradesmen of full age for four years, labourers for five years, & youth for six or more years according to their ages & circumstances."[33]

Most requests, however, were not couched in the language of social betterment or of the opportunity for poor workmen to rise and prosper but in the less-elevated terms of supply and demand. In 1774 Russell's agent Philip Fendell wrote from Port Tobacco, Maryland, that there was a good market for servants, and he requested urgently "40 or 50 indented servants, or as many as the ship will conveniently bring. I think they will turn out a profit. . . . Tradesmen and farmers will answer best, next to them common laborers, the fewer women the better . . . , and by all means let them be shipped off in good health." Two weeks later he was even more urgent, requesting that servants be sent over on his personal account and risk as well as on Russell's, that some be sent on every ship dispatched to the ports along Chesapeake Bay, and that "the more weavers, shoemakers, tailors, joiners, carpenters, bricklayers and farmers and the fewer women there are among them the better."[34]

Similar demands were voiced again and again in the middle colonies and the Chesapeake region. In Baltimore, Matthew Ridley wrote the convict contractor Duncan Campbell to keep sending him "good tradesmen" and able "country people," and John Smith & Sons told their ship captain to get "as many tradesmen as possible" at reasonable cost "but by no means w[ou]ld we have one woman, & the men not to exceed 35 years." The Carroll family, eagerly importing ironworkers for the furnaces and forges they had invested in, sought farmers and gardeners too and brought over whole families of Irish country people through their agent in Cork. Others sought weavers and spinners, especially after the non-importation agreement of 1774 made American textile manufacture an object of great political concern.[35]

But the key figures in many ways were the builders, private and public —men like William Buckland, who himself had been brought over as an indentured servant (but, being extremely skilled, a *salaried* indentured

[33] James and Drinker to Capt. Edward Spain, Philadelphia, Aug. 4, 1774, James and Drinker Foreign Letters. The same phrases appear in almost all their instructions, e.g., to Capt. Volans, Nov. 16, 1772, and May 23, 1774; Larsen, "Thomas Clifford," pp. 115, 111, 113, 114, 118. Cf. Galenson, *White Servitude,* pp. 102 ff.

[34] Fendell to Russell, Port Tobacco, Aug. 13, 26, 1774, Russell Papers.

[35] Matthew Ridley to Duncan Campbell, Baltimore, July 20 and Dec. 20, 1773, Ridley Letterbook; John Smith & Sons and William Smith, Sailing Orders for Capt. Dan[ie]l Lawrence, Baltimore, Dec. 3, 1774, Smith Letterbooks; Thomas O. Hanley, *Charles Carroll of Carrollton* (Washington, D.C., 1970), p. 177. On the market for spinners: Woolsey to Salmon, Dec. 8, 1775 ("if the[y] ware spinners they would have answered"), and Jan. 3, 1776 ("spinners would do"), Woolsey and Salmon Letterbook. For politically motivated efforts to stimulate the importation of weavers, worsted combers, and spinners, see *Virginia Gazette* (Pinkney), Oct. 27, 1774, and March 16, 1775.

servant) by the Mason family of Virginia to work on George Mason's new house, Gunston Hall. As soon as he was released from his indenture, Buckland set up his own construction business and began an important career building prisons, workhouses, churches, stores, and above all private houses, first in Virginia and then in Maryland. To his headquarters in Annapolis, a town in which, during his time, "there was scarcely a lot . . . that did not have signs of building on it," he brought large numbers of skilled British servants—carvers, bricklayers, carpenters, and plasterers. He seems to have formed them into building teams that traveled to various job sites throughout the Chesapeake seaboard. A number of these hired men worked with him for years, helping to produce some of the finest houses of the late colonial period. When Buckland died in December 1774 his executors listed among his financial assets two bricklayers, a painter, a carver, and a stonemason. None of this was new in the pre-Revolutionary years. The way to get a proper house built in Virginia, William Fitzhugh had written in 1687, was "to get a carpenter & bricklayer servants, and send them in here to serve 4 or five years, in which time of their service they might reasonably build a substantial good house . . . & earn money enough besides . . . at spare times from your work . . . as will purchase plank, nails & other materials, & supply them with necessarys during their servitude." The demand for such craftsmen-builders had grown steadily over the years; their importation had become common by 1774, and, in the hands of master builders like Buckland, systematic.[36]

The demand for indentured servants with skills of some sort, strong throughout the middle range of colonies because of the growth of the economy and the spread of settlement, was strengthened by a constant leakage in the available work force, a continuous draining away of trained workers recently recruited from abroad from the enterprises they were engaged in. If, as the Maryland census of 1755 reported, there were then approximately 9,000 indentured servants including convicts in that colony, something like 2,000 of them were being released from their bonds every year. Few of those 2,000 were willing to renew their contracts for bonded servitude. Many, like Buckland, sought to establish themselves as independent craftsmen or entrepreneurs, not always with satisfying results. But a large number drifted out of craft work altogether and attempted to secure

[36]Rosamund R. Beirne and John H. Scarff, *William Buckland, 1734–1774: Architect of Virginia and Maryland* (Baltimore, 1958), pp. 11, 99–100, 111; Fitzhugh to Nicholas Haywood, Jan. 30, 1687, quoted in William M. S. Rasmussen, "Designers, Builders, and Architectural Traditions in Colonial Virginia," *Virginia Magazine of History and Biography*, 90 (1982), 203. On convict servants in the construction trades, moving from place to place as new jobs arose, "whether it be a bridge, house, store, church, or barn," see Schmidt, "Convict Servant Labor," pp. 193–195. In general, on the increasing need for imported servant artisans, see Bridenbaugh, *Colonial Craftsman*, pp. 66–67, 134 ff.

themselves on the land, again with uneven results. One well-informed observer, Governor Moore of New York, attributed the high price of labor in the colonies in the late colonial period not to a gross shortage of workers but to this shift of former indentured servants away from "manufactures" to the land. "The genius of the people in a country where every one can have land to work upon," he wrote the Board of Trade in 1767, "leads them so naturally into agriculture that it prevails over every other occupation."

> There can be no stronger instances of this than in the servants imported from Europe of different trades. As soon as the time stipulated in their indentures is expired, they immediately quit their masters and get a small tract of land, in settling which for the first three or four years they lead miserable lives, and in the most abject poverty. But all this is patiently borne and submitted to with the greatest cheerfulness, the satisfaction of being land holders smooths every difficulty and makes them prefer this manner of living to that comfortable subsistence which they could procure for themselves and their families by working at the trades in which they were brought up.[37]

Given the constant demand for labor, compounded by this drainage of workers from the dependent labor force, the flow of indentured servants to the colonies continued through these years, and with it an increasing emphasis on specific skills. In the arrival notices, servants with trades were clearly distinguished from those without specified skills. Advertisement after advertisement in the newspapers—hundreds of them—told of the arrival not merely of "healthy SERVANTS, men, women, and boys," but of "tradesmen" skilled in specific, enumerated crafts—"carpenters and joiners, black and white smiths, braziers and copper-smiths, shoemakers, weavers, barbers, schoolmasters, a tailor, a cabinet-maker, a wheelwright, a house painter, a calico painter, a dancing-master, and several others. There are also farmers and other country labourers." The value of skills in this labor market was never in doubt. "Tradesmen hear lives like gentlemen," a struggling former indentured servant, William Roberts, wrote from Maryland in 1769 in one of the few letters from such bondsmen that have survived. For lack of training in a trade, he said with some bitterness, he had "followd planttasions, lookin over slaves and makein corne, wheat, and tobacco." His two brothers in London, he wrote, did not realize how lucky they were to have been educated in trades. He felt he must have been "born

[37]Barker, *Background . . . in Maryland*, p. 3; Moore to Lords of Trade, Jan. 12, 1767, *Documents Relative to the Colonial History of the State of New-York . . .*, ed. E. B. O'Callaghan (Albany, 1856–1887), VII, 888–889.

under a bad planet, or else i mite [have] had a trade two and not a sufferd the heate of sun from day break tell dark."[38]

It was fear of such a fate, as well as the desire for betterment, that led many servants to falsify, or at least exaggerate, their competences. "He was sold for a bricklayer," a master wrote of a runaway servant, "but knows nothing of the business." "The two men called carpenters in the servant list," James Cheston wrote an eager customer from Baltimore, "turned out otherwise. One lad of ab[ou]t 19 had worked with his father a year or two, but knew nothing of the business; the other was a farmer; and [they] are both sold at labourers prices. There was a joiner on board, who I believe understood his business, but as he knew nothing of rough carpenters work, which from my memorandum Mr. Hand and you only wanted servants for, I did not send him." William Eddis, writing from Annapolis in 1770, told at great length the story of an indentured servant who had not been trained in any "mechanical profession" but who, when informed by the ship captain that "it was absolutely necessary he should avow some particular calling, in order to secure a more comfortable situation," decided to call himself a gardener, an undemanding line of work, he thought, and thereby "avoid a more laborious servitude under the discipline of some rigid and inflexible planter." His deception succeeded. He was bought by an indulgent master who took him into his household, and there he flourished until, in a fit of discouragement, he ran away, was retaken, and was condemned "to the iron mines, there to reap the bitter effects of his conduct."[39]

Since fraudulent professions of skill were the natural result of the high demand for competences and the rewards they could bring, buyers of labor had to be constantly on their guard. John Augustine Washington was not fooled by the servant he bought who "called himself" a tailor. But vigilance was not enough. False claims of competence by indentured servants could lead masters into financial losses, especially when wages were advanced as an inducement for the servants' migration. A few buyers were in a position to demand specimens of work before agreeing to purchase skilled workmen, but in the booming sellers' market this was uncommon. Buyers, therefore, sought legal protection. In 1753 Virginia passed an elaborate Act for the Better Government of Servants and Slaves, in which it was explained that "many abuses have been committed by persons who under pretence of understanding trades and mysteries have procured large sums of money to be advanced to them, and entered into covenants with mer-

[38]*Virginia Gazette* (Pinkney), Oct. 19, 1775; *ibid.* (Purdie), Oct. 13, 1775; William Roberts to John Broughton, "in Woltnut Tree Walk, Lambeth, near Westminster Bridge in the County Surrey," Aug. 9, 1769, Aug. 16, 1768, in James P. P. Horn, ed., "The Letters of William Roberts of All Hollows Parish, Anne Arundel County, Maryland, 1756–1769," *Maryland Historical Magazine,* 74 (1979), 128, 126.
[39]*Virginia Gazette* (Purdie), Sept. 15, 1775; Cheston to Thomas Smyth, Dec. 24, 1773, Cheston Letterbooks; Eddis, *Letters,* pp. 42–43. Cf. Galenson, *White Servitude,* p. 238 n. 12.

chants and others in Great Britain or elsewhere for the payment of yearly
wages, though they were really ignorant of, and unable to perform, such
trades or mysteries." To deal with the problem the law provided that
anyone "imported into this colony as a tradesman, or [as a] workman on
wages, and shall be found not to understand such trade or employment"
could be sued by their masters in the county courts, and if convicted of such
fraud could be punished by "defalcation of . . . wages" or by extension of
time of service.[40]

The emphasis on specific skills was highly articulated, even in the
uncommon instances when farmworkers were ordered. One of Cheston's
customers defined his need, or desire, down to the last refinement: he
wanted, he said, "a westcountryman, that has been used to driving an ox
team and understands cattle grazing and mowing grass . . . I would chuse
him middleaged." He made out quite nicely: the "only one [Cheston had]
left that could drive an ox team" proved to be able to "mow and take care
of cattle besides reaping, sowing etc. and is 30 years old and [a] west country
man; his price £21." Another put in an order for someone "used to ditching"; still another asked for "a servant who understands ditching and bank-
ing." Only a few bothered to order servants simply "bread a farmer" or
workers "used to farming and that come from the country." For it was
assumed that most of the arrivals without specific skills could be put to work
in the field.[41]

Harry Piper, writing from Alexandria to his labor suppliers in the north
of England, expressed the typical overall priorities. The men and women
he received who were "brought up to no sort of business" were "very
sorry," and "very great blackguards"; he had all sorts of trouble disposing
of them and he wanted no more of them. On the other hand, tradesmen
of any kind he could sell even before they arrived, and "boys are the readyist
sale, if they are small, and can be got for a longer term." Further, despite
the fact that "few of my demand for servants are on those who make
tobacco," he could count on disposing of servants "used to farming" even
when the labor market he served was glutted with indentees. Similarly,
John Campbell of Bladensburg, Maryland, in a discursive essay on opportunities for British emigrants in America, premised on the belief that "a man
of slender fortune can live here much more easy and to his satisfaction than
he can in Britain," observed that the rewards were particularly high for
artisans. The greatest demand, he wrote, was for weavers, tailors, house

[40]Hening, *Statutes . . . of Virginia*, VI, 368.
[41]Smyth to Cheston, Langfords Bay, March 30, 1774, Cheston Incoming Letters; Cheston to Smyth, Baltimore, March 31, 1774, Cheston Letterbooks; Cheston to Peregrine Tilghman, Baltimore, April 13, 1774, *ibid*.; Turbutt Wright to Cheston, Love Point, April 11, 1773, Cheston Incoming Letters. "There's one thing in our favor," in a difficult market, Cheston wrote Stevenson, Randolph, & Cheston in Bristol, June 13, 1773: "the people here giving the preference to west country servants above all others."

carpenters, joiners, blacksmiths, shoemakers, and spinners—"in short, every branch of manufactures"—but there was a need too for "healthy stout fellows used to country work, particularly ploughing, threshing, mowing, reaping, ditching, etc. . . . few in this country being expert at these employments." And Matthew Ridley in Baltimore told the convict contractor Duncan Campbell that he might be able to get £10 sterling a head *more* for "good tradesmen" and "country people" than he could for servants with no specific skill. "Had there been any farmers in McCullock's load," he wrote, "I might have got more for them . . . these and tradesmen being the chief dependance."[42]

"Countrymen" who really "understood farming"—servants, in Cheston's phrase, "used to a spade"—though seldom ordered as such and never as sought-after as artisans, were usually in demand, but not to supply brute labor in the tobacco fields or on the more distant out-plantations where conditions were most primitive, where the opportunities for escape most numerous, and where the possibility of restraint weakest. Experienced farm hands, particularly in special lines of work, were relatively expensive, and they could be employed most profitably on well-developed farms of diversified crops, whose further cultivation required skill. They were bought and used most readily, therefore, in Pennsylvania (where as early as 1720 farmers had imported indentured servants to help produce hemp), in the backcountry of Maryland and Virginia, or in the tidewater areas where crop diversification had overtaken tobacco monoculture.[43]

Such was the demand for labor. Concentrated in the expanding middle colonies and the Chesapeake region, it was above all a demand for skilled workmen in the entire range of trades and crafts, especially in the trades related to construction and the materials of construction. It was a demand too, though to a lesser extent, for experienced farmworkers. And it was a demand, though least of all, for laborers without skills but with strong backs capable of contributing, like unskilled slaves, to the available sum of sheer manual power. Youth was at a premium and females at a discount, but almost any able-bodied person under the age of thirty-five could be found useful by the farmers, plantation owners, entrepreneurs, merchants, artisans, and tradesmen in the colonies between New York and North Carolina.

[42] Piper to Dixon and Littledale, Alexandria, Aug. 10, 1768, Jan. 7 and April 15, 1769, Piper Letterbook; John Campbell to William Sinclair, July 26, 1772, Freswick Muniments, GD 136/416/1; Ridley to Campbell, Baltimore, July 20 and Dec. 20, 1773, Ridley Letterbook.
[43] John Chisholm to James Chisholm, Aug. 16, 1759, Chisholm Letters; Cheston to Thomas Ringgold, April 13, 1774, Cheston Letterbooks; Lemon, *Best Poor Man's Country*, p. 215. For a particularly suggestive example of the priority of needs in eastern Pennsylvania in 1774, see the account of the sales of the servants aboard Richard Neave, Jr.'s *Dolphin*, discussed below, chap. 10, pp. 334–335.

8

Sources

To satisfy these unending and varied demands, many population sources were drawn on—local American, especially in the regions of the upper south, where long-settled land occupancy kept freed servants from easy access to land of their own; but chiefly foreign: slaves from Africa and from elsewhere in the Atlantic colonies, and white workers of all kinds, freemen and voluntary bondsmen, from the Protestant German principalities, from Ireland, and above all from Britain.

London

Of the potential sources in Britain, the richest by far lay in the working population of London. The great metropolis, with a population of approximately 750,000, was the largest urban center in the western world. It had expanded far beyond the ancient "cities" of London and Westminster. When the emigrants whose names appear in the Register were crowding into skiffs and lighters to reach the ocean-going vessels anchored in the Thames, London's continuous habitation stretched north through several miles of slums and suburbs to the north circular "New Road," built in the late 1750s to link several outlying villages, and south across the Thames into Southwark, Newington, Rotherhithe, and Lambeth. But that broad sweep of habitation constituted no more than London's central core. By 1776 the city had reached beyond that periphery to an outer ring of satellite villages forming a greater oval twice the size of central London—villages like Chelsea, Kensington, Islington, Hackney, and Stepney, which had become recognized parts of the metropolis though most of them still retained something of their original rural character. A detailed account of London in 1776

Central London, from John Rocque's map of 1769. Ocean shipping crowded the docks as far inland as London Bridge. Departing passengers could board ship at these wharves and later register officially at Gravesend, southeast of the city, close to the channel outlet to the sea.

put the dimensions of the metropolitan oval at roughly 7½ miles by 3, with a circumference of 18 miles. The legend of a map of 1769, comparing London's size favorably to Paris's, estimated the total area at 5,455 acres, or 8½ square miles.[1]

[1] M. Dorothy George, *London Life in the Eighteenth Century* ([1925], Penguin ed., Harmondsworth,

This sprawling conurbation—the center of government, commerce, industry, fashion, and art; the hub of a growing world empire; a tumultuous human agglomeration abounding in contrasts between wealth and poverty,

Eng., 1976), chap. 2; *The New Present State of Great-Britain . . .*, 2d ed. (London, 1776), pp. 178–180; "A Plan of London on the Same Scale as That of Paris . . . by J. Rocque . . . with Improvements to 1769" [London, 1769]. Paris was estimated at only 6⅓ square miles.

elegance and brutality, beauty and squalor—was the main source of recruitment for the American work force, and it had been since the colonies were
founded. This was in part the result of London's key role in Britain's
population history, its powerful magnetic force for migrant workers all
over the British Isles. The great metropolitan center devoured people. The
city was a graveyard. Disease devastated the slums, and epidemics deci-
mated the population. In the seventeenth century, when an estimated one-
third of the city's inhabitants were recent arrivals, plague wiped out some
15 percent of the total population, but the losses were made up by new
arrivals within two years. By the early eighteenth century London—a
pesthouse of malnutrition, disease, and early death, yet constantly increasing in size—must have been absorbing approximately half of the entire
increase in England's population. But "the waggon loads of poor servants
coming every day from all parts of this kingdom," as a correspondent to
the *London Chronicle* wrote in 1762, kept the great city growing despite the
devastating losses.[2]

The literary evidence supports the quantitative indications of the constant migration into greater London of a mobile, unattached labor force.
There is no more common theme in the writings of Fielding (a quintessen-
tial Londoner, who grew up in Dorset), Smollett (a Scot by birth), Richard-
son (from Derbyshire), or Sterne (a youthful wanderer who lived mainly
in York before arriving in London as a literary celebrity) than the story of
young country innocents seeking employment, migrating with stars in
their eyes to the great metropolis, there to struggle endlessly with corruption and temptation. Some of the thousands of country people who flocked
into London every year had connections to help them find their way in the
city, but most, "allured to London with the prospect of high wages," were
fleeing poverty—some were refugees from the malevolent pressure of the
poor laws—and had no way of finding security. They drifted quickly into
the mass of casually employed laborers and the abject poor, swarming in
the verminous, overbuilt ramshackle tenements and the garbage-strewn
streets of Cheapside, Houndsditch, Whitechapel, and Southwark.[3]

Hogarth vividly illustrated this migration process, as he did so many
other aspects of eighteenth-century London life. The first of the six plates
of his "Harlot's Progress" shows the innocent Yorkshire girl, Mary Hackabout, alighting excitedly and tremulously from a York wagon. Confronted
by the diseased procuress Mother Needham, and eyed by the rabid Colonel

[2] John H. C. Patten, *Rural-Urban Migration in Pre-industrial England* (Oxford Univ., School of
Geography, *Research Papers*, No. 6, 1973), 23, 27; E. A. Wrigley, "A Simple Model of London's
Importance in Changing English Society and Economy 1650–1750," *Past and Present*, 37 (1967), 44,
46–47, 49–50; Andrew B. Appleby, "Nutrition and Disease: The Case of London, 1550–1750,"
Journal of Interdisciplinary History, 6 (1975), 1–22; J. Jean Hecht, *The Domestic Servant Class in
Eighteenth-Century England* (London, 1956), p. 12.
[3] *Ibid.*, p. 13; George, *London Life*, pp. 83, 91.

William Hogarth, A Harlot's Progress, *Plate 1. (Mary Hackabout's
arrival in London.)*

Charteris and one of his pimps, she is caught up instantly in the vortex of
London's corruption. Such country girls, lacking reliable patrons in London, could hope at best to find employment as unskilled servants. But the
city was teeming with servants, many of them unemployed, and Mary's
doleful fate, foreshadowed in the figure of the goose she carries to her
"lofing cosen in Tems Stret in London," was predictable. In 1775 it was
estimated that one in every eight Londoners was a servant, most of them
recently arrived. If the city numbered 750,000, that meant a servant population of more than 90,000 men, women, and children.

Relatively few of these thousands of unskilled workers from the countryside, available for any kind of common labor or household service, would
ever find steady employment (a magistrate in 1796 estimated that "at all
times" there were more than 10,000 servants "out of place" in London), and
they formed a large pool of potential emigrants. For rarely, a contemporary
wrote, did they "go home again to be laughed at . . . but inlist for soldiers,
go to the plantations, etc. if they are well inclined, otherwise they probably
commence thieves or pickpockets." Many of the spinsters, laborers, and
artisans whose emigration from London was recorded in the Register were

drawn from this recently arrived, mobile, disoriented segment of the population. And in this sense London was not simply in itself an independent source of manpower for the colonies; it was also a selective conduit through which a particularly mobile part of the entire British and Irish work force was enabled to move westward to America. Precisely how this movement of country people took place, first into London in search of employment and then out of the city to the colonies, and something of the feelings of those who made such treks are documented in extraordinary detail in the case of one such voyager, who recorded his experiences in a daily journal.[4]

John Harrower, a forty-year-old shopkeeper and petty tradesman who lived on the outskirts of the remote port village of Lerwick in the Shetland Islands—130 miles off the north coast of Scotland, 300 miles north of Edinburgh, 700 miles from London—was literate, ambitious, and faced with grinding poverty, from which he was determined to rescue himself and his family. On December 6, 1773—three days before the orders were issued to register the emigrants from Britain—Harrower set out "to travel in search of business," wherever he could find it. He had no intention of emigrating to America; the Netherlands was the farthest he thought he might go. Equipped with almost no cash but with £3 worth of stockings and other woolen goods and a few trinkets, all of which, with a change of clothing, he carried in a box and in a bundle slung across his back, he made his way down the coast of Scotland looking for employment. At Dundee he tried to get passage to the Netherlands, and failed. The only opportunity he found in that northern Scottish town was an offer of indentured servitude by the master of a vessel heading for North Carolina, an offer he considered but rejected; "the thoughts of being so far from my family prevented me." After sixteen days of extremely penurious living in Dundee and some exquisitely calculated bartering to maintain the wherewithal he started with, he shipped south to Newcastle, where again he failed to get passage across the North Sea, and moved on once again, this time on foot through deep snow to nearby Sunderland, where again he failed to get shipping to the east. Peddling what he could at a profit, living on bread, cheese, and beer supplemented occasionally with fish, he finally got a free berth on a vessel bound either to the Netherlands or to London. In fact the vessel ended up in Portsmouth, on the far south coast of England, from which Harrower, box and bag in hand, counting every farthing, walked the eighty miles to London.

In London, "like a blind man without a guide, not knowing where to go being freindless and having no more money but fifteen shillings & eight pence farthing, a small sum to enter London with," Harrower settled into what proved to be a three-week stay full of frustration, ultimately of despair. He called at the Jamaica Coffee House, where he was told jobs might be

[4]Hecht, *Domestic Servant Class*, pp. 34, 25.

had, but found nothing (and drank three pennies' worth of punch that "I was obliged to make . . . serve me for dinner"). He followed up an advertisement for paid employment as a bookkeeper and clerk in Philadelphia, but his application was too late; then he failed to get a steward's berth on a vessel sailing between London and Maryland. Letters of response to advertisements for a messenger and an under-clerk to a London merchant proved to be useless, for the other applicants were "all weel acquanted and I a stranger." He took to roaming the streets randomly and attending church services, especially those of the Methodists. After one such visit, "solitarry in my room," he wrote hymn-like verses on his fate: "Now at London in a garret room I am,/ here frendless and foresaken;/ But from the Lord my help will come,/ Who trusts in him are not mistaken." Finally, after carrying around a general petition to any merchant or tradesman he encountered, explaining his background and experience and offering to work for anyone "for the bare support of life," and after spending his last shilling, he concluded that the situation was hopeless: "all pleaces here at present are intierly carried by freinds and intrest, And many hundreds are sterving for want of employment, and many good people are begging." After writing his wife a full account of everything that had happened to him since he left her, he signed on as an indentured servant, a bondsman, "to go to Virginia for four years, as a schoolmaster."

The *Planter*, which carried Harrower to his new life as a tutor on a tidewater plantation (he was exceptionally fortunate to get the work he wanted) was one of the vessels entered in the Register, and so we can identify most of the people it carried. Aboard, along with Harrower and several paying passengers, were seventy-one other male indentees, all but four (a father and three sons) traveling alone. Forty-two were from London and the Home Counties—artisans of all kinds: wigmakers, carpenters, clockmakers, bricklayers, cabinetmakers, hatters, weavers. But the other twenty-nine came from all over England and Ireland, and must have had itinerant careers similar to Harrower's. From Yorkshire came a groom and a farmer, from Leicester a weaver, from Birmingham a bricklayer, from Durham a breeches-maker, from Newcastle a pipemaker, from Chester a cabinetmaker, and from Ireland a bricklayer and a butcher.[5]

Harrower's career was distinguished from those of the thousands of indentured servants leaving the port of London for America in that, despite his poverty, he was not only literate but capable of literary expression; and though his experience had chiefly been that of a peddler of stockings and small household goods, he aspired to employment as a clerk or schoolteacher. Yet his bitter experience as a provincial trying his fortune in the

[5] *The Journal of John Harrower: An Indentured Servant in the Colony of Virginia, 1773–1776*, ed. Edward M. Riley (Williamsburg, Va., 1963), pp. 3, xiv, 7, 14–17. The *Planter*, David Bowers, master, which left London in the second week of February 1774, is entered in the Register at T47/9/55–57.

great metropolis, where he lacked connections to help him find his way, was typical of that of many thousands who swelled London's population and who eventually decided to sell themselves into temporary bondage in order to establish themselves in the colonies.

But the desperation Harrower felt in searching for employment in London was not restricted to provincials migrating to the metropolis, or to unskilled laborers only. London was the national center for skilled craft production of all kinds—the *only* center for some of the most highly skilled crafts—as well as for enterprises that used semiskilled and unskilled labor. For resident workers at all of these skill levels, only 5 or 6 percent of whom were self-employed, unemployment was a constant condition of life. It was so constant and common, even in the prosperous decade before 1765, that it was scarcely remarked on. Partly the irregularity in employment, or chronic underemployment, of resident workers—worst among the least skilled—was the result of deliberate overstaffing by employers to avoid labor shortages when business was brisk. Mainly, however, it was the result of constant and uncontrollable fluctuations in an economy highly vulnerable to short-term swings in external trade, which supported the nation's chief industry, textile manufacturing. The economy was vulnerable too to variations in the weather, to government intervention during war years, to the effects of an uncontrollable money supply, and to inflexible interest rates incapable of leveling out the repeated cycles of expansion and contraction. The downswings in the various economic sectors did not always coincide: the building industry tended to improve when the export trade declined. But in general the years 1755–1763 were prosperous, the late 1760s badly depressed, and the 3½ years from 1769 to late 1772 a period of recovery which ended in a severe economic collapse that lasted until late 1774.[6]

During the major, national "decays of trade," whole districts of London were "plunged into unemployment." But there were more localized reasons too for the irregularity of employment in the metropolis. When shifts in fashion suddenly cut the demand for certain kinds of consumer goods, specialist workers were immediately laid off. And seasonal cycles affected everything from schoolmastering (artisans' children were chiefly available for schooling during the summer) to shipping (during the two or three main seasons for ocean traffic, and when the winds were right, dockside workers were overwhelmed with work; on off-seasons, and when the weather was adverse, they were idle). The less skilled the trade "the most likely it was that a man would spend a great part of the year unemployed." Bricklayers were commonly unemployed during the winter, tailors could

[6]L. D. Schwarz, "Income Distribution and Social Structure in London in the Late Eighteenth Century," *Economic History Review*, 32 (1979), 257; George, *London Life*, p. 32; T. S. Ashton, *An Economic History of England: The 18th Century* (London, 1955), p. 203; idem, *Economic Fluctuations in England, 1700–1800* (Oxford, 1959), chap. 6, esp. pp. 152–160.

expect unemployment for a quarter of each year, and casual labor in general found employment only during the high point of the season. All trades, even the better-paid, high-skilled crafts, were affected in one way or another —to the extent that in East London an estimated 40% of the entire working population with families experienced a period of poverty at some time in the course of each year. And there were, too, the normal short-term fluctuations of the putting-out or domestic system of manufacture. London's domestic workmen, a pamphleteer wrote, commonly lose two working days in every six: "a great part of their time is spent in fetching home their materials, or carrying home their work, or in seeking after their money." And there were waits between jobs, determined by the masters, not the workers.[7]

Workers in almost all of London's trades and industries were affected by this irregularity of employment, and many of them adjusted to it—and also to the deadening monotony and physical strain of most kinds of work —by developing a willing, eventually habitual, alternation between spurts of intense labor and periods of inertia or bouts of dissipation. Even when employment was available, they worked only long enough to earn the next period of relief. But this was a destructive way of life, from which the more intelligent, ambitious, and imaginative sought to escape.[8] The most desperate of all, in the sixties and early seventies, were the thousands who labored in London's huge silk spinning and weaving industry.

Densely concentrated in an area four blocks square in the district of Spitalfields, just outside the ancient city walls at Bishopsgate in East London, the silk industry had been developed into a complex of small units by Huguenot refugees who had fled to London in the late seventeenth century. By the 1760s the industry formed an immense cluster of related enterprises, involving procurement of raw silk, thread spinning, cloth weaving in varying forms, and a system of distribution of finished goods that reached markets in Europe and North America as well as everywhere in the British Isles. Between 12,000 and 15,000 looms were in operation in the Spitalfields core of the industry and in the immediately adjacent areas of Mile End New Town, Norton Folgate, and Bethnal Green, which meant a working population of approximately 40,000 men, women, and children. Laboring, when

[7]M. Dorothy George, *England in Transition* ([1931], Penguin ed., London, 1953), pp. 53 ff.; O. H. K. Spate, "The Growth of London, A.D. 1660–1800," in *An Historical Geography of England before A.D. 1800*, ed. H. C. Darby (Cambridge, Eng., 1936), p. 545; Ashton, *Economic History*, pp. 202–203, 207, 219, 221–222; L. D. Schwarz, "Occupations and Incomes in Late Eighteenth-Century East London," *East London Papers*, 11 (1968), 95. In general, on seasonality in labor, see Ashton, *Economic Fluctuations*, pp. 4–11.

[8]Julia deL. Mann, *The Cloth Industry in the West of England from 1640 to 1880* (Oxford, 1971), p. 106; and see the vivid example of William Hutton, in George, *England in Transition*, pp. 61–63.

Roofscape of surviving eighteenth-century attic workrooms and weavers'
windows, north side of Fournier St., Spitalfields, London.

work was available, at the clattering machines twelve to fourteen hours a
day in the heat and humidity of sealed-off attic workrooms atop the master
weavers' houses (ground-floor workrooms were only beginning to be common) or in their own even more cramped home quarters, the journeymen
workers and apprentices suffered not only from exhaustion intensified by
the fetid air but from chest injuries that resulted from the pressure of the
loom bars. Their common resort to drinking, gaming, and idleness when
earnings were high is scarcely surprising.[9]

Once again Hogarth is a vivid illustrator. His drawing and engraving
of the idle and the industrious apprentices at their looms in Spitalfields are
accurate in every way, including the threatening presence of the master
weaver (who appears as a more malevolent figure in the original drawing).
Hogarth's scene is detailed, realistic, almost palpable; but one has to imagine, in addition, the banging and clattering din, the heat and deliberately
cultivated humidity in these airless attic workrooms, the numbing monotony of the work, and above all, the pervasive fear of reductions in wages
and of unemployment in a cutthroat industry extremely sensitive to
changes in fashion and to foreign competition, both technological and
commercial.

[9]A. V. B. Gibson, "Huguenot Weavers' Houses in Spitalfields," *East London Papers*, 1 (1958), 4,
13.

William Hogarth, "The Fellow 'Prentices at Their Looms," preparatory drawing for the engraving of Plate 1 of Hogarth's Industry and Idleness *series. The tyrannical face of the apprentices' master in this Spitalfields silk weavers' workroom is considerably softened in the final engraving.*

Labor unrest had existed for a century in this quickly growing industry. There had been riots by workers protesting employment conditions, layoffs, and poverty at least once a decade in the late seventeenth century and repeatedly thereafter: in the 1730s troops had to be sent in to control the weavers' violence. The journeymen, the poorest paid and most expendable of the weavers, notorious for their poverty but known too for their intelligence and literacy, had led these street protests, and they took the leadership too in the worst years of rioting, the mid- and late 1760s. The contraction of all consumer markets, especially the American market, after the Seven Years War, and the competition with the French, who could sell finished silks in England 25% cheaper than the English, led to a severe depression in the industry and mass protests by workers. When in 1765 the House of Lords defeated a bill to protect the industry from foreign competition, journeymen weavers mobbed St. James's Palace, followed the King with black flags, stormed the houses of mercers suspected of dealing with the French, and marched on Parliament in a mob of several thousand. The horse guards held them off, but it was only the distribution of relief to almost ten thousand men, women, and children, and the passage of a limited prohibition on imports, that eased the situation.[10]

But the underlying problems continued to multiply. More and more journeymen weavers arrived in Spitalfields from elsewhere in England; the use of child labor became even more common than it had been; engine looms, which reduced employment opportunities, became popular; and manufacturing centers in other parts of Britain became increasingly competitive. In 1769 violence erupted again. In August of that year Spitalfields was reported to have the aspect of a town "under military execution— bodies of men marching and counter-marching; whole streets blocked up by armed men at each end; the explosions of firearms; instant death threatened to all who show themselves at their windows." Gangs were hired to keep the workers from cutting the silk out of the looms. Peace, or a tense truce, returned only in October; by then five silk cutters had been killed by the soldiers and seven others were subsequently hanged. Shortly thereafter the Spitalfields workers turned to collective action. In the early seventies workers' clubs, originally mutual benefit societies, became unions threatening industrial sabotage to compel employers to pay standardized and publicized prices for work performed. They sought, too, restriction in the employment of women, girls, and "unlawful" workmen; strict and strictly enforced rules of apprenticeship; and more permanent protection from foreign competition. When in 1773 a new depression threatened a repetition of the upheaval of 1769 and a document called "The Weavers' Requests" gave highly specific terms to the relief that was sought, Parliament, upon the report of a select committee that investigated the silk industry, quickly enacted the protective statute that was demanded, the Spitalfields Act of 1773.[11]

[10]*Spitalfields and Mile End New Town* (F. H. W. Sheppard, ed., *Survey of London*, XXVII, London, 1957), 6; W. M. Jordan, "The Silk Industry in London, 1760–1830, with Special Reference to the Condition of the Wage Earners and the Policy of the Spitalfields Acts" (M.A. thesis, Univ. of London, 1931), chaps. 1, 3, 5; *Lloyd's Evening Post*, Dec. 6, 1769, for a typical account of the Spitalfields riots of that year.

[11]Jordan, "Silk Industry," p. 103 and chap. 5 generally. The official accounts of the agitation of 1773, the weavers' petition, and the government's response are summarized in *Calendar of Home Office Papers of the Reign of George III*, ed. Joseph Redington *et al.* (London, 1878–1899), IV, 39–42, together with Sir John Fielding's conclusion that the Spitalfields Act (13 Geo. III, c.68) had proved "a radical cure for all tumultuous assemblies from that quarter" (p. 65).

It is important to note the identification between the workers' cause and the political cause of the American colonies, which the Spitalfields weavers stressed and of which the government was well aware. The cause of all their troubles, the workers wrote, was the government's "insatiable venality." "The same spirit of rapacity originally laid the foundation of, and continues to cultivate, that destructive contention which has so long prevailed between the parent state and the British colonies in America, a contention which tends totally to alienate the affections of our distant fellow-subjects, is pregnant with every future commercial evil, and is the principal immediate cause of the present prevailing distress amongst the British merchants, and which, through them, extends to us, Your Majesty's miserable subjects who, for want of the usual circulation of their operations, are reduced to the utmost degree of destitution and wretchedness." *Gentleman's Magazine*, 43 (1773),

In these years the distress of the Spitalfields weavers became famous throughout the English-speaking world. Readers of the *Virginia Gazette* were told in March 1773 that six thousand Spitalfields textile workers were unemployed and that the workhouses and hospitals were crowded with them. In April the same paper reported that a benevolent nobleman was soliciting charity for the distressed and deserving weavers, arguing as he did so that only government action would really help them, or any of the rest of the nation's desperate poor, in a permanent way. Word received in South Carolina was more extreme: the distress of the silk weavers was indescribable, the *South-Carolina Gazette* reported, the markets for silk had collapsed, only a fifth of the work force was employed, and "forty thousand men are starving. Some of them have not a bed to lie upon, as they have been obliged to dispose of every thing they had to keep them in life."

There were sensation mongering and special pleading in these reports. Employers and other witnesses who appeared before the select committee of the House of Commons gave more moderate figures of unemployment and distinguished among conditions in the various branches of the complex industry. But even some of these witnesses told of the "cries of the poor creatures" and of "women with 8 or 10 children . . . crying and begging for work." A silk manufacturer with twenty years' experience testified that he had never seen the work force in such a shocking condition. Another reported that the distribution of relief money to four or five thousand unemployed weavers, which he had witnessed, hardly eased the problem; he estimated the whole number of unemployed in Spitalfields at 10,000. "What the poor people would do," another employer confessed, "he knew not."[12]

But there were those who did know what some, at least, of the unemployed would do. It had been clear as early as 1765 that one result of the employment problems in Spitalfields would be a large-scale exodus of weavers to America. The *Gentleman's Magazine* published such a prediction during the riots of that year, and it was soon fulfilled. In 1774 a report which circulated widely in the British periphery (identical notices appeared in Pennsylvania, Virginia, and Scotland) informed the public that numbers of Spitalfields' unemployed weavers were in process of emigrating to Boston, New York, and Philadelphia. Later that year two Yorkshire newspapers published a particularly detailed report on how some of the London weavers were managing the enterprise. A society called "The Emigrators," the

247. The workers' extreme discontent, emigration, and American political resistance merged in the minds of government officials and fed the fear that the entire fabric of civil society was threatened. Restricting emigration, quelling the domestic disturbances, and suppressing the American rebellion seemed parts of a general effort to maintain the nation's stability.

[12] *Virginia Gazette* (Rind), March 25, April 1, 1773; *South-Carolina Gazette; And Country Journal,* March 15, 1773, quoting a London report of Dec. 16, 1772; *Journals of the House of Commons,* XXXIV (Nov. 26, 1772, to Sept. 15, 1774), 239–241.

York Courant and the *Leeds Mercury* reported under a London dateline, had been formed in Spitalfields, "each member of which pays 6 pence weekly towards raising a sum towards carrying them to America, but none of them are to embark until the subscription will defray the expense of taking the whole society. The subscription of those members who die to be applied to the advantage of the survivors."[13]

What happened to the weavers and other workers in the silk industry happened in less dramatic and convulsive ways to workers in many of London's crafts, service trades, and industries in these years of chronic unemployment and repeated busts and booms. In 1772 the city's journeymen tailors petitioned for increased wages because of the escalating cost of living. In 1773 the cabinetmakers declared that they were "deprived of employment" because of illegal furniture imports, and that they and their families were reduced "to the most complicated distress." In the same year the artificers and laborers in the royal dockyards, one of the largest of the city's employers, sought "a very trifling increase of wages," a proposal Lord North "set his face against." At the same time coalheavers joined the weavers in petitioning the crown for relief from their depressed living conditions. Shortly thereafter the brewers struck in protest against low wages, and their strike had a ricochet effect on employment in the distillery and baking industries. In 1775 a leading hosiery manufacturer declared that the American crisis in general and non-importation in particular were making bad conditions worse and workmen were being laid off continuously. And at the same time the shipwrights in the naval yards struck in an effort to force wages up, and were fired for striking.[14]

All of these protesting, underemployed workers in London were in some degree available for emigration. Again and again "tradesmen and their families who [had] been out of employ for some time" were reported to be boarding ships riding at anchor in the Thames. For it was not simply, as the *Virginia Gazette* reported, that "the lower ranks of people" in general were emigrating "in prodigious numbers." Experienced artisans and craftsmen, who if satisfactorily employed would have been well-integrated members of society, were proving to be prime sources of recruitment into the

---

[13] *Gentleman's Magazine*, 35 (1765), 244; *Pennsylvania Journal; and the Weekly Advertiser*, Aug. 10, 1774; *Virginia Gazette* (Rind), Aug. 18, 1774; *Caledonian Mercury*, June 6, 1774; *York Courant*, Sept. 27, 1774; *Leeds Mercury*, Sept. 23, 1774.

[14] Ashton, *Economic History*, pp. 226–227; on the escalation of consumer prices during the years 1760–1774, S. H. Palmer, *Economic Arithmetic* (New York, 1977), p. 50; and on the fall in real wages in London, Elizabeth W. Gilboy, "The Cost of Living and Real Wages in the Eighteenth Century," *Review of Economic Statistics*, 18 (1936), 140. The petition and protests referred to are in *Gentleman's Magazine*, 43 (1773), 248, 148; *Cal. Home Office Papers*, IV, 39; *Annual Register*, 17 (1774), 85.

American work force. The numbers involved were small relative to London's working population as a whole, but the departures of these workers were noticed, and considered to be significant. Where the state was the employer, especially where skills of use in national defense were involved, emigration seemed conspiratorial. There was unmistakable evidence, the undersecretary of state for the colonies was informed, that the dismissed shipwrights at the royal dockyards were being enticed, even bribed, into emigration by supposedly respectable London businessmen working on behalf of elements "destructive of His Majesty's interest and the welfare of the public in general." Undercover agents circulating among the shipwrights discovered that the workers were being told that wages in their line of work were twice as high in New York as they were in London, and they were being shown—in a New York housewife's "book of house expenses" —that provisions were far cheaper in the colonies than they were in the metropolis.[15]

If such wooing of the shipwrights was a conspiracy, it involved no dissembling. The information on employment in New York was correct. Emigration was a rational option for workers facing low wages or periodic unemployment or both; it was a spillover, a specific expression of the general search by a labor force, skilled and unskilled, for stability in an unstable economy. London was the major source of recruitment because it was the economic center of the nation, to which workers from all over the British Isles flocked, and hence it was a virtual storehouse of underused skills and physical capacities, and, for many, a staging area for further migration. But the great metropolis was not the only source of recruitment for the American work force in Britain. What was happening on a large scale in London was happening in lesser degrees elsewhere.

The Provinces

There was no mass exodus of a starving urban, small-town, or rural proletariat anywhere in Britain. The British economy as a whole was growing, its product and population increasing steadily. But the "upward slope was not continuous" anywhere in Britain; it was "broken throughout by de-

[15] *Maryland Journal, and the Baltimore Advertiser,* June 11–18, 1774; *Virginia Gazette* (Pinkney), Nov. 24, 1774; *Cal. Home Office Papers,* IV, 398 (reports and documents on "efforts made to induce disaffected shipwrights, who had been discharged for petitioning the King, to emigrate to America"); C. R. Dobson, *Masters and Journeymen* (London, 1980), pp. 100–110 for a complete account of the shipwrights' strike. The household expense book was that of the wife of a merchant, Searle, circulated among the shipwrights to prove that New York was "a place in the world preferable to all the rest," Aug. 16, 1775, SP 37/11. The government's spies reported to Under Secretary John Pownall that Searle had assisted many men to emigrate "who had blessed him for so doing." The full narrative of this tangled episode is in SP 37/11/110–128.

clivities" in which a great deal of human misery was concentrated. Workers not only in London but everywhere in Britain faced uncertain conditions, periods of unemployment, and times of relatively low real wages. Cloth workers in the production centers in Gloucestershire, for example, lived precarious existences.

> Engaged by the piece [one authority writes] the Gloucestershire workers could never be certain of getting the next "chain" or "warp," and it was no uncommon sight to see a group of thirty or forty men standing outside some clothier's counting-house door for hours at a time, until only five or six would get any work. Those who worked for lesser clothiers might become involved in their failure or collapse. All were at the mercy of the weather. Work might be held up in the winter by frost, and in the summer by drought. But the greatest distress was caused by the "annual vibrations": in one year nine hundred men might be employed, while an increase in trade the next might require six or seven hundred more hands. However unwilling to dismiss them, the masters could not retain their men in times of slack trade.[16]

A similar uncertainty bedeviled the lives of workers in other trades. Reduced government contracts and overseas markets after 1763 hit the textile, hardware, coal-mining, and shipbuilding industries particularly hard, with severe drops in employment in all of the Midlands iron and iron-related industries and in the cloth-production centers in Wiltshire, Norfolk, and Yorkshire, as well as in Gloucestershire. Employment fell in all of the affected areas, and there were riots among the provincial poor—town dwellers, cottage workers, and farm laborers alike. Employers and prosperous farmers were threatened, and law enforcement took even more severe form than usual. The recovery was uneven and unsteady. Some of the distressed workers, their most acute problems eased somewhat by charity, "sank first into sullen resentment at the military repression, and then into apathetic resignation. . . . In a predominantly rustic society, natural scarcity seemed to be a divine retribution for past sins, which had to be endured." But those with the most initiative moved off, to regional centers where employment was said to be available, or to London; and many considered emigrating to what were said to be far better opportunities in America. Everywhere in Britain during the slump of the late sixties, artisans, shop workers, and laborers formed a mass, not of actual but of poten-

[16]A. W. Coats, "The Relief of Poverty, Attitudes to Labour, and Economic Change in England, 1660–1782," *International Review of Social History*, 21 (1976), 99–101; Ashton, *Economic Fluctuations*, p. 177; E. A. L. Moir, "The Gentlemen Clothiers . . . the Gloucestershire Cloth Industry 1750–1835," in *Gloucestershire Studies*, ed. H. P. R. Finberg (Leicester, 1957).

tial emigrants—a pool from which workers might be drawn into the American labor markets. And what was true of those postwar years was even more true of the two severely depressed years after late 1772.[17]

Witnesses before the House of Commons' select committee on the silk industry in 1773 explained that Spitalfields was not the only community whose silk workers were being laid off or were facing the prospect of desperately low wages. The silk industry in recent years "hath been removed to many places distant from London," and everywhere the story was the same. In Stockport and Macclesfield, near Manchester, between 50 and 80 percent of the workers in silk manufacture were reported to have been laid off. The same was said to be true in Blockley, Worcestershire; in Overton, Hampshire; in Congleton, Cheshire; in Burton and Wells, Somersetshire; in Ludlow, Shropshire; and in Derby. The select committee was finally convinced: the distress among the unemployed workers "in places distant from London," they reported to the House, "is very alarming."[18]

But Spitalfields' chief competitor in silk manufacture was none of these small English towns, but Paisley, the textile center near Glasgow that had developed swiftly in the course of the previous fifty years to the point where the many small factories, mills, and domestic units of manufacture in and around the town employed over fifteen thousand workers and turned out a variety of silk and linen goods worth over £250,000 a year. It had been here, in 1773, that a weavers' strike, backed by a threat "to goe off in a body to America," had stirred fears in Thomas Miller, the lord justice clerk, that Scotland was facing an "epidemical" spread of migration fever and had set in motion the search for information that resulted in the compilation of the Register of emigrants. Miller had felt that his handling of the strikers' trial had restored "peace & good order . . . and that all thoughts of goeing over to America are for the present laid aside." He was wrong, as he soon discovered. The source of the trouble had by no means been eliminated, and the exodus from Paisley, as from all over the Highlands and the outer islands, continued.

In February 1774 the *Caledonian Mercury* of Edinburgh, which printed enthusiastic letters from emigrant weavers settled in the colonies, reported that five hundred of Paisley's industrial workers were preparing to embark for America "as they can find no employment at home." A month later the town's "merchants, traders, and manufacturers" petitioned Parliament to send some kind of relief to the thousands of workers "reduced to the utmost distress for want of employ," many of whom had been forced "to emigrate . . . to distant countries to prevent them[selves] from starving." And the

[17] Walter J. Shelton, *English Hunger and Industrial Disorders . . . During the First Decade of George III's Reign* (Toronto, 1973), pp. 141–150, 158, 161. Dobson's list of labor disputes, 1717–1800, identifies 12 disruptions in 1764–1766, 27 in 1768–1769, and 17 in 1773–1775, *Masters and Journeymen*, pp. 159–162.
[18] *Journals of the House of Commons*, XXXIV, 239–241.

Pennsylvania Journal published a striking letter from "a gentleman near Glasgow" describing the "distress of the common people," the "almost total stagnation in our manufactures," and the flood of "labourers and mechanics, especially weavers in this neighbourhood . . . lately indented and gone to America." Anyone in the colonies, the letter writer declared, interested in setting up cloth manufactures [would] now have "an opportunity as favourable as they could wish for; they may immediately get from this country plenty of workmen as well skilled in these manufactures as any they will leave behind." And indeed, when that letter appeared in print, an enterprising twenty-two-year-old Derbyshire emigrant, Joseph Hague, who had been "brought up" in textile manufacture, was already following the writer's prescription. Shortly after his arrival in Philadelphia from Liverpool in the summer of 1774 he had launched a project to manufacture cloth, but he had found that the spinning of thread was so expensive in Pennsylvania that he would have to attend to that end of the business before he could proceed to cloth production. He therefore spent almost a year building, from memory, without "a plan or model of such machine," a spinning jenny, the first built in America, and then petitioned the Pennsylvania legislature to subsidize the initial use of the machine until his textile business could be established.[19]

Hague's experience had been in woolen and cotton weaving, which, like silk weaving, was a depressed industry in 1773 and 1774, especially after the effects of non-importation began to be felt. When Bristol, the commercial capital and communication center for the whole of western England, with excellent road and river communications to production centers from Yorkshire to Cornwall and east to London, cut back on its export trade, the city's broad hinterlands were severely affected. Woolen centers in Wiltshire, chronically plagued by unemployment, and in Gloucestershire, both regions served directly by the Bristol markets, slumped badly. In Chippenham and Devizes, two of the main production centers in Wiltshire, and in the surrounding countryside, "journeymen clothiers and their families are running about the country in a most miserable condition to seek bread." The condition of the poor was worsening too in Bradford, Wiltshire, and all of its surroundings. Of the mills in the Stroud district of Gloucestershire,

---

[19]"Account of the Progress and Estimate of the Present State of Manufactures in and about Paisley," *Weekly Magazine, or Edinburgh Amusement,* 32 (April 4, 1776), 44–46; Thomas Miller to the Earl of Suffolk, Barskimming [Ayrshire], Oct. 25, 1773, and Edinburgh, July 4, 1774, SP 54/46, 45: "I am sorry to inform Your Lordship that the spirit of migration still continues amongst the people of this country"; *Caledonian Mercury,* Feb. 12, March 23, 1774; *Pennsylvania Journal; and the Weekly Advertiser,* June 1, 1774; David J. Jeremy, "British Textile Technology Transmission . . . ," *Business History Review,* 47 (1973), 40–41. Hague's departure from Liverpool on the *Boston Packet,* together with 23 other emigrants—artisans and their families, drawn from all over England and from Scotland—is registered in T47/9/145; his petition to the Pennsylvania House is in *Pennsylvania Archives,* 8th ser., 8 (1935), 7215–16.

"some lie totally idle; others are little or not half employed." From both counties, journeymen clothiers were shipping out to the colonies. "More than five hundred hands in the woolen manufactory in the west of England," a report of February 1774 from London to South Carolina stated, "have embarked for North-America." In Bristol itself the normal level of unemployment and mobility in the working population rose significantly. The dangers of a continuing "stagnation of trade" in that capital of western England were manifest: "many thousands of [Bristol's] industrious poor," Parliament was told, "are and will be deprived of subsistance." Already, British steel workers "with their utmost industry can scarcely provide a sufficiency for themselves and their familys"; tobacco pipe makers were similarly affected by the deepening depression; tailors were striking for higher wages; and, inevitably, there were anxious reports of heightened emigration. If the several families known to have left Bristol for America in the spring of 1774, carrying with them "their arts and manufactures," succeeded in their resettlement overseas, "swarms will follow."[20]

Bristol's hinterland was one of the three major centers of the woolen industry, peculiarly sensitive to fluctuations in overseas trade. Of the other two concentrations, the more important was in Yorkshire, especially in the West Riding, which was in process of absorbing much of the woolen industry from elsewhere in Britain.[21] In 1773 reports from Leeds and the nearby Yorkshire towns—Dewsbury, Wakefield, Pontefract, Huddersfield, Halifax—were similar to those from Wiltshire and Gloucestershire. Substantial families were "finding it next to impossible, in the lamentable state of trade and dearness of provisions, to provide in any sort for themselves & their families"; unemployment was rising; the poor were facing destitution; farmers who depended on part-time work spinning and carding wool were failing to make ends meet; and they and others who were forced off the land by enclosures were compounding the troubles by moving to the industrial centers, where they faced further, and unsolvable, problems.

[20]R. G. Wilson, "The Supremacy of the Yorkshire Cloth Industry in the Eighteenth Century," in *Textile History and Economic History*, ed. N. B. Harte and K. G. Ponting (Manchester, Eng., 1973), p. 243; Walter Minchinton, *The Port of Bristol in the Eighteenth Century*, Bristol Historical Association, *Pamphlets*, no. 5 (1962), 5–6; W. E. Minchinton, ed., *The Trade of Bristol in the Eighteenth Century* (Bristol, 1957), pp. xii–xiv; E. Kerridge, "Agriculture 1500–1793," and Julia deL. Mann, "Textile Industries since 1550," in *History of Wiltshire*, ed. Elizabeth Crittall and R. B. Pugh *(Victoria History of the Counties of England)*, IV (London, 1959), 62–63, 162; *Virginia Gazette* (Rind), July 14, 1774; James Bischoff, *A Comprehensive History of the Woolen and Worsted Manufactures* . . . (London, 1782), I, 178; Jennifer Tann, *Gloucestershire Woolen Mills: Industrial Archaeology* (Newton Abbot, Devon, 1967), p. 40; *South-Carolina and American General Gazette*, April 22–26, 1774; [John Almon, ed.], *The Parliamentary Register . . . (1775–1780)*, I, 114–115; W. E. Minchinton, ed., *Politics and the Port of Bristol . . .*, (Bristol, 1963), p. 123; John Latimer, *The Annals of Bristol in the Eighteenth Century* (Frome and London, 1893), pp. 404, 414–415.
[21]R. G. Wilson, *Gentlemen Merchants: The Merchant Community in Leeds, 1700–1830* (Manchester, Eng., 1971), p. 37 and chap. 3 generally. The third area was East Anglia, especially Norfolk, which was quickly being outpaced by the West Riding.

Again, the inevitable result. From the industrial towns and villages of the West Riding and also from the North Riding and southern Durham came reports of a growing number of "manufacturers," "farmers and artificers" moving off to the seaports, especially Hull, to take passage overseas. The newspapers were full of letters from America describing conditions there, and public interest mounted steadily. "It is really surprising," the *York Chronicle and Weekly Advertiser* reported, "with what avidity they enquire for ships intending to sail [to North America], being desirous to embrace the first opportunity":

It touches ones heart [Virginians read in a letter from Norwich, England] to see our misery of the poor weavers. There used to be orders from the American merchants, but those being stopped by the apprehensions of the consequences of the acts against America now going on, prevents our manufacturers from being able to employ the poor workmen.[22]

Even more depressed than woolen production, especially as the effect of American non-importation was felt, was the linen industry, on which entire regional economies were dependent. A Parliamentary committee set up to investigate that industry—which was concentrated in the northeast in parts of Yorkshire and Durham, in the northwest in the Lancashire lowlands, and in the southwest in parts of Hampshire, Somerset, Dorset, Devon, and Wiltshire—received a flood of petitions from linen producers in all those areas and also from linen manufacturers in the Scottish Lowlands and Ireland. The pleas for relief were everywhere the same: the market had contracted, cuts were being made in the labor force, workers were facing a desperate situation, and people were emigrating, or talking about emigrating, or reading and hearing about people who were emigrating. "The spirit of emigration hath seized our people," ran a letter from the center of Irish linen production that appeared in the *Virginia Gazette*, "and the several counties hitherto famous for the residence of the linen manufacturers, are now almost dwindled into dreary wastes . . . scarcely a vessel sails from Ireland bound to any of the plantations, but what is filled with multitudes of useful artisans, their wives and children."[23]

So the textile industry in its many forms created a fluctuating redundancy of "useful artisans" throughout Britain—a population of experienced

[22] *Leeds Mercury*, May 17, March 1, 1774; letter from Wakefield, Yorks, April 2, 1774, reprinted in *South-Carolina Gazette*, June 3, 1774; Wilson, *Gentlemen Merchants*, p. 48; *York Chronicle and Weekly Advertiser*, March 4, 1774; *Virginia Gazette* (Rind), July 14, 1774.

[23] N. B. Harte, "The Rise of Protection and the English Linen Trade, 1690–1790," in Harte and Ponting, *Textile History*, pp. 102–103; *Journals of the House of Commons*, XXXIV, *passim*, esp. pp. 556–697; *Gentleman's Magazine*, 44 (March 1774), 137; *Virginia Gazette* (Rind), Nov. 11, 1773; *South-Carolina Gazette*, Oct. 4, 1773.

if not highly skilled workers, some of them part-time farmers, vulnerable to attractions of any kind, and habituated to think of emigration as one, if the most extreme, solution to economic pressure. But it was not only the large and scattered force of provincial textile workers that formed a pool of prospective emigrants. As in London and the Home Counties, there were throughout the British provinces unemployed or underemployed, restless, and mobile workers in the metal trades, in food production and distribution, in the building arts and crafts, and in the great array of service trades. Some were maintained in their home communities in an uncertain balance between occasional employment and public relief; others survived by patching together a pattern of local employment and seasonal migrations to work centers in nearby communities; still others, despairing of local solutions, joined the throngs moving off to London; a few pooled their resources, took fortune in hand, and voluntarily—as freemen, seeking paid employment for work in their crafts—joined relatives and friends in the colonies. And there were those who had no choice to consider anything voluntarily, but, like Harrower in London, "reduced to the last shilling," were "obliged to engage" themselves, when the opportunity arose, as bondsmen for four years of unpaid work in the colonies. And throughout the realm there were ordinary laborers, with even fewer choices than trained artisans, who added to the pool of potential emigrants.

To this population of available artisans, shopkeepers, and laborers— numerous in some places and in some trades and industries, scarce in others —must be added farmers and farmworkers, many of whom had occupied spare hours and supplemented their farm incomes by part-time work in local domestic industries, especially textiles, and, near woodland districts, in potting, tiling, coaling, and iron smelting. For the laboring population in many rural areas, agricultural employment, even when supplemented by part-time work in other occupations, had become highly unreliable. Commercial farming, enclosures, increased rents, and rising prices had forced out of customary rootages a growing number of farm laborers, who became "dependent on wages alone for their livelihood, often forced to wander from place to place till they found employment, or else to hire themselves out at the autumnal labour fairs held in many market towns." They could be found year after year at the hiring fairs, "where they stood in rows in the market-place, with ribbons in their caps to indicate their craft, waiting for some farmer to engage them." This "new population of migrant labour-ers . . . principally recruited from among the ranks of these disinherited peasants" were by no means all prone to emigrate. They were less commonly in touch with the process of emigration than town or city workers, and most often their needs could be satisfied by local and regional migrations. But some of them, particularly in regions otherwise involved in emigration, were susceptible to recruitment from abroad. They too—in their thousands in the Scottish Highlands, whose traditional economy was being transformed, in their hundreds in the coastal and suburban areas of England that were especially responsive to fluctuating commercial demands—were at least a partially redundant work force. Habituated to geographical movement and under pressure to find new roots and new sources of economic security, they too were available for recruitment.[24]

Convicts

Most available of all, of course, was the population of condemned criminals whose sentences had been commuted to banishment in the colonies, in effect to servitude, for periods of seven or fourteen years, in some cases for life. This source of manpower—despised by many but manifestly valuable to hard-pressed colonial employers—seemed particularly reliable. For the list of capital crimes, almost all of them offenses against property, approached two hundred in the later years of the eighteenth century, as Parliament sought "to make *every* kind of theft, malicious damage or rebellion an act punishable by death." The result was "one of the bloodiest criminal codes in Europe." But only in law, for while convictions under these statutes increased in number steadily through the century, the proportion of death sentences carried out declined, and the key to the discrepancy lies in the increasing commutation of capital sentences to "transportation" to the colonies. The combination of a savage, terror-inspiring criminal code and a discretionary, merciful magistracy, it appears, appealed to the rulers of British society as a balance well calculated to maintain social order in a tumultuous world.

The result, after the effects of the transportation act of 1717 were felt and with the encouragement of generous state subsidies to merchant contractors, was a rising tide of convict emigrants, most of whom, after their terms were completed, faded imperceptibly into the colonies' general white population. At the Old Bailey in London in 1755, for example, 240 men and women were convicted of felonies: 27 were let off lightly, 29 were probably executed, but the capital sentences of 184 were commuted to transportation. A multitude of similar court decisions siphoned off a random segment of the poor and unfortunate as well as of habitual criminals into the North American work force.[25]

Session after session, year after year, the formula was repeated. At the Old Bailey during the week in which the Treasury issued the order for

[24] Alan Everitt, "Farm Labourers," in *The Agrarian History of England and Wales, IV (1500–1640)*, ed. Joan Thirsk (Cambridge, Eng., 1967), pp. 425, 427, 399, 435.
[25] Douglas Hay *et al.*, *Albion's Fatal Tree* (New York, 1975), pp. 56, 18, 19; Ronald Leslie-Melville, *The Life and Work of Sir John Fielding* (London, [1934]), p. 44.

compiling the Register of emigrants, one Anthony Carnes was convicted for stealing goods, "val. 40s of George Peters. . . . jury say guilty—no goods —to be transported"; Timothy Featherstonehaugh Scutt, "for felony, stealing, & taking from the general post office two letters," transported; Henry Porte, "for stealing 10d. worth of goods," transported; Edward Coleman, "for ripping off a lead pipe of house of the East India Co.—to steal it," transported. The magnitude of the theft seems to have been irrelevant. John Harden, in that first week in December 1773, was condemned to transportation for stealing £11 6s. worth of goods; Richard Watson, for 10d. worth. And the next February Joseph Abrahams (alias Solomons) received the same sentence for stealing £131 6s. Some of those transported had not stolen but only connived as accessories: Jane Jones, Elizabeth Simmonds, and Thomas Sampson, for receiving goods worth £3 stolen by Mary Armstrong, "to be transported for 14 years." And some had only *tried* to steal and failed: years before, for example, Robert Halfpenny, "a young man, born of honest parents," who had successfully completed his apprenticeship, "unfortunately got intoxicated with liquor, and in that condition attempted to snatch a handkerchief from the body of a person in the street to him unknown, and was apprehended and convicted of the said attempt in April sessions last." His sentence of transportation was sustained despite Halfpenny's appeal to the Lord Mayor of London in which he pleaded his excellent prior record, his present misery and contrition, his master's willingness to "enter into recognizance for his setting [me] to work," and the financial sureties for his future good conduct by two upstanding London artisans. His career trails off somewhere in the records of the eighteenth-century American labor force.[26]

How deeply the experience of transportation entered into the consciousness of eighteenth-century Britons and into the fabric of British society and culture can only be surmised, but the evidence of a profound impact abounds. The mere idea of involuntary banishment, almost randomly imposed on the unfortunate and criminal—to some a miraculous and blessed reprieve from death, to others a savage deprivation of life as it had been known—together with the sight of coffles of manacled prisoners marching through the early-morning streets of London to the Thames or across the English countryside to pens in harbor prisons to await shipment —all of this had entered into popular awareness as early as the mid-seventeenth century.[27] And there were innumerable reports of the dread transat-

---

[26]General Sessions of the Peace for the City of London, Justice Hall in the Old Bailey, Dec. 8, 1773, Feb. 16, 1774, and Halfpenny's petition, 1725, Misc. MSS 38.3, Sessions Records.

[27]See the extraordinary petitions by people—some mere children, some half-blind, decrepit war veterans—praying for corporal punishment instead of the sentences to transportation just imposed. *Ibid.* On the scenes of the convicts moving from prisons to ships through the London streets and the English countryside, see Frederick H. Schmidt, "British Convict Servant Labor in Colonial Virginia" (Ph.D. diss., College of William and Mary, 1976), pp. 40–49.

lantic voyage under fearful physical conditions, the eventual sale of the prisoners to purchasers of labor (transactions considered to be indistinguishable from the sale of slaves), and years of drudgery in semitropical climates. As early as the late 1650s or 1660s the first of a series of popular ballads on the theme of transportation, *The Poor Unhappy Transported Felon's Sorrowful Account of His Fourteen Years Transportation at Virginia . . .* , appeared. In the later years of the seventeenth century, chapbook publishers ground out similar tales in prose and verse—*A Voyage to Virginia*; *the Trappan'd Maiden*; *Constancy Lamented.* Their evident popularity indicates a deep-felt response, and as soon as the newly authorized system of transportation went into full operation in the early eighteenth century, Daniel Defoe, ever alert to currents of thought and feeling in the swarming working population of London, wrote two novels, *Moll Flanders* and *Colonel Jack,* whose plots turned on the experience of transportation. This form of punishment became an important, ever-threatening fact of life for the whole of London's demimonde. Celebrated crime bosses like Jonathan Wild, of whom both Henry Fielding, a London magistrate as well as a writer, and Defoe wrote biographies, were known to base their gang operations on collusive manipulation of the transportation system.[28]

But though the phenomenon of transportation appears to have entered deeply into the awareness of eighteenth-century Britons, its psychological impact must remain conjectural. The demographic consequences, however, are more certain. The number of bodies—male and female, adult and child, able and incapacitated—produced for the American work force by the system has been estimated for the years 1718 to 1775 at 50,000. More definite is the figure of 18,600 convicts known to have been transported by the courts of London and the "home" circuit (Hertford, Essex, Kent, Sussex, and Suffolk) in the years 1719–1772. The convict contractors for this southeastern sector of England alone, therefore, were sending over, chiefly to Maryland and Virginia, an average of 326 convicts each year. And these figures represent only part of Britain's total: a reasonable estimate of the number of criminals made available by the courts in the other, provincial court circuits doubles the totals for southeastern England. Taking England as a whole, therefore, one finds that each year after Parliament extended and reinforced the system of transportation in the statute of 1717, an average of about 600 convicts were added to the pool of available men (and women and children) sent out to supplement the work force in America. In addition, as many as 16,000 convicts were estimated to have been added by

[28]John M. Jennings, ed., " 'The Poor Unhappy Transported Felon's Sorrowful Account of His Fourteen Years Transportation at Virginia in America,' " *Virginia Magazine of History and Biography,* 56 (1948), 180–194; Gerald Howson, *Thief-Taker General: The Rise and Fall of Jonathan Wild* (London, 1970), pp. 168–169; Hugh Jones, *The Present State of Virginia . . .* [1724], ed. Richard L. Morton (Chapel Hill, N.C., 1956), pp. 87, 210–212.

courts in Ireland, and about 800 by those in Scotland. The climax came in the decade before Independence. Each year between 1769 and 1776 about 960 convicts left the British Isles for the American colonies.[29]

In these shiploads of convicted felons were many hardened criminals— thieves, blackmailers, pimps, rapists, embezzlers, and thugs available for hire. But among them too were respectable tradesmen fallen on hard times, artisans who had forsaken their crafts out of desperation or dissipation or both, experienced farm hands, and capable laborers looking for a new life after a period of misadventure. Caught in the extraordinarily fine mesh of the eighteenth-century criminal laws, which classified equally as capital offenses both murder and the theft of a handkerchief, they formed a significant increment to the labor supply available for recruitment to the colonies.

[29]A. Roger Ekirch, *Bound for America: The Transportation of British Convicts to the Colonies, 1718–1775* (Oxford, Eng., Oxford Univ. Press, forthcoming) and Ekirch, "Bound for America: A Profile of British Convicts Transported to the Colonies, 1718–1775," *William and Mary Quarterly,* 42 (1985), 188. Abbot E. Smith, *Colonists in Bondage* (Chapel Hill, N.C., 1947), pp. 117, 311–312; A. G. L. Shaw, *Convicts and the Colonies* (London, 1966), p. 34. Ekirch has revised the earlier estimate of 30,000 for this period upward to 50,000.

9

Recruitment

T HUS, not only was the demand for labor powerful in the expanding middle colonies and in the Chesapeake region, but the supply was potentially plentiful in the chronically underemployed population of London and in the many areas of the British provinces, north and south of the Scottish border, where "declivities" in the upward slope of the British economy created the kind of misery and fear that impels people to search for radical solutions. But the demand, however powerful, was unstructured, and the supply remained only potential until mobilized. The conjunction between the two did not take place automatically. The American demand had to be focused and activated, some part of the British supply had to be organized, and the two had somehow to be brought together. This focusing, mobilization, and activation were the work of merchants and their correspondents, factors, and agents on both sides of the Atlantic engaged in business transactions impelled by the search for profits. Together they formed a network of labor marketers, whose reach stretched from cities, towns, villages, and farms throughout Britain to rough clearings on the Appalachian frontier, swampy plantations in Florida and Georgia, dusty grain and tobacco farms throughout the Chesapeake region, and villages, towns, and crossroads hamlets throughout North America, outside the New England colonies.

Precisely how large this network was, how many merchants, shipmasters, agents, factors, and other intermediaries were involved in this intercontinental transfer of labor, cannot be determined with any accuracy. In the years just before the Revolution the activities of at least thirty-eight colonial merchant firms that dealt in British servants, more than a third of them in Maryland, can be documented; but there were undoubtedly many others which traded less commonly or less publicly in the importation of workers from England and Scotland than these. For the trade in servants was almost always a sideline, incidental to the merchants' main business, profitable when conditions were right but erratic and risky when they were not. Only the merchants who held the exclusive contracts for transporting convicts had so reliable a source of supply that they could deal confidently in human "futures" and had, in effect, guaranteed profits. So many merchants took an occasional small "adventure" transporting a few indentured servants, and so many commercial vessels accommodated a few free workers as paying passengers that the commerce in the transfer of labor fades indistinguishably into commerce and shipping generally.[1]

But the precise numbers involved are less important than the pattern of this commerce and its bearing on the characteristics of the resulting immigrant population, and of that we can be more certain. For detailed business records of a number of the major merchandisers of imported labor, located at key transfer points on both sides of the Atlantic, have survived.[2] These papers, together with both British and American newspapers, public records, and personal documents, make possible the reconstruction of the process by which supply and demand were brought together—the process, that is, by which a labor force was gathered from the many parts of Britain, transported across the Atlantic, and marketed through broad reaches of coastal North America.

This process had evolved from origins that date back to the earliest years of colonization. By the 1770s the procedures were well established,

[1] Thus the merchant George Norton in London wrote his brother John in Yorktown, Va., Nov. 20, 1773, about recent shipments of goods, and then added: "As you are desirous of being concern'd in an adventure of servants, my father has engaged about half the number wrote for, chiefly Palatines [i.e., Germans], which [are] look'd on to be more civiliz'd & preferable in many respects to those of our own nation, the only objection will be their being less conversant with our language than natives. . . . The expence of equipping them &ca I fancy will exceed your calculation & the profit small. . . . I thank you for your offer that I may be a partner in the concern & readily acquiesce to the proposal." Norton then continued with his comments on "the goods you proposed ordering . . . blankets . . . candles" etc. F. N. Mason, ed., *John Norton and Sons . . .* (Richmond, Va., 1937), p. 362.

[2] The most useful collections for the years immediately preceding the Revolution proved to be the following: *In the Maryland Historical Society, Baltimore:* Smith Letterbooks; Russell Account Book. *In the Maryland Hall of Records, Annapolis:* Cheston-Galloway Papers; Johnson Letterbooks (published in part in *Joshua Johnson's Letterbook, 1771–1774,* ed. J. M. Price [London, 1979]). *In the Historical Society of Pennsylvania, Philadelphia:* Neave Account Book; James and Drinker Papers. *In the Massachusetts Historical Society, Boston:* Ridley Letterbook. *In the Library of Congress, Manuscript Division:* Woolsey and Salmon Letterbook. *In the Alderman Library, University of Virginia, Charlottesville:* Piper Letterbook; Russell Papers (microfilm). *In the New-York Historical Society, New York:* Lux Letterbook. And in addition, Thomas Clifford's correspondence, discussed in Grace H. Larsen, "Profile of a Colonial Merchant: Thomas Clifford of Pre-Revolutionary Philadelphia" (Ph.D. diss., Columbia Univ., 1955). For a study of the convict trade and its relationship to the Chesapeake labor market, based on the records of the Bristol firm of Stevenson, Randolph and Cheston, see Kenneth Morgan, "The Organization of the Convict Trade to Maryland: Stevenson, Randolph and Cheston, 1768–1775," *William and Mary Quarterly,* 42 (1985), 201–227.

and the problems were commonly understood. English and Scottish merchants, familiar with the needs of the American labor market and anxious to transmit any kind of profitable cargo, sought to gather some small part of the discontented and mobile labor force. The major British suppliers of servants—the firms, for example, of James Russell in London, Lancelot Cowper in Bristol, John Dixon and Isaac Littledale in Whitehaven, Cumberland, and John and George Buchanan in Greenock—were well aware that there was no organized national labor market in Britain nor even regional markets that could be drawn on in any systematic way in assembling groups of free workers or indentured servants for sale in the colonies. Even at the local level there were only two kinds of formal institutions that served as rallying points for available labor—intelligence or register offices and statute fairs or halls—and while both were involved in the transatlantic servant trade, neither provided the main mechanism of recruitment.

Register Offices and Statute Halls and Fairs

The intelligence, later called register, offices were private, profit-making employment agencies, which first appeared in London in the early seventeenth century and which quickly acquired a reputation for corruption. Applicants for employment on the one hand and for servants on the other paid fees for registering their needs, and the connections between them were made by the managers according to their own strategies or whims. Unscrupulous, involved in a variety of shady dealings, these operators often fleeced desperate job applicants of fees with false promises of available openings. Occasionally they trapped destitute women into prostitution, and as a consequence the intelligence offices in general became thought of popularly as "markets of pimps and procuresses" and "warehouses of iniquity." In the course of the seventeenth century these more or less corrupt offices became increasingly involved in the shadier aspects of the transatlantic servant trade. It was understood that the thoroughly naïve or the truly down-and-out who ventured into the central London intelligence offices were likely to end up as indentured servants in the colonies whether they wanted to or not. The managers sold them, in effect, to middlemen in the servant trade, who furnished them, for a fee, to merchants capable of transporting them overseas and profiting by their eventual sale. So Ned Ward in his salacious and sensational *London Spy* of 1699 described the plantation walk in the London Exchange as "kidnappers' walk," for there, he wrote, the colonial agents look "as sharp for servants as a gang of pick-pockets for a booty." The intelligence office just inside the back gate of the Exchange, he said, only pretends to help servants find jobs and masters find servants. "They have a knack of bubbling silly wenches out of their money, who loiter hereabouts upon the expectancy of work, till they are pick'd up by the plantation kidnappers and spirited away into a state of misery and whoredom."[3]

Ward played up the sensational aspects of the intelligence offices' traffic in the down-and-out, but their unsavory reputation was justified, and persisted despite an elaborate effort of Henry and Sir John Fielding in the mid-eighteenth century to transform the offices into public agencies, licensed and regulated by the government. The Fieldings' enterprise, part of a broad attempt on the part of these leading city magistrates and a few others to alleviate the misery and reduce the crime and disorder that so beset everyday life in central London, failed ultimately, and the labor exchanges they created, by then generally called register offices, drifted back into the old pattern.[4] In the 1770s the managers of these bureaus continued to solicit, as they had throughout the previous century, "any merchants that have occasion for servants to go beyond sea" and to inveigle the desperately poor and unemployed into allowing themselves to be sold into servitude abroad. One couple who kept a "lock-up house" in London were prosecuted in 1775 for kidnapping, incarcerating, and "conspiring to send into foreign countries" (in fact Maryland) a girl whose mother claimed she was seventeen years old. At the trial—almost a year after the girl had sailed to Maryland on one of the registered ships, together with 98 others to be sold upon arrival—it emerged that the kidnappers had received £9 7s 6d from middlemen to assemble in similar ways "near an hundred people." Such enterprises were notorious. They featured in a popular London theatrical farce, *The Register Office* (1758), in which the office manager, Gulwell, decides to indenture, secretly, an obnoxious Irishman ("He will fetch a rare price in the plantations"), but is caught and denounced: "You kidnapping rascal," the Irishman shouts, "you was going to send me into the other world to be turn'd into a black negro."[5]

However infamous, these shady dealers in human misery were too

---

[3] J. Jean Hecht, *The Domestic Servant Class in Eighteenth-Century England* (London, 1956), p. 31; *The London Spy by Ned Ward*, ed. Kenneth Fenwick (London, 1955), p. 56. Cf. M. Dorothy George, "The Early History of Registry Offices," *Economic History*, 1 (*Economic Journal* [*Supplement*], no. 4 [Jan., 1929]), 572–579.

[4] The registry offices in the provinces seem to have been considerably more respectable. The notices of Cross's Register Office in York, for example, advertised for housekeepers, cooks for well-known inns, butlers, gardeners, farmers, builders, wharfingers, etc.—but only people with appropriate skills and with "good characters" were asked to apply. *Etherington's York Chronicle*, Feb. 25, 1774.

[5] George, "Registry Offices," pp. 579–590; M. Dorothy George, *London Life in the Eighteenth Century* ([1925], Harmondsworth, Eng., 1976), pp. 150–151; Joseph Reed, "The Register Office," in *Cawthorn's Minor British Theatre* (1806), III, pp. 43, 53. The 17-year-old kidnapped girl, called Elizabeth "Brittleband" or "Brickleband" in the court records (George, *London Life*, pp. 150–151) was entered in the Register as Elizabeth "Brittlebank," a 21-year-old redemptioner servant aboard the *Nancy*, bound for Baltimore, June 1775 (T47/10/97).

disreputable and their wares too few and too unattractive and hence too difficult to market to become major contributors to the indentured servant trade. Nor were the statute fairs in the countryside or their urban variants, the statute halls, major mechanisms for recruiting labor for work overseas. For, though in the early eighteenth century the statute fairs, originally administrative sessions for enforcing wage regulations, had devolved into labor exchanges, by the end of the century that function had declined in most places, and the gatherings had become largely festive occasions, amusement fairs for farm servants relaxing from the year-long round of labor. And the statute halls in the cities too lost their primary function. Like the old intelligence offices, they had come to be viewed as—and in part were—run by "downright bullies and bawds, and old procurers." Though they were more open in their daily procedures than the register offices, they too operated at the disreputable margins of the huge but scattered and unorganized labor markets.[6]

Public Notification

To penetrate these markets and attract the kind of workers that would command good prices in the American colonies—always the prime consideration—the merchants and their agents relied primarily on public notification, in the expectation that interested individuals would make contact with them in ways they specified in their notices.

Public houses were important focuses of this form of communication. In London, and in the provinces as well, they were houses of call for artisans of all kinds. Some were almost private clubs for workers in particular trades, owned or kept by retired or part-time members of the trade concerned. The pubs, whose keepers were well acquainted with their customers and often extended credit to them in hard times, commonly became informal employment agencies where foremen in need of workmen were likely to call. Since the pubs were often used as clearing houses for casual workers' wage payments and since a considerable percentage of the workers' wages were spent in the pub, hiring agents and publicans commonly worked together closely. In such public houses, managed as informal employment agencies for artisans of ordinary skill—and in coffeehouses where somewhat more affluent or genteel workers congregated, and in inns of various degrees of gentility to which travelers and migrants of all sorts naturally gravitated—the merchants and the middlemen in the labor business posted notices of opportunities overseas, detailing information on

[6]K. L. McCutcheon, "Yorkshire Fairs and Markets . . .," *Publications of the Thoresby Society*, 39 (1939), 156–159; George, "Registry Offices," p. 585; Hecht, *Domestic Servant Class*, p. 30; Ann Kussmaul, *Servants in Husbandry in Early Modern England* (Cambridge, Eng., 1981), pp. 60–63.

trades or skills particularly in demand and schedules of ship departures.

So in April 1775 a visitor to one of the coffeehouses in Leith, the port of Edinburgh, found a typical notice posted. It informed the public that, at a specified time, in about three weeks from the date of the notice, a ship was to sail from Leith to Philadelphia. Young men and women willing to indenture themselves were asked to apply to the shipmaster, who left word where he could be found and where messages could be left for him. Such notices were an essential part of the system. The Philadelphia merchant Thomas Clifford, actively at work importing servants from Bristol, was confident that recruits would show up once his vessel, *Anna*, arrived in England and "her advertisements are up." In one form or another advertisements for indentured servants and free workers were up in the pubs, inns, and coffeehouses in all the main port towns of Britain, and in many of the minor ports too: Whitby and Scarborough in Yorkshire; Deal in Kent; Portsmouth in Hampshire; Poole in Dorset; Stranraer, Campbeltown, Kirkwall, and Dumfries in Scotland. And they appeared everywhere in London, "offering," wrote William Eddis, who had spent most of his life among London's petty shopkeepers and artisans, "the most seducing encouragement . . . to those who are disgusted with the frowns of fortune in their native land, and to those of an enterprising disposition who are tempted to court her smiles in a distant region." Notices were circulated in other ways too: in newspapers and in circulating handbills, copies of which commonly ended up on marketplace walls. And all of the information contained in these notices circulated by word of mouth in the countryside and among groups of city workers, reaching far beyond the ambit of the readership itself.[7]

Middlemen

At the same time as the merchants solicited servants impersonally through printed notices, they also undertook more direct and individual recruitment, most often through middlemen or agents of one sort or another. One enterprising merchant "who makes it his business to carry mechanics of all denominations to America as transports for 4 years" served as his own agent in a coffeehouse located at a strategic spot on the outskirts of London. There in November 1773 he managed to sign on "a hundred likely young men," certain, he said, "that he could make more money of them than he

[7] George, *London Life*, pp. 284 ff.; *Caledonian Mercury*, April 19, 1775; Larsen, "Thomas Clifford," pp. 118, 120; *Felix Farley's Bristol Journal*, March 12, 1774; William Eddis, *Letters from America*, ed. Aubrey C. Land (Cambridge, Mass., 1969), p. 37. For typical advertisements placed by American and West Indian employers seeking workers and workers seeking employment in America, see *Daily Advertiser* (London), Feb. 16, March 4, 19, 29, May 11, 1774.

could of double a quantity of blacks from the coast of Guinea." Some merchants sent their agents to places where the available poor were known to gather: to certain pubs, to the Spitalfields market square in London, where indigent silk weavers congregated, and to almshouses and poor-houses. In the last they bartered with the overseers, only too eager to unload their charges, and with the more attractive of the indigent charges them-selves in an effort to convince them to exchange their meager, hopeless existences for more promising lives overseas.[8]

These were respectable recruiters; but some—the so-called crimps—were known to be unscrupulous exploiters of human misery. The crimps' common practice, from which they made large profits, was to induce their impoverished victims, most often seamen, to pile up debts for drink, food, and clothes they could not afford, and then to confront them with the choice of debtors' prison or unwilling service—on naval vessels, on slaving ships, or as indentured servants in the colonies.[9]

The crimps' vicious tactics were famous, but they could not be success-ful on a large scale because their victims, for whom they were paid by the head, were likely to be the most miserable and unpromising, the least attractive, of human beings, and hence unlikely to command high prices in the colonial labor markets. Such unpromising human material came to the colonies in any case in the form of transported criminals, who at least had the attraction to employers of being committed to seven or fourteen years of labor, while the crimps' victims could be sold for only four or five. The highest prices always went for the most respectable indentees, the most highly skilled in useful trades, and the most versatile, promising, teachable, and adaptable. These were the servants the merchants chiefly sought, and to locate and engage them they sometimes made strenuous efforts.

The Philadelphia merchant Thomas Clifford, an idealistic booster both of America as the land of opportunity for the industrious poor and of indentured servitude as a socializing and educational process, hit on an unusual scheme to get "only such [as] we would wish to have to do with." Eager to import healthy, clever, industrious, young, and above all orderly

[8] *York Courant*, Nov. 23, 1773; T. S. Ashton, *An Economic History of England: The 18th Century* (London, 1955), p. 219. For reports that overseers of the poor in Yorkshire were paying the freight charges of the poor and of those "likely to become chargeable" in order to ship them off to "a distant clime," see *York Chronicle and Weekly Advertiser*, April 15, 1774.

[9] George, *London Life*, p. 302; Eddis, *Letters from America*, p. 37: Those who succumbed to the lures of these advertisements, Eddis wrote, "are referred to agents, or crimps, who represent the advan-tages to be obtained in America in colors so alluring that it is almost impossible to resist their artifices. Unwary persons are accordingly induced to enter into articles by which they engage to become servants, agreeable to their respective qualifications, for the term of five years, every necessary accommodation being found them during the voyage and every method taken that they may be treated with tenderness and humanity during the period of servitude, at the expiration of which they are taught to expect that opportunities will assuredly offer to secure to the honest and industrious a competent provision for the remainder of their days."

British artisans and to avoid troublesome and shiftless vagrants and Irish-men ("few but their own country men chuse to have them"), he sent over to Bristol one of his own indentured servants as living proof of the opportunities that existed in America and as a spokesman for his views. More commonly, Clifford sent to his regular Bristol factors the names of relatives of former emigrants who were well settled in Pennsylvania. Some of those contacted in this way had already been urged by letters from their families to join the emigration, and it was therefore not difficult to recruit them. In at least one case Clifford cooperated with a woman recently arrived in Pennsylvania in locating and bringing over her husband and sons as re-demptioners. Convinced of the "quality" of the family, Clifford trusted the woman to make every effort to have the necessary redemption money ready by the time her relatives arrived.

But Clifford's extraordinary efforts to locate precisely the kinds of immigrants that he wished (as he put it in 1768) "to contribute . . . to the peopling of His Majesty's colonies" never provided the numbers he hoped for; he was obliged to take many servants not up to his high standards. Some of those whom he found hopelessly below par he sent back to England, occasionally at his own expense. But there were few merchants on either side of the Atlantic as conscientious or as socially conscious as Clifford. The British merchants and their agents who were principally responsible for shipments to the colonies were mainly concerned with the prices the inden-tees could command in the American markets, and they made some, though not a great, effort to select with that in mind.[10]

Gravesend

One of the most convenient ways they found to do this was to travel, themselves, to Gravesend, twenty-six miles down the Thames from London, and supervise the final selection of indentees. The town of Gravesend, built on the shores of a broad basin in the river a few miles from the channel, was the ultimate departure point and customs clearance for vessels leaving England by the Thames. Since it was at Gravesend that final freight and passenger lists were drawn up and certified, and articles of indenture were completed and notarized, a labor pool formed there, made up of unem-ployed or discontented workers from all over southeastern England and in smaller numbers from elsewhere in Britain and Ireland. Shipmasters drew last-minute replacements of seamen from this pool and merchants com-pleted their cargoes of marketable servants.

The scene at Gravesend must have been busy, crowded, colorful. The

[10]Larsen, "Thomas Clifford," pp. 114–119.

Gravesend, the final registration and departure point for emigrants leaving London.

small town, which had numerous inns, taverns, and other houses of accommodation, was usually crowded with seamen, dockhands, travelers of all kinds, and unemployed workers seeking berths. The river basin was full of vessels, not only ocean-going ships but ferries and the more commodious "tiltboats," bearing passengers, horses, cattle, and carriages down from London and across the Thames from Kent to Essex. Customs bells rang out to announce arrivals and departures, musket shots resounded from the blockhouse as customs officials warned incoming vessels to stop and anchor for inspection, and cannonades drove back vessels attempting to leave without authorization. Occasionally alarms were sounded when convicts, incarcerated sometimes for weeks in the stifling holds of anchored vessels provisioning for the transatlantic voyage, jumped ship and attempted to swim the few hundred yards to freedom.[11]

Amid all this "bustle and continued hurry of business" doctors boarded the anchored transatlantic vessels to weed out passengers with infectious diseases, convict contractors issued cheap clothing to their human freight, clerks completed the indentures of the voluntary bondsmen, and the indentees made their own last-minute arrangements. One indentured servant wrote from shipboard "little below Grave[s]end Church" to his relatives in

[11]Edward Hasted, *The History . . . of Kent . . .* (Canterbury, Eng., 1797), III, 323; *A Tour thro' the Whole Island of Great Britain . . . by a Gentleman,* 5th ed. (London, 1753), I, 135–136; Frederick H. Schmidt, "British Convict Servant Labor in Colonial Virginia" (Ph.D. diss., College of William and Mary, 1976), pp. 49–51, 81.

London to redeem the clothes he had pawned in the city and send them to him as soon as possible. Harrower recorded the final preparations as his ship lay at anchor at Gravesend: clerks "fulling up the indentures," a doctor sending back two servants "haveing the clap," shiphands taking in provisions and water, and at the last minute a servant, struck down with a severe fever, being carried ashore.

It was during this stopover period of preparation at Gravesend that the merchants were able to inspect the transient labor gathered at the town's docks, pubs, inns, coffeehouses, and marketplaces and make their final choices. Only when he got to Gravesend, the London merchant George Norton wrote his brother John in Yorktown, Virginia, would he know the exact number of indentees he and their father would be able to send to Virginia. Similarly Joshua Johnson, a London merchant deeply involved in the Virginia tobacco trade, thought it worthwhile to make the trip to Gravesend himself "to indent what servants I can get." He recorded one occasion when he traveled the twenty-six miles to the exit port partly in hopes—unfulfilled, as it turned out—of indenting a single joiner ordered by one of his American customers and promised for delivery at Gravesend by an unreliable crimp.[12]

Supply and Demand

Matching the random British supply with specific American demands was always an uncertain business, and the more specific the demand the more uncertain the merchant's task became. Individual orders for particular kinds of workmen were seldom filled with anything like dispatch.[13] Workers of the highest skills and in greatest demand—particularly joiners, that is, skilled cabinetmakers and ornamental woodworkers—even if unemployed or poor, at times simply refused to accept the usual conditions of servitude. To Charles Wallace, the senior partner in an Annapolis, Maryland, firm then building the colony's new statehouse, Joshua Johnson wrote in 1771 that he had alerted his agent "to be on the lookout for two such servants as you describe," but he doubted that any of the skilled construction workers Wallace wanted could be had "without giving wages." "Daily conferences" with the agent proved his doubts justified. Building craftsmen, indeed, he wrote, "will not go without wages," and he refused to get into

[12][William Roberts] to John Broughton, March 10, 1756, in James P. P. Horn, ed., "The Letters of William Roberts of All Hollows Parish, Anne Arundel County, Maryland, 1756–1769," *Maryland Historical Magazine*, 74 (1979); 124; *The Journal of John Harrower: An Indentured Servant in the Colony of Virginia*, ed. Edward M. Riley (Williamsburg, Va., 1963), p. 19; George Norton to John Norton, Nov. 20, 1773, in *Norton and Sons*, p. 362; *Johnson's Letterbook*, pp. 122, 151.
[13]Orders such as that of "Mr. Jones, a very honest mechanic . . . to purchase of you a journeyman barber" were often simply ignored. *Norton and Sons*, p. 369.

that kind of recruitment without specific authorization from Maryland. Two particularly able and skillful craftsmen whom he eventually sent— "sober, honest, industrious men and well qualified"—took a particularly independent line. They agreed to go to Maryland and work for Wallace only with the understanding that their main aim was "to make trial" of the prospects of their eventually setting themselves up in their own construction business in Maryland, in effect in competition with Wallace, and only if Johnson advanced them £12 for their passage money.[14]

Such individual recruitment of servants was unusual. Most often the British merchants simply signed on the workers who came forward or whom their agents could produce, and made appropriate arrangements for the terms of their servitude according to commonly accepted criteria. The hope was that the American buyers would find sufficient satisfaction by locating among the variety included in shiploads of 20, 50, or 75 indentees an approximation, at least, of the particular kinds of workers they needed. But even this casual and wholesale method of recruiting servants could prove frustrating: there were all sorts of problems in gathering servants. Since the labor markets were narrowly local, the simultaneous loading of several ships could slow the whole process down for any one merchant and limit the numbers he could find. "Servants at this time of the year of any kind grow scarce," Johnson wrote in February 1774, "as there is such a number of ships going out."[15] Sudden, short-lived booms in employment —during seasonal upswings in manufactures or during harvest seasons— could temporarily stop recruitment altogether.

And there was, in addition, a complication beyond these palpable irregularities in the availability of recruits. There was at times a surprising casualness in the decisions of some of the workers to migrate to America. They could easily be swayed one way or another at the last moment, and securing their commitments could be difficult. Like Harrower, faced with unemployment and driven to the last extremity of poverty, they needed but a momentary upswing of fortune to regain their footing, and therefore often hesitated, glancing behind them, as it were, as they entered into the process of emigration. In the end, at times, the dramatic and life-determining decision to emigrate seems to have been subject to immediate, quite trivial-appearing pressures. Clifford, for example, writing his Bristol agent Cowper in the spring of 1768, attributed a sudden scarcity in the supply of indentured servants to the approaching general election. "The poor people rather inclined," he said, "to partake of the entertainment given on that

[14] Rosamond R. Beirne and John H. Scarff, *William Buckland, 1734–1774: Architect of Virginia and Maryland* (Baltimore, 1958), pp. 69, 100–101; *Johnson's Letterbook*, pp. 5, 13, 32–33. On forms of contract labor, see above, chap. 5, n. 17.

[15] *Ibid.*, p. 122.

occasion than to embark for America"—as if one or two drunken, meat-stuffing feasts were taken as seriously as permanent migration and transplantation overseas.[16]

Enticement and Kidnapping

So accident—whim, almost—seems at times to have played a significant role in the workers' decisions, and it is the impact of the merchants' determination to round up sufficient cargoes of servants, working upon the servants' tentativeness and uncertainty, that helps explain the repeated outcries of kidnapping, intimidation, and improper enticement.

The structure of the problem had been clear since the mid-seventeenth century, and was explained in detail in a sensational publication, "A Curious Discourse on Kidnapping" (1759). Merchants responding to suddenly rising prospects for profitable sales of servants in the colonies intensified their search for recruits and instructed their agents to collect specific numbers of indentees. Unemployed or destitute or discouraged workers were thereupon enticed by tales of the wonders of that "best poor man's country" and of the excellent prospects for prosperity they would find overseas. Adventurous, idle, and rebellious teenage boys were particularly susceptible to such blandishments, and they were always in demand. A temporary bargain would be struck with interested prospects by the payment to them of a small amount of money as an earnest of the benefits that lay ahead.[17]

Thereafter, while the recruits' doubts may have remained, the merchants' costs began to mount. Weeks would pass before the indentures were completed, the vessels freighted and provisioned, customs obligations satisfied, and the voyages begun. During all that time the merchants had to feed and provide living space for their charges if they expected to keep them, and they had also to take steps to prevent repudiation of the often still unformalized agreements. Various devices were used. In Bristol merchants were known to incarcerate the indentees in Bridewell for as long as three weeks, until they could be placed aboard ship. The author of the "Discourse" claimed that he had been enticed into servitude as an eight-year-old while "playing on the key" and kept below decks for a month before his vessel sailed. Servants maintained by the merchants pending departure were released to wander about only on payment of a sum for each

[16]Larsen, "Thomas Clifford," p. 120.
[17]Peter Williamson, *French and Indian Cruelty: Exemplified in the Life and Various Vicissitudes of Fortune, of Peter Williamson. Containing . . . a Curious Discourse on Kidnapping . . .*, 4th ed. (London, 1759), pp. 103 ff. (The pamphlet, without the "Curious Discourse," was first published in York, 1757.)

day they had been supported at the merchants' expense—a sum few of the servants could afford to pay.[18]

In such situations force easily became a part of the story. As the indentees began to experience the security of guaranteed sustenance, some of them came to doubt the wisdom of their decision, but found themselves committed, now against their will. Parents and masters who discovered that their footloose children had accepted indentures were also faced with commitments they wished to break. Struggles ensued, indentees were forcibly retained, and charges of kidnapping, spiriting, and illegal incarceration were made, and these charges were pursued, at times, into the courts. Such episodes multiplied significantly when particularly heavy demands for servants in the colonies coincided with a sudden improvement in conditions in Britain. At such times the merchants, bearing high shipping costs for vessels sent especially to collect large numbers of servants and finding their hoped-for supply severely reduced, were little inclined to question the methods their agents used to collect and to keep the manpower they sought.

No doubt there were instances of outright kidnapping in the trade in indentured servants. The late eighteenth century was an era when press gangs still swept through the streets of port towns seizing likely recruits for the royal navy and when vagrants could still be forced into servitude.[19] But there were probably few such cases in the indentured-servant trade— far fewer than there had been a hundred years earlier, when the colonies were universally regarded as a wild outback, a world of brutal exploitation beyond the boundaries of normal civility, and when the need for regulation of the servant trade was still being discovered.[20] In the 1770s, when the

---

[18]John Latimer, *The Annals of Bristol in the Eighteenth Century* (Frome and London, 1893), p. 153; Williamson, *French and Indian Cruelty*, p. 7. One merchant, a specialist in sending "mechanics of all denominations to America as transports for 4 years," allowed his charges to go "on shore to see their friends" only upon payment of "five shillings per day for all the time they have been on board." *York Courant*, Nov. 23, 1773.

[19]The Scottish poor law of 1672, which gave coalmasters the right "to seise upon any vagabonds or beggars wherevir they can find them and put them to worke in their coal-hewghs [open coal pits] or other manufactories," remained operative through most of the eighteenth century: "serfdom . . . was very much the norm in the coal industry until 1775." Baron F. Duckham, "Serfdom in Eighteenth Century Scotland," *History*, 54 (1969), 178–179.

[20]In London in the early 1660s the "wicked custome to seduce or spirit away young people to goe as servants to [the] plantations" had become so widespread that petty thieves had made a racket of voluntarily indenting themselves in order to collect "mony, cloathes, dyet, and other conveniences" from the merchants and then claiming they had been kidnapped to gain release. ("The Humble Petition of Diverse Merchants, Planters, and Masters of Shipps" . . . [1664], in Entry Book on Spiriting, CO 389/2, Public Record Office, London. In Bristol, too, charges of kidnapping had been common enough to cause riots in the streets and on the docks. Regulations were obviously needed and in time were mandated. Among them were the first national register of indentees referred to above, pp. 67–68 n.2, by which merchants could prove their innocence; a universal indenture form in which servants could certify their consent; limitation on the age of consent without parental approval; and customs scrutiny of all passengers on outbound ships. Documents in the Entry Book on Spiriting cited above. Cf. Abbot E. Smith, *Colonists in Bondage* (Chapel Hill,

gentility of life in long-settled parts of the colonies was commonly recognized and when a series of regulations helped guarantee the voluntary character of the servant trade, allegations of kidnapping mainly reflected the merchants' urgencies on the one hand and the ambiguities of the servants' responses on the other; but however they originated, such charges further complicated the process of recruitment.

It is this configuration that underlies the events that took place on the island of Lewis in the Outer Hebrides in the spring of 1774. Lewis and its southern extension, Harris, which together measure fifty miles in length by fifteen to thirty miles in breadth, had in 1774 a population of only nine thousand, but they had contributed a remarkable number of emigrants to the exodus of the previous two or three years. How many hundreds, or thousands, of the crofters, fishermen, weavers, and graziers of that bleak island of peat bogs, wet grassland, and small vegetation had left for America in the decade before 1774 is not known, but the exodus had become notorious, and it would climax in the departure in the single month of July 1774 of 840 men, women, and children.[21] To some, the island seemed to be in the process of complete depopulation, and that threat accounts for the sudden appearance on the island, in September 1773, of the landlord of Lewis, the Earl of Seaforth.

The entire island belonged "in property or superiority" to this thirty-year-old head of the Mackenzie clan, "a lively pretty young man," James Boswell had reported earlier, "with the most perfect elegance of manner, having been abroad a great many years." Seaforth's interest in Lewis, or in any part of Scotland, which he scarcely knew at all, was confined to rents, and his rents had failed to keep up with the rising costs of the fashionable existence he enjoyed in London and on the continent in circles famous for their extravagance. In 1770, deeply in debt despite an income from his lands of over £14,000 a year, he had jacked up the rents on Lewis. This had touched off much of the exodus, and in the face-to-face confrontation of September 1773 the tenants demanded a return to the old rents, refunds of the augmentations of rents paid over the previous three years, and the dismissal of Seaforth's agent, who had exacted the new rents. How much of this program Seaforth agreed to is not known, but news of the highly unusual confrontation of landlord and tenants circulated throughout the

---

N.C., 1947), p. 73 and chap. 4 generally. But charges of kidnapping continued to appear. The most famous case of the mid-eighteenth century was that of the author of the "Discourse on Kidnapping," Peter Williamson. When, upon his return to Aberdeen after years of bizarre and bloody adventures in North America, he charged that the city magistrates and leading merchants had kidnapped him, he was sued for libel. He won the case, and thereupon twice sued the merchants for damages. The affair is summarized in [Joseph Robertson], *The Book of Bon-Accord: Or, A Guide to the City of Aberdeen* (Aberdeen, 1838), I, 91–93.

[21] *York Courant*, Oct. 5, 1773. The *London Chronicle*, July 17–20, 1773, reported the departure of 700–800 people from Stornoway on the previous June 22.

British world: accounts appeared in newspapers in Edinburgh, York, London, and (in both German and English) in Pennsylvania.[22]

It was the fame of the migration from Lewis and the likelihood of many more departures that brought to the island's main harbor, Stornoway, on the 17th of March, 1774, the *Friendship* of Philadelphia, a vessel owned by the Philadelphia firm of James Stuart and Samuel Jackson and commanded by an apparently quite ruthless, or at least very tactless, captain, Thomas Jann. An experienced hand in the servant trade, Jann had brought with him as mate a native of Lewis, Colin McLeod, who had emigrated only the year before, and the two men immediately set about collecting all the servants they could get. Within a week they had signed on fifty men, women, and children, whom they presented to the customs officials to be "attested." And then they went after more. At that point Seaforth's steward on the island panicked. Though Jann and McLeod were not the only recruiters around ("no fewer than seven different companies," the steward reported, were at work on Lewis and the adjoining Scottish mainland), their operation was particularly threatening. Jann and his mate, the steward wrote in alarm to Seaforth's business agent in Edinburgh, were "taking in boys off the beach and shore without the consent of their parents or masters then they lock them up on board of the vessel, and the poor parents and masters are debarred from ever seeing them." The Pennsylvanians were engaged, in other words, in kidnapping, and something had to be done about it.[23]

The alarm spread. The agent in Edinburgh contacted Seaforth himself, who took time off from his amorous affairs (he was in the midst of preparations for a trip abroad with his mistress) to submit a memorial to the secretary of state, Lord Suffolk, asking for the only kind of help he thought would make any difference. Given the behavior of the various crews then in Stornoway harbor, particularly the crew from Philadelphia, which were "professedly employed in ensnaring & seducing the inhabitants to emigrate to America, and not only carry off persons who are lessees and under engagements for a future tract of time to the memorialist and the servants of such lessees, but also apprentices and infants under the age of 21 years without the consent of their masters and parents"—given all this, Seaforth

[22]Thomas Miller to the Earl of Suffolk, July 4, 1774, SP 54/45; Lewis Namier and John Brooke, *The House of Commons, 1754–1790* (London, 1964), III, 88–89; Loretta Timperley, "Landownership in Scotland in the Eighteenth Century" (Ph.D. diss., Univ. of Edinburgh, 1977), p. 154; *Caledonian Mercury*, Sept. 29, 1773; *York Courant*, Oct. 5, 1773; *Wöchentliche Pennsylvanische Staatsbote*, Dec. 21, 1773 (picking the story up from a London paper dated Oct. 6).
[23]A complete file of the Miller-Seaforth-Suffolk-Gillanders (Seaforth's steward) correspondence concerning the *Friendship* and Capt. Jann's behavior on Lewis is contained in SP 54/45/697–706. The episode is described in detail by the Stornoway customs officials, March 24 and May 2, 1774, Customs Collectors, Stornoway, to Board of Customs, Edinburgh, Stornoway Customs Letter Books.

asked that "a small command of the military" be stationed at Stornoway to back up the weak civil power in preventing the illegal recruiting.

With such a proposal, which he had heard before, Suffolk had no sympathy, but he forwarded Seaforth's memorial to Thomas Miller, the lord justice clerk, in Edinburgh, and asked for his opinion. Miller quizzed Seaforth's agent and made other inquiries, and was soon able to confirm the facts. Jann's conduct, he wrote Suffolk, was indeed "audacious"; his

> carrying off boys from this island aboard his ship without consent of their parents or masters . . . is highly injurious to his Lordship and to the people of that island and most provocking to every person interested in government . . . and if such practices were to prevail and pass unnoticed it would be attended with very bad consequences.

But were Jann and McLeod in fact kidnappers, seducers? By the time Miller wrote to Suffolk, the *Friendship* had arrived safely in Philadelphia and its cargo of servants was being sold at Stuart and Jackson's wharf. There is no question but that Jann and McLeod had concentrated on collecting boys separated from their families, and to a lesser extent girls too. Of the 106 registered passengers, 43, or 40.6%, gave no indication that they were emigrating in family groups; these were probably the main subjects of the steward's solicitude. The average age of the males in the group was 16.4 years; of the females, 21.3. Two-fifths of the males were 15 or younger (the youngest was 9), 92% were 19 or younger. And, if one eliminates all those whose surnames were the same as surnames of members of the family groups, thus isolating those who were almost certainly traveling alone, the figures are even more extreme: the average age of the twenty-one boys in this category is only 15.4, of the seven girls, 14.4. And, just as Seaforth's steward had reported, these children had been collected from all over the island—from thirteen of the hamlets that ring Lewis's misty coasts, desolate crofting settlements like Bayble, Lochs, Holm, Garrobost, Ness, Barvas, and Uig; only a fifth of the boys had come from the main port town of Stornoway.[24]

Seaforth's steward was certain that these children had been kidnapped or seduced; his agent too was convinced; and the lord justice clerk in turn was also convinced. But the furor over Jann's tactics had led the customs

---

[24] The *Friendship*'s arrival in Philadelphia (June 12) with its cargo of servants was advertised in the *Pennsylvania Journal; and the Weekly Advertiser* and the *Pennsylvania Gazette* on June 22, 1774, in the *Virginia Gazette* (Purdie and Dixon), July 7, and in the *New-York Journal; or, the General Advertiser,* June 30. By July 4, when the vessel's return voyage to Cork was advertised, all but a few of the Hebridean servants had been disposed of, *Dunlap's Pennsylvania Packet, or, the General Advertiser,* July 4, 1774. The vessel's voyage from Stornoway to Philadelphia and its 106 emigrant passengers are entered in the Register at T47/12/16–19.

officials in Stornoway to slow down the exit procedure and to enter into an especially close examination of the passengers. They had boarded the *Friendship* and had interviewed the emigrants "one by one." What they discovered was quite different from what the steward, the agent, and Miller had reported. Most of the emigrants, they found, were simply impoverished. They were "so poor that they could not pay for their passage, [and] therefore were obliged to indent themselves and to leave the country in order to procure bread elsewhere, as they could not do so here." No one had been kidnapped or coerced: "necessity obliged them to emigrate, without being induced to it by any person." And the officials warned that there were "a great many others in this country . . . reduced as low" as those they had found on the *Friendship*; there was every reason to believe that they too would emigrate as soon as more vessels arrived from America.[25]

But there were variations, seasonal and otherwise, in the availability of emigrants even in the Hebrides. Later in 1774 a former native of Stornoway, then settled in Ireland, who was said to have assembled earlier that year over 400 emigrants from the Western Highlands, contracted to furnish 300 more to the master of a New York vessel but failed almost completely to fulfill the bargain.[26] Jann probably knew that the situation in Lewis had become complicated. When he appeared in Scotland again, in March 1775, it was in Edinburgh not Stornoway, but again he ended in trouble. His tactics and the terms of his indentures were denounced in the *Caledonian Mercury*, and reports circulated that once again he was enticing people "to indent upon false pretences." The lord provost of Edinburgh arrested the ship, sent two magistrates aboard with an armed guard, and examined the status of every one of the passengers. This time Jann was caught. The magistrates found that about a third of the shipload of 90 servants were "either illegally indented or under age and consequently incapable of indenting." The 30 were sent back, and Jann was forced to sail off with a sadly incomplete cargo.[27]

[25] Customs Collectors, Stornoway, to Board of Customs, Edinburgh, March 24 and May 2, 1774, Stornoway Customs Letter Books.
[26] Customs Collectors, Stornoway, to Board of Customs, Edinburgh, Nov. 14, 1774, T47/12. Charles MacKenzie, the master of the *Peace and Plenty*, was so enraged by the failure of the promised emigrants to appear either in Stornoway or in the nearby mainland port of Lochbroom that he sailed off in a fury after waiting three weeks, leaving behind on the shore about 30 of those who had already paid for their passage. The abandoned passengers "got boats as quick as possible and went after him; he would not so much as ly too till they would come up with him, but crowded all his sail and pursued his voyage, leaving them all behind in a most destitute manner." T47/12/69. In 1775 MacKenzie was caught evading customs duties due on Irish provisions shipped with emigrants to Pennsylvania. Customs Collectors, Campbeltown, to Board of Customs, Edinburgh, June 16 and July 13, 1775, Campbeltown Customs Letter Books, CE 82/1/3.
[27] The story is told at great length and in rather lurid detail by "Hugh Manus," who, "stepping, the other evening, into one of the coffee-houses," found a handbill by Jann soliciting indentees. "This raised my curiosity a little, to know what might be the *terms* on which such persons were to be transported; and at last I happened to procure one which had been entered into between this

Indentures and Shipping

The likelihood of failure in recruiting the numbers desired was always present, even when there were no complications arising from excesses of zeal and charges of coercion or fraud. But most of the uncertainties were ended at the point at which the formal indenture was drawn up and notarized. By the late eighteenth century these documents had become printed forms filled out in duplicate, one copy for the servant, the other for the indentor, who was usually the ship captain, though occasionally an agent or the merchant himself. The servant swore before two witnesses to "well and truly serve" the indentor or his "executors, administrators or assigns" for a stated number of years, and testified that he or she was "no covenant or contracted servant to any person or persons." The servant swore also, in a special addendum, that he or she had not been "kidnapped or inticed, but [was] desirous to serve the above-named . . . or his assigns," for the agreed-upon term. The indentor on his part pledged for himself and his assigns to transport the servant to the named plantation and provide, during the voyage and for the stated term thereafter, "all necessary [clothes], meat, drink, washing, and lodging, fitting and convenient for [him] as covenant servants in such cases are usually provided for." Both parties pledged under heavy penalties to perform the enumerated duties. Later, in America, the document was completed by a notarized and carefully dated endorsement transferring the indentor's rights and obligations to his assignee as of the inscribed date. The assignee, the American purchaser of the servant, thereafter owned the servant's labor as a species of property, which he could sell, loan, bequeath, or mortgage as he could any other kind of property. The details of the expected treatment of the servant, including the small freedom dues given at the expiration of the contract, were seldom spelled out in the indenture; they were governed by "the custom of the country" established over the years by rulings of the local courts.

The indentures settled the legal if not the psychological question of the servants' commitment, but there remained an array of problems and uncertainties in shipping arrangements for which the merchants were responsi-

---

captain . . . and a young girl about 16 years of age. But upon perusal of its contents I confess my indignation was not a little raised. . . . By this agreement the poor creatures, who are deluded by fair speeches and a plausible story, are to be sold as slaves for no less a term than four years at the pleasure of this slave merchant, after which he is to give them two suits of apparel, *one* of which to be *new*—a mighty recompense for such a servitude! . . . Is not this a direct violation of all the laws of British liberty, that darling jewel?" *Caledonian Mercury*, April 19, 1775. The story is completed in the *Mercury*, May 13. Notices of the arrival of the *Friendship* in Philadelphia and the sale of the servants appear in *Dunlap's Pennsylvania Packet, or, the General Advertiser*, July 10, 24, 1775.

ble. They had to face, first of all, the problem of timing. Since maintenance charges were so high that servants could not be "stored" upon arrival in the colonies for later sale at propitious times but had to be sold almost immediately,[28] sales could be severely affected by the precise time of the servants' arrival. Certain kinds of servants could be sold at good prices at any time, and all healthy servants could eventually be sold at some price or other, but the profit margin varied significantly according to the immediate conditions of sale.

The seasonal variations were important. Matthew Ridley, in Baltimore, advised the convict contractor Duncan Campbell that cargoes of servants arriving in the Chesapeake during the July harvest season were almost certain to do badly, since purchasers were too preoccupied to come to the shipboard or dockside sales. The most prudent tactic Harry Piper could devise in handling a shipload that arrived in July was "to postpone the sale as long as I conveniently can till it [the harvest] is over." But every day's delay raised costs and cut profits. The best months for selling servants, George Woolsey wrote insistently from Baltimore, were April and May; one might still do fairly well in June, but thereafter the markets were likely to be poor until the fall, and after early November the season was too far advanced.[29] Harry Piper explained why. Even if sales of servants were brisk in the late fall, reloading vessels in winter was "very disagreeable," first, because after September the best tobacco was already sold and hence good returns were difficult to find, and, second, because even if cargoes could be found, they had to be loaded at top speed if the vessel was to get away before the weather became dangerous. Contracts allowed as much as ten weeks for the leisurely refitting and reloading of transatlantic vessels; that may have been excessive, but the turnaround could seldom be done in as little as three weeks (it took almost two weeks to prepare a proper sale of incoming servants). To cut down the time for a return voyage at the onset of winter, Piper said he would feel obliged "to take anything" for the incoming convicts in order to clear the ship for reloading. If the vessels *had* to be sent

[28]Thus Harry Piper wrote of one servant who seemed difficult to dispose of: "I must sell him . . . if I do not, he will soon cost me as much as he is worth, as I have no place to keep him at." Piper to Dixon and Littledale, April 15, 1769, Piper Letterbook.

[29]Matthew Ridley to Duncan Campbell, Baltimore, July 20, 1774, Ridley Letterbook; Piper to Dixon and Littledale, Alexandria, July 11, 1768, Piper Letterbook (cf. William Carr to James Russell, Dumfries, Va., July 6, 1774: he feared he would be stuck with three of the servants he received "if I cannot sell them, which probably I may after harvest," Russell Papers); George Woolsey to James Ford [Dec. 1774], to George Darly [Dec. 1774] ("push Kennedy out early in the spring . . . if he brings servants, the earlier he comes the better"), to Benjamin Titcomb [April 1775] ("they sell best the sooner they arrive here in the fall"), and to Robinson & Sandwith, Jan. 28, 1775 ("April & May is the two best months to sell servants, & next to them June, October, & the beginning of November"), all in Woolsey and Salmon Letterbook. The optimum timing was slightly different for emigrants settling on the land: departures in March or April were favored so that settlement could be made and planting begun in the spring and early summer.

that late in the year, he requested that they "not . . . have anything on board to prevent their immediately getting to loading." There seems to have been somewhat greater latitude in the timing of good sales in Philadelphia. James & Drinker believed February and March were not an inauspicious time to sell servants, and Clifford felt that servants arriving as late as September and October "were most easily placed out." But there was general agreement, especially in Virginia and Maryland, that April and May were the optimum time of arrival, with the very early fall (after the harvest and before the depletion of available returns and the onset of difficult weather) next best.[30]

The shipping figures bear this out. Tabulations of the departures of indentured servants from London show the most popular months to have been January and February: in March, April, and May these servants would have been available for sale in the American port towns. Over half of all the indentured servants who departed from London left between December and March; over 45% of the total leaving from all British ports shipped out during that winter and early spring season. The shipments diminished thereafter through the rest of the year: less than a quarter of London's emigrating indentees left in the spring and summer, and only 17% left in the fall.

The suppliers, well aware of this seasonality of advantageous sales, tried to time their shipments accordingly. But the erratic availability of servants in Britain made this timing difficult to accomplish, and, even more complicating, the merchants' success in reaching the markets at the optimum time could in itself compound the problems of sales if their cargoes arrived at the same time as others sent over by other merchants equally aware of the seasonal advantages. Four vessels unloading servants in the same weeks, even in so large a market as Baltimore, could seriously depress prices.[31] Sales are hopeless, Matthew Ridley wrote Duncan Campbell in mid-May 1775: "There are now several hundred servants here [in Baltimore] which are a mere drag; scarcely one being sold in a day." Occasionally the colonial marketers managed to get word to shipmasters just arriving off the American coast to delay their entrances until the markets cleared, and they repeat-

---

[30]Piper to Dixon and Littledale, Alexandria, Sept. 10, 1768, Nov. 8 and 17, 1772, and May 29, 1773, Piper Letterbook; Charles Grahame to Russell, Lower Marlboro, Md., Sept. 9, 1774, Russell Papers; Ridley to Duncan Campbell, Baltimore, March 9, 1775 ("Capt. Kid has [just] arrived with 131 servants . . . the sale is to be on the 22d"), to Somervell & Noble, Baltimore, June 25, 1773 ("I will take the servants out as soon as possible after her arrival . . . 10 days will be the shortest time I can do it in"), to John Campbell, Baltimore, Oct. 11, 1773 ("I think she may with ease take [on a load of lumber already prepared] in 3 weeks"), all in Ridley Letterbook; James and Drinker to Capt. Joseph Volans, Philadelphia, Nov. 16, 1772, and to Capt. Edward Spain, Aug. 4, 1775, James and Drinker Letterbook; Larsen, "Thomas Clifford," p. 123.
[31]Schmidt, "Convict Servant Labor," p. 96; James Cheston to Stevenson, Randolph, & Cheston, Baltimore, June 13, 1773, Cheston Letterbooks.

edly told their suppliers to move quickly at the start of each season in order to hit the markets when they were still fresh. But the best will in the world could not produce servants when few came forward, could not guarantee a specific arrival time, and could not anticipate the local economic conditions in the colonies—rates of exchange, availability of cash and credit, etc.—which would determine the purchasing power if not the labor needs of the ultimate American purchasers.[32]

In addition to all of these difficulties the British suppliers were faced with a peculiar problem of shipload size. While they felt in general that servants sent in good season would produce profits in proportion to their numbers, they were constrained by various factors in the numbers they could profitably send in any one shipment, and few dispatched more than one servant vessel at a time. Their ships were small—most were between 100 and 300 tons—and the steerage area in which the indentured servants traveled consisted usually of the 'tween decks, or upper hold, space that was used for freight on the inbound voyage. Hogsheads of tobacco and boxes, bags, and crates of other goods were unloaded from the 'tween decks area, which usually had head space of barely 5 feet (5½ feet was said to be "the greatest heighth of any vessel" in the 200-ton category; 4½ feet was considered excellent), and wooden slabs, often in two or three tiers, were substituted, to create a tightly jammed, airless dormitory. But it was not simply a question of physical space. The basic constraint on numbers per vessel was financial, dictated by problems of marketing. Do *not* cram in as many servants as possible, Harry Piper wrote his principals in Whitehaven. The danger of disease, which could cause drastic losses in sales, is increased, he said, if the hold is crowded. Further, when a vessel is loaded to capacity with servants there is "not room upon deck to muster them" in the American port for exhibition and sale with sufficient space for prospective purchasers to stroll, inspect, question, and bargain. And there was in addition the problem of "storage" costs, mounting steadily until the servants were sold. George Woolsey wrote one supplier that "your vessel will carry 100 servts but we think it would not be your intent to let her lye for more than 60 good servts, as the expense is great when youve many on board in port." Caution suggested that shiploads of servants or convicts for sale should not exceed 100; when a salesman or merchant disposed of a cargo of more than 100 at good prices he had cause for great satisfaction.[33]

[32]Ridley to Campbell, Baltimore, May 13, 1775, June 13, 1773 ("Here are now in the river not less than 300 servants. I wish he had kept out a little longer"), Ridley Letterbook; Johnson's Letterbook, p. xxiv; Cheston to Stevenson, Randolph, & Cheston, Baltimore, Aug. 31, 1774 ("These low prices of produce here will make it highly disadvantageous to us in the sale of servants, the high price which we have got heretofore has in great measure been owing to the great demand for wheat"), Cheston Letterbooks; Carr to Russell, Dumfries, Va., July 6, 1774 ("It was owing to a severe frost . . . that servants was not in demand this year"), Russell Papers.
[33]R. J. Dickson, *Ulster Emigration to Colonial America, 1718–1775* ([1966], Antrim, 1976), pp. 213–214;

Between-decks area, showing the cramped space in which bunks were built
or hammocks slung to accommodate emigrants. The drawing dates from the
early nineteenth century, when conditions had somewhat improved since
the pre-Revolutionary years.

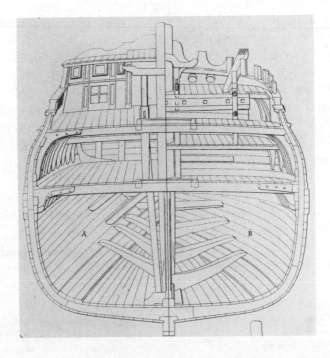

Cross-section of an eighteenth-century merchant vessel, showing the small
head space of the between-decks area.

The health of the human charges was a matter of constant concern, though little, it seemed, could be done to protect it. Epidemic disease could devastate the cold, damp, seasick, underfed passengers huddled in holds lacking sufficient ventilation or satisfactory sanitary facilities. Even full-fare-paying, "first class" cabin passengers had no more than buckets of sea water for their own waste disposal, and while they at least enjoyed continuous access to fresh air and sunlight and had the same rations as the ships' officers, they too were wet and cold much of the time. A few, but only a few, merchants made any real effort to improve shipboard conditions for the indentured servants and convicts. The idealistic Clifford instructed his ship captains to provide passengers with some room for baggage and with berths of what he considered to be reasonable size. Adults, he said, needed spaces "six feet long & 20 inches or two feet broad," and children less in proportion to their age—no great spaciousness, but far roomier conditions than steerage emigrants commonly had, "crowded together four in a bed, and those beds one upon another three deep, with not so much room betwixt each as to admit even the smallest person to sit up on end."[34]

Clifford—but no other merchant on record—insisted that the 'tween deck area of crowded vessels be washed down with vinegar, fore and aft, "every ten days if weather permits"; less crowded vessels might be washed simply with water. He told his captains to do their best to protect the servants' health, and he urged them to treat these future British Americans humanely. Occasionally other benevolent voices are heard. James Cheston in Baltimore argued at length with his colleagues in Bristol not to sell a rather clumsy, crudely constructed vessel of theirs because despite its sluggishness it was "well calculated for bringing servants healthy"; the vessel would cut down the "large sum of money which we generally lose by deaths and pay for nursing and doctors." He urged them too to keep on an annual retainer a particularly skillful doctor who had turned up on one of their ships, "for coming out in the spring and fall ships" every year. At the same time his partner, William Stevenson, in Bristol, had "gratings and air ports" cut in one of their vessels "which I hope will cause her convicts and servants to get in well and healthy." (Thomas Paine attributed the "putrid fever" that swept through the servants' quarters on the vessel he crossed on in 1775 to "the impurity of air between decks," and thought "ventilation would prevent it.") But Stevenson stopped short of installing

---

Piper to Dixon and Littledale, Alexandria, Oct. 24, 1767, Piper Letterbook; Woolsey to Titcomb [April, 1775], Woolsey and Salmon Letterbook; Ridley to Campbell, Baltimore, July 4, 1773 ("Enclosed you have an account [of] sales of 121 servants per the Thornton . . . you will find it one of the greatest [sales] ever made in this river"), Ridley Letterbook. Specifics on head space in steerage are given in *Newcastle Journal*, Jan. 22–29 (the *Endeavour*) and Feb. 12–19 (the *Providence*), 1774.
[34]Larsen, "Thomas Clifford," pp. 121–122; *Leeds Intelligencer*, April 19, 1774, quoted in *Publications of the Thoresby Society*, 38 (1937), 112.

forced ventilation: "I think pumping in such a torrent of fresh cold air when perhaps they are in a sweat must rather be a prejudice." It was for this reason, he supposed, that the African slave ships had no forced ventilation; the owners, he believed, quite reasonably "endeavor to give [the slaves] a more equal and moderate current of air."[35]

But such concerns are seldom found in the merchants' correspondences. There was far more prayerful hope for the servants' survival than practical efforts to assure it, and so conditions in the servants' holds remained primitive in the extreme. The voyages, averaging a week or two in port and seven or eight weeks at sea (they sometimes lasted three months), were commonly traumatic. The conditions of indentured servants and convicts differed mainly in the fact that the latter were shackled, either chained together in groups of six or manacled somehow to the vessel itself. Often the servants and convicts traveled together in the same holds, and they ate the same insufficient food. Weekly rations in steerage commonly consisted of a couple of pounds of oatmeal, four or five pounds of bread or biscuit, a pound of molasses, a pound of peas, and something less than a pound of beef or pork and of cheese, with daily rations of water. This meant, on a daily basis, oatmeal for breakfast, a scrap of meat and cheese with a few peas and some bread or biscuit for dinner, and biscuit or bread and molasses for supper. Emigrants who paid full fare received more of each item, and they commonly took some food of their own with them, but for the most part the diet was standard: meal of some kind, bread or biscuit, molasses, and small quantities of meat, cheese, and water. If all the food had been perfectly preserved and fresh, it would have been an insufficient diet: there is no mention of fruit and the only vegetables that appear are peas and potatoes. But the bread and biscuit were commonly wet and moldy, the meat spoilt, and the water brackish. When there was large-scale spoilage, which happened frequently, allowances of food were reduced; at such times the diet became in effect daily rations of bread and water.[36]

The servants, confined below decks, forty to a hundred or more men, women, and children, in a small, unventilated, cold wooden storage space with only a few candles or lanterns for light, must have suffered severely. The vessels pitched and rolled wildly in the Atlantic swells, and almost everyone, for at least the first week or so, was seasick. During the frequent ocean storms, which turned the 'tween decks areas into scenes of pandemonium and terror, the hatches were locked to keep the holds from

[35]Cheston to Stevenson, Randolph, & Cheston, Baltimore, Dec. 23, 1774, Cheston Letterbooks; William Stevenson to Cheston, Bristol, April 9, 1768, Cheston Incoming Letters; Thomas Paine to Benjamin Franklin, Philadelphia, March 4, 1775, in *The Complete Writings of Thomas Paine*, ed. Philip S. Foner (New York, 1945), pp. 1130–1131.
[36]Schmidt, "Convict Servant Labor," pp. 51 ff. For a lurid example of inadequate provisions for indentured servants in the course of a three-month voyage from London to Maryland, see *York Courant*, July 12, 1774.

*Foundering in a severe gale. "I was overwhelmed with an immense wave,
which broke my chair from its moorings, floated every thing in the cabin,
and I found myself swiming amongst joint-stools, chests, tables, and all the
various furniture. . . . The vessel which was one moment mounted to the
clouds and whirled on the pointed wave, descended with such violence . . .
it appears to me wonderful how her planks stuck together. . . . We heard
our sails fluttering into rags. The helm no longer was able to command the
vessel, tho' four men were lash'd to it, to steer her. We were therefore resigned to the mercy of the winds and waves." Janet Schaw, 1774.*

filling with the water that crashed over the low outer decks of the plunging
vessels. John Woolman, traveling in steerage in 1772, found it difficult to
breathe when the hatches were closed. During one storm he recorded in
his diary that he stood "near an hour with my face near the hatch door,
which was commonly shut down, partly to keep out rain and sometimes
to keep the breaking waves from dashing into the steerage."[37]

In the most detailed account we have of a vessel carrying indentured
servants through a severe Atlantic storm, Janet Schaw's *Journal* of 1774, the
waves are described as running "mountains high" and crashing into the
ship in floods that filled the cabins to the upper bunks. As the vessel,

[37] *The Journal . . . of John Woolman*, ed. Phillips P. Moulton (New York, 1971), p. 173.

overloaded and sailing heavily, alternately swept upward to the crests of the waves and then crashed down into the troughs, Janet and her maid hung on to anything they could grab to keep from drowning. The hogsheads of water fastened on deck came loose and went overboard, followed by all the poultry in their "hen coops," the kitchen utensils, and barrels of pickled tongues and hams. Four men struggled with the helm in the roaring gale but failed to control it. After fifty hours of constant high winds and drenching rain the crew lapsed into extreme fatigue. Their hands were "torn to pieces by the wet ropes" which were constantly snapping, causing the ship to convulse violently with each snap. The sails ripped off, and the foremast finally split. And then, in "a sudden and violent heel over," the ship "broached to"—turned over on its side—an accident that was usually fatal. Everything came loose—chests, beds, tables, stools, plates, lamps—all of which, together with the passengers, crashed "heels over head to the side the vessel had laid down on," and water poured in, in "a perfect deluge." The only thing that saved the ship was the loss of the masts, which went overboard; as a result the vessel righted itself, with a jolt as violent as the first. The passengers and all the gear were then "shoved with equal violence to the other side, and were overwhelmed by a second deluge of sea water."

All this was the experience of a cabin passenger, with the best accommodations aboard the ship. For the twenty-two or more indentured servants below the hatches the scene was an indescribable nightmare. Water beat down through the cracks constantly and flooded the dark, airless room. To keep from drowning in the deep pools, the emigrants were forced to sit up or stand, soaking wet, clutching their children, for days on end. "No victuals could be dressed," Janet Schaw reported, "nor fire got on, so that all they had to subsist on was some raw potatoes and a very small proportion of mouldy brisket [biscuit]." A young woman miscarried and passed into unconsciousness; her "absolutely distracted" husband broke "thro' all restraint, forced up the hatch, and carried her in his arms on deck, which saved her life, as the fresh air recalled her senses." The husband begged the cabin passengers for help. "But what could we do for her?" Janet Schaw wrote, "her cloaths all wet, not a dry spot to lay her on, nor a fire to warm her a drink."

The storm lasted twelve days, and when it subsided the ship was a wreck. The masts were gone, and the sails and rigging lay on the deck. Emergency masts had to be erected. Only then, the indentured servants, having been confined for nine days "without light, meat, or air, with the immediate prospect of death before them," were allowed to open the hatches and come up into the fresh air. The scene they left behind in the steerage must have been horrendous. Even in normal times, Miss Schaw reported, "the smell which came from the hole where they had been confined was sufficient to raise a plague aboard." And once on deck, shivering and half-starved, they discovered themselves dispossessed. All of their belongings had been stored in chests in the long boat. After a fortnight under water the chests had become unglued and their contents had been swept into the sea.[38]

The storm Janet Schaw described was severe, but there were worse experiences than hers and her shipmates'. Some of the wooden vessels were simply pounded to pieces by the wind and waves of the Atlantic gales. Notices of ships "lost at sea" and of people killed in storms appeared commonly in the colonial newspapers. Passengers or even crew members occasionally lost footing on the careening decks and were washed overboard. Food ran out, people starved, then ate anything: raw meal, rats, their leather clothes. And there was the constant threat of infectious disease. The possibility of smallpox, influenza, typhus, or diphtheria epidemics, and of a variety of "fluxes" and unidentified fevers haunted everyone involved in these voyages, and there was almost nothing that could be done to arrest an epidemic once it was under way. So death stalked these voyages. Paine, writing to Franklin as he left England aboard a ship carrying indentured servants, said simply that he "had very little hopes that the captain or myself would live to see America." The first question the receiving merchants in the colonies asked of the oncoming captains was the state of health of the indentured servants and convicts, and they became used to discouraging news. Captain MacDougal is safely arrived, Matthew Ridley was happy to report to Stewart and Campbell in London, and "the people are all remarkably healthy"—all those, that is, who had survived: "19 were buried upon the passage."[39]

The actual casualty rate aboard the vessels carrying indentured servants can only be surmised; there are no accurate figures. African slave ships voyaging to North America lost 10 to 15% of their human freight. One study of a small sample of the convict vessels traveling to the Chesapeake yields a similar estimate, but another puts the mortality rate much lower, at 2.5 to 4%. The casualty rate on vessels carrying indentured servants or mixed cargoes was undoubtedly low. The best-informed estimate is 3%, but that is on the high side, and the true figure may have been as low as the 1.8% loss among the convicts later shipped to Australia.[40] The more general

[38][Janet Schaw], *Journal of a Lady of Quality . . . 1774 to 1776,* ed. Evangeline W. Andrews and Charles M. Andrews (New Haven, 1921), pp. 47–52, 30, 55.
[39]Paine to Franklin, March 4, 1775, in *Writings of Paine;* Ridley to John Stewart & Campbell, Elk Ridge Landing, Md., July 19, 1770, Ridley Letterbook.
[40]Schmidt, "Convict Servant Labor," p. 62, finds an average loss of 14% in the early years of the eighteenth century, identical with an estimate for losses of convicts in transit in the 1770s: A. G. L. Shaw, *Convicts and the Colonies* (London, 1966), p. 35; testimony of Duncan Campbell summarizing his experiences as chief convict contractor just before the Revolution, *Journals of the House of Commons,* XXXVII (Nov. 26, 1778 to Aug. 24, 1780), 311. Smith, *Colonists in Bondage,* p. 118, estimates 10–15% loss among convicts shipped in the eighteenth century. The low estimate for the mortality

problem was not shipboard deaths but severe debilitation. Most of the indentured servants had been traveling under difficult circumstances for two or three months, and delays continued to the very end. Some ships ran aground as they approached the American coast, at times with disastrous results; there were serious accidents unloading; vessels found to have contraband goods were held up until legal issues could be settled; and those with diseased passengers were kept for a week or more in quarantine.[41] When, finally, the vessel actually drew up to a colonial wharf and its papers were cleared by customs and naval officials, the receiving merchants and agents came aboard, and preparations began for the final phase of mobilizing the labor force—selling the servants in the American labor markets.

---

rate of convicts to the Chesapeake is that of Morgan, "Organization of the Convict Trade," p. 213. But these figures are rough estimates and do not apply directly to the voluntary passengers on the registered vessels. The best discussion of the question, which concludes with the cautiously high figure of 3%, is Henry A. Gemery, "European Emigration to North America, 1700–1820: Numbers and Quasi-Numbers," *Perspectives in American History*, n.s., 1 (1984), 299–342. For the Australian figures (2,834 losses out of a total of 153,333 convicts sent to New South Wales and Van Dieman's Land), see L. L. Robson, *The Convict Settlers of Australia* (Melbourne, 1965), pp. 4–5.

[41]Williamson recalled arriving off Cape May during a storm and being shipwrecked on a sandbank. Finally on shore, the passengers "lay in a sort of camp made of sails of the vessel and such other things as they could get. The provisions lasted us until we were taken by a vessel bound to Philadelphia, lying on this island, as well as I can recollect, nearly three weeks." Williamson, *French and Indian Cruelty*, pp. 8–9.

I O

Sales and Distribution

A T ALMOST any time in the spring and fall months in pre-Revolutionary America a remarkable spectacle could be found unfolding on board newly arrived vessels tied up to the wharves in the port towns and the riverside villages south of New England. The scene—striking to almost every newcomer who witnessed it, yet to thousands of Americans an accepted part of life—marked the final episode in the process by which bound labor was transferred from Britain to America.

The servants or convicts, often mingled together, were brought up on the deck, males separated from females, and interested customers—merchants, planters, ordinary farmers, artisans, shopkeepers, and jobbers in the business of labor marketing—came aboard and began the process of inspecting and selecting the people whose labor they wished to buy. The apparent similarity of these auction sales of Britons to the auctions of enslaved blacks was shocking and commonly remarked on. Indentured servants, a letter in a Yorkshire newspaper explained, once arrived in America, are sold "for slaves at public sale, or [bartered] for country produce. They might as well fall into the hands of the Turks, they are subject nearly to the same laws as the Negroes and have the same coarse food and clothing." This trade, the letter declared, is "an infamous traffic," scandalous to the sensibilities of a free country and "disgraceful to humanity." In Philadelphia, an astonished British officer wrote back to his father, "They sell the servants here as they do their horses, and advertise them as they do their beef and oatmeal." Even some of the salaried salesmen found selling Britons into servitude a "disagreeable business" and felt they were entitled to extra compensation for conducting it. The mere fact that the convicts and indentured servants were often intermingled in these sales heightened the shock to outside observers.

Despite the fact that transported convicts had to be separately identified —because the law required the certification of their completed "transportation" and because their origins, crimes, and places of incarceration had to be made available for inspection—convicts and indentured servants were for the most part treated alike. Marylanders, William Eddis wrote, think "the difference is merely nominal between the indentured servant and the convicted felon," if only, he said, because they believe that no person of character above that of a criminal would voluntarily "abandon their friends and families and their ancient connections for a servile situation in a remote appendage to the British empire." In fact, he thought the colonists "rather consider the convict as the more profitable servant, his term being for seven, the . . . [indentured servant's] only for five years." Such an important marketer of convicts as Matthew Ridley commonly referred to all of his charges, felons and indentees alike, simply as "servants," in part, no doubt, to downplay the onus of criminality. In his sales accounts James Cheston listed together, without distinction of any kind, the "convicts and indentured servants" he sold, and referred to all of them as his "children," and the Annapolis firm of Thomas C. Williams & Co. advertised the convicts they imported simply as "healthy seven year men servents." In most situations both transported convicts and voluntary indentees shared similar fates, except for the length of their terms of service, determined by their age, skills, and experience.[1]

Shipboard Sales

The shipboard sales were carefully arranged. Every effort was made to spruce up the servants and convicts, many of whom, after weeks at sea and months of travel (Harrower spent almost seventeen weeks aboard the *Planter*) arrived sickly, filthy, and in rags. Sometimes it was difficult to make them look even vaguely respectable. Some were seriously ill, and many, as James Cheston wrote after inspecting one shipload devastated by smallpox and "the usual fever," were "excessively mangee and reduced."

[1] *Etherington's York Chronicle*, Jan. 27, 1775; "Extract of a letter from an officer in the 64th regiment, Boston, Aug. 5, 1773, to his father in Dublin," *Lloyd's Evening Post*, Oct. 4–6, 1773; Harry Piper to John Dixon, Alexandria, Va., Sept. 12, 1768, Piper Letterbook; William Eddis, *Letters from America*, ed. Aubrey C. Land (Cambridge, Mass., 1969), pp. 37–38; Matthew Ridley to Duncan Campbell, Baltimore, July 9, 1775 (referring to a shipload of convicts as "servants"), Ridley Letterbook; James Cheston to Thomas Ringgold, Baltimore, Dec. 30, 1773 ("Immediately after that is done and I have got rid of all my *children*, 25 of whom are still on hand . . ."), Cheston Letterbooks; Ringgold to Cheston, Chester Town, Dec. 16, 1773, Cheston Incoming Letters; various separate sales accounts of shiploads of indentured servants and convicts among the bills and receipts, box 19, all in Cheston-Galloway Papers; Williams's ad for the servants arriving on the *Star and Garter* in *Maryland Gazette* (Annapolis), July 20, 1775—the identification of the servants as convicts is in T47/10 between folios 71 and 72.

The women indentees in a shipment that Harry Piper was expected to sell arrived, he wrote, "very naked, their cloathes, especially their gowns, are very scanty and sorry and many of them had no handkerchiefs [i.e. necker-chiefs or bandana-like head cloths], the weather had been cold, they must have suffered." "They all was sett in a row," a London weaver recently settled in Williamsburg wrote in 1758,

> near a hundred man & women & the planter come down the cuntry to buy . . . I never see such pasels of pore raches [wretches] in my life som all most naked and what had cloths was as black as chimney swipers, and all most starved by the ill usidge in ther pasedge by the capn, for they are used no bater than so many negro slaves that are brought in hare and sold in the same manner as horss or cows in our market or fair.

Often sickly and undernourished, they wore the clumsy canvas gowns and trousers and the coarse dowlas shifts and petticoats issued by the merchants at Gravesend and other exit ports, or miscellaneous assortments of ragged shirts and waistcoats, disheveled overcoats and capes, battered hats and caps, and torn and patched-together gowns, bodices, and kilts. They were a woebegone, weary, largely silent crowd of men, women, and children, faced with a strange procedure they could not control but that would determine their fates. Hoping to be treated as valuable property rather than as refuse specimens good only for brute labor, they put on the best appearance they could. "We were wash'd and cleaned," James Revel, a former convict, recalled in labored verse, "That to our buyers we might better seem; / Our things were gave to each they did belong, / And they that had clean linnen put it on. / Our faces shav'd, com'd out our wigs and hair, / That we in decent order might appear, / Against the plant-ers did come down to view, / How well they lik'd this fresh transported crew."[2]

The buyers—strolling through the rows and groups of uneasy, shuf-fling, tatterdemalion servants on the small decks cluttered with ship gear, freight in crates and barrels, and bags of personal belongings; inspecting, questioning, probing, gauging ages and strengths and temperaments; chat-

[2]Cheston to Stevenson, Randolph, & Cheston, Baltimore, June 30, 1774, Cheston Letterbooks; Piper to Dixon and Littledale, Alexandria, Oct. 24, 1767, Piper Letterbook; Frederick H. Schmidt, "British Convict Servant Labor in Colonial Virginia" (Ph.D. diss., College of William and Mary, 1976), pp. 156, 123–124; John M. Jennings, ed., " 'The Poor Unhappy Transported Felon's Sorrowful Account of his Fourteen Years Transportation at Virginia in America,' " *Virginia Magazine of History and Biography*, 56 (1948), 190. The authorship and dating of Revel's "Sorrowful Account" are conjectural. It may have been written by a hack writer turning out popular tracts. But the author, whoever he was, was well acquainted with the details of the marketing of bondsmen in America.

ting with each other and checking with the ship captains and merchandisers about the health, origins, skills, and cost of those who struck their fancy—attempted to form sound judgments and strike profitable bargains. "Some view'd our limbs, and other's turn'd us round," James Revel wrote,

> Examening like Horses, if we're sound,
> What trade are you, my Lad, says one to me,
> A Tin-man, Sir, that will not do, says he.
> Some felt our hands and view'd our legs and feet,
> And made us walk, to see we were compleat;
> Some view'd our teeth, to see if they were good,
> Or fit to chew our hard and homely Food.
> If any like our look, our limbs, our trade,
> The Captain then a good advantage made.[3]

But "a good advantage" was often difficult for the sellers to make. Many elements had to be considered and difficulties overcome. Experience, up-to-the-minute information, and good judgment were required at every point. The first consideration was the location of the sale. Small "lots" could be disposed of at preliminary stopping places as the vessels entered American coastal waters. Harrower's ship captain, for example, managed to sell one servant, a boat builder, at their port of entry, Hampton, at the mouth of Chesapeake Bay, before proceeding forty miles north and seventy-five miles inland to Fredericksburg on the Rappahannock River where the main sale was scheduled.[4] And a certain amount of peddling could be conducted at stopovers along the river routes. But most cargoes of servants arriving from Britain were disposed of at one place, where the vessel was unloaded and where the receiving merchant or consignment agent could advertise and supervise sales and the reloading for the return voyage.

A choice of locations, however limited, was usually available, and the sellers considered the relative advantages carefully. They tried to avoid locations where markets were known to be glutted by recent ship arrivals; locations to which for some reason individual buyers might find it difficult to travel; and locations where the kinds of servants available for sale were unlikely to match the existing market. William Carr, one of James Russell's agents in Virginia, located at Dumfries, well up the Potomac River near Alexandria, puzzled repeatedly over whether to allow sales lower down on

---

[3] *Ibid.*, p. 190. For a similar account by a German redemptioner—"We had to strip naked, so that the prospective purchasers could see that we had perfectly developed and healthy bodies. After the purchaser had made a selection, he asked: 'How much is this boy or this girl?' "—see *Narrative of Johann Carl Buettner in the American Revolution* ([1828], New York, 1971), pp. 26–27.
[4] *The Journal of John Harrower: An Indentured Servant in the Colony of Virginia, 1773–1776*, ed. Edward M. Riley (Williamsburg, Va., 1963), p. 35.

the river or whether to insist that sales be held at his own station at Dumfries, near the backcountry markets. Sales on the James River, Harry Piper wrote his principals, were hopeless; he was not sure about the upper Potomac, but he thought it probably held out better prospects. Matthew Ridley knew enough about the crowded markets at Norfolk, opposite Hampton, at the entrance to Chesapeake Bay, where all vessels bound either for Virginia or Maryland entered American territory, to direct shipments away from there to Leedstown, a central market town near the fall line on the Rappahannock River. An error of judgment in the location or timing of sales could be costly. "I am hartily sorry," Thomas Ewing wrote the Neaves from Baltimore after selling a cargo of their servants, "that the sircumstances were such that I was oblidg'd for to sell the servants on cred't. Had Capt. Templeton have been fortunate enough to have arrived here three weeks sooner, it wold have made five hundred guineas more in your pockit, the servants wold have sold higher & for cash."[5]

But even the best judgment on location was only a guess, and the sellers stood by apprehensively when the servants were exposed to sale, waiting hopefully for the "backwoods waggons [to] come down," fearful that "extreme severity of weather" might prevent "people from coming in from the country" or that other cargoes of servants might suddenly arrive before their servants were sold. Once the sale was under way, a complicated interplay of two dynamically related sets of calculations—on the part of the buyers on the one hand and the sellers on the other—was set in motion. Each side worked with a rough equation for maximizing gain, and the relationship between the two equations was shaped in part by an independent factor, time. For the buyers the equation was relatively simple. Most wanted healthy young workers with particular skills; they sought to get as long a commitment as possible and for the lowest possible price; and they had to consider encumbrances like accompanying family members and unexpected peculiarities. Further, they had to make some judgment of character, which meant mainly guessing at the likelihood that the servant under consideration would be diligent, tractable, and willing to work out his or her time without attempting to escape. The time factor was obvious: from the buyers' point of view the longer they delayed the more likely it was that the prices would fall or the credit terms would be loosened, yet they had to move quickly enough to prevent the best prospects from being taken up by others.[6]

[5] William Carr to James Russell, Dumfries, March 30, 1774, Feb. 22, 1775, Russell Papers; Piper to Dixon and Littledale, Alexandria, Nov. 25, 1767, Sept. 6, 1769, Piper Letterbook; Ridley to Campbell, Baltimore, Oct. 5, 1772, Ridley Letterbook; Thomas Ewing to Richard Neave & Son, Baltimore, July 12, 1775, Emmet Collection, MS 5686, Special Collections, New York Public Library, New York City.

[6] Cheston to Stevenson, Randolph, & Cheston, Oct. 11, March 12, Jan. 5, 1774, Cheston Letterbooks;

The sellers' equation was more complicated. Seeking maximum profits, they had to juggle a variety of factors under a severe constraint of time, for the longer their "goods" were "stored"—fed, sheltered, nursed—the lower the profit margin ("he will soon cost me as much as he is worth") and the more likely the servants were to develop new disabilities ("I was glad to get rid of them on any terms for with the length of time they were aboard the ship they rather grew sickly").[7] Within this rigorous time constraint and with the obvious desire to sell their servants at the highest possible prices, the sellers had somehow to take into account the value of payments offered, the existing rate of exchange on colonial money, the creditworthiness of the buyers (the majority) who postponed payment to a later time, and above all—perhaps the most crucial decision of all—when to cut off retail sales altogether and "lump" the remainder in wholesale lots to "soul drivers." These jobbers would march the remaindered servants in groups through the backcountry, selling them off individually or a few at a time in remote markets out of contact with the major distributing centers east of the fall line.

Payment for servants in cash, in the form of colonial paper, at fluctuating rates of exchange, was not uncommon; but the most valuable form of direct payment (precious metals being practically nonexistent) was good bills of exchange payable on demand or at short notice, drawn on well-known and financially stable British firms. Such bills were not always available, however—ordinary farmers seldom had access to them—and their rarity in the colonial economy in itself increased their cost. Consequently the most common form of payment was goods—local produce, principally tobacco and wheat, but other commodities too—and the marketer of servants had to estimate the price he could eventually get for these commodities in relation to the price that the prospective buyer of the servant had set on them.

So the negotiations began, with the servants and convicts still on exhibit on board ship; with potential buyers coming and going, looking, talking, retiring, calculating, returning, and occasionally making offers; and with the sellers working every possible strategy for increasing the attractiveness of their wares, shortening the process of bargaining, and bringing the customers to the point of commitment. It was a nervous, unpredictable process, punctuated by quick decisions, sharp disappointments, and sudden successes.

John Page to Cheston, "Rockhall," March 24, 1774 (returning a servant "utterly averse to goe by water . . . he would by no means suit me"), Cheston Incoming Letters.

[7] Piper to Dixon and Littledale, Alexandria, April 15, 1769, Piper Letterbook; Ridley to Campbell, July 29, 1775, Ridley Letterbook. On the "warehousing" of German redemptioners, see note 21, below.

Calculations

The dominant concerns are clear in the pages of the merchants' letter books. The sellers were haunted, above all else, by the fear of disease. Everything depended on the health of their charges, which was unpredictable and uncontrollable. An incoming ship captain, Harry Piper reported, was believed to have caught "jail fever" from his convict servants, and "consequently many are afraid to see him, God grant that no other person may take it, for it is a shocking fever, poor Captain Smith has been out of his senses ever since he was taken and still continues so, so that it seems very doubtful whether he will live or not." One shipment of tradesmen that George Woolsey sold in Baltimore "would have done very well only for the fever that got among them, which will make a heavy expence on them." Smallpox, Matthew Ridley wrote Campbell, had swept through one of their vessels shortly after its departure from England, and though he was convinced that the infectious stage was past when the vessel arrived in Annapolis, the authorities insisted that it be quarantined for a week and that Ridley give bond and "let the purchasers know the smallpox had been on board." Ridley protested against what he took to be the "absurdities of this law— no pest house provided and a number of people confined together [for the week] who were not subject to this disorder might take other sickness merely from confinement." But though he railed against the inconvenience involved and designed ways to amend or get around the law, in the end he had to submit, removing from the ship those who had had the disease "at the risk of these people running away," and noting, when he finally sent the servants on to Baltimore for sale, that twenty had been "buried in passage."

When shipments arrived in good health the merchants' relief was palpable. Not one man lost, James Cheston rejoiced, "and all in so healthy a condition that the ship was immediately entered and is now on her way to Baltimore"; another batch "all well, and in top spirits, which gives me great hopes of soon getting them off." "Thank God," an incoming ship captain wrote, only "one man died, but it was with old age; he was 84 years old." All the rest were "in good health, and have had no sickness on board."[8]

[8]Piper to Dixon and Littledale, Alexandria, Oct. 10, 1767, Piper Letterbook; George Woolsey to George Darley [Baltimore, Dec. 1774], Woolsey and Salmon Letterbook; Ridley to Campbell, Annapolis, June 24, 1774, Ridley Letterbook; Cheston to Stevenson, Randolph, & Cheston, Baltimore, Dec. 5, 1774, Cheston Letterbooks; William Young, Jr., to Cheston, "Bush Town," May 16, 1771, Cheston Incoming Letters; Simon Bressett to Cheston, "off Patuxent," Dec. 10, 1773, *ibid.* Reports of disease among the servants came in to Cheston from all sides. Smallpox hit a cargo of 155 convict servants just after sailing, one ship captain wrote Cheston in a typical report; 10 died in the course of the voyage, 7 recovered, and 3 more were still suffering from the disease—and in

The first concern, at the receiving end of the process as at the sending, was thus always health: the best markets were for the "young, healthy, and not deformed"—a concern reflected in innumerable newspaper advertisements announcing the recent arrival and pending sale of "healthy servants —men, women, and boys." Only slightly less weighty was the stress on occupations and skills. The distinction between those who had and those who lacked skills was fundamental. When the *Pennsylvania Packet* arrived in Philadelphia in March 1775 a list of those on board was carefully prepared. Seven people were described as paying passengers, and 42 as indentured servants—27 "tradesmen" (average age, 23) and 15 "no trades." The tradesmen's occupations were carefully enumerated—18 trades and crafts were specified, ranging from watchmaker and watch finisher to stone mason, and from cabinetmaker to hairdresser. The indentees 20 years old and older were sold for four years, one 17-year-old for five years, and the two 15-year-olds (one of them bought by Dr. Benjamin Rush) for seven years. As one would expect, most of the "no trades" among the indentees were young laborers (average age, 15); but among them too were a clerk, a bookkeeper, 3 grooms, and 4 husbandmen (average age, 23). "Tradesmen," who seem to have mattered most to the sellers, apparently meant people who built things, made things, whether watches, loaves of bread, or houses, and nontradesmen were not only laborers but also those who worked with pens, those who took care of horses, and those who worked the land. A typical notice in the *Virginia Gazette* listing an incoming vessel's "150 healthy SERVANTS, men, women, and boys" specified 20 occupations, including not only the usual carpenters, joiners, shoemakers, tailors, and bricklayers, but also peruke makers, hairdressers, mantua makers, a printer, a copperplate printer, a surveyor, a dyer, and a tanner.[9]

William Carr, in Dumfries, Virginia, bemoaned his luck in getting stuck with two servants to sell who, in addition to being "sickly," had little in the way of skills to recommend them. One of them at least had "some notion of the carpenter's business, though very imperfect," but the other was a butcher who "never has been . . . out of London for he knows no kind of business but what he has been brought up to." Since "we have many of his trade," Carr thought it unlikely that he could ever sell him "to advantage." After attempting to sell the two for a month, he gave up, bought both of them cheaply himself, and dispatched them to work out

addition an unidentified fever was sickening, but had not yet killed, several others. Thomas Spencer to Cheston, June 15, 1774, Cheston Incoming Letters.
[9]Eleazer McComb to Cheston, Chester Town, Jan. 7, 1774, Cheston Incoming Letters; *Virginia Gazette* (Dixon and Hunter), March 18 and 25, 1775; *Virginia Gazette* (Rind), March 10, 1774; "A List of Serv[an]ts Indented on Board the Pennsylvania Packet . . . the 15th Day of March 1775," Indentures of Redemptioners. The published version of the list (*Pennsylvania Magazine of History and Biography*, 18 [1894], 379) is inaccurate: the 7 paying passengers are jumbled in with the "No Trades" servants.

their time on his own farm. Harry Piper hit an even worse patch of luck with a "sorry" contingent of servants he got from Dublin. Not only were they all, men and women alike, "very great blackguards"—regular "villains," the whole lot, he said—and not only did they dispute and change the number of years entered on their indentures, "which does not look well," but they were people "brought up to no sort of business," whereas tradesmen indented for five years he could dispose of perhaps even before they arrived.[10]

The merchants' letterbooks and their special-order memorandum books record an unending effort to satisfy their customers' special needs. They tried to fill individual orders of all kinds—for ordinary carpenters and for "rough carpenters"; for spinners and for weavers; for shoemakers, gardeners, and blacksmiths; for farmers and oxteam drivers; for a woolen and linen weaver "about 35 or 40 years of age"; for a middle-aged cook "from the west of England"; for a female household helper; for a "good fiddler"; for a ditchdigger; for a barber.[11] Special arrangements were made to guarantee satisfaction. Some sales contracts were written with conditional clauses to protect buyers against falsified skills. George Washington ordered some bricklayers, but only if their skills could be verified by an expert. A blacksmith was bought by another planter, but the price was left unsettled until the purchaser could "form some judgment of him." Another buyer sent an overseer to inspect a shipload of servants offered for sale and to judge their abilities personally. And special favors were done for friends and influential people: marketers of labor commonly reserved out of a shipload "the best men" for friends or patrons before the contingent as a whole was offered for sale. On one occasion an Englishman, the Reverend Dr. Dunford, leaving England for America, arranged in advance to have one person, a Henry Buckle, reserved for himself and "no other master" out of a shipload of servants and convicts en route to Maryland; the Reverend Dunford's brothers, the Bristol shippers explained to their Baltimore agent, "are justices and men of consequence in Hampshire who it is our interest to oblige."[12]

The prices offered, within equal terms of service, reflected the priorities of demand. When skills were absent, the prices for servants of equal age and length of indenture dropped. "The two men called carpenters in the servant

[10]Carr to Russell, Dumfries, Sept. 26, 1774, Russell Papers; Piper to Dixon and Littledale, Alexandria, Aug. 10, 1768, Piper Letterbook.
[11]Examples taken from a wide range of letters in James Cheston's Letterbooks and among his incoming letters and from other letters to individual customers and from customers placing orders.
[12]Robert O. Heavner, *Economic Aspects of Indentured Servitude in Colonial Pennsylvania* (New York, 1978), p. 82; Cheston to Thomas Smyth, Baltimore, Nov. 23, 1773, Cheston Letterbooks; Darby Lux to Cheston, "Mo. Airey," April 3, 1773, Cheston Incoming Letters; Cheston to James Brice, Nov. 30, 1772, Cheston Letterbooks; enclosure in Stevenson, Randolph, & Cheston to Cheston, Bristol, Sept. 1773, Cheston Incoming Letters.

list," James Cheston wrote of an incoming shipload to a customer who had ordered "rough carpenters," "turned out otherwise." One, aged nineteen, proved to know "nothing of the business," though he had once assisted his father in the trade, and the other was in fact a farmer. As a consequence, Cheston said, both were sold "at labourers prices." At one end of the spectrum were trained workers in building trades and other useful crafts and services, followed by experienced, respectable, and diligent young husbandmen and unskilled workers. At the other extreme were the "broken tradesmen," the elderly, the chronically ill, or anyone "ill suited for a gentleman's family or for hard labour in the country."[13]

The American marketers struggled in despair to dispose of the incompetents, the drunks, the violent, the sick, deformed, and elderly who ended up in their charge. The letterbooks in which these marketing problems are recorded reflect the worst kinds of human misery and misfortune. Nicholas Hobbs, one of James Cheston's customers, wrote back angrily to his supplier complaining of the "bad bargain" he had made. The girl he bought for the substantial price of £15, he told Cheston,

> is not worth one farthing, but [is a] very great expense. She has fitts almost perpetually, and has been under the doctors hand now a long while, and there is no hopes of getting her cured. She tells me that you and the captain both knew of her having fitts, for she had them often coming over sea. I think it was not quite generous to sell such a person without letting the buyer know of it, for it is just taking a man's money for nothing—besides the expense of doctoring, which will cost me near as much as the girl did at first.

Matthew Ridley solved a similar problem by giving away "a girl that was sick to prevent a continuation of the expense of 15/ [shillings] per week." But there was no such simple solution for the problem of another girl, who was insane. In that case the buyers threatened to publicize Ridley's bad faith in not warning them about her condition: "they say they can prove her to have been mad both before [she] shipd and after." Ridley promised to check with the other servants who had traveled on her ship, but if the charge proved to be justified, what, he asked, was he to do? He dreaded the possibility of having "to keep the girl." On another occasion Ridley found a woman among those he had to sell so afflicted with "a very bad leg" that he did not think he could "get anything" for her. Piper discovered in one shipment "an idiot," and in another, an old woman; "one [with] the clap"; a pregnant woman; and finally "a consummate villain," who had already

[13]Cheston to Smyth, Baltimore, Dec. 24, 1773, Cheston Letterbooks; James and Drinker to Capt. Joseph Volans, Philadelphia, May 23, 1774, James and Drinker Letterbook.

been transported to America "two or three times" and presumably had managed to escape back to England each time. George Woolsey too had to face the problem of trying to sell "a fool" and in addition "one woman that has a sore breast," as well as "a verry old convict woman that says she can spin."[14]

It was among the convicts that the most unfortunate, miserable, and least salable workers appeared—to the extent that at times even the British contractors were moved to compassion. One "unfortunate poor woman" ordered transported to America was such "a real object of pity" to Stevenson & Randolph in Bristol that they asked Cheston in Baltimore "to provide for her, if possible, a kind, humane master or mistress on her arrival in Maryland."[15] That the worst misfortunes were found among the convicts is significant, for the entire force of the merchandising mechanism for disposing of voluntary servants worked to promote the recruitment and emigration of youthful, healthy, and at least competent if not skilled workers, and to select out in advance the least autonomous and least productive among those available. While the American marketers had no choice but somehow to dispose of the convicts they were sent, many of whom had quite marketable skills, they constantly warned their principals in Britain of the difficulties they had in making any profit from voluntary indentees who would be useless or burdensome to potential American customers.

Prices, "Lumping," and Payment

All of these conditions—appearance, health, skills, temperament, general competence and promise, and length of commitment to servitude—together with sex, age, and the condition of the local economy and labor markets, entered into the complicated equation that determined the prices the servants fetched. One exhaustive sales record, covering a 3½-month period, of the servants of the *Dolphin,* which arrived in Philadelphia from London in early June 1774, is particularly valuable because the vessel is one of those whose passengers were entered in the Register of emigrants. Of the 46 registered servants on board, the sale of 26 is recorded between June 13 and September 30, 1774; for that group all the information that could be desired is available. The 14 males disposed of sold twice as quickly as the 12 females (9 males were sold in June but only 4 females), and the males

[14]Hobbs to Cheston, March 6, 1773, Cheston Incoming Letters; Ridley to Thomas Hodge, Baltimore, Nov. 29, 1773, May 26, 1774, and Ridley to Campbell, June 13, 1774, Ridley Letterbook; Piper to Dixon and Littledale, Alexandria, Oct. 24, 1767, and June 15, 1772, Piper Letterbook; Woolsey to Darley, Feb. 7, April 10, 1775, and to Messrs. Gaversay & Steward, Dec. 23, 1774, Woolsey and Salmon Letterbook.
[15]Stevenson & Randolph to Cheston, Bristol, April 26, 1775, Cheston Incoming Letters.

brought higher prices (an average of £18.5 vs. £15). The servants between the ages of 20 and 24 were more valuable than those either younger or older (£20 vs. £17.5 and £16.5); those who sold quickly sold most dearly (males sold in June averaged £19, after June £16.5; women sold in June averaged £19, and after June £13.5). If this sample is representative, the average amount a merchant could get for servants decreased approximately £4 for each month they remained unsold, a loss that was of course compounded by the mounting expenses of food, clothing, housing, and care. Of the 14 males sold in the 3½-month period, 5 were tradesmen, 4 were husbandmen, 4 were laborers, and 1 was a schoolmaster. The prices, except for that paid for the overaged (38-year-old) schoolmaster, who went cheaply (£15), were about the same (between £18 and £19), but the husbandmen sold more quickly than the artisans in this Pennsylvania market. The laborers were by far the youngest group (their average age was 15.8); the oldest were the husbandmen (23.5); the artisans fell between (21.4).[16]

The correlation of figures for the sale of the *Dolphin*'s servants suggests aspects of the juggling, judging, and guessing that the merchants had to do to maximize profits. Another element—one of the most crucial—is seen in the decision of the *Dolphin*'s merchandiser to sell five of the female servants in a "lump" for £55. The decision to "lump" (the word is used constantly in the business correspondences)—that is, to sell off a part or all of a shipment in wholesale lots, cheaply—was basic to the outcome of the sale as a whole. The most common reason for such a decision was the need for speed: because of anticipated competition; because of the threat of political problems; because of mounting illnesses or rumors of illnesses as the servants lingered about unsold; because of the fear that the lateness of the season might scare off wholesalers whom one would eventually have to turn to, since they had to have time to market their purchases retail; because a wholesale disposal at relatively low prices might bring cash or solid remittances quickly while retail sales at nominally higher prices would go only for credit or payment in kind, which in the end might mean less profit. The ultimate fear, which triggered all such decisions, was that servants kept on hand too long in a bad or confused market would in the end find no purchaser at all. Such disasters were not unknown. According to one report, the disgusted owners of a batch of indentees that did not sell quickly simply "threw them their indentures and bid them shift for themselves."[17]

---

[16]Neave Account Book; the *Dolphin*'s entry in the Register is T47/9/133–134. This account book also contains a sales record for the *Minerva*, another of Neave's vessels, whose voyage is recorded in the Register. But in the time covered in this account book only 4 of the *Minerva*'s 115 passengers were sold; the rest may have been disposed of in wholesale lots or entered into different account books. Neave's accounts list occasional expenses for clothing, lodging, and health care.

[17]Ridley to Campbell, Baltimore, July 20, 1773, Sept. 19, 1774, Ridley Letterbook; Cheston to Stevenson, Randolph, & Cheston, Baltimore, Nov. 26, 1770, July 11, 1774, Dec. 15 and 23, 1774, June

23

Dr. Cash in

1. To Ballance from June ———————— 904.8.4
5. To Sale of Servant ♯ Dolphin 1774 } for Ann Hurst — 16.—.—
7. To ditto ——— . Ford, in part — 6.—.—
8. To ditto ——— . Frewin — 18.—.—
9. To ditto ——— . Jefferson — 15.—.—
.. To ditto ——— . Hinch — 20.—.—
13. To Bond & Byrn — 13 Oct £50 & 70 — 85.—.—
.. To Sale of Servant ♯ Dolphin 1774 } for Selby & Wife in part — 16.5.—
14. To John James rec. Att Woolman full — 19.9.—
18. To Sale of Servant ♯ Dolphin 1774 } for Humberstone — 24.—.—
20. To Ditto rec'd of Jno. Black, for Bromfield, Fowler, Dawson, Gamble & Hopfield } — 55.—.—
23. To Bond & Byrn — 23 Octob £50 x 70 — 85.—.—
.. To Sale of Servant ♯ Dolphin 1774 } for Fowen — 15.—.—
28. To ditto ——— for Mollett — 16.—.—

£ 1295.2.4

Particulars of R. Neave's Charge
Capillaue 2/3. Almonds &c 3/. 3 Sheets sold 10/6 — .15.9
exp. to Chester b/d 19 Shoe. Toby 9/6 Black 3 4/. &c 42/2 — .18.5
Cash B 15/. 4/6. Tea 2/. Biscuit 6/ — £1.7.6
£3..1..8

A page from Richard Neave's Ledger, showing sale of indentured servants transported on the Dolphin, *departing London at the end of April 1774 (T47/9/133–134) and sold in Philadelphia in June–August. The five serv-*

The obvious strategy to avoid such defeats was to dispose of the most valuable servants individually and quickly, on the best terms possible, and then to "lump" the rest without undue delay while prices were still decent. The exact timing of when to take the wholesale plunge could be a matter of subtle calculation. Cheston, in an off-season sale in December 1774, had

21, 1773, Cheston Letterbooks (also April 21, 1771, *ibid.,* and the Company to Cheston, Jan. 25, 1773, Cheston Incoming Letters); *Caledonian Mercury,* May 13, 1775.

ants "lumped" on July 20 were women in their early twenties; other women on the page, sold retail earlier in the month, fetched much higher prices. Expenses for the servants are noted on July 7 and 31.

to consider, on the one hand, the likelihood that his high-quality charges might eventually bring good prices in retail sales, and, on the other hand, the poor condition of the roads that so reduced the flow of wheat into Baltimore and so increased its price that the eventual net profit from returns in wheat and flour would probably be low. He decided to hold out only "a few days longer in the retail way and then lump the remainder" before wheat prices rose precipitously.

At one point William Carr wrote James Russell that it was his judgment that the remaining servants in a particular shipment were "really troublesome and expensive" and that the best they could do was to get rid of them quickly in a lump, calculating all the exchanges involved most carefully. So Matthew Ridley sold off a cargo to a reliable wholesaler, Lux & Bowly, at the relatively low price of £10 sterling each, "£300 payable by the going of the ships with the remainder in six months and to ship 20 hogsheads of tobacco on which they are to draw £5 per hogshead." One of the most complicated "lumpings" was made by George Woolsey just after the news of the battle of Lexington threw "every thing in confusion." Fearful of a crisis that would stop all trade, he quickly sold off, in a series of "lumps," an entire cargo he was offering for sale. He sold "six [of the servants] for £16 p[er] piece at one month & seven months credit, eleaven for £14 p[er] piece a[t] three months credit to be p[ai]d in flour, & eight for £115 [at] six months credit, also one woman for £12 cash." And he sent the vessel back immediately, by way of Ireland, loaded with flour.[18]

Time pressure, which impelled agents and shipmasters to "lump" their sales of servants, especially when retail purchases were sluggish, was built into the overall planning of these transatlantic commercial voyages, since the speed with which a shipload of servants could be disposed of set the lower boundary of the turnaround time for the return voyage with salable commodities. Merchants were keenly aware of the problem ("it is not practicable," Harry Piper wrote, "to do anything at a ship while the servants are on board"), and they kept careful track of the turnaround schedules.

The progress of the *Hero,* bearing fifty-seven servants to be disposed of by Harry Piper in Alexandria in July and August 1768, can be followed day by day in his correspondence. Piper got word on the 11th of July that the vessel had registered at the entrance of the Chesapeake on the 8th and was refitting at St. Mary's, at the mouth of the Potomac, before proceeding up the river to Alexandria. It took over a week for the vessel finally to reach Piper, who advertised the sale of the servants for the 25th. On the 10th of August he wrote that all of the servants had been sold. The lapsed time of over two weeks for completion of the sale was somewhat longer than it might have been because, he reported, there had been sickness on board the vessel and the onset of the tobacco harvest had kept some planters from attending the sale.[19] The *Adventure,* from Newcastle, had a similar schedule; over two-thirds of its servants were sold within 10 days of its arrival

[18]Cheston to Stevenson, Randolph, & Cheston, Baltimore, Dec. 11, 1774, Cheston Letterbooks; Carr to Russell, Dumfries, P.S. to letter of Feb. 22, 1775, Russell Papers; Ridley to Campbell, Baltimore, July 20, 1773, Ridley Letterbook; Woolsey to Darley, May 4, 1775, Woolsey and Salmon Letterbook.
[19]Piper to Dixon and Littledale, Alexandria, Feb. 9, July 11, 19, Aug. 10, Sept. 10, 1768, Piper Letterbook.

in Maryland. A study of the sale of 319 "non-British" (largely German) male servants in Philadelphia in 1771–1773 produced a mean "storage time" of 11.7 days but a median time of only 3.98—which indicates that the great majority were sold off quickly, while a few remained unsold for weeks. The worst cases were still unsold after 80 days, though they were presumably long since removed from the vessel so that it could be loaded for the return trip.[20]

It was the pressure for speed in sales that led most agents to advise their principals in Britain to avoid taking on redemptioners, who had to be allowed time to search out relatives, friends, or sponsors to purchase the debts they had incurred in shipping costs. In some cases redemptioners were allowed to go as far from Maryland as Boston in search of the funds to buy their freedom, and that kind of delay involved costs that no merchant would willingly incur. It obviously postponed the receipt of funds with which to purchase goods for the return voyage, hence cut down profits on the overall transaction.[21]

The question of returns—the purchases made to load vessels for the return voyages, based on the income from the sale of servants—was one of the consuming issues for every merchandiser of servants, since the returns largely determined the ultimate profits. Every effort was made to get buyers of servants to pay in cash, which usually meant local currency or good sterling bills payable on short terms. But most of the transactions involved payment in kind of some sort—"cash, wheat, or flour," George Woolsey specified in advertising the terms of sale of "sundry tradesmen and farmers" and women who could spin and were used to "country or house work." These exchanges obliged the seller to know the current prices and values of a large range of marketable commodities—particularly grain, tobacco, and iron—and to be able to calculate realistically the likely profit in the later overseas sale of the commodity offered. Market information was therefore vital, even though communication was so slow that much of the information the agents were sent was likely to be out of date when acted upon.

Cheston's principals in Bristol sent him a constant flow of information useful in the decisions he would have to make. Scrutinize the bills of exchange you accept, they warned him in January 1773, and as for "ye state

---

[20] *York Courant*, Aug. 23, 1774; Heavner, *Indentured Servitude*, p. 36.
[21] Walter Hall to James Cheston and John Flanagan, Baltimore, Dec. 21, 1774, Cheston Incoming Letters; Legal Papers of James Cheston re: John Lynch & Daniel Carroll, box 18, Cheston-Galloway Papers. The unavoidable delays in recovering the costs of transporting German redemptioners were not the only problems that faced the shippers of these servants. Someone had to be found to "warehouse" them until they were disposed of—feed, house, and clothe them. In 1764 the Philadelphia German community organized a society to provide this aid for some of their countrymen, and a number of German residents of the city, especially widows, made a regular practice of housing the redemptioners until they could pay off their debts. *Wöchentliche Pennsylvanische Staatsbote*, Dec. 14, 28, 1773, Feb. 8, March 29, 1774; *Pennsylvania Gazette*, Jan. 12, Feb. 9, 23, 1774. No such facilities were available for British servant-immigrants, and so their upkeep, until they were sold, was a dead liability to the shipper.

of the market for wheat, Indian corn, tobacco, etc.," it continues as before "tho the prospect for tobacco seems worse, as there is little or no demand, and we think will be down to 1d 7/8 or lower for exports; you will therefore be best able to judge whether you shall load the *Restoration* with that article or grain." It was left to Cheston to make up the return load with the most salable commodity, some of it purchased by him with the income from the payments he received. So at one point he "lumped" off 55 convicts to an ironmaster in exchange for 100 tons of iron; the iron was loaded aboard the returning vessel together with 80 hogsheads of tobacco he received for another group of servants and with as much purchased tobacco and lumber as the vessel could hold.[22]

One could usually sell a cargo of servants easily if one took "any sort of country commodity for them." The trick was to load up, not with "any sort" of goods, but with goods bought at low rates that would sell well in distant markets, and to do that required judgment, information, experience, and luck. Failures could be costly. A classic case is the misfortunes of one of James Russell's shipmasters, Robert Miller. Ignoring the advice of Russell's agent, William Carr, Miller refused to wait out the usual negotiations, and not only sold the servants he brought in the *Diana* "very low" but negotiated such poor deals for returns that Carr feared he would "not get home above one-half the sum he has sold [the servants] for." Miller, Carr said, was "a simple body." "I advised him to wait till Wednesday and I would appoint that day for the sale of his servants and forwarded advertisements to the back counties. He altered his mind after leaving me and would not wait longer than Tuesday." The purchasers, who in any case, according to Carr, were poor credit risks, were thus freed from the usual pressure of competition, and took advantage of Miller. And beyond all that, Miller's "ignorance and obstinacy" were such that he bungled the reloading of his vessel, was fatally slow in getting the return voyage under way, and remitted only a minimal amount of tobacco, owing simply to "bad management in stowing."

Miller's defense revealed his comic-opera incompetence. When he had sold his servants, he explained to Russell, he had been promised iron in return, but the iron had not arrived when it was supposed to, and so he had sent off the ship's company to gather rocks for ballast, with which, together with some tobacco he had acquired, he had decided to fill the hold. No sooner had the ship been thus loaded—two months after it had arrived in Maryland—than the iron had been delivered, and so Miller had had "to unstow the stones to carry [them] ashore and stow the iron in [the] bot-

[22] *Maryland Journal, and the Baltimore Advertiser,* July 2–9, 1774; Stevenson & Randolph to Cheston, Bristol, Jan. 25, 1773, Cheston Incoming Letters; Cheston to Stevenson, Randolph, & Cheston, Aug. 5, 1770, Cheston Letterbooks.

tome"—at which point more tobacco had also arrived. He therefore had driven the crew to the limit, unloading and loading: ". . . we have no rest night nor day Sunday nor Saturday," he wrote; with the result that most of the crew quit. When Miller eventually sailed off, not only was he late, and not only was he carrying very poor returns, but he was short-handed as well.[23]

But Miller, it was agreed, was "a strange being." Most returns were handled more efficiently than this, though dangers of all sorts threatened to defeat the success of these transactions. One of the most persistent problems, which called for careful judgment and a knowledge of men, both of which Miller lacked, was the question of credit reliability of customers who delayed payment.

Though the agents and ship captains made every effort to sell their servants for cash or good bills, often, Harry Piper explained, "we are obliged to give credit, and sometimes trust people that one is not well acquainted with"; and he had found, he said, that even "the best deceives." Every effort was made to reduce the risk, however, by confining credit as far as possible to well-known, trustworthy customers. Cheston, being "unacquainted with [the] character and circumstance" of one applicant for the purchase of a servant, turned him down, but then relented when a former employer of the would-be purchaser testified to his diligence and honesty, and guaranteed payment if the buyer reneged. Four months later, however, not only had Cheston not been paid but the servant had run off with a neighbor's servant, who also had been sold by Cheston on credit. Both purchasers, the neighbor confessed, were "very much disappointed in getting money." Of the runaways, "one is [in] gaol now & is expected to be hanged, & he is a gran roag, Sir. If you will tarry a few months for your money you shall have security with interest till paid." In this situation the guarantee of a suretor willing to take responsibility for payment if the purchaser defaulted, was essential. But beating around after late payments and elusive guarantors was a time-consuming, frustrating, and expensive business, and it could easily end up in the courts. In July 1774 William Carr felt obliged to make a tour of Westmoreland County in an effort to collect bad debts, but for all his efforts "I could not get one penny." Recent tobacco sales, he reported, had been so poor that the planters were reluctant to ship

---

[23] Miller's travails are recorded in letters from Carr to Russell, Dumfries, May 26, June 28, Aug. 26, 1774; from Philip Fendell to Russell, Portobacco, Aug. 13, 1774; from Miller himself to Russell, "On board the *Diana*, Potomuck River Naval Office" and at "Easteren Brench," May 18, Aug. 8, 15, 1774; from Charles Grahame to Russell, "Lower Marlboro," Sept. 9, 1774: all in the Russell Papers. Miller's departure from London to Maryland at the start of his ill-fated voyage was recorded in the Register: T47/9/113–114; he carried with him 49 indentured servants. His bad luck, or bad judgment, persisted. On a similar voyage the next year three of his indentured servants, together with the boatswain, ran off from the *Diana* as it lay at anchor at Georgetown, Md., and disappeared in the direction of Baltimore. *Maryland Journal, and the Baltimore Advertiser*, July 26, 1775.

their plants, so out of necessity, he told Russell, "I have commenced solicitor for you, though I assure you it is a very disagreeable business."[24]

Certain rules of thumb in credit transactions could be agreed on. Cheston apologized for giving "more credit than I could have wished," but explained that most debtors were given only two or three months to pay; only a few were allowed as much as five. Six months' credit, he wrote, "is the longest credit I have given any person." But in many cases credit of some kind was absolutely essential—one had to make provision, for example, for the responsible planter who could only pay "early in the tobacco season"—and some kinds of risks were unavoidable. Ridley wrote Duncan Campbell that one vessel, whose servants he had sold at excellent prices, had largely satisfied the labor needs of his steady and reliable customers ("my people"). In selling the next cargo, already on its way, he would have no choice, he said, but to sell the servants to "strange hands whom I cannot depend on and increase too much the number of outstanding debts the consequence of which have already been too fatal."[25]

Concerned about terms of payment as well as simply about prices and sales; called upon to decide at what precise point to give up retail sales and to "lump" groups or whole shipments of servants; striving always to satisfy individual customers' needs with workers recruited almost randomly and whose professed skills failed often to correspond to their actual abilities; fearful of having somehow to dispose of willful, violent, crippled, elderly, or otherwise unsalable indentees or repellent convicts; subject always to the randomness of disease; and under constant compulsion to sell quickly and make returns promptly, the merchants, agents, and ship captains engaged in complex negotiations for which shrewdness, experience, knowledge, and luck were essential. Most outstanding successes were products of all of these qualities, together with imagination and the shrewd manipulation of consumer psychology.

Matthew Ridley wrote glowingly of a great success he had recently achieved—"one of the greatest ever made in this river." His "method," he explained, was the following. Noting a pent-up demand for his servants, he confined his convicts strictly to shipboard and allowed no visitors to come aboard to inspect them. No one therefore had any idea of what his

[24]Piper to Dixon and Littledale, Alexandria, Aug. 10, 1768, Piper Letterbook; Joseph Eason to Cheston, Baltimore, Aug. 27, 1770, and Alexander Crawford to Cheston, Jan. 9, 1771, Cheston Incoming Letters. For typical dunning letters, see Cheston to Reayen Penn and to Charles Conaway, Jan. 7, 1773, Cheston Letterbooks. Carr reported his perambulating solicitations to Russell on July 22, 1774, Russell Papers.
[25]Cheston to Stevenson, Randolph, & Cheston, Baltimore, June 21, 1773, to William Ringgold, Dec. 24, 1773, to John Page, Dec. 24, 1773: all in Cheston Letterbooks; Ridley to Campbell, Baltimore, July 4, 1773, Ridley Letterbook.

servants were like. Then, early on the morning he had appointed for the sale, he suddenly threw open shipboard sales, with the result that "the people flocked on board very early that day to have each his first choice. I let them gather till about 7 o'clock and then made my terms for about 80 the first day." In this tense atmosphere of heightened competition, the sales went quickly, and to the most reliable customers. "At present I do not know one bad debt in the whole."[26] But this strategy, combining secrecy with sudden sales, was quite unusual. The common practice was more leisurely: to allow a few buyers on shipboard without time restriction of any kind, and to allow negotiations to mature slowly.

Harrower's captain, once the *Planter* was moored at Fredericksburg, allowed two coopers and a barber and then a few others to go ashore "upon tryall." Harrower himself, favored by the captain and the mates, was permitted to roam through the town at will. Six days after the *Planter* arrived at Fredericksburg, the general sale, advertised in the *Virginia Gazette*, began. Several buyers, among them two "soul drivers," promptly "came on board to purchase serv[an]ts," Harrower recorded. Slowly, in the days that followed, purchases were made. First a cooper, a blacksmith, and a shoe-maker were sold; then a farmer and a cabinetmaker were taken on trial; then a middle-aged man and his three sons. A week after the shipboard sale began, the annual Fredericksburg fair opened, and the remaining servants were "ordred ashore to a tent . . . and severall of their indentures were then sold." That day, at "about 4 PM," Harrower himself was sold, to Colonel William Daingerfield, of the nearby Belvidera plantation, to serve as a schoolteacher to the planter's children. Harrower returned to the ship to gather up his belongings, and was ordered "to get all my dirty cloaths of every kind, washed at [Daingerfield's] expence in toun; at night he sent me five shillings on board by Capt. Bowers to keep my pocket." At 6 A.M. the next morning, May 24, 1774, Harrower "left the ship . . . having been sixteen weeks and six days on board her."[27]

What profits John Harrower and his fellow indentees brought to Captain Bowers and his merchant principals are not recorded, but profits there undoubtedly were. While there were great risks involved, many uncertainties, and unpredictable swings in the price of servants and the value of returns, it was generally agreed that selling servants, whether voluntary indentees or transported convicts, was a profitable if limited business— limited because only the monopolized trade in convicts and the chancier importation of German redemptioners involved sales in large volume. The figures on profit and loss, however, indicate a cost range of £4 to £10 to bring an indentured servant to America and a selling range of £6 to almost

[26]Ridley to Campbell, *ibid.*
[27]*Journal of John Harrower*, pp. 35–41, 179, n.48.

£30, with most sales in the £10 to £15 range. One Baltimore firm insisted that overall costs of servants shipped from Bristol not "exceed £5.10 stg p[er] head delivered here." A profit of £14 per head was considered good, and while it was generally agreed that "the most is made" by the sale of convicts, whose numbers could almost be guaranteed and whose expenses were minimal, there is evidence of net profits in the range of £650 to £700 for large shiploads of indentured servants.[28]

Distribution

Hoping for profits such as these, the ship captains and selling agents concluded the best terms for sales and returns they could, and the process of labor transfer entered its final stage. Harrower, sold to Colonel Daingerfield, left Fredericksburg on a horse provided by his new master to travel the seven miles to Belvidera, where he found "a neat little house" awaiting him as his home and schoolhouse, located "at the upper end of an avenue of planting at 500 yds. from the main house." There, on an estate "verry pleasantly situated on the banks of the river," this once desperate and impoverished Scotch islander, less than six months after he had left his home in the Shetlands and four months after he had sat alone in a London garret, "frendless and forsaken" and down to his last shilling, settled into a new life of plantation gentility, which he enjoyed until his death three years later.[29]

But Harrower's destiny was most uncommon. Few servants had the privilege of riding to their new homes on horseback, with money in their pockets, and fewer still had "a neat little house" awaiting them. Most, even highly skilled artisans, were committed to years of manual labor, and they reached their final destinations by foot or by wagon, river boat, or raft. These concluding passages in their long hegiras could take many days, even

[28]Abbot E. Smith, *Colonists in Bondage* (Chapel Hill, N.C., 1947), p. 39; Heavner, *Indentured Servitude*, p. 46; John Smith & Sons and William Smith, Sailing Orders for Capt. Dan[ie]ll Lawrence, Baltimore, Dec. 3, 1774, Smith Letterbooks; Woolsey to George Salmon [Baltimore], Dec. 5, 1774 and n.d. [Dec. 1774], and to Darley [Baltimore], March 1 and April 10, 1775 ("The servants are sold . . . the n[e]t proceeds £667; had there been no death or sickness we should have made a fine trip"), Woolsey and Salmon Letterbook; Piper to Dixon and Littledale, Alexandria, June 28, 1768, Piper Letterbook. The convict contractor Duncan Campbell summarized the price structure of his business as follows: he sold, in Virginia and Maryland, "common male convicts, not artificers, on an average for 10 pound apiece; females at about eight or nine pounds; those who were of useful trades, such as carpenters and blacksmiths, from fifteen to twenty-five pounds; the old and infirm he used to dispose of to those humane people who chose to take them, but with some he was obliged to give premiums." *Journals of the House of Commons*, XXXVII (Nov. 26, 1778, to Aug. 24, 1780), 310–311. For prices and sales of convicts, see A. Roger Ekirch, *Bound for America: The Transportation of British Convicts to the Colonies, 1718–1775* (Oxford, forthcoming), chap. 4.
[29]*Journal of John Harrower*, p. 41.

weeks, for the ultimate markets for their services were seldom clustered immediately around the port of sale but were scattered through the hinterland. Some of the final destinations were far in the interior—as far off as the trans-Appalachian lands of Kentucky and Ohio. Lord Dunmore's War, fought in 1774 against the Shawnee and Ottawa tribes in the Muskingum Valley and along the upper Ohio and Kanawha rivers, prevented James Cheston in Baltimore from sending servants to the backcountry of Virginia and Maryland "as usual." George Washington, in 1775, following the common pattern of western land speculators, "bought a parcel of servants" in Alexandria in January 1775, marched them, together with "hired men at considerable wages," to Mount Vernon, then sent the whole party off via the upper Potomac to western Pennsylvania and down the Ohio to a section of the 20,000 acres on the Great Kanawha River that he claimed. There, in an almost completely unbroken wilderness, they were told to join with the remnants of the "twenty odd servants and hirelings" Washington had sent off the year before, to put up houses, "get as much land as possible ready for corn," and in general to "seat the land" and hence validate Washington's tentative title to it.[30]

But these contested lands were at the ultimate frontier, far removed from contiguous British settlements. The inner, more populous periphery of continuous settlement was an arc formed by the Shenandoah Valley of western Virginia, the far west of Frederick County, Maryland, and the trans-Allegheny lands of Pennsylvania, west to Pittsburgh, on the upper Ohio River. British indentured servants had been marketed in the Shenandoah Valley as early as the first land boom of the 1730s. In the years that followed, a regular supply service had been worked out by William Preston, a leading valley land speculator, merchant, and magistrate, and a Richmond merchant, Edward Johnson, whose supplies of servants came from vessels penetrating to the fall line on the James River. Between 1755 and 1774 Preston sold scores of servants in the valley on his own account and as Johnson's agent. Though by 1774 the trade had slackened in the south of the valley, near Staunton, it continued to flourish elsewhere throughout these quickly populating western lands.[31]

To this western arc of contiguous settlements, and throughout the tidewater hinterlands whose boundaries it formed, servants were led out from each of the main distribution centers at or near the coast—Philadelphia, Baltimore, Alexandria, Fredericksburg, Leedstown, Richmond, Pe-

[30]Cheston to Stevenson, Randolph, & Cheston, Baltimore, June 21, 1774, Cheston Letterbooks; Roy B. Cook, *Washington's Western Lands* (Strasburg, Va., 1930), pp. 44 ff.; Instructions for James Cleveland and for William Stevens, Jan. 10, March 6, 1775, *Writings of George Washington*, ed. John C. Fitzpatrick (Washington, D.C., 1931–1944), III, 256–261, 268–272.
[31]Robert D. Mitchell, *Commercialism and Frontier: Perspectives on the Early Shenandoah Valley* (Charlottesville, Va., 1977), pp. 52–53, 125.

tersburg—along networks of wagon roads, foot trails, and waterways radiating into the countryside. Philadelphia fed a broad range of labor markets—in New Jersey, Delaware, all nine settled counties of Pennsylvania, and northern and western Maryland. The marketing system of the Chesapeake distribution centers has been described as three great intersecting loops flung out from the primary markets at or near the limits of ocean navigation at the fall line (see Map 10.A). First, southwestern Maryland and northwestern Virginia, as far west as the lower Shenandoah Valley, were supplied by the markets at Baltimore and Annapolis and the main Potomac trading centers at Dumfries and Alexandria. Second, a central Virginia loop, reaching back to the midsection of the Shenandoah Valley, was supplied from a series of small but active markets located along the Rappahannock River: Hobbs Hole, Leedstown, Port Royal, and above all Fredericksburg. And third, servants were distributed through a huge southern loop from markets on the James and Appomattox rivers—principally Norfolk and Hampton at the mouth of the Chesapeake, and Richmond and Petersburg at the fall line. Near the outer margins of these territorial loops there were well-established secondary markets—Lynchburg, Lexington, Staunton—where local auction sales were held for the servants still unsold after weeks or even months of being peddled in the backcountry.[32]

Most of these "remaindered" servants were sold by the notorious "soul drivers"—men, Harrower wrote, "who make it their bussines to go on board all ships who have in either servants or convicts and buy sometimes the whole and sometimes a parcell of them as they can agree, and then they drive them through the country like a parcell of sheep untill they can sell them to advantage." They drove us, Peter Williamson recalled of his early days as an indentured servant in Pennsylvania, "through the country like a parcel of sheep to the slaughter, exposing us for sale in all public fairs and markets, as brute beasts." There was something unforgettable, unnatural—something that stimulated elemental fears and a strange excitement—in this spectacle of "soul drivers" peddling coffles of white British servants and convicts through the countryside. The convicts were sometimes shackled, though most often not; but shackled or not, they and the indentured servants were clearly identified as human commodities available for purchase. Like slaves, to whom they were constantly if extravagantly compared, they seemed dehumanized, as they walked in groups, under guard, along the pathways or sailed up the rivers and streams to inland farms and to cross-

[32]Cheesman A. Herrick, *White Servitude in Pennsylvania* (Philadelphia, 1926), pp. 213–214. The marketing loops have been defined by Schmidt, "Convict Servant Labor," pp. 86 ff., in reference to the sale of convicts in Virginia from the mid-century on. But since the sales of convicts was always intermingled with that of indentured servants, the definition fits the broader marketing process and applies to the Chesapeake area generally in the 1770s.

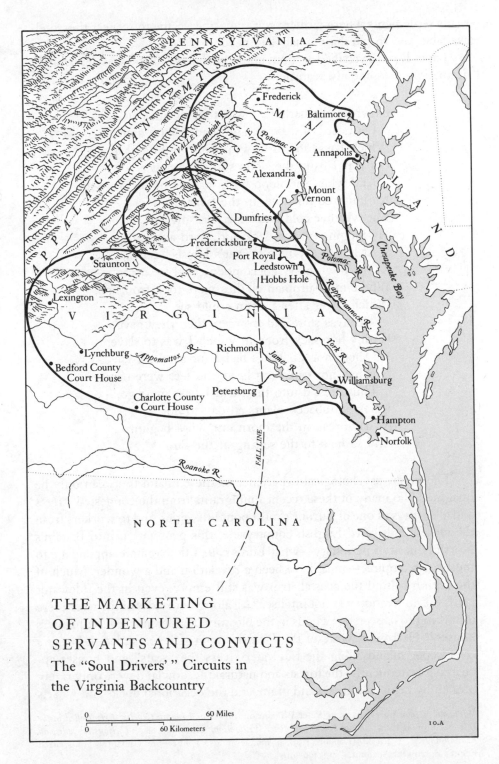

THE MARKETING
OF INDENTURED
SERVANTS AND CONVICTS
The "Soul Drivers'" Circuits in
the Virginia Backcountry

roads settlements where farmers and tradesmen came to inspect the goods available and to purchase what they needed.

James Revel's versified account of the final move inland was deliberately dramatic but essentially realistic:

> Down to the harbour I was took again,
>   On board of a sloop, and loaded with a chain;
> Which I was forc'd to wear both night and day,
> For fear I from the sloop should get away. . . .
>   And when the sloop with loading home was sent
> An hundred mile we up the river went
> The weather cold and very hard my fare,
> My lodging on the deck both hard and bare,
>   At last to my new master's house I came,
> At the town of Wicoccomoco call'd by name,
> Where my Europian clothes were took from me,
> Which never after I again could see.
>   A canvas shirt and trowsers then they gave,
> With a hop-sack frock in which I was to slave:
> No shoes nor stockings had I for to wear,
> Nor hat, nor cap, both head and feet were bare.
>   Thus dress'd into the Field I next must go,
> Amongst tobacco plants all day to hoe,
> At day break in the morn our work begun,
> And so held to the setting of the Sun.[33]

The inner, psychological experience of these inland treks can only be imagined. To many of these recent immigrants from the congested streets and alleyways of one of Europe's most populous cities, and to workers from the closely cultivated English countryside, this penetration into Britain's North American periphery—what Eddis called the "remote appendage to the British empire"—must have been a revelation and a wonder. Much of the region behind the coastal strip was still empty; even in the tidewater lands the cultivation was not intense. "All along both sides of the river there is nothing to be seen but woods in the blossom, gentlemens seats & planters houses," Harrower wrote of the *Planter*'s approach to Fredericksburg.

Deeper inland along the tidewater rivers the "seats" and houses appeared less frequently, the forests and natural meadowland were only rarely broken by fields of tobacco and grain, and the occasional docks and wharfs

[33] *Journal of John Harrower*, p. 39; Peter Williamson, *French and Indian Cruelty: Exemplified in the Life and Various Vicissitudes of Fortune, of Peter Williamson. Containing . . . a Curious Discourse on Kidnapping . . .* , 4th ed. (London, 1759), p. 106; Jennings, " 'The Poor Unhappy Transported Felon's Sorrowful Account,' " pp. 190–191.

became fewer and fewer and finally ceased to appear. Only now and then along the banks of these inland streams were there patches of cultivated land, where field workers, most of them black, waved or stared at the new arrivals; the only dwellings that were visible were cabins, workers' huts, and lean-tos. The backcountry that the servants penetrated along these water-ways was a silent world, exotic and mysterious.

And in the countryside itself, away from the streams, the form of community life was different from anything the servants could have known before. The tidewater plantations functioned as parts of neighborhoods "checkered with the homes and shops of tradesmen and ferry keepers, with ordinaries, churches . . . mills, courthouses, towns, and cross-roads ham-lets." Though individual plantations were sometimes miles apart from each other, they nevertheless formed an intricate social web "woven by family ties, geography, trade, industry, politics, social life, culture, and of course labor."

In the farther backcountry, the scene changed. The network of road-ways and paths thinned out, the complex if scattered neighborhoods faded, the landscape was largely of forests and unbroken fields. The occasional small market centers, each consisting of a mill, a store, a warehouse, and a primitive church, were isolated communities to which farmers, land developers, construction and iron workers, and hunters and traders came only on rare occasions for purchases, exchanges, and companionship. The more prominent of these isolated market villages had courthouses, hence were legal and administrative centers, and there the sale of servants was particularly convenient. Often the diminishing band of unsold servants—wandering through the backcountry, sleeping under the stars or occasion-ally in a convenient barn—was shunted through a circuit of these court-house towns, stretching from the upper tidewater to the frontier.

One group of servants whose dispersal has been traced entered Virginia through the James River and was bought by a Petersburg merchant, who peddled them through courthouse towns beginning in the Appomattox Valley and ending in the upper Shenandoah Valley. Advertisements were sent ahead to each of the courthouses on the route, and the drivers and their charges soon appeared—first at the Charlotte County courthouse, then at the Bedford courthouse sixty miles off, then at other similar centers along the upper James, then across the Blue Ridge Mountains, and finally in the valley. The rich countryside of the Shenandoah was different once again from what this remnant had seen before. This was no attenuation of the tidewater world, but an outer borderland, described by sophisticated visi-tors like Lord Fairfax's brother Robert as utterly primitive and uncouth. Though the region was growing rapidly in population and in the extent of cultivation, it was still a sparsely settled, isolated pioneer world of fron-tiersmen who were still opening the land. They were only beginning to emerge from a subsistence stage of agriculture into commercial farming, and to establish connections with the larger society that lay to the east. In all, the last remainders of this shipload of servants had wandered over two hundred miles along the southern Chesapeake route, and they had traversed three kinds of communities—tidewater, backcountry, and the pioneer valley—none of them similar to anything the servants had known before.[34]

So the workers, drawn from villages, farms, and cities three thousand miles away and from a culture that was dense, deeply rooted, and highly structured, were absorbed into the scattered farms and plantations, the small ironworks and foundries, and the village shops of a loosely organized, thinly populated, mobile, quickly developing society. So loosely were the American communities organized, so many and so wide were their interstices, that some of the servants simply disappeared—ran off, escaped, faded into the general population before they could be sold or before they had worked off all of their time.

How many indentured servants escaped from servitude is not known precisely—certainly less than the 5% of the Virginia convicts estimated to have run away in the course of the eighteenth century. Notices of runaway servants in the *Pennsylvania Gazette* suggest a maximum rate of loss in the early 1770s of just under 3%, but that seems extremely high. The same newspaper reported half that percentage in the 1760s.[35] Whatever the exact numbers, it was an accepted fact of the merchants' and agents' lives that some of the indentees would attempt to escape (the reports were almost perfunctory: "two or three of them have already run away") and that while some of them would be recovered, some would never be found and put back to work but would succeed in disappearing into the local population. The masters usually made some attempt to regain their losses. Runaways who were recaptured were forced to make up for their absences by extended periods of service: in Pennsylvania at the rate of 5 days for each day absent, in Maryland, 10 for 1, in Virginia 2 for 1, though often compromises were agreed to in cases where the standard ratios would add up to unreasonably long extensions of service. The costs of recovery were high, however, and

[34] Eddis, *Letters from America*, pp. 37–38; *Journal of John Harrower*, p. 37; Schmidt, "Convict Servant Labor," pp. 102–103, 197, 157–159; Mitchell, *Commercialism and Frontier*, pp. 230–232.

[35] Schmidt, "Convict Servant Labor," p. 234. The Pennsylvania estimate is based on the assumption that at any given time there were approximately 8,000 indentured servants and redemptioners in Pennsylvania—2,000 entering each year on 4-year terms (Smith, *Colonists in Bondage*, p. 377); the advertisements for runaways in the *Pennsylvania Gazette*, 1770–1775, indicate an average annual loss of 230. "Facts and Notes Relating to the Redemptioners and the Early Emigration of the Poor to America," Hunt MSS, VI, 37. For various figures on runaways and the punishment of those recovered, see Richard B. Morris, *Government and Labor in Early America* (New York, 1946), pp. 434–461.

some masters simply wrote the losses off as wastage: "the expense of getting her [back]," George Woolsey said of one runaway, "would be more than she would sell for."

The danger of escape was not high during the shipboard marketing period; only 10% of the convicts who escaped ran off during those first days and weeks in the colonies. Most escapes were made while the servants were en route from the market where they had been sold to their final destinations. It was with no surprise that Piper reported that "one of the rascals ran away the first night in carrying home," for the groups in transit were thinly guarded, watched over by only one or two guards; the servants were seldom chained or otherwise physically constrained; and they were not confined at night. Later, at work on the farms and in the shops, conditions were equally loose, and since there were no constabulary forces that could systematically search for runaways nor racial differences to distinguish these runaways from the free population, it is perhaps less surprising that some servants ran off than that the great majority did not.[36]

Laws were passed to control this leakage in the system of labor transfers. Provisions were made for vagrants and persons suspected of being runaways to be apprehended, jailed, and advertised (all at the expense of the masters), and statutory rewards were offered for the capture of runaway servants. But the main resource the masters had available to help them recover the runaways was public notification and the offer of special rewards inserted in the newspapers as advertisements. Often these notices, offering rewards for capture and recovery, were repeated week after week while there was still hope of recovery, and in them the runaways were described with remarkable exactness. Their physical characteristics were depicted: their hair, coloration, height, weight, stance, disfigurements, and facial expressions ("fierce," "roguish," "sour," and—over and over again—"a down look"). Frequently their characteristic behavior was indicated: aggressiveness, drunkenness, volubility; sometimes their accents, command of English, and distinctive turns of phrase were given; commonly their skills, occupational and avocational, were described; and often their attitudes and personalities were sketched. They were said to be surly or obsequious or ingratiating, insinuating, artful, sly, hypocritical, villainous, boastful, blasphemous, slow-witted, or clever.

The precision of the individual descriptions is at times astonishing, and it represents some careful planning. Washington, for example, kept notes on the precise personal characteristics of the servants he bought, to be drawn on for advertisements in case any of them escaped. Many others must

[36]Piper to Dixon and Littledale, Alexandria, July 20, 1772, Dec. 23, 1770, Piper Letterbook; Woolsey to Thomas McCabe, May 31, 1775, Woolsey and Salmon Letterbook. For a report that a small group of convicts en route to Hagerstown, Md., in an effort to escape turned on their new owner along the road and robbed and murdered him, see *Lloyd's Evening Post*, Oct. 6–8, 1773.

have done the same, and they kept careful track too of the clothes the servants wore and the clothing and equipment they had available to steal. And, more than these individual descriptions, the owners often attempted, in a few phrases, to depict the escape itself, the groups that may have been involved, and the plan of action that the escapees were liable to follow. They were likely to run off north, the notices said, or to the nearest seaport; they would undoubtedly stop off somewhere long enough to strike off manacles or the studded iron collars that inveterate escapees were made to wear; they would try to find a sailboat to escape downriver to the sea; they would try to find a berth on a vessel sailing back to Britain; they would try to pass themselves off as gentlemen or as gentlemen's valets; they would attempt to enlist in the army, the navy.[37]

Here, in the hundreds of advertisements for runaways that appeared in the newspapers south of New England, lies the physical presence, vividly described, of a sample of the thousands of British servants who were recruited into the American work force in the years before the Revolution. In these descriptions the servants come vividly alive. One can picture the clothes, the expressions, the characteristic stances, the "down looks," the boozy half-smiles, the aggressive postures. One can almost hear the boisterous laughs and the grog-shop songs that are mentioned. And one can imagine the scenes as the fugitives furtively saddled up horses in the dark, silently pushed boats or canoes away from the riverside wharves, struck off shackles and collars, talked their way onto naval vessels or into British army regiments, cut off their hair and put on wigs, and mingled with the crowds in the towns to which they had fled.

A thousand portraits could be sketched from these notices, a thousand scenes and groups. The pages that follow contain a sampling of these newspaper notices, together with excerpts from a merchant's ledger book, itemizing expenses incurred in searching for the runaways.[38]

[37] Herrick, *White Servitude*, pp. 217–221, 227–229; Smith, *Colonists in Bondage*, pp. 264–270; Schmidt, "Convict Servant Labor," pp. 233–237; Washington, Instructions for Stevens, *Writings*, III, 271.
[38] The first, hardcover edition of this book contains a portfolio of 21 sketches illustrating the people and scenes depicted in these advertisements. They are imaginative reconstructions based on careful examination of every descriptive word in these notices. This small sketchbook, eliminated from the present paperback edition, includes a sketch of a scene that impressed itself unforgettably on the minds of contemporaries and that was described again and again: the sale, at the American docks, of shiploads of indentured servants and convicts—weary and sickly from two or three months aboard small, pitching, overcrowded vessels, many of them despondent and in rags, but all of them tricked out by the ship captains and merchants to attract buyers.

VOYAGERS IN FLIGHT

A Sketchbook of Runaway Servants

1774–1775

John Cass

The Pennsylvania Journal   July 19, 1775

Four Dollars Reward.

R A N A W A Y on Sunday last, from the Subscribers, A Servant Lad, named JOHN CASS, born in the city of Wells, in England, and has been in America about nine months, may pass for a Printer or Book-binder, as he understands a little of both; he is about 5 feet 5 or 6 inches high, rather thick built, 19 years of age, very likely, smooth faced, with a fresh colour, black eyes, very black hair, which he mostly wears tied behind in a club, curled at the sides and turned up before, and is a tolerable likely fellow when clean dressed, but is in general much of a sloven. —Had on, when he went away, an half worn beaver hat, a dark olive coloured fustian coatee, a red and white striped linen jacket, white shirt and stock, an old pair of leather breeches, almost black, being much dirtied with his work, white cotton stockings, good shoes and pinch-beck-buckles.—Whoever takes up and secures said servant, so that his masters may have him again, shall receive the above reward, and all reasonable charges, paid by

WILLIAM AND THOMAS BRADFORD.

John Watts

The Pennsylvania Journal   May 10, 1775

Five Pounds Reward.

RAN-AWAY from the Subscriber, in Third-street, near Race-street, an English Servant Man named JOHN WATTS, a Brass-founder by trade, about 22 years old, 5 feet 5 inches high; he came to this place in December last with Capt. Cook, from London; he has a long face, white grey eyes, black curled hair very thin on his head, a childish but hoarse voice; and says, since he has been here, he ran-away from his uncle in London, to come to this country. He had on when he went away, a felt hat, a black silk cravat, Check Shirt, an old peachblossom-coloured waistcoat, of cotton velvet, the back parts of different stuff, and a coating upper-jacket, the lining of white woollen stuff, blue duffil trousers, blue and white mixed stockings very little worn, new neat's leather shoes with silver plated buckles.—Whoever takes up said Servant, and secures him so that his Master may have him again, shall have the above Reward of FIVE POUNDS, and reasonable charges, paid by me

FREDERICK WECKERLY, Brass-founder.

*§*All Masters of Vessels and others, are forbid to take him off at their peril.

May 9, 1775.

Catharine Moserin

Der Wöchentliche Pennsylvanische Staatsbote   March 22, 1774

Zwanzig Schilling Belohnung

Den 19ten März, 1774.

Um 12ten dieses Monats ist von dem Endsbenamten, wohnhaft in Passyunk Taunschip, eine Deutsche verbundene Magd weggelaufen, Namens CATHARINE MOSERIN; als sie wegging hatte sie eine weisse Haube auf, ein rothlecht Seiden Halstuch um, und einen roth Flanellenen Schort-Gaun an mit schwarzen Blumen, einen dunkelbraunes Unterrock mit Schnüren von einer hellen Farbe eingefasst, neue Schuh, mit Weissmetallenen Schnallen; sie ist etwan 5 Fuss lang, hat eine frische Farbe, kan kein Englisch sprechen; trinkt gern rum, und ist sehr schwazhustig. Wer sie aufnimmt und ihrem Meister wieder bringt, soll obige Belohnung haben, nebst Erstattung billiger Kosten, von mir

CHRISTIAN DERICK

Jan Peterson

Der Wöchentliche Pennsylvanische Staatsbote   April 19, 1774

Dreyssig Schillinge Belohnung.

Philadelphia, den 6ten April, 1774.
Es ist gestern Morgen dem Endsbenamten weggelaufer, Ein verbun-
dener Knabe, er ist etwan 13 Jahr alt, ungefähr 4 Fuss und 6 Zoll lang,
schmächtigen Leibes, hat ein hellfärbicht oder Flachsen haar, und ein
blass Angesicht; er ist ein Holänder, Namens JAN PETERSON, erst leztern
Herbst in dis land gekommen, und dem Martin Noll abgekauft worden.
Da er wegging hatte er an ein Camisol von blauem Duffield mit einem
rothen Kragen, und lange Hosen von dem nämlichen Zeuge, welche an
den Knien geflicht sind, alte Schuh und Strümpfe, glatte messingene
Schnallen, und eine blau und weisse feinwollene Kappe, aber keinen
Huth auf. Wer ihn aufnimmt, und zu dem Endsbenamten bringt, der
soll obige Belohnung haben von Dreyssig Schillingen, nebst Erstattung
billiger Kösten, von mir

WILLIAM DEWEES

NB. Allen Schiffern, und andern, wird auf ihre Gefahr verboten, ihn
wegzuführen.

George Newton

The Virginia Gazette (Pinkney)   June 1, 1775

RUN away from the subscriber, in *Spotsylvania*, the 20th of *May*, a
convict servant man, named GEORGE NEWTON, a farmer, born in *Yorkshire*, and imported in the *Justitia* this spring, a stout man, about 6 feet
high, much freckled, has a very red beard, and walks clumsily. I am
informed he has a scar on the fore part of his head, and some scars on
his left arm, which he says was occasioned by shot. He has been in some
office about the customhouse in *London*. He took with him two oznabrig shirts, almost new, one of them died of a purple colour, a pair of
oznabrig trowsers, rather too small for him, a felt hat, bound, a pair of
old country shoes, a jacket without sleeves, much worn, a *Dutch* blanket,
a white linen shirt, a stock, and brass stock buckle, a pair of new worsted
hose, mixed brown and white, and one pair of white yarn stockings. I
suspect he has other clothes with him. He also took away with him a
negro man, named GEORGE, about 5 feet 3 inches high, well made, and

understands working in stone and wood; his fore teeth in the upper jaw is a good deal worn; the finger next to his little finger, on his left hand, is stiff in the first joint, occasioned by a cut, and when the others are shut, stands out; he has lost part of a toe, and, as well as I remember, it is the toe next his great toe, and on the left foot. He took with him some oznabrig shirts, a kersey jacket, with yellow metal buttons, a pair of white yarn stockings, a blanket, a pair of country made shoes, with some other clothes. They say they intend getting on board some ship, but I suspect they will endeavour getting on board the man of war. All masters of vessels, or other persons, are forewarned from harbouring or taking them on board. I will give FIVE POUNDS reward for both, or THREE POUNDS for *Newton,* and FORTY SHILLINGS for *George,* besides what the law allows, if conveyed to me, near *Fredericksburg,* or FORTY SHILLINGS each if secured in any gaol, so that I get them again. If they are not well secured they will make their escapes, being both cunning, artful fellows.

JAMES TUTT.

N.B. I suspect a negro man, named *Tim,* belonging to the honourable *John Tayloe,* is gone off with them.

Richard Dawson & Solomon

Dunlap's Maryland Gazette; or, the Baltimore General Advertiser.
July 18, 1775

Thirty Pounds Reward.

R A N A W A Y from the subscriber, living in Baltimore county, Maryland, about twelve miles from Baltimore town, a white servant man, and a negro man, viz. RICHARD DAWSON, an English convict, came into the country last winter, about 55 years of age, was a soldier under the King of Prussia last war, is given to liquor, upwards of six feet high, brown hair, round face, fresh coloured, has been hurt in his left thumb, which occasions it to be stiff: Had on when he went away an iron collar double rivitted, old castor hat dark frock, much tarred, old dark grey German serge jacket, mended with black lincey, brown role shirt, white fulled cloth breeches, coarse white yarn stockings, and old country made shoes with strings.

SOLOMON, a negro, about twenty-two years of age, has been in the country about four years, and talks pretty good English: Had on when he went away an iron collar, a darby on each leg with a chain to one of them, all double rivitted, a new felt hat, old brown cloth coat, blue cloth jacket lined with red, brown role shirt, white fulled cloth breeches, old white yarn stockings, and old country made shoes.

It is supposed they will make for Boston to the soldiers, as they have often been talking about them, and it is likely they may get their irons off, get other cloaths, change their names, and deny their master, as the negro has always done; has been in New Castle upon Delaware twelve months and upwards; he went from thence in July last and got in goal in Somerset county, Maryland, and was brought home in November last; he has been in Philadelphia, he is of a middle size, somewhat upon the yellow, has some marks upon one of his cheeks like the small pox, has lost part of the side of his right thumb, that makes the end of it look sharper than the other. Whoever apprehends them, or either of them, and secures them in any gaol, so that their masters may have them again, shall have Twenty Shillings; if above ten miles Forty Shillings; if above forty miles Three Pounds, if sixty miles Five Pounds; if two hundred miles Ten Pounds; if five hundred miles the above reward, and reasonable charges if brought home, paid by

THOMAS COCKEY, Sen.
THOMAS COCKEY, Jun.

William Smith

The Virginia Gazette (Pinkney)   January 5, 1775

Newcastle, *December 22, 1774.*

R U N away, on the 10th day of *December,* 1774, WILLIAM SMITH, a *Scotchman,* who is about 23 years of age, and about 5 feet 6 or 7 inches high, speaks very bad *English,* has a yellowish complexion, a long visage, a down look, dark coloured hair, and a mould on his right cheek. He had on, when he went away, a light coloured broad cloth coat, which is broke at the elbows, and with very few buttons on it, a pail blue duroy waistcoat, a pair of deep blue sagathy breeches, coarse shoes, several pair of stockings, steel buckles, coarse felt hat, a *Newmarket* coat of light bath coating, not bound, but stitched on the edges, with death head buttons on it, a pair of wrappers, rather of a darker colour than the *Newmarket* coat; and a large spur, plated with silver; he likewise carried off with him a black sattin capuchin, a piece of new *Virginia* cloth, containing eight yards, striped with blue and copperass, and emptied a boulster of feathers to carry them in. He is very sickly, and stole out of my stable a black horse, with a great many white hairs about his head, neck, and rump, with remarkable long ears, which stand straight up, and very near together, and branded on his near shoulder R C, and likewise on his near buttock R C, with the same mark above it, and is about 4 feet 8 inches high. He also stole a saddle, and double rein bridle, about half worn, a saddle cloth, striped across with red, and bound with red ferret. He has a discharge from the earl of Dunmore's clerk, which he is very fond of shewing. I hereby offer a reward of FIFTY SHILLINGS for apprehending the said *Smith,* and securing the horse, so that I may get him again, or FIVE POUNDS if taken out of the colony. It is expected that he will make for *Wilmington,* in *North Carolina,* as he has a brother's widow living there, that moved from *Virginia* some time since.

JOHN COCKBURN.

James Hickman

The Maryland Journal, and the Baltimore Advertiser
February 24 to March 3, 1774

TEN POUNDS REWARD.

February 12, 1774

R A N away, last night, from the subscriber, living in Baltimore County, about twelve miles from Baltimore-Town, in Maryland, a convict servant man, named JAMES HICKMAN, straight, well made, and of a fresh complexion; about 23 years of age, five feet 6 or 7 inches high, has short dark hair, dark eyes, a blemish in his left eye; is pitted with the small-pox, and has had his collar bone broke, which makes a bump; had on and took with him, a felt hat about half worn, a blue great coat, the cap to the cape made of the same cloth, white country cloth jacket and breeches, mostly new, the jacket has pieces set on the elbows and a pocket inside the skirt, the breeches made with a large flap, and buttons to the knee-bands, light coloured fearnought under jacket, coarse white yarn stockings, strong country made shoes, with strings, and well nail'd; the said fellow ran away last June, and was taken up at the mouth of Juniata; he will probably change his name, and perhaps his clothes, and 'tis likely he may have a pass: Whoever takes up said servant and secures him, so that his master may get him again, shall have FORTY SHILLINGS, if 50 miles from home, FOUR POUNDS, if 100 miles SIX POUNDS, if 150 miles EIGHT POUNDS, and if 200 miles the above reward, including what the law allows, and reasonable charges if brought home, paid by

THOMAS OWINGS

Joseph Ingram

The Virginia Gazette (Pinkney)

September 14, 1775

R U N away from the subscriber, in the upper end of *Spotsylvania*, the 20th of *May* last, JOSEPH INGRAM, an *English* convict servant man, 27 years of age, about 5 feet 7 inches high, rather smaller built than the common size of men, with dark hair, his complexion rather pale, has a sly cast with his eyes, a round face, a peaked nose, wears whiskers, and a kind of a dimple, or something like it, on his chin; he has a scar on one of his arms below his elbow, talks something quick, and much of it when a *little groggy,* and can sing well. He understands farming, and can use a scythe well. He carried away with him a *Devonshire* kersey brown coloured coat, with metal buttons, and pieced in the sides, two oznabrig shirts, roll trowsers, an old felt hat, and a pair of shoes with strings. He went off with one *Reuben Cave,* an apprentice, who is returned, and says that the said *Ingram* altered his name to *Joseph Wagpels,* but perhaps he may alter that name, as he is very artful. Whoever will bring the said servant to me shall have FIVE POUNDS reward, and all reasonable charges paid.

HENRY COLEMAN.

John Shaw

The Pennsylvania Ledger: Or the Virginia, Maryland, Pennsylvania, & New-Jersey Weekly Advertiser   April 22, 1775

R A N A W A Y from the subscriber, living in Hannover Township, Lancaster county, An English Servant MAN, named *John Shaw,* of a swarthy complexion, has a scar on his right cheek: Had on an old felt hat, an old blue coat, an old light coloured jacket, red flannel double breasted jacket, old white breeches with holes in the knees, old blue rig and firr stockings, old shoes with shoe packs, a pair of odd buckles, and an old coarse shirt; he is about five feet six inches high, about twenty years of age. Whoever takes up the said servant and secures him so that his master may have him again, shall receive Four Dollars reward, and all reasonable charges paid by me

WILLIAM CREAN.

SEARCHING FOR THE RUNAWAYS

Expenses

from the Ledger Books of
CAPT. CHARLES RIDGELY
Baltimore County, Maryland
(*courtesy*: Maryland Historical Society)

1775 John Arven & Wm Jones Dr Serv^{ts}

To printer for Advertise^{mts}	-10.0
To puting them in Phil^a papers	10 –
To putting them in Maryl^d papers	-10 –
To Thos Nukles for 6 Days Rideing After them & his Expences & Crosing the bay from Chester to Balti^m	4. 0.0
To Somutch p^d for a horse 6 Days	1. 2.6
To 2 Days Samul Stanbury Riding After them & his Expences	1. 5.0
To 2/3 of 3 men & [James?] Bowen Boat 5 Days Each Brin[g]ing them home & their Expences	
To 39 Days Prision feils [fees?]	7. 3.9
To Commitment & Releasem^t	.– 7.6
To Somutch p^d She[ri]ff for Putt^g them in Annapolis paper	– 7.6
paid Reward	7. 0.0
To Vachel Dorsey 1 Day & horse & Expences getting the Advert^s printed	–12.6
To a man & horse one Day Riding After them	-10 –
To 50 days Each from the time they went away till Returned	

To Runaway time 3 days	
To my Oversheer 2 Days & a horse two days & his Expences	
To Runaway time 3 days	
To 2 hands one Day After him	
To my Over Sheer one Day After him .... }	
To my Oversheer 2 Days & a horse 2 Days	
To Cash p^d for Taken him up	1.10 –
To Sundrys Expences p^d By my Over Sher _____	1. 5 –
To Advertising him the first time he runaway _____	- 10 –
To Advertising him the second time he Runaway _____	- 10 –
To Runaway time When he Runaway from the Works Expences &C Which Howard has an Acc^t of	
To Runaway time the fourth time he Run away from May 22 to June 11	
To 2 Blanketts took w^t him & my Boat which was away from May 25 to June the 10—	
To Cash paid for taken him up	3. 0.0
To Cash p^d Mr Christie For fees .... }	
To 4 hand 1 Day After him	
To my Overseer one Day after him & horse }	
To Advertiezments	-10 –
To Advertiesments When I found out he had stold the Boat _____]	-10 –

Supra _ C^r

By Profit & Loss ....

William George _ Solomon Burnham _ Samuel Chapman

The Virginia Gazette (Pinkney) January 5, 1775

Maryland, *September 25, 1774*

FIFTEEN POUNDS REWARD.

R U N away last night, from *Dorsey's* forge, 3 servant men, *viz. William George,* born in *England,* about 34 years old, about 5 feet 7 inches high, has a down look, light coloured short hair, pock marked, round shouldered, and has had his left wrist broke, which occasions it to be much larger than his right; he is a carpenter and joiner by trade; had on and took with him, 1 check and 1 oznabrig shirt, old leather breeches, light blue jacket without sleeves, a small round hat, bound with black worsted, and has a small piece of crape tied round the crown, a pair of ribbed worsted stockings, and a pair of pumps, with steel buckles; he had on an iron collar.

   Solomon Burnham, born in *Yorkshire,* and speaks in that dialect; he is about 26 years of age, about 5 feet 10 inches high, swarthy complexion, down look, short black curled hair; had on and took with him, 1 oznabrig shirt, blue grey jacket without sleeves, leather breeches, a coarse hat about half worn, a pair of yarn stockings, and 1 pair of shoes and buckles, professes himself to be a complete farmer, and had on an iron collar.

   Samuel Chapman, an *Englishman,* 28 years of age, 5 feet 7 inches high, a lusty well made fellow, a little round shouldered, swarthy complexion, has a large boney face, thick lips, and a very full set of teeth; had on and took with him, a cloth jacket, 1 oznabrig and 1 check shirt, oznabrig trowsers, a pair of stockings, new shoes with buckles, and a new felt hat. Whoever takes up said servants, and brings them to the subscribers, shall have, if 20 miles from home, 30s. if 30 miles, 40s. and if 60 miles, 5£. for each, including what the law allows, and reasonable charges.

SAMUEL DORSEY, junior,
EDWARD NORWOOD.

William Chase

The Pennsylvania Ledger: Or the Virginia, Maryland, Pennsylvania, &
New-Jersey Weekly Advertiser November 23, 1776

TEN DOLLARS Reward.

R A N away on Monday morning last, the 4th instant, an English
servant man named WILLIAM CHASE, by trade a stuff shoemaker, about
23 years of age, about 5 feet 4 inches high, grey eyes, round face'd, a little
pitted with the small pox, a scar under his right eye, brown hair curled;
a smiling way of speaking to strangers; had on a wilton Coat of a lightish
colour, a masquerade bengal jacket, nankeen breeches mended on the
knee knit thread stockings, black grain'd shoes, carvid brass buckles,
check'd shirt, black silk neck-cloth, felt hat, but it is likely he may
change his cloaths as he is a very artful fellow. The person that takes
him up must take care he does not deceive him, as he values himself upon
being a compleat villain. Whoever apprehends and secures the above
servant, so that his master may have him again shall be paid the above
reward by

ROBERT LOOSELY.

N.B. It is hoped masters of vessels will not carry him off.

John Scott

Dunlap's Maryland Gazette; or, the Baltimore General Advertiser.
September 12, 1775. *Postscript Extraordinary to Dunlap's Maryland Gazette.*
Baltimore, September 18, 1775.

Talbot County, August 2, 1775.

R A N A W A Y last night, from the subscribers, an English servant
man named JOHN SCOTT, a square well made fellow, about five feet four
inches high, a good complexion, something sunburnt, wears his own
brown straight hair; took with him a blue cloth coat with a red plush
cape, a good scarlet knit jacket with callimanco back, old buckskin
breeches, a pair of double channelled pumps capped at each toe, but may
change his cloaths, as he stole a very good dark claret coloured coat with
yellow buttons; he is a very artful scoundrel. Also a white woman,
something taller than the fellow, of a very dark complexion, a ring-
worm on her upper lip, a small scar on one cheek; she has left behind

a mulatto bastard, for having which she is bound to appear next court; It is probable they will pass for man and wife. TWENTY SHILLINGS Reward for each if taken in the county, and FORTY SHILLINGS each if taken fifty miles from home, will be paid by

WILLIAM BORDLEY, and
WOOLMAN GIBSON the 3d.

William Webster ✕ Charles Tippin

Virginia Gazette (Pinkney) November 23, 1775

Annapolis, November 5, 1775.

R A N away last night, from the subscriber, the two following servants, viz. William Webster, an Englishman, a hatter by trade, about 5 feet 8 or 9 inches high, 23 years of age, long dark brown hair, cued behind, turned up before, and curled at the ears, thin faced, thick lips, and walks parrot-toed, is a forward, talkative fellow, and can be very complaisant when he pleases; had on, and took with him, a light blue cloth coat and waistcoat, the coat has been turned, a red cloth waistcoat, a pair of white Russia drab breeches, a white linen shirt, two brown Russia sheeting ditto, a good castor hat fan-tail'd, cocked in the military fashion, lined with new white linen, plain pinchbeck knee and shoe buckles.

Charles Tippin, or Tippins, by trade a gardener, and can work a little at the carpenter's business, about 5 feet 6 inches high, remarkably thick set, full face and short brown hair; had on, and took with him, a short brown working coat, with metal buttons, a blue cloth jacket, with sleeves and metal buttons, good buckskin breeches, a white pair of Russia drab ditto, a white shirt, two brown of Russia sheeting ditto, and may have sundry other cloaths.

The above servants went off in a two mast boat, and four oars, in company with some others. They took a pair of oznabrig sheets, which it is supposed they intend to make sails of. Whoever will secure the above servants, so that their master may get them again, shall receive twenty shillings for each if 40 miles, forty shillings for each if 100 miles, or if out of the province, five pounds for each, and if brought home, reasonable charges paid by

WILLIAM REYNOLDS.

Charles Piller

Dunlap's Maryland Gazette; or, the Baltimore General Advertiser.
March 12, 1776

March 7th, 1776.

EIGHT DOLLARS REWARD.

R A N away from the subscriber, the 6th inst. (March) an indented servant man, named CHARLES PILLER, by trade a Barber, came from London about four months ago, but says he is a Scotchman; he is about 5 feet 3 inches high, fair complexion, is much pitted with the small pox, short sandy coloured hair, had on when he went away, a light blue greasy coat and waistcoat, deep blue breeches with flat mettle buttons, white yarn stockings, new soaled shoes, with small pinchbeck buckles, an old castor hat, and a new striped Holland shirt; likewise took with him several razors, strap, shaving box, a diaper towel, and his comb and curling iron; he is a very great drunkard, and is very talkative and abusive when drunk. Whoever takes up said servant and brings him home to his Master in Baltimore town, shall have if in town 2 Dollars, and if out of town 10 miles 4 Dollars, and if out of the province the above Reward, and reasonable Charges, paid by

PHILIP MILLER.

Thomas Welsh

The Virginia Gazette (Purdie)   June 30, 1775

FINCASTLE, *June 1, 1775.*

R U N away from the subscriber, last night, within 9 miles of *English* ferry, on *New* river, an *Irish* servant man named THOMAS WELSH, about 21 years old, about 5 feet 8 inches high, is well made to his height, of a fair complexion, and speaks bad *English.* He was clad in a hunting shirt filled with wool, buckskin breeches, linsey leggins, a wool hat, and his shoes nailed all round, both heels and soles. He has a smooth-bore gun with him, and is supposed to be along with *Nathaniel Morgan*'s servant man. Whoever secures the said servant, so that he may be got again, shall have 50s. reward, if taken in the county, if out thereof 5£ paid by

SAMUEL INGRAM.
JOSEPH MEARS.

Thomas Hardy

Dunlap's Maryland Gazette; or, the Baltimore General Advertiser.
October 17, 1775

July 28th, 1775.

FIVE POUNDS REWARD.

RAN AWAY last night from the subscriber living near the Northampton Iron-Work, Baltimore County, Maryland. A convict servant man, an Englishman, named THOMAS HARDY, about five feet eight or nine inches high, grey eyes, short grey hair, about fifty-two years old, limps in his walk; he has a small hole in one of his lips, lost most of his teeth, talks in the North Country dialect; Had on and took with him, a white country cloth jacket, country tow linen trowsers, good English shoes, two oznabrig shirts, old felt hat; he may have other cloths. Whoever takes up the said servant and secures him, so as his Master gets him again, shall have 20 Shillings if 10 miles from home, 30 Shillings if 20 miles, 40 Shillings if 30 miles, 3 Pounds if 50 miles, and the above reward if one hundred miles from home, and reasonable charges if brought home, paid by

JOHN ROBERT HOLLIDAY.

Ralph Chillingsworth

The Virginia Gazette (Purdie)   December 29, 1775

Richmond, *December 26, 1775.*

RUN away, on *Sunday* the 3d instant, an *English* servant man, named RALPH CHILLINGSWORTH, of the middle stature, slim made, thin visaged, has had the smallpox, is very fond of spirituous liquors, a plaisterer by trade, and a very artful sensible fellow. He had on a good frieze coat, red cloth waistcoat, worsted stockings, strong *London* made shoes, white shirt, brown wig, which is rather too large for him, and a beaver hat, that has been dressed, after being some time wore. He has been seen, since he made his escape, selling some osnabrugs, and I hear purchased a gun, with which it is probable he will endeavour to get on board some of the men of war at *Norfolk*. Whoever conveys the said servant to me shall have 40s. reward, but if he returns to his duty he will be received kindly.

RICHARD ADAMS.

John Williams

The Virginia Gazette (Purdie)   August 4, 1775

R U N away from the subscriber, in *Peytonsburg, Pittsylvania* county, the 24th of *June,* an *English* convict servant man named JOHN WILLIAMS; he carried with him a claret coloured frieze coat, a light coloured *New-market* d[itt]o, either bearskin or beaver coating, two osnabrug shirts, and a pair of osnabrug trousers, a pair of leather breeches, and a rackoon hat lined with green persian. He is a thick well set fellow, about 5 feet 9 or 10 inches high, light hair, a brazen look, and is very fond of spirits, has several large warts on his hands, and a very remarkable scar on his upper lip, right under his nose, thus X. He formerly teached a reading school at this place, for about six or eight months past. As he understands the *Prussian* exercise very well, I expect he will endeavour to pass for a deserter from general *Gage,* or some of his majesty's troops. I will give 5£ reward for him if taken in *Virginia,* and 10£ if taken in *Carolina, Maryland,* or *Philadelphia,* or secured in any of his majesty's jails, so that I get him.

HENRY WILLIAMS.

George Han ⌐ Friedrich Broner

Der Wöchentliche Pennsylvanische Staatsbote   April 12, 1774

Philadelphia, den 4ten April, 1774

GESTERN NACHMITTAG SIND VON MIR dem Endsbenamten Schumacher in der Zweytenstrasse, nahe bey der Reedsstrasse, zwey verbundene Deutsche Burschen weggelaufen, beyde Schumacher. Der erste heisst Georg Han, ist ein dicker, starker Bursch, hat ein fett rund Angesicht, dicke Augen, ist etwan 5 Fuss und etliche Zoll lang, spricht sehr gebrochen Englisch. Als er wegging, hatte er einen Rock und Camisol von blauem Tuch an, mit gelben Knöpfen, Hirschlederne Hosen, blaue wollene Strümpfe, umgewandte Schuh mit silbernen Schnallen, einen guten Bieberhuth auf, und sein weis Hemd an; er hat schwarzbraune Haare, die er hinten gebunden trägt. Des andern Name ist Friedrich Broner; er ist so gross wie der erste; hatte auch einen blauen Tüchenen Rock und Camisol an mit blauen Camelhdrenen Knöpfen, Hirschlederne Hosen, blaue Strümpfe und ein Paar leichte Schuh mit gelben Schnallen, ein Kelschen Hemd, und einen Wollhuth auf. Er spricht gut Deutsch und Französisch, aber sehr gebrochen Englisch; er hat kurze schwarze Haare. Es wird vermuthet sie seyn beyde bey einander. Wer sie aufnimmt und in einig Gefängniss bringt, oder einen von ihnen, oder gibt solche Nachricht von selbigen, dass ihr Meister sie wieder bekommen kan der soll für jeden Fünf Pfand zur Belohnung haben, nebst Erstattung billiger Kosten, von mir

JOHANNES RUP.

NB. Allen Schiffern wird verboten sie wegzuführen.

John Ducrect

The Virginia Gazette (Purdie)   July 21, 1775

Twenty Dollars Reward.

R U N away the 16th ult. JOHN ECTON DUCRECT, a native of *Berne* in *Switzerland,* who speaks very good *French* and tolerable *English* and *Italian.* He is about 5 feet 9 inches high, pitted with the smallpox, and very swarthy, almost as dark as a mulatto; wears his own hair, with a false tail, and is generally powdered, being a barber by trade. I have heard, however, since he went off, that he intended to cut off his hair, and wear a wig. He has been used to travel with gentlemen, and will probably try to get into employ that way, or with some of the barbers in *Williamsburg,* as he was seen at doctor *Todd's* tavern, on his way there, the 22d ult. He took with him a suit of brown and a suit of green clothes, the brown pretty much wore, and has had some rents on the back of the coat, the green almost new, a pair of new buckskin breeches, trousers that button down the legs, some white thread stockings and white shirts, a powder bag and some shaving materials, a prayer-book in *French,* and some old commissions for officers in the *Swiss* militia, by which he will probably try to pass. One of his testicles was swelled, which he says was occasioned by a kick he got on board the *Justitia,* capt. *Kidd,* the ship he came out in. Whoever secures the said convict, so that I can get him again, shall be paid the above sum by

RICHARD GRAHAM.
Dumfries, July 3, 1775.

I V

Peopling the
Peripheral Lands:
The Extremities

INTRODUCTION

THE demand for labor, in the expansive years after 1760, accounts for a major segment of the migration flow to North America reflected in the Register of 1773–1776, but not for the whole of it. While the Register documents the exodus of thousands of indentured and free workers—most of them unencumbered male artisans in their early twenties or late teens drawn from metropolitan, southern England—it also records the movements of families from northern Britain, from Yorkshire and Scotland particularly, most of them associated with farming rather than with trades and crafts, and they traveled to different destinations. Drawn mainly from the land, they were seeking reinstatement on the land under circumstances different from those they were leaving behind. Discontented, disoriented by changes taking place around them, and threatened with a radical diminishment of their lives, they responded to the attractions offered by a battalion of recruitment agents serving the needs of land speculators in every region of British North America. Some of these entrepreneurs of migration were long-established American landowners, substantial figures in the local scenes. They were seeking to populate, and profit by populating, new land acquisitions of their own, extensions of their central holdings or additions they hoped to exploit. Others were less respectable speculators, native Americans operating alone or in companies, whose major enterprises were dealings in relatively small parcels of unopened land. And still others were high-flying operators, British and American, whose imaginations took fire in the 1760s when the peace treaty with France flung open a vast new periphery for settlement.

Large-scale land speculation in the American borderlands was nothing new in American history. It had been present from the earliest years of British settlement, but it had reached a climax and achieved a new scale in the 1740s, before subsiding at the outbreak of the mid-century war with France. It had developed in response to population pressure on cultivated land. With the British North American population growing after 1713 at an average rate of approximately 35 percent per decade, those with access to large parcels of land or with the means of gaining access had risen to exploit the situation. Wherever, in these years, men had gathered to talk about crops, government, and business, and wherever men of property and position had met to discuss the trends of the time and the opportunities that lay ahead, plans had been made, groups formed, and the first steps taken in enterprises whose scale could not have been seriously considered twenty years before.

The most successful enterprises of the mid-century had taken little effort to organize. Land claims dating back to the seventeenth century had been legally activated and in some cases proved to be immensely lucrative because of the press of population. It had required only a small outlay of capital on the part of the diplomat and politician John Carteret, Earl Granville, to validate, in 1744, his claim to the inheritance of the northern half of North Carolina, then becoming a major field for frontier settlement, and to appoint agents to extract an income from rents and land sales there. Similarly in 1745 Lord Fairfax had legally established his claim to the Northern Neck of Virginia, a property of some five million acres that he had inherited from the recipients of a grant made a century before by Charles II, property that stretched west into the northern half of the Shenandoah Valley and hence included a region just then being occupied by migrants moving south from Pennsylvania and Maryland and west from tidewater Virginia. These inherited titles had been quite easily established in law, and settlers already had been available on these lands, or had been voluntarily moving into them, or had been easily diverted to them. The same had been true of some of the enormous properties claimed as inheritances by the Penn family in their colony and by the Calverts in Maryland.

These were practical successes in land speculation. Other efforts were visionary, grandiose, and futile. But even the most visionary land projects of the 1740s—the Ohio Company's claim to 200,000 acres between the Appalachians and the Ohio River and the Loyal and Greenbriar companies' grants totaling nearly a million acres in the same region—were accurate indicators of the swiftly moving trends of the times. In the early 1750s—as immigrants continued to arrive in large numbers in the port towns, as they and domestic migrants moved off to fresh, uncultivated land—the colonies were seized by a fever of land speculation. Enterprising men listened carefully to traders and woodsmen returning from the west, laid out their maps, considered the ever-rising tide of population growth and the constant movement and resettlement of people everywhere, and projected extraordinary new plans. By 1754, when war erupted in western Pennsylvania,

Benjamin Franklin was beginning to promote a scheme for two huge colonies along the Ohio; a group of Pennsylvania merchants had projected an immense new province just north of the Tennessee River; and there were stirrings of a similar sort elsewhere—in almost every colony and commercial center.

A vision had been glimpsed, in these mid-century years, of the possibilities of extensive and fabulously profitable land settlements on the frontiers —possibilities largely created by continuing population growth. But then, in 1754, conflict with the French over control of the western lands exploded, and the mounting entrepreneurship came to a sudden halt. The wartime interruption was creative, however. For when these efforts were revived after 1760, they had acquired new and powerful accelerators.

The continuing growth of the American population during the long war—it grew by a third in the 1750s—had created even greater population pressure than had existed before. And at the same time pressures of another sort were also created by an increasing number of influential and ambitious Britons who had become aware of the commercial possibilities of exploiting the American west. British army officers, as well as a large number of civilian officials, had served in North America in the late 1750s, had seen some part of the western territories for themselves, had heard of plans for western development, and had brought all this back to Britain with them. Further, the war increased the awareness on the part of other Britons, who had never lived in or visited the colonies, of the magnitude of the landed empire the nation had acquired: members of the Board of Trade, secretaries of state, lords of the Treasury and Admiralty, certain members of Parliament, and leading naval and customs officials. But these major figures in government, together with influential merchants who had profited handsomely from government contracting during the war, were not the only ones in Britain aware of the new possibilities that were opening up in America. A number of officials at the subministerial level, men who earned their livings by handling some part of the flow of information to and from America, together with their advisors and hangers-on who passed as experts on colonial matters, were also eager to put their expertise in American affairs to profitable use.

Beyond all of these quite visible new elements in the pressure toward the expansion of settlement and the continuing growth of population, a less palpable force had also developed during the war years that contributed much to the explosion of enterprise and the spread of population that followed in the 1760s and '70s. The war stimulated the ambition and magnified the confidence and the scale of activities of many of the leading colonists. In the summer of 1754, twenty-five delegates from seven colonies met at Albany and considered not only the immediate issue of common defense but westward expansion, Indian relations, and the overall state of

British North America. Though their recommendation for a continent-wide political union was ignored, the mere fact that they met together to consider problems of continental scale was important. In the years that followed, prominent American politicians, merchants, and planters—Thomas Hutchinson, John Penn, Benjamin Franklin, James DeLancey, William Shirley, George Washington—shared in the planning and supplying, if not in the actual direction, of the extensive military operations that resulted in Britain's victory. In the process they stretched their abilities as managers and planners, raised their sights, and shared an atmosphere of great affairs and the excitement of mobilizing men and equipment to accomplish something that mattered in the larger world abroad.

It was not simply that the war for empire provided leading Americans with opportunities for profit that were not otherwise available. Beyond that, the struggle enlarged the experience and stimulated the ambitions of these men, otherwise provincial, otherwise restricted in their activities to the limited scale of the colonial world. When the fighting ended there were men in every colony whose experience and horizons had been broadened, who had been involved in the international struggle for control of the west, who were aware of the disposition of the American population generally, and who had connections with British military and commercial organizers.

The combination of all these circumstances—an enlarged colonial population poised for movement to the frontiers, the heightened involvement of British officials and entrepreneurs in North American affairs, and the broadening of the horizons and ambitions of native American leaders—created an irresistible force for expansion when released by the terms of the Treaty of Paris of 1763.

Complex, often the product of elaborate, shadowy intrigues, and intricately interrelated, the colonization projects and migration schemes of the decade before the Revolution, even now, after generations of assiduous scholarship, can scarcely be sorted out and clearly depicted. Everyone with any ambition and capacity, it seems, on both sides of the Atlantic, sought some profit from what promised to be the greatest land boom in history. Plans were drawn up, revised, expanded, abandoned; companies formed overnight, sometimes quickly disappeared, sometimes grew into syndicates; and connections between American and British groups were universal, conceived of by everyone as a requirement for ultimate success.

The sheer volume and intricacy of the scheming and the proliferating confusion of the related migrations and settlements are monumental. Simply to sketch the developments is to impose order where little existed. Two regions, however, can be distinguished from the rest. They stood out as prime targets for exploitation because most easily accessible to Atlantic shipping. Both Nova Scotia and the Floridas, at the extremities of the great new peripheral arc, were *coastal* frontiers. Unlike the older colonies, they were not thickly settled at the ocean fringes. The opening of new land for settlement did not involve deep penetration into the interior, far from the transatlantic routes of transportation. Acquired by Britain at different times —Nova Scotia in 1713, the Floridas in 1763—they were nevertheless equally open for initial coastal exploitation in the mid-1760s, and they stimulated equally some of the most elaborate speculative schemes. They also, in different ways, involved the overseas resettlement of provincial Britons, some of whose lives were caught in transit in the pages of the Register and whose fortunes may be traced through that powerful, if flawed, prism.

These are ordinary, obscure people moving to uncultivated land on the North American periphery made available by profit-seeking entrepreneurs. Their private histories are multitudinous, and cannot easily be generalized. Their individual backgrounds are too diverse, their experiences too dissimilar, the geographical circumstances of their settlements too varied, to allow easy summaries or sweeping conclusions. Only an immersion in the details of many careers, in the everyday events of many of these long-forgotten lives, based as far as possible on their own testimonies, makes possible an understanding of what this passage in the peopling of North America meant for the people who experienced it.

So, in the chapters that follow, the entrepreneurial—speculative— efforts that directed the movements of these thousands of migrants are sketched, the entrepreneurs themselves identified, and the lives of the voyagers involved in their ventures explored in narrative form. The narratives are based on letters, diaries, business records, land titles, state papers, official documents of all kinds—on every scrap of documentation that could be found. And each of these narratives is associated in some manner, directly or indirectly, with the central Register of emigrants created by the government's concern for the departure of precisely these migrants—not "surplus" artisans and laborers individually seeking better markets for their labor or drifting helplessly with the movements of the economy, but family people from farming areas in the north of Britain, traditional producers of the rental incomes that made possible the leisured existence of the nation's rulers. They were people who in some degree were attempting to determine their own fates.

I I

Yorkshire and the
Maritime Northeast

Nova Scotia, in the years before the American Revolution, was the northeasternmost point of the great arc of borderlands that swung west and south from Canada to Florida to form the outer boundaries of the settled communities of British North America. A 270-mile-long promontory lying parallel to the mainland across the Bay of Fundy and attached to the mainland at the north by a 17-mile-wide isthmus, Nova Scotia is extended in two directions by closely adjacent islands: Cape Breton, which reaches 110 miles east out into the Atlantic, and St. John (now Prince Edward) Island, a narrow crescent that nestles close to Nova Scotia's northern shore in the Gulf of St. Lawrence. Comprising in all a land area of 22,500 square miles (over 14 million acres), Nova Scotia and the adjacent islands had a total population of less than 18,000 in early 1774 when the voyagers whose names appear in the Register arrived from Britain.

PRELIMINARIES

Origins

However small the population, it constituted a society of remarkable ethnic complexity. Part of the base population remained the Acadians, themselves an extraordinary amalgam of peoples. Descended from the seventeenth-century French settlers drawn from many regions of France, they had intermingled with Portuguese, Scots, English, and Micmac Indians, and in time, living in isolation on the marshy fringes of the Bay of Fundy, they had developed a unique folk culture and language. By 1713, when Britain took possession of Nova Scotia (but not Cape Breton) by the terms of the Treaty of Utrecht, the Acadians numbered 2,000; in the course of the next forty years the figure more than quintupled. But then, in 1755, came the decisive event in the Acadians' history. The British commanders on Nova Scotia, frightened by reports of Braddock's defeat in western Pennsylvania and fearful that in renewed warfare the Acadians would favor the French and Indian enemies, deported the entire Acadian population. Ten thousand of this long-settled population—men, women, and children— were rounded up and exiled. Their property confiscated, they were shipped in small groups here, there, and everywhere in the seaboard colonies and the Caribbean islands; many—the future Cajuns—eventually settled in Spanish Louisiana. A thousand or two managed to escape deportation by disappearing into the countryside, and emerged from hiding after the war officially ended in 1763. Slowly, others returned from the diaspora to join them. But those who survived and those who returned, though they were able to reconstitute a new Acadian community, found their properties confiscated and themselves restricted in where they could live. They were relegated to marginal lands and special government reserves, and while their numbers again rose, they remained outside the central life of the province. In the 1770s they formed a substratum of the Nova Scotia population, living in small, defensive, inward-looking communities united by close-woven ties of kinship, by a shared folk culture and language, and above all by the collective memory of hardships endured and of a golden age, long since destroyed, whose nostalgic glow grew brighter with the passage of years.[1]

Their displacement had been the result not only of military decisions taken in time of war. In part, too, this drastic deracination had been the product of the government's desire to repopulate the province with politically reliable Protestants; and it was the result as well of New Englanders' consuming hunger for fresh land. The government's plans for peopling Nova Scotia and some of the surrounding lands were first formed in 1748 when the peace treaty of Aix-la-Chapelle had restored to France the fortress of Louisbourg on Cape Breton, which had been captured by Anglo-American forces three years before. To offset Louisbourg, not only was a new British naval base and provincial capital built at Halifax on the south shore of Nova Scotia, but at the same time the government announced in London that it would give free transportation, land, and supplies to foreign Protestants who would settle on the peninsula.

[1] N. E. S. Griffiths, "The Acadians," in *Dictionary of Canadian Biography*, ed. George W. Brown *et al.* (Toronto, 1966–   ), IV, xxvi; Marcus L. Hansen, *The Mingling of the Canadian and American Peoples*, ed. John B. Brebner, I (New Haven, 1940), pp. 27–29.

The result was an influx of over 2,700 immigrants from the small states of southwestern Germany, particularly the Palatinate, Württemberg, and Hesse-Darmstadt; from the French Protestant enclave of Montbéliard, a dependency of Württemberg adjacent to the Swiss canton of Bern; from Bern itself and the other Protestant cantons of Switzerland; and in smaller numbers from a few locations in northern Germany and the Netherlands. Some 1,500 of these foreign Protestants were settled, at great expense to the government, in a new township, Lunenburg, ninety miles by road, sixty by sea, south of Halifax. New Englanders too, though in smaller numbers, responded to the government's call for Protestant settlers. Then the onset of the Seven Years War temporarily cut off all responses to the government's efforts to repeople the land. But when the fighting ended in 1760, the confiscated lands of the Acadians, now being reclaimed from the marshes along the Bay of Fundy, were added to the attractions of the region, and interest rose dramatically.[2]

In the early 1760s agents of land companies and of groups of prospective settlers, encouraged by the government, toured the peninsula and eyed the most promising sites. The fertile, recently abandoned farmlands along the Bay of Fundy were especially attractive to associations of farmers in the colonies to the south, while fishing and lumber interests turned to the Atlantic shoreline south of Halifax and along the southern tip of the peninsula at Cape Sable. Fleets of small transport vessels carried land-hungry New Englanders to newly designated townships along the shores of the Bay of Fundy; there the Acadians helped repair the dikes their people had originally built and prepared the abandoned marshes and fields for reclamation. At the same time new lands were opened or claimed for development at both of the two deep waterways that extended northward into the narrow isthmus like fingers from the hand of the bay. To the eastern finger, formed by Minas Basin and Cobequid Bay, came Protestant Irish to join the New Englanders entering the region and to help found a range of new townships. The lands of the western finger, formed by Chignecto Bay and its northern extensions, Shepody Bay and the Cumberland Basin, were reserved for major projects: a settlement for large-scale migration from Ireland and a colony for war veterans. At the same time fishermen, lumbermen, and farmers from Cape Cod and Nantucket projected a series of townships on the southern Atlantic shores of the peninsula, where the combination of meadows, forest, and fishing waters promised a well-balanced economy. New Englanders began to move too to the continental mainland opposite Nova Scotia and north of Maine, the region that later would become the province of New Brunswick, to establish farms near the

---

[2]Winthrop P. Bell, *The "Foreign Protestants" and the Settlement of Nova Scotia* (Toronto, 1961), pp. 284, 304–305, Table X, chap. 5.

mouths of the St. John and St. Croix rivers and to found a lumbering industry in the midst of the untouched forests.[3]

The "Carnival of Land Grabbing"

These were the first enterprises of the early sixties. But the possibilities of exploiting Nova Scotia were enormous, and people with volatile imaginations and large ambitions responded accordingly. The mid-sixties saw a wild land boom, "a veritable carnival of land grabbing." Speculation in Nova Scotia lands swept like an epidemic through the British world, infecting impoverished Pennsylvanians and affluent New Englanders alike, Cape Cod fishermen as well as London merchants, obscure farm folk on the American frontier as well as politicians in Britain. Above all, the fever struck the officials of the Nova Scotia government, who, with easy access to the choicest land and an income of fees from all land transactions, were consumed with ambition. Granting townships of 100,000 acres left and right to individuals or syndicates promising to settle specified numbers of people in a short period of years, and at the same time issuing smaller grants both in Halifax and London, the government gave away over 3.5 million acres in a decade; 2.5 million acres were granted in the single fortnight before November 1, 1765, when the Stamp Act, which would have increased legal costs, was to have gone into effect. In all, by 1773, over 5 million acres had been granted away.[4]

Some of the speculators, like the frenetic and unscrupulous Irish-American Alexander McNutt,[5] were typical fly-by-night operators such as had surfaced in every uncontrolled land boom in the history of the colonies. But much more substantial figures were also involved in the Nova Scotia bubble of the 1760s. John Perceval, second Earl of Egmont, the first lord of the Admiralty and a prominent politician, whose father had been instrumental in founding the colony of Georgia and who had large landholdings in

[3] Hansen, *Canadian and American Peoples*, pp. 30–34.
[4] William O. Sawtelle, "Acadia: The Pre-Loyalist Migration and the Philadelphia Plantation," *Pennsylvania Magazine of History and Biography*, 51 (1927), 270; John B. Brebner, *The Neutral Yankees of Nova Scotia* (New York, 1937), pp. 94, 99; Norman Macdonald, *Canada, 1763–1841: Immigration and Settlement* (London, 1939), p. 71.
[5] On McNutt's bizarre, indeed megalomaniac, and fruitless career as a land speculator, see W. O. Raymond, "Colonel Alexander McNutt and the Pre-Loyalist Settlements of Nova Scotia," *Proceedings and Transactions of the Royal Society of Canada*, 3d ser., 5 (1911), sect. 2, 23–115; Bell, *"Foreign Protestants,"* pp. 122–123; Brebner, *Neutral Yankees*, pp. 96–99. Three of the fifteen grants to which McNutt managed to attach his name involved the Philadelphia group that attempted a settlement at Pictou and of which Benjamin Franklin was a prominent member. On Franklin's elusive land maneuvers in Nova Scotia, see *Papers of Benjamin Franklin*, ed. Leonard Labaree *et al.* (New Haven, 1959–), XI, 186–187; XII, 345–350; XIII, 123; XIV, 291–293, 202–204; Sawtelle, "Acadia," pp. 273–283; Raymond, "Alexander McNutt," pp. 86–87.

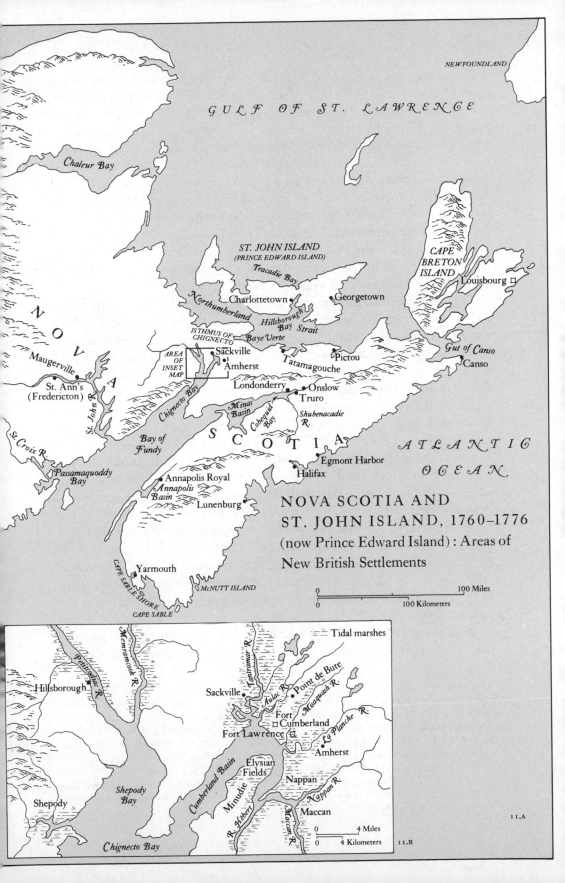

NEWFOUNDLAND

GULF OF ST. LAWRENCE

Chaleur Bay

CAPE BRETON ISLAND

Louisbourg □

ST. JOHN ISLAND
(PRINCE EDWARD ISLAND)

Tracadie Bay

Northumberland

Charlottetown • • Georgetown

Hillsborough Bay Strait

Baye Verte

ISTHMUS OF CHIGNECTO

AREA OF INSET MAP

Sackville • • Pictou

Amherst • Tatamagouche

Maugerville •

N O V A

Gut of Canso
Canso

St. Ann's
(Fredericton)

Londonderry • Onslow
Truro

Minas Basin

Shubenacadie R.

St. Croix R.

Chignecto Bay

Cobequid Bay

S C O T I A

Bay of Fundy

A T L A N T I C

O C E A N

Egmont Harbor •

Halifax •

Passamaquoddy Bay

Annapolis Royal •

Annapolis Basin

Lunenburg •

NOVA SCOTIA AND
ST. JOHN ISLAND, 1760–1776
(now Prince Edward Island): Areas of
New British Settlements

CAPE SABLE SHORE

Yarmouth •

McNUTT ISLAND

CAPE SABLE

0   100 Miles

0   100 Kilometers

—·— Tidal marshes

Petitcodiac R.

Memramcook R.

Hillsborough •

Tantramar R.

Sackville • Point de Bute

Aulac R. *Misaquash R.*

Fort □ Cumberland

Fort Lawrence 日

La Planche R.

• Amherst

Cumberland Basin

Elysian Fields

Nappan •

Shepody Bay

Minudie

Shepody •

R. Hébert

Nappan R.

Maccan •

Maccan R.

Chignecto Bay

0   4 Miles

0   4 Kilometers

11.A

11.B

Ireland as well as in England, had staked out claims in two of the newly opened borderlands of British America. In the early 1760s he established title to 65,000 acres in East Florida, and in Nova Scotia between 1768 and his death in 1770 he engaged actively in developing a 22,000-acre grant reaching back inland from the Atlantic coast just east of Halifax, while asserting less firmly a claim to another unspecified 100,000 acres. A man of far-flung interests and romantic imagination, whose name would be memorialized in New Zealand as well as in Nova Scotia and Florida, he was mocked by his political opponents for his sometimes fantastical neo-feudal ambitions. Characteristically, he devised his 22,000-acre plot in Nova Scotia for descent within the Perceval family, and planned with great care the physical layout of his personal estate—at that point a thick forest broken by a single clearing with a squatter's hut.[6]

This private establishment near the sea at Egmont Harbor was designed to include a "mansion house, park, castle, etc." (Egmont was said to have rebuilt his house in peaceful Somersetshire "in the guise of a castle, moated round, and prepared it to defend itself with cross-bows and arrows"). And he made elaborate and equally unrealistic plans to attract a general population of tenants. The whole property, aside from the mansion estate, Egmont wrote on the margins of a detailed terrain map of the 22,000 acres, would be divided into "grand divisions" of 9 square miles, or 5,760 acres. He planned to grant out "in fee" four 1-square-mile blocks (640 acres) at each corner of the 9-square-mile "grand divisions" to "any four gentlemen who will plant each four families of five to a family on his respective square mile." In this way he would subdivide four-ninths of the 5,760-acre blocks into 160-acre family farms, from which he would collect rents; all the rest he would reserve for later sale when the initial development would have enhanced the value of the land. Dividing the property into basic units of 640 acres particularly appealed to Egmont because, he wrote, they were "the exact size of one fief as granted by William the Conqueror in England to the gentlemen who made the conquest of England with him—and was called a knight's fee which was always esteemed a very honourable degree of property and rank." And he jotted down on the terrain map the "ancient names" used in the eleventh century for the smaller subdivisions of the land

[6]For a sketch of Egmont's public career, see Lewis Namier and John Brooke, *The House of Commons, 1754–1790* (London, 1964), III, 266–268. The main documentation for Egmont's speculations in Nova Scotia and East Florida lands is in the Egmont Papers, Add. MSS 47053, 47054A and B, especially the letters in 47054A, 1–38. Egmont's properties in England and Ireland are documented in Add. MSS 47049–47051. For Horace Walpole's waspish view of this curious antiquarian and colonizer, see his *Memoirs of the Reign of King George the Third . . .*, ed. G. F. Russell Barker (London, 1894), I, 308, and his *Memoirs of the Reign of King George the Second*, ed. [Henry Fox] Lord Holland, 2d ed. (London, 1846–1847), I, 35–37. It was Capt. Cook in 1770 who named Cape Egmont and Mount Egmont in the north island of New Zealand after the earl, though Egmont had long since left the admiralty.

as a kind of *aide mémoire* to his agents—carucates or plowlands (160 acres each), virgates or yardlands (40 acres), ferdells or ferlings (10 acres).[7]

Egmont's own calculations were romantic, and useless. His agents in Nova Scotia were more down-to-earth. While Egmont ruminated on feudal estates, his representatives on the scene considered the realistic problems of actually obtaining settlers for these wilderness properties. One agent advised Egmont to "chequer" the layout of the square-mile units so that they would join only at the corners, and hence ethnocentric "sets of people" could settle on the land without fear of continuous contact with each other. Another agent made plans to attract Germans, a third devised schemes for the Irish. The most knowledgeable of Egmont's agents, Charles Morris, Jr., son of Nova Scotia's official surveyor, argued that road construction was the key to success. "We may compare this province to a rough diamond of immense value but little lustre at present"; but if roads were built it would fill up with inhabitants, and, "like that well polished jewel, would yield as bright a lustre as any gem in the British crown."[8]

Similar hopes sparked the speculative interests of many substantial figures. Eleven prominent individuals claimed blocks of land just north of Egmont's property in Nova Scotia. Among them were two Scottish merchants, Robert and Sir Alexander Grant; two prominent Halifax merchants, John and William Henry Newton; Henry Ellis, scientist, *philosophe*, and colonial "expert," who had been governor of both Georgia and Nova Scotia; Montague Wilmot, then the governor of Nova Scotia; and Alexander Lord Colville, the naval commander in North America. It was only a matter of time before Lord Dartmouth, secretary of state for the colonies after August 1772—who had also, like Egmont, acquired land in East Florida as soon as that province had been thrown open for settlement—would invest in Nova Scotian land. His cousin, Francis Legge, whom Dartmouth had appointed governor of Nova Scotia in 1773, reminded him that "many of the nobility are soliciting for grants of land within this province," and he urged him to do so too as soon as possible. "Considering your numerous family, it may be of some advantage hereafter to some of your younger sons if they could obtain grants within this province." It was simple common sense. "Most of the great estates in America arise from purchases at first of wild lands which are continually rising in value as the adjoining lands become settled." He recommended that Dartmouth obtain 20,000-acre plots "for four or five of your sons" in the valuable territory close to Halifax and

---

[7]Egmont's heavily annotated map of this 22,000-acre plot, stretching back from Egmont Harbor to the Shubenacadie River, with his comments, sketches, and land distribution scheme (Oct. 22, 1769) written in the margins, is in Egmont Papers, Add. MSS 47054B. See pp. 368–369.

[8]Letters to Egmont concerning his Nova Scotia property from Joseph Gerrish, Gov. William Campbell, Joseph Woodmass, Michael Francklin, and Charles Morris, Jr., 1769–1770 (the most detailed is that of Morris, Feb. 6, 1770), in Egmont Papers, Add. MSS 47054A.

Manuscript map of Egmont's 20,000 acres in Nova Scotia, looking north (top) from the harbor entrance. The map precisely identifies topographical features, forestation, and settlement plans. Egmont's ideas on the future peopling of the area are outlined in his handwritten notes in the right margin.

Elm
Ash
Beech.
Plane Tree.
Maple
Birch
White Pine

or Ellis

N° 5

N° 5

...R Y

...m Habites in Cobequit or Truro
...out Watered

27 October 1767

The Red for a large Town in future, will be
set out on the Plan of that Capital sord. & laid —
Streets & Miles & Lanes to be left, paving the setting
of the first Ground of each House & do
and all & first to be built out of this family &c.

the East side & between before the same side
compleat, together if there were but one & do it in all comer
mon Places — the different proposes to be for ever
one moiety of 5th or 1 Acre — the Last Lot — one half to
be paid at do — 15 years — the Half at d.— 9 do
10 years from date of 5 Kings grant —

To pay one peppercorn or so as
for the large — only to pay a Kings Grant under for that
them to 13 d

For the Farms & Settlements without a head.

The Grand Divisions of the Lands
are to be in Squares 3 Miles on each side
containing 9 Square Miles in the whole 5760 acres

The Central Square to be settled by the Grantor
The 4 regular Squares to be granted away in Fee
to any 4 Gentlemen who will plant each 4 Families
of 5 to a Family on his Respective Square mile — for we
The 4 Gentlemen are to draw lots

by the 4 Square Miles may be granted to one
Set of 16 Families of 5 each — viz. 4 to each Square
mile who had best Engage at once together in order
to draw lots — & will give 160 acres to each Family
The 4 other Square Miles are to be reserved for
the Reception of new Inhabitants

One Square Mile contains 640 acres and is of
exact Size of one Fief as granted by William the Conqueror
in England to the Gentlemen who were his companions
with him — and was called a Knights Fee or who was always
esteemed a very honourable Fee or Knights Rank

The Subdivisions of a Knights Fee down as follows and
the Antient Names to such Allotments are intended, at such
as of Like proportions in these parts

viz. One Entire Fee —— 640 acres
One Carucate 160 acres —— 4 Carucates make one Fee.
One Virgate 40 acres —— 4 Virgates make one Carucate
One Ferdell or Farthing 10 acres, —— 4 Ferdells make one Virgate

There is no Exception in the Grant to any Person
who has resided two years in America —

Crossed this River on a Raft which we made of dry
dead Trees bound together with twisted with...

From this proposed Settlement at...
Pic out 7 miles to a Kings high Road
to Halifax —
But 10 miles to the Shubenacadie River
by Land & thence carried down 5 miles River from
that about 32 —
also Part to 11 miles over a Shubenacadie
to the Falls of Avon & at town to the Falls
Ships & Sloops & above 30 foot water can
come up — from the Head the navigation of both
Bay of Fundy — & their own

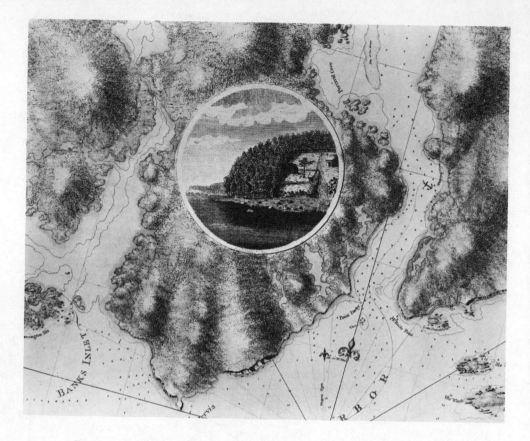

Egmont Harbor, near Halifax, Nova Scotia. Detail from J. F. W. DesBar-
res' Atlantic Neptune *(c. 1774). The inset shows the single primitive settle-*
ment to be found on Egmont's 20,000-acre claim when the drawing
was made, probably 1776.

adjacent to Egmont's property—land, he said, that he happened to know
was due to revert to the crown. "I shall take care," he wrote dutifully to
his powerful kinsman, "to have them located in such places as they must
of course in time become valuable."[9]

In the same years as these claims and settlement plans were being
formed for Nova Scotia, the adjacent island of St. John was thrown open
for development. The first proposals came from the irrepressible Lord
Egmont. In an intricate, anachronistic, and ultimately notorious memorial
to the King, he suggested that he be created "Lord Paramount" of the
island, which he proposed to divide into 50 hundreds or baronies of 40,000
acres each, which would be subdivided, first in 400 manors and then into
800 freeholds. An estate of just under 400,000 acres was to be reserved for
Egmont "and his nine children, his friends and dependents and others at
the pleasure of the said Earl." The barons and lords of manors would hold

---

[9]The plots adjoining Egmont's are outlined in Egmont's map, n. 7, above; Legge to Lord Dartmouth, Aug. 18, 1775, Dartmouth Papers, Canada, III, 2872–2874.

their property by military tenure, and would be obliged to supply Egmont with 1,200 vassals for defense. All of this was based on the assumption that St. John contained 2 million acres; on the chance that that estimation proved too high, Egmont included a contingency plan to augment the proposed St. John grant with a sizable piece of the newly conquered Caribbean island of Dominica.

In the event, in 1767, St. John's 1.4 million acres, divided into 67 large townships, were offered to a selected group of applicants in a carefully managed lottery. The result was that a broad range of merchants, officials, politicians, military officers, and private gentlemen with funds to invest— most of them well-connected Scots, almost none of them interested in anything but quick sale for profit—became the first owners of the island's land.[10]

All of these speculations depended in the end on people—on settlers willing to subdue the wilderness and render it profitable. But settlers were rare in all of these newly opened territories. The migrants, encouraged and partly subsidized by the speculators or the government, who came north to Nova Scotia from New England and, in smaller numbers, from other mainland colonies, were far too few. The Pennsylvania group that was granted the "Philadelphia Plantation," a wilderness spot near Pictou on the north coast of Nova Scotia, could induce only six families from Pennsylvania and northern Maryland to settle there in 1767, and most of those who went were not American-born colonists but recent arrivals from Scotland and Ireland on the second or third leg of their travels. A few others from Pennsylvania joined that small band in subsequent years, but many of these former Pennsylvanians suffered severely from lack of provisions; they returned home, it was said, "with great complaints against the severity and length of the winter." Benjamin Franklin, one of the investors in the

---

[10]Memorial of John, Earl of Egmont [Dec., 1763], CO 226, P.E.I., ser. "A," I, pp. 10, 35, 15, 41 ff., Public Archives of Canada, Ottawa; Andrew H. Clark, *Three Centuries and the Island . . . Prince Edward Island, Canada* (Toronto, 1959), pp. 42, 48, 50, app. B. Egmont's proposal, harking back to semifeudal proprietary arrangements that had become anachronistic a century earlier, resonated in Scotland as well as in England, partly for ideological reasons, partly for economic. Thus a London merchant (James Hammond?), writing (Oct. 12, 1765) to Lt. Col. James Robertson, barrack-master-general for North America, then in New York, about their plans to acquire and exploit a substantial land grant in East Florida, spoke of the great stir Egmont was making in London in renewing his proposal "with great eagerness" though it had been rejected by Hillsborough two years earlier because of its "feudal tenors for military service." "The late disturbances" over the Stamp Act, Hammond reported, are "made use of as a great argument for this mode of settlement, as if you have not a proper subordination it is quite impossible to expect you can have any form of government that can be depended on." Egmont was so sincere in his belief that this kind of feudal system could alone guarantee order that he said he did not care who actually got the grant of the island, "provided it is under that mode of settlement." Fordell Muniments, GD 172/2556/1. For a positive reaction in Scotland and the flat rejection of any such ideas by men of affairs in London, see below, pp. 436–437. Cf. Lewis Namier, *England in the Age of the American Revolution*, 2d ed. (London, 1961), pp. 271–272.

company, was disappointed not merely for financial reasons—he and his Philadelphia colleagues had had social goals too in developing land in Nova Scotia. There are, they wrote, "in the interior parts of all the old colonies thousands of poor people that w[oul]d be glad to meet with a little encouragement to transport themselves & family to a new colony." The investors had no doubt that the company's shareholders with their wide "acquaintance and interest" in the colonies, could easily procure "many hundred poor families to remove [to Nova Scotia] shortly, where they will not only be usefull to themselves but advantagious to Brittain . . . & thereby make for[tune] to themselves and help inrich others."[11]

By the end of the decade migration to Nova Scotia was increasing, but only very slowly. A number of developments, besides the region's increasing reputation for severe winters, prevented the hoped-for surge of population from taking place.[12] The peopling of Nova Scotia and St. John continued as before—a small, gradual accretion drawn principally from the older colonies. A census of 1767 covering all the settlements in the present maritime provinces, but principally Nova Scotia, listed a total population of only 13,374.[13]

The New Migration: North Britain

It was then, in 1772, at this low point in Nova Scotia's fortunes, that the first significant shiploads of voyagers direct from Britain arrived in the peninsula to take up promised parcels of land or otherwise to pursue their search for betterment in this suddenly revealed corner of "the best poor man's country." Their arrival marks a new stage in the population history of this northeastern coastal borderland.

Migration direct from Britain to Nova Scotia was not altogether new. In very small numbers migrants from England and Scotland had long contributed to the ethnic mixture developing on the peninsula. But in the early 1770s immigrants from Scotland and the north of England began appearing in far larger numbers than before. And their numbers increased

[11]Benjamin Franklin, John Foxcroft, and John Hughes to Alexander McNutt, Philadelphia, July 10, 1764, Hughes Papers, box 11, Historical Society of Pennsylvania, Philadelphia; [Samuel Wharton], "Reply to the Board of Trade's Report, 1772," *Works of Benjamin Franklin . . .* , ed. Jared Sparks (Boston, 1836–1840), IV, 355. For a general account of the settlers' suffering in Pictou, see Charles Baker to John Hughes, "Summersat," July 24, 1769, Hughes Papers, box 1.
[12]The Privy Council, responding to fears of Irish landlords, vetoed McNutt's plan for a large-scale migration from Ulster; the Fort Stanwix treaty diverted migration to newly opened land in the west; the military headquarters, a prime market, was transferred from Halifax to Boston; and hundreds of thousands of acres of recently granted but unsettled land reverted to the crown.
[13]"A General Return of the Several Townships . . . ," in Raymond, "Alexander McNutt," table facing p. 114.

steadily despite the growing belief in government circles that such emigration should be discouraged if not altogether stopped.

From newspaper notices, government reports, private papers, and above all from the Register of 1773–1776, the magnitudes involved can be estimated. In the four years between 1772 and the end of 1775, 20 vessels, carrying some 1,400 people from Britain to Nova Scotia and St. John, can be definitely identified, their voyages dated, and the numbers of their passengers established. Of these, 7 vessels, carrying no more than 60 passengers, were only incidentally involved: they were small commercial vessels, all but one from London and southern England. The 13 vessels that accounted for all the rest carried more than 100 emigrants each, and they all left from northern ports: in England, from Newcastle, Sunderland, Stockton, Scarborough, Hull, and Liverpool; in Scotland from Dumfries and Aberdeen. And just as these voyagers were heavily concentrated in geographical origins, so were their departures concentrated in time. Two-thirds of these northern emigrants left for Nova Scotia in the three-month period of March–May 1774.

None of this was accidental. The movement of farming people to Nova Scotia from the northern regions of the British Isles, which would continue and increase in later years, had been stimulated and organized by a number of hard-headed entrepreneurs, who had managed to mobilize, and had helped transfer to newly opened land on the peninsula, elements of the farming population of Yorkshire, Durham, and southern Scotland. Some of these organizers were prominent in public life and are easily identifiable; some were obscure and emerge only fleetingly from the records. They are a strangely assorted group, with only one thing in common: the desire to profit by transferring to what is now maritime Canada some small segment of the north British population.

Francklin and Yorkshire

Michael Francklin, a hustling, scrappy, widely disliked wheeler and dealer, was the most prominent. Born to modest circumstances in Poole, England, he had made a fortune, with the help of family contacts, in supplying troops and in privateering during the last colonial war, and then, in the decade preceding the Revolution, exploited to the full his position as lieutenant governor of Nova Scotia. In the early 1770s, connected by a network of trading deals to the province's main merchants, by marriage to leading commercial families in New England, and by kinship and intense application to influential politicians and merchants in England, Francklin had his hand in overseas trade, local merchandising, mining, political patronage, and above all land speculation. He had been acquiring land for years, and

by the late 1760s he was land-poor, hit hard by the discouragement and
departures of the New Englanders, and heavily in debt for, among other
things, quit rents to the crown. Ignoring for the moment most of his other
properties, he concentrated his efforts on "Francklin Manor," a choice tract
on both sides of the River Hébert near its mouth at Cumberland Basin,
seven miles from the nascent hamlet of Amherst. The "manor" consisted
of "above 1300 acres of rich marsh land . . . and many thousand acres of
excellent upland . . . [lying] very conveniently to the marsh." Ocean-going
vessels could sail directly to this tract, which contained—besides fertile,
well-diked marshland, mill streams, "an almost inexhaustible quarry of
free-stones," and great stands of timber—"an extensive bed of very good
coal . . . which may be worked with great ease and at trifling expense
. . . as the coals are thrown at once from the bank into the vessel."[14]

It was to attract settlers to this property, which once he had hoped to
populate with New Englanders, that Francklin, early in 1769, traveled to
England, where he remained for over three years. He concentrated his
efforts at recruitment in Yorkshire—not the semi-industrialized West Riding but the farmland in the dales and on the moors of the East and North
ridings, a large region stretching from the Humber River north to the
Durham border at the River Tees and from the Westmorland border in the
Pennines east to the North Sea coast. Here a virtual revolution in agricultural economics was in process, and a population of substantial farmers and
farmworkers had become susceptible to attractive offers from outside. How
well and from what sources Francklin knew of conditions in Yorkshire, we
do not know; but one source, in all probability, was Robert Monckton, a
soldier active in Nova Scotia during the Seven Years War and lieutenant
governor of the province from 1755 to 1761. Francklin had known Monckton
well in the late years of the war and through him, if from no other source,
he must have known what was happening on the Yorkshire estates of the
Duke of Rutland, who was Monckton's father-in-law. For Rutland was a
leader in the nationwide movement to modernize agricultural production
and increase profits by combining and enclosing the scattered parcels of
open-field tillage together with common land into consolidated farms under
single management, and to bring into these more efficient agricultural units
wastelands hitherto neglected. Modernization through enclosure had long

---

[14]On Michael Francklin: *Dictionary of Canadian Biography*, IV, 272–275. The key figure in Francklin's career was his kinsman Joshua Mauger, who made a fortune through naval supplies and other
businesses, including privateering, in Nova Scotia, and remained influential in that province after
his return to England (Namier and Brooke, *House of Commons*, III, 119–120). The description of
Francklin Manor is taken from the *Weekly Chronicle* (Halifax), July 2, 1813, where the property was
advertised for sale. For another description of Francklin's property, see John Robinson and
Thomas Rispin, *Journey through Nova-Scotia* . . . (York, 1774), reprinted in Public Archives of Nova
Scotia, *Report for the Year 1944* (Halifax, 1945), p. 36. (Further citations to the *Journey* will be to
this reprint rather than to the original volume.)

YORKSHIRE, 1770–1776
Villages of Emigrants in the
East and North Ridings

NORTHUMBERLAND

Newcastle
South
Shields

DURHAM

NORTH SEA

0   30 Miles
0   30 Kilometers

Tees Mouth

WESTMORLAND

Barnard
Castle

Stockton

Tees River

Yarm

Whitby

CLEVELAND HILLS

Robin Hood's Bay

Swale River

Northallerton

NORTH YORK
MOORS

Coverham

N O R T H   R I D I N G

COVERDALE

BILSDALE

HAMBLETON HILLS

Helmsley

Rye River

Scarborough

Ripon

Easingwold

Rillington

Sutton on
the Forest

Derwent River

Acklam

FLAMBOROUGH
HEAD

Ouse River

W E S T

Y O R K

E A S T

York

YORK WOLDS

R I D I N G

Escrick

R I D I N G

Leeds

Aire River

Selby

LANCASTER

Humber River

Hull

Huddersfield

Cross Land

Don River

Sheffield

CHESHIRE

YORK

LINCOLN

STAFFORD

DERBY

NOTTINGHAM

II.B

been in process; it rose swiftly in the years after 1765. Of 147 Yorkshire enclosures before 1776, 70% were awarded in the decade after 1765, the largest made in the East Riding. At the same time "improving" landlords were also undertaking extensive renovations of country properties.[15]

Beilby Thompson, M.P., typical of a generation of enterprising manor lords, contributed substantially if unwittingly to the peopling of Nova Scotia. He rebuilt the village of Escrick, just south of York, not only by enclosing open fields and commons but by diverting roads, turning strip fields into parkland, and tearing down old houses in the village and building new (in fewer numbers). And like all the "improving" landlords Thompson, who had an annual income of £8,000, raised rents, for in the end the purpose of modernization was greater profits. On the average, rents on newly enclosed properties doubled in the eighteenth century. Thompson raised his rents so high and so quickly that he drove substantial farmers, like his tenant John Bulmer, 45, his wife and three sons, off the land, drove them to the ship *Two Friends,* one of the registered vessels, riding anchor in the harbor of Hull, thence to Nova Scotia—to Amherst, one of the three new townships on the Chignecto Isthmus at the head of Cumberland Basin, ultimately to land owned by Michael Francklin. Similarly severe were the rent hikes of William Weddell, Esq., M.P., whose improvements in his splendid Newby Hall, near Ripon on the border of the West Riding, included a new wing, in which he housed his great statuary collection, "the best private collection of ancient sculpture in the kingdom." A veritable village of Weddell's former tenants jostled with those of Thompson aboard the *Two Friends* bound for Nova Scotia.[16]

[15] James D. Snowdon, "Footprints in the Marsh Mud: Politics and Land Settlement in the Township of Sackville, 1760–1800" (M.A. thesis, Univ. of New Brunswick, 1974), pp. 70–74; Brebner, *Neutral Yankees,* p. 119; J. D. Chambers and G. E. Mingay, *The Agricultural Revolution, 1750–1880* (London, 1966), p. 77 and chap. 4; K. J. Allison, *The East Riding of Yorkshire Landscape* (London, 1976), p. 150, chap. 6; W. E. Tate, *A Domesday of English Enclosure Acts and Awards,* ed. M. E. Turner (Reading, 1978), pp. 285–311.

[16] Namier and Brooke, *House of Commons,* III, 523–524; on the transformation of Escrick: Allison, *East Riding,* pp. 184–186, with map of Thompson's changes, [p. 185]. Bulmer's statement, one of many to the same effect, that he emigrated "on account of his rents being raised by Beilby Thompson Esq. his landlord" is in T 47/9/78; for his settlement in Amherst, see Esther C. Wright, *Planters and Pioneers: Nova Scotia, 1749 to 1775* (Hantsport, N.S., 1978), p. 61. On the opening of the Chignecto townships, Brebner, *Neutral Yankees,* pp. 60–61. On Weddell and Newby Hall, with interiors designed by Robert Adam and landscaping by Capability Brown, now restored to its late 18th-century elegance, see John Cornforth, "Newby Hall, North Yorkshire," *Country Life,* June 7, 14, and 21, 1979, Dec. 25, 1980. There are also modern books on the estate and buildings by W. Harrison and Ernest I. Musgrave, and a near contemporary description of the interior of the main building, with a listing and appraisal of all the decorations and art objects, room by room, ending with a rhapsodic account of the statue gallery, "the admiration of all connoisseurs," in John Bigland, *Yorkshire . . .* (London, 1815), pp. 711–714. The Newby Hall Papers in the Leeds Archives are voluminous but lack details on rent hikes and the displacement of tenants in the early 1770s. The quotation is taken from a sketch of the buildings and the descent of the property in Thomas Langdale, *A Topographical Dictionary of Yorkshire . . .* [1809], 2d ed. (Northallerton, Eng., 1822), p.

Rent increases imposed by Yorkshire landlords like Weddell, Thompson, the Duke of Rutland, Lord Cavendish, Lord Bruce, and half a dozen others identified in the Register by their former tenants as they boarded ship for Nova Scotia were typical of the time. They took place at a time when the rural population was increasing faster than agricultural growth, and along with this population rise came an upswing in the cost of basic commodities. As a result the least secure of farmworkers, the poorest and least adaptable—their lives disrupted or threatened with disruption by agricultural improvements and hit hard by increased rents and rising costs— came under great pressure. The old and infirm, one pamphleteer wrote, fell first, to become burdens to parochial charity "till death's merciful hand . . . by degrees easeth the parish of its burthen, which in a few years is generally accomplished, as the young and healthy have dispersed themselves, those that could pay their passage having transported themselves to America." But it was not only the old and infirm: "small farmers who have been thus deprived of their livelihood have sold their stock in trade and have raised from fifty to five hundred pounds, with which they have procured themselves, their families, and [their] money a passage to America."[17]

Five hundred pounds, or even fifty, was an enormous sum for working people, and indeed not all of the "small farmers" who left the land in

<hr>

364. I have relied heavily on this invaluable guide to Yorkshire's towns and villages as they were in the late 18th century. In the pages that follow, all topographical details not otherwise noted are taken from this book.

[17]Chambers and Mingay, *Agricultural Revolution*, pp. 88–104; *Cursory Remarks on Inclosures . . . by a Country Farmer* (London, 1786), pp. 5, 6.

Lord Dartmouth, during the years when he was speculating in wild land in Nova Scotia and East Florida, was systematically raising rents on his estates in west Yorkshire. Among his estate papers preserved in Leeds are moving letters from his tenants and subtenants appealing to him over the head of his resident agent, Edward Elmsall. One letter, from a subtenant named Thomas Hopkins, who apologizes for his "plane way of expression . . . as I have not been used to address noblemen," informs Dartmouth that he as subtenant pays the principal tenant "double the rent Your L[ordshi]p receives," and that he understands that when his lease is up he will be faced with a rent rise or eviction, "which I think is a very hard case." Hopkins had worked the land for 19 years and the tenant had never lived on the property, let alone worked it, though he collected as much rent as Dartmouth did. Hopkins begs to be taken on as a direct tenant, and promises to pay a reasonable rent "under a lld [landlord] that haith sum bowels of mercy, and might spend the remainder of my days in quietness on that account." But an endorsement on the letter states that the property had already been requested by someone else. Another tenant, William Lister, writing his "dear, dear landlord" on June 14, 1774, declared that he would "rather go to my bear and bended knees" than do anything to offend. But if Dartmouth could see the tears running down his cheeks his heart would melt. Elmsall is heartless, raising rents and ejecting tenants he did not like until people like the Listers' neighbor Robert Dixon are "gone to America." In fact, however, Elmsall's letters to Dartmouth make clear that the agent was advising *against* further rent rises and that Dartmouth was insisting that the present rents did not reflect the true value of the land. A meticulous series of rent rolls of Dartmouth's properties in the manors of Slaithwaite and Lingards, near Huddersfield in the West Riding, shows rises over the years 1774–1778 of a shilling or more in almost every case; in a few instances the rents almost doubled. And a marginal note, probably by Elmsall, sketches plans to rent out certain new enclosures of bad land as soon as tenants could be found who would pay "a sufficient rent." Leeds Archives, DT 305/5.

Yorkshire were poor or threatened with poverty. Some were tenants-in-chief of large properties rented by their families for generations and worked with teams of servants. Many of the more substantial tenants could in fact pay the new rents—some later invested hundreds of pounds in North American land—but to do so would mean a lowering of living standards and of family prospects or an injury to their self-respect. For farmers such as these, an alternative was possible. If opportunity presented, they could move off the land with their entire households including servants, and reestablish themselves in more promising circumstances elsewhere. It was precisely this opportunity that Francklin and the other speculators in American land held out to them.

Francklin was favored too by another circumstance. By the 1760s Methodism—that populist religion of the heart, officially conformist but in fact socially disruptive and devoted to endowing the lives of ordinary working people with dignity in the eyes of the Lord if not of the landlords—had burned deep into the communities of the Yorkshire countryside. An estimated fifth, perhaps a fourth, of the entire Methodist fellowship lived in Yorkshire—some 8,000 to 9,000 communicants, increasing almost 5% a year—and not only in the manufacturing districts of the West Riding. There were "inner light" preachings, "passionate eucharistic love feasts," and networks of communicants in the Yorkshire dales and on the moors as well as in the towns. The starkly beautiful countryside of the North and East ridings, under pressure from economic reorganization, was a "burnt-over district." Flames of evangelical enthusiasm swept across the villages, singed isolated farm hamlets, and shot up in great explosions in the larger towns when John Wesley and other itinerants preached their hopeful doctrine of universal redemption to parched and anxious congregations. The distressed—tradesmen, craftsmen, farmers, and the laboring poor, seeking security, spiritual and psychological as well as economic—found relief in this religion of evangelical renewal. And the abuse they received for their deviance from the world at large—the condemnation, physical intimidation, and contempt they endured—confirmed them in their sense of isolation and made them even more susceptible than they otherwise would have been to blandishments from abroad.[18]

It was to this distressed population of Yorkshire country folk, faced with an uncertain economic future, many in a high state of religious agitation and eager to withdraw into a separate community of like-minded

[18]Robert F. Wearmouth, *Methodism and the Common People of the Eighteenth Century* (London, 1945), pp. 165–238, figures on p. 182; Roy Porter, *English Society in the Eighteenth Century*, Penguin ed. (Harmondsworth, Eng., 1982), p. 194; W. A. Speck, *Stability and Strife, England 1714–1760* (London, 1977), pp. 114–115. Details on the number of Methodists in each locality of Yorkshire, annually in the 1770s, are in Wesleyan Methodist Church Conference, *Minutes of the Methodist Conferences, from . . . 1774*, I (London, 1813), 99.

worshipers, that Francklin directed his recruiting campaign. He appointed agents in seven towns in the North and East ridings and put at least one in charge of shipping, in Liverpool. In newspaper ads he praised the climate of Nova Scotia and the absence of game laws, taxes, tithes, and political disturbances, and he offered generous terms to those who would inhabit his land. A settler would discover that he could get "as much land as he pleases" and would be charged only a trivial annual quit rent for the first ten years, for the next five years only sixpence an acre, thereafter one shilling an acre. Further, Francklin offered loans to settlers sufficient to enable them to buy two cows, two calves, one sow pig, and enough seed corn for two years. But he was selective—or hoped to be selective—in his clientele. He would take, he announced in the *York Courant,* only Protestants (though in that he was merely conforming to the law), only husbandmen or artificers, and only "such as are possessed of at least £50 in money."[19]

His efforts succeeded. When on March 16, 1772, the *Duke of York* left Liverpool for Nova Scotia it carried among its 62 passengers a sizable contingent committed to taking up land on Francklin's Manor.[20] They came from a scattering of villages in a central strip of the North Riding— villages set in deep, fertile dales that run like dry river beds between the plateaus and moors: a countryside that looks like the work of some cosmic giant that had torn at the land with its fingertips, leaving behind parallel gorges and valleys separated by steep hills and highland plains tufted with grassy turf and scraggly bushes.

There was Thomas Coates, from Sutton-under-Whitestonecliff, a farming hamlet of ten dwellings separated from the market town of Thirsk by a 3½-mile footpath that led across the desolate Bagby Moor. He would settle, eventually, at Nappan, a short distance from Francklin's Manor, where he would marry another Yorkshire native and establish a family important in the affairs of Nova Scotia. Aboard too was James Metcalf, sixty-six, and his son James, Jr., twenty-seven, farmers and Methodists. The father had come from his native farm, "Eppy Head," near Hawnby, five miles northeast of Coates's house, the son from his place of employment, Thomas Wilkinson's farm at Marton Lordship, twelve miles south of "Eppy Head," in some of the richest farmland of the North Riding.[21]

Of James Metcalf, Jr.'s initial experiences in Nova Scotia something is known by virtue of an enthusiastic letter he wrote his fiancée four months after his arrival. The fiancée, Ann Gill, a farmer's daughter from the hamlet

---

[19]Snowdon, "Footprints," p. 74. The terms of Francklin's recruitment are set out in great detail in the *York Courant,* May 19, 1772.
[20]Details of the voyage are in Charles Dixon's Memoir, written for his children, Sept. 21, 1773, in Dixon Papers.
[21]Coates genealogy; BMD Records; Thornton H. Lodge, comp., "The Metcalfe Family," genealogy in Webster Collection, 7001/347. "Eppy Head" is still a name known in Hawnby; at the post office in that village it is identified as a plot of land in the near vicinity.

William Weddell's Newby Hall, North Yorkshire, showing front entrance façade, library, and statue gallery. The gallery, designed by Robert Adam in 1767, was scaled to accommodate the art assembled by Weddell with perfect spatial harmony. Seven years after the gallery was built, when still further refinements were being completed at Newby Hall, fifteen Yorkshire emigrants boarded the Two Friends *in Hull "in hopes of a better livelihood, & on account of their rents being rais'd by Wm. Weddell, Esqʳ, their landlord."*

of Huby, 2½ miles from Marton Lordship, was still employed, as James had been, at Wilkinson's place. The prospects in Nova Scotia, James wrote her, were excellent. He had already bought 207 acres of land and shared with two others in the purchase of 45 acres more. He foresaw no problems in producing "wheat and other grane" in a few years, and there were already orchards in bloom. The people he had met were "naturally kind one to another, even the Indians," and though they were chiefly Presbyterians and Baptists, he was confident that if a single one of "our Methodist preachers" appeared in Nova Scotia, people of all persuasions would welcome him. Eventually, he believed, "religeon in its purity will be preached here." Indeed, aside from the ravages of "a little flye caled a misketo that . . . bites like a midge," he had nothing bad to say about the country. And so he reminded her of her promise to come and join him. "My dear, I shall be very glad to see you fulfill your promise to mee, and I will fulfill mine to you if you come. I will be a kind husband to you, and will take you before aney other, for I must marry, for I cannot live well as I am." Do not fear the ocean passage, he wrote: "you will have plenty [of people] from York-shire to acompaney you. O would I wear in the place of these lines and that I might be your companion." But he was confident that she would keep her promise, and went into details. Be so good, he wrote, as to bring a bushel of four different kinds of wheat seed (he specified which) and be careful to keep the bag dry: "lay it like a pillow in your bed." He advised her also to take along with her a little tea or something else nourishing in case she got seasick, and he warned her not to listen to adverse comments about Nova Scotia. "Ye country," he insisted, "is good." Even the "trobel-some misketos" could be kept out of the houses by smoke pots, and they would in any case disappear when the wild wet meadow grass was cut down and settlement spread. She should leave from Liverpool, as he had done, and if she did not have all of the passage money when she arrived at the dock she should ask her friends for help; James promised to repay them. Or she could borrow from Francklin's Liverpool agent, James Shanks. Her vessel would undoubtedly arrive at Fort Cumberland, at the far end of the deepest subinlet of the Bay of Fundy, not far from James's farm; if she sent word ahead he would meet her there. "May ye Lord bles you," he ended, "and conduct you safe hither."[22]

Ann was as good as her word. The farmer's daughter from Huby in the parish of Sutton-on-the-Forest, close to Marton Lordship and just south of the North Riding dales from which, day after day, farming families were leaving for America, joined Metcalf the next year. She was married to him in the crude church within the stockade of Fort Cumberland, bore a brood

---

[22]Metcalfe to Ann Gill "with Mr Thomas Wilkinson at Martin Lordship near Easingwould in Yorkshire, England," Aug. 1772, Webster Collection, 7001/336.

YORKSHIRE, 1760–1776
The Main Region of Emigration

NORTH SEA

DURHAM

AREA OF MAP
YORK

Stockton

Tees River

Yarm

Kirk Leavington

Crathorne   Rudby   Leven River

Hutton Rudby

CLEVELAND HILLS

Northallerton

Arden   BILSDALE   Helm
Hall   House
New Hall

HAMBLETON

SWAINSWORTH

Hawnby

HILLS

Hodge Beck

Dove River

NORTH YORK MOORS

Thirlby   Rievaulx
Cod Beck   Helmsley

Thirsk   Duncombe Park

Sowerby   Sutton under
Whitestonecliffe

NORTH   RIDING

Nunnington   Ness
Stonegrave

Swale River   Hovingham

Skakleton   Amotherby   Swinton   Rillington

Rye River

OF   Easingwold   Marton Lordship   Malton

Castle Howard

ipon

Ouse River

Huby

Newby   Sutton on the Forest
Hall

Acklam

Derwent River

WEST   Haxby

RIDING   Skelton   Earswick   EAST

Huntington   RIDING

YORK

0   6 Miles

0   6 Kilometers

York

II.C

of children, worked alongside him on their wilderness farm until his death fourteen years later, died on the farm herself, and was buried there, next to James, on the banks of the Maccan River.

Of others on the *Duke of York*—with one important exception—much less is known. We know that Thomas Bowser, twenty-eight, traveled with his wife and two sisters; that immediately upon his arrival he leased a 500-acre farm, 45 acres of which were well-diked marshland, 20 acres of cleared upland, for which he paid with 22 days of service a year; that he prospered; and that he fathered twelve children, who scattered throughout the land. Some of them intermarried, inevitably, with the children of another voyager of 1772, George Bulmer, a thirteen-year-old apprentice mason when he boarded the *Duke of York*. He eventually bought 1,000 acres, got a grant for 300 acres more, and produced thirteen children, all but one of whom established families of their own. Both Bowser and Bulmer paved the way for others of their families, tenants of either Beilby Thompson or William Weddell, who came over later, on the registered ships of 1774. And George Bulmer, twelve years after his arrival, made a notable marriage. The seventeen-year-old girl he married in 1784 had also crossed on the *Duke of York*. She had been one of several small children in the family of Charles Dixon.[23]

Dixon, of all the Nova Scotian immigrants of 1772, is the best known. Not only was he the leading figure, socially and economically, among the emigrants on the *Duke of York*, and not only did he prove to be a magisterial figure in Nova Scotia, but he also left behind the most detailed account of the process of departure that has survived in the records of these migrants. In 1773, a little over a year after he arrived in Nova Scotia, he wrote a memoir for the instruction of his seven-year-old son Charles and Charles's four little sisters (one of them Bulmer's future wife), that they might "remember the rock from whence ye was hewn" and recall, when "I & thy mother shall be called home and laid in the silent grave," that it was "for your sakes we crosd the ocean, so that you [would] out strip us in purity of heart and holiness of life." In the torn pages of Dixon's memoir, with its crude spellings and jumbled syntax, one finds a picture, however blurred, of the state of mind, the motivations and experiences, of some, at least, of the men and women of Yorkshire who first responded to Francklin's appeal.

Born in the hamlet of Kirk Leavington, in the northern extremity of Yorkshire, Dixon had spent his life, before his departure at the age of forty-one, in the villages of that district of the North Riding. He had

---

[23] W. C. Milner, *History of Sackville, New Brunswick* (Sackville, N.B., 1934), pp. 129–132, 150, 153; Robinson and Rispin, *Journey*, p. 39; Graeme Wynn, "Late Eighteenth-Century Agriculture on the Bay of Fundy Marshlands," *Acadiensis*, 8 (1979), 87.

followed his father's craft of bricklaying until, at the age of twenty-nine, he had turned to paper manufacturing in the nearby hamlet of Hutton Rudby. He had prospered in business, and had prospered too, or so he had then thought, in spiritual things. A member of the Church of England, sober, righteous, and godly, he had been confident that he would "obtaine heaven at last." But then his complacency had been shattered. On a visit to Robin Hood's Bay near Whitby on the North Sea coast, he heard a Methodist sermon. Such preaching he had never before experienced. Instantly he realized that he was "condemned by the laws of God, for it says whoever offends one point is guilty of all." His "pretence" of being a member of God's church "fell to the ground." He had, he realized, "broke my batismall covenant" and was no better than a "babtised heathen." And so he cried out, "in ye bitterness of my soul, What must I do to be saved?" For a full year he lived in despair, mourning the condition of his soul "under a sence of guilt" and praying to God that he might "rejoice with his chosen." And then one day—September 21, 1759, he noted—"seeking and striving upon my knees," he found deliverance. The Lord forgave his iniquities "and set my soul at liberty."

And he remained in that blessed state, a fervent member of the Methodist Society in Hutton Rudby. But if his inner life was secure, the outer world seemed to be crumbling. He saw all about him "the troubles that was befalling my native country—opresshion of every kind abounded, and twas very difficult to earn bread." He struggled to maintain his position in the world. Then one day Michael Francklin's proposals for resettlement in Nova Scotia came his way. An acquaintance of Dixon's, probably someone in Thirsk, was Francklin's agent for the district, and he discussed the possibilities in Nova Scotia with Dixon. But Dixon was deeply committed in Yorkshire; he could not just abandon everything he had worked for and run. He did, however, see the promise of Nova Scotia as a refuge, and "frequently recommended" Francklin's advertisements to others. Then once again there was a sudden intervention from without. Two months before the *Duke of York* was due to leave Liverpool, "a gentleman"—apparently a complete stranger, but no doubt someone informed by Francklin's agent—called at Dixon's house and proposed to buy him out: his business, his stock, and his other property. This changed everything for Dixon. He immediately began consultations with his wife and friends, and in the end decided to accept the proposal, leave Yorkshire, and live out his life in Nova Scotia.

Time was short. He and his family were barely able to pack and get to Liverpool before the *Duke of York* sailed. The passage, he recorded, was "rouf," but not half so rough as the information they received when they arrived in Halifax, six weeks and four days later, concerning their ultimate destination. The account they were given "was enough to make [the] stoutest heart give place." But he comforted his wife, who was in despair, "for I was sure we sh'd meet with good success at our jorney's end." Three weeks later, disembarked at Cumberland, a few miles from Francklin's land, they discovered that conditions were even worse than they were reported to be. Everyone they met wanted to sell out and return home. The Dixons put up temporarily in "the barracks" while Dixon himself studied the situation carefully. There was nothing wrong with the land, he decided; the cause of the universal discouragement was "indolence and want of knowledge." And so, confident of his own industry and capacity, he bought 2,500 acres in the township of nearby Sackville, for which he paid £260, and animals and equipment which may have cost him another £210, and settled down to carve out his fortune in the new land. He settled, too, into an enthusiastic if badly splintered religious community. There were parties and schisms everywhere, and everyone seemed to be "ready to say to each other, Stand off, I am holier than thou," which robbed the whole community, Dixon wrote, of "that universality so conspicuous in a Christian spiritt & so agreeable to God's attributes, who wo'd that none sho'd perish but that all men sho'd be saved." Despite this contention and despite all the discouragements that had gone before, Dixon gave thanks to a generous Providence that had preserved him and his family "and given us a lott in a strange land, and an earthly inherittance that we neavour expected or deserv'd."[24]

Dixon's "lott," even in 1773 when he wrote the memoir, was no mere scrap tossed to him by an indulgent deity. An investigating party in 1774 reported that of his 2,500 acres, 100 were well-diked, fertile marshland and another 100 were cleared upland; that he also had "a good house and barn, twelve cows, four oxen, and other cattle"; and that by renting half the farm he was already producing an income of £30 8s a year. Furthermore, he had been appointed a justice of the peace. Truly, as the investigators said, "he seems to have fallen in very well." And this was only the beginning. As the years passed, Dixon's affairs flourished. He bought more land: parcels shrewdly chosen in various locations. As a leading figure in and around Sackville he served as agent for others who had been "men of property at home," was called upon repeatedly to authenticate land deeds and the testimonies concerning boundaries, and served in Nova Scotia's first House of Assembly. Charles Dixon, the bricklayer's son from the north Yorkshire village of Kirk Leavington, died in 1817—in his 87th year, 45 years after his arrival in Nova Scotia—a respected magistrate, a patriarch, a founding

[24]Dixon, Memoir, cited above n. 20; Robinson and Rispin, *Journey*, p. 39. The transcription of the memoir in James D. Dixon, *History of Charles Dixon . . .* (Sackville, N.B., 1891) is full of errors, but the book contains useful genealogical material.

father, the lives of whose progeny (94 in all, he recorded in 1810) were woven into the fabric of North American society.[25]

DesBarres

In Charles Dixon's transformation from a devout Yorkshire papermaker to a land-rich Nova Scotia patriarch, the hustling Michael Francklin had been the critically effective agent. But he was only one of several entrepreneurs at work recruiting a population for the vacant lands of Nova Scotia, and his success was limited by the competition. His main rival was a remarkable figure, J. F. W. DesBarres, who, though no less a land speculator than Francklin and no less a colonial politician, was the principal draftsman and artist of the great hydrographic survey of the eastern coasts of North America, *The Atlantic Neptune* (1777–1784). This immense collaborative work of great technical accuracy and artistry consists of four huge volumes of charts, maps, views, and miscellaneous documentation—178 plates in all, many of them separately printed in various editions—at least 40% of which pertain to the coasts and harbors of Nova Scotia. DesBarres himself did most of the technical work on the Nova Scotia charts and adorned them with aquatint sketches of the coastal waters and shoreline settlements, sketches that are now as valuable as the technical charts themselves.

The routes and passages of DesBarres's career are curious. A settler in Lunenburg, Nova Scotia, he was a Huguenot whose family had come from Montbéliard, the remarkably prolific Protestant enclave in southeastern France. He had been well educated in Switzerland and the British Royal Military Academy, and while serving in America as an engineer in the British army during the Seven Years War had become involved in the government's hydrographic project. That work had occupied him throughout the decade preceding the Revolution—but not exclusively. In the same years he started his career as a speculator in Nova Scotia land. How much land in all DesBarres acquired before 1776 is not known, but it is certain that he had clear title to at least 78,000 acres. The chief properties were a 20,000-acre plot at Tatamagouche on the north shore (the residue of a much larger grant he had once sought in partnership with Michael Francklin) and two 8,000-acre plots close to Francklin Manor, one of them actually adjoining Francklin's land, the other a few miles off, in the expertly diked marsh-

[25] Robinson and Rispin, *Journey,* p. 39; Westmorland County 1788, #7, Westmorland County CB, New Brunswick Museum, St. John, N.B.; J. E. Humphreys, "Some Account of the Settlement of Salisbury Parish by English Speaking Settlers," Ganong Collection, box 20, pkt. 3, pp. 3–4; J. E. Humphreys, "Some Account of the First Settlers on the Pollet River, in Salisbury Parish," *ibid.,* pp. 86–87; Milner, *Sackville,* pp. 150–160.

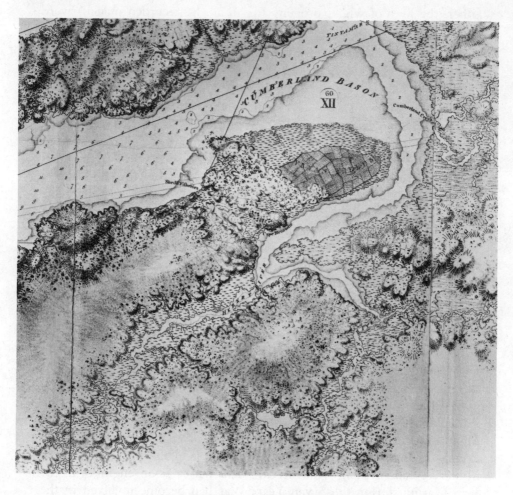

The Cumberland Basin area at the Isthmus of Chignecto, Nova Scotia, showing the Elysian Fields and the tidal marshes along the Hébert, Maccan, and Nappan rivers being reclaimed for farmland by Yorkshire families in the 1770s. Detail from J. F. W. DesBarres' Atlantic Neptune (c. 1774). The lacework precision is typical of DesBarres' depiction of settlement areas that interested him.

Shipwreck in the approaches to Nova Scotia. Aquatint drawing in J. F. W. DesBarres' Atlantic Neptune *(c. 1774).*

Beach scene and view of the sand hills, Isle of Sable, off the Nova Scotia coast. Aquatint drawing in J. F. W. DesBarres' Atlantic Neptune *(c. 1774).*

lands of Minudie, a tract so fertile that DesBarres called it the Elysian Fields. Both tracts, along with Francklin's adjacent lands, he sketched in an exquisitely detailed segment of one of the *Neptune* charts.[26]

DesBarres lacked Francklin's ability to reach directly into the disturbed and restless population of Yorkshire, but he was able to capitalize on other advantages. His ethnic association with the Montbéliardians in Lunenburg made it relatively easy for him to entice a number of them to his Tatamagouche lands, which he did in 1771, and his agents were shrewd enough to see that they could compete effectively with Francklin in the Cumberland Basin area by reducing rents sharply and furnishing livestock and seed to the settlers in exchange for a portion of the product. By such means DesBarres managed to recruit fifteen of the Yorkshire families that arrived in the spring of 1772, a group that proved to be the forerunner of many others, in the exodus of 1773–1775, who would eventually settle on his lands.[27]

Witherspoon, Pictou, and the Voyage of the *Hector*

But however cleverly DesBarres managed things, he remained at a disadvantage in not being able to reach directly into the British sources of migration. For the closer one came to the potential migrants and the more intimately involved one was with their affairs, the more effective one's recruitment was likely to be. So in these same years John Witherspoon, for many years a Presbyterian preacher and controversialist in the depressed town of Paisley in the Scottish Lowlands, recently appointed president of the college at Princeton, New Jersey, capitalized on his lifelong associations in Scotland to help populate some of the north shore lands once claimed by the Philadelphia Company. Witherspoon had been involved in land

[26]John C. Webster, *The Life of . . . DesBarres* (Shediac, N.B., 1933), pp. 23–24; G. N. D. Evans, *Uncommon Obdurate . . . J. F. W. DesBarres* (Salem, Mass., 1969), pp. 21–22, 27–28, chap. 1.
[27]Bell, *"Foreign Protestants,"* pp. 550–552 n.21a; Evans, *DesBarres,* p. 31; Report of Capt. John Macdonald to DesBarres on his Estate on the Rivers Maccan and Nappan, 1795, DesBarres Papers, series 2. This section of Macdonald's elaborate report on all of DesBarres's properties as of 1795 (Evans, *DesBarres,* p. 102) contains a shrewd analysis that uncovers the essence of the structural problems of land speculation in a wilderness world. The rental rates for these lands, Macdonald told DesBarres, had originally been set unrealistically high, though the rates were the same as those Francklin had asked. DesBarres's agents, Macdonald discovered, had "found it necessary to abate the demand in order to prevent the people from falling into Francklin's hands," indeed to obtain any settlers at all. The reduced rents he was receiving, Macdonald said, "however trifling and short of your original demand, is still something, and infinitely preferable to losing the lands by the total want of settlers, particularly," he added, in a conclusion that touched the central springs of speculative profits, "as there are 1,500 acres in reserve for being left [let] upon better terms at some future period, when the province is better peopled and new lands in greater demand. . . . the interior parts will be eligible enough in twenty or thirty more years, as the soil and wood are good."

transactions—for profit, or for the relief of his Lowlands countrymen, or both—almost from the day of his arrival in America in 1768. In 1770 he and a family of prosperous Glasgow merchants and shipowners with the unpropitious name of Pagan had managed the transportation of 200 Scots to Boston; the group had already invested in wild land far up on the Connecticut River. And then in 1772—as the *Duke of York* was transporting Francklin's recruits to Fort Cumberland and as DesBarres was bargaining with settlers on the terms for renting plots in his two 8,000-acre tracts—Witherspoon and the Pagans became active in the affairs of the moribund Philadelphia Company, and the famous preacher began his most elaborate, and controversial, effort at land settlement.

There is nothing mysterious in Witherspoon's involvement with the lands at Pictou, on the north shore of Nova Scotia, left undeveloped by the failure of the Philadelphia Company. Some of the merchants who had been instrumental in bringing him from Scotland to head the New Jersey college had also been shareholders in the company. Faced with loss of title to their entire grant for noncompliance with the settlement requirements, they turned for help to the energetic Witherspoon, with his many ties to an especially mobile segment of the Scottish population, and to the Pagans, whose business operations already touched New York, Boston, Maine, Halifax, Quebec, and the West Indies. Together Witherspoon and the Pagans took over approximately 40,000 acres of the company's north shore land for £225, provided by John Pagan, and they set to work immediately. They appointed recruiting agents in five strategic locations in Scotland: Inveraray in Argyll, 30 miles west of Greenock; Portree on the Isle of Skye; and the three main towns along the string of narrow lochs that slice diagonally through the Highlands from sea to sea: Fort William, Fort Augustus, and Inverness. Most of the business was conducted in Glasgow, however, and it was from there, in September 1772, that the associates issued their advertisements to "all farmers and others, in Scotland, who are inclined to settle upon easy terms in the province of Nova Scotia in North America."[28]

In these notices, which appeared in the Edinburgh and Glasgow newspapers and which were reprinted in the *Scots Magazine*, Witherspoon and the Pagans praised the fertility of the land they were offering on the north shore of Nova Scotia, the richness of the nearby fishing grounds, and the wealth of timber available—all of which, they said, were peculiarly suitable for a Scots settlement. They also set out a schedule of special enticements. All families that agreed to settle would receive outright, in fee simple, 150 acres, and in addition would have available to rent 50 acres more for each family member. The rent for these additional acres would be 6 pence per

[28]Varnum L. Collins, *President Witherspoon, a Biography* (Princeton, 1925), I, 149; Sawtelle, "Acadia," p. 282; Donald MacKay, *Scotland Farewell: The People of the Hector* (Toronto, 1980), pp. 78–79, 214–215, 76; "Lands to Be Settled in North America," *Edinburgh Advertiser*, Sept. 18, 1772.

acre for the first 20 families that committed themselves; 1 shilling per acre for the second 20 families; and 1 shilling 6 pence for the third 20. No rents, however, would be collected for two years. Further, they promised to provide excellent transportation conditions, at the "easy rate" of £3 5s per adult (with half fares for children two to eight and no charge for children under two). They specified, further, exactly how much food they would provide for each passenger, and they promised to stock enough supplies to last for twelve weeks, though most trips to Nova Scotia took only four weeks. And they added that the land was by no means uninhabited. Twenty families were already settled at Pictou, they said; a school had been started, and there was a good prospect for the establishment of a Presbyterian minister. In all of these arrangements, the notices stated, especially in the distribution of land, "Dr. Witherspoon will take particular care that the strictest justice be done."[29]

It may have been the prominence of Witherspoon's name in these announcements that touched off a flurry of attacks on the project—for Witherspoon had been involved in public controversies before, and had enemies—or it may simply have been the nervous concern of certain land-lords that their own land would be affected. Whatever the immediate trigger, the barrage of attacks was heavy, and it led Witherspoon to justify at length, to himself if not to the world at large, the whole enterprise of emigration to North America. In an essay written in New Jersey for publication in the *Scots Magazine*, Witherspoon replied to the attacks. To the charge that by encouraging emigration he had become "an enemy to his country," he replied that his involvement was strictly the result of a desire to see to it that those among his countrymen who emigrated would receive fair treatment. He cited instances of credulous Britons, ignorant of actual conditions in America "where land is so cheap and labor so dear," being bilked by the "ensnaring proposals" of shrewd speculators. Emigrants should not have to *buy* land at all, or if they did they should pay only trivial prices. For the real reward for honest land dealers lay not in the initial sale price of wild land but in the eventual rise in its value created by the cultivation of a few tracts by pioneers. Hence the propriety of his and the Pagans' terms.

Beyond this personal justification, he argued that the numbers involved in all of these population movements were small. But even if emigration *did* in part depopulate Britain, why should poor or oppressed people *not* go to a situation "where they may have a happy and plentiful provision, and their posterity be multiplied as the sand of the sea"? The migrants them-selves were obviously better off for their move, but so too were the people they left behind, since the exodus could only relieve the pressure on the rest

[29] *Scots Magazine*, 34 (Sept. 1772), 482–483.

of the population. Perhaps the immediate interest of a handful of landlords might suffer. But surely, Witherspoon wrote, it is never right for the happiness of one class of men to depend on the misery of another. If the landlords freed themselves from "narrow, selfish views" they would realize that masses will never leave unless driven out by the most extreme oppression; and that in any case Britain, and especially Scotland, derived immense wealth from America's growth. They would realize too that attacks on generous schemes such as his and the Pagans' only focused attention on the issues and therefore proved to be self-defeating. The more anxious landlords were to restrain their people, the more eager the people would be to leave. Emigrants, he concluded, are motivated only by "the hope of bettering their circumstances. It is both unjust and impossible to hinder them if they be so minded, and . . . I am persuaded it will not be the least injury to those of any rank whom they leave behind."[30]

In fact the associates found recruitment rather more difficult than they had expected, and they ended by subcontracting to John Ross, their chief agent in the 1770 expedition to Boston, the entire enterprise of enlisting 250 Scots and settling them on the land at Pictou. Ross, a Highlander from Lochbroom in the far northwest, contracted to gather the emigrants, supervise their settlement at Pictou over a period of a year, and pay the quit rent due on the grant; in return he would receive half of the associates' 40,000 acres. When, late in June or early July 1773, the Pagans' old transport, the *Hector,* a brig of 200 tons acquired years before from the Dutch, left Greenock, the season was far advanced, and most of the passengers were not yet aboard. Only 10 people boarded at Greenock. The rest were Ross's Highlanders awaiting the *Hector* 300 miles to the north, beyond the hundreds of jagged inlets, scattered isles, and oceanside mountains that adjoin the shipping lanes of western Scotland.[31]

During the first week of July the *Hector,* anchored within the entrance to Loch Broom, near the present ferry landing at Ullapool, took on its Highland passengers. The scene, which would prove to be a vivid moment in the collective memory of Scottish Canada, was, in its poignancy and in the ordeals that would follow, reminiscent of the departure of the *Mayflower* from Leyden a century and a half before.[32] A collection of farmers,

---

[30]Collins, *Witherspoon,* I, 150, 152–155; *The Works of the Rev. John Witherspoon . . . ,* 2d ed. (Philadelphia, 1802), IV, 281–288.

[31]This account of the *Hector*'s voyage follows MacKay, *Scotland Farewell,* esp. chaps. 5, 6, and George MacLaren, "Passenger List of the Ship Hector," *Nova Scotia Historical Quarterly,* 3 (1973), 121–129.

[32]"That stream of Scottish immigration which, in after years, flowed, not only over the county of Pictou, but over much of the eastern part of the Province, Cape Breton, Prince Edward Island, portions of New Brunswick, and even the Upper Provinces, began with this voyage, and even, in a large measure, originated with it, for it was by the representations of those on board to their friends, that others followed, and so the stream deepened and widened in succeeding years. We

artisans, gentlemen's sons, and herders and their families had gathered, some on the hillsides along the loch, some in rough shelters set up on the Broom estuary. More were assembling from all directions—from over the northern hills; from the impoverished parish of Assynt and other disturbed farming districts of Sutherland; from east coast farms forty or fifty miles away: properties near Dornoch, Dingwall, Beauly, and Inverness; and from Gairloch, 24 miles south across the mountains, twice that far by sea; and from the crofts scattered south of Gairloch along the coastal strip of southern Ross. "They strode down the mountains with their piper playing as if they were bound for battle," a recent chronicler of this legendary voyage has written. "Some arrived on horses, leading Highland ponies with panniers stuffed with belongings. Most walked, 40 miles from Beauly and beyond, carrying a few possessions on their backs and their babes in arms, over cattle tracks which had never seen a wheel." After the Reverend James Robertson of Lochbroom held a last communion in the churchyard, the emigrants were ferried in small groups to the *Hector,* and the old, small vessel—crammed now with 189 passengers and with barrels and crates of supplies and mountains of bags and chests—weighed anchor.[33]

The voyage started well as the *Hector* cleared the bay, sailed south through the Minch Channel between the Hebrides groups and then southwest out into the Atlantic; but in the end it proved to be a nightmare. The hold quickly became a frightful pesthole. Measuring only 83 feet long, 24 feet wide, and 10 feet deep, it was lit by a few fish-oil lamps and by the light that filtered through the hatch. Such ventilation as it had also came through the hatch, and the only sanitary facilities available for the 189 passengers, almost all of whom were seasick for the first week or two, were a few wooden buckets. The voyagers were literally shelved: assigned narrow wooden straw-covered pallets stacked in tiers two feet apart. While the good weather held, most people went on deck and learned to keep their balance as the *Hector,* rolling from side to side in the heavy sea, rose at sharp angles, then buried its prow in the waves while the decks were drenched and drenched again by great sheets of spray. Then, a few days out, disease swept through the ship—first dysentery, which debilitated, almost eviscerated, its victims and made them vulnerable to deadlier diseases; then smallpox. The chills, fevers, nausea, and erupting pustules of that deadly affliction hit the children first (71—over a third—of the passengers were below the age of nine); they lay stricken in the dark, stinking hold, their parents helpless as they watched them suffer and fade.

---

venture to say that there is no one element in the population of these Lower Provinces, upon which their social, moral, and religious condition has depended more than upon its Scottish immigrants, and of these that band in the Hector were the pioneers and vanguard." George Patterson, *A History of the County of Pictou, Nova Scotia* (Montreal, 1877), p. 82.
[33] MacKay, *Scotland Farewell,* pp. 86, 98, 211–212.

In the midst of this deepening disaster, a hurricane struck. The tiny
vessel was flung about the sea like a cork. Its despairing passengers reeled
in their filthy, jam-packed barrack and fell together in heaps on the wet
floor as the vessel rolled wildly from side to side. In groups or in isolation
they prayed for relief or an easy death. Death came only too easily: 18,
almost 10% of the group, died on shipboard. Relief came slowly, after two
weeks of unremitting horror. By then, as the vessel regained its course in
a calm sea, they discovered that the bread and drinking water had been
spoiled and the other food supplies were running out. When the *Hector*
finally limped into Pictou harbor it was September 15, two and a half
months after the departure from Lochbroom; and the survivors—debilitated by their ordeal, bereaved and utterly exhausted—were faced with new
trials altogether.

In a reaction common among the voyagers to the British borderland in
the 1770s, and especially among the Scots, they were shocked at what they
saw as the *Hector* entered the narrow neck of Pictou harbor and rounded
the promontory that juts into its middle. Before them lay not the more or
less civilized frontier they had romantically imagined, with farmland and
villages, schoolhouses and roadways, in recognizable form, but an almost
untouched wilderness in which dense forests, the like of which was nowhere to be seen in the Scottish Highlands, grew down to the water's edge.
As the *Hector* drew closer to the shore and the voyagers stared at the scene
before them, they could make out only a few log houses in small clearings
—dwellings, they proved to be, of some of the sixteen families that remained from the Philadelphia Company's original efforts at colonization.
A number of these residents now gathered on the beach to greet the *Hector*,
and in response the voyagers (it would later be said) drew themselves up
on the deck as the vessel dropped anchor, some in kilts and some with
broadswords, while the ship's bagpiper pierced the silence with a shrill
song.[34]

That romantic recollection may be fanciful: it comes from an oral
tradition recorded in print a century after the event. But some such show
of bravado would have been needed to hearten the disembarking passengers, some still recovering from the voyage, a few lingering toward death.
Everything was wrong. It was too late to plant crops even if there had been
arable fields to plant in, and their arrival quickly exhausted the supplies of
the earlier settlers, and soon too their hospitality and good will. But the
newcomers had to have shelter, and so, since the Philadelphia Company's
resident agent could not provide accommodations for them, they were
forced to learn some of the skills of woodsmen quickly. They cut down
trees and improvised, not solid log houses but rough lean-tos, the flimsiest

[34] *Ibid.*, pp. 135–139; Patterson, *Pictou*, p. 82.

kinds of huts, whose roofs were nothing but piles of bark and branches. Then they turned to Ross for the assignments of land they had been promised—only to discover that the harborside properties, the only easily accessible land, had been reserved for others (yet to appear), and that the land to be parceled out to them lay two or three miles back of the harbor, in an area covered with thick stands of pines.

Conflicts quickly developed: between the voyagers and the earlier settlers, concerned about their own survival; between the voyagers and Ross, who was supposed to be supervising their now chaotic settling but who had no control over the situation and who could not supply their most elemental needs; and between Ross and the Philadelphia Company's resident agent. Autumn was upon them, and provisions had to be made for the winter. Groups formed around particular approaches to the problems they faced. Some fled, seeking refuge forty miles away in the three recently settled communities of Londonderry, Onslow, and Truro. To these easternmost offshoots of the Fundy settlements, reached from Pictou by a two-day trek southwest through the woods, these Highlanders took their families and belongings. The men worked through the winter as laborers, the women and children as domestic servants. A few of these families never returned to Pictou, settling into the nascent towns or moving on later, south to Halifax or farther west to the Yorkshire settlements on Francklin's and DesBarres's lands or to the Cumberland villages of Amherst and Sackville. But most returned to the Pictou region the next spring to rejoin the sixty or seventy who had remained through the winter.

These, the hardiest or most stubborn of the voyagers, had suffered greatly. The *Hector* had returned from a voyage to the south with promised supplies, but the Highlanders were told they could not receive them free, as they had expected, unless they returned to the lands they had been assigned; if they remained at the harbor they would have to pay cash. But the cash of most families had been depleted, so some sold their belongings for necessary supplies. Two desperate householders simply took over the storehouse by force and seized the food they needed, a "rebellion" the militia in the nearest towns refused to put down. During that first winter the Highlanders learned to store clams before the snow fell, learned too to fish through the ice and hunt deer and moose in the snow; and they learned also, sometimes at great cost, how to protect their own bodies against the bitter and prolonged cold. Gradually, as the snow melted and their companions who had fled to settled communities drifted back, the Highlanders came to terms with the situation they faced, staked out property they might legitimately claim, and began their transformation into frontier farmers and American woodsmen.

By 1775 they had settled into this strange land, so different from their imagining. Householders from the *Hector* then comprised half of the permanent residents of the region, and their property—temporary or permanent, claimed or rented or owned—was scattered along the river valleys south and west of Pictou. Fifty years later a local historian and genealogist could locate the final establishments of the *Hector*'s Highlanders—those who had responded to Witherspoon's and the Pagans' advertisements and had survived the voyage—throughout what had become a rich and open farm country along the river valleys that run like spokes into Pictou harbor. Some he traced out into other regions—to nearby points in northern Nova Scotia; others to more distant points: Halifax and New Brunswick. But most lived out their lives on farms of their own creation in a fan-shaped territory around Pictou harbor. A few, the most favored of them, had settled in a particularly fine span of property on the shores of the harbor itself—a district they fondly called, and which is still known as, Loch Broom.[35]

But none had remained clients of the Philadelphia Company or of the Witherspoon-Pagan associates. The associates' agent Ross never asserted the control he was given over the settlement, and there is no evidence that Witherspoon ever visited the area, to adjudicate land grants or for any other purpose. The Highlanders simply ignored their would-be sponsors and squatted on likely properties; in time many of them applied to the government for land grants, and received them. Later, after the Revolution, the younger Pagans renewed the family's interest in the land, and sent over another small contingent of Scotch emigrants, while Witherspoon exchanged his shares for land the Pagans owned in the United States. Finally, in 1809, the entire episode was concluded when the British government took back all of the unappropriated land in the Philadelphia Company's original grant for noncompliance with the settlement terms. The final accounting showed that the Pagans, over the thirty-six years of the project, had incurred a net loss of £701 1s 6d.[36]

Montgomery: Georgetown and Tracadie Bay

Such a loss was relatively small for such enterprises, for profits from associated land speculation and immigration management could only develop in the long term—not by initial land purchases or by steady rents, but, as Witherspoon had realized, by the increase in the value of residual land after settlers were given free rein, and that process could take years. Yet in the early 1770s the hope of profits continued to stimulate projects—some real-

---

[35]MacKay, *Scotland Farewell*, chap. 9; Patterson, *Pictou*, app. C.
[36]MacKay, *Scotland Farewell*, pp. 214–215. On the relation of these maneuvers of Witherspoon and the Pagans to their landholdings in Vermont, see below, chap. 16, pp. 610–612, 614, 616, 618.

ized, some not—to transport settlers to this new northern borderland and through them to make the land profitable.

The powerful lord advocate of Scotland, Sir James Montgomery, a shrewd businessman, invested in emigration and overseas land as he did in any enterprise—for a substantial profit on his capital. He picked up, for nothing but the cost of passing title, four of the "lots" into which the island of St. John had been divided, a total of over 100,000 acres, and in 1770 sent over from Scotland fifty indentured servants to start producing flax and collecting fish and timber for shipment. The mere "start-up" cost of establishing, on the island's east coast, this experimental beginning of what was expected to become a larger enterprise was £1,200, and the problems and costs multiplied quickly. The whole undertaking had to be shrouded in secrecy since Montgomery was Scotland's chief law officer and hence was himself officially responsible for discouraging emigration from Britain. (His successor, Henry Dundas, would take this duty more seriously.) Understandably, he instructed his business agent to manage the affair so "as to incur as little observation as possible." Sending reinforcements to his advance party would be very difficult, and in fact never happened. But the fifty servants did arrive safely and began their settlement on the shores of the east-coast harbor that would be called Georgetown.

None of Montgomery's servants knew the ways of the American wilderness, and their "seasoning" was painful, in some cases lethal. Some drowned, some succumbed to disease, one was killed by a tree he was attempting to fell. Montgomery's overseer did manage to get enough land cleared in two years to support the surviving servants, but their indentures expired before profits could be produced, and they drifted away from the settlement. A second project, to establish a trading center on the island in partnership with a well-connected New England shipmaster, cost Montgomery, by 1774, over £4,000. Though the lord advocate did manage to retain title to his land on St. John into the nineteenth century, his losses, in all, exceeded £10,000. By 1774 his direct contribution to the peopling of the island was merely the few survivors of the original fifty servants and a few storekeepers in a trading post at Georgetown.[37]

Montgomery was indirectly involved in a more successful venture in the same early years, which resulted in the transplantation to Tracadie Bay, on the north shore of St. John, of over 200 Scotch Highlanders, both Catholic and Protestant. The origin of this project lay far off, in one of the most remote corners of North Britain. A bigoted Protestant landlord on the small, wet, windswept island of South Uist in the Outer Hebrides, the

[37]J. M. Bumsted, "Sir James Montgomery and Prince Edward Island, 1767–1803," *Acadiensis,* 7 (1978), 76–102. This excellent essay illustrates in detail "that settlement of a North American wilderness was simply not a viable *business* proposition for any private entrepreneur."

young MacDonald of Boisdale, was known to be using economic coercion to force his Catholic tenants into religious conformity. Fearful that he would succeed in this, and that once successful this technique would be used by other Protestant lairds, the Scottish Catholic Church raised special funds to create a refuge in America for its persecuted people, and found a determined lay leader for its project in the devout John MacDonald of Glenaladale, an influential and able tacksman (tenant-in-chief) on the mainland coast opposite the Hebrides. While the church leaders negotiated, surreptitiously, with Montgomery for one of the best of the 20,000-acre lots on St. John's north shore, Glenaladale made contact with other threatened farmers on the western mainland and started preparations for an emigrant expedition. It turned out that the mere threat of the depopulation was enough to force Boisdale to relax his pressure on the Catholics, and in the end only eleven families of his tenants left on Glenaladale's *Alexander* when it cleared the Highlands for St. John in May 1772.

But there were other harassed families on Uist, and others elsewhere within the range of Glenaladale's influence who were interested in emigration. In all, the *Alexander* carried 210 emigrants—100 people from Uist, most of them Catholics, and 110 from Glenaladale's country on the mainland coast. The expedition was unusually well supplied—one of the best equipped of the time—partly because the church invested heavily in providing for the indigent Catholics, partly because the rest of the passengers, recruited by Glenaladale, were relatively prosperous and provided for themselves comfortably. In one way or another approximately £30 was raised for the transportation and settlement of each family aboard. But while these settlers, who arrived at St. John in good season, opened up small farms in the virgin larch forests inland of Tracadie Bay with relatively little difficulty, they too, like the Highlanders at Pictou, were deeply disillusioned by life in a forested wilderness and settled into their new lives with foreboding.[38]

The starting point of this unusual expedition had been the church's undercover purchase of one of Montgomery's lots on the north shore of the island. Thus, Montgomery had been responsible, directly or indirectly, for the settlement by a few hundred Scots of two tiny areas in this outer fringe of an opening borderland. Other entrepreneurs in the same years were even less successful, in that they failed, despite desperate efforts, to establish any viable settlements at all.

[38] J. M. Bumsted, "Highland Emigration to the Island of St. John and the Scottish Catholic Church, 1769–1774," *Dalhousie Review*, 58 (1978), 511–527; John Macdonald of Glenaladale to Alexander Macdonald, Greenock, March 7, 1772, in Iain R. MacKay, "Glenalladale's Settlement, Prince Edward Island," *Scottish Gaelic Studies*, 10 (1963), 17–20.

Desbrisay and St. John

Thomas Desbrisay, the indefatigable lieutenant governor of St. John, whose recruitment efforts had touched off the lord justice clerk's appeals for an end to emigration, was boiling with enterprise in those years and determined to settle the lands he purchased on the island. His chief appeal was to prosperous farmers in Ireland, but despite unusual financial inducements, and despite his notorious campaign of newspaper advertisements and a remarkable network of agents (most of them, usefully, tavernkeepers rather than merchants)—despite, indeed, his desperate promise to rename the island New Ireland—he had little success. Nine families in 1771, 188 people who scattered through the island in 1772, and a few more in 1773 were all that he managed to collect. He failed to establish any permanent settlement. His settlers of 1772 were, in fact, so disillusioned with what they found on the island and so angered by what they believed were Desbrisay's deliberate misrepresentations that they discouraged all other prospective emigrants they knew from following them. But when in 1773 the authorities, led by the lord justice clerk, cracked down on Desbrisay, preventing him, he said, "from tenanting my lands in St. Johns with either English, Scotch, or Irish settlers," neither his determination nor his ingenuity was exhausted.[39] In May 1773 he sent forward to Lord Dartmouth a detailed and comprehensive proposal to populate St. John, a proposal he had received from a German, a former Brunswick major, Emanuel Lutterloh, then resident in London. Lutterloh proposed to send to the island within three years no fewer than 4,000 families, presumably German Protestants, each family containing at least four persons, three of them "capable of labour"—to transport them to the island and supply them there for six months. In return he asked for £20,000 and the fifth year's rents. Desbrisay was confident that Lutterloh's program would work and that in twelve years' time the owner of the land on which Lutterloh's people settled would be able to sell off 20,000-acre lots for an estimated £10,000 each. He therefore bought up more land—by 1775 he claimed title, in all, to almost 70,000 acres—and tried to ingratiate himself with Dartmouth by advising him to buy land too.[40]

[39]Desbrisay to Dartmouth, Dublin, Feb. 12, 1774, Dartmouth Papers, Canada, III, 3143–3146. On Desbrisay's troubles with the authorities, see above, pp. 59–60, 62–63; R. J. Dickson, *Ulster Emigration to Colonial America, 1718–1775* ([1966], Antrim, 1976), pp. 152–164.

[40]Desbrisay to Dartmouth, London, May 13, 1773, enclosing Lutterloh's undated but printed *Proposal . . . to Furnish Four Thousand Families as Tenants or Settlers . . . in the Said Island,* and same to same, Feb. 12, 1774, Dartmouth Papers, Canada, III, 3117–3118 and 3143–3146; Clark, *Three Centuries,* pp. 261, 265–266. Lutterloh was deeply involved in land speculation in East Florida, having visited there personally as a prospective settler in 1767. Daniel L. Schafer, "Early Plantation Development in British East Florida," *El Escribano,* 19 (1982), 42. In 1777 he joined the American army and later

THE GREAT SURGE OF
1773-1774

Desbrisay's and Lutterloh's ingenious maneuvers came to nothing. But, like all of these entrepreneurs—Francklin, DesBarres, Witherspoon, the Pagans, Montgomery, Glenaladale—Desbrisay helped publicize the possibility of emigration from distressed areas of northern Britain to Nova Scotia and St. John. In the three years between 1770 and 1773 these adventurers had spread the word throughout a wide area of northern England and Scotland —an area stretching from York and Leeds on the south through all three ridings of Yorkshire, through parts of Lancashire, Cumberland, Durham, and Northumberland, and into the Scottish Lowlands, the western and northern Highlands, and the Hebrides. They and many who worked for and with them had gained experience in mobilizing groups and distributing supplies, and in confronting the strange and at times deadly problems of settling British farmers into a new life on one of the wilderness peripheries of British North America.

So active had these recruiters and speculators been that by mid-December 1773, when the British customs officials began compiling the Register of emigrants, the newspapers in these regions were full of notices of various kinds concerning emigration to Nova Scotia and St. John. Most common were advertisements of vessels planning to leave Yorkshire or Lancashire ports for Halifax or Fort Cumberland—ads like that for the *Thomas and William*, due to leave Scarborough for Nova Scotia in mid-March 1774 and prepared to take on passengers at £5 per head for adults, £2 10s for children under ten, and "sucking children gratis"; agents were named in four towns in the hinterland of Scarborough. Some notices were straightforward and businesslike, full of details of land available for sale, sailing plans, costs, accommodations on board, advice on what to bring, and procedures for booking. But others mixed business information with high-blown promotional material. Nova Scotia was called "that famous and flourishing country . . . that land of liberty where there are neither game laws nor land tax" and where ordinary people, "particularly those skillful in the husbandry business," can make their fortune.[41]

Such notices were often repeated week after week, beginning long in

---

became a colonel. Horst Dippel, *Germany and the American Revolution, 1770–1800*, trans. B. A. Uhlendorf (Chapel Hill, N.C., 1977), p. 271 n.
[41] *Etherington's York Chronicle*, Jan. 7, 1774; *York Courant*, Dec. 7, 1773, March 29, 1774.

advance of a vessel's sailing and ending with news of the actual departure and eventual arrival. Departure and arrival notices appeared not only in the papers of the regions directly affected but elsewhere as well, often in far-off places throughout the Atlantic basin. The range of this circulated shipping news originating in northern Britain, printed whenever it came to hand, is at times astonishing. It is as if a huge but rather inefficient communication network centered on Yorkshire and the Scottish Lowlands had been in continuous operation, spreading news of population movements randomly throughout the British world. Impulses received at any one point would eventually be felt elsewhere—not necessarily where it mattered—as the printers recirculated material received at second, third, or fourth hand. The arrival of the *Hector* in Pictou, for example, with an account of its disastrous trip from Lochbroom, was noted, in German, in the *Wöchentliche Pennsylvanische Staatsbote* five months after the event. On one occasion the *Nova-Scotia Gazette*, whose pages were full of news of emigration and resettlement, reprinted a notice published in Quebec reporting the arrival in New York of an immigrant vessel from Scotland.[42]

The central theme of most of these notices was the magnitude of the emigration from northern Britain. The subject was inexhaustible and to some extent sensational; the larger the numbers that could be reported, the more prosperous the emigrants, and the more vivid the depiction of the exodus the more extensive the coverage. It must have seemed interesting to the editor of the *Scots Magazine* to reprint the story circulating widely in April 1774 that some of the passengers then leaving Scarborough for Nova Scotia were "of real and substantial property, particularly one of them, with thirteen in family, said to be worth £3,000, £800 of which is left in security in England and the rest taken with him." So too London's *Lloyd's Evening Post* devoted most of a column to a letter from "A Lover of his Country, and a Friend to Old England" reporting that hundreds of men, women, and children were crowding into the inns of York, Malton, and other mid-Yorkshire towns en route to Hull and Scarborough to find shipping to Nova Scotia. These were people, the letter stated, who had "quit their farms without great disadvantage to themselves" and hence were able to remove substantial sums from the country. "All the principal inhabitants" of one township were reported to be leaving, taking with them not

---

[42] *Wöchentliche Pennsylvanische Staatsbote*, March 22, 1774; *Nova-Scotia Gazette*, Aug. 24, 1773. The *Gazette* reported not only on significant local events like ships arriving with emigrants in Halifax, and Francklin's and DesBarres's land sales, but also on the arrival in Virginia of a vessel from Ireland whose passengers proved to be "mere skeletons so weak they could hardly walk or stand"; on the settlement of land along the Mississippi by war veterans from Connecticut; on land grants in Georgia; on the massive emigration from northern Ireland; on depression and hard times among any number of groups in Britain who were considering emigration; and on anything the printer could lay hands on connected with Lord Hillsborough: his efforts to keep his tenants from emigrating; his land policy as secretary of state, his retirement to his estates in Ireland.

only their own funds but some of the neighbors' "in order to purchase [land] for them" if the region lived up to its reputation.[43]

To some, such reports, together with news of active recruitment of emigrants among the north British farming population and notices of emigrant ship departures, represented a threat to social stability and economic security, and they responded with various kinds of counter-propaganda, which too filled the newspapers in the months when the Register was being compiled. Nova Scotia and St. John were singled out for abuse, along with the people who were foolish enough to go there. Every negative aspect of the migration to those settlements was given full play. Not only was the transatlantic voyage declared to be fearful in itself, but fare-paying passengers, it was reported, were treated like transported criminals. And the country that was finally reached could hardly be worse. The inhabitants of Nova Scotia, one young woman recently arrived in Halifax wrote in a letter published in the *York Chronicle*,

> seem to be poor miserable beings, which was very mortifying to me, who had always been used to good living at home. It is a desolate, oppressed, and almost uninhabited country, and their food is chiefly fish, which is not very delicate, but cheap. Flesh is very scarce and dear, [and] if anyone should inquire after my situation here [in Halifax], pray describe the country as I have done, every word I have wrote being truth.

Emigrants would be fools, a correspondent to the *Leeds Intelligencer* said, if they did not consider carefully the consequences of being cooped up on shipboard for two months, "crowded together four in a bed, and those beds one upon another three deep, with not so much room betwixt each as to admit even the smallest person to sit up on end." The emigrants who flock to the exit port of Scarborough, another correspondent wrote, seeking to make their fortunes "in the wilds of Nova Scotia . . . will be miserably mistaken." They leave in high spirits, deluding themselves "that when they arrive in the wished for land they will every day have the pleasure of climbing up large mountains of roast beef & after that to swim in oceans of wine and rivers of rum."

Voyagers were warned against being "too precipitate in their resolution of leaving their native home"; rumors were deliberately circulated to the effect that certain vessels were "totally unfit to perform the voyage, and that

[43] *Scots Magazine*, 36 (April 1774), 217; *York Chronicle or Weekly Advertiser*, April 15, 1774; *Lloyd's Evening Post*, March 18–21, 1774. The "Lover of His Country" 's letter is full of circumstantial detail and ends with the question, "What will become of poor Old England when left destitute of its principal inhabitants, having only the poorer sort of people, without money and most of them with large families?"

therefore the persons going therein must do it at the hazard of their lives and fortunes"; and word was passed from person to person and published repeatedly that emigrant vessels were returning from Nova Scotia "with nearly as many passengers on board as went out . . . the situation of the country [not being] equal to the favorable idea they had formed of it." The entire enterprise of emigration was declared to be disastrous, and even the inhabitants of the poorhouses said to have shipped out, willingly, at the expense of their parishes in hopes of better prospects abroad—even these destitute and hopeless people, to say nothing of the prosperous farmers whom the land speculators chiefly sought to attract, were bound to be bitterly disappointed.[44]

So it was said, by those threatened by the emigration, in newspapers and broadsides that circulated throughout the northern counties. But to the victims of economic instability and to people facing discouraging futures, the advertised prospects of land ownership or cheap rentals in a world free from the power of landlords were far more effective than the dire warnings and dark rumors. The result, in the months during which the Register was being compiled, was a surge of migration from northern Britain to the easternmost corner of the North American periphery, a surge, well known throughout the colonies as well as throughout northern Britain,[45] that took off from the preliminary, unsure experimental voyages of the previous three years and rose to a climax just before the American war brought all such transfers of people to a halt. Of the vessels leaving northern Britain for Nova Scotia and St. John in 1774 and 1775, six were entered in the Register. Through these lists, supplemented by information on the other emigrant vessels to Nova Scotia, we can discover much about the voyagers to the

[44] *York Courant,* Aug. 30, 1774; *Leeds Intelligencer,* April 19, 1774 (and more fully, *York Chronicle and Weekly Advertiser,* March 18, April 15, 1774); *Daily Advertiser* (London), April 8, 1774 (reprinted in *Virginia Gazette or, Norfolk Intelligencer,* June 9, 1774); *Leeds Mercury,* April 26, 1774; *Etherington's York Chronicle,* Feb. 25, Sept. 23, Nov. 4, 1774 (the latter's notice of counter-migrations is reprinted in *Leeds Intelligencer,* Sept. 27, 1774; the same sentiment in *York Courant,* Oct. 11, 1774). *Etherington's York Chronicle,* Jan. 27, 1775, carried a particularly emphatic letter from North America, dated Aug. 10, 1774:

> a great many farmers are quitting the northern parts of Yorkshire for America. I fear that most of them will change for the worse. They little know what they must suffer from change of soil and climate, and the toil they must endure before they can make bread to eat; and if, by their industry, they, at the last, attain to live free from want, they need never expect to grow rich, for they must settle so far inland that the produce of their land will bear a very low price, and in all the back settlements cash is scarcely known amongst them, the merchants giving them clothing, work-tools, salt, sugar, etc., etc. for their produce, at two, three or four hundred percent advance. Those who are gone to Nova Scotia will have five or six months winter.

[45] So, in the characteristic circuitry of news dissemination, the *Virginia Gazette* (Purdie and Dixon), July 7, 1774, reprinted a notice published in a Philadelphia newspaper that had been reprinted from the *Nova-Scotia Gazette,* to the effect that five vessels from Hull, Scarborough, and Newcastle, with 662 passengers, had arrived in Halifax.

northeasternmost extremity of North America—their origins, their social character, the groupings in which they traveled, and their ultimate destinies.

This was a migration of families. In all, three out of four of the passengers aboard these registered vessels traveled as members of families, and these families were not simply husband and wife. The average size of the families aboard these vessels was 4.4, and some of the families were exceptionally large. The *Jenny,* which left Hull for Halifax and Fort Cumberland in April 1775, carried eighty passengers, 82.5% of whom were traveling as members of families; the average size of these families was 5.5. Aboard the *Jenny* was the Peck family of Yorkshire, led by a forty-seven-year-old husbandman, Richard Peck; his family numbered ten; all eight of his children, the eldest twenty, the youngest two, were leaving with him. Aboard the *Jenny* also was the prosperous forty-five-year-old farmer, Christopher Harper, from Barthorpe-Bottoms near Malton in Yorkshire, with his wife and seven children; the Johnson family: husband, wife, four children, and two servants; and Mrs. Elizabeth Anderson, traveling with all five of her children to join her husband in Nova Scotia. Among the fourteen families on the *Two Friends* were the Parkers: husband, wife, two children, the husband's widowed mother, and a maidservant. The *Lovely Nelly*'s departure from Dumfries was delayed, in fact, because of preliminary stops at the Isle of Man, Whitehaven, and Kirkcudbright to pick up particular families in those places that had booked passage in advance and that were prosperous enough to pay for this service.[46]

The occupational pattern reflects the problems that had dislodged these people and the desires of the land speculators who were managing the exodus. Of the registered voyagers to Nova Scotia and St. John whose occupations are known, half had been employed in agriculture, almost every one of them either independent farmers or tenant yeomen of some substance. A further 26.9% were artisans, the largest number of them in textile work. Laborers constituted only about 20% of those whose occupations were listed. The voyagers' ages too reflect the central character of the migration. These are mature people, not footloose young adventurers. The average age of the farmers who migrated to Nova Scotia and St. John in these years was 31.8; of the artisans, 30.3. Even the laborers migrating to these provinces were older—on the average almost five years older—than those leaving central and southern England for the Chesapeake colonies and Pennsylvania.

[46]The *Jenny*'s entry in the Register is T47/10/59–60; the *Lovely Nelly* is T47/12, 87, 90; the *Two Friends*, T47/9/77–79.

Blinkhorn

But such averages, revealing as they are, do not convey with any clarity the extent to which the movement to the northeastern periphery was dominated by established householders, farmers for the most part, not destitute at the point of their migration, not forced out by abject poverty, but dislodged by shifts in the organization of the economy, impelled in many cases by the desire for religious independence, and ambitious for greater security and better prospects for the future. One must reach into the fine details of individual lives among these voyagers of 1773–1776 and trace lines back from known eventualities in America to obscure origins in Britain, in order to grasp the human realities involved.

The *Two Friends,* the first of the crowded transport vessels to leave for Nova Scotia in the early spring of 1774, recruited its 103 passengers primarily from among the substantial farmers in the eastern third of Yorkshire.[47] Among them was William Blinkhorn, 33, his 29-year-old wife, Ann, and all four of their children, ranging in age from seven to one. They came from Hovingham, a parish village of some 600 souls situated in the alluvial Vale of Pickering, the fertile valley (a lake in prehistoric times) that stretches 30 miles east from Helmsley along the Rye and Derwent rivers to the North Sea port of Scarborough. Hovingham was one of a string of small villages that had grown up along the road that ran parallel to the east-west river line, and it was in the center of a farming area in which much modernization had taken place. Surrounded by a ring of recently enclosed properties—in Amotherby, Swinton, Nunnington, Ness, Stonegrave, Skakleton (the last a manor owned by that indefatigable improving landlord Beilby Thompson)—Hovingham was surrounded too by lands of the Earl of Carlisle, whose magnificent estate, Castle Howard, lay only four miles to the southeast.[48] But the most immediate development had been the building, in Hovingham itself, of the strange Italianate mansion of Sir Thomas Worsley, M.P., close friend of the Earl of Bute and of George III, surveyor general of the Office of Works, horse breeder, art collector, and amateur of architecture and of science. His Hovingham Hall, which one entered through stables and a riding school, had quickly become recognized as a private art museum of distinction. Where, precisely, in the lands around the village of Hovingham Blinkhorn's tenancy had been located, and which of

[47] Of the 45 passengers whose occupations were identified in the registration of the *Two Friends,* 35 were farmers or husbandmen.
[48] John Rushton, *The Ryedale Story* [York, n.d.], p. 10; a survey of Yorkshire enclosures compiled by Virginia DeJohn Anderson from *The History of York (The Victoria History of the Counties of England)* (London, 1907–1925), vols. I–III. Cf. Tate, *Domesday of Enclosures,* pp. 285–311.

the several improving landlords in the region had been his, are not known. But rents everywhere in the immediate neighborhood had been raised so sharply that the local farming population had become highly susceptible to the appeal of emigration—a fact Michael Francklin knew well when he selected Hovingham as the location for one of his recruiting agents. It was precisely the recent rent increase, Blinkhorn told the customs officials at Hull, that had been the cause of his own and his family's emigration.[49]

Aboard the *Two Friends*, Blinkhorn and his family found farming people from all over the dales and vales of eastern Yorkshire, almost every one of whom gave as the cause of their emigration either a recent elevation of rents or their desire "to seek a better livelihood." Most of these statements are succinct; a few are discursive ("in hopes of a better support for himself and family every necessary of life being so dear"; "provisions, rents, and every necessary of life being so very high they cannot support their family"). And specific landlords whose rent increases had driven the voyagers out are named: twenty-one of the passengers had been tenants of either Beilby Thompson or William Weddell, builders of new estates at Escrick and Newby Hall.

In Nova Scotia, after a difficult transatlantic voyage and a second trip through the Bay of Fundy to Fort Cumberland on the Isthmus of Chignecto, Blinkhorn and his family made a final removal to join the fifteen Yorkshire families that had settled in 1772 on DesBarres's well-diked lands above the tidal marshes along the Maccan River. There, ten miles from Fort Cumberland, the former Yorkshire husbandman created a farm of over three hundred acres, for which he paid only a nominal rent (if any at all) until, in 1780, he took possession of the property he had developed, with all its buildings and improvements, on a perpetual lease. His annual rent thereafter was stated to be £7 18s 18½ d Nova Scotia money, though how much of it was ever paid is not known. It proved to be an admirable property. On this recently opened farm just above the dikes that held back the tidal waters, Blinkhorn and his family thrived. In addition to the four children he had brought with him, he had seven more born in Nova Scotia, the youngest by a second wife he married in his late forties. By the time of his death in 1813, aged seventy-two, Blinkhorn had seen his children marry into other English families that had settled into the same rich, marshy riverland of the Cumberland Basin, and had seen his farm develop still further and flourish. In 1795 an agent reported to DesBarres that Blinkhorn's farm was one of several, under the management of Yorkshire men, whose

[49]G. Bernard Wood, *Yorkshire Villages* (London, 1971), p. 184; Namier and Brooke, *House of Commons*, III, 659–661; Arthur Young, *A Six Months Tour through the North of England . . .* , 2d ed. (London, 1770–1771), II, 88n.–91n., lists all the statuary and paintings, room by room, with occasional comments on the quality of the art.

appearance was "beautiful"; the houses look "as well as the considerable extent of verdant fields which they have made. The marsh extends along the sides of the rivers—each has the portion thereof belonging to his front dyke. The soil is good—a little springy and strong—good for grass—not complained of for corn—the wood is also good."[50]

Fertile, profitable, autonomous, and full of promise for the future, Blinkhorn's farm was, however, isolated and remote, still at the edge of a half-wild world, a universe away from the intensely cultivated, coveted, overrented lands of eastern Yorkshire, lands possessed and worked by tiers of landlords and tenants. And it was a world apart too from the deeply structured, close-woven, and highly interactive society these people had known before.

The Harrisons

Blinkhorn's outline biography, classic in its structure, must be extracted from the impersonal documents that have survived. It is an inarticulate story: there are no traces of his feelings or of the social role he assumed in the nascent community that he helped found. Others who traveled in the fleet that departed from Yorkshire for Nova Scotia in the spring of 1774 left more complete evidence of their settling into the land, in some cases of their inner experiences as well.

The Harrisons, for example. The departure of that huge family—the fifty-four-year-old farmer, his wife and nine children—must have been a major expedition in itself. The family's fare on the *William and Mary* alone could not have cost less than £35; the entire trip probably cost five or ten times that much, especially if there is truth in the family tradition that they came heavily laden with household possessions. John Harrison, whose wife was said to be well-to-do, was undoubtedly one of those "passengers . . . of real and substantial property" whose emigration so troubled the establishment—though he listed his occupation and "quality" as only that of farmer. They came from Rillington, a village in the same Vale of Pickering from which the Blinkhorns had come, and another of the towns in which Francklin had appointed a recruiting agent. It was only a dozen miles east of Blinkhorn's Hovingham and a stone's throw from the turnpike that led to the port of Scarborough, twenty-two miles to the east, where the *William and Mary* took on its passengers.[51]

[50]DesBarres's lease of land to William Blinkhorn, Oct. 17, 1780, DesBarres Papers, series 5, vol. 18. Macdonald's Report on DesBarres's Estate on Rivers Maccan and Nappan, 1795 (n. 27, above).
[51]Wright, *Planters and Pioneers*, p. 139. This vessel, unnamed but probably the *William and Mary* with its 193 passengers, is listed at T47/9/121–123.

Having joined the throngs of east Yorkshire farming folk who traveled, on foot, on horses, and in heavily loaded carts, along that turnpike to Scarborough in the spring of 1774, the Harrisons followed the usual course in Nova Scotia, disembarking in Halifax and then reshipping to Fort Cumberland. There they negotiated the rental, for £20 a year payable in farm goods, of a fully equipped farm along the River Hébert ("A Bare" it was spelled in their letters), from Edward Barron, probably acting as agent for Michael Francklin. Though the farm was remarkably well supplied (ten cows, four oxen, twenty sheep, one sow, and one breeding mare) and though it was in operation within a month of the Harrisons' arrival, they found the place full of miseries and they hated everything about it.

We "do not like it at all," the Harrisons' twenty-year-old son Luke wrote home to his cousin William in Rillington, and neither do "a great many besids us," most of whom, he said, were planning to return to England as soon as possible. Furthermore, they never *would* like the place. For one thing, the whole marshy area was swarming with fierce "muss keetoes." "You may think," he wrote his cousin, "that muss keetoes cannot hurt a deal, but if you do you are mistaken, for they will swell one['s] legs and hands [so] that some is both blind and lame for some days, and they grow wors every year . . . and they bite the English worst." Hay mowers suffer especially: "the muss keetoes will bite them verey often [so] that they will throw down . . . their syths and run home almost bitten to dead, and there is a black fly wors than all the rest. Every one in this contry has trowsers, and sevral women, for they fly up their petacoats and bite them terabely." But it was not only the mosquitoes. The winters were so cold one is "almost frozen to dead." The past winter, he reported, was supposed to have been mild, but "the frost was not gone out of the ground the 20 day of June"—to that he could personally testify. And he added a P.S. for his friend Mathew Cook: "I could wish to be with you again, loving friend, for I do not like the contry we are in now."[52]

But the Harrisons did not leave. The family worked the farm along the River Hébert for a decade, and then made the break into full independence. In 1783 twenty men, thirteen of whom had come over from Yorkshire in the spring of 1774, petitioned the government for a 10,000-acre grant nearby, in the unclaimed land behind the tidal dikes along the Maccan River, four or five miles east of the Hébert. The grant was awarded in 1785, and in the years that followed, each of the twenty men—among them John Harrison, Sr. (then aged 65) and his three eldest sons, Luke (then 31), John, Jr. (25),

---

[52]Luke Harrison to William Harrison, "at the river a bare [Hébert] nigh Fort Cumberland," June 30, 1774, Harrison Papers, folder 12, 187–192.

and Thomas (23)—took up a 500-acre plot of wilderness land, to bring it under cultivation. They never forgot the experience. A quarter of a century later, in 1810, young John, his father only recently dead, recalled the details of settling those "lands that never has been cultivated, all a wilderness. Wee cut down the wood of the land and burnt it of[f] and sowed it with wheat and rye so that we have made out [of] it [a] very good living." By then the family had spread throughout the rich, well-watered lands which the Acadians, a century before, had first broken open and diked against the tides, and they had married into the leading English families of the region. They had become indigenous to the region, though the memories of their origins remained fresh.

In 1803 Luke wrote a long letter of New Year's greeting to the same "Cousin Billy" in Rillington he had written to in 1774. Luke lamented the great "carnage death has made since we left you," but he was happy to say that the family along the Maccan had become "larger then old Jacob's was when he went down to Egypt . . . nay some women that had left of[f] bearing in England begun again in Nova Scotia." Twenty-nine years after his shocked arrival in Nova Scotia, Luke was proud of everything about the place. He wrote glowingly of the great stands of timber, especially the black birches, like mahogany when made into furniture, and the rock maples, from which his younger brother William had made 600 pounds of sugar the previous year. Berries, fruit, and grains of all kinds grew lushly—and potatoes: no praise was too much for the potatoes they produced, which were particularly good when eaten with the fish that abounded. There were fowl of all kinds ("our partridges sit in trees, & pidgeons too"). Cattle were comparable in size to Rillington's. There was no need for market days since each farm did its own slaughtering and raised most of what it consumed. Wages were enormously high. He himself would pay much to get a cloth fuller so that he might add a fulling mill to the grain and saw mills he already had. And he wrote too of personal affairs: about whom Billy might have married (he gave his opinion of the woman he thought had been the likeliest candidate); about his own family (he had been married fifteen years to the same woman, who had borne eight children still alive and one who died); and about the people in Yorkshire they used to gossip about. And then he turned to the future. Billy had invited Luke to return home to Rillington and "purchase a place in my native country." Luke's answer was unequivocal: "I had rather, ten to one, stay where I am, unless," he added in a simple but profoundly revealing phrase, "I could live in it independant." Much more likely, he thought, would be the reverse prospect, that Billy might come to Nova Scotia. "Nothing could give greater satisfaction then to see you here—5 or 600 pounds would purchase a good place." And though he warned him of the old complaints—especially the hot summers and the long, cold winters—he told him that Englishmen usually liked the country well enough, lived to a great old age, and found the land and its resources bountiful. And he assured him that he would be welcome: the whole family would assist in his relocation.

So the world had greatly changed since Luke first wrote his cousin so many years before, within a month of the Harrisons' arrival. But they had not forgotten their origins. "In my mind," Luke wrote, "I oftimes visit Rillington." And his brother John, Jr.—who had bought five hundred acres more adjoining the five hundred he had got from the grant, and had a family of ten—confessed to another Yorkshire cousin that he "could wish to see you once more, to talk with you face to face." True, he had scarcely known his cousin in the old days (he had only been fourteen when they left), but he wondered if they should not now, thirty-six years later, establish a regular "coraspondance." For he wanted to know "how all my play fellows comes on, John Stephenson in peticuler, and William Welbran, and Darke Richard England and John." But the nostalgia was fleeting. These were deeply engaged people, rooted in the land, and there was business to be done. "I have too sons, [grown] up young men," John, Jr., concluded in his letter to his cousin. "Pray send them, each of them," he wrote, perhaps facetiously, "a good industres wife. One of them is 24 and the other 18." And then: "Pray send out a ship load of young wemen, for there is great call for them that can card and spinn. The wages is from five to six shillings a week."[53]

Affluence

The articulation, the subjective detail, of the Harrisons' story is rare—made possible by the chance survival of family letters. More commonly, the central characteristics of these transplanted lives must be inferred from inert, fragmentary information scattered in local archives that may be brought together and fitted into patterns around the names that appear in the Register. Circumstances differed greatly, and so too do the dominant themes that emerge from these biographies.

Some of these obscure emigrants from the East and North ridings of Yorkshire, almost all of them farmers, were surprisingly affluent, especially in view of their commonly stated reason for leaving, that they could not afford the new rents, or that expenses were otherwise so high "they cannot support their families." Christopher Harper is an intriguing example. His home village, Barthorpe-Bottoms, was a crossroads hamlet consisting of

[53] Petition of William Pipes, Jr., and Others, Dec. 10, 1783, endorsed by Edward Barron, and Report of Survey of 10,000 Acres for William Pipes and Others, Jan. 17, 1785, NS Land Papers; John Harrison, [Jr.] to John Harrison, Maccan River, June 24, 1810, and Luke Harrison to William Harrison, "at Maccan," Jan. 1, 1803, Harrison Papers, folder 12, 189–191.

two or three farmhouses a few miles south of Rillington in the East Riding. He described himself at one point as a "farmer," at another as a "yeoman," and was one of those who gave as their reason for emigrating their hopes for a better livelihood and "on account of their rents being raised by Wm. Weddell, Esq. their landlord." Alone, in 1774, he crossed the Atlantic on the *Two Friends* for the purpose of surveying the possibilities, and set his eye on two pieces of choice property in the land near Fort Cumberland. One was owned by Lord William Campbell, the former governor of Nova Scotia. Harper negotiated with Campbell directly, but fruitlessly, as it turned out, since Campbell still hoped to rent his wild land rather than sell it. Harper then turned to John Huston, a New Englander who like many of his countrymen in Nova Scotia was selling out. Harper paid Huston £530 for 143 acres of what two contemporaries described as "fine cleared land, with a good house upon it, elegantly furnished, with barns and other conveniences, besides woodland at a distance, and twenty cows, with other cattle." Having arranged the purchase, Harper then returned to Yorkshire, packed up his large family (wife, four daughters and three sons) and re-turned, on the *Jenny*, to his property in Cumberland. A month before he left, however, he wrote to Lord Campbell, then in London, asking His Lordship "please to let me know your proposal of leting; it may sute sum people that are going along with me." Then he added, with rather cool condescension, in this unsolicited letter to the son of the Duke of Argyll, that "if there is anything I can do for you in that country [I] shall be glad and willing to do anything in my power."

Harper, the "over-rented" farmer from Barthorpe-Bottoms in the East Riding of Yorkshire, prospered on his handsome property in Cumberland, Nova Scotia, opened a store in or around the fort itself, and then, when his house was burnt by American raiders during the war, sold out (to his son-in-law), and bought valuable property in nearby Sackville. There he remained, embroiled in lawsuits to retain title to his property and to expand it, prosperous and enterprising. There he raised his family, and there he died, in 1820, aged ninety.[54]

Harper's initial prosperity was unusual, though the more one explores these biographies the more one is impressed with the evidence, if not of affluence then at least of the absence of poverty among these emigrants. The Harri-

[54]Christopher Harper to Lord William Campbell, Barthorpe-Bottoms, March 4, 1775, DesBarres Papers, series 5, vol. 18; Deed of Land, John Huston to Christopher Harper, June 6, 1775, Book C, Deed Book 24, Cumberland County Deeds; Robinson and Rispin, *Journey*, p. 38; Harper Petitions, in Westmorland County, 1788 (note 25 above); Milner, *Sackville*, pp. 167, 169; David G. Near, "A Decade of Yorkshire Occupation on Chignecto: 1772–1782" (unpub. essay, 1977, Mt. Allison Univ. Library, Sackville, N.B.), app. I (Sackville burial records).

sons, who claimed that they had been "forced to leave the kingdom" because of the increases in rents, must have spent several hundred pounds on transportation and resettlement. One group among the settlers of 1774 and 1775 from the North Riding of Yorkshire seems to have included some particularly prosperous people. Arriving on the *Albion* in 1774, they settled initially to the west of their countrymen—not along the rivers that empty into the Cumberland Basin (especially the Hébert, Maccan, and Nappan) but along the banks of the Petitcodiac and Memramcook rivers, which flow into Shepody Bay, the other upper arm of the Bay of Chignecto, twenty-five miles or so to the west of Cumberland. In this rich area, once reserved for war veterans and long a target for land speculators, Michael Francklin had established a land claim equivalent in size to his land on the Hébert, and it was undoubtedly Francklin who encouraged these voyagers aboard the *Albion* to settle there. They had an advance agent and property scout in the person of John Weldon, from the North Riding village of Crathorne, close to—almost adjoining—Charles Dixon's Hutton Rudby, and, like that hamlet part of the district, recently "burnt over" by Methodism.

Weldon, one of Francklin's recruits of 1772, had selected for himself a promising parcel of land in what became Hillsborough Township along the Petitcodiac River and had equipped it with livestock and other necessities. Then he had sent for his family. His wife of twelve years, Ann Dale, thirty-eight, and their four children arrived in April 1774, and the Weldon family began their well-financed entry into life on the northeastern borderland. A year later a census of Hillsborough reported that Weldon's livestock included 22 oxen, 26 cows, 6 horses, 32 sheep, and 18 swine—a remarkable collection for a frontier farm—and that he was producing 90 bushels of wheat and 185 bushels of other grains and vegetables—barley, pease, oats, turnips, and potatoes—and 10 pounds of flax. Further, he quickly changed his status from that of tenant to that of landowner. In 1780 he sold what claim he had to the land he had worked on the Petitcodiac to another of the Yorkshire emigrants of 1774 and moved to property of his own, a few miles east, in Dorchester, on the Memramcook. There he remained (though he acquired land elsewhere), head of a family of eight, a justice of the peace, and a founding member of the Methodist church in Point de Bute.[55]

Some of the Yorkshiremen who followed Weldon to the western branch of these settlements off Shepody Bay seem to have been even more affluent than Weldon. Joshua Gildart, a forty-eight-year-old husbandman from Carlton, in Coverdale in the North Riding, traveling with his nephew John, nineteen, also rented land from Francklin on the Petitcodiac—150

[55]Brebner, *Neutral Yankees*, pp. 61, 114; Weldon Family Genealogy, enclosure in Carrie B. Weldon to J. Clarence Webster, Sept. 21, 1945, Webster Collection, 7001/114; A General Return of Families . . . in the Township of Hillsborough . . . June 1783, box 21, pkt. 4, and Humphreys, "Settlement of Salisbury Parish," Ganong Collection, box 20, pkt. 3, pp. 3, 9, 10.

acres, two-thirds of which during the first ten years he actively cultivated. But he was no ordinary farmer. Within a year of his arrival he had acquired even more livestock than Weldon, and was engaged in a variety of enterprises. The upright Charles Dixon, endorsing a petition of Gildart's for land grants in 1787, testified to the governor of Nova Scotia that Gildart had been "a man of property at home"; that he had brought three servants with him to Nova Scotia; that in addition to renting land from Francklin he had bought more than 500 acres farther up the Petitcodiac, at Monckton—he had been the first person enterprising enough to open up that still remote area; that he had sunk no less than £300 in improvements in the land he controlled in the province and had spent another "suppose 159 pounds" in repairing the damage done by American "merodors" (marauders) during the war; and that his affairs in Yorkshire were such that he was obliged to return there on business during the years 1784–1787, leasing his Nova Scotia land, through an agent, to his nephew John. Gildart received the grants he sought—a total of 753 acres on both sides of the Petitcodiac, near its juncture with a river he called, after his native region, the Coverdale. In 1800, back in England once again, he sold that property, which had been granted to him for his earlier investments, for £260, probably to relatives in Nova Scotia.[56]

No doubt a large number—perhaps most—of the Yorkshire settlers on the Petitcodiac and elsewhere off the Bay of Shepody were in fact ordinary farmers in financial straits, but the enumeration of their livestock and production in the Hillsborough census of 1775[57] reveals an unusually high level of affluence for a working population of farmers one year after their arrival, and the leading figures in the group were certainly people of means.

So too were the leaders of that special group of Scotsmen that sailed from the Lowlands to the island of St. John on the *Lovely Nelly* in May 1775. Theirs was a clannish, quite private expedition. The passengers aboard the *Lovely Nelly* consisted of 30 families comprising 127 people, traveling together with only 23 unaffiliated individuals. Almost every one of these 150 voyagers came from communities clustered in a short span of the southwest coast of Scotland. This was no ragtag collection of desperate Highlanders like those who had emigrated on the *Hector*, but substantial fare-paying Lowlands farmers, clerks, and artisans; even the laborers among them paid their own way. Their leader, Walward or Wellwood Waugh—who described himself to the customs officials as a joiner, was well educated and related, it was generally believed, to a landed family, the Lairds of Barnbarrock—had come from Brownmoor in Annan, but he appears to have had

[56]Humphreys, "Settlement of Salisbury Parish," pp. 3–7; Humphreys, "Settlers on the Pollet River," p. 2; Humphreys, "Some Account of . . . the Geldart Family . . . ," pp. 1–10: all in Ganong Collection.
[57]Included in the General Return of . . . Hillsborough . . . 1783 (note 55, above).

property in nearby Lockerbie. Traveling with his wife and five children, Waugh was responding to enticements, probably from the lord advocate, Montgomery, to settle at Georgetown on the island of St. John. He and his half-brother William Campbell organized the expedition, hired the ship, and, with the support of the other heads of families, stocked it with provisions, household possessions, and even books.

The *Lovely Nelly* stopped like a taxi boat first at the Isle of Man, then at Whitehaven, and finally at Kirkcudbright to pick up designated family groups, and it deposited its well-supplied passengers, as planned, at Georgetown, St. John. But thereafter nothing went as planned. The Scotsmen were hit by fatal disasters in the winter of 1775 and the early spring of 1776: first a plague of rodents that destroyed both provisions and crops, then a destructive raid by drunken American sailors. They would have starved to death if they had not been helped by friendly Acadians in the neighborhood. In the late spring of 1776 the community, its members sickly and debilitated, dissolved. Some dispersed through the countryside. The main group, now reduced to fifteen families led by Waugh, crossed the Northumberland Strait to Pictou, Nova Scotia, and threw themselves on the mercy of the *Hector*'s Highlanders, then just beginning to secure themselves in the land. Treated hospitably, most of the Lowlanders remained there, on property once claimed by the Philadelphia Company and the Witherspoon associates; but the leaders moved once more, seeking greater opportunities. Waugh ended up some thirty miles to the west, on DesBarres's land at Tatamagouche, where he quickly reestablished a superior position.

In 1785 DesBarres's representative, John Macdonald, after visiting the Tatamagouche area and talking with all the tenants, described Waugh as DesBarres's "principal setler and agent there." Waugh and his two recently married sons leased 1,000 acres a few miles up the Tatamagouche River, for which they paid the highest rent of any of DesBarres's tenants, £15 a year. When you approach Waugh's land from the sea, Macdonald wrote, it had "a wild and raw like appearance; but in good weather it is not destitute of romantic beauty." And the Waughs, he reported, were industrious and full of enterprise, "strenuously . . . clearing and improving this difficult soil." They were, in fact, "as fit for any business by sea or land as any in America. They do their own iron work—have erected a small grist mill for their domestic use on the farm," and in partnership with others were building a sawmill. Their enterprise extended beyond Tatamagouche itself: they drove their cattle through seventy miles of primitive roads direct to the Halifax markets, and dealt with the merchants there. They were "hospitable and obliging to strangers, as myself have experienced." And, in addition to all of this, one of them served as a justice of the peace. In sum, Macdonald wrote, the Waughs "excite all the life or stirr that appears to be in the place, which indeed is no great matter, but without them it would be dead to all intents." Naturally, they were not content to remain tenants indefinitely; they were in the midst of complicated negotiations with DesBarres's legal representative to purchase the property they worked. And to protect their own sizable stake in the land they had acted strenuously to defend the whole of DesBarres's estate at Tatamagouche, including the cattle he had leased to the tenants, from seizure and dispossession by DesBarres's creditors.

But the Waughs' stake was not confined to their lease and eventual purchase of DesBarres's thousand acres. They had "more promising wood lands in other parts." As the leading inhabitants of the region, they were looked upon by the other resident farmers with envy and some resentment, especially when they acted, as they did from time to time, as *de facto* landlords, seeking to protect DesBarres's as well as their own interest in the land. But they did not appear to mind the resentment they stirred. They knew they were dealing with what Macdonald called "a number of ignorant people" whom no one, no matter how cautious and reasonable, could please all the time. Waugh knew his rights and something of the law. When "the ignorant court of common pleas for the county" ruled against him despite the evidence in his favor, he went straight to the supreme court in Halifax and won a quick reversal.

Well-educated, sophisticated, self-confident, active, and enterprising, Waugh, like a surprising number of the emigrants of 1774–1775, had been a man of some property before he left Britain, and, despite all the misfortunes that befell the voyagers on the *Lovely Nelly*, he managed to re-create that position in the Nova Scotia borderland.[58]

Competence and Emergence

But such initial affluence and its successful transference to the wilderness world of Nova Scotia is not the most common theme in these many emigrant biographies. The typical history is, rather, the story of a modest competence largely absorbed in the process of transplantation, and then the development, through years of labor, of substantial property and minor prominence in the New World. Of such quite typical and modest careers, that of William Pipes, Jr., may be taken as a model. And the peculiar skill he brought with him from Yorkshire, or quickly learned from his countrymen in the marshlands bordering the Bay of Fundy, is an important part of the story.

[58]MacKay, *Scotland Farewell*, pp. 154–155; Patterson, *Pictou*, pp. 94–97; Macdonald, "Information Respecting the [DesBarres] Estate of Tat[a]magouche in Nova Scotia . . . [1795]," Public Archives of Nova Scotia, *Report for the Year 1945* (1946), pp. xxviii–xxix, xxx, xxxiii, xxxv, xli, xlii.

His father, William Pipes, Sr., a farmer, was one of the 188 men, women, and children who left Yorkshire on the *Albion,* from Hull, in early March 1774, explaining their emigration as the result of "advances" in their rents.[59] Then 49 years of age, he was traveling together with two sons, both "husbandmen"—William, Jr., 22, and Jonathan, 20. The family followed the usual route of the Yorkshire emigrants, from Halifax to the Cumberland Basin and the marshy farmlands along the rivers that flowed into it. For several years they lived in Amherst Township, working "with great spirit," as other Yorkshiremen were doing, at the edge of the marshland, ditching, draining, and reclaiming arable fields from soil constantly washed by tidal waters.[60] How skilled Pipes became at this specialized work, necessary throughout the Fundy shorelands, is not known. Other Yorkshiremen from the Vales of Pickering and York proved to be experts. William Cornforth, for example, one of Pipes's shipmates aboard the *Albion,* during the same years not only diked and drained the lands he himself rented but was hired to supervise similar efforts elsewhere on the isthmus.

Such expertise was not accidental. Yorkshiremen were commonly familiar with the problems of wetland farming, as New Englanders were not. For large areas of the lower East Riding were salt marshes and fenland in process of reclamation, and to the north, where most of the emigrants came from, streams running sluggishly through flat-floored valleys with slight gradients flooded frequently, creating waterlogged clays and strips of "carrs," spongy peat marshes that held water even in dry seasons. An estimated 17,500 acres along the banks of the Rye and Derwent rivers, prime centers of emigration in the mid-1770s, were known to be either "greatly damaged or rendered entirely useless by the overflowings of those rivers," and a variety of techniques were used to contain this waste, as well as control some of the bogs on the moorlands. Many Yorkshire farmers, Pipes among them, in all probability, were experienced in, or at least knew something of the technique of, ditching, draining, and building floodgates to create arable land out of the water-soaked fields and to maintain the land's utility.[61]

So the Pipeses began by helping to reclaim farmland from the tidal marshes in and around Amherst. Then the family divided. In 1783 William, Sr., led the list of twenty applicants for the ten-thousand-acre government grant on the Maccan River; his son Jonathan was an applicant too. Two

[59]The *Albion:* T47/9/84–90.
[60]Robinson and Rispin, *Journey,* p. 37. These two investigating farmers came from the Yorkshire villages of Bewholm and Fangfoss, which were at the edge of an area of active reclamation in these years. Their account of Nova Scotia has a heavy emphasis on ditching, draining, and reclamation.
[61]Wynn, "Bay of Fundy Marshlands," p. 87; John Tuke, *General View of the Agriculture of the North Riding of Yorkshire . . .* (London, 1794), p. 20; June A. Sheppard's two pamphlets for the East Yorkshire Local History Society: *The Draining of the Hull Valley* (1958) and *The Draining of the Marshlands of South Holderness and the Vale of York* (1966).

years later they probably took up their five-hundred-acre grants, either separately or in a combined enterprise. William, Jr., meanwhile, had rented land, at the usual nominal cost, a few miles south of Amherst, part of the property owned by DesBarres. There, along the third of the rivers that empty into the Cumberland Basin, the Nappan, he built his farm. Twenty years later, married (to a woman from the West Riding), and the father of five daughters and three sons, he still worked that farm, and had become a prominent figure in the district. His farm on the Nappan was one of those "beautiful" establishments that so impressed DesBarres's agent, Macdonald, when in 1795 he reported to DesBarres on the condition of the property he owned on the Nappan and Maccan rivers. Pipes, Macdonald reported, was "an intelligent, respectable farmer."

> His place bears every mark of spirit and hard labor. His marsh is dyked—a considerable extent of ground cleared—one orchard planted and a larger one under preparation. He has a good house, which he means to enlarge, as his family has increased. This year he has erected one of the best barns I have seen in the country, with the best conveniences, at an expense which cannot be under £150. It is 52 feet long, 32 wide, and 20 high . . . and he regrets not having made it twenty feet longer, for the purpose of containing more hay. The situation of it is admirably judicious. Its lower story is for the cattle, the upper is for corn and hay and the threshing floor, with contrivances for conveying straw and hay to the stalls below, and the bullock may easily draw a load of hay or corn into the upper story. The work is very substantial.

But Pipes was not simply a prosperous farmer whose "large family and the people he employs consume 2,000 weight of pork and beef annually." He had successfully concluded a large-scale public enterprise with another Yorkshireman, Thomas Coates. Coates, one of the emigrants of 1772, had come from the village of Thirlby, a dozen miles west of Hovingham, at the southern end of the long ridge of dark, desolate, and particularly wet moors known as Black Hambleton; he was certainly acquainted with the techniques used in Yorkshire for wetlands reclamation. Pipes and Coates had been frustrated for years by the tidal currents in the Nappan Valley; "they cannot stir a mile or two from home," Macdonald wrote, "without being obliged to wait for the return of the next favorable tide." They had therefore decided to construct what proved to be "a handsome, useful bridge" over the Nappan River and its water-soaked margins. They collected subscriptions amounting to £180 from the other farmers in the district, invested substantially themselves, and after much difficulty attempting to sink and secure timber pilings in marshland swept by huge tidal flows, managed to get the bridge built. Not only were their own lives made easier as a result, but the whole region was greatly benefited since the road from Halifax to the isthmus—much of it still a crude bridle path and blazed trail but nevertheless the major overland link from the metropolis to the Yorkshire settlements—could now go directly north, in fact along Pipes's farm, rather than having to circle far east, via a ferry, to the left bank of the Hébert.

Pipes's success was modest but impressive. A prominent resident of the Nappan region, he was consulted by Macdonald, and indeed his views are reflected in Macdonald's recommendations to DesBarres. But none of this had come easily. When Pipes first broke ground on the Nappan, Macdonald reported, he had had a terrible time simply surviving. Often, Pipes recalled to Macdonald, he had trudged miles into the woods to collect a bushel of grain "and carried it over the snow upon his back to the mill." It took him years to figure out ways of bringing his animals and fowl safely through the severe winters. And there had been periods when he could not pay his rent, small as it was. At one point he had been three years in arrears, and if then the overdue rent "had been peremptorily exacted, he had never been able to get over it." But now the great struggle was over. He is, Macdonald wrote, "upon the even of being comfortable for life. Once he shall have finished his houses and renewed the fences he will have no more jobs to call him off the working of the lands all the year over."[62]

The initial exhaustion of assembled resources, the struggle for survival, and the eventual establishment, after years of labor in primitive conditions, of a secure position in this open, chaotic frontier world—all of this was typical of the lives of most emigrants to Nova Scotia in the 1770s. Not everyone succeeded, of course. Some never recovered from the initial shock; some returned home. In 1776 Thomas Wheatley, a fifty-three-year-old farmer from the neighborhood of Northallerton in the North Riding, who had arrived the year before on the *Jenny*, managed to get a free trip back to England aboard a military transport. As companions he had the young Hill family from Sutton-on-the-Forest near York (father, mother, and three small children) who had arrived on the *Albion* in 1774. But it is significant that both Wheatley and the Hills had been tentative, experimental, in the first place ("going to purchase *or return*," Wheatley had told the customs officials; "in *hopes* of making a purchase of lands," the Hills had said). And it is significant also that when they appealed to the commanding general in Halifax, Eyre Massey, for transportation, explaining that they had met "no encouragement in America" and were unable to support themselves, General Massey thought their "distresses" offered a special opportunity to help the government fight emigration. He explained to the

[62]Draft of Grant to William Pipes and 19 Others . . . Dec. 1783, NS Land Papers, vols. 13–15; BMD Records; Macdonald's Report on DesBarres's Estate on the Rivers Maccan and Nappan (n. 27, above); Coates Genealogy; Young, *Six Months Tour*, II, 88–89.

secretary of state that, since they "seemed heartily sick of their jaunt," sending them back "might have a proper effect at home, to prevent the old country from losing so many of her subjects."[63]

The Evangelical Impulse

Such returns, much talked about, were in fact infrequent. The overwhelming number of voyagers remained in Nova Scotia and established themselves, however modestly, after struggles during the first few years. In these difficulties a large number were fortified, as Dixon and others of the earlier years had been, by religious faith—impelled, like so many settlers in America before them, by the passionate desire to draw apart from a corrupt and abusive world and to create a refuge for themselves and their community on the far margins of the British periphery.

In the three years before the Revolution the Methodist influence was spread widely through the English emigration to Nova Scotia, but it concentrated with a peculiar intensity in the emigrants from the northernmost districts of Yorkshire—from a string of villages in the dales that began at the far western end of the Rye Valley and reached north along the east side of the Hambleton Hills, across some of the most rugged of the North York Moors, into the Cleveland Hills, down the valley of the Leven River, ending in the low flat land along the Durham-Yorkshire border at the River Tees. How many of the emigrants to Nova Scotia from these north Yorkshire villages—Hawnby, Snilesworth, Bilsdale, Rudby, Hutton Rudby, Crathorne, Kirk Leavington, Yarm—were Methodists is not known. But it is a suggestive fact that, while the number of Methodists in Yorkshire as a whole rose approximately 19% in the peak years of the emigration, 1774–1776, the membership in the Yorkshire Dales alone *fell* 26%. And to these north Yorkshire villages must be added other centers of Methodist emigration to Nova Scotia in neighboring Durham, and especially villages in the vicinity of Newcastle, like Swalwell, already a hothouse of Wesleyan Methodism and soon to nourish a succession of evangelical offshoots and secessions: Primitive Methodists, New Connexion Methodists, Tent Methodists, Methodist "reformers" of all kinds.[64]

It was from Swalwell that one of the most eloquent testimonies to the evangelical spirit in the Nova Scotia emigration derives. "Dear Loving Niece," wrote Francis Allen in December 1774 to Mrs. George Forster, recently settled in Nova Scotia, "I hope . . . you are pleasantly and agreeably situated." But "it is no matter," he comforted her, "where we are situated if GOD is with us. His presence makes our Paradise. It is but a little while

[63] Major General Eyre Massey to Lord George Germain, Halifax, June 27–28, 1776, CO 217/52.
[64] *Minutes of the Methodist Conferences*, I, 99.

before we shall be called hence, being only strangers, pilgrims, and sojourners upon earth, and then I hope we shall take possession of an house, not made with hands, eternal in the heavens." Most things back in Swalwell, he said, were unchanged. He reviewed the state of the preaching circuits and explained who was active and who was not; and he sent greetings from the whole sisterhood and brotherhood that his niece had left behind. She was now remote from them all, and he deeply felt her absence ("I wish [the muskatoes] would bite you so as to make you come back to Old England for a cure"), but he told her not to regret the loss of the "means of grace and the valuable privileges you enjoyd in Old England." If the Lord is with you, he reminded her, you will find the way to salvation, and if you are faithful "who knows what a blessing you may be to those that are near you." The great prize is all that counts: a crown of eternal life for all who are faithful unto death. So be constant in faith, he exhorted her, be pious. True piety, Allen wrote,

> carries its own reward with it. Example and precept together, thro[ugh] the Lord, will have a happy effect on yourselves and others. Let your dear Redeemer and Best Friend tell of His goodness and invite all you can to Him. Be watchful, resist the Devil and he must flee from you. Yea, your Captain will bruise him under your feet. May the LORD bless you with constant peace, true happiness, and contentment, power, humility, and love, a heaven within and eternal glory in the world to come, and if we never meet in this world may the LORD grant that we may meet at His right hand, to part no more. Amen and Amen.[65]

The exalted tone, the exhortation to fortitude in the faith, and the elegiac expression of human loss and potential spiritual gain—all of this is typical of the surviving writings of the Methodists among the emigrants, especially of their correspondence with their co-religionists in England. Of Mrs. Forster nothing is known, save that in 1773 she and her husband had bought land on a "fine dry hill" on Fort Lawrence Ridge overlooking the marshes and bogs that surrounded the forts, and that they had begun their farm on that ridge, "much exposed to winds & weather."[66] But of others of her persuasion who arrived in Nova Scotia in 1773 and after, much is known. The Truemans, the Chapmans, and especially the Blacks, together with a few of the earlier arrivals like the Dixons and the Weldons, were the leading figures in this transplanted religious community, and of their affairs the records are full.

---

[65] Francis Allen to [Mrs. Forster], Swalwell, Dec. 18, 1774, Webster Collection, 7001/337.
[66] Robinson and Rispin, *Journey*, pp. 37–38.

The Truemans had lived in the North Riding, in what the family called "the old habitation," Helm House, a gray stone farmhouse, whose foundations are still standing, where members of their family and their kin the Chapmans had lived for generations. The house was located just off the road that runs north through the long, deep, narrow valley of Bilsdale, a sinuous cleavage that winds between hills a thousand feet high topped by miles of rugged moorland. A few miles to the south of Helm House lay the ruins of the ancient Cistercian abbey of Rievaulx, even in the eighteenth century a popular tourist attraction, and the market town of Helmsley at the head of the broad Rye Valley. To the west lay Snilesworth Moor where the Truemans' kinsmen the Flintofts lived; and to the north lay some of the wildest moor country east of the Pennines, eventuating in the lowland towns where the Dixons and Weldons had lived.[67]

William Trueman, at fifty-two a senior figure in a farming community of enthusiastic Methodists in and around Bilsdale, described himself as a miller to the customs officials when he boarded the *Albion* with his wife and twenty-two-year-old son. But he had farmed too, on land in Bilsdale owned by Thomas Duncombe, Esq., another "improving" landlord who, like Beilby Thompson, Thomas Worsley, and William Weddell, was engaged in developing a "noble seat." His mansion at Duncombe Park, eight miles south of Trueman's Helm House, had been designed by Vanbrugh and was one of the most elegant country houses in England: a work of art, both outside and in. Its ornamented grounds, with broad lawns, carefully crafted terraces, artfully placed hillside temples, and magnificent vistas, inspired Arthur Young to rhapsodies in his *Six Months Tour through the North of England* (1771). The enormous interior rooms, with their Corinthian pillars, their ceilings covered with "very delicately executed" bas-reliefs, and above all their spectacular paintings—by Rubens, Rembrandt, Titian, Correggio, Leonardo, Poussin, Lorrain, and a dozen others—gave Young "the most rapturous delight" and in the end overtaxed his powers of description. But all of this magnificence had to be maintained, and while Duncombe had various sources of income, one of them was rents, and it was his rent increases that drove his tenant Trueman, among others, off the land.[68]

The small, mature Trueman family followed the usual route of these emigrating Yorkshire farmers—from their moorside farms and ancient villages to an east coast port, Hull in this case, then, after a six- or eight-week ocean voyage of some danger and great discomfort, to the small, bustling

[67]For a descendant's detailed and romantic description of the eighteenth-century physical setting of the Trueman family in Yorkshire, see George J. Trueman (then president of Mt. Allison Univ.) to J. C. Webster, Sackville, N.B., May 24, 1939, Webster Collection, 7001/143; Elinor Trueman to [her cousin], Helmhouse, Bilsdale, March 7, 1805, in Howard Trueman, *The Chignecto Isthmus and Its First Settlers* (Toronto, 1902), p. 104.
[68]Young, *Six Months Tour*, II, 73–87; Bigland, *Yorkshire*, pp. 272–277.

colonial harbor town of Halifax, thence by schooner to the stockaded fort at Cumberland, and finally to the uninhabited and uncultivated countryside on or near the Chignecto Isthmus, where they began their new lives on rented land.

The Truemans too went through the characteristic initial shock and despair in confronting a wilderness world, and then recovered as they found their way. Within a year of their arrival, word got back to relatives in Snilesworth that they were "in a very poor situation," that they had found "no where to sattle," and that they "would have returnd back to Old England but had nothing to pay [their] pasage with." Their friends and relatives immediately rallied to raise money for their return, but then in November 1775 word arrived from the Truemans themselves that all was well, that they were in good health, and that in fact they liked "Nove," as the family referred to Nova Scotia, very well. But the relatives were still anxious, for the Truemans' souls as well as for their bodies. Do you have a proper place to worship in? they wrote. Do you "meet amongst your selves acording to the usuall way of the Methedests"? "Dear brother and friends," Sarah Bentley wrote Trueman in February 1776, remember that "the means of grace is profitable if they be used aright and to the glory of our God; and if you have them not, remember you have a God to go to that is allways ready to hear the prayers of all them that call upon Him in sencerity and truth." Call upon Him in time. In the end we will all "have to give an acount for the tallants that we have been intrusted with."

> So let us be like the wise virgans, with oyl in our lamps and our lights shining, so that when ever the Lord shall call us out of this world we may be made partakers for the next. Dear brother and sister, if you find dificultes here below, as I expect you do, cast not away your shield but look unto Jesus, who art the author of your faith, untill He become the full finisher of your salvation. Let not the world nor the things of the world ever cheat any of us of our better part, but let us always watch unto prayer and keep close to God that we may be made happy here in time and happy here after for ever more; and if we never have the opportunety to see each other here below, grant that we may all meet at last in the persute of rest to our poor souls, to praise God for ever more.[69]

The relatives in Snilesworth need not have been concerned for the Truemans' welfare, either physical or spiritual. After they recovered from the initial shock and found their bearings, they flourished. Three years after

---

[69]Sarah Bentley to William and Ann Trueman, Feb. 9, 1776, and Andrew and Mary Flintoft to same, Feb. 9, 1776, Webster Collection, 7001/313.

their arrival, having worked on rented land, they bought their first parcel of American property, indirectly from Joshua Mauger, M.P., once Nova Scotia's leading entrepreneur and now a merchant in Poole, England, but still involved in the colony's affairs. From him they bought, for £90 of Nova Scotia money, 134 acres of upland and marshland on the north side of the isthmus, close to the shores of Northumberland Strait. There, fifteen miles removed from the central settlements on the isthmus, they lived and worked for twelve years, until in 1789 they made their major purchase. For the equivalent in local money of approximately £585 sterling they bought 800 acres, 500 of them uncultivated, only four miles north of Fort Cumberland. On this choice property, which became known as Prospect Farm, the Truemans lived in increasing prosperity—and indeed the family continued to live there for at least five successive generations, into the twentieth century.

To general farming they added milling, with equipment powered first by horses, then by wind, finally by water. Acre by acre, arable fields were worked out of the wild land, and between 1797 and 1799 a handsome new brick house and a large barn were added: the house was still lived in by Trueman's descendants in 1900, who declared it to be "as comfortable a dwelling as it has ever been." By the time that house had been completed (1799) William Trueman, Sr., was two years dead; his wife followed him in 1800, aged eighty-four. Their successor at Prospect Farm, William, Jr., had married a distant relative, Elizabeth Keillor, the daughter of a large family of Methodists who had emigrated from Skelton, near York, and had settled near the Truemans on the isthmus. She bore William six sons and two daughters, and it was probably she and her husband who received the last recorded letter from the Truemans at Helm House, Bilsdale. In response to letters from the Truemans at Prospect Farm, their cousins John and "Helling" (Helen or Elinor) wrote from the old stone farmhouse in the Yorkshire dales, not exhorting their relatives to maintain the love of God but listing impersonally the family marriages, the names and fortunes of their five children, and the physical condition of the older folk the Americans might still remember. Their landlords, the Duncombes, as another cousin had reported five years earlier, had continued to make "general rasements" of rent, but "since the peace the times are pretty good"; crops were plentiful, despite wet weather and flooding, "and we have a fine season for reaping the same."[70]

But the original Methodist fervor had not faded; it remained strong in

[70]Trueman, *Chignecto Isthmus*, pp. 88–89, 99, 94, 97–98 (John and Helling Trueman to "Cousins" [Trueman], Helmhouse, Bilsdale, Aug. 15, 1789); Harmon Trueman to William Trueman ("at Prospect [Farm] near Cumberland, Nova Scotia, West Indies"), Kirby Malzard "nigh Rippon, Yorkshire," Oct. 12, 1783, Webster Collection, 7001/314. On Mauger, see above, n. 14.

the Trueman family and their kinsmen for at least three full generations. The immigrants of 1774 and 1775 worshiped first in houses and barns. And then in 1788, after the first meeting of the Methodist Conference in the Maritime Provinces and after the creation of a Cumberland Circuit, a church building was constructed, at Point de Bute, less than a mile from Trueman's Prospect Farm.

The land for this "preaching house and burying-ground" was given by William Chapman to "John Wesley and his successors in the Methodist line forever." Chapman, then fifty-eight, had arrived with his wife and their nine children fourteen years earlier, in the shipment of north Yorkshire people aboard the *Albion,* and they had settled near their friends the True-mans on the isthmus. They had come from Hawnby, less than three miles as the crow flies from Helm House, four or five miles along the footpaths over the moors and along the lower slope of the intervening thousand-foot height known as Easterside. In earlier years in Hawnby the Chapmans had shared the life of the spirit with the whole communion of Methodists in the rugged northern strip of the North Riding, and in later years their kin in Hawnby kept the Cumberland community informed of the "Hawnby love feasts," of the lives and deaths of the original Methodists, and of the home family's continuing struggle, "feebly creeping towards the mark for the prize of our high calling of God in Christ Jesus."

Along with William Chapman and his prolific wife, Jane, as subscribers to the building of the Methodist stone church at Point de Bute in 1788, were all the prominent names of the Methodists in the North Riding emigration of the 1770s—Dixon, Trueman, Coates, Weldon, Keillor, Wells, Harrison, Ripley, Metcalf. But to contemporaries the most resonant name on that list of twenty-eight members of the church was that of William Black, a boy of fourteen at his emigration in 1775 but by 1788 the spiritual leader of the entire Nova Scotia Methodist communion.[71]

Black's religious vocation had been born in agonizing struggles to overcome a sinfulness he felt as early as the age of five. Son of a devout Huddersfield linen draper and grocer wealthy enough to have visited Nova Scotia and to have bought property at Amherst a year before the family emigrated, and son too of a mother once agonized by sin and then ecstatically redeemed, young William went through years of soul-searching in Nova Scotia. He struggled with his love of pleasure while sharing the Yorkshire settlers' devotions and their countless "love feasts," prayer sessions, and joyful exhortations.

[71]Indenture between William Chapman and John Wesley, Sept. 18, 1788, and James Chapman to William Trueman [Yorkshire, 1789], in Trueman, *Chignecto Isthmus,* pp. 76, 187; George J. Trueman, "Church History of Point de Bute," typescript, Pine Hill Divinity Hall Archives, Halifax, Nova Scotia.

At the age of nineteen he began to see a clearer path to holy life, and, stimulated by an elderly Methodist of powerful conviction who came from Prudhoe, outside Newcastle, he devoted himself to prayer. "For some months," he wrote in his journal, "we met almost every night, to sing and pray; generally continuing from a little after sun-down, until midnight. Frequently, I with another remained till day-light. To weep—to fast—to pray—was now become as my meat and drink. . . . I thought, I talked, of Jesus; nor could I bear to hear of any thing but what had a tendency to lead my soul to him." Finally, he felt himself saved, and his life was transformed.

Convinced of God's redemptive powers, he turned to his family and sought to save them too. Then at the age of twenty-one he became a public preacher. He concentrated first on the world he knew best, the Yorkshire settlers on the isthmus, then turned to the surrounding areas, traveling as an itinerant preacher south to the farmers in the Hébert-Nappan-Maccan district, west to the Petitcodiac, then down the west coast of the Bay of Fundy and over the bay once again to Annapolis and Halifax. By the time the church at Point de Bute was built, he was known far and wide as a powerful proselytizer and a zealous organizer, and had become a regular correspondent of John Wesley, whose salutations quickly progressed from "My Dear Brother" to "Dear Billy." In 1789, aged twenty-nine, Black was appointed superintendent of the Methodist societies in Nova Scotia, New Brunswick, and Newfoundland, and thereafter became one of the most important Methodist leaders in North America. Known as Bishop Black, he was commonly referred to, long before his death in 1834, as the father of Methodism in Nova Scotia and New Brunswick.

His roots lay in the passionate evangelicalism of north Yorkshire Methodism, now transferred to the Isthmus of Chignecto and elsewhere in Nova Scotia, and he never lost touch with that transplanted community. One of his greatest satisfactions lay in the help he was able to give to his brother John, who in 1786 settled on a large but entirely wild property on the River Philip, twenty miles east of the isthmus, and who struggled there for years under the most primitive conditions. Like so many of these immigrants of the seventies from the North Riding of Yorkshire, John proved to be not only a capable frontier farmer, a small-time merchant, and a local magistrate, but, with his brother's strong encouragement, a preacher as well. His strenuous religious faith suited well the demanding physical struggles he endured until he succeeded in conquering a small portion of the North American environment and in creating a measure of security for himself and his family.[72]

---

[72]Matthew Richey, *A Memoir of the Late Rev. William Black* . . . (Halifax, 1839), pp. 6–8, 22–25, 35, 47, 158, 201, 253, 365, 202–203; Black's Narrative.

The Forming of a New Society

So, in the years of the Register's compilation, voyagers from Yorkshire helped settle a portion of the northeastern corner of the British-American borderland. Drawn largely from the county's East and North ridings—from the broad valley of the Rye, from the bleak, jagged moorlands of the Hambleton and Cleveland Hills and the North York Moors, and from the gentler countryside along the Tees—they were farmers of some little substance, not young, traveling with entire, sometimes quite large, families. In their exodus they became deracinated, but once settled in "Nove"—a distant region of the world that became part of Yorkshire's life[73]—they became rootless no more. Most of them eventually prospered on farms they created out of wilderness land, and over the years became part of a new, derivative society. It was a society far less intricate, structured, and continuously interactive than the one they left behind, but one that allowed them autonomy—the "independance" that Luke Harrison discovered had become essential to his life. But if independent, they were not isolated individuals moving alone in the world, without human context. Communities formed out of complex networks of Anglo-American intermarriages spread throughout a large, thinly populated farming region. The children of these large families married children of others derived from the same Yorkshire emigration, and children too of the very few other English, and occasionally New England and Scottish, families that had otherwise arrived. The range was small and the network, consequently, tight. The same names recur repeatedly in the records of births, marriages, and deaths.

For thirty-three years Luke Harrison was the town clerk of the districts of Francklin Manor, the Elysian Fields, Maccan, and Nappan, and he kept careful records. They revealed a community of almost tribal endogamy. In 1781 Luke's brother John married Dinah (Diana in the customs Register) Lumley, the twenty-one-year-old daughter of Thomas Lumley who had emigrated from the Harrisons' own village of Rillington in the same month in 1774 for the usual reason, that his landlord, Mr. Knowsley, had raised the rents too high. Five years later John's sister Ann married Dinah's brother John, age six at the time of the migration. Harrisons married also Lodges, from Whitby, on the Yorkshire coast; Browns, from New Malton, four miles from Rillington; and Coateses from Thirlby, near Thirsk, a dozen miles west of Hovingham, two dozen miles from Rillington. The Weldons,

---

[73]The interpenetration of the two regions was so common that a farm in southeastern Yorkshire was officially known as "Nova-Scotia" in the early 19th century, and there is a farmhouse on the outskirts of Hawnby, in the heart of the north Yorkshire emigration region of the 1770s, that is still known by that name. Langdale, *Topographical Dictionary*, p. 185.

father and eldest son, both married Killians, mother and daughter. Two of William Trueman, Jr.'s seven sons married Ripley sisters, two others married Bent sisters. Two of William Chapman's sons also married sisters. The Keillors married into both the Trueman and Weldon families, and the Blacks and the Chapmans intermarried several times in the second American generation.

As the generations passed, the same names continued to recur, though new ones appeared too; but the identifying residences became local: no longer Rillington, Whitby, New Malton, Hovingham, Bilsdale, Hutton Rudby, Crathorne and Yarm, but Maccan, Halifax, River Hébert, Cobequid Mountain, River Philip, Shepody, Sackville, Point de Bute, and Barronsfield.[74]

The new world of the northeast borderland was developing swiftly. Stump-filled wilderness clearings at the edge of the massive forests were becoming well-fertilized farmlands, clusters of shacks that earlier had been falling into ruins were becoming stable crossroads hamlets, villages were becoming towns, and footpaths everywhere were broadening into a network of wagon trails and drovers' roads that laced the settlements together. But visitors in 1774 and 1775 still told of going for miles "through nothing but dreary wastes or forests of rocks and wood" without seeing a single inhabitant or sign of cultivation. Everyone on the farms—men, women, and children—went barefoot in the summer, and the women "instead of stays . . . wear a loose jacket like a bedgown" and trousers for protection against mosquitoes. The passengers on a vessel shipwrecked on the north shore of St. John in 1775 almost starved to death before contact could be made with the few settlers scattered through the island, and when they finally came on a building they "thought it had been a cow house or place for cattle but [were] informed it was a dwelling house." Crude log cabins, even wigwams, were still common on that island, and the settlers, living through the severe winters on salt fish and potatoes, were only beginning to create a life above the merest subsistence level.[75]

[74]BMD Records, supplemented by genealogical material cited in notes above.
[75]Robinson and Rispin, *Journey*, pp. 29, 49; "A Narrative of the Voyage of Thos. Curtis to the Island of St. John's in . . . 1775 . . . ," in *Journeys to the Island of St. John or Prince Edward Island 1775–1832*, ed. D. C. Harvey (Toronto, 1955), p. 38. Curtis's narrative of his voyage "as a steerage passenger" from London to Prince Edward Island on the *Elizabeth* in the fall of 1775 (the passengers are partly listed in the Register at T47/10/139), though written some years after the events depicted, is an extraordinarily vivid and detailed account of the difficulties of departure, of the peddling stopovers on the way out, of storms at sea and the conflicts among passengers of different social standings cooped up on a small vessel for weeks on end, of a shipwreck in a winter gale and the desperate effort of the survivors to keep alive on a deserted shore of the island, and then of the survivors' dismay at the utter primitiveness of the island's few settlements. There is no way of verifying the accuracy of Curtis's story, but if the mass of vivid details was invented, Curtis must have had a spectacular imagination and somehow memorized from others' tales the last twists and turns of circumstances on the *Elizabeth* and on the largely barren island in the years 1775–1777.

But the mixed population of the Nova Scotian core of this maritime marchland—Yorkshiremen and Scots, New Englanders and Acadians, Germans and Irish—recognized that they were at the beginning of a great surge of development, which "English farmers of substance" could easily impel forward. Fortunes in trade were being made in a few years and farmers were beginning to prosper. For the soil and all the resources of the land were rich, and "there are vast tracks of land at present unoccupied." Rents were trivial, taxes did not exist. The main problem was the lack of population. But that would soon change since energetic people would have "a better opportunity of supporting themselves more comfortably [in Nova Scotia] than they are ever likely to have in England." Why should anyone continue to struggle at home, "racked up till bread can scarce be got to supply the wants of their children"? The next twenty years were certain to see vast improvements in Nova Scotia, it was said, and those who undertook those developments "have greatly the advantage of those in England, as the land cleared and improved by the former is generally their own property while the latter are for the most part tenants, and, as is too frequently the case, after all the pains and expense they have been at for the improvement of their farms, are deprived of the enjoyment of the fruits of their industry." A new world and a new society: between masters and servants "there seems to be no distinction, and you scarce can know one from the other. They are all Misters and Sirs, and their maidens all Misses." It was a "land of liberty and freedom," where ordinary people like Luke Harrison, once of Rillington, Yorkshire, now a farmer along the River Maccan, found they could live "independant."[76]

[76]Robinson and Rispin, *Journey,* pp. 35, 46, 48, 47, 50, 27.

12

Failure in Xanadu

While in Nova Scotia, in the northeast corner of Britain's North American empire, a distinctive new world was forming from the movement westward of people from the north of Britain, a far stranger, more exotic society was emerging 2,000 miles to the south. In the same interwar years in which the Nova Scotian borderland was being peopled, efforts were being made to exploit and populate the far southern fringe of Britain's enormous new land acquisitions in North America: the coastal lands of Florida, and the gulf and river shores of the later states of Mississippi and Alabama. The crude settlements that were newly founded on these far margins of the deep south or that were taken over from the Spanish were Britain's first penetrations into a little-known land, utterly different from the maritime region in the far northeast.

What little the English had known before the 1760s of the semitropical territory south and west of Georgia had come from the leaders of military skirmishes with the Spanish in Florida, from the few British merchants who had bartered with the Spanish on the shores of the Gulf of Mexico, and above all from the Carolina traders ranging deep into the interior from the coastal entrepôt of Charleston. Year after year, since the late seventeenth century, these traders had organized caravans of packhorses which they had led or sent deep into Indian territory to trade, first with the nearby Creek tribes, then across Georgia, across Alabama, and eventually across Mississippi, on treks that took a year or more, to reach the Chickasaw tribes on the Mississippi River. By 1715 an average of 54,000 deerskins were being exported annually to England from the still primitive settlements on the southern Carolina coast—cargoes worth a small fortune; by the 1760s the number had almost tripled. It was from this Indian trade—with its half-savage trappers and woodsmen, many of them accepted members of the

430

Indian tribes in which they lived for most of each year; with its caravans of packhorses coming and going; with its log and bark warehouses serving as transfer centers at strategic points along the rivers; and with its fleets of canoes and flatboats piled high with animal skins—it was from this exotic trade that word had first been received of the rich semitropical wilderness that lay deep in Indian territory and behind the barriers of the Spanish forts.[1]

When in 1763 virtually all of the land east of the Mississippi became British, the forces of greed, ambition, and high entrepreneurial adventure, boiling up in the triumphant nation, spilled out into this unknown region of the south. The result was a hectic boom in land speculation, and a series of strange episodes in overseas migration—so strange, some of them, that they seem more likely to have sprung from the imagination of a Faulkner or a Poe than to have actually happened in the past. The purpose of these extraordinary efforts was the same as those of Francklin and DesBarres in the north, to profit by managing the transfer of Europeans to unopened lands in North America to which these entrepreneurs had claim. But while in the northeast the managers of migration succeeded in attracting sizable numbers of farming families from northern Britain, in the south such efforts failed, and these failures are as revealing of the forces at work as the successes in the north. For only gradually did the characteristics of an exotic society emerge—a world, not of family farms, worked and eventually owned by north British emigrants, but of plantations, large and small, worked by gangs of black slaves and nurturing a distinctive culture. Despite the proximity of these lands to the West Indies plantation islands, this outcome had not been predicted and had not been expected. Much wealth and hundreds of lives were lost as a result, until gradually the imperatives of the situation became clear. The process of this unanticipated emergence provides a dark backdrop for the successful transatlantic transfers of Europeans which took place elsewhere, and reveals in miniature, in one small corner of the British Atlantic world, something of the entrepreneurial effort and the complex filiations of influence and interest that lay behind the peopling of America.

Promotion, Visions, and First Plans

The initial steps in opening to settlement the newly acquired southern fringe of Britain's North American possessions were confident enough.

[1]Verner W. Crane, *The Southern Frontier, 1670–1732* (Durham, N.C., 1928), pp. 111, 330, chap. 5. For contemporary views of the savagery of the traders—"monsters in human form, the very scum and outcast of the earth . . . more prone to savage barbarity than the savages themselves"—see Cecil Johnson, *British West Florida, 1763–1783* (New Haven, 1943), p. 73n.

Shortly after the signing of the peace treaty of 1763—by which Spain ceded Florida to Britain in exchange for the return of Cuba, and France gave up its claim to the land east of the Mississippi—the British government divided the trans-Appalachian territory into three new provinces north and south of an immense Indian reserve: Quebec, East Florida, and West Florida. West Florida covered the southern half of the present states of Mississippi and Alabama, Louisiana east of the Mississippi, and most of the western panhandle of modern Florida. East Florida included all of the present state except the northwestern strip. Governors were appointed, both of them Scotsmen, and the apparatus of civil government was created in the pattern of the older colonies. But the main necessity in transforming this semitropical wilderness into a prosperous appendage of the British state was to open the land to settlement and draw into the area a substantial number of people capable of making the land profitable.

Procedures for land distribution were quickly adapted from established patterns. Land in both Floridas would be acquired either as township grants of up to 20,000 acres each, bestowed directly by the Privy Council in London, or, in smaller quantities, as "family" grants given by the governor and council in Florida to actual settlers in proportion to the size of their families. In both cases grants took the initial form of patent rights—the right to undertake a survey by which to locate a specific tract, the survey in turn to be submitted to the governor and council for confirmation as an actual title of possession. In both cases, too, grants were revocable unless one-third of the land was populated within three years with one white person for each hundred acres; after ten years any land not thus populated would revert to the crown. Special terms were offered to veterans of the late war, the benefits graduated by rank, from field officers down to private soldiers.[2]

The terms of land distribution were immediately advertised. In a notice that circulated widely in November 1763 the Board of Trade stated that it was aware that "many persons" were seeking land in the Floridas to raise "silk, cotton, wine, oil, indigo, cochineal, and other commodities to which the said lands are adapted." To facilitate such settlements it informed the public that it would survey quickly and make available the 20,000-acre grants to all applicants who would commit themselves "to settle the lands within a limited time, and at their own expence, with a proper number of useful and industrious Protestant inhabitants, either from His Majesty's other colonies or from foreign parts"—Protestants, that is, from anywhere but the British Isles.

As soon as the terms of the peace treaty were known, the possibility of

---

[2] *Ibid.*, pp. 1, 5, 118; Charles L. Mowat, *East Florida as a British Province, 1763–1784* (Berkeley, 1943), pp. 54–55.

large-scale land acquisitions in the Floridas excited interest throughout Britain. After the board's notice appeared and was reprinted in the *Annual Register*, the *Scots Magazine*, and newspapers throughout the English-speaking world, the flurry turned into a storm, especially in Scotland. In October 1763, from Megerny Castle, Perthshire, Archibald Menzies, an energetic pamphleteer, issued a leaflet praising the soil and other resources of the new British territories (which he apparently had never seen) and produced an instant scheme "for the peopling of Florida, and the rest of his Majesty's southern colonies on the continent of America, with inhabitants fit for the cultivating the natural produce of that country." William Knox, recently returned from five years as an official and landowner in Georgia, and as agent for both Georgia and East Florida considered an expert in colonial affairs, wrote a paper—"Hints Respecting the Settlement of Florida"—that circulated among influential officials. In it he explained the superiority of Florida's soil over Georgia's and South Carolina's and the colony's potential for producing cotton, indigo, silk, wine, and naval stores. He too explained how a population could be quickly recruited. At the same time the newly appointed governor of East Florida, General James Grant, who had served in the Indian war in South Carolina, knew that colony well, and dreamed of duplicating its prosperity in the new colony, issued a proclamation praising Florida's soil and climate and explaining the easy terms on which families could acquire land. His glowing statement circulated widely as a separate document and was reproduced in books and gazettes. The wonder of Florida's climate and soil—its sheer exoticism—was so popular a subject, so universally intriguing, that John Wilkes used it in December 1762 in an elaborate spoof in *The North Briton* to ridicule the ignorance of the government's paid publicists.[3]

But these were only the earliest manifestations of a growing fascination with the exotic opportunities opening up in the Floridas. One of the key public documents was a pamphlet published in 1766 by a German, Dr. William Stork. Stork, a physician and botanist, had probably established contact with British war contractors in Germany in the fifties, and after the war had become an agent of some of the would-be colonizers of Florida.

[3] *Annual Register*, 6 (1763), 111; *Scots Magazine*, 25 (Nov. 1763), 627; Archibald Menzies, *Proposal for Peopling His Majesty's Southern Colonies on the Continent of America* ([Perthshire], 1763), p. 1; [William Knox], "Hints Respecting the Settlement of Florida" [1764], Knox Papers, 9:3; Charles L. Mowat, "The First Campaign of Publicity for Florida," *Mississippi Valley Historical Review*, 30 (1943), 363–364; George Nobbe, *The North Briton* (New York, 1939), chap. 12. Knox's "Hints" remained unpublished, but it was known in the right circles. Knox wrote his friend Gov. James Grant of East Florida that the prime minister, George Grenville, "took me aside & told me he had read my paper respecting East Florida with much pleasure, & that any thing the Board of Treasury could do to further the colony he should be very ready to attend to whenever I thought proper to apply." William Knox to [Gov. James Grant], London, July 22, 1764, MacPherson-Grant Papers, bundle 313.

At their behest he visited the colony briefly in 1765–1766 and reported his findings in a rhapsodic pamphlet, *An Account of East Florida. with Remarks on Its Future Importance to Trade and Commerce.* Blasting the popular "prejudices" that held Florida to be unhealthy and infertile, "little better than a sandy desert," he gave a lyrical account of the fertility of the land, its mild winters, its freedom from all "fogs and dark gloomy weather," the moderation of the heat ("mitigated by a never-failing sea-breeze in the day time, and a land-wind at night"), and above all the rich possibilities of the soil for producing rice, cotton, silk, sugar, indigo, and wine. And in successive expansions of the pamphlet Stork included the first technical study of the environment of Florida by an experienced naturalist, the Pennsylvanian John Bartram, who held appointment as botanist to King George III. The journal that this self-trained but keenly observant naturalist kept of his two-month exploration of Florida (December 1765–February 1766) was vivid, detailed, and above all readable ("fine warm morning, birds singing, fish jumping, and turkies gobbling"). The effect of Stork's enthusiasm ("Puff General" of Florida, he was called) and of Bartram's technical details was stunning. The pamphlet, Lord Adam Gordon reported in London, "has sett us all Florida mad."[4]

The enthusiasm was further stoked by the publication shortly thereafter of a digest of Stork's pamphlet together with "Observations" on the colony's potential by Denys Rolle, M.P., one of the first British colonizers of East Florida, who had recently returned after a year's effort to establish his own plantation on the peninsula. "This happy province," he wrote, "the most precious jewel of His Majesty's American dominions," could cultivate "the productions of the whole world" in one place or another. Rolle also refuted negative rumors that were circulating—ravenous beasts, deadly insects, hostile Indians, excessive heat—and explained how Englishmen with very little capital could settle independently there, and how those without funds could join him as indentured servants.

It was probably Rolle too who wrote or inspired a widely noticed article that appeared in the *Gentleman's Magazine* shortly after the appearance of the two inspiring pamphlets. Entitled "An Exhortation to Gentlemen of small Fortunes to settle in East Florida," it explained how "the middling gentry of England, and the younger sons of good families" could make

[4]George C. Rogers, Jr., "The East Florida Society of London, 1766–1767," *Florida Historical Quarterly*, 54 (1976), 489, 483; William Stork, *An Account of East Florida* . . . (London, 1766), pp. ii, iii, 40, 42; *idem, A Description of East-Florida, with a Journal, Kept by John Bartram of Philadelphia* . . . , 3d ed. (London, 1769), *passim*, quotations at pp. i, 2, 3; John Bartram, *Diary of a Journey through the Carolinas, Georgia, and Florida from July 1, 1765, to April 10, 1766*, ed. Francis Harper, *Transactions of the American Philosophical Society*, new ser., 33, part 1 (Dec. 1942), pp. 4–5, 36–49 (quotation at p. 43). For a summary of Stork's curious career, see *Papers of Henry Laurens*, ed. Philip M. Hamer et al. (Columbia, S.C., 1968–   ), VI, 73n.–74n.

good profits in Florida only two years after investing £1,000. Gentlemen, the "Exhortation" said, faced with "the impossibility of preserving rank without a fortune, and the mortification of finding our accustomed respect in life daily diminish, and our circumstances more and more confined," should get a tract of land in East Florida. There, on an estate with only five white servants and ten blacks, they would be "happy, independent, and in a few years rich."[5]

The availability of a wholly new, untouched British world in the American deep south gripped the imagination of people everywhere, in the provinces as well as in the metropolis. The sheer exoticism of this strange universe of cypress swamps and grassy savannas, of spectacular natural fountains and hidden lakes, of jungles of live oaks, palmettos, and towering pines crowded with screaming birds, of roaring alligators in muddy creeks, of endless sand barrens and "black, rich, soapy earth"—all of this exoticism, revealed in the reports, oral and written, received after 1763, stimulated in Britons dreamlike visions of Xanadus, in one form or another, long before Coleridge fixed its ideal image in permanent form, and stirred latent longings for the feudal past.[6]

Rolle, whose family had been the richest landowners in Devonshire for a century, dreamed up his Florida projects in Stevenstone House, his "fine old mansion" set in broad parkland well stocked with deer. He began in 1763 with a vision of a huge semifeudal proprietary colony, which he located north of the Gulf of Mexico, deep inland, near the present Georgia-Alabama boundary. The community he envisaged was to serve British trade by sending Indian goods and exotic products south to the gulf and also east by portages to the rivers leading to the Atlantic coast; and it was to provide a refuge and rehabilitation center for the impoverished masses of Britain. When nothing came of this proposal, Rolle designed another, this one for two settlements, totaling 100,000 acres. One of the settlements was to be established in the west of East Florida, near present-day Tallahassee, the other in the east, near the Atlantic coastline; he blandly promised to connect the two by safe communications he would construct through what was in fact 200 miles of almost impenetrable wilderness. Two years later, frustrated by the squalid plantation he actually founded on the St. Johns River, he dreamed of an even greater estate, this time a swath of land approximately 40 miles wide and 100 miles long (2½ million acres) stretching east from the Gulf of Mexico at Tampa Bay across almost the whole of the peninsula. The colony—"one entire country"—was to be held of the crown by mili-

[5]Charles L. Mowat, "The Tribulations of Denys Rolle," *Florida Historical Quarterly*, 23 (1944), 13; *Gentleman's Magazine*, 37 (1767), 21, 22.
[6]*The Travels of William Bartram*, ed. Francis Harper (New Haven, 1958), pp. 148, 75–82, and chap. 7 generally; John Bartram, *Diary*, esp. pp. 38–46.

tary tenure (he promised to put 1,000 men into the field at the summons of the crown), and to be governed, not by the "arbitrary" powers of justices of the peace appointed by petty-minded governors like James Grant (with whom he had quarreled), but by the "ancient and known constitutions" of "county, hundred, and manor courts with courts leet and courts baron."[7]

Some of the grandest visions of Florida's future came from an even more remote region of Britain than Devon. In the lonely austerity of Monymusk House, a tall, turreted mansion alongside a lake 20 miles northwest of Aberdeen, Scotland, Sir Archibald Grant, the elderly successful proprietor of a recently modernized estate of 10,000 acres in the adjacent countryside, brooded on the huge territories in the distant American south that Britain had acquired, and found his ambitions soaring. In March 1764 he confided his thoughts to his kinsman Sir Alexander Grant, a London merchant and Member of Parliament, in a long letter, a veritable treatise, to judge from the scribbled, half-legible record he kept of what he had written.

Sir Archibald complimented his kinsman on the efforts he had made in developing his properties in Scotland. But there were more challenging, more exciting, and more public-spirited things to do. Sir Alexander would recall, of course, Archibald wrote, the great proprietary grants of Lord Baltimore, the Earl Granville, William Penn, and Lord Fairfax—valuable properties "and yearly improving"—and he would undoubtedly have heard that the Earl of Egmont had applied for a similar grant of semifeudal proprietary rights over the whole of the island of St. John. "Since ever I could read on these subjects, I have been convinced, and am daily more and more confirmed in opinion, that America will at a periode, I don't presume to say when, be the grand seat of Empire and all its concomitants." Everything pointed to America's future greatness: the soil there, the minerals, the navigation, and simply the "variable nature and constant rotation of human things." If all this is so, "why should those who see, be blind and continue too far behind?" In the past he had been wrong to allow the "pinch" in his private affairs to keep him from acquiring "some large tracts there." The opportunities now available in the new provinces were extraordinary: huge properties almost for the asking, quit rents small, forfeitures unlikely. Furthermore, and most important, people were available for settlement. Every country, "and especially [the Scottish] highlands, have people [who are] ambitious, avaricious, or some how uneasy or whimsical"; most often they "ramble [off] to [the] army, or somewhere abroad"—and where better could they go than to Britain's own new colonies? He could personally guarantee

[7]W. G. Hoskins and H. P. R. Finberg, *Devonshire Studies* (London, 1952), p. 335; William White, *History, Gazetteer, and Directory of Devonshire* . . . ([1850], Newton Abbot, Devon, 1968), p. 746; Lawrence H. Gipson, *The Triumphant Empire . . . 1763–1766* (*The British Empire before the American Revolution,* IX, New York, 1956), pp. 191–194; Wilbur H. Siebert, *Loyalists in East Florida, 1774 to 1785* (Deland, Fla., 1929), II, 367–368.

one hundred families from Scotland "of sufficient substance to move and settle themselves, each of whom would carry some underlings with them to manage subgrants or leases." And it would be easy too to get people from Ireland, Germany, Switzerland, "Civenns [i.e., Cévennes] [and] Provenze." He was sure that Sir Alexander, with his connections in London, could get a grant of land for them to develop together, and though he himself was quite strapped for funds, he would be prepared to put up £5,000 to £6,000 —not for his own eventual benefit (at sixty-eight he was too old to hope for that) but for his children and his children's children.

As to where to locate such a grant or grants, he favored going *both* north and south—both to cool climates and to warm: "2 strings to the bow is prudent." In the north he would recommend "something on either or both sides of the Bay of Fundy, especially on or near St. Johns River, and oposite to Hallifax or the Istmus [of Chignecto]," not only for the land and minerals but also for the proximity to Lord Egmont's property. In the south "anywhere near Pensicola, Mobile, or on River Missisippi as high as Ohio might do very well." And he closed with a request that Sir Alexander get hold of a copy of Egmont's "constitution and plann" for the island of St. John, which he had read about in the newspapers, and send it to him.[8]

"Settling a Colony over a Bottle of Claret"

So in Monymusk House in the eastern Highlands, as in Stevenstone House in Devon, a successful landowner, squire of hundreds of acres, dreamed of far greater proprietary estates than any he had ever actually seen, estates to be peopled by farming families from northern Europe, in a land he could scarcely imagine, and professed himself eager to establish them. Hardheaded businessmen, however, were more cautious. In response to Grant of Monymusk's letter, Sir Alexander Grant dutifully sent north the text of Egmont's scheme for St. John, but he took the opportunity in replying to Sir Archibald to denounce the whole idea of proprietary grants. "Imperium in imperio is a solecism in government," he informed his kinsman in a phrase that would ring through the approaching Anglo-American controversy. Instead of granting more such proprietary grants as Baltimore's and Penn's, he wrote, "I wish to God it were in our power to draw back all those already granted." Sir Alexander did, however, see the point of *temporary* jurisdictional and territorial grants to enable investors to make shortterm profits in exchange for developing barren land. And, though he felt himself too busy, too committed to other things, and too poor to join Sir

[8] *Selections from the Monymusk Papers (1713–1755)*, ed. Henry Hamilton (Edinburgh, 1945), intro.; Archibald Grant to [Alexander Grant], Monymusk, March 7, 1764, Seafield Muniments, GD 248/49/2, Scottish Record Office, Edinburgh.

Archibald in acquiring and developing a grant in the new colonies, he did not rule out an eventual "scheme of an American settlement."[9]

In fact Sir Alexander wasted little time in getting in on the Florida land boom, a boom even larger than the great Nova Scotia speculative bubble then swelling to its climax, though destined to produce far fewer permanent results. Applications for the 20,000-acre grants began arriving at the Board of Trade as soon as they could be legally received—but not from people likely to lead settlements themselves. The applications came from speculators—large-scale speculators, with grand synoptic visions like Archibald Grant's, which included Nova Scotia and the two Floridas, Quebec, and Georgia, as well as new acquisitions in the Caribbean.

Names already familiar, or soon to become familiar, in land development in Nova Scotia appeared also as applicants for grants in the Floridas, principally East Florida. The irrepressible Earl of Egmont, famous not only for his nostalgia for a feudal world long since vanished but for his "assiduous application in prosecution of any undertaking he embarks in," turned his "attention, precision, [and] method" to land acquisition in the mainland south as well as in the maritime north. In the same years that he advanced his notorious proposal to be created the feudal "lord paramount" over the island of St. John and was designing the "grand divisions" of his 22,000-acre estate near Halifax, Nova Scotia, he invested heavily in East Florida land. He began as co-investor in an inland plantation, Mount Royal, far up the St. Johns River, which he hoped to settle as his family's estates in Ireland had been settled, "by younger sons of gentlemen, and tenants in England." After investing over £12,000 in the project, he abandoned it and concentrated his efforts on a slave plantation, of which he was "exceeding fond," on Amelia, or Egmont, Island, a 13-mile-long strip of land just off the Florida coast near the Georgia boundary. In all, Egmont established claims to 65,000 acres in East Florida. The Earl of Dartmouth got grants totaling 100,000 acres in East Florida shortly before his cousin, Governor Francis Legge of Nova Scotia, drew his attention to large parcels of land available on that northern peninsula. Richard Oswald, the future negotiator of the American peace treaty of 1783, a Scottish merchant of great wealth gained as a government contractor and in general trade during the war and developed in West Indies planting, debated carefully whether he should invest in Nova Scotia or in East Florida or in both, before finally deciding on East Florida. He became one of the major absentee landowners in Florida, while his associates, in the several overseas land syndicates he dominated, secured claims in both places.[10]

[9][Alexander Grant] to Archibald Grant, London, April 22, 1764, *ibid.*
[10]Rogers, "East Florida Society," pp. 481, 485–87; [Richard Oswald to Grant, c. 1770], and same to same, London, May 17, 1765, MacPherson-Grant Papers, bundle 295. For Egmont's Florida

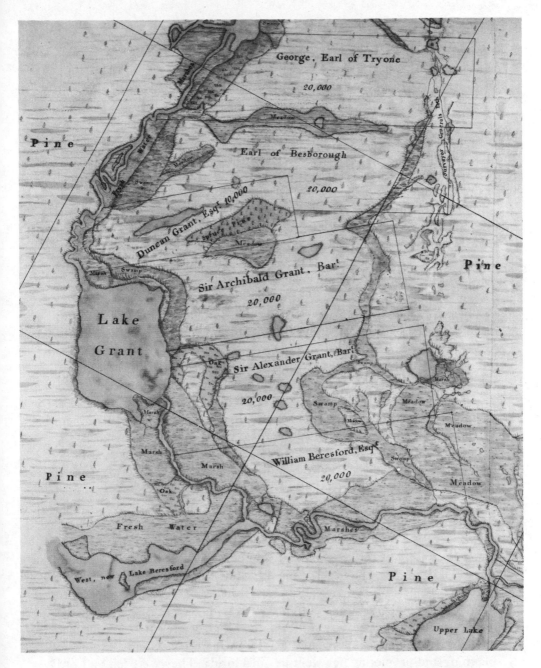

Land claims deep in East Florida by absentee British speculators. Detail from De Brahm's carefully colored, extremely detailed, 21'-long map of East Florida entitled "A Plan of Part of the Coast of East Florida. . . ." At a scale of about an inch to a mile, it shows every known detail of terrain features, and plots all known land claims, but confesses to a great vagueness in the interior regions. The entire area west of the St. Johns River is described as "land which as yet is not surveyed, but by the attempts to go through it, proves to be large swamps, cypress, savannas, and sunken pine land."

Indeed, of the whole range of new territories, north and south, East Florida in the 1760s proved to be by far the most attractive to British land speculators and investors. In those years the Privy Council issued 227 grants of land in East Florida but only 41 for land in West Florida and 82 for Nova Scotia; the East Florida grants totaled over 2.8 million acres; all other Privy Council grants combined—for land in Nova Scotia, New York, Quebec, and West Florida—totaled only 2.1 million acres. In all, between 1764 and 1774 the Privy Council issued 242 grants for East Florida land, 121 of which were presented in St. Augustine for actual surveying, resulting ultimately in confirmed land titles to over 1.4 million acres.

Never, wrote Alexander Grant, was there a colony "in which so many of the first rank were concerned." The list of the East Florida applicants to the Privy Council reads like a selection from the Almanach de Gotha and an eighteenth-century Who's Who. It includes 13 members of titled families, 11 baronets or knights, 2 prime ministers (working through proxy applicants), a chancellor of the exchequer, the lord lieutenant of Ireland, the solicitor general, the secretaries to the Treasury, the barracks master general, one of the King's physicians, the London agent of the colonies of Georgia and East Florida, the deputy paymaster general of the army in Germany (who had returned home from the war with £400,000 in profits), 21 officers of the army and navy, 5 lesser government officials, several members of Parliament, 4 physicians, and 49 merchants, almost all of them government contractors. Some of the most influential applicants managed to inflate their claims by seeking grants for several members of their families. Lord Dartmouth's record total of 100,000 acres in East Florida was the assemblage of five separate grants of 20,000 acres each, to himself and his four sons; the Earl of Tyrone and his two sons together received 60,000 acres.

Most of these applications were the products of individual ambitions and enterprise, but the most powerful impetus behind the settlements in East Florida, and most of the financing, came from the membership of a curious organization known as the East Florida Society. A group of 40 to 50 merchants, noblemen, and entrepreneurs with capital to risk, all bullish on developing new properties in America, the society operated not as a business unit but as a discussion and lobbying organization devoted to planning and promoting new ventures in Florida. They were led by Lord Adam Gordon, an enterprising younger son of the Duke of Gordon, who had recently returned from a tour of the colonies with considerable interest in American land speculation (he obtained a grant of 10,000 acres along the Mohawk in New York); and they held rather bibulous meetings once a

ventures, see Daniel L. Schafer, "Plantation Development in British East Florida: A Case Study of the Earl of Egmont," *Florida Historical Quarterly*, 63 (1984), 172–183.

month at the Shakespeare Head tavern in Covent Garden. There, under Gordon's chairmanship and that of the vice-president, Peter Taylor, M.P., an unscrupulous newly rich "German" war contractor and former deputy paymaster general, they planned their strategies, discussed ways of establishing personal estates in Florida, and drank toasts to everyone's health— Governor Grant's health taking precedence over all others' except George III's.[11]

The East Florida Society, Oswald wrote, made "a very respectable figure" at their monthly meetings; and indeed it must have done, any time a sizable percentage of the membership appeared. For the main clusters of associations represented in the society constituted a significant segment of the British establishment. Oswald himself was a key figure in a circle of former war contractors turned merchant-entrepreneurs, and he apparently drew into the society a group of his former wartime associates, all immensely enterprising and still involved in government contracting. Oswald also linked the society to the powerful Scottish faction involved in overseas settlements, though they were represented also by Gordon and others, and to a less formally organized group of speculators in Nova Scotia real estate, which included Benjamin Franklin and the former Massachusetts governor Thomas Pownall. Further, Oswald had remarkably close ties to a physically remote but central figure in all of these enterprises, Henry Laurens of Charleston, South Carolina.

Laurens was the main American credit manager, adviser, and general facilitator of most of the major settlement efforts made in the southeast during these years. Plantation owner (one of his properties was an inland rice plantation owned jointly with Oswald), merchant, and politician, Laurens was the personal business manager of all of Governor Grant's affairs, the transfer agent for shipments into and out of Florida, as well as the transmitter and negotiator of bills of exchange between Florida and London. He maintained correspondences with almost everyone involved in settlements in East Florida, provided a staging area in South Carolina for expeditions into the peninsula, took in the settlement leaders' children when necessary, and proved to be a reliable if pessimistic one-man information bureau on the state of affairs in East Florida—affairs financial, agricultural, demographic, and geographic. In 1766 he made a personal inspection tour of the peninsula, whose possibilities he assessed more shrewdly than most: coolly, and in the end gloomily.

[11]Mowat, *East Florida*, p. 59; Alexander Grant to [Archibald Grant], London, July 3, 1767, Monymusk Muniments, GD 345/1171/1/68; List of the Grantees of East Florida, *ibid.*, GD 1/32, 38; Lewis Namier and John Brooke, *The House of Commons, 1754–1790* (London, 1964), II, 510–512, III, 517, 106; Daniel L. Schafer, "Early Plantation Development in British East Florida," *El Escribano*, 19 (1982), 49; Rogers, "East Florida Society," pp. 480, 485.

Another key figure in the East Florida Society, though personally less influential than Oswald, was Thomas Thoroton. His importance derived largely from his marriage to the illegitimate daughter of the Duke of Rutland, that modernizing landlord whose "overpopulated" estates in Yorkshire were providing so many settlers, through Michael Francklin, to Nova Scotia—a colony over which another of Rutland's sons-in-law, Robert Monckton, had presided as governor. Thoroton, prominent in East Florida affairs from the start, was Rutland's chief "man of business" in politics and secretary of the duke's son, the Marquess of Granby, who had been the commander in chief in Germany from 1759 to 1763, and whose wartime entourage "swarmed with future Florida speculators."

Thoroton was intimately involved not only with Florida affairs but also with speculation in Nova Scotia land, and he was a mediator between the two groups of entrepreneurs. He needed such a range of contacts—needed all the contacts he could make—since he had at that point no fewer than nine children to provide for; ultimately his progeny numbered thirteen. In a gossipy letter to Governor Grant, Oswald recalled a dinner party at the duke's house where the guests speculated, amid some hilarity, about how many colonies in America it would take to satisfy the needs of Thoroton's hungry brood.[12]

Indeed, there was a general air of hilarity about all of these enterprises —a reckless, exuberant zest, as these neo-Elizabethan appetites for wealth, landed properties, and sheer entrepreneurial adventure began to feast on the new British territories. The whole uproarious tumult of enterprise within the East Florida Society and its affiliated groupings is revealed vividly in two sentences of a letter from Oswald to Governor Grant when the Florida undertakings were getting under way. Oswald had just received a grant of 20,000 acres in Florida, which he was apparently planning to share with Grant, and was explaining his plan for combining that parcel of land with those of two other grantees, a proposition that somehow overlapped with plans for settling six townships in Nova Scotia. All of this business, he wrote, was extremely confusing; he could scarcely keep it all straight in his own mind. But then, what could one expect? You have to make allowances, he said, "for gentlemen settling a colony over a bottle of claret. For so this plan has proceeded—by way of a joke."[13]

[12] *Ibid.*, pp. 485–488; Namier and Brooke, *House of Commons*, III, 526–527.
[13] Oswald to Grant, July 27, 1764, MacPherson-Grant Papers, bundle 295. Oswald himself was slightly puzzled by the group's offhand attitude. His colleagues in the society, he reported to Grant, "were amused with the prospect of having two fine settlements." But he could not be sure what to make of their amusement, and so he "waited untill I could be more certain that the gentlemen were serious." Oswald to Grant, London, May 17, 1765, *ibid.* On the group's involvement in Nova Scotia land speculation, see John B. Brebner, *The Neutral Yankees of Nova Scotia* (New York, 1937), pp. 62–63.

De Brahm: Mapping the Terra Incognita

A joke, perhaps, to him at the moment he wrote, with his usual high spirits, to his friend and countryman Governor Grant. But his and the society's business was serious, and risky, especially since it proceeded in the face of profound ignorance of what kind of a land Florida actually was, aside from the popular panegyrics: what its physical contours really were; and where costly settlements might best be located. All of the existing maps were worthless. The few available in 1763 were pastiches of rumors, travelers' accounts, and the mapmakers' fantasies. The map Dr. Stork issued in 1767, for example, was based in part on his own observations; but it was declared by an unfortunate planter who actually tried to use it in Florida to be a wretched work of imagination; it "might as well serve for any part of Germany as for East-Florida." The degree of ignorance was intolerable, the Board of Trade informed the King. Maps and coastal charts would have to be made, with great exactitude, and quickly.[14]

As a result of these urgencies two surveyors general of North America were appointed: in the north, Samuel Holland, and in the south, William Gerard De Brahm. A well-born and well-educated German military engineer, De Brahm had led a group of Protestant refugees from the southern German states to Ebenezer, Georgia, in 1751. Within a year of his arrival he was turning out valuable maps of Georgia, and he was quickly appointed one of the colony's two surveyors general. In 1764, by then an important figure in both Georgia and South Carolina, he was appointed not only, in parallel with Holland, surveyor general of the southern district of North America but surveyor of the colony of East Florida as well. His somewhat conflicting tasks were to provide surveys of individual grants in East Florida and at the same time to survey and map the whole of North America south of the Potomac, with special priority to East Florida, from St. Augustine south to the Florida keys.[15]

De Brahm set to work with a team of assistants, with whom he sailed south from St. Augustine early in 1765 on the first of a series of surveying expeditions. By the summer he was sending back to England preliminary

---

[14]William P. Cumming, *The Southeast in Early Maps . . .* (Princeton, 1958), nos. 333, 334, 336, 379; Mowat, "First Campaign," p. 375. Louis De Vorsey, Jr., "De Brahm's East Florida on the Eve of the Revolution . . . ," in *Eighteenth-Century Florida and Its Borderlands*, ed. Samuel Proctor (Gainesville, Fla., 1975), pp. 79–82; *De Brahm's Report of the General Survey in the Southern District of North America*, ed. Louis De Vorsey, Jr. (Columbia, S.C., 1971), intro., p. 5. The map referred to, reproduced on p. 444, is in the Public Record Office, London (CO 700, Florida/34) and described in P. A. Penfold, ed., *Maps and Plans in the Public Record Office* (London, 1967–1982), II, #2302.

[15]*De Brahm's Report*, pp. 6, 9–33.

William Stork's "New Map of East Florida" (1767).

sketches, verbal descriptions, and small-scale surveys, which he continued to produce for six years, until, as a result of controversies with Governor Grant, he was forced to return to England. By then he and his assistants had mapped or sketched every inlet on the east Florida coast, and for the inlets north of Key Biscayne had prepared charts of extraordinary accuracy, drawn to a standard scale, showing land features, shoals, soundings, and bottom characteristics. From these charts and De Brahm's other sketches and surveys, John and Samuel Lewis, expert draftsmen in the Plantation Office in London, were able to compile as early as 1769 a magnificent map, twenty-one feet in length, five feet in width. This splendid work of cartography and freehand sketching locates the main land claims, which then extended only irregularly halfway down the east coast and along the banks of the St. Johns River and the adjoining lakes, and concentrates on verbal and graphic portrayal of terrain features. Mangrove swamps, salt- and freshwater marshes, pine barrens, savannas, streams, hills, and shelly bluffs are all drawn in color, deftly, where the information was available; where it was not, the draftsmen occasionally recorded their guesses.[16]

Upon his return to London De Brahm himself set to work on a summary of his cartographical labors. In 1772 he presented to the King, who had a personal interest in cartography, an immense map, in three sheets, each five feet in width, in all more than twenty-five feet in length, covering in detail the whole east coast of the colony. Different from the more illustrative map the Lewises had prepared from De Brahm's sketches and charts three years earlier, it is a highly technical rendering of the East Florida coastal terrain, crowded with tiny lettering, minutely nuanced tracings of the shoreline contours, the coastal waterways, and the nearby inland streams, and peppered with depth soundings over all the water areas. At the same time De Brahm submitted his "Report of the General Survey in the Southern District of North America," a meticulous account in two volumes of the region's topography, climate, flora, fauna, and settlement. Included too was a hydrographical map of the Atlantic Ocean, which, with the accompanying section of the "Report," De Brahm published separately as *The Atlantic Pilot* (1772). In addition, the "Report" contains a list, by name, of every head of household who had inhabited East Florida from 1763 to 1771, showing their "employs, business and qualifications in science."[17]

[16] *Ibid.*, pp. 34, 37–38, 268 n. 158; De Vorsey, "De Brahm's East Florida," pp. 85–86, 92–93; Roland Chardon, "A Best-Fit Evaluation of De Brahm's 1770 Chart of Northern Biscayne Bay, Florida," *The American Cartographer*, 9 (1982), 51, 57, 60. The map of 1769 is catalogued as K CXXII, 81 in the Map Collection, British Library. Two sections of it, particularly relevant for settling efforts, are reproduced on pp. 439, 456. Over the huge sweep of land west of the St. Johns River the draftsmen wrote the words "Land which as yet is not surveyed, but by the attempts to go through it, proves to be large swamps, cypress savannas, and sunken pineland."
[17] *De Brahm's Report*, pp. 45–46. The map presented to the King is now in two sections mounted on rollers in the Public Record Office, CO 700, Florida/53, and CO 700, Florida/3. As De Vorsey

De Brahm's maps and descriptions are exceptionally exact, reliable, and comprehensive, and since some of them circulated in manuscript and were quickly reproduced as engravings, they provided the basis for coastal navigation and for locating many of the individual grants, hence they significantly shaped the process of settlement. But his maps were only the most professional of a number of remarkable geographical studies and representations produced in a few years in response to the surge of settlement plans. De Brahm's assistant surveyor general and bitter rival, a Dutchman, Bernard Romans, turned out his own *Concise Natural History of East and West Florida* (1775). A long, rambling, but informative travelogue, technically descriptive yet anecdotal, it contains not only detailed accounts of topography, flora, and coastal waters, but also depictions of the social life of both Indians and whites and a map, twelve feet by seven feet, engraved in two sheets by Paul Revere, showing all of East Florida, West Florida as far north as Natchez, and part of the Caribbean. But by the time Romans's map appeared, West Florida had been provided with a series of detailed land surveys showing every bend and twist of the Mississippi from the Yazoo River (at modern Vicksburg) south to New Orleans, and the gulf shoreline east from the Mississippi—past Biloxi, into and around Mobile and Pensacola bays and up the rivers that empty into them—to the province's eastern boundary at the Apalachicola. Most of these large West Florida maps (some of them ten feet long) were the work of Elias Durnford, West Florida's surveyor general and lieutenant governor, in collaboration with Samuel Lewis in London, and they served to reveal both the topography of the settled areas and the land claims and grants, parcel by parcel, grantee by grantee, year by year. By 1775 similar surveys of lands granted were being produced for East Florida at similarly huge scales.[18]

So ignorance was overcome—but only gradually. In 1768 the knowledgeable William Knox wanted "exceedingly to begin a settlement," but he refused to do so until he knew more about the communication, if any, that existed between the colony's two main northeastern waterways, the St. Marys River and the St. Johns. In the same year De Brahm told Oswald —wrongly—that there was a water route straight across the middle of the peninsula from the Atlantic to the gulf, a circumstance Oswald declared to be "most glorious . . . for the province." But though ignorance persisted, by the early 1770s East Florida was no longer what Oswald had called it in

suggests (*De Brahm's Report*, p. 273), these two segments fit together to form one immense map, by my measurement 29 feet by 5 feet. The list of settlers appears in De Vorsey's splendid edition of *De Brahm's Report* on pp. [180–186]. *The Atlantic Pilot* has been reprinted in facsimile (Gainesville, Fla., 1974) with an introduction by De Vorsey.

[18] Romans's *Natural History* and the accompanying map, which was sold separately, have been reprinted in facsimile (New Orleans, 1961). The three most comprehensive maps of the settlements in West Florida are identified below, chap. 13, n.7. Cf. Johnson, *West Florida*, pp. 119 n., 141.

1764, "in a manner a terra incognita," and serious efforts to populate it were well under way.[19]

Rollestown: "Shoe Blacks, Cheminy Sweepers . . . Cinder Wenches, Whores and Pickpockets"

Denys Rolle's plantation, the actuality that emerged from his dream of princely domains in "the most precious jewel of his majesty's American dominions," was the first notable undertaking, and its fortunes and those of the people who settled it were prophetic. Rolle, faithful to his dream of populating Florida with the dispossessed of England, took ship with fourteen vagrants, beggars, and debtors he had collected in London; stopped off in Charleston, South Carolina, where a family of five he had rescued from prison deserted him; and, thus reduced, arrived in Florida in September 1764. He stayed first in St. Augustine, where he immediately tangled with his host, Governor Grant. Then, reequipped, his party supplemented by hunters and guides, Rolle headed off up the St. Johns River, the colony's central waterway running north and south parallel to the coast fifty miles inland. There, on a bluff overlooking a bend in the river fifty miles downstream from the river's main source, Lake George, he established his headquarters. The place came to be called Rollestown, and there Rolle's troubles began.

First, there was the land. Rolle's grant gave him the right to claim 20,000 *contiguous* acres; but he quickly discovered that any such block would contain hundreds of acres of swamps, pine barrens, or otherwise useless soil, and so he proposed to Grant that he be allowed to scatter his 20,000 acres among small, selected parcels along the river. In anticipation he had his people throw together huts at promising places to establish rights of possession. But Grant refused: Rolle's plan would violate the terms of the grant, and, more important, preempt choice parcels which others would be prepared to settle and develop. Rolle was furious. He declared that the governor was deliberately thwarting his efforts, and then proposed that his block extend on both sides of the river, which, while counting water as land, would double the riverfront acreage he would have. Grant again refused —the land west of the river was an Indian reserve, and in any case water was not land. Rolle, his rage compounded, denounced the governor as a

[19]Knox to Grant, London, March 4, 1768, MacPherson-Grant Papers, bundle 313. (It took another five years to plot the capillary rivulets that link the two rivers.) Moultrie to Grant, St. Augustine, June 3, 1773, Knox to Grant, London, Aug. 20, 1768, Oswald to Grant, London, May 17, 1765, all in *ibid.*, bundles 370, 313, and 295. In 1770 even De Brahm did not know what lay between Lake George, in northeastern Florida, and the ocean, only 40 or 50 miles to the east. He called the whole area a "great swamp whose inside as yet unknown." *De Brahm's Report*, map facing p. 199.

duplicitous villain determined to frustrate his settlement plans, and fired off charges to the government at home. Grant replied coolly, describing Rolle as a cranky, suspicious, litigious malcontent—"he hates, indeed never forgives a man who differs in opinion with him"; he would never be satisfied with any reasonable portion of land. And Grant grew more and more irritated as months went by and Rolle continued to delay locating his grant, thereby holding up the governor's efforts to get others to stake out plantations on the upper St. Johns and to bring in a population of settlers.[20]

But land was a minor part of Rolle's troubles. A more important difficulty was presented by the people he had brought with him and whom he had indented to repay the cost of their transportation. Unused to hard farming work, unused perhaps to work of any kind, these derelicts of Britain's greatest city were horrified by the swampy jungle scene they found in inland Florida, and refused Rolle's orders to start digging up palmetto roots to prepare the land for cultivation. Where, they asked, was the half-share of the crops they had been promised? When Rolle blandly told them they could sell half of the palmetto roots they dug up, some fled to St. Augustine; but Governor Grant refused to release them from their indentures and sent them back. Rolle then denied food to those who refused to work—and not occasionally or selectively: he deprived, Grant reported, "whole families for ten days or a fortnight at a time, and that in a wilderness where it was impossible for them to get any thing to eat, unless it was in charity from the other servants out of their allowance." Some gave in and began digging out roots and shrubs, but others slipped off into the woods to scrabble for themselves or to find their way back to civilization.

So Rolle's work force faded away to ineffectiveness, even when supplemented by "vagabonds" to whom, Grant said, the squire offered "protection as a Member of Parliament," and by a second small contingent of recruits that soon arrived from England. Rolle remained unrelenting, "complaining and wandering upon the River St. John's during the winter of 1765—wherever a place pleased his eye he built a log house by way of taking possession, upon islands as well as on each side of the river indifferently, without asking my consent." He worked out a scheme by which his workers would claim "family" grants from the Florida government; when issued, they would be handed over to him by prearrangement. Grant refused to sanction such deals, and again the two fell into bitter recrimination, and still Rolle refused to settle for any specific tract. By the time a year had gone by, Grant was fed up and began allowing surveys in the area

[20] *The Humble Petition* [*to the Privy Council*] *of Denys Rolle . . .* ([1765], facsimile reprint, Gainesville, Fla., 1977), pp. 2 ff., 66; Mowat, "Tribulations," p. 3; Carita D. Corse, "Denys Rolle and Rollestown, A Pioneer for Utopia," *Florida Historical Society Quarterly,* 7 (1928), 117, 118, 123, 124, 126–129 (containing the texts of two important letters about Rolle written by Gov. Grant in St. Augustine: one to Lachlan MacLeane, Feb. 13, 1767, the other to the Earl of Hillsborough, Aug. 13, 1768).

favored by Rolle. The proprietor, frustrated, angry, but still determined to establish a princely domain in East Florida, returned to England to renew his political support and gather a fresh contingent of recruits.[21]

In London Rolle detailed his grievances in a monstrously prolix, scarcely readable *Humble Petition* he sent to the Privy Council, repeated his pleas for a proprietary grant, publicized his plantation in extravagant terms, and arranged for the transportation of prospective voyagers. In January 1767 this modern Don Quixote, as a contemporary referred to him, reappeared in Florida with forty-nine more English vagrants and debtors—Stork said they were a pack of "shoe blacks, cheminy sweepers, sinkboys . . . cinder wenches, whores and pickpockets"—and once again threw himself into battle with the governor and with nature, physical and human. Rollestown had not developed in his absence. "Mr. Rolle's crackertown," as Laurens called it, was still no more than a scattering of log cabins thrown up in a riverside clearing hacked out of a forest of scrub oaks and pine trees; and it was now surrounded by land grants claimed by others. But it was not land that chiefly bothered Rolle at this point. He had learned how to take care of himself on that score, and indeed he eventually managed to accumulate, by private purchases and minor grants, a total of 80,140 acres, an estate he later valued, together with equipment, slaves, and buildings, at over £28,000.

Rolle's "great and constant complaint" upon his return, Grant wrote, was "the loss he sustains by his indentured servants, who he says are seduced away by other people." This was a perfectly natural development, Grant explained to him, and not a conspiracy of villains, but Rolle compounded the problem by lengthening the terms of his servants' indentures in exchange for small favors. Discontented, shocked by the living conditions and at the work they were supposed to do, Rolle's newest contingent of "idle and starving" settlers, like their predecessors, refused to work and simply disappeared from the scene, struck down by disease and accidents or drawn away by the attractions of St. Augustine, by better working conditions elsewhere on the peninsula, or by the possibility of escape and return to their former lives. The population Rolle had expected to establish in Florida simply could not be secured even if it could be recruited.[22]

The situation appeared to be hopeless, at times farcical. In November 1768 Henry Laurens got word from Rolle that he was sending another twenty-six indentured servants from England to Charleston, to be transshipped to the St. Johns River. No sooner had the ship docked at Charleston, the disgusted Laurens reported, than "the whole body march'd on

[21] *Ibid.*, pp. 120, 132, 133, 131, 124, 125; Mowat, "Tribulations," p. 5.

[22] *Ibid.*, pp. 2–3, 11–14; *Laurens Papers*, VI, 121 n., 122, V, 203; Schafer, "Early Plantation Development," p. 42; John Bartram, *Diary*, pp. 37, 46; Siebert, *Loyalists*, II, 287–297; Corse, "Rolle and Rollestown," pp. 131, 132; Mowat, "Tribulations," p. 8.

shoar & scatter'd themselves in twenty different parts of the town. Some
went a begging, others to seek for employment, & the remainder eating &
drinking as they had money or could obtain credit." With great difficulty
the ship captain managed to recapture twelve of the escapees, for which he
charged Rolle twenty shillings a head in recovery costs plus the price of the
"rum &ca. to induce them to go on board." You cannot compel these people
to go to Florida, Laurens wrote Rolle's agent; and indeed, so great was their
cost—not only for transportation but for maintenance thereafter—and so
feeble the prospect of their productive labor, that their permanent disap-
pearance would be "an absolute gain" to Rolle. Four days later Laurens was
still rounding up the runaways, using a recaptured carpenter to reveal the
hiding places of the others. The whole business was ludicrous to Laurens,
who had a poor opinion of Florida in any case, and he swore he would never
get involved in such transactions again.

How many derelict English servants in all Rolle imported to his plantation is not known—he claimed at one point to have committed himself to
importing two hundred. But Laurens was right as to their uselessness. In
1768, after the escapees had been returned, there were over fifty white
people in Rollestown, but all of them were reported to be idle. The only
work under way was being done by slaves, twenty-two in all. A year later
Rolle, still seeking a population of white settlers, switched his tactics and,
instead of rounding up indigents, advertised in London for recruits who
would be proprietors of the land, not laborers: independent farmers capable
of paying twelve guineas each for their transportation and for a parcel of
land on Rolle's property. He had few if any takers. In the end he brought
in a permanent work force of slaves, and in the decade that followed, what
had been envisaged as a princely estate manned by impoverished but
rehabilitating Englishmen devolved into a cluster of scrubby cattle ranches
and turpentine manufactories, together with a three-hundred-acre farm, all
of it worked by slaves and managed by overseers. But by then, in the 1780s,
Rolle himself had left. He had returned to Devonshire and had resumed the
management of his properties there. When in 1783 East Florida was returned to Spain, Rolle evacuated all of his movable possessions to the
Bahamas and claimed losses of over £19,000; the Claims Commission
awarded him £6,597. A generation later, when the colony became part of
the United States, Rollestown had entirely disappeared.[23]

The demise of Rolle's settlement was the result neither of financial
constraint nor of neglect. Rolle's initial failure flowed from his inability to
mobilize a population of British settlers capable of turning the wild over-

[23]*Laurens Papers*, VI, 152–153, 157; Siebert, *Loyalists*, II, 370, 371; Knox to [Grant], London, April
12, 1769, MacPherson-Grant Papers, bundle 313; Mowat, *East Florida*, p. 71. For Rolle's "engagement" to import 200 white settlers, and his plans for developing a civilized community, "well
stocking it with white inhabitants," see his *Humble Petition*, p. 66.

grown land along the St. Johns into a profitable plantation. His high-minded plan to people the colony with indigents collected from the slums of London proved utterly impractical, and when he set about recruiting small property owners he had no means of reaching significant numbers of them, as Francklin had done in Yorkshire, or of inducing those he did reach to emigrate to Florida. The problem of recruitment was unsolvable by Rolle —but not by him alone. Everyone involved in the exploitation of the newly opened lands in East Florida faced the same problem in one form or another, and their failing efforts to solve it constitute the main substance of the colony's history in the years between the wars. All sorts of strategies were used, all sorts of devices and ingenious schemes. One common approach—reflecting a curious view of human ecology—proved to be particularly disastrous.

New Smyrna: a "Transplanted _Bashawship_ from the Levant"

The first indication of the approach that would result in the largest single settlement of the era, and the most wasteful of human and material resources, appeared in Menzies' brief pamphlet issued a bare two weeks after the colony of East Florida was formally created. Menzies had recently visited the Middle East, and there he had discovered a race perfectly suited, he believed, for the peopling of Florida. "The Greeks of the Levant," he wrote, were a naturally frugal and industrious people, used to a hot climate, familiar with the cultivation of exotic products—vines, olives, cotton, tobacco, madder, silk—and subject to the brutal tyranny of the Turkish conquerors. In addition, they were excellent oarsmen, hence potentially useful for inland navigation. Further, Menzies had discovered the Armenians—honest tradesmen and artisans, he believed, not likely to fleece the Indians as the British did. They too lived under Turkish despotism, and like the Greeks would gladly flee to the New World. All that was needed to attract these Greeks and Armenians, who were already emigrating to Naples and to Minorca, would be individual allotments of land. Everything favored their settlement in British North America. They hated the Roman Catholics, hence would be impervious to the lures of the French and Spanish, and their women were so "remarkably handsome" that they would quickly intermarry with the British, and all distinctions would disappear. The project could start slowly—just a few Greeks and Armenians at the beginning—but if they received a "good reception" they would draw over their countrymen "to partake of their happiness."

Menzies' ideas were shared by others, some of them people in positions of great influence. Knox, in his "Hints," sketched a similar plan. He too praised Florida's soil and climate and listed the exotic crops that could be produced there, and then he added,

ye kind of settlers who ought to be encouraged to sit down in Florida . . . are Greeks or any other of the inhabitants of the archipelago who profess the Christian religion. I am well assur'd that great numbers of those people might be induced to become our subjects if their mode of worship was tolerated and the expence of their transportation defray'd. Their priests who are the proper persons to employ might be easily brought to persuade y^m to emigrate, and our island of Minorca would be a convenient place for y^m to rendezvous at.[24]

This, conceptually, was the start of the largest single shipment of emigrants from Europe to North America since the Puritan migration of the 1630s—and the most disastrous. The central figure was a Scotsman, Dr. Andrew Turnbull, well connected in London and an acquaintance and client of the Earl of Shelburne. Long a resident of Smyrna in the Levant (now Izmir, Turkey), he had married a Greek and had become convinced that "the Greeks would be a very proper people for settling in His Majesty's southern provinces of North America," both because they were used to producing semitropical crops and because they were eager to escape their "hard masters."[25]

Returned to England, he had become involved in the affairs of the East Florida Society, and threw himself into organizing precisely the emigration from the Mediterranean described by Menzies and Knox. From the begin-

[24]Menzies, *Proposal for Peopling His Majesty's Southern Colonies*, pp. 2–4; Knox, "Hints," pp. [8–9]. These were not the first geo-climatological theories of population recruitment that were acted upon. In 1718 a Swiss entrepreneur, Jean Pierre Purry, concluded on the basis of "scientific" calculations that the 33d parallel everywhere around the globe was ideal for colonization. The result in 1734 was the settlement of Purrysburg, S.C., by 600 Swiss imported by Purry, who tried and failed to develop silk culture, olive orchards, and wine production believed to be appropriate for that latitude of the globe. W. Stitt Robinson, *The Southern Colonial Frontier, 1607–1763* (Albuquerque, N.M., 1979), pp. 167–168.

[25]"Narrative of Dr. Turnbull," Sept. 1, 1766, Lansdowne MSS, LXXXVIII, 133.

Turnbull, a graduate of Edinburgh University, was a physician and naturalist, though he was entered in the list of East Florida grantees as "clerk of the crown." Others in England besides Isaac Barré thought of him as "a man of enterprise & extream good sense" (*Laurens Papers*, VI, 71n.), but those who had to deal with him in Florida thought otherwise. For "all his cleverness," Lt. Gov. Moultrie wrote Gov. Grant (June 10, 1771), Turnbull was a nervous, somewhat paranoiac man, occasionally "full of the horrors"—though Moultrie admitted that he continued to have "a great and sincere regard for him and his family." MacPherson-Grant Papers, bundle 242. On Turnbull's associations with the leading naturalists, see Alexander Garden to John Ellis, Feb. 2, 1767, in *A Selection of the Correspondence of Linnaeus and Other Naturalists . . .*, ed. James E. Smith (London, 1821), I, 551–552.

ning his energy and imagination were fevered, dilated, overreaching—altogether beyond the ordinary range of colonizing enterprise—and the resulting settlement was proportionately outsized in its soaring promise and tragic reality. Everyone interested in Anglo-American colonization knew of this strange undertaking: it fascinated one of the spokesmen of the French Enlightenment. The Abbé Raynal, writing in Paris in the late 1770s, reported in his famous history of the Indies that Turnbull's settlement in Florida astonished the whole world. It had become an asylum for the oppressed, and a place where, after one bad summer, people enjoyed perfect health, men grew taller than they did elsewhere, women were more fruitful, and "the spirit of concord" prevailed. It was a new "Athens and Lacedaemon," he said. He saw no reason why "the city of Turnbull [should not] become in a few centuries the residence of politeness, of the fine arts, and of elegance." Distance from the centers of civilization was no problem: Turnbull's colony was no farther from Europe, Raynal said, than "were the barbarous Pelasgians from the fellow citizens of Pericles." Think what South America might have become if it had been settled, not by "avaricious, extravagant, and sanguinary men," but by "wise and pacific" men like Turnbull. "Will not nations learn by his example, that the foundation of a colony requires more wisdom than expense?"[26]

Thus Turnbull carried with him to Florida, in the first flush of enthusiasm for his extraordinary enterprise, the hopes of the *philosophes* as well as of his co-investors; and he was heartily endorsed too by the British government. "No measure," wrote the Earl of Hillsborough in 1768, "that has been thought of for the improvement of East Florida, appears to me to afford a fairer prospect of rendering it a valuable and rich province." "His Majesty considers [it] to be both an example and effect of great publick utility." And the Earl of Shelburne, Turnbull's principal patron, not only supported the venture but, when secretary of state, urged Turnbull to expand it beyond its original dimensions.[27]

[26]Quoted in E. P. Panagopoulos, *New Smyrna, an Eighteenth Century Greek Odyssey* (Gainesville, Fla., 1966), p. 34. A check of the various editions of Raynal's famous book shows that the *philosophe* picked the story up rather late, sometime between 1774 and 1783. It had long been famous in English circles—"*famous,*" Bernard Romans wrote in his *Natural History*, p. 179, "on account of the cruel methods used in settling it, which made it the daily topic of conversation for a long time in this and the neighbouring provinces." Panagopoulos's book, the best account available on the whole bizarre story, is especially valuable for the information it contains drawn from Greek and Italian sources.

[27]Hillsborough to Grant, Whitehall, Feb. 23 and Sept. 14, 1768, MacPherson-Grant Papers, bundle 290; Turnbull to Shelburne, Minorca, Feb. 27, 1768, Lansdowne MSS, LXXXVIII, 147. On Hillsborough's support of the project generally, see the documentation collected by a descendant of Turnbull's, Carita Doggett [Corse], in her *Dr. Andrew Turnbull and the New Smyrna Colony of Florida* (n.p. [Florida], 1919), pp. 64 ff. Turnbull wrote directly to both Hillsborough and Shelburne to keep them abreast of developments; Hillsborough was particularly interested. Hillsborough to Grant, March 10, May 12, 1768, MacPherson-Grant Papers, bundle 290.

The undertaking had begun in 1766 when Turnbull had joined with another medical practitioner, Dr. William Duncan, physician to the King and son-in-law of the Earl of Thanet, to petition for separate grants of 20,000 acres in East Florida, which they expected to develop together and to populate with emigrants from the Mediterranean. Shortly after they received the grants, Turnbull traveled to Florida, settled his family in St. Augustine, ingratiated himself with Governor Grant, who hoped the project would begin the effective peopling of the colony, and with the help of the governor selected a spot for settlement, behind Mosquito Inlet 75 miles south of St. Augustine. There Turnbull laid out the two land grants in huge adjacent blocks; and on a bluff behind a large mangrove swamp on the bank of the Hillsborough River, which flows into the inlet, he stationed a few workmen to begin erecting crude shelters for the immigrants. He then returned to England, where his enthusiasm and newly acquired knowledge of the land in Florida inflated the sails of the East Florida Society. He also took on as a third partner—involuntarily, he would later say—the former prime minister, George Grenville, who had read Knox's paper with such interest. With Grenville, Turnbull and Duncan formed a new, tripartite agreement. Duncan and Grenville would put up a maximum of £9,000 to recruit the settlers and launch the plantation, and they would obtain from the government a subsidy of £12 for each of 500 emigrants, as well as some surplus shipping; Turnbull would personally do the recruiting, oversee the settlement in Florida, and manage the property thereafter.[28]

These plans drawn up, Turnbull headed south to the Mediterranean on the crucial business of gathering the desired settlers. He remained there for ten months, and despite opposition by the Turkish government, the Levant Company, and various Italian officials, he succeeded—indeed, oversucceeded—in his task.

His recruits were a bizarre collection of ethnic groups drawn, largely in family units, from all over the Mediterranean; all of them were refugees from political and religious oppression and from hardship and the threat of starvation. The first large group Turnbull attracted were not Greeks but Italians—110 north Italians, laborers and their families, whom he recruited in Leghorn (Livorno) over the strenuous objection of the town's governor. A second, larger group was, as planned, composed of Greeks: refugees from the villages of Mani in the southern Peloponnesus, villages "built like eagles' nests high on the cliffs of a rocky peninsula," which had been ravaged by

---

[28]Panagopoulos, *New Smyrna*, chap. 1; Shelburne to Grant, May 14, 1767, enclosing the favorable report of the Board of Trade, April 16, 1767, MacPherson-Grant Papers, bundle 303. For Turnbull's "unlucky and involuntary partnership with the Grenvilles," Turnbull to Shelburne, Charlestown, S.C., May 30, 1783, Lansdowne MSS, LXXXVIII, 189. Grenville did not himself deal directly with the venture but used his kinsman Sir Richard Temple, commissioner of the navy and comptroller of the excise, to front for him. For De Brahm's description of Mosquito Inlet together with an excellent map of the site, see his *Report*, p. 206 and the facing page.

plagues, family feuds, poverty, and above all by the savage persecution of the Turkish conquerors who, just before Turnbull arrived, had snuffed out an incipient rebellion by beheading the Maniotes' most beloved leader and by slaughtering an entire community returning from a religious pilgrimage.

Word spread through this grieving population that an English doctor was offering a life of freedom, security, and peace in a sunny land of orange groves where the coasts were gentle, where their religion would be tolerated, and where each householder would own his own plot of land. Several hundred responded, and so from among the refugees of a rugged mountain land of the southern Peloponnesus Turnbull filled his vessel. He was never in doubt about the kinds of people they were, though only later would he come to realize what this would mean for his settlement. For they were "only such Greeks as the Turks wish out of their way"—fierce freedom fighters from the mountains whom the Turks had never been able to subdue and who "continue free to this day," preferring to struggle for survival on infertile mountain farms than to "live under tyranny in the fertile and extensive plains under them."[29] After bribing the appropriate Turkish port officials he sailed off with these recruits to continue his Aegean and Mediterranean perambulation.

Further stops at Crete, Smyrna, Melos, and the volcanic island of Santorini yielded a few more emigrants. And on the island of Corsica, 1,000 miles to the west, then in its tormented transition from Genoese to French rule, Turnbull was able to gather another large contingent—again of Greeks, but this time of *Corsican* Greeks, descendants of a migration from Mani to Corsica that had taken place a century before. Still loyal to the Genoese who had protected them over the years, these second- and third-generation Corsican Greeks were considered enemies by the Corsican independence fighters, and were scattering for their lives when Turnbull arrived—to Spain, to nearby Leghorn, to the adjoining island of Sardinia (where many of them would be massacred), and to Minorca.

With these Italians, Greeks, Aegean islanders, and Greek-Corsicans, Turnbull had many more than the 500 settlers he sought. But still they came. In the end it was the Minorcans, whose island, British territory since 1713, was in the midst of a severe crop failure, who crowded his vessels to the limit of their capacity. Hundreds of native Minorcans and recent arrivals from Italy and Greece pleaded with Turnbull to take them too, and by March 1768 he had agreed to an overall total of about 1,200 men, women, and children. But he soon discovered, as he sailed to Gibraltar en route to Florida, that this was only the official figure: he was carrying too, he found, close to 200 Minorcan stowaways. When on April 17, 1768, his fleet of eight

---

[29]Panagopoulos, *New Smyrna*, chap. 2 (quote at p. 30); Turnbull to Shelburne, Minorca, Feb. 27, 1768, Lansdowne MSS, LXXXVIII, 147.

Mosquito Inlet (New Smyrna) East Florida, site of Turnbull's tragic settlement of Greeks, Italians, and Minorcans. Detail from De Brahm's "Plan of Part of the Coast of East Florida. . . ." (1769).

vessels sailed out into the Atlantic it bore a total of 1,403 men, women, and children.

It was a polyglot population of refugees from persecution, misery, and starvation, none of whom were even remotely aware of the reality of the land they would inhabit—its primitivism, its humid semitropical climate so different from the Mediterranean coasts they had left behind, its unfamiliar disease environment, its strange animals, reptiles, and flora. And few of them were capable of grasping the meaning of the complicated contracts of indentured servitude and sharecropping they were obliged to sign upon their departure.[30]

But reality soon closed in on them. At the start, Turnbull wrote Shelburne, they were all "healthy and very fit for a new colony . . . not a deformed nor maimed person among them."[31] But the three-month voyage was a nightmare: one in ten died on shipboard. And when in July 1768 the fleet finally sailed into the still harbor behind Mosquito Inlet, and in the sweltering heat the exhausted and debilitated survivors climbed to the shacks on the bluff, they knew they faced hardships none of them had ever dreamed of.

The scene at New Smyrna, as Turnbull called the settlement after his wife's birthplace, must have been strangely beautiful, and fiercely forbidding. The swampy lowlands between the small upland clearing and the ocean were covered with palmettos, salt marshes, and pine barrens. The upland clearing itself was cut out of a thickly overgrown tangle of cabbage palms, pawpaw trees, and semitropical plants. From the clearing, in the distance, the edge of an extensive orange grove could be seen, left behind by earlier Spanish and Indian settlers. The settlers' main tasks were to clear the swampy lowlands, full of snakes and swarming with mosquitoes, in order to make indigo fields—and to tear out the palmettos where the land was dry, and plant corn, which would be their main food crop. Somehow, too, they were to make vegetable gardens on the bluff, though the soil was sandy and full of shells.

For a month the settlers, driven by British army veterans and Italian foremen now employed as overseers, and driven too by hunger and fear, struggled to clear the land and begin the planting. They were disoriented, bewildered; they were tortured by the heat and by the clouds of mosquitoes that swarmed over the settlement both day and night; and they were

---

[30]Panagopoulos, *New Smyrna*, chaps. 2, 3. The formal contract terms were complicated, but in general stipulated that Turnbull and his company would take half the product of the land after all the expenses had been repaid, and that the immigrants would work for him for at least ten years. *Ibid.*, pp. 46–47. As he put it less formally to Gov. Grant, "the families are engaged to stay on our grounds ten years after they have paid the expense of settling in the province, so that it carries them for thirteen or fourteen years at least." Turnbull to Grant, "in sight of the Madeira," April 29, 1768, MacPherson-Grant Papers, bundle 253.

[31]Turnbull to Shelburne, Gibraltar, April 4, 1768, Lansdowne MSS, LXXXVIII, 145.

shocked at the ferocity of their overseers who, themselves half-crazed by heat and fear, drove them like beasts in the field. Some progress was made, but after four weeks it seemed clear to many of the settlers that they were caught in a fearful death trap and that they would perish if they did not escape while they were still relatively strong. On August 19, a month after their arrival, while Turnbull was off visiting Oswald's plantation to the north, some 300 of the settlers revolted. Under the leadership of one of the more aggressive overseers, they seized a vessel, plundered the warehouse of arms and supplies, drank up much of the rum and wine they could not take, butchered animals for food on the voyage ahead, and captured the overseers who opposed them. The most hated of these drivers they dealt with by cutting off an ear and two fingers.

But in the end the escape was frustrated. Two loyal Italians alerted Turnbull, who in turn alerted Governor Grant. Fearful as always for the success of the colony, Grant was not entirely surprised at this turn of events. He had been afraid of trouble from the start—fearful of riots among "so great a number of people, collected together in so many different parts of the world and imported into an infant colony," and fearful also for the safety of the settlers. For "the Indians will not be fond of either their language or complexion, as both resemble the Spanish, which the Indians have a mortal antipathy to." But he did what he could, quickly. He immediately sent off the provincial frigate with troops and ammunition and dispatched a contingent by land as well. The rebels were caught and brought to St. Augustine, where they were tried for a variety of crimes. Three were condemned to death, one of whom was reprieved when he agreed to serve as the executioner of the other two. The intimidation was successful; there were no more overt revolts. But the settlement took on a strange character. Profitable crops were only slowly forthcoming and the costs shot up astronomically. By 1769 Grenville and Duncan had invested not £9,000 as planned, but £52,000, and had forced Turnbull to reduce his share in the ultimate division of assets and to give in to the common fund his original 20,000 acres plus another 21,400 acres he and his four children had subsequently acquired. In addition the government had increased its cash subsidy to £3,000, and it had thrown in equipment and services as well.

Progress continued, painfully and slowly. High swampland was cleared of palmettos and tangled vegetation, and then drained; indigo and corn were successfully planted; and experimental crops of all sorts were sown. Exports of indigo averaged 6,000 pounds annually by 1771, and New Smyrna had become a small village with stores, a windmill, wharfs, canals, boats, and well over a hundred dwellings.[32]

---

[32]Panagopoulos, *New Smyrna*, chaps. 4, 5. On the mutilation: Corse, *Turnbull*, p. 55. (Panagopoulos, p. 60, says the rebels cut off the ears and the nose of the obnoxious overseer; Romans, *Natural History*, p. 181, agrees with Corse.) Grant's reaction: Grant to [Hillsborough?], St. Augustine, Aug.

But for all its improvements, the settlement was a death camp—a scene of horror, a "transplant[ed] *Bashawship* from the Levant," an eyewitness reported.[33] In the first six months after the settlers landed, one of every four people died—305 in all—of malnutrition and diseases that swept through bodies severely debilitated by malaria. The original huts could not keep out the wind and rain, and they swarmed with insects. No effective provision was made for sanitation, and food was so scarce that everyone in New Smyrna would have starved to death if emergency supplies had not been sent in from St. Augustine.

These were problems enough, but they were greatly compounded by the severe discipline imposed on the workers, directly by the overseers, indirectly by Turnbull. The enterprising doctor, faced with mounting costs and the prospect of a catastrophic failure that would ruin him and his partners, drove the workers like animals. His overseers horsewhipped them when they took time off to fish, beat them with clubs when they were suspected of malingering. In this florid concentration camp Turnbull, despite his enlightened views, became the law. Enforcing a criminal code of his own devising, he had his drivers flog, starve, and chain to logs and heavy balls those who attempted to escape. An unknown number, debilitated and incapable of work, were beaten to death. When workers requested their freedom after their terms of service were completed, they were confined and forced to sign on for further work.[34]

Two years after New Smyrna was founded, half the settlers were dead. When the American Revolution loosened the ties of all civil authority, most of the surviving settlers fled to St. Augustine and to the protection of the new governor, a pugnacious Irishman, Patrick Tonyn, who had quarreled with Turnbull and threatened his property and personal safety. On November 9, 1777, the last of the settlers, a priest from Minorca, left New Smyrna for St. Augustine. The deserted village, which had witnessed

---

29, 1768, CO 5/549/281–285. Hillsborough was indignant when he heard of the revolt—indignant to think that "an undertaking of great public utility and advantage" should be obstructed by colonists "collected at so large an expense" who thus made "so ungratefull a return for the kindness and tenderness with which they appeared to have been treated." Hillsborough to Grant, Whitehall, Dec. 10, 1768, MacPherson-Grant Papers, bundle 290.

The precise level of prosperity the settlement achieved in its best years is not clear. Turnbull described the colony on Sept. 24, 1769, as a line of palm huts strung evenly along eight miles of river front, which created "a resemblance of an Eastern or Chinese plantation." And on Oct. 3, 1774, he believed everyone was in perfect health, the whole project certain to succeed "in a very large way," especially as he had adopted an "Egyptian" irrigation system to handle future droughts. Letters to Shelburne, Lansdowne MSS, LXXXVIII, 155, 157. But an objective observer of the Florida plantations in the same year reported Turnbull's settlement "not at all promising": the indigo crop was poor, the supply of seeds falling short, the good land in the back swamp area not yet cleared, some of the better land already worn out, and once again the "people become troublesome." David Yeats to Grant, St. Augustine, May 24, 1774, MacPherson-Grant Papers, bundle 369.
[33] Romans, *Natural History*, p. 179, part of his vivid summary of the affair, pp. 179–182.
[34] Panagopoulos, *New Smyrna*, pp. 64, 82, 87–91.

bloodshed, death, and degradation, was soon overgrown by a jungle of weeds. Of Turnbull's great migration of 1768, drawn from all over the Mediterranean, 80% had perished. In St. Augustine the survivors and their children, 291 in all, merged with the Spanish when they returned in 1783 and, with their descendants, formed part of the mixture of peoples that make up the permanent population of modern Florida. Turnbull himself, having failed in an effort to unseat Tonyn, and embroiled with creditors and political enemies in Florida, including the heirs of his former partners, worked his way north to Charleston. There he lived out his life, a British subject to the end, still struggling to recover his earlier losses, a respected physician and one of the founders of the South Carolina Medical Society. His beautiful Greek wife, the last legacy of his earlier adventure, survived him.[35]

Behind the spectacular failure of Turnbull's New Smyrna lay a vicious descending spiral, impelled, ultimately, by greed. Turnbull, a man of mercurial temperament and more enthusiasm than good judgment, took in almost three times as many settlers as had been planned for, in the hope of speeding up the development of the settlement and with it the realization of his share of the profits. But the cost of shelter and provisions for such numbers far exceeded the available funds and put such pressure on producing profitable crops as to lead, first, to the neglect of subsistence produce necessary for survival, and then to the imposition of a brutal work regime that drove the settlers into a state of chronic exhaustion, fatal in a debilitating environment. As the human and financial losses mounted, the situation became more desperate and the regime more severe. By the time an export crop was being produced the population had been severely reduced, resistance smoldered continuously, and the reputation of the enterprise was badly fouled. While in the salons of the French intellectuals New Smyrna was being praised for its enlightened and benevolent intentions, in the wilderness clearings of Florida and elsewhere in the deep south it was condemned for its terrible waste and brutality. After all, Lieutenant Governor John Moultrie wrote in a caustic appraisal of the whole affair, settlers in Florida no less than those in any other British territory must be allowed

---

[35] *Ibid.*, pp. 91, 174, chaps. 9, 10. Turnbull's bitterness at the wreck of his fortunes was directed chiefly at Gov. Tonyn, whom he considered "an inveterate and insidious enemy" determined to destroy him, and secondarily at Lord George Germaine, the colonial secretary, 1775 and after, to whom he wrote insulting letters accusing him of deliberately neglecting his, Turnbull's, interests. Turnbull to Germaine, St. Augustine, March 16, 1780, Lansdowne MSS, LXXXVIII, 181–182d. As for his former partners, whose heirs in 1783 were attempting to sue him, they were, he said, a craven, money-grubbing lot. "Money never was my object," Turnbull wrote, "much less an idol to which one moments peace of mind was to be sacrificed. I am generally engaged in pursuit of objects of purer metal than ever the Grenvilles were remarkable for." Turnbull to Shelburne, Charlestown, S.C., May 30, 1783, *ibid.*, p. 189.

to "taste some of the sweets of a constitution that even to slaves allows some freedom."[36]

A Train of Failures:
from New Bordeaux to Biscayne Bay

Much in the New Smyrna settlement was unique—the recruitment of Mediterranean peasants, the bizarre work regime, the rebellion of the workers. But in essential ways Turnbull's plantation village typifies the general failure of settlement efforts in early East Florida. Time and again absentee land grantees sought to import a population of white settlers and sustain them in order to satisfy the terms of land acquisition. Time and again such recruitment efforts failed.

The very first recruitment plan proposed for East Florida had been that of Governor Grant, written in July 1763 at the request of the Board of Trade. Do not recruit the idle or craven poor, Grant wrote. "The most reasonable and frugal methods of peopling and settling the new established colonies in America," he said, was to draw over a population of French Protestants, who were neither unenterprising nor poor and whose only desire was to live under a free government. East Florida, he proposed, should be populated initially with 500 Huguenots, supported by a work gang of 100 Negro slaves to attend to public enterprises like road-building, house construction, and fuel production. The plan was attractive enough in the eyes of the government, and practical in that in September of the same year 1,000 Huguenots did in fact arrive in England from Bordeaux and were available for resettlement. But Grant also reported, realistically, that the transportation, equipment, and settlement of 500 Huguenots and 100 slave laborers would cost the government £16,000 the first year and £8,000 a year for the next four years, after which " 'tis to be hoped the province will be no longer a load upon the public except for the salaries of the civil officers." At a cost of £48,000 the government was not interested. Two hundred of the available Huguenots were in fact settled in America, not in Florida but in South Carolina, where, subsidized by the province government, they established the upcountry community of New Bordeaux.[37]

If Grant was cast down by the government's refusal to support his own

[36]Panagopoulos, *New Smyrna*, pp. 82, 84, 155; Knox to Grant, London, Aug. 20, 1768, and Moultrie to Grant, St. Augustine, June 10, 1771, MacPherson-Grant Papers, bundles 313 and 242.

[37]The text of Grant's plan is printed in Alastair M. Grant, *General James Grant of Ballindalloch, 1720–1806* . . . (London, [1930]), pp. 72–74; the original, with financial details, is CO 5/540/1–7, with a copy in MacPherson-Grant Papers, bundle 262. For the fortunes of the Huguenots, *Laurens Papers*, IV, 118 n.3, 333 n.6; Johnson, *West Florida*, p. 152 n.3.

proposal he left no record of the fact. In the years that followed he gave his wholehearted assistance to a series of plans—some sensible, some not— to import a sizable population of white settlers. In his first year in office he responded jubilantly to an inquiry from a Bermudian entrepreneur who proposed to resettle several hundred families of poor whites from that island to the east coast of Florida. Grant immediately conjured up a vision of Bermudians becoming the foundation of East Florida's society—2,000 of them, he somehow came to believe, would eventually settle in the colony; and his hopes were further stimulated by word that "a great number of people" from North Carolina were planning to settle near the Bermudians. So he cleared away all rival claims to 40,000 acres the Bermudians' agent favored, and assigned De Brahm to design a street "plat" for their town, which he called "New Bermuda." But the first small contingent approached East Florida by way of Georgia, and though Grant was certain they would press on to their reserve in Florida, in fact they stopped in their progress south only 25 miles from Savannah, at a place called Sunbury, and there they and the few who followed remained. Their putative neighbors from North Carolina never appeared.[38]

While this possibility was running its course, another even less promising prospect was unfolding under the auspices of the Grants—Sir Archibald of Monymusk, Sir Alexander of London, and Duncan of Bristol. Despite Alexander's earlier misgivings, Archibald's enthusiasm of 1764 for developing overseas properties had carried the day, and in 1767 each of the three clansmen received a large grant—Archibald and Alexander for 20,000 acres each, Duncan for 10,000—and the triumvirate engaged in an extensive correspondence about plans for locating and developing the immense territory legally available to them.[39] Many difficulties had to be cleared away. Sir Archibald, then seventy-one but overbrimming with youthful zeal, had to be dissuaded from voyaging to Florida himself; an agent or two had to be sent to Florida to assess the land and locate the grants (the fantastically detailed nineteen-point set of instructions the tireless Sir Archibald wrote for their agents illuminates the ambitions, hopes, and ignorance of this whole generation of colonizers); and a supervisor had to be stationed in the colony to oversee the project. By August 1768 Dr. Stork, agent to the Grant associates as well as to more than twenty other land claimants, laid out the Scotsmen's grants in adjoining blocks deep inland, at the far end of the St. Johns River, along the shores of what he flatteringly called Lake Grant (now Lake Monroe).[40]

[38]Ephraim and John Gilbert to Grant, Sunbury, Ga., Jan. 14, 1766, MacPherson-Grant Papers, bundle 402; *Laurens Papers*, IV, 451–454, 530; VI, 118 n.8.
[39]The correspondence consists of 13 letters in the Monymusk Muniments, GD 345/1171/1, 2.
[40]Instructions [from Sir Archibald Grant] to Francis Lunan and Alexander Anderson of Monymusk, "Going to East Florida, Monymusk Town," June 20, 1767, *ibid.*, GD 345/916/4; *Laurens*

By then the main business of population recruitment was under way. Archibald's early assurances that he could easily induce 100 Scottish families of substance to emigrate or could gather a contingent of Irish, Germans, Swiss, or French had proved to be a delusion. There is some evidence that an effort was made to recruit 500 Highlanders, and apparently the Grants sent two vessels to Hamburg to pick up German Protestants for their properties. But if anything came of these efforts, no record of it survives.

The Grants continued to be aware, however, that "population is the soul of a new country," and Sir Alexander hit upon a remarkable plan to help resolve the problem. He decided to introduce into the colony "young women in the hopes of their becoming very useful & agreeable inhabitants." But not *any* women, or women randomly chosen—rather, a special group for whom Sir Alexander had direct responsibility. Among the merchant-politician's offices was the vice-presidency of Magdalen House, a charitable organization recently formed to rescue from degradation, disease, and early death some of the several thousand prostitutes who walked the streets of London. And not only to rescue them—to redeem and rehabilitate them as well. The society had been a great success, Sir Alexander explained to Governor Grant. " 'Tis true," he admitted in a striking understatement, the society's charges "are not virgins." But he could assure the governor that "they are comly, good tempered, reformed penitents, whose youth & inadvertency plunged into misfortunes which brought them into sad sufferings." Hundreds of them had been rescued from wickedness and misery, and "restored to virtue & industry & became very useful members of society." Many had been sent abroad, "where they behave well as mothers of familys." With these precedents in mind Sir Alexander had proposed to the East Florida Society that they dispatch to the colony "some of them on trial as a specimen." Sir Alexander himself had had the honor of making the choice of the trial group. With the advice of Dr. Stork he had chosen four women "of the middle rank" since Stork felt that they "will be most useful & have the best chance of geting husbands amongst the tradesmen or overseers settled in the country." If this sample contingent succeeded, many more would follow, and to secure Governor Grant's responsibility

---

Papers, VI, 74; Schafer, "Early Plantation Development," pp. 43–45. Among a host of detailed instructions concerning the soil, flora, fauna, and climate of East Florida, the Grants' agents were told to keep a careful journal ("get two good pencils each, with books or paper to use them"); to spy out the land shrewdly and decide where the three Grant properties might best be located; to show "all possible signs of friendship and confidence" to any Indians they ran into "by bowing and putting hands to mouth"; and to learn everything they could about local lore, from how to handle alligators to the best ways of cutting timber. And on top of all that—and on top of specified courtesies they were told to extend to a list of people they were likely to meet—they were to start a garden of one or two acres and build some huts. For the layout of the Grants' Florida claims, see the section of the Lewis map of 1769 based on De Brahm's surveys (K CXXII, 81, British Library), reproduced above, p. 439.

in the matter, Sir Alexander had him elected one of the governors of the charity—a very illustrious company indeed, Sir Alexander assured him, which included "Her Sacred Majesty." So he hoped the governor would "adopt & protect them as your childeren, place them properly out as servants & protect them from mischief." All of this would be of great utility to the colony and "greatly add to your fame."[41]

What happened to the four young women of redeemed virtue is not known. Stork escorted them to Florida, and there, like so many others, they disappeared in the confusion of the settlements. Stork himself died in the colony at the end of August 1768, and with his death went the Grants' hopes for a quick development of their Florida claims. Somehow they had not been able to hit upon the right people to send over. Sir Alexander was convinced that it was simply too expensive to import people "accustomed to southern climates and cultivation"—Turnbull was proving that to be sadly true. On the other hand, Scots were too inexperienced in semitropical farming to develop properties profitably in Florida; and as for Londoners, "coruption of morals prevailes so much in this place that verry few indeed cann be found [worthy] of trust." Committed as the Grants were to projects in the West Indies, in the Scottish Highlands, and elsewhere, they would have to content themselves with doing just enough to hold on to their new lands in East Florida, a territory they believed clearly "capable and worthy of improvement and which will soon be a most desirable and flourishing collony—producing wealth worthy of the care and attention of the greatest men in this country." They had no intention of impoverishing themselves by attempting to populate their Florida lands, but they did continue to think that maintaining these extensive tracts "was absolutely necessary before the most convenient scituations were engrossed and occupied."[42]

But if the Grants, for all their energy and wealth, proved unable or unwilling to populate their distant territory, other, younger Scots were brimming with hope. While the Grants were learning the difficulties of settling Florida and were dispatching rehabilitated prostitutes to the colony, a well-connected and well-financed young Glaswegian, John Bowman, Jr., was taking up the cause. Son of the wealthy lord provost of Glasgow, he had been trained in the law, but after making a tour of Europe had decided

[41] Wilbur H. Siebert, "Slavery and White Servitude in East Florida, 1726 to 1776," *Florida Historical Society Quarterly*, 10 (1931), 14; Alexander Grant to [Gov. James Grant], London, June 19, 1767, MacPherson-Grant Papers, bundle 402; John H. Hutchins, *Jonas Hanway, 1712–1786* (London, 1940), chap. 5 ("The Magdalen House").
[42] Alexander Grant to Gov. Grant, Feb 8, 1770, MacPherson-Grant Papers, bundle 402; same to [Archibald Grant], July 3, 1767, Monymusk Muniments, GD 345/1171/1/68.

on "an adventure abroad." On the advice of Richard Oswald, Bowman decided "to be a Florida planter." Well funded, his way smoothed for him by letters from his father and Oswald to Grant and Laurens, he took on a small group of servants, arranged for the purchase of slaves, tools, and land, and set sail on his great adventure in North America.

Governor Grant was once again enthusiastic. There was no telling what benefits the wealthy young man would bring with him. If he succeeded, Oswald had informed the governor, "youl probably have many more from Glasgow. They are rich, & really clever—not inferior to any sett of people in ye mercantile way in Britain . . . no sett of people are so well calculated to give the Florida settlem^t such a push as those of that town could do." But Bowman, like the Bermudians, approached Florida through South Carolina and Georgia, and there he found far less enthusiasm for the new colony than Oswald had had. Once arrived in Florida he was shocked at the difference between the picture he had been given in Scotland and the reality before him. "Too sanguine in his expectations," as Oswald had predicted, "too quick & rapid in his temper for an undertaking of this nature," he found the difficulties of organizing a labor force and of establishing a plantation discouraging. His disillusion led to clashes with Grant, ever the booster, and he moved off—first to Georgia, then to South Carolina, where he eventually settled and prospered as a planter on the Santee River.[43]

So it went, year after year. In 1769 Francis Levett, Sr., a wealthy Georgia planter and another connection of Richard Oswald's, took up his ten-thousand-acre grant on the St. Johns River with the intention of following Turnbull's lead and importing settlers of his own from the Morea, in Greece. Levett did manage to carve a farm of some sort out of his wilderness grant, but such cultivation as took place there was the work of the slaves he took with him from Georgia and not of householding Greeks or Italians or Asians or freemen of any description; no such settlers ever appeared at Levett's plantation.[44]

Even less successful were the hopes of Jean Daniel Roux, a Swiss from Lausanne and Morges in the canton of Bern, who in 1772 petitioned for, and received, a 6,000-acre grant in Florida for himself, his wife, nine children, and a contingent of neighbors, with the intention of creating there "an asylum for himself & Mrs Roux & of making or begining an establishment for the young branches." His target was far south of the then existing East Florida settlements—off the shores of Biscayne Bay, just south of the pre-

[43] *Laurens Papers,* VI, 593 n.; Oswald to Gov. James Grant, Auchincruive [Ayrshire], Jan. 29, 1769, MacPherson-Grant Papers, bundle 295; John Bowman, Jr., to Richard Oswald, Glasgow, Nov. 13, 1768, and John Bowman, Sr., to same, Glasgow, Nov. 15, 1770, Bowman Letters.
[44] *Laurens Papers,* VI, 577n.; Mowat, *East Florida,* pp. 44, 66, 71.

sent city of Miami. But en route Roux too stopped off in Charleston, and he got no farther. He died in Charleston eight months later, still planning his trip south.[45]

He was not, however, alone in looking to Biscayne Bay 270 miles south of St. Augustine, 200 miles south of Turnbull's isolated New Smyrna; nor was his interest in the region accidental. It had been stimulated by the promotional efforts of De Brahm, who also directed to the same region the attention of one of the great London merchants. Samuel Touchett, engaged in world-wide trade and high-level politics, had obtained a 20,000-acre grant in 1766. Five years later, embroiled in severe financial difficulties from which he saw no safe exit, he commissioned Bernard Romans to locate the grant for him, and the result was a huge wedge-shaped plot whose broad base included much of the present city of Miami and whose length extended south along the coast for eleven miles. But Touchett's affairs were too pressing, too contorted, to allow him time to develop the grant (he committed suicide in 1773), nor was another recently surveyed plot just to the north of Touchett's, claimed by an Anglo-German, John Augustus Ernest, developed before the Revolution.[46]

De Brahm was involved in all of these tentative probes in the Biscayne or, as he called it, the Cape Florida, region, for he had long been convinced that that region was particularly promising for European colonization. He had produced detailed charts of the bay area first in 1765 and again in 1770, stressing among other features the attractiveness of the sand of Miami Beach for growing crops like indigo and cotton. It was to this region, consequently, that he directed his main efforts at colonization in attempting to develop the greatest property claim of all, the massive land grant, or set of grants, totaling 100,000 acres issued to Lord Dartmouth and his family.

In 1772, when Dartmouth was appointed secretary of state for the colonies and De Brahm, then in London, was entirely dependent upon his favor for reinstatement as surveyor in Florida, he threw himself into the work of locating and populating Dartmouth's property. With the help of a functionary of Dartmouth's in Florida, De Brahm set off his patron's claim just south of what he flatteringly designated Dartmouth Inlet (Bear Cut) and Dartmouth Stream (northern Biscayne Bay between Miami and Miami Beach) and opposite Dartmouth Sound (southern Biscayne Bay), and he mapped in detail a central segment of 40,000 acres. It was this central block, running 6½ miles along the shore just south of Touchett's claim and extending inland almost 10 miles, that De Brahm hoped to populate for his patron. He cast about for colonists, running down every lead he could find. At one

[45]*Laurens Papers*, VIII, 372n.–373n., 418.
[46]Namier and Brooke, *House of Commons*, III, 533–536; James C. Frazier, "Samuel Touchett's Florida Plantation, 1771," *Tequesta*, 35 (1975), [75]–88; Schafer, "Early Plantation Development," p. 42.

point he hoped to locate on this property the Swiss Roux, already en route to Florida, together with his family and associates; at another point he sought the cooperation of a well-connected Anglo-Swiss intellectual, Johann Rodolph von Valltravers, who already had obtained a personal grant in Florida and who declared himself interested in bringing over to Dartmouth's land Protestants from Poland, Germany, and Switzerland, some hundreds of whom, expert in husbandry and various crafts, he said he would himself be willing to recruit. But the main possibility, which De Brahm pursued with a characteristic, and fatal, excess of zeal, was to persuade a strange polyglot organization which became known as the Cape Florida Society to settle on Dartmouth's surveyed grant.[47]

Organized by a French-Swiss Protestant, Daniel Bercher, the society was an idealistic communal venture of English, Scots, Swiss, and Italians, initially to consist of twenty families, that proposed to settle in Florida and produce for export the commodities believed natural in southern climates —wine, silk, cotton, indigo, and "other fruits very useful to the happiness of a reasonable society." As described in the society's code of thirty-two detailed regulations, all official members, without respect to previous condition, would be treated equally and "view themselves as brothers," support each other in need, help each other build houses, choose "directors" by ballot, and receive two fifty-acre lots free, with the possibility of buying more land at will. Laws would be made by unanimous consent, and the communal commitment would be maintained for at least ten years. In March 1773 the society, after protracted negotiations with De Brahm as Dartmouth's agent, reached a preliminary agreement for the acquisition, at delayed rents, of a 6,000-acre plot in the middle of Dartmouth's surveyed

[47]Chardon, "Best-Fit Evaluation of De Brahm's . . . Biscayne Bay," p. 51; Roland E. Chardon, "The Cape Florida Society of 1773," *Tequesta*, 35 (1975), 3, 10–13, figs. 1, 2; *Laurens Papers*, VIII, 372n.–373n., 316n. Assigning patrons' names to newly settled or discovered terrain was universal. Just as Egmont's name is still memorialized in Nova Scotia, Florida, and New Zealand, so Dartmouth's was placed by De Brahm all over the Biscayne Bay Area. And not by accident or casual whim. Settle or lay out—Knox wrote Gov. Grant, Jan. 4, 1768—"a Hillsborough on St. Mary's River." The colonial secretary, he continued on Sept. 29, "is in raptures with the province . . . and if Your Excellency should change the name [of a town on the St. Marys] to Hillsborrough [*sic*], you would both flatter His Lordship and engage his patronage. . . . I always tell him that East Florida is his child, and that thro' his support & Your Excellency's good management he will see it rise to maturity before any other colony could ever have walk'd with leading strings. He is exceedingly fond of presents from America. Any bird or animal that's curious, or any of the products of the country, would be a grateful offering" (MacPherson-Grant Papers, bundle 313). And so Hillsborough's name is duly memorialized not only in Florida (where there are today a Hillsboro inlet, lighthouse, river, county, and bay) but in the backcountry of every other east coast state. But some objected to this practice. The alteration of long-familiar place names to flatter the great, Bernard Romans wrote in a tirade against his rival and the main sinner, De Brahm, has created great confusion. "Can the arbitrary imposition of the names of *Dartmouth, Littleton, Pownal, Hawke, Egmont* . . . and about a legion more . . . make up for the mistakes they may occasion? Or can these statesmen and heroes owe him thanks for the confusion occasioned by the jumbling of their names like dice in a box?" Romans, *Natural History*, p. 198.

land. At this point De Brahm extended himself still further and produced an exhaustive report on life in Florida, which he presented to the society in order, he said, to prevent the "confusion, discouragment and miscarriage" that might overtake them in Florida.

In tangled prose and exquisite detail (invaluable now as an account of life in wilderness Florida) De Brahm warned them against believing the myth, so fatal to Turnbull, that "emigrations of man and transplantations of vegitation do best succeed in the same climate"; instructed them in the agricultural possibilities of the Cape Florida region; described for them the local climate zones, water currents, and soil conditions; advised them on "diet and regimen," on hygiene, exercise, sleeping arrangements, work habits, body temperatures, sun protection, dress, and perspiration; told them how to protect themselves against "nats," that is, mosquitoes, and how to build houses; identified the native Indians, animals, and reptiles; and gave them tips on handling cattle in Florida and on buying and managing Negro slaves.

It was all informative—but also, it seems, intimidating. The society decided to expand their number to twenty-five or thirty families, which would require more land, and to take on more servants, who would also be entitled to land. When De Brahm, for reasons unknown, discouraged them from applying for a larger grant from Dartmouth, they began to question his good faith, and when Dartmouth, innocent of all this, backed De Brahm as his spokesman, the members fell to bickering on whether or how to continue. Differences deepened and grew bitter, and in the end, as one disgusted leader reported, "the intended society and all the mighty projects belonging thereto, have exhaled themselves away into smoke." From the beginning there had been confusion and in the end conflict among "the respective interests of the united tribes of English, Scots, Swiss and Italians." And so, in view of the disarray that had developed, the leaders decided "to get rid of the united tribes" entirely by dissolving the existing organization, raise new capital, and choose a new membership that would have "no mixtures of nations, but all Swiss only." But if they were serious about the reorganization, they were doomed to further disappointment. The moment for action had passed, and the ambitious project followed into limbo the other major enterprises thrown up in the initial enthusiasm for East Florida—those of Rolle, Turnbull, the Grants, the Bermuda entrepreneur, Bowman, Levett, Touchett, and Roux.[48]

[48]Chardon, "Cape Florida Society," pp. 6–7, 24, 29–30, 15, 16, app. A; *The Manuscripts of the Earl of Dartmouth, II: American Papers,* Historical Manuscripts Commission, *Fourteenth Report, Appendix,* part 10 (London, 1895), 144, 149, 159, 160.

"The Forlorn State of Poor Billy Bartram"

In 1776 the Cape Florida (Biscayne) region, like most of the rest of the colony of East Florida, was still in the pristine state it had been in when the British acquired it thirteen years earlier. Not a single permanent habitation or settlement was to be found anywhere in that region of De Brahm's highest hopes—not on the shores, the islands, or the keys. Occasionally fishermen from the Bahamas, only forty-seven miles away, appeared, and wanderers from Cuba, Providence Island, or elsewhere along the nearby sea lanes stopped off for turtling, timber cutting, or ship salvaging. But they did not stay, and a voyager sailing along the Cape Florida shores and up the peninsula as far as Mosquito Inlet would have seen no houses, not even a hut or a shelter for Indian hunting parties—only long lines and clusters of mangroves, palmettos, and pines, salt-water marshes, tall grass, tidal flats, sand, and rocks.[49]

Within the entire 50,000 square miles of the province of East Florida settlements could be found only in a narrow strip approximately 25 to 30 miles wide and 125 long, extending from New Smyrna on the south to the Georgia border on the north, and west only to the St. Johns River and the lakes and streams that feed into it. And even that narrow strip was only thinly settled. The areas actually populated formed an inverted U, north along the coast, west at or near the Georgia boundary, and south along the St. Johns. In these areas settlements were scattered at five-, ten-, or even twenty-mile intervals. The only concentration of contiguous farms formed a ring around St. Augustine, and those establishments numbered only around twenty. A contemporary's estimate that in the whole of the province outside St. Augustine there were scarcely one hundred white families was probably correct.

At least as many plantations and cattle farms had been abandoned as were still in operation, and of those only a few were flourishing. Most were scruffy clearings, described in a survey of 1774 as "rather backward," "too weak handed," or "not at all promising." No one could claim that the colony, whose total population in 1776 was certainly no more and probably less than it had been under the Spanish in 1763, had been a success. It had proved no attraction whatever to the many thousands of voyagers from Britain seeking employment or new lives in the American west.[50]

[49]Roland E. Chardon, "Northern Biscayne Bay in 1776," *Tequesta*, 35 (1975), 37, 64–65.
[50]Mowat, *East Florida*, pp. 58, 64, 69, 70; [William Drayton], An Inquiry into the Present State and Administration of . . . East Florida . . . (1778), Peter Force Collection, MS 17137, Series 8D, Manuscript Division, Library of Congress. Egmont had died in 1770, but his island plantation off the north coast of Florida, after years of mismanagement and other vicissitudes that had drained

Why? What had happened to the high hopes and elaborate plans for this best-advertised and initially most-attractive new land acquisition of Britain? What accounts for this outcome? Laurens, a shrewd businessman, had predicted it from the beginning. Even before his five-week trip to Florida in 1766 he had seen enough "bars" to the colony's development to suspect that it would prove to be "only a frontier garrison" and not "a flourishing country of merchants and farmers." After that trip he was certain of it and adamantly and consistently opposed all investments there. There were no roads, he wrote his friend and business partner Oswald, who insisted that Florida could be developed, no neighbors, no decent navigation, no markets, and no ports. Lacking neighbors and a surrounding community, isolated in the cypress groves and swampy farmland "your negroes will be exposed to the arbitrary power of an overseer & perhaps sometimes tempted to knock him in the head & file off in a body." But what chiefly bothered Laurens was the land, much of which he said was "mean" and "base," so scruffy and deficient that it would be inhabited, if at all, only by such people "as will be a pest to your settlements." Vast stretches of it produced, he wrote, "chiefly pine trees of an inferior growth & some swamps of bay & cypress of a sandy foundation hence in my opinion its inhabitants will never be numerous." Here and there, to be sure, there were wetlands suitable for rice growing and some decent planting soil, but he never relented in his general view—"I do not think East Florida will ever be valuable to Britain as a *plantation*"—and he argued that position in every way he could to every interested correspondent and business associate, even to those like Oswald and Governor Grant who in fact in the end did manage to develop their land profitably.[51]

To some extent Laurens was right—not because there was no fertile land: in sum, there was a great deal of it; but because the arable fields were scattered among swampland and marshes, interrupted by lakes and streams widening out into shallow ponds, surrounded by virtual jungles of mangroves and cypresses, and interspersed among sandy pine barrens. At best

---

Egmont of over £12,000, had finally begun to show a profit, as had Richard Oswald's "Mount Oswald" on the Tomoka River, just north of Mosquito Inlet. And there were a few other successes —Moultrie's "Bella Vista" near St. Augustine and his "Rosetta Place" far to the south; Capt. Robert Bisset's "Mount Plenty"; and the properties of the former governor, Grant, of the military engineer James Moncrief, and of the absentee entrepreneur Peter Taylor. Trustees of the late Earl of Egmont to Grant, Feb. 21, 1771, and Yeats to Grant, May 24, 1774, MacPherson-Grant Papers, bundles 264 and 369; Egmont Papers, Add. MSS 47054A.

Settlers—independent householders similar to the Harrisons and Truemans and Pipeses in Nova Scotia—did arrive, but they left quickly or did not continue as planters. In De Brahm's enumeration of all arrivals in East Florida from 1763 to 1771, the names of 288 white adult males are listed, in addition to Turnbull's settlers at New Smyrna. But by 1771 all but 75 of the 288 had either died, left the province, or turned from planting to shopkeeping or officeholding. *De Brahm's Report,* pp. [180–186].

[51] *Laurens Papers,* IV, 430; V, 155, 156, 158; VI, 122, 135, 153, 156, 424; VII, 268, 360, 410, 501.

good farmland would have had to be developed carefully out of patches of fertile soil scattered through this complex terrain. But that possibility was inhibited by two limitations. First, an Indian reserve, negotiated in 1765, set the western boundary of east coast settlement at the St. Johns River; a few especially enterprising or restless souls like Rolle found that to be a constraint. Second, and more important, the Privy Council's land grants, which so excited the bonanza mentality of the East Florida Society, withdrew from practical use huge parcels of the best land east of the Indian boundary.

The summary figures are revealing. While of 242 Privy Council grants of East Florida land only 114 were actually processed in the colony, those 114, almost all to absentees, totaled 1,443,000 acres. In fact only 16 of the 114 grantees actually settled some part of their land, but the other 98 grants continued to represent legal titles and in effect kept from circulation well over a million acres—precisely how much cannot be known since the surveys were inexact and there was no way of policing encroachments. In contrast to these large grants made by the Privy Council to absentees, the total acreage awarded to residents, presumably actual farmers, by the East Florida Council was small. While the English authorities were parceling out initial rights to a total of about 3 million acres to absentees, in units that averaged 12,000 acres, the colony's council was issuing to residents in "family" grants, which averaged 366 acres, a total of only just over 200,000 acres. How many of the 576 small grants that the colony's council awarded were ever surveyed and settled is not known—perhaps 80 if the same proportion of settlements to surveyed grants prevailed at this level as it did among the larger grants.[52]

Yet even all of this—the dispersal of arable land in an extremely difficult terrain, much of which was tied up in absentee holdings—is not sufficient to explain the unexpected outcome. Given these circumstances, the decisive element was the necessary character of the labor force. The situation,

---

[52] *De Brahm's Report*, pp. 255–256; Mowat, *East Florida*, pp. 59–62. The dangers of tying up large parcels of land in absentee proprietorships had been understood by some from the beginning. Governor Grant, in his general scheme of development of 1764, had warned that "no lands ought to be granted but to people who are actually to reside in the country." Knox, fresh from his experiences in Georgia, had been more explicit in his so-called "Hints" of 1764. If large tracts were granted in England even to people with "plausible pretences" of transporting settlers, "that province can never become of any value to Great Britain, for such grantees very seldom fulfill their promises, but instead of doing so keep their lands unoccupy'd in expectation of their becoming more valuable by the settlement of the other parts of the province." And later, when these predictions came true, Bernard Romans deplored the "monopolizers of East Florida" who could not tell pine barrens from savannas, and Lieutenant Governor Moultrie, one of the most successful of the resident planters, regretted "to see so good a part of the colony run out in large tracts for grantee's at home who likely do not mean to cultivate them, and have not left room for other settlers, for many miles on the rivers." Grant, *Gen. James Grant*, p. 73; Knox, "Hints," p. [10]; Mowat, *East Florida*, p. 61; Moultrie to Grant, St. Augustine, June 3, 1773, MacPherson-Grant Papers, bundle 370.

environmental and legal, was not conducive to the recruitment of a population of free householders. The staggeringly difficult labor required to create
farmland or even cattle ranges out of tangled thickets of mangroves and
palmettos would be done only under duress. Freemen with any alternatives
whatever would not suffer the brutalities of such labor, nor would they
willingly engage in the miserable work required to produce the region's
most reliable cash crop, indigo. Only bondsmen—chattel slaves—under
physical duress could be made to do this work. Slaves were therefore
essential, and while few Anglo-Americans had compunctions about buying
and using slaves, they were expensive, and emigrant householders seeking
independent properties like those being developed by family labor out of
wild land in Nova Scotia were rarely in a position to acquire them.

Every informed observer sooner or later became convinced that a slave
labor force was essential to developing profitable agriculture in Florida.
Even before he arrived in Florida Governor Grant assumed this when he
planned a slave force to support the free Huguenots he hoped to bring to
Florida, and he promoted the importation of slaves by including them in
the headright system of land distribution. For while advancing every
scheme, however unlikely, to settle whites in the colony, he knew that
"Africans are the only people to go to work in warm climates." Indentured
servants, he believed, could scarcely be made to work for their own survival.
Even the Germans, famous for their industry and enterprise, were worthless in East Florida. "Upon their landing they are immediately seized with
the pride which every man is possessed of who wears a white face in
America, and they say they won't be slaves and so they make their escape."
Once the land was opened to cultivation by slaves, however, whites might
be able to prosper on small farms.

Oswald, a successful West Indian planter and investor in South Carolina properties, was even more insistent. It took "a gang of seasoned
negroes," he believed, to start a plantation in Florida; later it might be
sustained by new slaves fresh from Africa. As for indentured servants, they
were simply unobtainable "at almost any wages." Rolle learned the same
facts only at great expense. What little productive work was done at Rollestown was done not by the indentured servants Rolle brought over—and
failed to keep on his farm—but by the slaves he soon began to acquire;
Rollestown became profitable only when it became a slave plantation. All
the successful plantations were based on slave labor, and even Turnbull had
known about this apparent fact of life in East Florida well enough to have
used slaves to prepare the ground for his settlers, and he planned the
purchase of a large number of slaves to support the Mediterranean laborers.
If he had not himself realized this necessity he had his supplier Laurens at
hand to instruct him that "in these southern climes," "negroes are the most
useful servants." New Smyrna might have had a very different history if

a large shipment of slaves that Turnbull ordered had not miscarried.[53]

Laurens, Grant, Romans—all close students of life in East Florida—learned that indentured servants, resistant to the heavy labor most needed on the plantations, were scarcely worth their cost. Since the transit from bondsman to established householder required capital they did not have, they had little to look forward to, were insolent, unmanageable, and often unwilling to serve out their terms of service. Romans, in his advice to northerners thinking of migrating to Florida, made the point dramatically. In three months, he wrote, your white servants would refuse to call you master "in a country where the most dirty vagabond you can hire at six dollars per month would think his honour touched by hearing any body call him to you with less civility than, *Sir, your employer would be glad to speak to you.*" So the numbers of indentured servants declined while the slave force increased. In November 1767 seventy Negroes were imported directly from Africa, the first recruited in this way. The word in Charleston that autumn was that 2,000 more were on their way to East Florida. Grant estimated that there were 600 working slaves in the province in 1767; De Brahm's figure for 1771 was 900.[54]

In such a world, what were the prospects for an ambitious householder with little but his own and his family's labor to help him establish himself? Fertile land that could be readily developed was not easily available; when it could be acquired there were substantial fees for gaining title; and a necessary labor force could only be bought at a very high price. Beyond all of this, the physical conditions of life in most places were fearful, and there was always the danger of a complete defeat, of utter demoralization, and of sudden barbarization. The danger of such a collapse was palpable, and examples were notorious.

William Bartram, the future naturalist, barely escaped. Aged twenty-seven, he had accompanied his father to Florida in the winter of 1765–1766, and, when his father had returned to Philadelphia, had petitioned for and received a grant of 500 acres, which he located on the St. Johns River. There Henry Laurens, on his inspection trip of 1766, found him. "That poor young man," he reported with shock to William's father, was living in a small "hovel" that was "not proof against the weather," that was extremely hot ("the only disagreeably hot place that I found in East Florida"), and that was located on a sandy pine barren at the edge of a swamp that had formed in a small cove of the river. The river's current did not flow through this swampy inlet, and as a result the water there, covered with decaying

[53]Siebert, "Slavery and White Servitude," p. 8; Schafer, "Early Plantation Development," pp. 49–50, 47, 39, 41; *Laurens Papers*, VI, 155; Corse, *Turnbull*, p. 44.
[54]Romans, *Natural History*, p. 130; Mowat, *East Florida*, p. 67.

vegetation, was "almost stagnated, [and] exceedingly foul & absolutely stank when stirred up by our oars." William had been attempting to cut down trees and clear the swamp, but without much success, Laurens wrote, "for want of strong hands. He assured me that he had but two among the six negroes that you gave him that could handle an axe tolerably & one of those two had been exceedingly insolent." The situation was grim, Laurens concluded. William's provisions were "scanty even to penury. . . . His own health very imperfect, he had the fever when I was first with him & looked very poorly in the second visit." He hoped he was not exaggerating in his description of "the forlorn state of poor Billy Bartram":

> A gentle mild young man, no wife, no friend, no companion, no neighbour, no human inhabitant within nine miles of him the near-est by water, no boat to come at them & those only common soldiers, seated upon a beggarly spot of land, scant of the bare necessaries & totally void of all the comforts of life except an inimitable degree of patience . . . an unpleasant unhealthy situation. Six negroes rather plagues than aids to him, of whom one so insolent as to threaten his life, one a useless expence, one a helpless child in arms, one a pregnant woman without prospect of any female help, distant 30 long miles from the metropolis, no money to pay the expence of a journey there upon the most important occasions, over a road al-ways bad & in wet weather wholly impassable. . . . These I say are discouragements enough to break the spirits of any modest young man & more than any man should be exposed to without his own free acceptance, unless his crimes had been so great as to merit a state of exile.

Laurens was not surprised to learn that William had grown despondent and was hoping to be able to "decamp." At the very least he needed emergency supplies and an "exchange of good negroes in place of almost useless ones that are wanting." Laurens hoped William's father would quickly supply these necessities "to make his banishment less galling & present him with some prospect of reaping the fruit of his labours."[55]

Young Bartram was in due course rescued, and he returned to Philadel-phia to fulfill his ambitions and live a long and fruitful life. But other adventurous and independent young men in the situation Bartram found himself in in 1766, facing a brutal environment without resources or assist-ance or homes to return to, were not rescued, and they succumbed to an environment they could not control.

[55] *Laurens Papers*, V, 151–155.

13

Gulf and Delta

EAST FLORIDA from the beginning had a peculiar fascination for writers, speculators, and adventurers alike, but the western province had no such exotic attractiveness, and its population history in this crucial decade of expansion was more businesslike, less dramatic, and for many involved more successful. While it too became dominated by slave-worked plantations rather than family farms, it differed significantly from East Florida in its human recruitment and in its relation to the population movements of the time. Behind these differences lay several highly favorable circumstances.

First, the colony lay adjacent to the territory of a rival power, Spain, which by the treaty of 1763 gained possession from France of the entire trans-Mississippi west, "Louisiana," which included the so-called Isle of Orleans, a 125-mile strip east of the Mississippi at its mouth (see map). The Spanish border areas closest to West Florida, especially the Isle of Orleans, had been populated by France, and there was good reason to think that the settlers established there could be brought over into British territory to help settle the new province. Second, the colony's proximity to Spanish territory meant that the home government was concerned with the colony's military security and hence would be prepared to invest in its garrisons, riverways, roads, and population growth far more than it would otherwise have done. Third, the remoteness of this far borderland colony from familiar sea lanes and trade routes, its obscurity and lack of glamour, meant that the metropolitan entrepreneurs plunging into overseas land speculation were relatively uninterested in its possibilities and hence tied up less of its land in absentee grants. A mere forty-one grants were issued for that colony by the Privy Council in the 1760s, averaging less than 10,000 acres each; the Privy Council's total commitment to grants of this kind in West Florida

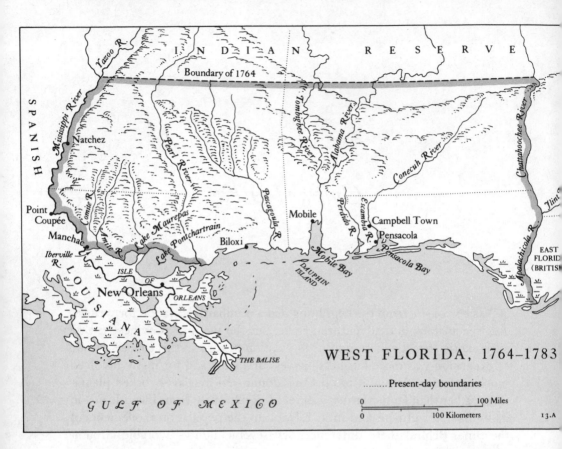

Boundary of 1764

WEST FLORIDA, 1764–1783

.... Present-day boundaries

0 — 100 Miles

0 — 100 Kilometers

13.A

amounted to less than a fifth of the number issued for East Florida during the same years, and less than a seventh of the acreage. And only about half of all the grants awarded in England were ever presented for surveys in the colony. Most important of all, though only gradually revealed, was the fact that the amplitude, accessibility, and richness of the arable land in the western province were far greater than in the eastern, despite all the praise that had been given East Florida's resources. All of these differences helped shape the process of population recruitment and the resulting demographic pattern.[1]

[1]Cecil Johnson, *British West Florida, 1763–1783* (New Haven, 1943), pp. 31–32. The precise number of orders in council for West Florida land grants is not clear. Johnson finds 45 (p. 119), but Charles L. Mowat, in his careful calculation, finds only 41 (*East Florida as a British Province, 1763–1784* [Berkeley, 1943], p. 59). But the insignificance of large-scale grants to absentees in West Florida was generally recognized. Clinton N. Howard, *The British Development of West Florida, 1763–1769* (Berkeley, 1947), pp. 37–38.

Entry

The first British to inspect the province were the military commanders, who in 1763 took over the Spanish garrisons at Pensacola and Mobile and toured the adjacent land. They were dismayed at what they found. The land they first encountered, along the gulf shorelands, was sandy and infertile, useful if at all only for pasturage. The fort at Pensacola was dilapidated and the barracks a mere collection of windowless bark huts. As for Mobile, Governor Johnstone reported, "the state of the town in filth, nastiness & brushwood running over the houses is hardly to be credited"; it was surely, he said, "the most unhealthy place on the face of the earth." Neither the Spanish nor the French had developed farms or even useful gardens around the forts, and disease was rampant among the few hundred inhabitants. A year after the British takeover, little had improved. Most of the Spanish had left and the few who remained were mainly adventurers and "riffraff," with here and there an "indentured servant, a rare slave, and a few wandering Indians begging bread or trinkets."[2]

Johnstone immediately set to work improving the situation. He had a ground plan drawn up for building a proper town at Pensacola, assigning sections for public purposes and lots and garden properties for private inhabitants. At the same time he set in motion two major engineering projects which would help open up to British penetration the little-known lands along the Mississippi. He sent his engineers to clear the debris and uprooted trees that clogged the short Iberville River, which led from the Mississippi to Lakes Maurepas and Pontchartrain and thence to the gulf. For if the Iberville were open to shipping, Britain could funnel off to Mobile and Pensacola all of the Indian trade that flowed down the Mississippi before it could reach the Spanish in New Orleans, and at the same time facilitate the movement of settlers south from the Illinois country into the gulf shorelands and north from the gulf into the Mississippi delta. And to protect this vital short-cut route from the gulf to the Mississippi and up through that river to the trans-Appalachian northwest, he began investigating the possibility of building a fort at a spot called Manchac, where the Iberville joins the Mississippi. In the end neither of these projects succeeded, but in the process of investigation and exploration, the river routes were carefully traced, the extraordinarily rich delta lands were at least in part recognized for what they were, the first land grants were laid out along the river, and under the keen eye of Elias Durnford, the colony's surveyor

[2]Johnson, *West Florida*, pp. 7, 9, 12, 25; Robert R. Rea, " 'Graveyard for Britons,' West Florida, 1763–1781," *Florida Historical Quarterly*, 47 (1969), 346, 349.

general, the first of a series of detailed land-grant maps of the province was drawn up.[3]

In the midst of this first flurry of activity, Johnstone pursued the possibility of drawing over to British territory the former French inhabitants, now under Spanish rule—and not only the French. A large community of Germans and Swiss had been settled early in the century in a section called the "German Coast" on the Isle of Orleans, and an encampment of refugee Acadians had taken stable form just above the Germans on the same stretch of the lower Mississippi. Word received in London and conveyed to the colony was that more than 400 Swiss and German families would move east with their stock if they were protected by British troops. Johnstone's first direct contact with these groups revealed that they were indeed interested in migrating to British territory, but also that they correctly believed the lands on the margins of the gulf were infertile, that they were uncertain of the British government's attitude toward Roman Catholics, and that they saw no way of selling their present property for negotiable funds. Johnstone was able to reassure them on some points, but their distrust continued until, later in the decade, the rich delta lands were opened up; but by then it was clear that the Spanish regime was unexpectedly mild and reasonable, and the propulsion of fear diminished. In the end, some of the inhabitants of Spanish Louisiana did come over to British territory, but though the West Florida government continued to exploit every sign of discontent in Louisiana, refugees from that Spanish province did not constitute a major element in the colony's population.[4]

Greater hopes were held for the success of the small contingent of French Huguenots whom the colony's first lieutenant governor, Montfort Browne, brought with him when he arrived in the colony in January 1766. Like the French Protestants who had been sent to South Carolina instead of to East Florida two years earlier, these refugees had been subsidized by the British government in the hope that they would establish silk manufactures in the colony and begin the cultivation of vineyards. Browne, an ambitious, avaricious, and cantankerous man, first confused them by attempting to settle them as tenants on his own property on Dauphin Island near Mobile, then established them in a new village called Campbell Town located in a peculiarly unhealthy spot north of Pensacola Bay. The little

[3] Johnson, *West Florida*, pp. 29, 33–36. For a contemporary's careful analysis of Johnstone's strategy in attempting to clear the Iberville to advance the peopling of the colony, see Philip Pittman, *The Present State of the European Settlements on the Mississippi . . .* (London, 1770), p. 26. This important survey, containing the first detailed description, maps, and illustrations of the newly acquired province, written by a young army officer, has been twice reprinted in excellent facsimile editions, by Robert R. Rea (Gainesville, Fla., 1973) and John F. McDermott ([Memphis], 1977).
[4] Pittman, *Present State*, pp. 22–25; Howard, *British Development*, pp. 28–30 (for specific instances of the resettlement of Spanish/French nationals, pp. 93, 100); Johnson, *West Florida*, pp. 35, 33, 151, 135.

community, poorly led, had no success in developing its assigned products, and was maintained only by a subsidy from the provincial government. By 1770 all but two or three of the Huguenots had died or were scattered through the province. Their pastor ended up in Charleston, South Carolina, attempting to support himself by teaching French.

There are traces too of a group of German emigrants that planned to settle in the colony in the same year as the French, but their movements cannot be followed in the colony's scant records. And from time to time ships from England, arriving at the main port of Pensacola, brought with them settlers from Britain. The Register of 1773–1776 records five departures for West Florida—emigrants who were typical of a small influx from Britain that continued throughout the years of British rule. One of the registered emigrants to West Florida was a twenty-nine-year-old "clerk" from Gloucestershire, who left from Bristol to take up a minor post in the colony's government. The other four, three artisans and a spinster, left from the port of London. Free people in their twenties, traveling alone, two from Scotland, one from London, one from Kent, they intended, they said, "to settle" in the far western province. They were not unique; such migrations, in small numbers, were continuing throughout these years. So in 1769 one John Haigh had arrived from England with his wife, four children, and two servants; desiring, he said, "to settle," he petitioned for 1,000 acres of land for grazing. As late as 1774 plans were being projected to bring over a hundred families from Scotland.[5]

Discovering the Delta

While such episodes were hopeful signs of migrations that might contribute substantially to the colony's peopling, the major sources were developing in other ways. The process is encapsulated in the short career in West Florida of the cranky but energetic lieutenant governor, Montfort Browne. His arrival in 1766 had been preceded by a letter informing the government that he, his father, and two brothers had together received a Privy Council grant for 20,000 acres. Some of this entitlement Browne located on Dauphin Island off Mobile Bay. But two years later, in the spring and summer of 1768, Browne made one of the first extended explorations of the western parts of the province, and his interests shifted. Traveling in the flood season, he was able to navigate through the lakes and the Iberville to reach the Mississippi, and then he ascended the twisting, debris-filled river at least as far as the dilapidated fort at "The Natches."

[5] *Ibid.*, pp. 57, 151, 62, 152–153; Howard, *British Development*, p. 101; Cecil Johnson, "Expansion in West Florida, 1770–1779," *Mississippi Valley Historical Review*, 20 (1933–1934), 491.

What he found there was a revelation, and he wrote excitedly to Lord Hillsborough about it. The soil along the Mississippi, he wrote, was extraordinarily fertile. The Natchez area, about a third of the way up to the colony's northern border, was so rich and so attractive that he would happily spend the rest of his days there. Everywhere he had found "the most charming prospects in the world, extensive plains intermixed with beautiful hills, and small rivers; here are, my lord, fruit trees of most excellent kinds, the grape, peach, plum, apricot, pear, figs, mulberry, cherry, persimmon, medlars, and strawberries as good in their kind as any in the world and in as great abundance."

Other explorations followed quickly. In the spring of 1770 Governor Chester sent Elias Durnford, who had become the lieutenant governor, to inspect the country. Durnford's report fully confirmed Browne's, in regard not only to the lands along the Mississippi but also to those along the colony's southern border from the Mississippi east to the gulf. These were lands, he reported, "superior in goodness to what I have ever imagined," and he recommended the immediate nullification of all unused land grants issued to absentees and the establishment of new townships along the rivers to attract settlers.

But the most rhapsodic, ecstatic report came from another investigator of 1770, Edward Mease, a councilor long settled on the gulf coast and in Pensacola, who set out on his own exploration of the lower Mississippi later in the year. His praise of what he found, recorded in a long and detailed "Narrative" he sent to Hillsborough, was unbounded, and highly circumstantial. "No lands in North America can possibly exceed the banks of this noble river in fertility," he wrote. "The situation is inconceivably beautifull. . . . Looking eastward [from Natchez] you see *a country* land not gradually rising into hills but a fine undulating country which even the celebrated Campania of Rome cannot exceed in beauty." And the timber —"no country on earth," Bernard Romans wrote after his exploration of the province, "can surpass it either in quantity, quality or variety. The quantity is such as makes it absolutely impossible to describe to an European who has not seen the like, and indeed it is beyond the conception of an inhabitant of any part of that quarter of the world [Europe]; where such vast and continued forests and desarts are utterly unknown every where." And it was all within easy reach of rivers leading to excellent markets.[6]

[6]Howard, *British Development*, pp. 56, 63, 69, 107, 58; Johnson, *West Florida*, pp. 61–62n., 64–65; Chester to Hillsborough, Pensacola, June 20, 1771, and Durnford to Chester, Pensacola, June 23, 1771, Dartmouth Papers, Canada, V, 5767–5768, 5773–5776; Edward Mease, "Narrative of a Journey through Several Parts of the Province of West Florida in the Years 1770 and 1771," and Bernard Romans, "An Attempt towards a Short Description of West Florida," in Eron O. Rowland, "Peter Chester, Third Governor of . . . West Florida . . . 1770–1781," *Publications of the Mississippi Historical Society*, 5 (1925), 67, 69, 77, 176. So, similarly, Pittman, *Present State*, p. 37: "the *Natches* . . . the finest and most fertile part of West Florida."

By the time Mease returned to Pensacola, in March 1771, the movement of settlers was under way, in response to these discoveries of the extraordinarily rich Mississippi delta, with its deep black alluvial soil and its vast stands of timber. These priceless resources would provide the basis for the colony's rapid population growth.

The local officials moved first. At the very first opportunity Browne staked out his claim to choice lands along the Mississippi. In December 1768 he surveyed and confirmed one plot of 17,400 acres and another of 2,000 in a bend of the river just north of Baton Rouge; his brother William laid claim to two islands in the river nearby. Similarly, Mease, within a month of his return from his river trip, took possession of a plot of 5,000 acres in a protected cove near Natchez, and a month after that he added another of 200 acres just south of Baton Rouge. At about the same time Durnford took out 9 plots totaling 14,513 acres scattered along the river bank. Peter Chester, the colony's second governor, took 7,300 acres in 7 grants similarly dispersed, and the military commander, General Haldimand, claimed 3,000 acres in 4 grants along the river. But the most significant aspect of Browne's land acquisitions lay in the fact that one of his kinsmen associated with him in the Privy Council grant was "of New York." For the opening of the Mississippi delta lands in the late sixties was the impetus for a major movement of people west and south from the backcountry of the older colonies into the new colony of West Florida. It is this migration, prefigured in the Brownes' connections in New York, that largely accounts for the peopling of Britain's westernmost province.[7]

First Settlers

It had started in 1767 with a seepage of people from the seaboard colonies, not at first to the Mississippi delta but to the fertile upper valley of the Tombigbee and Alabama rivers, which empty into Mobile Bay and whose sources, almost 300 miles to the north, connect, directly or indirectly, with the Tennessee and the Ohio tributaries. Through that river system emigrants from the older colonies flocked in increasing numbers south into the lands above Mobile Bay to begin opening the colony's central sector. And

[7]The acreage and dating of these grants have been derived from the reference tables accompanying two of the remarkable maps of West Florida produced by Elias Durnford; the maps show every twist and turn of the Mississippi and the location of every grant along the river: "Plan of the River Mississippi, from the River Yasous to the River Ibberville in West Florida" [1771] (4 mi./inch), CO 700, Florida/45, Public Record Office, and "Plan of the Rivers Mississippi, Iberville, Mobile and Bay of Pensacola in the Province of West Florida . . ." (1772), K CXXII, 90, British Library, London. The exact locations of the grants are drawn in greatest detail (1½ mi./inch) in a third of Durnford's maps, approximately 10 feet long, CO 700, Florida/38 [c. 1774]. Howard, *British Development*, p. 56; for specific examples of this domestic migration, pp. 97, 99, 100–101.

then, when the Mississippi lands were better known, the flow turned west and south to the delta, and especially to the area around Natchez. By 1770 what had begun as a thin, irregular trickle of wagons and barges, of carts and rafts and canoes moving tentatively, in isolation, through a vast wilderness, was becoming a small but steady flow, directed by experienced guides, along well-marked paths to destinations well canvassed in advance.

Governor Peter Chester, newly arrived in the colony in 1770, understood the situation clearly. In a long, masterful letter to Lord Hillsborough he explained the desperation of newly arriving migrants from the east, their need for help from the government, their importance to the future of the colony, and the likelihood that others from the older colonies would continue to arrive in increasing numbers. "When they first arrive on the Mississippi, they are with their wives and children destitute of almost every thing, and without a little assistance from hence of powder, shot, salt and corn, which it will be unavoidable to give them, they will be driven to the greatest distress during the winter." He hoped Hillsborough would appreciate the importance of helping these people. If supported over this initial period and thereafter encouraged, they would populate the Mississippi lands in large numbers. For inhabitants of the backcountry of the older colonies, Chester wrote, "find their lands either so barren, or are obliged to pay such high prices for them to the different proprietors that many of them have been waiting with impatience for an opportunity of removing." Some, of course, had been hoping that England would create new provinces in the immediate trans-Appalachian west, but since that was clearly not to be, "they will naturally flock to the Mississippi, some down the Ohio, and others by sea, the soil and climate of that country having the highest character through the whole continent." And as producers of timber, rice, indigo, hemp, and corn, and as transshippers of the huge inland Indian trade, they would fulfill all the mercantilist requirements of colonization.

They were not men of property, to be sure, Chester recognized, but neither were they the outlaws and thuggish riffraff that infested the backcountry of all the colonies. They were industrious people who "either could not subsist upon the barren lands on the back parts of the provinces from whence they came, or could not afford to pay to proprietors such sums as they demanded, and were therefore induced to emigrate into a country of whose fertility of soil and temperature of climate they had received such favourable accounts, in order to better their circumstances." Such people could not contribute capital to the development of the province, but they "can labour, and will make very good *first settlers*.... These sort of people, however insignificant they may appear, are the only persons we can expect that will first attempt to settle an uninhabited country, surrounded on all sides by numerous tribes of savages." Once these people break open the land to settlement "we are then to expect some people of *real property* who will have it in their power to make useful improvements . . . and would not themselves become the first adventurers, nor trust their property, untill they see that protection and encouragement will be given to them." The pace could not be forced, nor could the settlements be arbitrarily selected. The natural flow, already in motion, settling where it would in West Florida, would provide a basic population for the colony, Chester wrote, given "the natural disposition for emigration that prevails in all the old colonies."[8]

His prediction was accurate. They came, in the years that followed, from everywhere: from central and western New York via the Ohio; from the backcountry of Pennsylvania via Fort Pitt and the Ohio; from western Maryland and Virginia via the Holston and Tennessee rivers; and especially from western North Carolina through gaps and passes in the Appalachians to the Tennessee, Tombigbee, and Mississippi valleys. But they came not only from these closest, western parts of the established colonies: they came too from some of the most distant and least accessible places—from New England, particularly Connecticut, by ship through the Gulf of Mexico, and, in surprising numbers, overland from New Jersey. And some came from Britain.

The reach and sweep of these hegiras—along river routes hundreds of miles long, across portages, through fords, and over makeshift ferries, along Indian trails and on rough, rocky wagon roads only recently cut through the woods—are extraordinary. Most were small group movements, many of single families or of clusters of families that came together at staging points like Fort Pitt. The traces of these small-scale intercolonial migrations are largely lost to historical sight in the exiguous records of the time. But notices of a few survive—enough to form a chronology of major episodes that exemplify this process of recruitment, so different from the failing efforts being made in East Florida.

One of the first large groups to migrate from the eastern colonies to West Florida were backcountry Virginians for whom the Chesapeake markets were inaccessible and who had moved in large numbers to the disputed borderland of western Pennsylvania. They began their investigation of West Florida in 1768. Two years later, in May 1770, when the roads to the western Pennsylvania frontier were filled with settlers' wagons, they asked Durnford to reserve for them a strip ten miles long on the Mississippi River. In July of the same year another group consisting of 79 whites and 18 black slaves, mostly from Redstone Creek, just south of Fort Pitt, were led by an experienced guide down the Ohio to Natchez. Carrying with them equip-

---

[8] *Ibid.*, p. 36; Chester to Hillsborough, Pensacola, Sept. 26, 1770, in Rowland, "Peter Chester," pp. 19, 20, 23, 24. For Hillsborough's approval of settlement along the Mississippi up to Natchez and his willingness to subsidize the first settlers, see Chester to Hillsborough, June 20, 1771, Dartmouth Papers, Canada, V, 5767–5768.

ment to build a sawmill and a gristmill, and numbering among them artisans as well as farmers, they were in a position to exact protection and
support from the colony, especially since they could give assurances that
at least 100 families would follow them from western Pennsylvania, Virginia, and North Carolina if their reports were favorable. A year later the
intention of 200 families in the quickly populating Holston River valley of
eastern Tennessee to settle in West Florida was sufficiently positive for the
colony's council to agree to furnish them with provisions until they could
support themselves.

A year after that, in October 1772, Captain Amos Ogden of New Jersey
—a veteran Indian trader, land jobber, and bush fighter who had been
defeated in the "Pennamite War" launched to expel the Connecticut settlers in Pennsylvania's Wyoming Valley—located and surveyed a personal
grant of 25,000 acres near Natchez. He reserved another strip of 15,000 acres
for those who, he said, would soon follow him from his native colony. His
promise was good: within a year enough people had followed him to justify
family grants of 3,550 acres. By the time that information came in, another
New Jersey leader, the Reverend Samuel Sweesy, who had already led
people from that colony to West Florida, was also laying claim to a 25,000-
acre block near Natchez. And almost simultaneously three groups interested in bringing settlers in from New York—one led by the Rapalje family,
the second by the Livingstons, the third by a group of Pensacola merchants
—reserved blocks of the same size for the settlers they hoped to attract.
Soon thereafter notice of the arrival, or the intention to settle, of several
other large groups, mainly from Pennsylvania and New Jersey, were received, while a Colonel Anthony Hutchins and his associates reserved a
tract of no less than 152,000 acres near Natchez for families from Virginia
and the Carolinas.[9]

Connecticut Yankees on the Mississippi

In these cases the documents are scant, the details missing. But in the case
of the largest single group of migrants to settle in the delta before the
Revolution, much more is known, and the details illuminate the background of the other migrations. The origins of this group go back to the
mobilization of Connecticut farmers, under Major General Phineas Lyman
of Suffield, Connecticut, and Captain (later General) Israel Putnam, to fight

[9]Johnson, *West Florida*, pp. 136–140; John McIntire to Chester, Fort Natchez, July 19, 1770, and the
Deposition of Daniel Huay, Aug. 20, 1770, Rowland, "Peter Chester," pp. 25–27. On Ogden's
flamboyant career, see J. P. Boyd, "Connecticut's Experiment in Expansion, the Susquehannah
Company, 1753–1803," *Journal of Economic and Business History*, 4 (1931), 47–50; William Brewster,
The Pennsylvania and New York Frontier (Philadelphia, 1954), pp. 159–161.

in the campaigns in upper New York in the 1750s and then in 1762 to share in the successful siege of Havana. That military engagement, which resulted in the conquest of Cuba (later exchanged for Spanish Florida) was dangerous enough, but not half so dangerous as the conditions in the army camps where the provincial troops were confined, after the siege, through a tropical summer. It was the malnutrition, contaminated water, absence of sanitation, and vitiating labor in the camps that mainly accounted for the fearful death toll. Two-fifths of the 1,050 Connecticut men who had sailed for Cuba died before the regiment was disbanded six months later. The survivors were disoriented, dissatisfied with the terms of their discharge, and frustrated by the prospects that faced them at home. In June 1763 they formed a "Company of Military Adventurers" to seek land "sufficient for a government, in some of the conquer'd lands in America." Dues were collected, officers and a standing committee were appointed, and General Lyman, well acquainted with leading figures through his war service, was sent off to England "to solicit His Majesty for said grant."[10]

Favored by the promise in the Proclamation of 1763 that veterans of the late war would receive cheap or free land in the new colonies in America, Lyman applied for a major grant in West Florida. But London was full of schemers, British and American, promoting land deals in the newly opened west, and Lord Hillsborough, Lyman correctly reported, was adamantly opposed to all substantial settlements in the west, to say nothing of the founding of trans-Appalachian colonies. So several years went by with no sign of success, and Lyman occupied himself in advancing his own interests, receiving in 1770 a personal grant of 20,000 acres in West Florida. When, finally, in 1772 Hillsborough resigned, his "ill will . . . [no longer] so likely to injure me [Lyman] by preventing the emanation of royal goodness," and was succeeded by the more sympathetic Dartmouth, Lyman was able to return to Connecticut confident that the Adventurers' grant in West Florida would soon be forthcoming. The company was reconvened, a formal roster of members, old and new, was drawn up, terms for newcomers to join the organization were specified, a committee was appointed to go to West Florida to "explore and reconnoitre" the land, and it was decided to advertise "the doings of this meeting" in the newspapers of Connecticut, Massachusetts, New York, and Pennsylvania.[11]

The reconnoitering committee, led by Israel Putnam, two of his sons,

[10]Lawrence H. Gipson, *The Great War for Empire: The Victorious Years, 1758–1760,* (*The British Empire before the American Revolution,* VII, New York, 1949), pp. 79–80, 154, 157, 224, 232–234; *The Two Putnams . . . with Some Account of the Company of Military Adventurers,* ed. Albert C. Bates (Hartford, 1931), pp. 3–11.
[11]Lyman to Earl of Loudoun, Suffield, Conn., Oct. 21, 1772, Papers of the Marquess of Bute, NRA(S)/0631, Scottish Record Office, Edinburgh; *Two Putnams,* pp. 18–27. For Lyman's personal grant, see William L. Grant and James Munro, eds., *Acts of the Privy Council of England, Colonial Series* (Hereford, 1908–1912), V, 594.

and Lyman's son Thaddeus, sailed into Pensacola Bay on March 5, 1773. They were welcomed by Governor Chester and were given every encouragement by him and the council to explore the Mississippi lands on the assumption "that the lands they should choose and fix upon should be granted to them and their associates, in townships of about 20,000 acres each." The established terms for free family grants were extended to them, and they proceeded to the Mississippi, where they discovered, as had those who had preceded them, that the delta lands, "for fertility and the variety of produce it would afford upon cultivation appeared to be equal, if not superior to any in North America"; it was, they said, "a very easy country to live in, and independent fortunes may be made there equal to almost any country in the world." And so they reserved a tract of land extending more than ten miles along the Mississippi south of the Yazoo, providing space for nineteen townships (380,000 acres). All of this was duly registered in Pensacola, and the nineteen townships were drawn in large yellow blocks in Durnford's largest and most detailed map of West Florida, undated but completed in all probability in 1774.

By August the exploring committee was back in Connecticut and reported jubilantly to the company. The Adventurers were clearly moving toward the satisfaction of their ambitions, but the time was now short. "The adjacent country was settling in the most rapid manner," the committee reported, "settlers flocking to it from all quarters," and the huge reservation could not be held indefinitely. In November four townships were selected for initial settlement, and on December 19, 1773, the first party of about 30 settlers left Middletown, Connecticut, for Pensacola. General Lyman and his son led a second party soon thereafter, and the general's wife followed with a third contingent from Massachusetts that left in the summer of 1774. In all, in these two years, some 400 New England families, drawn chiefly from the lower Connecticut River valley, joined this migration to the Mississippi.[12]

So the New Englanders, more than 2,000 miles from home, struck roots in the soil of West Florida. Who were these migrants? Why had they left for this distant frontier? Letters from Lyman to Lord Dartmouth, upon whose good will everything depended, and to Lord Loudoun, Lyman's former commander-in-chief, now retired in Scotland, explained the background and the Adventurers' hopes for the future. "The lands in Connecticut," Lyman wrote these patrons in almost identical letters in December 1772, "have long since been all granted out, and by division to the numerous children of families, reduced to very small tract[s] owned by individuals." Connecticut's population, he estimated, was growing by 8,000 a year, the

[12] *Two Putnams*, pp. 32–45, 261; Jack M. Sosin, *The Revolutionary Frontier, 1763–1783* (Albuquerque, N.M., 1967), pp. 39, 62, 64. The map referred to is Durnford's, 1½ mi./inch, identified above, n.7.

whole of New England's by perhaps 30,000. "This forces a constant emigration for a livelihood." At present, he wrote, the main target of emigration was an area he had once campaigned in, between Crown Point and the Connecticut River (an area which a map of 1779 locates more precisely in the Green Mountains of central Vermont near the present town of Randolph). But this was a country "so cold in winter and of such continuance, that they can't have more than six months in a year that answers for agriculture." Further, the soil was poor and the isolation disastrous for commerce, which in any case they could not advance since in that region they could not produce goods appropriate for sale within the mercantilist empire. But despite all this, "the numbers that have settled in that country since the late war is allmost incredible."

This, Lyman said, was the present, difficult situation. But all of these misfortunes could be avoided, he wrote, "If this emigration . . . could be diverted and directed to the Mississippi." In West Florida, by producing raw materials for manufactures and exotic goods that would otherwise have to be purchased abroad, each person could contribute "ten times as much to the support of the national commerce, as he can do in the afores^d northern, frozen . . . comparatively barren climes." It had been to accomplish this that the Military Adventurers had petitioned the government for the establishment of a new colony extending from the gulf to the Ohio River, "perhaps 150 or 200 miles" wide, a government, he wrote, that he would be pleased to head as its first governor. But even if the Adventurers had to operate under the jurisdiction of West Florida, whose seat of government was "at too inconvenient a distance," they were eager to proceed. The number of potential settlers increases daily, and if the plan were supported, it would "soon form a strong settlement in that country." The company proper numbered "several thousands," including "many in the southern colonies," and if they were encouraged by the government they would "soon form a settlement in the Mississippi country of eight or ten thousand inhabitants," for never, he declared, had he known "any scheem for colonization [to] engage the attention of the people so much as this does." He hoped at the least that orders would be sent from England to West Florida to assure the Adventurers of the land they sought. He himself, he said, intended to "begin a settlement there next summer and fix my abode [there] for life."[13]

[13]Lyman to Dartmouth, Suffield, [Conn.], Dec. 8, 1772, Dartmouth Papers, Canada, V, 5819–5823; Lyman to Loudoun, Oct. 21 and Dec. 10, 1772, Papers of the Marquess of Bute, NRA(S)/0631, Scottish Record Office, Edinburgh. Dartmouth had no interest in creating a separate province on the Mississippi, let alone in appointing Lyman to govern it. "Report . . . upon a Proposed . . . Colony on the Banks of the River Mississippi," Jan. 22, 1773, Dartmouth Papers, Canada, III, 3391–3395. The map referred to is Claude Sauthier's superb "Chorographical Map of the Province of New York in North America . . . Exhibiting . . . All the Private Grants of Land . . . Compiled from Actual Surveys . . ." (London, 1779), reprinted in *The Documentary History of the State of New*

How many of the Military Adventurers in fact went to the nineteen designated townships on the Mississippi between 1773 and 1776, when the Revolution put an end to the flow, is not known. Undoubtedly more than the 400 families of the first two years, though not all were successful. Lyman, the key figure in the whole adventure, survivor of the Havana campaign and of years in London's unhealthy environment, died within a year of establishing a plantation on the Big Black River near its juncture with the Mississippi. His son died there too within the same year, and his widow, who had followed him in the summer of 1774, succumbed only a few days after she arrived in Florida. Many survived, however, to constitute part of the permanent population of the great fertile crescent of the Mississippi delta.

An Enlightened Scot at Manchac

The organization and migration of Connecticut's Military Adventurers is the best-known, largest-scale episode in the transfer of people from the eastern colonies to West Florida in the pre-Revolutionary years. But though led by people of some local prominence in New England, this migration too was a movement of obscure people, anonymous except for occasional entries in official documents—unselfconscious people who left few traces of their personal circumstances, perceptions, or feelings. In one case, however, late in the period, the documents are different—more intimate, more detailed, more revealing.

William Dunbar, seen through his letters and diary, appears to be more fictional than real—a creature of William Faulkner's imagination, a more cultivated Colonel Sutpen but no less mysterious. He too, like that strange character in *Absalom, Absalom!*, was a man in his early twenties who appeared suddenly in the Mississippi wilderness to stake out a claim to a large parcel of land, then disappeared to the Caribbean, to return leading a battalion of "wild" slaves with whose labor alone he built an estate where before there had been nothing but trees and uncultivated soil. But he was more complex than Sutpen, if no less driving in his early ambitions, no less a progenitor of a notable southern family, and no less a part of a violent biracial world whose tensions could lead in strange directions. For this wilderness planter was a scientist, who would later correspond with Jefferson on science and exploration, a Mississippi planter whose contributions

---

York . . ., ed. E. B. O'Callaghan (Albany, 1850–1851), I, 525, which shows an L-shaped plot of over 30,000 acres entered in the name of Phineas Lyman just west of Tunbridge and Royalton, Vermont, on the eastern slopes of the Green Mountains. The settlement of this area, bitterly disputed between New York and New Hampshire, is discussed below, chap. 16. Lyman's settlement on the Mississippi was widely publicized: e.g., *Nova-Scotia Gazette*, June 29, Oct. 26, 1773.

to the American Philosophical Society (to which Jefferson proposed him for membership) included linguistics, archaeology, hydrostatics, astronomy, and climatology, and whose geographical explorations were reported in widely known publications. Like Sutpen an exotic figure in the plantation world of early Mississippi—known as "Sir" William as Sutpen was known as "Colonel"—he too imported into that raw, half-savage world the niceties of European culture: not chandeliers and costly rugs, but books, surveyor's equipment of the finest kind, and the latest instruments of science.

Dunbar was a Scot by birth, the youngest son of Sir Archibald Dunbar of Morayshire. He was educated first by tutors at home, then at the university in Aberdeen, where his interest in mathematics, astronomy, and belles-lettres took mature shape. What happened to him after his return home and later in London, where he circulated with young intellectuals, what propelled, or led, him out of the metropolis on the first leg of his long voyage west is not known. But whatever his motivation may have been, in April 1771, aged only twenty-two, Dunbar appeared in Philadelphia with trading goods bought in London. With that capital he crossed the mountains to Fort Pitt where for two years he traded alone, in that violent frontier outpost, until he formed a partnership with another Scotch merchant, John Ross of Philadelphia. That arrangement apparently freed him to move still farther west, and in 1773 the young man, now experienced in the ways of the American frontier, joined the movement to the rich lands of West Florida. From Fort Pitt, he descended the Ohio River by flatboat, then floated down the Mississippi. He stopped first at Baton Rouge, then selected land in the fifteen-mile strip between that populated bend and Manchac, the juncture of the Mississippi and the Iberville. To secure his grant and register title he traveled to Pensacola, and then, with this accomplished, sailed off to Jamaica, where he bought slaves, with whom he returned, via the Louisiana lakes, to his wilderness home. There he remained for a decade, until, after the peace treaty of 1783, he found himself on the Spanish side of the new United States border and moved north to a point near Natchez, where he built an estate, "The Forest," on which he lived until his death twenty-seven years later.[14]

It was at the earlier plantation, "New Richmond," near Manchac, with his slaves fresh from the Caribbean, that Dunbar established himself and created the way of life he would follow ever after. Of his life there he left

[14]For biographical information and a sketch of Dunbar's scientific work: Franklin L. Riley, "Sir William Dunbar—the Pioneer Scientist of Mississippi," *Publications of the Mississippi State Historical Society,* 2 (1899), 85–111; also the chronology and introduction to *Life, Letters and Papers of William Dunbar of Elgin, Morayshire, Scotland, and Natchez, Mississippi, Pioneer Scientist of the Southern United States,* ed. Eron Rowland (Jackson, Miss., 1930). On his education and background in Scotland, see Arthur H. DeRosier, Jr., "William Dunbar: A Product of the Eighteenth Century Scottish Renaissance," *Journal of Mississippi History,* 28 (1966), 185–227.

a record in the form of a diary covering the years 1776 to 1780. It is almost entirely a record of plantation work and of his relations with his slaves. Work engrossed him almost completely at that stage of his life. In creating and maintaining the plantation, he was experimental, diligent, and, for all his humanistic and scientific interests, a strict disciplinarian as he forced his team of slaves to tame the wilderness and wrest from it commodities vendible in the British mercantile world. His production was varied: rice, some indigo, tobacco, and cotton; and for home consumption, corn, which he milled himself, and a variety of vegetables and fruits. But his chief product throughout the years of his diary was small timber products, staves and headings for the barrels and hogsheads essential to the sugar and tobacco industries in the West Indies. For this commodity the demand was high and steady, the raw material was profuse in the nearby forests, production was simple for any able-bodied worker, and transportation to excellent markets was easy and inexpensive. So he emphasized stave making, and his diary in the early years is largely a record of the problems he faced in producing that convenient commodity and the amounts his people were able to provide. By keeping at least half of his slave force of between 17 and 25 blacks at work felling trees, sawing them into proper lengths, and splitting the logs into staves, he could turn out as many as 5,000 staves a week. From time to time he totaled his production, and the numbers he recorded are in the tens of thousands. An average month's production was 17,000 barrel staves and 1,000 headings. At one point he had about 100,000 staves piled up on the riverbank for shipment to the West Indies.

Dunbar's plantation was a work camp, an agricultural factory, and his own role was that of a vigilant supervisor and manager required to make careful judgments, day after day, in shifting a quite limited work force among a variety of productive tasks. But despite the crudeness of life in this westernmost borderland of Britain's world empire, devoted to pell-mell exploitation far from the constraints of the civilized world, the attributes of gentility were recreated even in the earlier years. Dunbar visits constantly with "the gentlemen of the settlement," who are his friends on neighboring plantations. They dine together "with mirth & good humor, our spirits being elivated by the moderate use of good Madeira wine & claret." He celebrates holidays with them at one plantation or another. He turns work into sport by arranging a week-long "trial of skill" in stave production among the slaves on the local plantations. And he is constantly at work beautifying his property, at one point cutting "an avenue thro' the swamp about 70 yards broad, opposite the house which has a fine effect in producing an excellent prospect."[15]

Ever eager for gentility, this well-educated product of the Scottish

[15] Life, Letters and Papers of William Dunbar, pp. 47, 52, 56–57, 26.

enlightenment and of London's sophistication—this bookish young *littérateur* and scientist who, only five years earlier, had been corresponding about scientific problems—about "Dean Swifts beatitudes," about the "virtuous and happy life," and about the Lord's commandment that mankind should "love one another"—was yet strangely insensitive to the suffering of those who served him. In July 1776 he recorded not the independence of the American colonies from Britain, but the suppression of an alleged conspiracy for freedom by slaves on his own plantation.

"Judge my surprise," he wrote on July 12, 1776. "Of what avail is kindness & good usage when rewarded by such ingratitude; 'tis true indeed they were kept under due subordination & obliged to do their duty in respect to plantation work, but two of the three [suspected conspirators] had always behaved so well that they had never once received a stroke of the whip." He immediately took one of the accused ringleaders to a neighbor's plantation to confront the slaves who had informed on him. Despite the informers' testimony, Dunbar's slave "still persisted in his inocence & ignorance & mentioned as an argument why it must be impossible; that he had now b[een] considerable time with his master, that he had fed & clothed him well & had never once struck him & of course it was absurd to suppose him guilty." After this unsatisfactory confrontation, Dunbar tied up the slave and put him in the bottom of the boat in which the party returned home "to seize the rest of the criminals."

Then something strange happened. Dunbar's accused slave, sitting in the bottom of the boat "with his arms pinioned," managed, when the boat was in the middle of the river, "to throw himself overboard & was immediately drowned." For Dunbar there could be only one interpretation of this desperate act—not that the slave was reacting to the hopelessness of the situation (four of the other suspects were hanged within twenty-four hours) but that he was demonstrating "evidence of his guilt." For, Dunbar reasoned, the slave must have been so "stung with the heghnousness of his guilt, ashamed perhaps to look a master in the face against whom he could urge no plea to paliate his intended diabolical plan," that his only recourse had been suicide. The whole business was disappointing and disagreeable, it "occasioned such fatigues both of body & mind, that stave making hath been discontinued." Furthermore, when it was all over, Dunbar was distressed to learn that it was impossible to enforce the colony's law providing that when Negroes were executed by a proper court their owners were entitled to compensation for their loss at the public's expense.

Dunbar was constantly bewildered by his slaves' behavior. When he recovered two runaways and "condemned them to receive 500 lashes each at 5 dif[feren]t times, and to carry a chain & log fixt to the ancle," he puzzled over their motivation. "Poor ignorant devils," he wrote, "for what do they

run away? They are well cloathed, work easy, and have all kinds of plantation produce at no allowance." But he was a humane man and let them off
"after a slighter chastisement than was intended." His slave Adam was a
perpetual enigma. Found drunk, he was "confined in the Bastile," where,
under threat of 500 lashes, he confessed to having stolen some rum. Dunbar
"ordered a large chain to be fixt to his leg which he carried untill today [five
days later]; [I] had it taken off, his leg being swelled." Two months later
Adam made trouble again; this time he ran away, for fear of a flogging.
When a slave, Bessy, got into a fight with another named Hob, and bit off
a piece of his ear, Dunbar threw them both into the "Bastile," and when
another slave girl was convicted of killing a white, her hand was cut off
before she was hanged.[16]

Dunbar, the young *érudit*, the Scottish scientist and man of letters, was
no sadist. His plantation regime was, by the standards of the time, mild; he
clothed and fed his slaves decently, and frequently relented in his more
severe punishments. But 4,000 miles from the sources of culture, alone on
the far periphery of British civilization where physical survival was a daily
struggle, where ruthless exploitation was a way of life, and where disorder,
violence, and human degradation were commonplace, he had triumphed by
successful adaptation. Endlessly enterprising and resourceful, his finer sensibilities dulled by the abrasions of frontier life, and feeling within himself
a sense of authority and autonomy he had not known before, a force that
flowed from his absolute control over the lives of others, he emerged a
distinctive new man, a borderland gentleman, a man of property in a raw,
half-savage world.

The Pattern of Plantation Life

Unique in his expressive self-consciousness, Dunbar was in other ways
typical of the hundreds of individuals who in these years pushed southward
into the Mississippi delta from here, there, and everywhere: from the
French-Spanish borderland, from the failing plantations of East Florida,
from all the eastern colonies, and from Britain itself. Together, these migrants, whose trails into West Florida form a network of criss-crossing lines
throughout the cis-Mississippi west, account for the opening of a sizable
portion of the riverfront land on the eastern bank of the Mississippi, from
the Yazoo River 235 miles south to the Iberville, along the Iberville and its
tributaries to Lake Maurepas, and along the gulf coast and the lands surrounding the two main bays. The spread of settlement was swift. Durn-

[16]*Ibid.*, pp. 20, 21, 27, 28, 46, 47, 55, 59, 51, 72.

ford's land-grant map of 1771 shows 107 grants along the Mississippi proper; his map of 1774 shows 250 grants covering the same area and another 79 located on the Iberville and its tributaries, the Comite and Amite rivers. At the same time the properties in and around the main gulf towns were being developed by people from the same places. As early as 1769, 131 plots around Mobile and Pensacola bays were claimed and surveyed; and by 1781, 249 plots were registered and surveyed in Pensacola alone.[17]

Still, all of this development only scratched the surface of the available resources. The total population of the colony in 1774, Durnford estimated, was just under 5,000, 25 percent of whom were slaves. There were very few land claims north of Natchez, and even below Natchez, according to Durnford's last pre-Revolutionary maps, there were many miles at or close to the eastern bank still unclaimed, while almost no settlements are identified between the band of land claims on the eastern bank of the Mississippi and the river valleys of what is now central Mississippi.

The province as a whole—over 56,000 square miles, or around 36 million acres—was still thinly inhabited. But a decade earlier there had been almost no white inhabitants there. In the intervening years over 3,000 people—more than the entire population of East Florida—had settled on the eastern bank of the Mississippi River alone. Nor was this the work of absentee landowners who, like the Grants in East Florida, were simply holding on to their titles to huge parcels in the expectation of a rise in land values. That had, in fact, been a fear of responsible officials. Governor Chester, discovering soon after his arrival a number of large grants along the lower Mississippi made "to persons many of whom are utterly unable, and others unwilling, to cultivate them," sought permission to revoke the grants and reissue them "to such petitioners as will realy cultivate them."

Two years later he was still seeking permission to confiscate the idle grants, and while such permission was not forthcoming, he rigidly enforced the existing council policy of confining new grants, as far as possible, to 2,000 acres or less and awarding them only to those who gave "the strongest assurances . . . of their intentions to cultivate and improve them." The result was striking, especially in comparison with what had happened in East Florida. Durnford's map of 1771 lists only four surveyed grants of 10,000 acres or more; a similar map of 1772 lists six such grants; the map of 1774 shows only a few more. On all of these maps, moderate-size holdings predominate. And everywhere there were signs that the land was being opened, that cultivation was under way, that resident householders and not absentee landlords were at work on the land, and that their successes were

[17]Maps identified above, n.7; Howard, *British Development*, pp. 16, 42, and frontispiece map. For the relation between Mobile's growth and the inland fur trade, see Johnson, *West Florida*, pp. 190–191.

acting like a magnet to draw more and more migrants from the older colonies—colonies, paradoxically, whose populations in the same years were being steadily supplemented by voyagers from Britain.[18]

When after 1775 West Florida was designated an asylum for refugee loyalists, what had begun as a modest transference of people from the older colonies and Britain developed quickly into a major land boom, and the population figures soared.[19] But the basic migration pattern had developed before the Revolution, and with it a characteristic mode of life.

[18] *Ibid.*, pp. 155, 169–170; Chester to Hillsborough, Pensacola, June 23, 1771, Dartmouth Papers, Canada, V, 5769–5770; Chester to Hillsborough, Sept. 18, 1771, and to Dartmouth, May 19, 1773, in Rowland, "Peter Chester," pp. 98, 169–170; Howard, *British Development*, pp. 37–38.
[19] Johnson, "Expansion in West Florida," pp. 491–496; Johnson, *West Florida*, pp. 145–149.

V

Peopling the
Peripheral Lands:
The Great Inland Arc

INTRODUCTION

Nova Scotia and the Floridas were the exposed coastal extremities—the most easily accessible end points—of the huge inland periphery of settlement bulging west across the Appalachians in the 1760s and '70s. When the fighting ended, in 1760, the great surge outward into the now open arc of inland territories behind the screen of coastal settlements began in a veritable explosion. Along the upper Connecticut River Valley into northern New England, into upcountry New York in the region of the Mohawk River and Lake Champlain, into western Pennsylvania and through the Appalachian valley system south into the backcountry of the Carolinas and Georgia, came thousands of migrants—some Americans, some recently arrived emigrants from Europe, intent on finding some space for themselves, some property of their own, and an independent way of life.

All of these voyagers were risk takers, traveling as they did "without even a previous path to direct their steps," as Crèvecoeur said, "and without being in any number sufficient either to protect or assist one another." Not oblivious of the dangers of what they were doing but defiant of them, not fearless, but strengthened against danger by an unspoken desire for an open future, they by-passed even the little security and the elementary services of organized society that would have been available to them in the east as they traveled out into these little-known lands.

But if all of these migrants to the inland periphery were in some degree gamblers, willing to forsake a known present for an unknown future, the greatest risk takers among them were the thousands who crossed the sea. These transatlantic voyagers knew little or nothing of what might lie ahead a hundred or two hundred miles inland from the coastal communities. They were the least able to retreat, return, and recover if things went wrong; and they faced, knowingly but helplessly, physical dangers in the process of relocation far more severe than those that confronted migrants who moved simply from tidewater to backcountry or from downriver to upriver, or who took the rocky, pitted wagon roads from north to south. Yet they were not simply plunging adventurers, footloose and feckless, rootless and isolated. However mobile, they were people closely tied to the lands of their birth, family members who expected to extend their families further or to build their own new families, people who intended to recreate the stability they had known before or that they had believed in as a living ideal.

For these voyagers, seeking security, and seeking too, as the Yorkshire Nova Scotian Luke Harrison wrote, "to live independant," the possible losses, as they began the trek to remote points on the inland arc, could be total, absolute, beyond all possibility of recovery. Why did they take these extraordinary risks when others in the same situation did not? What drove them out, or drew them away? What rootage had they had in the land of their birth? And what was the process of their relocation in these inland territories? How did they find their way in the massive periphery that swung west and south from Nova Scotia to the Appalachian plateaus and the Florida borderlands? How did they in fact—did they at all—resecure themselves? What in the end was the cost of the great move—the yield and the gain? Was it true, as Dr. Johnson said, that there was some catastrophic cultural loss in their emigration, in that their power had consisted in their concentration in the lands of their birth, and that, dispersed "in the bound-less regions of America . . . they have no effect"? What "effect" was lost in their dispersal? Was there no *re*construction of cultural power in the new environment?

None of these questions can be fully answered. For these voyagers were ordinary and obscure people, part of the mass population in motion throughout Europe and America in these years. But though the records of their lives are scattered and incomplete, some careers can be traced through the Register of 1773–1776, back into origins and forward into destinies. For each of the main regions into which the provincial migrants from the north of Britain moved, documents survive that supplement the Register's listings and allow glimpses of individual lives in transit, of family sagas, and of the entrepreneurial efforts of particular organizers of emigration and resettle-ment. These scenes, these tracings of careers and passages of careers, though discontinuous and at times fragmentary, are vivid and full of the strange coloration of a distant reality.

14

North Carolina:
The Wreck of the _Bachelor_

THERE IS, first, the saga of James Hogg—the story of his effort to resettle over 200 Scottish Highlanders in the backcountry of North Carolina, a region that had been opened to European colonization by Scots and that had become a veritable nova scotia by the 1770s. No one could have predicted the outcome of Hogg's great enterprise—either the tragic failure of the group migration he supervised or the brilliant success of his and his family's personal careers. But in part because the failure was so spectacular and because the resulting litigation was so elaborate, the documentation is profuse and the tale can be told with a degree of detail unsurpassed in the histories of the pre-Revolutionary migration.

The Frustrations of an Ambitious Tacksman

James Hogg was a native of East Lothian in the Scottish Lowlands. In 1765, at the age of thirty-six, he moved with his young family to a farm in the far northern Highlands, which he took over as principal lessee, or tacksman. Why Hogg leased this property, with its servants and subtenants, in the remote north coast hamlet of Borlum at the western edge of the stark, treeless, infertile, and impoverished county of Caithness—so "very bleak, heathy, & mossy"—is not known. But he was, as the pages of American history would soon prove, an entrepreneur of extraordinary energy, a canny businessman who knew how to make his way; and he was, as he said, "fond of improvements in agriculture." He therefore must have seen possibilities in developing Highlands farmland that drew him to this bleak outpost.

An improver, a developer, somewhat crude in his relations with others,

Caithness, Scotland. Smallholder's "longhouse."

Hogg launched a program of agricultural renewal in Borlum, and then his problems began. He sowed field turnips, "but they were stolen before they came to perfection." He sowed pease, potatoes, and carrots, and they suffered the same fate. Large-scale theft and petty pilfering, "the constant attendants of slavery and poverty," he said, were everywhere, but that was not the worst of it. When he sought to "check such misdemeanors" by dismissing the servants and subtenants he believed were involved, they turned to the protection of other tacksmen and landlords. Hogg could only turn to the law. He sued a well-known farmer for sheep stealing, got him convicted and sentenced to a whipping and banishment, only to find that when he returned after serving his sentence he was taken under the protection of a clansman—"a gentleman of his name"—acting "in compliance with a popular maxim of that place, that a gentleman ought to protect from punishment all of his name, as well as his tenants and connections, whatever be their crimes." What could Hogg do? Having failed at some cost to stop the petty thievery of his "licentious neighbours, supported by gentlemen of wealth and influence," he could only make the best of a bad situation grown worse by the resentments his efforts had stirred.

But he found no peace. In the winter of 1771–1772 a crisis was reached. In October 1771 a cargo ship was wrecked on the nearby rocky shore. Hogg and a few neighbors rescued some of the sailors and tried to save too some of the ship's cargo, despite the local belief in the ancient right of pillage. To his amazement and disgust, Hogg saw country people from the entire region swarm to the shore and make off with everything they could carry.

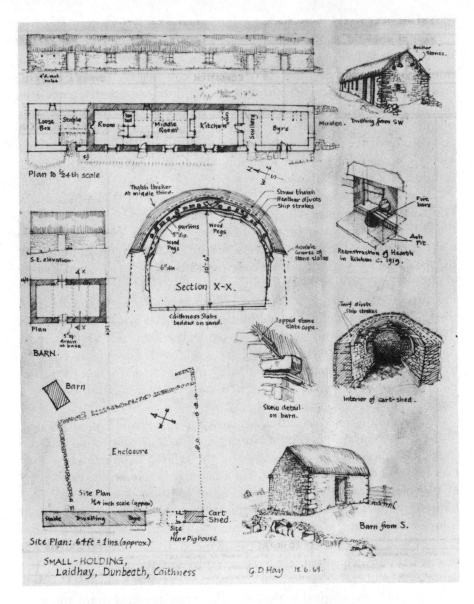

Caithness, Scotland, interior plans and site of smallholder's "longhouse."

Hogg and a neighbor took out search warrants, and in the weeks that followed recovered from the houses of western Caithness "a considerable quantity of goods." But the cost was high. The scavengers were enraged at "that dog Hog" and cast about for ways to recover their "losses."

Since Hogg was, as they said, "of a superior station," they could not make him repay them legally, and so they took direct action. On the night of February 21, 1772, "seven desperate ruffians, armed with pistols and dirks," attacked Hogg's house, ransacked part of it, terrorized his aged mother-in-law, beat up her maid, and set the thatched roof on fire. By an immense effort and at a cost of over £55 Hogg managed to identify the attackers and bring them to court. But then he discovered that "a party soon formed to protect them," a party led by the acting sheriff himself, who openly acted as the suspects' counsel and agent. After elaborate maneuvers and counter-maneuvers in a series of minutely recorded court proceedings, Hogg got the criminals convicted and the acting sheriff officially reprimanded. But this was the end.

The situation was hopeless. It was not merely the lawlessness of the Highlands that defeated Hogg and the danger he and his family found themselves in as they sought to improve their property. The basic problem was the cohesion, the imperviousness, the tightly woven inner bindings of the local society, with its private code of ethics, which as a newcomer he could not enter or control, that drove him out. Ambitious, capable, thrusting, he could not act, expand, grow, reach out in a land "where the thief, the robber, the murderer, and wilfull fire-raiser never . . . wanted a gentleman, or rather a party of gentlemen, to patronize them." He sought a more open world for his expansive energies, a world where difficulties could be by-passed when they could not be directly overcome, and where the imagination was released rather than impacted and twisted in frustration back into the generative source.[1]

He found this open world, as so many Scotsmen before him had done, in the sandy pinelands of central North Carolina. The connection between Scotland, especially the Highlands, and the remote borderland of North Carolina had been formed almost half a century before, in the early years of the administration of Governor Gabriel Johnston (1734–1752). A Scot himself, Johnston had promoted immigration into the colony from all sources, had sponsored legislation to encourage settlement, and had stimulated especially the immigration of his own countrymen after the upheaval of 1745. And he helped redirect the geography of settlement. Avoiding the dangerous sand reefs that formed natural barriers to the northern sounds behind which the original settlements clustered, the immigrant traffic of

[1]Petition of James Hogg to the Lord Advocate (for the recovery of expenses incurred in pursuing the scavengers), endorsed April 27, 1773; Memorial of James Hogg . . . to Postpone the Trial of Alexander Morrison and Alexander McDonald . . . to Enable Him to Use Their Testimony in Prosecuting the Persons Concerned in Setting Fire to His House, Feb. 21st, 1772; Testimony of Witnesses, Aug. 25, 1772: all in Hogg Papers. The fullest account of Hogg's background and of his tribulations in Borlum is in his petition of 1773, but he published a shorter version in the form of a letter to William Balfour, March 29, 1774, in *Scots Magazine*, 36 (July 1774), 345–346, which was reprinted in the *Weekly Magazine, or Edinburgh Amusement* (1774), 107, and in a modern version in William K. Boyd, ed., *Some Eighteenth Century Tracts Concerning North Carolina* (Raleigh, N.C., 1927), pp. 421–424. On thievery and gangsterism in and around Borlum, see Robert Mackay, *A History of the House and Clan of Mackay* . . . (Edinburgh, 1829), pp. 546–547.

Johnston's time and after entered the colony in the south, through the Cape Fear River. There, arriving vessels had no reefs to contend with, and could sail directly to a key port of entry, Wilmington, sixteen miles inland, where the voyagers could easily transfer to long boats, lighters, and large canoes to move slowly inland. Their destination increasingly became Cross Creek and its surrounding areas, one hundred miles north on the upper Cape Fear, where the pine forests provided an excellent source of naval supplies and the bottomlands of the sandhills proved fertile for the growing of grain.

How many Highlanders entered this inner region, which became Cumberland County, after the first large contingent arrived from Argyllshire in 1739 is not known. One estimate, of a total Highland community of 12,000 in the upper Cape Fear region in 1776, is probably low, especially in view of the repeated reports of large numbers of sailings in the 1760s and '70s. But the geographical concentration of the Highland population at the time of Hogg's involvement is clearly indicated in the location of 1,003 individual land grants and purchases secured by Highlanders between 1733 and 1775. The map locating these properties (Map 14.A) shows a thick clustering along the main stem of the upper Cape Fear, and thinner groupings along every one of the streams and creeks that feed into it. Constituting, in that inland territory, approximately half of the total population, the Highlanders, though surrounded by the typical British North American mix of Scotch-Irish, Germans, Swiss, English, Welsh, and French, were yet the most distinctive and numerous community in the region, and their contacts with their home communities, maintained with extraordinary persistence, kept their ethnic identity alive and the recruitment of their fellow countrymen continuous.[2]

How active, how vital and effective, this communication between inland North Carolina and the Scottish Highlands remained through all these years can be illustrated in a hundred ways—in letters and notices printed in the Scottish newspapers, in the communications of officials on both sides of the ocean, in local records, above all in family correspondences maintained for decades by members of families divided between the two continents. Such transatlantic networks of communication were common in the eighteenth century, and were well known to everyone familiar with the process of emigration. The letters that passed between the Yorkshire and the Nova Scotian Harrisons were typical. But among the Scots, whose clannish instincts remained intense despite the wrenching social changes after the '45 rebellion, the links were especially strong and consequential. They helped determine the routes of Scottish migration. "Wherever some friends or clansmen from the same glens or islands had happened to precede

[2]Duane Meyer, *The Highland Scots of North Carolina, 1732–1776* (Chapel Hill, N.C., 1961), pp. 79, 69, 77, 75, 85, 100, 117, and maps VIII and IX.

them, there the rest followed, when they moved at all. Thus almost each separate district of the Highlands had its own preference."[3] So the Georgia Scots tended to be from Inverness; a large proportion of the New York Scots were from Perthshire, Badenoch, and Strathspey. And from Argyll-shire and the western islands, and above all from Sutherland and the far north, came the central core of North Carolina's Scotsmen.

The correspondence of the Argyllshire MacAllisters is particularly detailed. The first of the family to settle in North Carolina was Alexander, who arrived in 1736, brought over his wife, three sisters, and his brother Hector, and prospered as a landowner and mill proprietor. Hector, however, returned home, and for thirty-five years thereafter he and his brother Alexander corresponded, mainly about Hector's endlessly pending but never realized return to Carolina and about the condition of life on both sides of the Atlantic. Their lengthy and graphic letters and those of the other members of the family describe the Carolina countryside, its climate, crops, and land; analyze wages, prices, and the state of the labor force; discuss the desperate need for artisans; and offer advice on shipping arrangements, goods to be brought over, and the process of settling.

Repeatedly the emigration decision is praised. Carolina was "the best poor man's country I have heard in this age." "You would do well to advise all poor people whom you wish well to take courage and come to this country." For here most people, even humble people, become "leards," such was the ease of getting land. One could leave land in equal proportions to all one's children, and no one, no matter how poor initially, ends up begging. Few even remain servants: they "get above serving when they come to the country" because they are paid "such extrav[agant] wages." It was stupid to delay emigrating from a land where a lifetime of labor would never produce "one farthing ahead," where whatever a man possesses his "landlord will sure be master of," and where "the face of the poor is kept to the grinding stone." The Carolina backcountry was filling up quickly,

[3] [George Douglas Campbell, 8th] Duke of Argyll, *Scotland As It Was and As It Is* (Edinburgh, 1887), II, 132–133. The power of continuous correspondence in determining the direction of migration was well known. In innumerable letters from the settlers in North Carolina "to their friends and acquaintance in the Highlands," one pamphleteer wrote in 1773, "we find parents inviting over children that were left behind, children their parents, husbands their wives and families, and brothers their sisters, all describing their state there as far preferable to what they ever knew before in every respect, and earnestly wishing their relations and connections of every tender tie would go and partake of the same happiness, and no longer remain under home oppression." *Informations Concerning the Province of North Carolina, Addressed to Emigrants from the Western Highlands and Western Islands . . .* (Glasgow, 1773), in Boyd, *Tracts,* p. 436. The landlords were well aware of the force of this communication network. The Sutherlands' factor James Campbell wrote Alexander Mackenzie, Feb. 22, 1773, that the spirit of emigration was reviving on the Sutherland estates "owing to letters lately rec[eive]d f[ro]m those that went to Carolina last season." Sutherland Papers, Dep. 313/III/box 16.

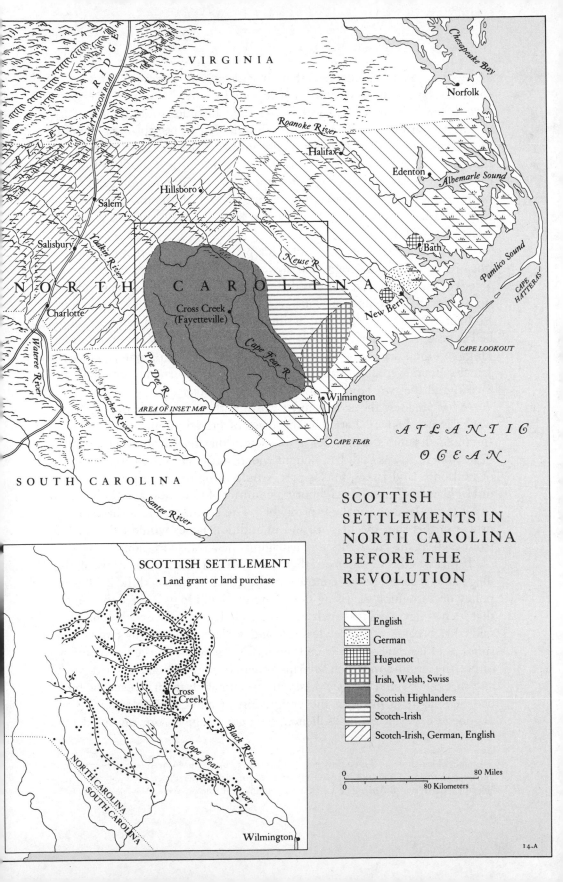

VIRGINIA

BLUE RIDGE

GREAT WAGON ROAD

Norfolk

Roanoke River

Halifax

Edenton

Albemarle Sound

Hillsboro

Salem

Salisbury

Yadkin River

Bath

Pamlico Sound

NORTH CAROLINA

Cross Creek
(Fayetteville)

Neuse R.

New Bern

CAPE HATTERAS

Charlotte

Pee Dee R.

Cape Fear R.

CAPE LOOKOUT

Wateree River

Lynches River

AREA OF INSET MAP

Wilmington

ATLANTIC OCEAN

SOUTH CAROLINA

Santee River

CAPE FEAR

SCOTTISH SETTLEMENTS IN NORTII CAROLINA BEFORE THE REVOLUTION

SCOTTISH SETTLEMENT
• Land grant or land purchase

Cross Creek

Black River

NORTH CAROLINA

SOUTH CAROLINA

Cape Fear River

Wilmington

English

German

Huguenot

Irish, Welsh, Swiss

Scottish Highlanders

Scotch-Irish

Scotch-Irish, German, English

0   80 Miles
0   80 Kilometers

14.A

and with so many Highlanders that "it will soon be a new Scotland." Act soon, Alexander urged his kinsmen repeatedly; speed counts—"everyone says if they had come ten years sooner their fortune would be made."[4]

So the Carolina MacAllisters, like a hundred other transplanted families, kept contact with their homeland and with their kinsmen, called the day they had decided to emigrate blessed, and told of a new quality of life in the sandy pineland of the upper Cape Fear—an open country, full of promise. There, in that loose, ill-organized world on the margin of European civilization, one could "breathe the air of [li]berty, and not want the necessarys of life."[5]

It was this openness, this outlet for pent-up energies, that caught the imagination of James Hogg; and again, as in so many other cases, it was a network of family connections that drew him into the process of emigration. In 1756 his brother Robert had emigrated from their first home in East Lothian to North Carolina, and in time had established with Samuel Campbell a prosperous merchant firm in the port town of Wilmington. The Hogg brothers had kept in touch, and in the winter of 1771–1772, when James's affairs were most deeply troubled, Robert returned to Scotland for a visit, and the two brothers concerted their plans.

What precisely the arrangement was that they concluded during those weeks is not known. Later, in the mass of litigation and publicity that surrounded James's departure, it was stated that they had struck a secret deal. Robert, it was said, had bought 12,000 acres near the inland entrepôt of Hillsboro, and James, for his part, would bring over a large contingent of Highlanders from the neighboring counties of Caithness and Sutherland to settle the land and make it profitable. The brothers would share in the profits of this land speculation, and in addition James would collect a fee from each of the emigrants for managing their transportation.

If this was the arrangement they concluded, it was neither unusual nor illegal, but it certainly was contrary to the government's and the landlords' policy of restraining the rising tide of emigration. Hogg insisted, however, that he had never devised such a scheme. He had merely decided, he later said, that because of the lawlessness and violence he and his family had suffered in Caithness they were leaving for a new life in the backcountry of North Carolina, to which so many others from the Highlands had gone, and that they would take six or seven servants with them. Never, he said, had he sought to instigate the emigration of Scotch Highlanders or of anyone else; never had he "solicited, took advantage of, nor inveigled any

[4] Alexander MacAllister to [his cousin], n.d. and Nov. 29, 1770, to James MacAllister [1771–1772], and to [Alexander MacAllister, 1770–1771 and 1771–1772], all in MacAllister Papers.
[5] Hector MacAllister to Alexander MacAllister, Monnyquill, Isle of Arran, May 31, 1774, *ibid.*

person." Indeed, he had "rejected hundreds who warmly intreated me to find them a passage."[6]

His procedure was in fact quite standard; even the outcome was not unique. What is unusual about Hogg's departure from Scotland and the voyage of the vessel, the *Bachelor*, which he hired, is that the records have survived in such completeness that the story can be reconstructed down to the last detail. In the entire annals of the peopling of British North America in the eighteenth century there is no fuller account of the process of departure, with all its confusion, delays, costs, miseries, and dangers, and no more complete documentation of the background and motivations of the emigrants than can be found in the record of this vessel and in the personal papers of its contractor, James Hogg. The story, in all its particularity, forms a prototype, save for its conclusion, of one set of procedures by which voyagers from Britain helped settle the peripheral arc of inland territories in North America in the years before the Revolution.

Planning and Organization

The process began when James Hogg, the Borlum tacksman, made known, after his brother's return to North Carolina, that he and his family intended to leave for that colony in the near future. At the same time Robert Hogg, on his way back to America, stopped in Edinburgh to visit his main business correspondent, James Inglis, and arranged to have a vessel sent north to transport James and his family. As soon as word of James's decision to emigrate circulated in Caithness and Sutherland, Hogg was besieged by requests of people who wanted to join him, begging him, he later recalled, to make room for them and their families. They arrived, Hogg reported, "by scores & dozens together, cringing a fawning & begging to have their passage in the ship with me." His family, he said, was bothered by them, and his business suffered because he was so "pester'd with them night & day . . . besides expences of entertaining many of them."[7]

At first, to judge from his later statements, Hogg was determined to

---

[6]"Answers and Replies for James Inglis, Jr., Merchant in Edinburgh, Defender, to the Petition and Answers of James Hogg . . . , July 24, 1774," Admiralty Papers; Hogg to Balfour, March 29, 1774 (note 1, above); James Inglis to James Hogg, Edinburgh, April 10, 1773, Inglis Letterbook. The surviving correspondence seems to bear out Hogg's contention. In his earliest letter on the subject Hogg said only that he intended "to carry out with him a number of servants," later specified as 6 or 7. But he observed that "there is many people applying to emigrate that is able and willing to pay for their passage." Inglis to Hogg & Campbell, Edinburgh, Feb. 26, 1773, and to James Hogg, Edinburgh, April 10, Inglis Letterbook.

[7]"Unto the Honourable the Vice Admiral of Zetland, Answers and Defences for James Hogg . . . against the Petitions & Complaints of Alexr Mackay & Others," Nov. 5, 1773, pp. 1–2, Hogg Papers (hereafter: "Answers and Defences for James Hogg").

ignore these would-be emigrants and simply provide for his own family. But he was apparently encouraged to change his mind by certain local leaders with whom he talked and by the Edinburgh shipowner, James Inglis. The views of his minister in the parish of Reay, the Reverend Alexander Pope, were unequivocal. Hogg should be thankful, Pope wrote, to be leaving "the miserable parish of Reay." If he himself had some encouragement, "heartily would I also bid farewell to all Caithnes and Strathnavern and all their gentry and commons."

The views of William MacKay were especially emphatic. A lesser member of the powerful MacKay clan, kinsmen of the Lords of Reay, whose influence blanketed a territory of about 1,500 square miles stretching from Caithness to Assynt, and whose major estates directly shaped the lives of hundreds of tenants, subtenants, and ordinary laborers, MacKay was himself determined to emigrate. He told Hogg, in discussing the emigration, "which was the sole topic of conversation, all over that part of Scotland," that letters received from those who had left the district for Carolina only the year before described the colony as rich in resources and cheap to live in, and that it held out for those who settled there "the certain prospect of bettering their fortunes." Later it would emerge that MacKay's brother and sister had both emigrated to North Carolina and had quoted facts and figures to him to prove that any "sober industrious man could not fail of living comfortably" there, and that "if a man could bring a small sum of money with him, he might make rich very fast." "Half the people of this country," MacKay told Hogg, "would emigrate if they were able," and he urged him to organize a large-scale shipment of people, to leave, not from the distant shipping ports of Greenock or Leith, which the subtenants of Caithness and Sutherland could reach only by reducing themselves to beggary, but directly from one of the many nearby north-coast lochs or ports.[8]

In the end it was probably Inglis, the shipowner, who persuaded Hogg to lead and organize an expedition of emigrants. Inglis was quite willing, he wrote, to transport Hogg, his family and servants, even if he made nothing on the voyage. But he asked Hogg to note that, since the vessel would have to go north to pick up the Hogg party, "I could wish at [the] same time to take at least 100 passengers in order to make something of the freight outwards." Whether out of good will, or self-interest, or as a favor

[8]Pope to Hogg, Reay, May 13, 1774, *Scottish Gaelic Studies*, 11 (1966), 106; Mackay, *Clan of Mackay*, pp. 1–2; "Answers and Defences for James Hogg," pp. 2, 3; "Report of the Examination of the Emigrants from the Counties of Caithness and Sutherland on Board the Ship Bachelor of Leith Bound to Wilmington in North Carolina," April 15, 1774, T47/12/29–39; quotation at 37–38. This last document, which will be cited hereafter as "Examination of the *Bachelor* Emigrants," is of great importance, and has been twice reprinted: in *North Carolina Historical Review*, 11 (1934), 130–138, and in Merrill Jensen, ed., *English Historical Documents*, IX (*American Colonial Documents to 1776*, London, 1955), 469–476.

to Inglis—or all three—Hogg agreed, and so he became the organizer, manager, and sponsor of a shipment of emigrants to inland North America.

He wrote Inglis to send the vessel, fitted for transporting a large number of emigrants, to the port of Thurso, Caithness, ten miles or so east of Borlum. He intended, he explained, to "take with me as many [people] as she could conveniently hold." And he put MacKay in charge of preparing a preliminary list of prospective passengers. Hogg, however, responding to suggestions from Inglis, set the conditions of recruitment. To qualify, prospective emigrants must, first, be "free of foul & infectious diseases." Second, they must be of proven "good character." And third, and most important, they must be able "to pay their freight with an overplus for accidents."[9]

What the freight charge would be was to be determined by Inglis. But he agreed with Hogg that this basic charge should be kept as low as possible —lower than the £4 usually charged for an adult emigrant. They settled on £3 10s for a full freight (age eight and above) and approximately half that for those younger than eight, except "sucking children," who would go free. But Inglis soon realized that these charges, calculated rather casually on the basis of a shipload of 100, were too low. The costs of outfitting and provisioning an emigrant ship, he discovered, were much higher than he had anticipated. To compensate, he began to increase the number of emigrants he would have to take in order to make the voyage profitable. His first figure of 100 emigrants quickly became 150, then 200. In the end he settled for 200-plus: that is, a minimum of 200 and as many more as could be "easily stowed" on board. And to secure himself further against loss he insisted that the passengers not clutter up the available space with excessive baggage (he expected them to take only their body clothes and some bedding), and he insisted too that half the freight costs be paid before the vessel left Edinburgh's docks at Leith for Thurso, and that the rest be remitted before the vessel left Thurso for America.[10]

In these ways, Inglis sought to protect himself against loss. But he was not one of the notorious shippers determined to squeeze every farthing from the transportation of emigrants at whatever cost to their health, safety, and comfort. His correspondence reflects a genuine concern for the welfare of the passengers. Even in his preliminary planning he made clear that he did not intend to crowd the vessel to excess ("the poor people ought to be properly accommodated for fear of any disease happening among them");

[9]Inglis to Hogg, April 10, 1773, Inglis Letterbook; "Answers and Defences for James Hogg," p. 3. For a general discussion of tacksmen as emigration contractors in the Highlands—"the key to the emigration" before 1775—largely based on the example of Hogg, see Meyer, *Highland Scots*, pp. 54–59. For specific charges of the tacksmen's "oppression" as the cause of emigration, see James Sutherland to [?], Feb. 17 and March 2, 1772, Sutherland Papers, Dep. 313/II/BV4.
[10]Inglis to Hogg, Edinburgh, Feb. 22, April 10, and May 10, 1773, and to Alexander Ramage, Edinburgh, Aug. 25, 1773, Inglis Letterbook.

he was careful to provide healthy food ("barley brothe without a proper quantity of beef would never answer for these poor people"); and he planned to lay in provisions that would last, not simply for the usual nine or ten weeks but for twelve weeks, even though the individual food allowances were to be larger than those normally provided.[11]

So during the early months of 1773 Inglis was busy with the preliminary planning for the voyage; and he also selected a vessel. He chose the *Bachelor*, a vessel of 260 tons built in Philadelphia ten years earlier and refitted in 1771, which he had been using for carrying cargoes of rice from North America to Britain. Its captain, Alexander Ramage, had a rather ominous record of "misfortunes in shipping," but he knew the vessel well (he had apparently been the builder) and Inglis was hopeful that this time he would be more attentive to his duties than he had been before—and would be luckier. The *Bachelor* was due to return from its current voyage in early June. Inglis, with what proved to be tragic optimism, planned to have it unloaded, refitted, in part rebuilt, and then reloaded in time for it to get to Thurso in "June or July." He was well aware that by September one could expect Atlantic storms, which, he said with remarkable understatement, "would be a great inconvenience with passengers aboard." He planned to have the vessel complete the six-week voyage before the summer was out.[12]

Selection: Background and Causes

While Inglis in Edinburgh was ordering the supplies he needed—barley, beef, biscuits, fish, oatmeal, pease, and molasses—from all over central and northern Scotland and while he awaited Ramage's arrival in Leith, Hogg, on the Caithness coast two hundred miles to the north, was busy with MacKay and others, selecting the passengers for the voyage. It was not a simple task: the situation was in fact quite confusing. MacKay first came up with a list of 120 names, but then kept adding others. At the same time "great lists" started to come in from all over Sutherland and Caithness. In order to "fix their numbers, and get security for their freight," Hogg posted a notice on the church door in Reay calling for a meeting of all those interested. At this point, when it came to a formal commitment and the payment of half freight in advance, many withdrew; some withdrew even later, after they had paid their security, and Hogg released them from their pledges. For there were many others to take the places of those who

[11]Inglis to Hogg, Edinburgh, April 21, May 10, 1773, and to William Calhoun, May 28, 1774, Inglis Letterbook.
[12]On the *Bachelor*: Inglis to Hogg, April 21, 1773, to Andrew Conan, Aug. 16, 1774, and to Peter Lawson, Aug. 30, 1774; on Ramage: Inglis to Ramage, Aug. 25, 1773; on the schedule of departure: Inglis to Hogg & Campbell, Feb. 26, 1773, and to Hogg, April 21, 1773: all in Inglis Letterbook.

withdrew, and so by filling in and substituting, the shifting of names eased and a firm list of fully committed emigrants was compiled.

But it was easier to fill the list with paying passengers than it was to enforce the first two of Hogg's conditions, good health and good character. William Gun, for example, could not have been more serious in his commitment, more respectable, or more responsible financially. He traveled twenty-four miles over roadless hills from the inland parish of Kildonan simply to register his family of seven. But when later they all arrived at Thurso to board ship, it developed that the children had recently had smallpox. Hogg tried to persuade Gun not to go, "told him how cruel it would be to introduce into the ship so grievous a disease," and urged him to sell his places to others waiting at Thurso. But Gun refused, insisting that the children were fully recovered, and demanded that Hogg fulfill his commitment. Reluctantly he did.

Alexander MacKay presented a disagreeable problem of another kind. He came over to Borlum from his home in Strathy, eight miles to the east along the coast, as soon as he heard of Hogg's plans. But he was "beastly drunk," Hogg later recalled, "and boasting of his gentle connections, and of his wealth & worth." Hogg was repelled by his "behavior & appearance," and turned him away. But MacKay was not to be put off so easily. By the time he returned to press his case he made sure that Hogg knew that he was a cousin of that "worthy gentleman" James MacKay, tacksman of Skerray, an estate farther west along the north shore. And James of Skerray, "a gentleman who, from his singular and uniform correctness of habits and manners, was a credit to his name" and who had been appointed custodian of the incapacitated sixth Lord Reay, was a man for whom Hogg himself "had a great regard." Hogg still refused to enroll the wretched Alexander, though now he felt obliged to treat him civilly. In the end, however, he had to give in: he had no choice, he felt, when Alexander produced a letter of recommendation from his genteel, influential, and affluent cousin of Skerray.[13]

So the passenger list was compiled. When completed it contained 280 names. First listed was Hogg's party of 16 (wife, mother-in-law, 5 children, 6 personal wage servants, and 2 indentured servants). Their accommodations were special. Not only were all but the male servants in the party housed in the ship's cabin, but they were allowed to bring their own food and beer and their own "live sheep, hogs, goats, etc." For this they paid £6 per adult, £3 per weaned child, £1 10s per personal servant, and £6 per indentured servant—a total of £51 for all 16. Of the 264 emigrants shipped in the hold, which only recently had been filled with barrels of rice, 174 were

[13]"Answers and Defences for James Hogg," pp. 3, 4, 9, 2; Mackay, *Clan of Mackay,* pp. 543, 545; Angus Mackay, *The Book of Mackay* (Edinburgh, 1906), pp. 216–217.

8 years old or older, 60 were under 8, and 30 were "sucking children." Their total transportation cost was £714, plus £15 6s more to Hogg as a commission or fee "for his trouble in finding the ship and entering into a formal contract with the shipmaster or owner of the vessel" (1s 6d per full freight, 9d for half freights).[14]

Who were these emigrants collected by Hogg? What was their background, their condition, and their motivation? Inglis always referred to them as "the poor people." How poor were they? Why, specifically, did they leave? The records are surprisingly full, uniquely detailed. For the emigrants were subjected to the routine inquiry mandated by the Treasury for the Register of departures—but not in a routine way. Instead of the casual and quick questioning about background, condition, and purpose that was taking place at the docksides throughout Britain during these months, the emigrants on the *Bachelor* were interviewed intensively and at leisure, apparently on the instruction of the deputy vice admiral of the Shetland Islands, William Balfour, when in the spring of 1774 they were stranded on those northern islands, were idle, and had become public charges. By then the group had begun to scatter. But 31 heads of households representing 126 individuals, or 48% of all the *Bachelor*'s emigrants, responded in detail. Hogg himself replied in a lengthy statement, which was published and widely circulated and discussed.[15] These interviews, to-

[14]The list of passengers, grouped by families and with fares enumerated, exists in several forms in the Hogg Papers. The figures used here are based on those published in Hogg's letter to Balfour, referred to above, n. 1, supplemented by two checklists in the Hogg Papers. The special provisions for the accommodation of the Hogg family, sketched in Inglis to Hogg, April 10, 1773, Inglis Letterbook, were written into the formal contract between Hogg and Inglis, Aug. 24, 1773, Hogg Papers; the costs, as part of the total freight charges, were itemized in Inglis to James Davidson, Edinburgh, Oct. 16, 1773, Inglis Letterbook. On Hogg's fee: "Petition of John Bruce Stewart and Others of Shetland to William Balfour, the Deputy Vice Admiral of Shetland, Nov. 9, 1773," Hogg Papers (hereafter: "Stewart Petition"). The clearest statement of the freight costs is in the Admiralty Papers. The sums involved became matters of public interest: e.g., *York Courant*, July 5, 1774 ("near £700 sterling").

[15]The 31 interviews constitute the "Examination of the *Bachelor* Emigrants" referred to above, n.8. Hogg's reply to the questionnaire took the form of his letter to Balfour, March 29, 1774 (note 1, above). His blistering condemnation, in this letter, of the violence and general disorder that prevailed in Caithness ("A list of the murders, robberies, and thefts committed with impunity there . . . would surprise a Mohawk or a Cherokee") and his attack on the "oppression . . . of these haughty landlords" touched off a series of outbursts in the *Weekly Magazine, or Edinburgh Amusement*: Aug. 4, Sept. 1, and Oct. 13, 1774. The Sept. 1 piece is a long and detailed essay insisting that Caithness landlords were humane and that the fault lay strictly with the Sutherland estate owners. The Oct. 13 essay is a remarkable production—a dialogue in heavy Scotch dialect that begins as an apparently indignant reply to Hogg but ends as an ironic defense. "Mr. Hogg . . . hae proclaim'd ye a' murderers, thieves, robbers and oppressors! Gin [If] ye hae na seen them, if ye kep in wi' me, I'll tell ye what they say, and how it came. Mr. Hogg (my auld neighbour) sent it in the prents frae Shetland to my master; and he tells murderers, thieves and rogues are rife in Caithness, and will hae us a' wretches like the fouks [folks] he ca's Sherokees or Mohacks (they say that's wild heathens or Indians); and he tells we poor fouks hae nae mair to do but turn robber, thief or fire-raiser (that's a house-burner), and then we are protected by our gentry—Sicken impudence!—I hae been a

gether with other information in the legal records and in Hogg's personal papers, throw a flood of light on the precise circumstances of these 280 voyagers to the west.

The former residences of 212 of the 234 non-infant emigrants can be established, and they prove to be scattered through seven parishes of the county of Sutherland and five parishes of Caithness, a territory stretching all across the far northern peninsula of Scotland. They came from Wick and Latheron on the North Sea coast and from Eddrachillis on the Minch Channel in the west, from Lairg in the south, and from a string of farms and communities on the far north coast facing out to the Orkney and Shetland Islands. But though there were thus representatives of the entire circumference of northern Scotland aboard the *Bachelor*, the great majority (about 70%) of those who sailed on the vessel came from three parishes close to Hogg's tack at Borlum: the immediately surrounding parish of Reay, and Kildonan and Farr, adjacent to Reay on the south and west. And since the whole of the parish of Reay formed a single estate, the Bighouse estate owned by George MacKay, and since most of the rest of the properties abandoned by the other emigrants were parts either of the estates of the sixth Lord Reay, administered by the same Bighouse Mackays, or of the even vaster Sutherland properties, then administered by a committee of Tutors for the infant Countess of Sutherland, the emigrants were responding to conditions shaped by a very small number of great landlords or their administrators.[16]

The holdings of these estate owners were immense—the Sutherland family estates alone included three-quarters of a million acres, well over half the entire county of Sutherland, and accounted for 47% of the county's property value—and all of these properties were troubled by economic dislocations and distress. The estate papers of 1772 and 1773, especially those of the Sutherland properties, are full of cries of despair at the difficulties of the time and of the direct effect of the distress on the spread of emigration. From the parish of Assynt in the west to Kildonan in the east—and especially in those two localities—the alarm was sounded again and again by the Sutherlands' estate agents. Economic conditions, especially after the severe winter of 1771–1772, were atrocious. Crops, they reported, were a

---

tenant this thretty year, and under seven different masters, and I never heard till shortly of house-burners; but I hae kend my auld masters banter thieves, and threaten to herry [harry] them, when they steal'd frae themselves." And then: "Gin they . . . stop our slavery, it wad be Christian charity: But, ah! the master's officer cries us out to muck the laird's byres [barns]. The wife and I maun gang [must go]. He poinded [seized] our bed-claiths yesterday for not being out in time."

[16]Twenty-two of the 31 interviewees can be identified as tenants on 9 estates; 12 of the 22 came from Sutherland; 64% of the *Bachelor*'s passengers whose homes can be located came from that shire. On the Bighouse estate, see Mackay, *Clan of Mackay*, pp. 2, 545; Pope to Hogg, May 13, 1774, p. 106 (note 8, above). On the Countess of Sutherland's estates, see Eric Richards, *The Leviathan of Wealth: The Sutherland Fortune in the Industrial Revolution* (London, 1973), pp. 161–162.

disaster, cattle were dying and their selling price had collapsed. "Our poor people are in a starving condition," they wrote; "the distress of the poor people is inexpressible." The southern properties especially had "the most deplorable aspeck I ever beheld." "Without a miracle there will not be six tenants in [the parish of Kildonan] another year able to pay his rent."[17]

The economic situation was *very* grave and its effect on emigration, it seemed, was palpable. In the west the people were threatening to imitate the recent large-scale emigration from the Isle of Skye, oppressed as they were, the agents reported, by the want of victuals and the oppression of the tacksmen. The idea of emigrating to America had become "a sort of madness among the common people"—it "spreads like a contagion." The *Edinburgh Evening Courant* claimed that despite all the efforts that had been made to limit emigration from Sutherland, 1,500 had left that county for America between 1771 and 1773—a figure that seems reasonable if not low in view of the certain exodus of between 700 and 800 from the Sutherland family estates alone in only 7 parishes in the single year 1771–1772. One estimate of the county's losses for the year 1772–1773 was 735, another was 400 to 500—and this from a total population of just over 20,000.[18]

The emigration, it seemed, was an obvious response to severe economic distress. But was it simply that? In the end the exodus proved to be rather mysterious: the agents themselves were puzzled at "what can have possessed the people to the madness they now labour under," and blamed the tacksmen, either for oppressing the subtenants to the point of desperation or for leading groups out for their personal profit. For despite widespread charges that the Highland landlords were "Egyptian taskmasters"—absentees intent on squeezing the poor tenants into bankruptcy and beggary in order to live lives of riotous extravagance in distant cities—the people must have known that the major landlords, like the Countess of Sutherland's Tutors, were responsible, concerned, and conscientious. They brought in emergency food supplies for the poorest of the subtenants, created jobs for

[17] *John Home's Survey of Assynt*, ed. R. J. Adam (Edinburgh, 1960), pp. xxiv ff.; James Campbell to Thomas and James Arbuthnot, Peterhead, June 16, 1772, to Alexander Mckenzie, June 29 and Aug. 10, 1772, to Capt. Sutherland, June 13, 1772, all in Sutherland Papers, Dep. 313/III/box 16. The value of the Sutherland properties has been calculated from the valuation roll of 1771, in Loretta R. Timperley, ed., *A Directory of Landownership in Scotland c. 1770* (Scottish Record Society, new ser., 5, Edinburgh, 1976), p. 338. By the same measure, Lord Reay's estate represented 12.3% of the county's total property, the Bighouse estate 3.4%.
[18] James Sutherland to [?], Feb. 17, March 2, 1772, and James Campbell to Alexander Mckenzie, July 16, 1772, Sutherland Papers, Dep. 313/II/BV4 and Dep. 313/III/box 16. Meyer, *Highland Scots*, pp. 55, 49; misc. paper inserted before minute for March 11, 1773, Minute Book and Letter Book of the Tutors of the Duchess-Countess [of Sutherland], 1766–1782, Sutherland Papers, Dep. 313/II/BV4. The emigration estimates are from the report of the Steward of the County of Sutherland summarized in Thomas Miller to the Earl of Suffolk, Barskimming [Ayrshire], April 25, 1775, SP 54/45, and Collectors and Comptroller of Customs at Inverness to Board of Customs, Edinburgh, Jan. 3, 1774, T1/500.

them in public-works projects, and demanded and studied report after report on who the emigrants were and why they were leaving. They discovered that it was not the poorest always, or even commonly, who left. Some of the most secure small farmers, led by some of the most prominent tacksmen, left too, and they did not go in rags, penniless, nor were they fleeing in desperation. They were in no sense a "surplus" population. The 1,500 said to have left Sutherland between 1771 and 1773, the *Courant* claimed, took with them funds equivalent to more than a year's rent for the entire county.[19]

That some such drainage had accompanied the departures is not surprising. The *Bachelor*'s passengers were not unemployed laborers, drifters, cotters without secure roots in the land, or isolated adventurers, and they were not traveling alone. Only 8 of the people who crowded into the small, dark hold of the *Bachelor* may have been unaffiliated with migrating kinship groups. All the rest were organized into 46 households. Similarly, of the 126 individuals represented in the 31 interviews, only 4 were traveling independent of families. The mean family size in the shipment as a whole, excluding the 30 infants, was 4.2; of the interviewed families, 4.15. And these were not young and heedless newlyweds, but mature families—astonishingly mature families in an era when the average life expectancy at birth in Scotland was approximately 40.[20] The average age of the heads of households on the *Bachelor* who were interviewed was 41.4, the median age 37. While just over 60% of these were under 40 years of age, 29% were over 50: 5 were in their sixties, 2 in their seventies. The largest number of children per household was 6; but, as the average family size of 4.15 indicates, most married couples took with them only 1 or 2 children beyond infancy. Only 3 families were "extended" in the sense of including the married couples' parents or siblings, and only 3 of the 31 families included servants.

A population, then, of families far enough into their cycle of development to have acquired settled modes of life—experienced people not likely to abandon security for delusive dreams—they were, almost all of them, rooted in the soil. Twenty-three of the thirty-one interviewed identified themselves as farmers, and gave evidence of the specific kinds of farming work they did. Of the rest, four were artisans, not in highly skilled or ornamental crafts but in the basic trades of shoemaking and tailoring. One had been and another hoped to be a teacher, one was a shopkeeper, and one was a 29-year-old servant. There were no casual laborers (though one particularly discouraged farmer hoped to recover his fortunes in farming

---

[19]James Sutherland to James Campbell, June 22, 1772, Sutherland Papers, Dep. 313/III/box 16; *Home's Survey of Assynt*, pp. xxx–xxxiv; *Informations Concerning the Province of North Carolina*, pp. 433–434; Meyer, *Highland Scots*, p. 55. The total rent of the Sutherland estates was slightly over £3,000 a year. *Home's Survey of Assynt*, p. xxviii.
[20]Michael Flinn, ed., *Scottish Population History* (Cambridge, Eng., 1977), p. 270.

by working for a time as a "day labourer" while his wife did spinning and sewing). No one, except possibly the spinster, was without a specific occupation; and there were no transients. Only one of the 31 interviewed—a 60-year-old shoemaker from Lord Reay's estate in Strathnaver—confessed to being so "exceeding poor" that he could not pay for his passage. But his friends, he said, had contributed the money he needed; they had hoped "he would find better employment in Carolina."

With this exception, abject impoverishment did not exist among the emigrants on the *Bachelor*. Even the farmer who was willing to work as a day laborer referred to "his little stock," and the servant was not destitute or even unemployed. She was leaving, she said, because she had been assured by friends who had gone before her that "she would get much better service and greater encouragement in Carolina than in her own country." Hogg, after all, had seen to all of this by accepting only those able to pay for their passages "with an overplus for accidents." What drove out almost all of those interviewed and drew them to Carolina, where they had relatives or friends, was not starvation or the immediate prospect of it but threats of another kind to their well-being and security.

Subtenants and artisans with a narrow margin of security, small farmers unaccustomed to substantial profits but unaccustomed too to the fear of degradation, they were caught up in changes they could not control, changes that, by any sensible projection into the future, threatened to debase their settled way of life. They quoted precise figures and named names.

William Gordon, a farmer "aged sixty and upwards" from the far southern border region of Sutherland, fifty or more miles from Borlum, was emigrating with his wife, six grown children, and two daughters-in-law (at the substantial cost of £35). He had witnessed in his own lifetime an escalation of rents on the property he worked in southeastern Sutherland, owned by William Baillie of Rosehall, from the 8 marks his grandfather had paid to the 60 marks he had last paid (the mark was worth just over a shilling sterling). As a result of these successive rent rises, lurching up with each of the many changes in ownership that had taken place in recent years, and as a result too of the great loss of cattle he had suffered in the severe winter of 1771–1772, "his circumstances were greatly reduced." He said nothing about impoverishment, and he had little to gain for himself, being "an old man and lame so that it was indifferent to him in what country he died." It was the long-term future he was concerned about—the next generation. He was emigrating "for the greater benefit of his children . . . in hopes that his children would earn their bread more comfortably elsewhere." For he saw no hope that things would improve on the farm he subrented. The tacksman who had the major lease from the landlord "must also have his profits." The whole system seemed to be closing in, dark and portentous.

Two of his sons were already settled in Carolina and had written to him glowingly about the prospects there, encouraging him to make the move. There, in that distant world, he hoped his other children too would be able to create independent lives for themselves and be "a help and support to him."

This was the dominant note of the thirty-one interviews: not impoverishment but diminished circumstances and the prospect of further reductions in the future; not present ruin but the fear of future deprivation—severe deprivation relative to the standard of life known before—as one watched one's "little stock daily decreasing." For "in such circumstances" Hugh Matheson, a thirty-two-year-old farmer emigrating with his wife, sister, and three young children, explained to the interviewers, "it seems impossible for farmers to avoid ruin"; hence his hopes, "encouraged by his friends already in America" "of bettering his condition in that country."

Such was the general background. The specific precipitations to uprooting, the immediate incitations, were not only rent rises—a doubling or tripling of rents in a few years' time, specified in these interviews down to the last shilling—but also a precipitous drop in the selling price of cattle, one of the region's chief products; disastrous harvests; and sudden advances in the purchase price of grains, in part because of the greater profits derived from distilling. There were many variations: the shopkeeper who faced ruin because his customers—"the common people," he called them—were so poor they could not pay their debts to him; a farmer certain the rent rises were due to the return of soldiers with too much money in their pockets; a tenant whose rents had risen 150% but who was devastated not by the rents but by the conversion of his pasture to the "parking and placing" of new tenants, which "rendered his farm useless, his cattle died for want of grass, and his corn farm was unfit to support his family, after paying the extravagant tack duty."

But there was another, subtler theme wound in among these explanations of immediate precipitants, besides the steep rent rises, the collapse of cattle prices, and the soaring cost of basic food supplies. The farmer who complained about the loss of his pastureland, John Catanoch, age fifty, traveling with his wife and four children, made the issue clear. His landlord, notorious in the region, was the Reverend Alexander Nicolson of Thurso. He and his tacksman were squeezing his property at Shebster, three miles east of Hogg's tack at Borlum, for all it could yield. Not only had Nicolson jacked up the rents and converted common pastureland to rent-paying tenancies, but, what seemed to oppress his subtenants even more, he had enforced all the "arbitrary and oppressive services" that his property rights entitled him to. Such unpaid labor services, once expected of most subtenants throughout Britain, had long since disappeared almost everywhere except on certain estates in these far northern Scottish counties. Catanoch, already caught in a severe economic squeeze, had been forced

> to labour up [Nicolson's] ground, cart, win, lead, and stack his peats, mow, win, and lead his hay, and cut his corn and lead it in the yard which took up above 30 or 40 days of his servants and horses each year, without the least acknowledgement for it, and without victuals, save the men that mowed the hay who got their dinner only.

William Sutherland, forty, leaving with his wife and five children, had faced almost identical demands on the Bighouse estate. In addition to his rent of sixty marks,

> he was obliged to find two horses and two servants from the middle of July to the end of harvest solely at his own expence, besides plowing, cutting turf, making middings [manure heaps], mixing dung and leading it out in seed time, and besides cutting, winning, leading and stacking 10 fathoms of peats yearly, all done without so much as a bit of bread or a drink to his servants.

Similar complaints came from the subtenants on the Sutherland estates. Hector McDonald, age seventy-five, traveling with his three sons and two grandsons to join his married daughter in Carolina, calculated that he had put in at least forty days a year, with his people and his cattle, on the Sutherlands' fields at Langwell, in the far southeast of Sutherland County, near the North Sea. And young William Sutherland (the clan name is ubiquitous), on the Sutherland's remote Forse estate, just off the North Sea coast thirty-five miles northeast of Hector McDonald's tenancy at Langwell, found the services he owed so numerous and so "arbitrary," especially "in seed time & harvest, that he could not in [the] two years he possest it, raise as much corn as [would] serve his family for six months."[21]

[21] The same theme is sounded in the responses to Hogg's letter to Balfour (note 1, above) published in the *Weekly Magazine, or Edinburgh Amusement.* "Probus," defending the Caithness landlords (Sept. 1, 1774), had to admit that in these northern counties tenants still had to perform personal services on the landlords' farms, a practice that had been eliminated elsewhere and that the writer wished "for the sake of the country . . . was totally abolished." But the practice was not wholly unreasonable. "Each tenant has the particular number of days he has to work in seed-time and harvest stipulated to him, or his particular piece of work assigned him, according to the extent of land that he possesses. He takes his farm with that express burden; and it is in fact a part of the rent he pays for it. He cannot, therefore, be said to be *oppressed* by these services. He is far from thinking so himself; and I know landholders in Caithness who proposed to convert the services of their tenants at a rate incredibly low, infinitely less than the value of their work; and yet the tenants chose to continue their services. So far are these people from looking on themselves as hurt or oppressed by the services they perform to the masters!" But the dialect piece of Oct. 13, 1774, had no such benign view: "We maun gang [must go] wi' his carriage twenty miles, if but wi' a

It was to escape these services—demeaning, costly, and universally described as "arbitrary"—and to escape the progressive constriction of life taking place around them and the deprivation that seemed clearly to lie ahead, that these subtenant farmers and tradesmen made the momentous decision to uproot themselves from a settled way of life and transplant themselves to the pineland of inland North Carolina. Few of them had substantial surplus funds to draw on. Almost all of them must have liquidated their entire stock—cattle, farm equipment, current crops, stores, and tenancy rights—to raise the passage money and the "overplus" that Hogg required. It was estimated that an ordinary north Scottish subtenant could raise £10 by a total liquidation, but many of the sums raised were considerably more than that. The passage money for large emigrant families like the Catanochs (£35) approached the sum the affluent Hogg paid for the cabin accommodations for his party. At least nine of the family groups paid £20 or more for their passages, and the total transportation cost of the whole expedition, £765, which with the required "overplus" undoubtedly totaled over £1,000, was a substantial drainage of the liquid capital available in the two northern counties that were mainly affected. And the *Bachelor* was one of three such vessels that left directly from Sutherland or Caithness in 1773, each of which carried off at least £650 in freight costs.[22]

Departure

How slim the "overplus" these emigrants carried with them to cover unexpected expenses, how risky their venture, and how dependent they were on Hogg's management and on Inglis's efficiency and good will emerged even before the voyage began. The original plan, based on Inglis's estimate of when he could refit, provision, and partly rebuild the *Bachelor* and get it to Thurso, called for departure for Carolina in early July, and that in turn rested on when the *Bachelor* would return to Leith from its current voyage. By late June the voyagers were gathering in Thurso; by early July most of them had arrived. But there was no sign of the *Bachelor* off the coast of

---

letter, till and harrow his mains [domains], carry dung (and sometimes war [worse]) upon our backs, cast and carry his peats, lead his middings [heaps of manure], thack [thatch] his houses, shear and thrash, mill, and kill his crop, and carry his victual and farms when and where he orders, at our ain charges, and this stops nothing of our rents; yea, stop it! they're heezing [rising] ilka [every] day."

[22] The passengers on the ill-fated *Nancy* (chap. 16, no. 2, below) paid over 650 guineas in freight charges, the *Virginia Gazette* (Rind) reported on Dec. 16, 1773; those on another storm-tossed Highlands emigration vessel (the *David and Ann*) paid £650. Some such sum seems to have been the usual freight cost of a fully loaded emigrant vessel, and it represented almost all the pooled resources of emigrants—people who, "by selling their stock, could realize a sum sufficient to cover the expense and to start the family with some little capital in America." Argyll, *Scotland As It Was*, II, 131.

Caithness. Where the emigrants stayed and how they managed while they waited is not known. Few of them could have afforded to put up in taverns or had friends in the area; many must have camped, as so many other emigrants awaiting shipment had done, in rough shelters or vacant buildings. Some may have taken casual employment in Thurso, though there is no evidence for this and the local economy was hardly hospitable. But no matter how primitive their accommodations and no matter how frugal their subsistence, they were already beginning to consume the "overplus" that Hogg had insisted on. Later it would be said that the long wait in Thurso had reduced the emigrants "to a state of indigence and want."

As the weeks went by and Ramage and the *Bachelor* still failed to return from their voyage, Inglis began to shift his plans. On May 10 he said the emigrants would be able to leave in "the latter end of July." But the *Bachelor* did not arrive in Leith until the very end of June; only then could Inglis start unloading and refitting it and rebuilding the hold to provide sleeping platforms and a few other facilities for the emigrants. On July 2, at approximately the time the emigrants had expected to leave Thurso, Inglis wrote that the vessel would be ready by mid-August and could therefore be expected to arrive in Carolina in October. Everything took longer than expected, he explained. On August 2 he predicted that the *Bachelor* would be able to clear Leith around August 20. Finally it did leave—on August 26, only partly provisioned; the rest of the supplies were to be picked up at Thurso.[23]

By August 28, when the vessel arrived in Thurso, all the preliminaries had been completed. The provisions were all accounted for if not all taken on board. The vessel had been insured by underwriters in Glasgow. Hogg and his wife had traveled, at considerable expense and trouble, to Edinburgh to sign an exhaustive contract with Inglis, which they circulated among the emigrants. And the voyagers, who had been waiting in and around Thurso for approximately six weeks, began to go aboard. Inglis by then was quite pleased with things—as well he might have been. Having managed the quite complicated task of fitting up an emigrant ship, which he had never done before, he discovered the magnitude of the profits involved. The entire cost of outfitting and victualing the *Bachelor* amounted to £461 7s 7d, and since the freight charges paid by the emigrants and Hogg brought in £765 he stood to gain 65% on his money—just on the emigrants alone. But he had also arranged with Ramage to return to England with naval stores from North Carolina and with rice from South Carolina, cargoes which in themselves would produce a profit beyond all the other

[23]"Stewart Petition" (n.14, above), pp. 1, 2; "Answers and Defences for James Hogg," p. 6; Inglis to Colin Campbell and Co., June 28, July 13, 1773, to Hogg & Campbell, Feb. 26, July 2, 1773, to James Davidson, Aug. 2, 1773, to James Hogg, April 21, May 10, 1773, to James Baird, Jr., Aug. 26, 1773, all in Inglis Letterbook.

operating costs: insurance, seamen's wages, and depreciation. So, now experienced in the emigrant shipping business and highly optimistic about the profits, Inglis asked Hogg to recommend him to any others he happened to know who were planning such expeditions. Transporting emigrants seemed a most welcome supplement to his usual line of trade.[24]

Yet the progress of the *Bachelor* continued to drag, extending into early fall. It took eighteen days to load all the provisions stored at Thurso and get the emigrants checked and rechecked, as to their correct ages and payments, and safely lodged aboard. When the *Bachelor* finally weighed anchor and headed out into the north Atlantic on its way to Carolina, it was September 14. Inglis was greatly relieved to get word in Edinburgh that the emigrants had finally left, though he was annoyed at some of the details. Hogg had paid part of what he owed Inglis for the emigrants' transportation with a bill on Hogg and Campbell in Wilmington instead of with cash, and other parts of the payments due Inglis were late in coming in. He was convinced too that Hogg had not taken in as many emigrants as he might have; 10 or 20 more could have been fitted in, he wrote, "without incumbrance." Still, things looked promising, and on October 2 Inglis wrote Hogg, in care of Hogg and Campbell in Wilmington, that despite the little annoyances he was satisfied. "I hope before this reaches you that you'll be safe arrived with all your fellow passengers after an agreeable voyage."[25]

Disaster

On the day Inglis wrote these cheery words the 280 emigrants aboard the *Bachelor* were experiencing unimagined horrors and must have despaired of their lives. The September storms that Inglis himself had feared had moved in almost immediately after their departure from Thurso on the fourteenth. The vessel battled "high & contrary winds" for five days, only to be blown so sharply backward in the roaring seas above Scotland that they were forced to take refuge in the port of Stromness in the Orkneys, only twenty-eight miles due north of their starting point. There they waited, along with two other storm-tossed emigrant vessels from the Highlands, for six days, repairing the damage, sorting things out, and waiting

[24]"Stewart Petition," p. 2; Inglis to James Baird, Jr., Aug. 26, 1773, Inglis Letterbook. The contract, an exhaustively detailed document dated Aug. 24, 1773, is in the Hogg Papers. The details of expenditure and income, hence of Inglis's expected profit, are in the Admiralty Papers. For the return cargo and Inglis's optimistic request for more emigrant business, Inglis to Hogg & Campbell, July 2, 1773, and to James Hogg, Oct. 2, 1773, Inglis Letterbook.
[25]Hogg's two-page undated sketch of events leading up to the shipwreck, prepared in the course of arbitration proceedings, and the legal controversies that followed, in Hogg Papers; Inglis to Hogg, Oct. 2, 1773, Inglis Letterbook.

for the storm to subside. On September 25 they finally ventured out again. This time they got as far as the Outer Hebrides, ninety miles or so from Thurso. Off the Butt of Lewis, in a notoriously dangerous stretch of water, they met with another storm, even more severe than the first. The longboat was smashed, the rudder controls and pumps were damaged, and the vessel went out of control. It was blown back north and east helplessly, in a week of what must have been horrendous turmoil and fear. Smallpox appeared and began to spread, fatally among the children, Inglis later explained, "on board a ship crammed together in such numbers in so narrow a space." But it was even worse than that. "Some of their children crammed in the hold" (a well-informed contemporary recorded) "were said to be stifled to death and thrown overboard into the sea." The *Bachelor* plunged and pitched in a great loop back to the northeast, ending finally, on October 3, in the fishing village of Walls on Vaila Sound in the Shetlands, 137 miles north*east* of Thurso.[26]

By then eleven of the emigrants had died, most of them children but also a few adults, including Hogg's elderly mother-in-law. And now the emigrants, disembarked at Walls, were in real economic as well as physical distress. They had little if anything left of their "overplus" to buy supplies for their subsistence, and so they turned to Captain Ramage with a plea that he distribute the *Bachelor*'s provisions while they waited for the repairs to be completed. He refused, saying that the stores were only for shipboard use and that the owner and he had no responsibility for the passengers once they had disembarked. He then unloaded part of the ship's provisions and stored them on shore for safekeeping—his casks of bread would remain in the church most of the winter—retaining the rest himself under lock and key. After four days Hogg drew up a legal protest against Inglis and Ramage—the first of a succession of legal processes that would trail in the wake of the *Bachelor*—demanding that they supply the passengers during the stopover in the Shetlands. Nothing came of this, and the emigrants were thrown on the charity of the Shetland Islanders, through the good offices of the deputy vice-admiral of the Shetlands, William Balfour, who had witnessed their arrival.

The help they received was assumed to be temporary, to last only while the vessel was being repaired. By October 24 the work was complete and

[26]Hogg's sketch of events (see preceding note); *Caledonian Mercury,* May 2, 1774; "Answers and Replies for James Inglis, Jr.," July 24, 1774, Admiralty Papers; *The Diary of the Rev. John Mill, Minister . . . in Shetland, 1740–1803 . . .* (Edinburgh, 1889), p. 40. For newspaper accounts of the storm that hit the three emigrant vessels, see *Lloyd's Evening Post,* Nov. 1–3, 1773, and *Leeds Mercury,* March 15, 1774. The violence of this stormy season became famous. "In eight weeks we have rarely had twenty-four hours together without a storm," a letter from Orkney stated on Nov. 30. "We have had more excessive gales of wind since the 7th of September than has been known in the space of twelve months in any period for seven years past, and at present the weather is as threatening as ever. Six ships have been lost within these six weeks." *Lloyd's Evening Post,* Dec. 15–17, 1773.

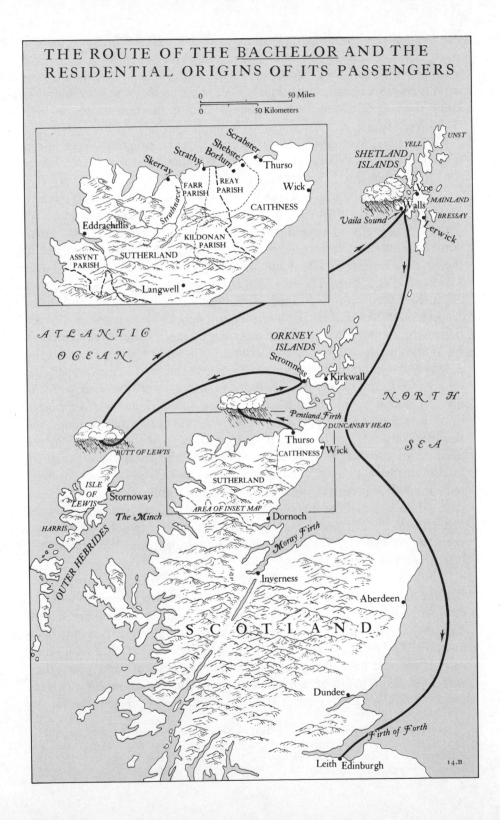

THE ROUTE OF THE BACHELOR AND THE RESIDENTIAL ORIGINS OF ITS PASSENGERS

0   50 Miles

0   50 Kilometers

Scrabster
Shebster
Strathy
Skerray
Borlum
Thurso
FARR PARISH
REAY PARISH
Wick
CAITHNESS
Eddrachillis
KILDONAN PARISH
ASSYNT PARISH
SUTHERLAND
Strathnaver
Langwell

SHETLAND ISLANDS
YELL
UNST
Voe
MAINLAND
Walls
BRESSAY
Vaila Sound
Lerwick

ATLANTIC OCEAN

ORKNEY ISLANDS
Stromness
Kirkwall

NORTH

Pentland Firth
DUNCANSBY HEAD

BUTT OF LEWIS
Thurso
CAITHNESS
Wick

SEA

ISLE OF LEWIS
Stornoway
SUTHERLAND
AREA OF INSET MAP

HARRIS
The Minch
Dornoch

OUTER HEBRIDES
Moray Firth

Inverness

Aberdeen

S C O T L A N D

Dundee

Firth of Forth

Leith Edinburgh

14.B

the emigrants were preparing to reboard the *Bachelor* and resume the voyage. But on that day the most violent gale of this extraordinarily stormy season hit the North Sea. Sweeping over the Shetlands, it tore the *Bachelor* from its two anchors, both of which were lost, and threw it onto the rocks along the sound, which ripped through the bottom. The vessel was now severely damaged, and there was no hope of a speedy departure.[27]

What state, psychologically and physically, the emigrants were in can only be imagined. What is clearly recorded is that the storm of October 24 set into motion three clusters of activities.

First, Balfour, working through a network of parish organizations and local gentry, intensified his efforts to mobilize charitable assistance and place the emigrants in local homes until they could leave the islands. Small contributions came in from all over the windswept Shetlands, from Yell in the north to Bressay in the east and from half a dozen villages scattered over Mainland Island. But these were poor communities. Only £13 2s in cash was collected ("their resources in this kind," Balfour told Hogg on November 7, were just about exhausted); and the food supplies amounted to thirteen or fourteen hundredweight of potatoes and oatmeal. He was more successful in housing the emigrants. By December it was known that the refugees, as they had become, had been lodged one way or another in various parishes where, according to one published account, they were "treated with the greatest humanity and hospitality," and would continue to be supported until the *Bachelor* could proceed. But this had not been easy to arrange and was not without conflict. When Balfour tried to send ten or so of the neediest of the emigrants to a nearby island, the inhabitants panicked, fearing smallpox. Balfour had to visit the place himself and arrange for them to be located "where the danger of infection may be avoided." More important, while some of the emigrants were able to pay their own way—the venerable William Gordon and his party of ten, for example, who lodged with the minister in Walls—others were destitute, and the burden fell heavily on the few residents of means.

On November 9 eight landowners in and around Walls petitioned Balfour to order Hogg and Ramage either to supply the emigrants with the *Bachelor*'s own provisions or hire another vessel and get them off the islands. The people of Walls and its vicinity, they pointed out, had not been uncharitable. If it had not been for them, they said, "most [of the emigrants] certainly would have died of hunger and cold." But for three years, they explained, there had been a food shortage in the islands, and the current crop was unlikely to give relief. Why should this hard-pressed community

[27]"Stewart Petition," pp. 2–4; Hogg's payment to Notary Malcolmson to frame "a long protist . . . agst Mr. Inglis & Mr. Ramages," Oct. 3, 1773, Hogg Papers. For the final disaster on the rocks at Walls in Vaila Sound, see *Caledonian Mercury*, May 2, 1774, and *Lloyd's Evening Post*, Dec. 13–15, 1773. For Ramage's rental of storage space: Minutes of the Kirk Session at Walls, CH 2/380/3.

"be oppressed by these emigrants"? "There lies no obligation on them to provide them when those obliged to do it are able and actually have a large stock of provisions on hand bought with the emigrants money." Furthermore, Ramage's dilatory conduct suggested that he had no intention of saving the *Bachelor* and continuing the voyage. They suspected that he hoped to have the vessel legally declared a wreck and so be released from his obligation to complete the voyage. If that happened, "it is not to be doubted but both he and Mr. Hogg will desert the emigrants and leave them an insufferable burden on the country"—a country, they said, "which has nothing to do with them."[28]

Balfour had little difficulty in dismissing this petition. Not only was the document technically deficient, but the whole issue was already "subjudice." For while Balfour and others were organizing charitable donations and housing, a second cluster of activities formed. A group of the emigrants, led by the disreputable Alexander MacKay, filed a lawsuit with the Vice Admiralty Court, which was presented by the schoolmaster Patrick Ross; they sued Ramage for release of the supplies and Hogg and Ramage on a series of broader charges.

They alleged, first, that Hogg had exploited the "spirit of emigration" and the general discontent in northern Scotland to inveigle the emigrants into his plan "merely with a view of getting [his] freight paid by them." In a twelve-page rejection of all the charges, Hogg easily refuted this allegation. He detailed the clamor for emigration that had long been in process in precisely the areas of Scotland from which the emigrants had come, quite independent of anything he had done. And he explained exhaustively how he had first resisted the pleas of would-be emigrants, including most of the complainants; how, when he had decided to serve them as contractor, he had turned many back; and how he had let through his screening only a small number of the many applicants. Far from being entrapped unwillingly by him, the complainants had applied for admission "and looked on it as a favour to be enrolled in my list." Surely the deputy vice-admiral knew "that scarcely a ship goes from Brittain to America but advertizes for & promises encouragement to passengers and mechanics," and since when is that "culpable or illegal"?

[28] A full itemization of goods and money collected by Balfour "for the use of the distressed emigrants," early Nov. 1773, is in Hogg Papers; Balfour to Hogg, Lerwick, Nov. 7, 1773, *ibid.*; *Pennsylvania Journal; and the Weekly Advertiser*, March 9, 1774; *Caledonian Mercury*, May 2, 1774; "Stewart Petition," pp. 2–4. The dispersal of the shipwrecked emigrants may be traced in part through church records. The minister of the kirk in Walls, James Buchan, writing to a ministerial colleague (March 2, 1774), explained that William Gordon, the first of the 31 emigrants to be interviewed at length, was living with his large family with Buchan in Walls and paying for all his expenses. Of those sent off to the fishing isle of Bressay, across the harbor from Lerwick, most lived with one "Gaerdie & Lady," and they too were causing little trouble "at least by way of pocket expense." Church Sessions Records, Presbytery of Lerwick, CH 2/1071/33.

As to lining his own pockets, the small payment the emigrants had made to him for organizing the expedition did not begin to repay him for his trouble and expense; it was less than what was usually paid to such contractors; and it scarcely made up for an easily overlooked cost to him, "the disagreeable necessity of taking my passage in the same ship with so many of them." He refuted too their charges that the tardy departure was his fault and that he had ever told them that they could expect the owner to feed them while in port ("I told them in words and letters not to expect it, on the contrary desird all and every one of them according to their abilities to lay in stores for themselves—which accordingly they did—for fear of being put in anywhere"). He willingly assigned to the complainants the contract's provision for £200 damages due him if the owner failed to fulfill the terms, and he explained that far from trying to "elope" from the Shetlands and abandon them, as they had charged, he was planning to go to Edinburgh for the sole purpose of straightening the mess out with Inglis and getting the voyage under way again—and he was doing this quite openly and with the hoped-for concurrence of the emigrants themselves, whose interests were surely identical with his own.

In truth, he concluded, the source of the suit against him was in no way mysterious. Before the complainants left home, he wrote,

> they had filled their heads with towring hopes of wealth & idleness & having a conceited opinion of their own merit they could not allow themselves to think that ever they would be crossd in thier high expectations by storms & tempests. But alas! the winds & the waves have contended against us, and like common mortals they as well as I are reduced to difficulties & distress. Unthankful to providence for saving us from the dangers of the sea when so many others perishd around us, and wanting fortitude to support their share of distress . . . they are too fond of themselves to believe that on their own account they could be so hardly dealt with. They look about for one on whom to throw the blame of their misfortunes, and how can they find a more proper object of their resentment than the man who found them the means of leaving their own country? If a ship had not been got for them they could not have gone to sea and if they had not gone to sea they could not have met with storms and if they had not met with storms they could not now have been reduced to live on charity.

He begged the court's forgiveness for such testy language. "I know their misfortune and I feel for them." He shared their troubles but he too deserved sympathy. Instead of acknowledging his losses, the complainants "have filld this island with murmurs & complaints, and by falsehoods & vile insinuations have done all in their power to hurt my character & interest, and to prejudice the gentlemen of this country against me." He was indignant at what they had done, and blameless of their charges.

Balfour, for the vice-admiralty court, agreed. Even if the facts alleged were true, he wrote in his decision, they would not have warranted the inferences drawn from them. He dismissed the case against Hogg, and assigned court costs to the complainants. He dismissed too, on legal technicalities, their charge that Ramage's navigation had been incompetent, but he declined to rule on whether the owner was obliged to supply the passengers while in port. The contract was silent on that point, and so it would depend on the parties' intent at the time of signing the contract, or, failing that information, on the common practice in such matters. And he concluded his ruling by requiring Ramage to report in writing on the present state of the *Bachelor*, on what repairs were necessary, and on how long it would take to make the repairs.[29]

For Balfour himself had taken a direct role in the third cluster of activities that formed after the storm of October 24, the attempt to get the vessel repaired and the voyage resumed. He had quickly formed a poor opinion of Ramage. "With ordinary activity & spirit," he told Hogg, the captain could have secured the vessel on the 24th and kept it from harm. And since then, for a fortnight, he seemed to be doing nothing at all, caught up, apparently, in a fit of irresolution, procrastination, or despondency. Balfour himself, therefore, wrote Inglis to inform him of what had happened and the state of the ship and its passengers. And he advised Hogg that if Inglis did not take "the most speedy & effectual means of puting the ship in a condition to prosecute the voyage" Hogg and the emigrants could sue for the full value of the ship and its contents. And he advised Hogg how to proceed if he wished to take that course. As to timing, he felt that if Inglis did his "indespensible duty, unless the ship is a rag not fit to repair," it could be made ready for a transatlantic crossing by the early spring.[30]

Rescue, Repair, and Abandonment

Inglis heard the news of the wreck not from Balfour but from a commercial correspondent in the town of Wick, Caithness, whose letter reached him

[29]"Stewart Petition," p. 6; "Answers and Defences for James Hogg," pp. 5, 7, 11–12; "Depositions of James Hogg in the Process Against Him at the Instance of Alexander MacKay & Others"; "Findings of Deputy Vice Admiral Balfour, re Petition of Alexander MacKay and Others . . . ," Lerwick, Nov. 19, 1773; and "Claim of Expenses by Mr. Hogg," Nov. 1773: all in Hogg Papers.
[30]Balfour to Hogg, Lerwick, Nov. 7, 1773, Hogg Papers.

on November 2, the day Ramage finally got around to writing. He cursed Ramage, the "most unlucky man as ever sailed on salt water," grieved at "the great death and confusion that must have ensued from that disaster and the poor emigrants who had no other enducement than the mending of their fortune," and set to work preparing a rescue vessel, the sloop *Mary*, with equipment to make the repairs in the Shetlands. As letters arrived from the north during November and December (Ramage's complete account only got to him on December 10) he was busy hiring a master carpenter, providing him with the tools and materials needed to make the repairs, preparing casks of food to replace those that were lost, and having two new anchors cast. All this took not only money—over £100—but time, and winter storms further delayed the departure of the *Mary*. It arrived at Walls on February 10, three-and-a-half months after the storm, and only then could the serious repair work get under way. This labor consumed two more months, and so it was in April 1774—seven months after the original departure date—that the *Bachelor* was once again able to set out to sea. But not out into the Atlantic. Only the most necessary repairs could be done in the Shetlands. The structural damage had to be more carefully assessed before a major voyage could be undertaken. The *Bachelor* therefore set out, not for North Carolina but for the Edinburgh docks at Leith—and with a significant deviation from its orders.[31]

Inglis's orders to Ramage were included in a long, detailed letter he wrote the shipmaster on January 1. This latest disaster, he informed the captain, was such a "crowning" of Ramage's many misfortunes "that no individual possibly can bear it. . . . A man in this world without activity and pushing with prudence will never succeed." But he hoped for the best, and was at least able to compliment Ramage on holding fast against the "absurd," "nonsensical" claim that the owner was obliged to feed the passengers while in port. Make all the repairs immediately, he ordered Ramage. If they are completely successful "you are immediately to proceed in the voyage." If not, take the remaining emigrants on board, "land them at Thurso and proceed thereafter directly for Leith." When the ship was refitted it would call back at Thurso and pick the emigrants up. But he encouraged Ramage to get rid of as many of the emigrants as possible by giving any who would accept a settlement eight weeks' worth of provisions in exchange for "their discharge in full of all claims." And Inglis repeated his orders that Ramage land the emigrants "at Thurso" in separate letters to both Balfour and Hogg, and asked Balfour, a man he believed to be of

[31] Inglis to William Woodbine, Nov. 2, 1773; Alexander Miller to Inglis, Wick, Oct. 24, 1773, referred to in Inglis to Miller, Nov. 3, 1773; Inglis to Ramage, and to John Martin *re* emergency repairs and the rescue sloop *Mary*, Jan. 1, 1774: all in Inglis Letterbook. Ramage wrote Inglis, after some delay, on Nov. 2, 9, and 20. The Admiralty Papers show Inglis's costs in recovering the vessel and bringing it back to Leith to have been over £100.

"honour, probity and humanity" and a wise judge, to supervise the whole transaction.[32]

On April 25, 1774, the *Bachelor*, with all but twenty-eight of the surviving passengers aboard, limped not into Thurso but into Leith, without ever having stopped at the Caithness port. Apparently, however, Ramage had been faithful to his orders, for when the *Bachelor* was off the coast of Caithness he had called the emigrants together and offered to drop them at Thurso. "But they to a man absolutely refused to comply therewith." They insisted on being taken to Leith. They had, it seems, no desire to lose contact with Inglis or the vessel since they fully intended to see their venture through. There was nothing for them to do in Thurso, no possibility of help there, and no way there for them to force Inglis's hand if that became necessary. And to return to their homes at this point would have been a disaster. They had burned their bridges, and they had no interest in exchanging their future for eight weeks' worth of provisions. The twenty-eight who accepted Inglis's discharge offer—eighteen of them children below the age of eight—did so in the Shetlands before the *Bachelor* set out.[33]

The arrival of these 228 emigrants (the original 280 minus the eight who had died and the 28 discharged, and minus Hogg's party of 16, who took care of themselves) proved to be a notable event in Edinburgh and Leith. Almost all of the emigrants were now completely destitute, through no fault of their own, and their cause had become famous. Scarcely a week after their arrival in Leith the *Caledonian Mercury* carried a column describing their misfortunes, explaining how Balfour had mobilized charity for them in the Shetlands, and asserting that 200 of them "who have nothing to maintain themselves on, are just now reduced to the greatest extremities, and unless some speedy relief is afforded them, they must certainly perish. Many of them are able and willing to work, but cannot find employment." A group of ministers and merchants organized a charity drive for them, and Sunday collections in the churches were soon under way. Many people, of course, were against emigration altogether, but the question, the *Mercury* declared, is not "whether their emigration is right or wrong, wise or unwise. . . . At present they are in the most destitute circumstances, and call for the pity and assistance of every feeling, benevolent mind." And in successive weeks, as the story was picked up first by the *Scots Magazine* and then by London's *Annual Register*, the *Mercury* informed the readers of the charitable gifts made to the refugees (£29 2s 6d collected in South Leith one

[32] Inglis to Ramage, to Balfour, and to Hogg, all Jan. 1, 1774, Inglis Letterbook. Inglis continued to denounce Ramage: "that man who shall never go to see in my employ again" (to Edie and Laird, March 18, 1774); "there never was a more unlucky man than Ramage in every respect" (to Balfour, May 13, 1774), *ibid*.

[33] "Answers and Replies for James Inglis, Jr.," July 24, 1774, Admiralty Papers.

Sunday, £20 from a "young nobleman . . . distinguished for humanity") and exhorted the inhabitants of Edinburgh itself to contribute too.[34]

As the weeks passed, the emigrants began scattering across the countryside and into various corners of Leith and Edinburgh seeking employment. But the results were poor: "if speedy relief is not afforded," the *Mercury* insisted, "they must die in the streets." Four did die—in an accident in an abandoned house which a group of them had expropriated, suffocating from fumes when a chimney vent failed during the night.[35] Inglis reached far afield in the emigrants' behalf, writing a friend in Falkirk, twenty-five miles west of Edinburgh, that a number of the stranded emigrants were "stout able people and willing to work for very low wages." One could get work done by them "on the easiest terms," and he hoped his friend would employ a "parcell" of them, since their survival depended on such help. Later, in court proceedings, he would attribute some of their failure to find work to their own behavior, a mixture, he said, of pride and indolence— but undoubtedly too a reflection of their humiliation at the condition into which they had fallen. Some, he said, when offered 8 pence a day for "ordinary labour," replied "they would rather beg alleging that others were allowed more. It is a question if they ever had that much at home, and in their situation they ought rather to have thankfully accepted of the offer than made the insolent reply." Others were apparently chased out of town for illegal employment or for begging with forged testimonials.[36]

But these were later recriminations. In the early weeks Inglis was sympathetic to the emigrants' plight. He was, however, adamant in refusing to admit any legal responsibility for them while they were on shore. And a more serious issue soon emerged. As the work on the vessel went on— slowly & carefully, to satisfy the insurers that good-faith efforts were being made to reclaim the vessel and that the damage was not being exaggerated —it became clear from the testimony of experts that the vessel was not

[34]The exact number of the *Bachelor's* emigrants who arrived in Edinburgh varies somewhat in the documents in the Admiralty Papers, probably because "freights," full fare-paying *adults,* were sometimes wrongly equated with people: one "freight" referring to children meant two individuals; "sucking children" went free and were not counted among the "freights" at all. The figures given here are the most likely. For the publicity, see *Caledonian Mercury,* May 2, 9, 18, and June 18, 1774.

[35]*Ibid.,* June 18, May 4, 7, 1774. The victims were Alexander Morison, 60, formerly a farmer on the Sutherland estates, his wife, son, and maidservant. Morison was one of the 31 heads of households who had been interviewed at length in Lerwick. The story of the Morisons' death circulated widely: *York Chronicle and Weekly Advertiser,* May 20, 1774; *Scots Magazine,* 36 (April, 1774), 222.

[36]Inglis to Alexander Stiven, May 14 and Aug. 15, 1774, Inglis Letterbook; "Answers and Replies for James Inglis, Jr.," July 24, 1774, Admiralty Papers. For the fate of Lucy Mackay, one of the refugees from the *Bachelor,* who was caught begging in Edinburgh with a forged "certificate of her distress" from one of the city's ministers and two church elders, see *Caledonian Mercury,* Jan. 11, 1775.

likely to be usable in transatlantic shipping.[37] Hogg, who had acquired power of attorney for the emigrants, began to doubt Inglis's intentions, though Inglis continued to say "that the ship was to proceed as soon as she could be refitted." But time passed, and Hogg pressed Inglis for a definite commitment. He demanded to know what the prospects were. If the ship was officially declared a wreck, he said, Inglis was obliged either to repay all of the freight money he had received or provide another vessel to carry the emigrants to Carolina. If Inglis refused to do either, Hogg threatened to sue him in the high court of admiralty. On May 7 Inglis, his irritation rising at this "d——d unfortunate affair," at "this d——d misfortunate fellow Ramage and these d——ls of emigrants," replied, and his reply launched a complex, sprawling, costly contest in law.[38]

Inglis was deeply sympathetic to the plight of the emigrants, he wrote in a critical letter of May 7, but he had more than fulfilled the terms of the contract. Since the vessel "lies almost a wreck" and experts said it could not proceed across the Atlantic, there was no more he could do: he had "fulfilled and implemented every part of the contract incumbent upon me. Therefore I look upon myself as no longer bound to proceed the voyage." It was no fault of his if Hogg and the emigrants had failed to cover their risks with insurance. Everyone suffered from misfortunes like this. He himself was well covered by insurance, but even so he would take a large loss. He noted that some of the ship's original supplies were still intact. As a sign of good will he was prepared to distribute this remnant equally among the emigrants, or sell it and distribute the income. What he would not do was agree that he still had an obligation to take Hogg and the others to Carolina. That would require an entirely new contract, which he would not undertake unless it was understood that he owed them nothing under the terms of the original contract. If Hogg wished to sue him for the freight charges they had paid, and for which they had not received the return they had expected, well and good. But he was sure his position was correct and would be willing to save Hogg the trouble and expense of a lawsuit by submitting the controversy to arbitration.[39]

Hogg was in no mood to compromise. As soon as he received this reply of May 7 from Inglis he concluded that Inglis had reneged on his contract, got in touch with a Greenock shipper to transport himself and his family

[37]For explanations of the delays in repairs, see "Petition of James Inglis, Jr., to the Judge of the High Court of Admiralty," [c. June 24–Aug. 5, 1774], Admiralty Papers. On the appointment of damage inspectors by the underwriters and Inglis, see Inglis to John Sine and Robert Dryburgh, April 30, 1774, and on his efforts to collect the insurance, Inglis to James Baird, Jr., and Co., June 14 and 24, 1774, Inglis Letterbook.

[38]Hogg's sketch of events (note 25, above); Inglis to Peter Innes, May 23, 1774, and to Alexander Ferguson of Craigdarroch, May 7, 1774, Inglis Letterbook.

[39]Inglis to Hogg, May 7, 1774, Inglis Letterbook.

to Carolina, and then forthwith began court proceedings against Inglis to recover the money they had given him before they had left Thurso. Speed was essential. The emigrants could not afford to attend the lengthy court proceedings. If they could not resume their voyage to America, and soon, they would have to accommodate themselves somehow in Scotland. When to their dismay the admiralty court adjourned until June 3, Hogg and the emigrants turned to the arbitration proceedings that Inglis had proposed. Two arbitrators were selected, position papers were drafted, and elaborate depositions filed.[40] To bolster his case, Inglis wrote letters to three firms that were long established in the business of shipping emigrants or that were in touch with merchants who had such experience: William Calhoun and Co. in Glasgow; Edie & Laird in London, with whom Inglis had regular dealings on other matters; and Coysgarne & Lloyds in Rotterdam, whom Inglis asked to forward his inquiries to "sundries from your place . . . concerned in carrying Palatines to America." To all three he asked the same two questions: first, was he "still bound to proceed on voyage on the terms of the original contract or does it cease on my part from this disaster"; and second, if he was obliged to proceed, was not the *contractor*, that is, Hogg, obliged to supply the needed provisions? Surely he, Inglis, as the shipper could not be expected to supply and resupply the vessel every time there was a delay or misfortune—he could not be held responsible for an endless supply of consumable goods.[41]

Apparently the replies Inglis received from the experienced firms were more or less satisfactory, though he had differences with some of the views of Edie & Laird. But then, for reasons unexplained, he withdrew from the arbitration, and early in June, when the admiralty court reconvened, the legal case began to erode. He suddenly commenced a feverish effort to have the *Bachelor* "instantly repair'd," and tried to explain away his responsibility for the earlier delays in repairing the *Bachelor* when it had returned to Leith. Further, he began specifying the terms under which he would resume the voyage. But by then, Hogg insisted, the damage had been done. The emigrants could not have been expected to sit around and starve. They had either booked passage on other vessels or had begun the long trek home, or had begun to settle elsewhere. Their losses had already been incurred, definitively, and remained losses no matter what Inglis *now* proposed to do for them.[42]

[40]"Replies to James Inglis, Jr.," Aug. 15, 1774, Admiralty Papers; Hogg's sketch of events; legal advice to Hogg from Mr. Stewart, Gossford's Close, Edinburgh; draft of charges against Inglis; draft of suit for arbitration; Hogg's deposition and assignment of lawyers: all in Hogg Papers.
[41]May 28 and 30, 1774, Inglis Letterbook.
[42]Inglis to John Sine, Jr., and to Thomas Kinnear, June 4, 1774, Inglis Letterbook; "Answers for James Hogg . . . to . . . James Inglis, Jr. . . . ," June 9, 1774; "Replies to James Inglis, Jr.," June 15, 1774; "Replies for James Hogg," June 17, 1774: all in Admiralty Papers.

With this position the court, in its decision of June 24, 1774, agreed. Inglis, the court stated in a decision that was widely publicized, was fully liable for the transportation costs of all except those who had died or had been discharged, a total of £684 10s, plus interest accumulated from May 7, and also for court charges and a token payment for damages. This decision held, but the legal proceedings were by no means over, though carried on solely by lawyers, most of the principals in the case having left the scene. A few days after the decision Inglis's lawyers declared the *Bachelor* seaworthy and ordered Hogg (already at sea) and the scattered emigrants to board the vessel, by which announcement, they claimed, the merchant was discharging his full responsibility.

Hogg's lawyers responded with a petition for higher damages than the token amount (£4) that had been awarded. Inglis replied to that with an array of new arguments, including the charge that Hogg had never had the interest of the emigrants at heart; the whole enterprise had been a scheme of the Hogg brothers to populate a large tract of land in North Carolina they had bought for speculation. And he submitted new and higher figures for the expenses to which he had been put (£915 7s, he now said) and insisted that his losses were continuing to mount as long as the newly refitted *Bachelor* lay idle in Leith, equipped to transport not cargoes but emigrants. And so it went, with charges and counter-charges, petitions and "condescendences" forming a thickening tangle of legal involvements through the summer and early fall.[43]

There is no record of a concluding payment by which Inglis discharged his debt. But the effect on him became evident. On July 9 he announced that he was "going out of shipping" and would sell the *Bachelor*, which he advertised publicly and in a series of private letters. On September 9, 1774, the *Bachelor* and "a quantity of provisions ... viz., beef, biscuit, meal, barley, pease, molasses, [and] a number of puncheons and pipes" were put up for auction at Lawson's Coffeehouse in Leith. A little over a year after that, on November 6, 1775, James Inglis, merchant, died at his house on Princes Street, Edinburgh.[44]

[43] Decision of the Admiralty Court, June 24, 1774, signed by James Philip, J: A: [Judge of Admiralty]; Statement of John Irving, attorney for Inglis, June 27, 1774; "Petition of James Hogg and Others . . .," July 15, 1774; "Answers and Replies for James Inglis, Jr.," July 24, 1774; "Accompt of Expences of Outfitt & Provision for Ship Bachelor . . . ," 1774: all in Admiralty Papers. The decision of the Admiralty Court was summarized in the *Caledonian Mercury*, June 29, 1774; the *York Courant*, July 5, 1774; and the *Annual Register*, 17 (July 1774), 137–138.
[44] Inglis to George Barclay, July 9, 1774, to Andrew Conan, Aug. 16, 1774, to Peter Lawson, Aug. 30, 1774, all in Inglis Letterbook; *Caledonian Mercury*, Aug. 27, 1774, and Nov. 8, 1775.

Hogg's Establishment

Inglis had been destroyed by the wreck of the *Bachelor*. And for many of the emigrants, now scattered to the Lowlands labor markets, back to the northern Highlands, or into the anonymity of Edinburgh or Leith, it had been a disaster too.[45] But some of them—we do not know how many— managed to complete the voyage to North Carolina, either with Hogg or by themselves, and they must have witnessed, in subsequent years, the extraordinary later fortunes of their former emigration contractor, James Hogg, tacksman of Borlum, Caithness, turned merchant of Hillsboro and Cross Creek, North Carolina, land dealer, politician, and civic leader.

The speed of his ascent in America, the responsiveness of the colonial environment to his energy, enterprise, and boundless ambition, may be judged by the fact that scarcely a year after he had arrived in North Carolina he was negotiating in the Continental Congress, first with John and Samuel Adams of Massachusetts, and then more intensively with Thomas Jefferson and George Wythe of Virginia and with Silas Deane of Connecticut, for the admission of "Transylvania" as the fourteenth colony. His connections with the visionary judge Richard Henderson, the organizer and leader of the Transylvania Company, one of the most articulate, grandiloquent, ideo- logically lofty, and yet materially voracious speculators in trans-Appala- chian land, and with the other sponsors of that enterprise, had been estab- lished almost immediately.

Hogg and his party had sailed from Greenock at the end of June, 1774, almost exactly a year after they had first expected to leave from Thurso,[46]

[45]"Petition of James Hogg and Others . . .," July 15, 1774; "Answers for the Assignees of James Hogg . . .," Aug. 12, 1774; "Answers for James Inglis, Jr.," Aug. 22, 1774: all in Admiralty Papers. One of the abandoned families can be partially traced through to an interesting conclusion. Among the *Bachelor*'s shipwrecked emigrants was a young couple, the Sutherlands, who returned to Edinburgh to await the outcome of the lawsuits. There they remained, and there, in 1777, their son David was born. Prepared for the ministry in a charity school, David suddenly received, at the age of 25, an invitation "from a Scottish farmer who had settled in Barnet, Vt." to serve in the ministry in that community far up the Connecticut River. He accepted, arrived there in 1803, perambulating for a time among the neighboring settlements, many of them settled by Scots—Ryegate, Groton, Peacham, Danville—where he found, to his dismay, that "the Church was nothing but a worldly sanctuary where the most ungodly men were welcomed and retained." Nevertheless he accepted a permanent call to the town of Bath, where he remained as minister until his death fifty years later. On the Scottish settlement of Ryegate and Barnet, traced through the entries in the Register, see below, chap. 16. The Rev. David Sutherland's career, linking two otherwise separate developments among the registered emigrants, is sketched, with excerpts from his diary, in *An Historical Pam- phlet*, ed. Frank C. Wright (St. Johnsbury, Vt., 1931), pp. 47–51.
[46]Inglis to Hogg & Campbell, to James Hogg, to James Gemel and Co., June 30, 1774, all in Inglis Letterbook.

and they had arrived at the mouth of the Cape Fear River in mid or late August. What Hogg made of the "dreary waste of white barren sand, and melancholy, nodding pines" which a contemporary found at that first point of contact with North Carolina, is not known. If he, like that observant visitor, Janet Schaw of Edinburgh, found the entrance "dreary, savage and desert," and Wilmington, about twenty-five miles up the river, a mere clearing in the woods consisting of a dozen or so sandy streets within an area of a few hundred yards, broiling in the summer heat and swarming with mosquitoes, with livestock roaming freely about, he left no record of it. What is known is that he remained there, in that crude, bustling little riverside town, long enough to get his bearings and to make arrangements with his brother Robert to extend the trade of his firm, Hogg and Campbell, more securely into the backcountry.

None of that took very long. A few weeks after his arrival, in the early fall of 1774, Hogg made his first move, 100 miles inland, to the flourishing little inland center of Scottish and Scotch-Irish immigration, Cross Creek (renamed Fayetteville, after Lafayette, in 1784). There, at that crossroads village built on the lower slopes of sandhills with excellent access to the inland wagon roads and creeks, and close to the Cape Fear River exit—a raw but vital little community alive with mills, smith shops, taverns, and tenements for its few hundred inhabitants—Hogg opened a store, one of half a dozen satellite outlets of Hogg and Campbell of Wilmington. Like the other branches of Wilmington firms, Hogg's store would collect the country produce, some of it processed by the local mills, and ship it downstream by raft or other small craft to the Wilmington headquarters, taking back imported goods and supplies for sale to the inland farmers.[47]

But Hogg, an entrepreneur and man "of a superior station," had not come 3,000 miles to settle as a Cross Creek storekeeper. Within a few weeks, or at the most two months, he moved again, this time 70 miles north to the major inland "metropolis" of Hillsboro, the very epicenter of backcountry Scottish settlement, the seat of the Orange County government and courts, and a major thoroughfare located on the Great Wagon Road. Around this town a thick cluster of hamlets had developed almost overnight—"numerous beyond belief," the colony's governor reported in 1772, though still in "infantine rudeness." Rude or not, the proliferating farms and hamlets, nourished by a constant flow of new settlers moving south from Virginia and west from the coast, meant booming real-estate values, and it was there,

[47][Janet Schaw], *Journal of a Lady of Quality . . . 1774 to 1776*, ed. Evangeline W. Andrews and Charles M. Andrews (New Haven, 1921), pp. 141, 179–180, and app. VI; Harry R. Merrens, *Colonial North Carolina in the Eighteenth Century: A Study in Historical Geography* (Chapel Hill, N.C., 1964), pp. 151–153; Lawrence Lee, *The Lower Cape Fear in Colonial Days* (Chapel Hill, N.C., 1965), pp. 132–137. For a contemporary's description of Cross Creek's trade—40 to 50 wagons arriving daily from the backcountry and timber rafts floating down river to the entrepôt of European trade in Wilmington—see *Informations Concerning the Province of North Carolina*, pp. 448–449.

on the southern outskirts of Hillsboro, that Hogg, through his brother, had bought land—1,160 acres along the bank of the adjacent Eno River.[48] And it was there, in those busy weeks of resettlement in America, that he met the remarkable former judge and visionary land speculator, Richard Henderson, and his small group of affluent collaborators in one of the grandiose schemes of the era.

Transylvania

Henderson had had his eye on the Kentucky territory, west of the Appalachians and south of the Ohio, for at least a decade. Since 1764 he had supported the annual expeditions of Daniel Boone and other "long hunters" into that land of fabled natural richness, and had collected what lore he could from their reports of the trans-Appalachian wilderness. Much had been learned from these backwoodsmen as they had emerged each year with their packhorses loaded with furs and their imaginations and ambitions fired by what they had seen. The few pioneer homesteaders who had ventured into this Indian reserve also told tales that quickened the pulses of the speculators. By 1772 Virginia, which claimed all of this land as within its chartered boundaries, was sending out surveyors to designate "bounty lands" for the colony's war veterans, while affluent planters like George Washington instructed their personal land agents to scout the land and stake out claims. The roaming of the sharp-eyed hunters doubling as advance men for land speculators, the activities of the first settlers, and the arrival of official surveyors all had the expected effect on the Indians whose prized hunting ground this territory was. As the pressure on them increased, bloody incidents, some of them deliberately provoked by the white hunters, took place, and in the summer of 1774, as James Hogg was arriving and settling in America, the skirmishes became a war—Lord Dunmore's War it was called, after the Virginia governor who authorized and directed it—which ended in the early fall with the complete abdication of claims by the Shawnee tribes. Their forced concession left only the Cherokees, who had not fought in the war, as effective native occupants of the land.[49]

Henderson understood the drift of events perfectly. He knew that a whole population of land-hungry farmers was poised at the western edges of the coastal colonies; he knew the extraordinary richness of the Kentucky

[48]Merrens, *Colonial North Carolina*, pp. 162–164. For the precise location of Hogg's property, see Francis Nash, *Hillsboro* (Raleigh, N.C., 1903), p. 38.
[49]William S. Lester, *The Transylvania Colony* (Spencer, Ind., 1935), pp. 4–5; Ray A. Billington, *Westward Expansion: A History of the American Frontier,* 4th ed. (New York, 1974), pp. 164, 165. On Dunmore's War and its relation to land speculation, see Thomas P. Abernethy, *Western Lands and the American Revolution* (New York, 1937), pp. 106–113.

lands; and he believed that a lease if not a purchase might be arranged with the Cherokees. If he was aware of the complete illegality of such a move —first, because it violated the Proclamation of 1763, even as later revised; second, because it ignored the jurisdictions of Virginia and North Carolina, within whose boundaries Kentucky was believed to lie; and third, because the crown had the ultimate legal title to all the undistributed land in America—he gave no indication of it. In August, when Hogg was setting up his store in Cross Creek and surveying his property in Hillsboro, Henderson met in that town with five other affluent North Carolinians, most of them Scots by birth or derivation, and formed the Louisa Company to negotiate a lease of some part of the Kentucky territory. Early contacts with the Indians were promising, and by December, before anything had even been broached officially, the company was advertising for settlers to buy or lease parcels of its still unacquired land. Further contacts with the Indians increased Henderson's confidence, and on January 6, 1775, the company made a series of basic decisions. The partners reorganized themselves as the Transylvania Company, and they decided that they could, legally enough, buy rather than lease an immense trans-Appalachian territory from the Cherokees. They decided too, without authorization from anyone, crown or colony, hence without a shred of legality, that as proprietors of the region they would sponsor, as the Carolina proprietors of the seventeenth century had done, an entirely new colony in the west, complete with a constitution, a government, a legal system, and a land office. And they decided, finally, to expand their membership. Among three new members included in the now nine-man partnership of the Transylvania Company was James Hogg, who only six months before had been struggling with the Edinburgh merchant Inglis for the fulfillment of the contract they had signed to transport the Sutherland and Caithness emigrants.[50]

What precisely Hogg contributed to the company's capital in exchange for his full membership is not known, but it is reasonable to assume that he contracted to supply a sizable share of the great store of trading goods that was being stockpiled in Cross Creek for the eventual land purchase from the Indians. By mid-January that stockpile and the magnitudes of the enterprise in general were becoming known, and protests were arising quickly on all sides. Rival land speculators like George Washington were alarmed, and officials like William Preston, Virginia's surveyor of western lands, were horrified. The governors of both interested colonies issued sulfurous proclamations condemning as outlaws "Henderson and other disorderly persons, his associates" and enjoining all loyal subjects of the King to help "prevent the execution of his design." But by the time these

[50]Lester, *Transylvania Colony*, pp. 17, 21–28. The text of the new charter, which included Hogg as a proprietor, is printed in Shaw Livermore, *Early American Land Companies* (New York, 1939), app. B.

fiery denunciations were published and even more dramatic protests were received in London, Henderson and three of his partners were deep in the western wilderness, at Sycamore Shoals in northeastern Tennessee. There, in mid-March, in exchange for a reputed £10,000 worth of trading goods, equipment, guns, and cattle, they acquired from the Cherokees a putative title to about 17 million acres of land. Their tract included the entire triangle between the Kentucky River on the east, the Ohio River on the north and west, and the *sources* of the Cumberland River, which reached down into northern Tennessee, on the south; and it was supplemented by an access strip leading in from the southeast.[51]

This accomplished, Henderson dispatched Boone and thirty axemen to hack a settlers' trail—the Wilderness Road, it would be called—out of the bridle paths, Indian trails, and animal traces that led 220 miles from south-western Virginia and northeastern Tennessee across the mountains through the Cumberland Gap and north into central Kentucky.[52] Once this access route through rocky, mountainous, river-laced, heavily forested ter-rain was completed and a tiny fort-settlement called Boonesborough was built on the banks of the Kentucky River, Henderson began to organize his colony. He had long contemplated creating a separate colonial government in Kentucky; this had now become an urgent necessity. Rival land claim-ants and unaffiliated settlers were arriving daily, and some means had to be found to incorporate all of them into the Transylvania scheme if it was to succeed. If only to adjudicate destructive conflicts and to guarantee land titles, but also to assert the company's jurisdiction and its overall land claim, some sort of general government was needed, and Henderson moved quickly. On May 23, 1775, he convened a House of Delegates made up of seventeen commissioned representatives of the settlers in the four main contending settlements in central Kentucky, already rivals in land claims though mere frontier hamlets. To this body, gathered under a massive elm tree, whose branches shaded a circle 400 feet in diameter and which was "placed on a beautiful plain surrounded by a turf of fine white clover"— in this open-air amphitheater that "is to be our church, state-house, [and] council chamber"—Henderson proclaimed the wave of the future.[53]

The ecstatic oration with which this self-educated lawyer and back-country judge, a man of heroic and yet pragmatic imagination, opened the delegates' proceedings must have thrilled the former Borlum tacksman. For it had been only a year earlier that Hogg had declared to the Scottish public, concerned about the magnitudes of the emigration, that far from being an

[51]Lester, *Transylvania Colony*, pp. [vii], 20, 23–24, 29–32, 35–36, 39, 41, 44. On the opposition to the company's purchase, see Abernethy, *Western Lands*, pp. 126–132.
[52]William A. Pusey, *The Wilderness Road to Kentucky* (New York, 1921), pp. 56–65, map following p. 50.
[53]Richard Henderson's Journal, entries of May 8 and 14, 1775, Kentucky MSS, 1-2CC.

enemy to his country for carrying to America so many people, he was, he believed, an agent of liberty. He was, he had declared, "the instrument, in the hand of Providence, to punish oppression, which is by far too general; and I am glad to understand, that already some of these haughty [Scottish] landlords now find it necessary to court and caress these same people, whom they lately despised, and treated as slaves, or beasts of burden."⁵⁴ Just so, fourteen months later, the assembled delegates of the Transylvania colony, gathered under the great elm tree outside the stockade at Boonesborough, were declared to be agents of liberty. They were perhaps establishing, Henderson declared, "the palladium, or placing the first corner stone of an edifice, the height and magnificence of whose superstructure is now in the womb of futurity, and can only become great and glorious in proportion to the excellence of its foundation." Remember, he declared in this opening charge, that "we are all Englishmen, or, what amounts to the same, ourselves and our fathers have, for many generations, experienced the invaluable blessings of that most excellent constitution." So be animated and inspired, he said, "with sentiments worthy the grandeur of the subject." Pass laws by the consent of the governed "without giving offense to Great Britain, or any of the American colonies"; establish courts; provide for the recovery of debts and for determining disputes over "property, contracts, torts, injuries, &c"; form a militia; and protect the region's game and other resources from exploitation by outsiders.⁵⁵

To this peroration, as if from the throne, a committee of the house responded with "a very sensible address," Henderson said, agreeing that they did indeed possess "an absolute right, as a political body, without giving umbrage to Great Britain or any of the colonies, to frame rules for the government of our little society." And this they forthwith proceeded to do. In addition they formally accepted a constitution, or compact, that had been prepared by the proprietors. This instrument defined the dele-

⁵⁴Hogg to Balfour, March 29, 1774 (note 1, above). The theme that "the tyrannical, oppressive, and impolitic conduct of landholders" had driven the laboring poor of Scotland to despair and forced them to choose between starvation and emigration was a commonplace in the periodical publications of the English-speaking world. E.g., *South-Carolina Gazette*, April 11, 1774; *Pennsylvania Journal; and the Weekly Advertiser*, March 23, 1774.
⁵⁵Henderson's opening speech to "The House of Delegates . . . of the Colony of Transylvania . . . 23d of May in the Year of Our Lord Christ 1775 . . .," in *American Archives . . .*, ed. Peter Force (Washington, D.C., 1837–1853), 4th ser., IV, cols. 546–548. Henderson's ecstasy at his creation of this Rousseau-esque democracy, carefully controlled by the proprietors, was boundless. "Thank G—d," he confided to his Journal (May 14, 1775), the great elm tree "is mine, where I often retire and oh! were my famaly & friends under it with me it would be a heavenly tree indeed." But his wilderness elysium was seen differently by others. Harrodsburg, the most prominent of these Kentucky settlements, was described by a Baptist minister who visited there in 1776 as "a poor town . . . a row or two of smoky cabins, dirty women, men with their britch clouts, greasy hunting shirts, leggings and moccasins. I there ate some of the first corn raised in the country, but little of it, as they had a very poor way to make it into meal; we learnt to eat wild meat, without bread or salt." Quoted in Lester, *Transylvania Colony*, p. 253.

gates' role as a lower house, mandated "perfect religious freedom and general toleration," created a structure of government in which the proprietors would participate as a group executive, and provided that the land office, through which the proprietors would sell off their princely realm, would "be always open" and that the quit rents they would charge would never exceed two shillings sterling per hundred acres.[56]

Hogg and the Continental Congress

All of this took place at Boonesborough in May 1775. When the proprietors met again in September, in North Carolina, they went further. They passed a flock of resolutions bearing on all aspects of the colony's life, and, assuming quasi-sovereign authority, appointed James Hogg to be the colony's delegate to the second Continental Congress then meeting in Philadelphia. His orders were to present to that body, and negotiate for the acceptance of, a memorial announcing the existence of the Transylvania colony and asking for its acceptance as the fourteenth member of the continental union; if successful he was to take his seat in the Congress until permanent representatives could be sent. He was also authorized to sell land to any purchasers he might encounter.

The memorial that Hogg carried with him to Philadelphia and attempted to present to the Congress is as remarkable as all the rest of the company's materially ambitious and magniloquent statements. It informed the Congress of the company's purchase; explained the "difficulties and dangers," the expense and sacrifice, they had endured in establishing the new colony "without the violation of any British or American law whatever"; and affiliated the Transylvania Company with the Congress by referring to "ministerial usurpations" and "the late arbitrary proceedings of the British Parliament" and mentioning their own fear of the consequences if "the United Colonies are reduced, or will tamely submit to be slaves." Despite all this, they declared their continuing "allegiance to their Sovereign, whose constitutional rights . . . they will support, at the risk of their lives," and expressed the hope that the crown would soon accept them as a new legitimate colony. However that might be, they insisted that "their hearts warmed with the same noble spirit that animates the United Colonies" and that they wished "to be considered by the colonies as brethren, engaged in the same great cause of liberty and mankind." They therefore prayed the Congress to "take the infant colony of Transylvania under their protection" and admit Hogg to a seat among them.

[56]Henderson, Journal, entry of May 25, 1775, Kentucky MSS; "Answer . . . to the Proprietor's Speech" and subsequent legislation, *American Archives*, cols. 548, 551, 552.

The result, Hogg informed Henderson in a long letter written as soon as he returned to North Carolina, was not altogether satisfactory. He had spoken first to Samuel and John Adams. They were friendly, but they quickly put their finger on a serious problem, which the proprietors had feared might arise. The Congress, the Adamses pointed out to Hogg, was petitioning the King for a redress of grievances and hoped for an accommodation; to accomplish this they had to avoid the appearance of "that independent spirit with which we are daily reproached." How would it look in London if they now adopted a body of people "who have acted in defiance of the King's proclamations"? Further, they pointed out to Hogg, a glance at the map showed that Transylvania lay within the extended boundaries of Virginia as defined in the original charters, and so they advised Hogg to discuss the matter with the delegates from that colony. Privately John Adams noted that the Transylvanians were "charged with republican notions—and utopian schemes."[57]

It took Hogg some days to arrange a meeting with the Virginians, but he finally did meet with Jefferson and George Wythe and later with Richard Henry Lee. This time Hogg was more discreet and more modest in his presentation, and he encountered a far more complex response. He was careful to make much of the Transylvanians' interest in "the cause of liberty, &c., &c., but said nothing of our memorial, or any pretensions to a seat in Congress." Jefferson and Wythe questioned Hogg and examined the map; they then observed that Transylvania indeed lay within Virginia's boundaries, "and gently hinted" that by its chartered rights Virginia might well one day "claim the whole." Jefferson seemed to be rather accommodating, however. He seemed willing, Hogg wrote, to accept the colony if it were properly united to Virginia. His main interest, he explained to Hogg, lay in preventing the establishment of an arbitrary and oppressive government to the west of Virginia which might threaten them from the rear. He personally would have no objection to a "free government" to their west, indeed to a government that stretched all the way from the western settlements in Virginia to the Mississippi River. But nothing could be done, he told Hogg, without the approval of Virginia's Provincial Congress, and he suggested that the Transylvania Company send delegates to the Congress's next meeting.

At this point in the conversation Hogg fell silent, and then gradually in the days that followed came to realize what the central issue was. He first discovered, as he mingled with the delegates and talked informally with them, what looked like good legal grounds for the company's land purchase; then he discovered, through Silas Deane—that "enthusiast in lib-

[57] *Ibid.*, cols. 553–555, 543–546; *Diary and Autobiography of John Adams*, ed. L. H. Butterfield *et al.* (Cambridge, Mass., 1961), II, 218.

erty"—that "a party of Connecticut adventurers" headed by Deane himself might join the Transylvanians in Kentucky. And Deane, in his enthusiasm, recommended the Connecticut constitution as a model for Transylvania and presented Hogg with a small treatise on the Connecticut government and on the principles of liberty to guide the new colony in its proceedings. And that was part of the biggest discovery of all. "You would be amazed," Hogg wrote to Henderson,

> to see how much in earnest all these speculative gentlemen are about the plan to be adopted by the Transylvanians. They entreat, they pray, that we may make it a free government, and beg that no mercenary or ambitious views in the Proprietors may prevent it. Quit-rents, they say, is a mark of vassalage, and hope they shall not be established in Transylvania. They even threaten us with their opposition if we do not act upon liberal principles when we have it so much in our power to render ourselves immortal. Many of them advised a law against Negroes.[58]

Later he would feel the practical force of this Revolutionary idealism. For Jefferson was utterly committed to the development of the west as a land of opportunity for independent small farmers; he wanted settlers to be able to appropriate at least a small parcel of this western land for their own use, free of charges of any kind. Unknown to Hogg, he had already written this doctrine into his constitution for Virginia, and he was prepared to lead a major battle in the Virginia legislature to defeat any and all attempts of land speculators—the Transylvania Company included—to exploit the un-opened land for profit at the expense of the small farmer.[59]

The Ascent of the Borlum Tacksman

Hogg's mission to Philadelphia in October and November 1775 was the high point of his entry into American life—his one, and sudden, involvement with the great men and the grand national affairs of the era. But though he remained thereafter in North Carolina and though the affairs of the Transylvania Company never fulfilled the proprietors' hopes because of the opposition of the quickly growing population in the west as well as of the states of Virginia and North Carolina, Hogg's personal affairs prospered. Having been involved in this way in attempting to create a free and liberal

[58] *American Archives,* cols. 544–545.
[59] *Papers of Thomas Jefferson,* ed. Julian Boyd *et al.* (Princeton, 1950–   ), I, 564–569; II, 64–110.

American colony, having represented the principles of liberty before the Continental Congress, and having met its leading figures, he could hardly follow his brother Robert into loyalist opposition to the Revolution and the new nation. While Robert and his family fled under difficult circumstances to the protection of the British army in New York, James remained in Hillsboro and Cross Creek and became an active member of Orange County's Committee of Safety and a local official.[60]

While promoting the war effort, he did what he could to protect Hogg and Campbell's property and his brother's personal safety. He emerged in the eighties a highly influential merchant, closely allied to the state's leading politicians, in trade for himself and with his cousins, with his headquarters largely in Fayetteville. After the war his business interests fructified. He invested in canals, at one point as a member of the North Canal Company, organized to extend the navigability of the Cape Fear River deep into the backcountry; and he kept up his interest in land speculation. By the 1790s his prosperity was such that he was sending surplus funds in the form of gold and local currency to Philadelphia to be invested in bank stock and Treasury bills, and his revolutionary ardor had succumbed to his affluence. For a brief period he apparently shared the popular enthusiasm for the French Revolution, but by the mid-nineties he had become a solid Federalist with a low estimation of the "great mass of the people."[61]

By then he had developed an interest outside of trade altogether, an interest that became an abiding commitment in the last two decades of his life. Even before the war ended he had turned to the advancement of education. When Science Hall Academy was organized in Hillsboro in 1779, Hogg made the largest single contribution to its support, and in 1784 he became chairman of the academy's board. By then he was deeply involved in the politically controversial founding of the University of North Carolina. One of the small group of Federalist leaders responsible for its establishment, he was particularly influential in locating the institution on 1,390 acres contributed by some of the survivors of the Scottish emigration of the 1770s at "New Hope Chapel Hill" near Hillsboro. When the university was chartered in 1789 Hogg was one of the trustees, and he remained a trustee for thirteen years. His interest in the university never waned. He helped nourish it in its infancy, shared in the plans for its educational

---

[60]Schaw, *Journal*, pp. 180, 323–324; Archibald Henderson, "The Transylvania Company: Study in Personnel," *Filson Club History Quarterly*, 21 (1947), 14. On the demise of the Transylvania colony and the proprietors' land schemes, see Abernethy, *Western Lands*, pp. 131–133, 162–166; Livermore, *Land Companies*, p. 95; Lester, *Transylvania Colony*, chaps. 8, 11.

[61]Henry M. Wagstaff, ed., "Letters of William Barry Grove," *James Sprunt Historical Publications*, IX, no. 2 (1910), 48, 63–64, 67–73, 77–78; Kemp P. Battle, ed., "Letters of Nathaniel Macon, John Steele, and William Barry Grove," *James Sprunt Historical Monographs*, no. 3 (1902), 86.

program, and as a member of the trustees' visiting committee presided for a time over the students' final examinations.[62]

Through all these years of constant application in business and in the advancement of higher education, Hogg kept up his involvement in the complicated and protracted negotiations of the Transylvania Company to redeem something of value from its land purchase of 1775. After elaborate maneuvers, including a successful campaign led by Jefferson to defeat the land speculators and incorporate Virginia's trans-Appalachian lands into three new western counties, the two states that had established jurisdiction over the company's land were induced to present the proprietors with a total of 400,000 acres as payment for their investments and their efforts in first securing the property from the Indians. But legally clearing the Indians' claims to the land was another matter, and Hogg and the other surviving proprietors pursued that problem into Congress. There, year after year, it lingered, one of a number of such title problems.

But in the end the issue was resolved. In 1797 the company's Virginia acres were surveyed and became the town and county of Henderson (Kentucky); Hogg was one of only three of the original proprietors who lived to see that single material result of their efforts. The next year the company's Tennessee lands were divided among the proprietors and their heirs, and Hogg, in his seventieth year, traveled west and inspected the share he had received. Four years later he suffered a stroke. He died in 1805, a prosperous seventy-six-year-old North Carolinian, the founder of a prominent American family. The former Borlum tacksman was buried in the midst of the Scottish-American community he had helped create.[63]

[62]Henderson, "Transylvania Company," pp. 17–20; Jurgen Herbst, *From Crisis to Crisis: American College Government, 1636–1819* (Cambridge, Mass., 1982), pp. 187–188, 220–221; Archibald Henderson, *The Campus of the First State University* (Chapel Hill, N.C., 1949), pp. 12, 42.
[63]Henderson, "Transylvania Company," pp. 14–17, 20; Lester, *Transylvania Colony*, chaps. 11, 13, 14; Wagstaff, "Letters of . . . Grove," pp. 50–53; Battle, "Letters of . . . Macon, Steele, and Grove," pp. 94, 100, 114, 87, 15.

15

Georgia: Exploiting the Ceded Lands

HOGG's great enterprise—his life-transforming transit from the obscure Caithness hamlet of Borlum, on the bare, bleak north shore of Scotland, to Cross Creek and Hillsboro, in the sandy pinelands of backcountry North Carolina—is an infinitesimally small speck in the great galactic blur of human movements that spread across the Atlantic world in the years before the Revolution. But his saga contains within it a remarkable range of experiences common to the transatlantic migrants in those years; its American episodes touch on both the high idealism and the driving opportunism that dominated the lives of the Revolutionary generation. Yet Hogg's carefully recorded enterprise as an organizer of emigration illustrates only one of several ways in which these transfers from Britain into the inland arc of North American settlements were managed. The emigration Register of 1773–1776 reveals other modes, in the details of other obscure constellations barely visible in that remote and complex universe of voyagers. They involve other points of departure and other regions of settlement.

The Browns of Whitby

The Register brings into focus the small fishing village and market town of Whitby on the North Sea coast of Yorkshire. In the 1770s it was one of the many minor ports in the north of England whose merchants were involved in small ways in trade with North America. And, since it was located on the coastal edge of the North York Moors, it shared with two nearby minor ports—Scarborough on the south and Stockton on the north —a portion of the east Yorkshire emigrant traffic that sought ports of exit closer than the major regional shipping centers of Newcastle and Hull. The numbers involved are small. The Register documents only two voyages, with 155 emigrants, from Whitby—via Kirkwall in the Orkneys—to North America. But these voyages, and their extensive ramifications involving other, later voyages, illuminate vividly the peopling of a remote corner of the inland arc; and in both cases the same vessel was involved, the *Marlborough*.

Precisely how Jonas Brown, the owner of the *Marlborough*, whose two voyages, of 1774 and 1775, carrying emigrants from Whitby and Kirkwall to the so-called Ceded Lands of upcountry Georgia, became involved in the emigrant trade to that southern province is not known. But the outlines of Brown's story are clear, and like Hogg's it spins out into some of the most celebrated events of the American Revolution.

Jonas Brown's main business in Whitby—prosperous enough to enable him to build his own "seat," Newton House, outside the town—was the production and sale of alum, a substance commonly found in the hills surrounding Whitby and used in dyeing, tanning, wine making, fish curing, and medicine.[1] But he also traded in a variety of other products, in coastal voyages and overseas. In 1764 his ship, the *Flora*, commanded by William Manson, after a stopover in the Orkneys, Manson's home islands, sailed to New England to trade at the fishing stations in Casco Bay, Maine. Two years later the same vessel was engaged in more extensive trade to South Carolina, exchanging a shipload of Newcastle coal and miscellaneous manufactured goods for rice and deerskins. In the years that followed, Brown's commercial operations broadened out to include Nova Scotia, New England, Georgia, and Barbados. Contacts with Georgia became especially important.

In 1772, even before Governor Wright had concluded his purchase of the Ceded Lands—the huge wedge of over 2 million acres in the backcountry that he extracted from the Indians—Brown, with his son Thomas, the enterprising Orkney Islander James Gordon, and two others, "embarked on a scheme of forming an extensive settlement on those lands."[2] Before

[1] Lionel Charlton, *The History of Whitby* . . . (York, 1779), pp. 339, 357, 359; G. H. J. Daysh, ed., *A Survey of Whitby and the Surrounding Area* (Eton, Windsor, Eng., 1958), pp. 59–66. For Brown's Newton House, seven miles south of Whitby, and the obelisk later erected there to commemorate his "industry and perseverance, in converting wild moors into pleasure grounds," see George Young, *A History of Whitby* . . . (Whitby, 1817), II, 655.

[2] Richard Weatherill, *The Ancient Port of Whitby and Its Shipping* (Whitby, 1908), pp. 40, 57, 73, 75, 76; *Collections of the Georgia Historical Society*, VIII (1913), app.; "Accompts for a Voyage to New England in the Flora of Whitby, per Capt. William Manson, Commander," Aug. 31–Nov. 27, 1764, and "Accounts for a Voyage to Charleston in South Carolina Anno 1766–7," Balfour Papers, D2/16; Memorial of James Gordon, March 21, 1786, Loyalist Transcripts, XIII, 79, 80.

The original plan for the Brownsborough settlement company was later described by the Hull merchant Jonas Brown, Jr., Thomas's brother. (Jonas Brown, Jr., to Loyalist Claims Commissioners, Hull, Dec. 13, 1788, Loyalist Transcripts, XIII, 141–144). The elder Brown, his son Thomas, James Gordon, and two others, Walter Stuart and Mungo Baikie, contracted to share equally in

the year was out the financial responsibility had fallen entirely on Jonas Brown. Gordon, financed by Brown, set out for the colony to make preliminary arrangements while Brown sought political support. In April 1773 he wrote Nathaniel Cholmley, M.P., a native of Whitby, for help in obtaining for young Thomas, "a gent[n] of education and fortune," a crown office of some kind in either South Carolina or Georgia. His son, Brown explained, had had a liberal education, had traveled much abroad, and in recent years had managed Brown's colonial affairs with "prudence & judgment scarce to be expected from a person of his age." After a residence of two years in the colonies, Thomas had resolved to settle there and was preparing himself for public office by studying law. But his father's plans moved ahead quickly, before any office could be obtained.[3]

In the spring of 1773 the two Browns and Gordon, now acting as the resident manager, acquired warrants for 5,350 acres of the richest soil in the Ceded Lands, for a deposit, or down payment, of 8 pence per acre (£162 10s 8d) and an eventual purchase price of 3s 6d per acre (£936 5s—but never paid). The plot was located along the Broad River in the north of the cession, approximately 80 miles northwest of Augusta and 180 miles inland from the closest seaport, Savannah. Gordon, located temporarily with a first shipment of emigrants just outside Augusta on the South Carolina side of the river, promised to bring in within twelve months "a sufficient number of inhabitants" to populate the grant in the Ceded Lands "at the rate of 50 acres for each person and 100 acres for the head of each family"—a calculation which obliged the partners to recruit approximately 75 to 80 settlers, assuming some of them were family groups. They set to work promptly. Within six months of their acquisition of land in Georgia, Jonas Brown's advertisements began to appear in the Yorkshire newspapers, and thereafter a "printed paper" of his, expanding on the newspaper notices, began circulating in northern England and in the far north of Scotland, including the Orkneys, as well.[4]

---

the expenses and profits of the settlement. But Stuart and Baikie failed to produce the required capital and almost immediately dropped out, and Gordon's relatives in Orkney, whom he had counted on for the funds he needed, in the end also failed to make the necessary advances. The financial responsibility for the entire venture thus quickly fell to the senior Brown; Gordon's role became that of plantation manager, and his later claim for a share of the recompense for the company's losses was hotly disputed by the Brown family. He made separate claims for the loss of property he had acquired on his own in Georgia and South Carolina. *Ibid.*, pp. 79–81.

[3] Wilbur H. Siebert, *Loyalists in East Florida, 1774 to 1785* (Deland, Fla., 1929), II, 323; Jonas Brown to Nathaniel Cholmley, April 23, 1773, Dartmouth Papers, Stafford, D(W) 1778/II/604; Gov. Patrick Tonyn to Gen. Sir William Howe, St. Augustine, Feb. 24, 1778, Historical Manuscripts Commission, *Report on American Manuscripts in the Royal Institution of Great Britain*, I (London, 1904), 198.

[4] Loyalist Transcripts, XIII, 91, 92; Grace G. Davidson, comp., *Early Records of Georgia, I (Wilkes County)* (Macon, Ga., 1933), 15; Alex M. Hitz, "The Earliest Settlements in Wilkes County," *Georgia Historical Quarterly*, 40 (1956), 275, 276; Siebert, *Loyalists*, II, 323. For characteristic enthusiasm for the richness of the Ceded Lands and the likelihood of quick settlement and profits, see

Jonas Brown's 300-ton ship, the *Marlborough*, the advertisement stated, "completely fitted and accommodated for passengers," would sail from Whitby to Georgia on August 1, 1774, and would take on board anyone wishing to settle in the "new-ceded valuable lands in that province." Those interested in the "situation, quality, and mode of purchasing" these newly available lands should apply to Jonas Brown at Whitby, who would not only reply in detail ("post-paid") but would also send a copy of Governor Wright's proclamation describing the land and encouraging settlement. The detailed provision of Brown's project appeared in his "printed paper" and in later newspaper notices. He was hoping to fill the *Marlborough*, in part with independent family groups who would be useful to him as land purchasers and help him satisfy the terms of the land grant, but in greater part with indentured servants who would develop the personal plantation that he, his son, and Gordon planned.

Workers unable to pay their passage, Brown announced, would on their arrival in America become "covenant servants for not less than three years," and would be fed, lodged, and clothed by Brown during that time. At the end of their service to him they would be given the following benefits to begin their independent lives in Georgia. Single men would receive fifteen acres of good land complete with a newly built house; would be provided with seed, cattle, instruments of husbandry, and other specified necessities; and in addition would be supported by Brown until they were able to raise their first crops. A married man would receive ten more acres for his wife and five acres more for each child, plus additional livestock and equipment according to the size of his family. Once the settlers took over their land they would be exempt from all fees and taxes for five years. Thereafter, however, they would be charged an annual rent of one shilling sterling per acre, but Brown and Company would assume the burden of the quit rents due the crown. Complete title of ownership to the land would pass to the former servants after five years. At that point they could sell the land, divide it, bequeath it, or make any other disposition of it they wished. And this was land, Brown informed his readers, "esteemed the richest in North America"—and land, furthermore, he added with fatal optimism, located a thousand miles from Boston and New England and hence with "no connection or concern in the troubles now subsisting with Great Britain."[5]

James Habersham to the Earl of Hillsborough, Savannah, April 24, 1772, *Collections of the Georgia Historical Society,* VI (1904), 173; and "Memorial of James Wright to the Earl of Hillsborough, Dec. 12, 1771 . . . Proposing an Indian Land Cession to Georgia . . .," in Kenneth Coleman and Milton Ready, eds., pt. 2 of *Original Papers of Governor Wright, President Habersham, and Others, 1764–1782* (*Colonial Records of the State of Georgia,* XXVIII, Athens, Ga., 1979), 354–357.
[5] *Etherington's York Chronicle,* May 13, July 29, 1774; *Newcastle Journal,* July 16–23, 1774. Brown's "printed paper" has not been located, but its contents were undoubtedly repeated in the detailed advertisement he placed in *Etherington's York Chronicle,* June 16, 1775, from which the conditions of settlement cited here are taken. But the circular must have been much more elaborate than the

The terms had been carefully calculated. For penniless farm workers an annual fee of one shilling sterling per acre would seem high. But on the other hand such charges would begin only eight or ten years in the future, and the capital investment in transportation, in land purchase with all its attendant costs, and in the seed, livestock, and equipment needed to start up independent farms would all be provided by Brown. The prospective settler's total contribution would only be his labor in opening a portion of Brown's land and a fee in perpetuity, after some years of no charges at all, paid for out of the profits of the land.

It was an attractive proposition, and the question is less why Brown was able to gather a full load of emigrants for the *Marlborough* than why he did so in such a roundabout way. When the vessel left Whitby in early August it had aboard only twenty-nine emigrants, all but four of them members of seven family groups, several of which were sizable. These were not impoverished farm workers capable of developing Brown's wilderness plantation. The eleven heads of households or independent travelers, all but a few of whom indented themselves to Brown for bonded service, were almost all artisans—bookbinders, canvas weavers, carpenters, gardeners, and blacksmiths. They were people of mature years (average age: 29.3), burdened with families, and very few of them used to heavy field work. Nor were they driven by desperate need: they professed not poverty as the cause of their migration but a desire "for better employment." And the terms of their indentures must have been loose, since they told the customs officials that they intended to stay in Georgia "or return," depending on what they found.

This was scarcely the labor force needed to man the Browns' plantation deep in the Georgia backcountry. To recruit such workers, Jonas Brown directed the *Marlborough,* when it left Whitby, to sail 350 miles north, around and beyond the Scottish mainland, to the Orkney Islands, Gordon's

businesslike ad. The *Caledonian Mercury,* concerned about the paper's effect on the restive population, stated that the paper gave "a very flattering description of Georgia, which, to the sad experience of many who have left this part, has been found exceedingly unhealthy, and has proof [proved] the burial place of some hundreds of unhappy people who have been induced to leave this and the neighboring county." Brown's careful dissociation from the troubles in Boston was aimed at counteracting warnings such as appeared in a letter from Savannah printed in *Etherington's York Chronicle,* Nov. 18, 1774, against anyone's going to America "at least till the Bostonian affairs are settled and America and England are come to a right understanding."

Wright's famous proclamation, dated Savannah, June 11, 1773—only ten days after the land cession had been concluded with the Creeks and Cherokees—also praised the Ceded Lands in the most glowing terms and specified unusually attractive conditions of settlement which were widely advertised (e.g., *Lloyd's Evening Post,* Sept. 8–10, 1773). In addition to the proclamation, Wright published a map of the newly available territory, reproduced here on the following page, showing terrain features and soil conditions. The original map, from which the present illustration was taken, is in the Public Record Office, London. For Wright's detailed instructions to the land commissioners on the terms of sale of the Ceded Lands, see *Early Records of Georgia,* I, 4.

Governor Wright's descriptive map of the newly ceded lands of Georgia, 1773. Widely distributed, the map was essential to Wright's efforts to people the newly available land. The legend contains a lettered key to topography, soil, and vegetation.

native land. There, in the main port of Kirkwall, the *Marlborough* remained for a month collecting a contingent of indentured servants; and a very different group they were from the twenty-nine who had been taken on in Whitby. In all, fifty-five people (fifty-three indentured servants) boarded the *Marlborough* at Kirkwall, according to the emigration Register, twenty-four of them heads of households or independent voyagers. Only two of the twenty-four were artisans (unmarried weavers in their mid-twenties) and six were farmers, who carried with them wives and children. Of the others, twelve stated their occupations as servants, in almost every case servants to farmers—precisely the sort of laborers Brown needed for his plantation. Two were sailors, one was a laborer, and one, a ten-year-old, was a beggar. The sailors (average age forty) were grizzled veterans of the struggle for existence: one said he could not support his family in this country, the other that he could not "get bread here." The other servants, the labor force Brown was chiefly interested in, were young (median age sixteen) and unmarried. Most had drifted into Kirkwall from farmlands scattered through the central islands of the Orkneys and the neighboring isle of Rousay.[6]

On September 9, 1774, its hold filled, the *Marlborough* left the Orkneys for Savannah. It was the first vessel, an Orcadian reported to the *Caledonian Mercury*, that had "purposely stopped here for emigrants since emigration began to be so frequent in Britain." Georgia's climate, the correspondent added, was known to be far from ideal; nevertheless, Brown "would have got three times the number come had he occasion for them."[7] The eighty-four on board were enough, however, to validate the grant and to start the Browns' and Gordon's plantation just south of the Broad River.

Brownsborough

Brown and the emigrants joined Gordon, first in South Carolina, then, after some preliminary organization, on the Georgia grant, where an initial clearing was made and the first temporary buildings were quickly erected. What happened thereafter during the first year of settlement in what they called Brownsborough is not known in any detail, but it is at least certain that a large permanent dwelling was built on the plantation, that a number

---

[6]The first leg of the *Marlborough*'s voyage of 1774, from Whitby to Kirkwall, is entered in the Register at T47/9/207; the second leg, from Kirkwall to Savannah, at T47/12/56. The legal status of the emigrants from Whitby is somewhat ambiguous, since the Register does not refer to them, as it does to the emigrants from Kirkwall, as indentured servants. But later testimony by Gordon and the Browns makes clear that most of them were indentured. The conclusive evidence is a muster roll of the indentured servants who shipped aboard the *Marlborough* in 1774 and 1775 which Thomas Brown submitted to the Loyalist Claims Commissioners, Jan. 1, 1788. A comparison of the names on this muster roll with those in the Register's 84 entries for the *Marlborough* on its 1774 voyage shows a perfect correspondence, name for name, except for 5 adults traveling alone and a family of 6. In this later reckoning for the Loyalist Claims Commissioners, Brown included even very young children among the indentured servants. He stated that the charges for "procuring & indenting" these servants together with the "cost of their cloathing, the expence of their passage out to America, & the charges on landing there & removing from the port of Savannah to the plantations on the Ceded Lands . . . [was] £3,001 7s 8d," or slightly more than £20 each. Loyalist Papers, AO 13/34/122–124.
[7]*Caledonian Mercury*, Sept. 21, 1774.

of small separate farms were opened on adjoining tracts on which, in all, thirty-eight small buildings were constructed, and that the initial harvest in the whole settlement was expected to yield nearly 2,000 bushels of wheat.[8] And it is also certain that Brown and Gordon, like so many other importers of bonded servants, discovered during those early months how difficult it was to maintain a work force of indentured servants in a situation where labor was extremely scarce, where land was abundantly available and cheap, and where the ordinary constraints of civil society were practically nonexistent. Almost all of the emigrants who arrived on the *Marlborough* simply faded into the general confusion of backcountry Georgia and can be identified only in passing references in the documents of the time. But one face, one voice, does emerge clearly, to testify to the complexity of the central problems of labor.

Baikia Harvey, who registered on the *Marlborough* as a sixteen-year-old servant from Kirkwall, was an orphan. His godfather, Thomas Baikia, Esq., who lived nearby in the Orkneys, had tried to discourage him from signing on with the Browns and shipping off to Georgia "to seek a better way of living." A year later the results were clear. Baikia confessed, in a letter he wrote back to his godfather, that he had made a mistake: "I ought not to have slightig your advice." James Gordon had treated him well enough, but Thomas Brown had "us'd me vere ill." So Baikia had run away, he reported, simply by crossing the Savannah River into South Carolina. There he had come on a large band of patriot troops "mar[c]hing up to the back parts of South Carolina against a sett of people they call Torrys in this country." He had tagged on to that makeshift army, and had been deeply impressed by what he had seen. Wide-eyed, he reported to his godfather that the American sharpshooters, all armed with rifled guns, "can kill the bigness of a dollar betwixt two & three hundreds yards distance." All the boys of his own age had rifles and knew how to use them. They marched side by side with their fathers, "& all thir cry is Liberty or Death."

> Dear Godfather tell all my country people not to come hear, for the Americans will kill them like deer in the woods & they will never see them. They can lie on their backs & load & fire & every time they draw sight at anything they are sure to kill or criple, & they run in the woods like horses. I seed the Liberty Boys take between two & three hundred Torrys and one liberty man would take & drive four or five before him just as the shepards do the sheep in our country, & they have taken all their arms from them and putt the

---

[8]Gordon, "Memorial," Loyalist Transcripts, XIII, 80, 91, 93, 101; Gary D. Olson, "Loyalists and the American Revolution: Thomas Brown and the South Carolina Backcountry, 1775–1776," *South Carolina Historical Magazine*, 68 (1967), 202.

head men in gaile so that they will never be able to make head against them any more.

After the army raid Harvey had gone, not back to Georgia but to the low country of South Carolina, where he had been taken on as a servant by a merchant named Hammond. With Hammond his luck had changed: "he & his lady uses me vere well & gives me cloaths & I ride with my master & loves them both." But he needed money, for a particular purpose, and he asked his godfather to send him everything that was rightfully his. That was the chief lesson he had learned in America. He, like all the other British emigrants to the colonies, he said, had been hopelessly ignorant at the start —as ignorant as "the new negros that comes out of the ships at first whin they come amongst them." But experience had taught him that in this "good poor mans country" anyone free of servitude and willing to work could prosper; and so, having simply run off in rebellion from the tyrannical Browns he searched for ways of extricating himself legally from his present benevolent masters, the Hammonds, who, he acknowledged, had rescued him in his need.[9]

So the months passed on Brown and Gordon's cluster of newly opened farms as the proprietors drove their small labor force to clear the ground, break open the soil, plant and harvest the first crop, build crude shelters and then more substantial buildings, and ditch and fence the fields. But to succeed they needed more of everything—more labor, more land. Thomas Brown, for his personal use, soon acquired an additional 200 acres, and in January 1775 the partners petitioned—unsuccessfully—for "a further reserve" of the Ceded Lands. At the same time arrangements were being made in Whitby for another shipment of servants. By June 1775 advertisements were being placed in the newspapers of the English north country and of northern Scotland, the "printed paper" with the detailed terms was being recirculated, and the *Marlborough* was being readied for a second voyage.[10]

The recruitment pattern in 1775 was almost identical to that of the previous year. When the *Marlborough* left Whitby on this second voyage, it had on board only eighteen people intending to settle in Georgia, eight of them heads of families or independent voyagers. They were a mixed group from all over the north of England—two laborers, several artisans,

[9]Baikia Harvey to Thomas Baikia, Esq[r], "Snowhill, near Augusta in Georgia," Dec. 30, 1775, Breckness MSS, D3/385. Mungo Baikie, one of the original planners of the Brownsville settlement, was probably a relative of Thomas Baikia and his godson. Loyalist Transcripts, XIII, 142.

[10]*Early Records of Georgia*, I, 28; Georgia Council Meeting, Jan. 3, 1775, *Collections of the Georgia Historical Society*, X (1952), 8; *Etherington's York Chronicle*, June 16, 1775; *Newcastle Journal, Or, General Advertiser*, July 29, Aug. 5, 1775 (repeating verbatim the terms of settlement offered in 1774).

a bookkeeper, and Jonas Brown's young agent and attorney "going to superintend a plantation." Fifteen of them were indentured servants, but, as in 1774, this contingent from Whitby was scarcely a useful supplement to the labor force in Georgia. So again the *Marlborough* sailed north to Kirkwall in the Orkneys to take on the needed workers. This time fifty-three people (fifty indentured servants) were added (Brown later claimed there were sixty), including two full families, one with four children, the other with six. And once again the indentured servants were mainly farmers, farm servants of unspecified experience, and laborers. Some were desperately hard up ("could not live by his trade"); some were unemployed drifters ("NB," the customs officials recorded of one such idle servant, "this man has a very bad character"); others were discontented ("hard labour and small wages"); two were mistreated dependents ("used ill by his parents"; "used ill by her master"). But many were adventurous and optimistic: "could not live so well at home as he thought he would do abroad"; "to try to better his fortune." Not all were natives of the Orkneys; twenty-four of the fifty-three had traveled across the narrow Pentland Firth from Caithness on the mainland in search of employment or betterment. Almost all were young—in their late teens or very early twenties.[11]

With this collection of unemployed, discontented, and adventurous farm hands, servants, and laborers, the *Marlborough* finally left Britain, only days before news of the ban on emigrant shipping from Scotland reached the Orkneys. But the impact of the war, which had occasioned the ban, could not be evaded. By the time the new workers arrived in Savannah and were shipped up from Savannah to the Broad River (then called the Dart, after Lord Dartmouth), and then west along that stream to Brownsborough, the world had turned upside down. The Browns' property, far from having "no connection or concern in the troubles now subsisting with Great Britain," as Jonas Brown had assured the would-be emigrants, proved to be in the eye of the storm. In fact the very epicenter of the upheaval in the backcountry of Georgia was Thomas Brown himself. His career as a Tory guerrilla leader and loyalist troop commander made him one of the legendary and notorious figures of the war in the south. His courageous, enterprising, but apparently brutal and ruthless campaigns were praised extravagantly by his superiors and so savagely denounced by

[11]The entries for the two legs of the 1775 voyage are at T47/10/139 and T47/12/124. The *Newcastle Journal. Or, General Advertiser*, Oct. 7, 1775, reported the vessel's departure incorrectly as from Stromness. Brown's muster roll of the indentured servants in this shipment is in Loyalist Papers, AO 13/34/123. The three passengers from Whitby whose names are on the Register but not on the Browns' muster roll of indentured servants are Isaac Herbert, 23, Jonas Brown's agent and attorney, destined to become a prominent figure in Georgia; John Wainwright, 25, from Nottingham, "late bookkeeper to William Cartwright, Esq."; and a 32-year-old laborer, George Bennington. Five of the 53 emigrants who boarded at Kirkwall are not on the muster roll: three single women servants in their twenties, and two boys, 12 and 7.

his enemies that his name became synonymous with viciousness and brutality in the histories of the time and, later, in a popular novel.[12]

The Wartime Fortunes of Bloody Colonel Brown

Brown's wartime career began with a traumatic event which he always insisted shaped it decisively. In the summer of 1775, after Lexington and Concord and the Battle of Bunker Hill, while the indentured servants imported from Whitby and the Orkneys were still opening the plantation to cultivation, Brown found himself caught up in the bitter struggle between loyalists and revolutionaries for control of the Georgia backcountry. He attended some of the meetings of the local Committee of Safety in Augusta, opposed their measures, ridiculed the rustic patriots he found in charge, and joined an association of Tories in the region to oppose them. In early August the vigilante soldiers he too easily despised came after him, took him prisoner, tried, according to his later report, to torture him into compliance, and ended, when he continued to resist, by tarring and feathering him. As a contemporary wrote, "He was knocked down with the butt-end of a musquet, then laid like a calf across a horse, and tied to a tree while yet insensible, and tarred and feathered." In that condition he was carried through the town and displayed.[13]

The next morning, in pain and fearing for his life, he capitulated—said he repented of his conduct and promised to support the American cause and discourage the Tory force forming in backcountry South Carolina. But once freed, burning for revenge, he planned an assault on Augusta, then joined the loyalists in South Carolina in their struggle with Whig emissaries

[12]Tonyn to Howe, Feb. 24, 1778, cited above, n.3; Henry Lee, *Memoirs of the War in the Southern Department of the United States* (Philadelphia, 1812), I, 204, 207; David Ramsay, *The History of the Revolution of South-Carolina* . . . (Trenton, 1786), II, 2, 237–238; Thomas Brown to David Ramsay, Nassau, Bahamas, Dec. 25, 1786 (his "Vindication against Atrocities Charged Him in Our History"), in *Journal and Letters of the Late Samuel Curwen* . . . , ed. George A. Ward, 3d ed. (New York, 1845), pp. 649–657. The novel is William Gilmore Simms's *Mellichampe* (1836), in which Brown, whom Simms calls "one of the most malignant and vindictive among the southern loyalists," appears as the evil Capt. Barsfield, esp. in chap. 37.
[13]Extract from *Lloyd's Evening Post and British Chronicle*, Feb. 26–28, 1776, in *Letters on the American Revolution, 1774–1776*, ed. Margaret W. Willard (Boston, 1925), p. 246. There are various versions of precisely what punishment the patriots inflicted on Brown. It was generally agreed that he was tarred and feathered: Allen D. Candler, ed., *Colonial Records of the State of Georgia*, XII (Atlanta, 1907), 434; Siebert, *Loyalists*, II, 324; Lorenzo Sabine, *Biographical Sketches of the Loyalists of the American Revolution* . . . (Boston, 1864), I, 260. But Brown himself, in his "Supplemental Memorial" to the Loyalist Claims Commission, stated that his skull was fractured by a blow from a rifle barrel and thereafter, tied to a tree, he was tortured "in the most inhuman manner by applying burning torches of lightwood to the soles of his feet." Loyalist Papers, AO 13/34/100. Whatever the details may have been, Brown never ceased saying that everything he did during the war was a response to this initial trauma.

from the low country. Thereafter he moved off to Charleston to seek support from the governor, and by January 1776 was in St. Augustine. There with Governor Tonyn of East Florida he worked out a comprehensive plan for using the Cherokee Indians to support the loyalists and bring first the backcountry and then the whole of South Carolina and Georgia back into British control. Though the plan was never put into effect, Brown lived for several months among the Indians in preparation for the campaign. While there he was commissioned lieutenant colonel of the Carolina King's Rangers, a force of over 500 men at its peak, which he recruited and which was assigned the task of defending the East Florida–Georgia border area. Later he would be appointed one of the superintendents of Indian affairs in the south.[14]

It was his exploits over a period of six years as leader of the Rangers —in effect a commando unit described even by a British commander who relied on them as "a mere rabble of undisciplined freebooters"—that formed his flamboyant and malign reputation. The fighting in the backcountry was bitter and brutal—contemporaries called it "a war of extermination"—and Brown's tactics seemed excessively brutal, even in that bloody environment. Whether it is true that, after his capture and successful defense of Augusta in 1780, after having fought on during the siege while wounded in both thighs and reduced to drinking urine to keep alive, he hanged seventeen of the wounded prisoners of war, hanged them inside his own garrison house "that he might have the satisfaction of seeing [them] expire," and then handed over others to the Indians to be burned alive— whether all or any of that is true cannot be definitely established. But that all of this was said at the time and was generally believed to be true is certain. By 1781 Brown's reputation was such that when he was forced to surrender Augusta a special guard of Georgia militiamen had to protect him from the fury of the local inhabitants, who threatened to tear him limb from limb. He survived the war, and when his Rangers were disbanded he moved to the Bahamas, where he began a new and successful career as a planter and colonial politician. In 1809 a land grant on the tiny island of St. Vincent in the southern Caribbean brought him to that distant tropical outpost; and there, more than 4,000 miles from Whitby and 2,000 from the Broad River,

[14]Berry Fleming, *Autobiography of a Colony: The First Half-Century of Augusta, Georgia* (Athens, Ga., 1957), pp. 118–119; James Grierson to Gov. James Wright, Augusta, Aug. 6, 1775, *Colonial Records of the State of Georgia*, XII, 435; Siebert, *Loyalists*, II, 324; Olson, "Loyalists and the American Revolution," pp. 210, 215, 219, 208; *ibid.*, [part II: *South Carolina Historical Magazine*, 69 (1968)], 49, 54; John R. Alden, *John Stuart and the Southern Colonial Frontier* (Ann Arbor, Mich., 1944), pp. 139–140. Brown's plan for the use of Indians to control the backcountry is excerpted in Edward J. Cashin, Jr., and Heard Robertson, *Augusta and the American Revolution: Events in the Georgia Back Country, 1773–1783* (Darien, Ga., 1975), pp. 12–14. On the strength and changing title of the Rangers, see Paul H. Smith, "The American Loyalists . . .," *William and Mary Quarterly*, 3d ser., 25 (1968), 272.

Georgia, he died, in 1825, 50 years after the tarring and feathering which he insisted had driven him into his years of vengeful warfare.[15]

Long before that—four decades earlier—he had liquidated his interest in the Georgia plantation that had brought him to America in the first place. When he had fled from the Liberty Boys in 1775 he had left the company's agent, James Gordon, in charge of the plantation and its servants on the Broad River. Gordon was a better politician than Brown, a justice of the peace and a local dignitary, but by the time the second shipload of emigrants arrived in Georgia later that year the entire venture was out of control. Brown had been declared a traitor in the *Georgia Gazette,* and this alone was a signal for some of the servants to repudiate their obligations and drift off into the countryside, to work for other planters or to carve out small independent farms as squatters on land whose legal status had become indeterminate. Some remained with Gordon, however, until word arrived that the plantation would be plundered by the militia and their hangers-on. At that point Gordon gathered up the servants and moved off to a safe refuge on a plantation of his own in South Carolina, "endeavoring by that means to keep the white servants together and to save any further expence upon their account." But it was hopeless. "The rebels," he later reported to the claims commission, "from time to time inveigled those servants from him, and the whole concern with Messrs Browns was at length entirely sunk & lost." Alone, Gordon made his way back to Britain. What remained of his and the Browns' property was confiscated by the state of Georgia, and the servants merged with the general backcountry population, moving here and there in inland Georgia and South Carolina, their origins in the two voyages of the *Marlborough* gradually fading from memory.[16]

So Jonas Brown's Georgia enterprise came to an end. The last vestige, in the mid-eighties, was a flurry of petitions to the loyalist claims commission for the Browns' personal and company losses in Georgia. The total came to £10,196, for which, in the end, Brown was allowed £3,500. Gordon's claim to one-third the sum allowed the Browns was vociferously and successfully challenged by the family. For his personal claim of £6,735 the Scot had to be content with a mere £117.[17] As for Jonas Brown's initial invest-

[15]Clyde R. Ferguson, "Carolina and Georgia . . . Militia in Action, 1778–1783," in *The Southern Experience in the American Revolution,* ed. Jeffrey J. Crow and Larry E. Tise (Chapel Hill, N.C., 1978), p. 180; Lee, *Memoirs,* II, 94n., 101n., 115, 89, 117; I, 207; Cashin and Robertson, *Augusta,* pp. 41–47; Fleming, *Autobiography,* pp. 141, 138; Sabine, *Loyalists,* I, 262–265.

[16]*Collections of the Georgia Historical Society,* X, 23; Siebert, *Loyalists,* II, 324; Gordon, "Memorial," Loyalist Transcripts, XIII, 81 ff.

[17]"Schedule of the Real and Personal Estate which Belonged to Lt. Col. Brown . . . Confiscated by . . . the Georgia Legislature . . .," Loyalist Papers, AO 13/34/116–117; "State of the Claim of Jonas Brown of Whitby, Colonel Thomas Brown, and James Gordon . . .," Loyalist Transcripts, XIII, 88–91; Jonas Brown, Jr., to Loyalist Claims Commissioners, Kingston upon Hull, Dec. 13, 1788, Loyalist Transcripts, XIII, 141–147; "Muster-Rolls of Lieut. Colonel Brown's Indented Servants

ment in the two shiploads of indentured servants he had recruited in Yorkshire and the Orkneys and had settled on the Ceded Lands, nothing was allowed. Gathering these emigrants in Whitby and Kirkwall, shipping them to Georgia in the *Marlborough*, transshipping them from Savannah to Augusta and then to the settlement on the Ceded Lands, and clothing and maintaining them for two years had cost in all, Thomas Brown testified, £3,001 7s 8d. They had all hoped this investment in the settlement of American land would make their fortunes. But all was "sunk & lost."[18]

Manson's Enterprise

Yet, if the Browns' personal venture failed after they had carried over to Georgia from Yorkshire and the Orkneys approximately 150 emigrants, bond and free, its indirect role in the peopling of the Ceded Lands did not end there. The emigration enterprise—impelled by discontent, constriction, and the fear of future deprivation; inspired by a desire for betterment, renewal, and fulfillment—once undertaken, spread. And each promoter, each organizer, moving independently, devised significant variations on a common theme.

So it was that while the Browns' and Gordon's work force was scattering in the wartime confusion of the Georgia backcountry, a related enterprise of one of Jonas Brown's former employees, his ship captain William Manson, was taking root in that same remote area of the deep south.

Manson was a deeply religious and rather sanctimonious Quaker who lectured his "dear aged parents" in long, passionate, sermonlike letters on the sin of pride ("a monster that ravages our country and hinders the progress of the gospell"), enjoining them to remember their immortal souls and to "strive with God in prayer & supplication as Jacob strove with the angel," and reminding them that "without holiness of life none shall see the Lord or can enter into the new Jerusalem." He was also a capable seaman, whose contacts with the southern colonies had probably been continuous after the voyage of Jonas Brown's *Flora* in 1766–1767.[19] It may have been he, a native of the Orkneys, who had suggested to Brown that he recruit

... & the Expenses of the Same," Loyalist Papers, AO 13/34/124. The final claims and settlements are listed in Loyalist Transcripts, XI, 92–93, 164–165.

[18] The cost of settling the emigrants was variously estimated; on one occasion Brown said £3,001 7s 8d (Loyalist Papers, AO 13/34/124); on another, £2,490 (Loyalist Papers, AO 13/34/116); on another £2,319 19s 2d (Loyalist Transcripts, XIII, 88). But the range is not great. The average cost must have been somewhere between £15 and £20 a person.

[19] William Manson to Mr. and Mrs. William Manson, Philadelphia, Dec. 16, 1772, Balfour Papers, D2/9/15. Manson is identified as the "commander" of Brown's *Flora* on its voyage to New England in 1764; the accounts of the *Flora*'s voyage to South Carolina in 1766–1767, unsigned, is in the identical form and handwriting. For the two accounts, see above, n.2.

his plantation workers in those northern islands. But when, in September 1775, he himself became an active entrepreneur in emigrant shipping, his recruitment pattern was different. Manson's enterprise, though related to Brown's, developed different possibilities, involved different approaches, and it reflects, in the details of two account books that have miraculously survived, different uses of human resources.

Manson's involvement with Jonas Brown's commercial voyages to the American south would in itself have been enough to direct his attention to the possibilities of settlements on the Ceded Lands, but in addition he and his family in the Orkneys were friends of both Isaac Herbert, Jonas Brown's attorney and agent in Georgia, and the Browns' partner in the Broad River plantation, James Gordon. Manson must have been well aware of Gordon's migration to Georgia in 1772, even though he was then employed by the firm of Horne & Kemp of London on long sea voyages looping along the borders of the Atlantic basin from London to Philadelphia to South Carolina and to Spain before touching at several Baltic ports and returning to England. By 1774 he had heard much, one way or another, about the fertility of Georgia's soil, and knowing that "many of my old acquaintances [were] settled in that country," he decided, during a stopover in Savannah in December of that year, to tour the interior and "see and judge for myself." What he saw of the Ceded Lands far surpassed even the most favorable reports he had had. When the governor and council, ever eager to promote settlement in that border area, made "advantageous proposals" to him, he came to a decision. He resolved, he later recalled in a narrative he wrote for the loyalist claims commission, "to become a settler amongst them." So, late in 1774, immediately after that inspection tour of the interior, he bought a 300-acre plantation not far from Savannah and settled a family there to raise provisions in anticipation of his return the following year. In addition he made arrangements with the Georgia Council to hold for him on an informal basis a reserve of 3,100 acres in the Ceded Lands, which he would formally claim and locate when he could produce the requisite number of settlers.[20]

All of this done, he returned to England and set to work on the project. His most pressing need was for capital, and for that he turned to William and John Chapman, merchants in Newcastle, who were old family ac-

[20]Thomas Taylor to Mrs. [William] Manson, Philadelphia, Nov. 9, 1777; William Manson to same, Savannah, Ga., April 8, 1777, and to Mr. and Mrs. William Manson, Philadelphia, Dec. 6, 1772, and aboard the *Arundel* in Dover Road, July 5, 1773; "Narrative of William Manson" [c. 1788]: all in Balfour Papers, D2/9/15, D2/18/12, D2/9/10. For the land reserve, see *Collections of the Georgia Historical Society*, X, 10; for Manson's tour of the interior, see his "Narrative." Robert S. Davis, Jr., "The Last Colonial Enthusiast: Captain William Manson in Revolutionary Georgia," *Atlanta Historical Journal*, 28 (1984), 23–24, cites different figures for the reserve land and Manson's own tract. This informative article stresses Manson's wartime tribulations, and unaccountably attributes the collapse of the Friendsborough settlement to Manson's mismanagement.

quaintances, commercial correspondents of his recent employers, Horne & Kemp of London, and speculators in East Florida land, and possibly also, in a preliminary way, in Georgia land as well. They agreed to help Manson if he would extend the scope of the venture. Manson's ambitions swelled. He decided to join with the Chapmans in "a more extensive plan" than he had originally intended. The contract he and the Chapmans signed called for the Chapmans to finance not only a plantation in the Ceded Lands but a trading establishment there as well. The merchants would receive in exchange for their investment four-fifths of the profits of both plantation and store. Manson and his family, for one-fifth of the profits and a salary of £100 a year, would settle on the plantation and manage both enterprises. The Chapmans' financing, in addition to covering all costs in England, would take the form of a bill of credit of £2,000, which Manson could draw on for his expenses in setting up the plantation and trading emporium and in providing for the needs of the servants and other settlers they would send.[21]

Once the contract was signed, Manson set to work fitting out the ship they would use, the *Georgia Packet*, which regularly made runs to Savannah, and recruiting the emigrants he would need to open and sustain the plantation and to validate the provisional land grants he had obtained. He estimated he needed about one hundred emigrants, and he was confident he could get them all in Newcastle: "we get people here very fast," he wrote. Of course it was possible he would fail to get the number he wanted. In that case he would stop off in the Orkneys, as the Browns had done; there he could be sure of getting any number of people. But he did not expect that to be necessary.

In the summer of 1775 Manson and the Chapmans were hard at work organizing the business side of the venture. In addition to direct recruitment in the area of their contracts, the associates placed a carefully written, curiously conceived advertisement in five issues of the *Newcastle Journal*, an ambitious paper that boasted of its 600-mile circulation range and its distribution in over 250 towns, some of which never saw another Newcastle newspaper. The back settlements of Georgia, the notice stated, like "all high countries in the same latitude"—"Judea," for example, "or Canaan, &c"—"are universally allowed by all authors to enjoy a perpetual spring and the most agreeable temperature of climate, as well as to produce with the least trouble the most valuable products of the world. And to these so happily situated back settlements of Georgia the greatest encouragement is

[21]Manson, "Narrative." The contract has not been found, but a later summary of it (Loyalist Papers, AO 13/36/654–659) states that Manson agreed to remain in Georgia for 30 years to manage the land as the company's factor and agent, a stipulation he did not mention in his "Narrative." Peter W. Coldham, comp., *American Loyalist Claims* (Washington, D.C., 1980), I, 87. On the Chapmans' earlier land ventures, see Davis, "Last Colonial Enthusiast," p. 24.

given for indented servants to go out, who, after their term of servitude is expired, will be enabled to settle on these lands as proprietors and acquire to themselves, or leave to their posterity, an easy competency."[22]

But to Manson the enterprise was not exclusively a commercial undertaking. It was also a personal and family affair. His brother Tom, 16, whose welfare and prospects had long concerned him, was with him in Newcastle, and he intended to take him along. But his wife, also in Newcastle, was five months pregnant with their second child, and while he assumed she would join him in Georgia, he did not think she should risk the sea voyage at that stage. He therefore wrote two of his sisters in the Orkneys—Elizabeth, 26, and Barbara, 23, apparently spinsters who lived with their widowed mother —explaining his intention to go to Georgia and "please Providence . . . to leave off the sea and settle in that country with my brother Tom & our servants." Since he did not want his wife to go until later, he asked his sisters if one or both of them would "immediately set out for this place with all speed." They would be "very useful and serviceable to me to manage the affairs of my house in that country—and without one of you I shall be much at a loss for a person to confide in as a housekeeper. Besides we shall be company for one another. My family that you will have the management of will be myself, brother Thomas, a doctor, two or three maid servants, and your two selves. I have no doubt that you will [not] refuse this offer as I think it will be for both your goods and better than being in service, as I shall take care that you want for nothing." To cover their expenses in getting from the Orkneys to Newcastle, he sent them an advance of five guineas, and he urged them to respond immediately. The *Georgia Packet*, he said, was due to leave exactly a month later, on September 5. For his mother, who would be left alone, he arranged a small annuity to be paid by the Chapmans.[23]

When the ship left, on the 8th, the sisters were aboard, but so too were Manson's wife and daughter, his young brother, Tom, and a loyal friend, a doctor, Thomas Taylor, who came from the nearby town of Sunderland. The rest of the 100 passengers aboard formed a curious group, whose characteristics make clear why Manson was so confident he could find in Newcastle the full complement of emigrants he needed for his project in Georgia. The ship list in the Register reveals the existence in that North Sea port, twenty-two miles from the Scottish border, of a double pool of unemployed or discontented people seeking resettlement in the colonies. One group consisted of Scots, farmers and artisans who had moved south

---

[22] *Newcastle Journal. Or, General Advertiser*, July 29, Aug. 5, 12, 26, 1775. The newspaper's elaborate circulation boast—including "the JOURNAL is conveyed ONE HUNDRED MILES south west and north on the day of publication"—was printed in each issue during these years.

[23] William Manson to Elizabeth Manson "or her sisters," Newcastle, Aug. 6, 1775, Balfour Papers, D2/52/2.

across the border to this nearest port of exit just before the ban on emigration from Scotland went into effect. The other group was made up of urban artisans from Newcastle and its surrounding towns—not only shoemakers, breeches makers, barbers, butchers, and carpenters, but also workers in more specialized urban crafts like watchmaking, upholstering, dyeing, ribbon-weaving, and rope-making. Together the two groups on board the *Georgia Packet* formed not a gang of hired laborers appropriate for exploiting a frontier outpost, but the nucleus of a normally structured community. Almost half (44) of the 94 who joined the Mansons on the *Georgia Packet* were members of eleven family groups, which included 23 children below the age of 14; thus one-fourth of all the passengers were children of those ages. The occupational distribution—farmers and low-skill artisans from Scotland, urban artisans and skilled craftsmen from greater Newcastle— was also that of a settled society, even though the group had first come together on the decks of Manson's vessel.[24]

With this community of emigrants, who praised the treatment they received from the organizers, Manson left Newcastle, stopped over in the Orkneys to pick up provisions (but not more emigrants), and sailed off to Savannah. He arrived there on December 12, after 82 days at sea, and by early January 1776 the emigrants were established on the Ceded Lands. The property Manson selected was a tract of two adjoining plots totaling 4,100 acres along Rocky Creek, a tributary of the Little River, which marked the southern boundary of the new land cession. The location, thirty miles or so south of the Browns' main settlement on the Broad River, was well selected. It had easy access through the Little and Savannah rivers to Augusta (fifty miles away by water) and to the port of Savannah, and it was only eight miles or so north of the Quaker community of Wrightsborough, a recently founded and flourishing township and village of over 500 Quakers, just south of the Little River, which was linked to Augusta by a newly constructed wagon road. Manson, the Quaker, named this settlement on Rocky Creek Friendsborough, and there he established the company's store and plantation—but not without difficulty.[25]

---

[24]The *Georgia Packet* is entered in the Register at T47/10/153–155. The *Georgia Gazette,* Dec. 20, 1775, announced that the *Georgia Packet* had arrived with "about 200 servants, who are to be settled . . . on the Ceded Lands." The *Newcastle Journal,* Sept. 16, 1775, said the emigrants numbered 105, "all in high spirits." But the Register's figure of 100 passengers is undoubtedly correct. In his later petitions to the Loyalist Claims Commission, when it might have been to his advantage to exaggerate the number of servants he had imported, Manson still gave the figure of 100. "Schedule No. 1, Containing an Account and Valuation of the Real Estate of William Manson . . ." [c. 1787], Balfour Papers, D8/1/4.

[25]*Newcastle Journal. Or, General Advertiser,* Sept. 16, Nov. 11, 1775. Manson's account of the voyage, on which four children died of smallpox and three were born, appears in the issue of Feb. 17, 1776. The approximate location of Friendsborough, which disappeared during the Revolutionary War, can be established by Manson's "Schedule No. 1" and the surveys of two adjoining plots of land, dated March 15, 1776, in the Balfour Papers, D8/1/4. The surveys, one of a 3,500-acre plot, the other

Though Manson assured his mother in Kirkwall that all was well, that they were properly settled, and that the "troubles" did not affect them much since they were 180 miles from the coast, in fact they had scarcely arrived when the war impinged on their isolated settlement. Within a month a recruiting officer of the Georgia Council of Safety swept through the settlement and "enticed" away four of the young unmarried indentured servants Manson had brought from Newcastle. When Manson complained bitterly at this treatment, the Council of Safety backed him, instructing the recruiter that the Continental Congress never intended to enlist people recently brought in to the "frontier parts" of the province; they ordered him either to return the servants forthwith or repay Manson for the cost of indenting and transporting them. When the recruiter refused to comply, two militia officers were sent after him, with what effect is not known.[26]

There were other troubles too. Manson's wife proved to be a trial. In ways that are not clear she managed to alienate almost everyone she came in contact with; later the Chapmans would claim that Mrs. Manson had influenced her husband to behave in such a way that he drove all the servants away.[27] But however she may have compounded the difficulties, the essential troubles Manson faced in maintaining a work force were typical of the time and place and less disruptive than might have been expected. In fact, the accidental survival of some remarkably detailed evidence reveals a flourishing backcountry agricultural and commercial operation at Friendsborough, in which advantage was taken, through most of the years of the servants' indentures, of the full range of their varied skills.

Friendsborough as a Business Enterprise

Still preserved, 200 years later, in the Orkney County Library in Kirkwall, are two account books that Manson maintained during his years as manager of the Chapman-Manson venture in the Ceded Lands of Georgia.[28] The

---

of a 600-acre plot, place the property on both sides of the short Rocky Creek, which flows south into the Little River. He valued the property, in 1788, at £3,587 20s. It is possible that the Browns led Manson to this spot, since the surveys show that Thomas Brown claimed land immediately adjacent to it. For a useful sketch of the history of Wrightsborough and a list of the first landowners there, see Alex M. Hitz, "The Wrightsborough Quaker Town and Township in Georgia," *Friends Historical Association, Bulletin,* 46 (1957), 10–22; also R. C. Scott, Jr., "The Quaker Settlement of Wrightsborough, Georgia," *Georgia Historical Quarterly,* 56 (1972), 210–223.

[26] Manson to "The Widow Manson," Savannah, April 8, 1776, Balfour Papers, D2/18/12; Meeting of the Council of Safety, Jan. 2, 1776, *The Revolutionary Records of the State of Georgia,* comp. Allen D. Candler (Atlanta, 1908), I, 82–84.

[27] William and John Chapman to Mrs. Marion Manson, Newcastle, Oct. 26, 1778, Balfour Papers, D2/9/15.

[28] Both are in the Balfour Papers: the Cash Book of the Copartnership of William & John Chapman & [Co.], Dec. 1774–July 1779, is catalogued as D2/25; the Ledger of the Accounts of William Manson & Co., Friendsborough, 1776–1779, is D2/26.

first is a cash book in which he recorded in parallel chronological sequences all the cash expenditures (as distinct from commodity exchanges) that he made and all the cash income (bills drawn on the Chapmans and their bankers and debtors in England and cash payments made by customers in Georgia) that he received in behalf of the "Copartnership" during the four years of the company's active existence, December 1774–July 1779. The second is a ledger containing the company's individual accounts in Georgia with 107 customers—presumably all of its customers in 1776 and 1777. The ledger shows, in separate balances for each customer, every transaction the company made, as creditor or debtor, and the balance of the accounts as they stood at the end of each year. This ledger, which was apparently the first of two such books that Manson kept, covers comprehensively the year 1776 and includes entries for the three following years mainly to show the closing of accounts that were active during the first year of settlement.[29] Together the cash book and the ledger reveal much of the character and range of the company's enterprise in its most active phase and something of the fate of the servants Manson brought with him to settle this small speck of land in the great inland arc.

The ledger is particularly revealing. At first glance it appears to contain no surprises: it seems simply to document the transactions of a typical farmland emporium. Credited to an ordinary account are small deliveries to Manson & Co. of wheat, timber, butter, flax, "hogs fatt," sole leather, potatoes, tobacco, beef, and deerskins as well as deliveries of turkeys and other fowl, "a sow and 5 shouts," and, occasionally, a horse. Also on the credit side of the ledger are many entries showing the employment of the neighboring backcountry farmers by Manson as he built up his plantation, made purchases in Augusta and Savannah, and marketed goods there. "By his wages for waggoning at sundry times . . . £4," is a typical entry; "By carriage of 5 loads of corn from Aintleys . . . £1 12s," is another; similarly, "2 loads from Watsons . . . £1" and "1 days drawing from Baldwins . . . 10s." There are frequent creditor entries too for "waggon hire from [or to] Augusta," for "5 days drawing at the plantation," and for "52 days work at the upper house [@] 4/ [per day] . . . £10 8s" and for "29 days work at the lower house [@] 5/ [per day] . . . £7 5s." Occasionally Manson's customers paid cash, in small amounts, into the credit side, and in a few cases they were creditors by land sales; in one or two cases, also, they were creditors for land transactions of substantial size, though the largest overall account totaled only just over £170.

All of this is what one might have expected in the accounts of a country storekeeper. But there are at least two aspects of the ledger that are not typical and show the peculiar nature of Manson & Chapman's enterprise.

[29]Of the total, 49 accounts extend into 1777, 9 into 1778, and 4 into 1779.

First, the deliveries of farm products, made day after day in the early months, begin to taper off after the summer of 1776, decline still further in 1777, and then dwindle away to insignificance in 1778 and 1779. Partly, no doubt, the decline was the result of the war in the backcountry, which disrupted all normal activities. But mainly it reflects the reduced need for such supplies. Manson's ultimate aim was to profit not by storekeeping but by planting and eventually land sales, and the heavy importation of farm products into Friendsborough in 1776 was an effort to keep his plantation supplied with food and necessary farm equipment until the first crops were harvested and the rest of the agricultural enterprise was set on foot. By late 1776 the need for farm products slackened. The plantation was producing its own supplies and had enough equipment, cattle, and seed to continue on without supplies from outside.

But it is in the entries on the other side of the ledger that the special quality of life at Friendsborough is most clearly revealed. Again, many items seem quite normal. There are, for example, entries charged against various accounts for quantities of nails sold by Manson, for unworked iron and steel, for sugar, salt, knives and forks, a weeding hoe, rum, butter tubs, lengths of cloth, rugs, blankets, an anvil, metal files, a "camp oven," and iron pots. And occasionally Manson balanced the books on the debit side with cash payments drawn indirectly from the capital advanced by the Chapmans. But there are also frequent entries on the debit side, not for *selling* clothes, but for *making* them, and also for performing skilled services of various kinds. Thus Manson's servants made for Isaac Herbert, Jonas Brown's agent and attorney at the Broad River plantation, a suit of clothes (£1 5s), a waistcoat and breeches (12s 6d), and a morning gown (6s). Others paid for "a pair of leather breeches," "a short coat & breeches," women's gowns, and also for smith's work, for mending a plow, and for labor on the fort being built at Wrightsborough. And the "making" in each case was the work of the artisans Manson had imported.

Among the indentured servants on the *Georgia Packet* had been 5 shoe-makers, 4 joiners, 3 tailors, 3 smiths, 3 carpenters, 2 mantua makers, a breeches-maker, a weaver, and a ribbon-weaver. Friendsborough was not simply a plantation whose owners expected to profit by its produce, and it was not merely an emporium for the exchange of supplies and manufactures for farmers' services. It was also a handicraft manufacturing center— a production and service center—made possible by the work, skilled and semiskilled, of the indentured servants Manson had brought over from Newcastle. Their total production is impressive. Quite aside from what they must have produced for their fellow workers at Friendsborough, they made for sale, on behalf of the company in 1776–77, 16 pairs of breeches, 8 waistcoats, 8 outercoats of one sort or another, 2 complete men's suits, 2 pairs of trousers, a riding dress, a morning gown, a pair of gloves, and unspecified numbers of handkerchiefs, stockings, and shirts. In addition, on thirteen occasions they performed "smithwork," and there are frequent entries too for the repair of clothes, shoes, and farm equipment.

There is no way of totaling precisely the financial value of these contributions to the solvency of the enterprise, but they formed a major part of the debit side of the 107 accounts during the first year. This craft production of the indentured servants was a fading resource, valuable chiefly during the expensive and risky period when the Friendsborough enterprise was getting under way. For the indentures of many of the servants began to expire in the third year, and in several cases their services failed prematurely as Manson experienced the usual difficulties of keeping such a labor force intact and functioning. On five occasions the books reveal payments to the local constables and others for "hunting serv ts," with what success is not recorded. Further, the servants themselves—that is, their unexpired labor —became commodities in such demand that it was more profitable to sell them than to use them.

The ledger records the sale of 11 indentured servants within the first eight months of settlement. One other sale is noted two years later, in August 1778, and there may have been others recorded in the second, missing ledger. In 10 of the 12 documented transactions the buyers can be identified, and with one or two exceptions they are all prominent Quakers from nearby Wrightsborough. One of the purchasers, John Walton, "Esq.," the leading figure in that community—justice of the peace, tax collector, delegate to the General Assembly and the Provincial Congress[30] —bought three of the servants, all artisans (a barber, a smith or joiner, and a shoemaker), whose average age was 19 or 20. Half of the servants sold were women, most of whom sold for £12 each. The men's prices varied. Three of the six sold for £25 each; two sold for less (£18 and £12); and one was a very special case. He was Whitaker Shadforth, a 21-year-old Scotch watchmaker who was sold to a silversmith, probably from Augusta or Savannah, for the unusually high sum of £40. In all, Manson's accounts show a credit to the company of £206 for the sale of 11 of the 12 servants.

So in the ledger book kept by Manson, one sees something of the actual operation of the Manson-Chapman enterprise at Friendsborough during its early months and years, and catches at least a glimpse of the use made of the indentured servants imported in the *Georgia Packet*. The cash book reveals a different facet of the venture. Manson or someone employed by him maintained the book faithfully, from December 1774 (before the company even existed legally, when he recorded an expense of £10 10s for traveling up the Savannah to inspect the Ceded Lands) until July 27, 1779, when he entered, as a final item in the book, an expenditure of £15 for the

[30]Fleming, *Autobiography*, pp. 96, 100, 102, 112, 113.

purchase of a coffin. No item was too small to be entered ("Mrs. Jarvis for washing &c . . . 2s 3d"; "sailors for drink money . . . 1s 6d") or too large ("James Thompson in part [purchase] of Y^e [ship] Katherine . . . £230 17s 6d"; "plantation in St. Matthews parish, paid . . . £552 10s"). The items purchased for cash (with bills, for the most part; occasionally with gold or silver) almost defy classification. They include food supplies, personal services, animals, equipment of all sorts, wagon hire, slaves, coffins (for two of the indentured servants, Thomas Tulip, a tailor from Newcastle and his wife Jane, both dead within eight months of arrival), house rentals, saddle cloths, "snuffers," and, repeatedly through the four years, parcels of land.

The income side of the cash book is less varied. It consists largely of entries of cash received from the Chapmans' bookkeeper, of sums paid in cash by the company's more affluent customers (the Quaker leader Joseph Maddock, for example, and the wealthy Savannah merchant and president of the council, James Habersham, and his English-educated son Joseph), and of money received in small amounts at the store in payments for goods and services. The last category—cash sales in the Friendsborough store— was by no means trivial. For eight months Manson entered monthly totals of the many small purchases made in cash, and while the average monthly total was only £77, such receipts rose to over £200 in the best months. In all, the meticulous Manson recorded cash expenditures over the four years of £6,898 1s 17½d and cash income of only £6,261 7s 11d. But the cash deficit was more than balanced by the book transactions and the appreciated value of the land the company purchased. Years later, in England, Manson worked out for the loyalist claims commission a complete overview of the company's finances as of the date of the claim, 1788. He estimated the company's total assets, lost as a consequence of the Revolution, at £9,255 17s 6d; of that sum, £6,417 10s was the value of their confiscated real estate.[31]

Manson's Demerit

By then, 1788, the world had long since by-passed the Manson-Chapman project. Pressure on the Manson family had built up quickly after the start of the war in 1775. The upheaval in the backcountry had forced Manson to move his family to a house within 200 yards of the British fort in Augusta.

[31] "Schedule No. 1" and "Schedule No. 2 . . . Personal Estate . . .," Balfour Papers, D8/1/4, which correspond perfectly with the figures presented in Manson's "Narrative." Manson's calculation of lost assets is not only comprehensive but imaginative as well. He included not only obvious assets like livestock, farm equipment, food stores, and "a very valuable negro man," and not only less palpable values like "a small library of books," but also the uncollected rental income from the company's property; the principal and accrued interest on £327 9s 3d he had paid in 1774 for a mandamus to survey 5,000 acres, which was never accomplished; and the assumed value of the return cargo on the *Georgia Packet*, which the revolutionaries had prevented him from loading.

But it was precisely that fort that was the main target of the guerrilla fighting in the backcountry, and when the American troops took the fort they "plundered, and destroyed all my personal property, and everything in my house, which they razed to the ground, had I been there my life would certainly been taken." By then his young brother, Tom, had left him, first to work for a merchant in Augusta, then to go to Florida, and eventually to serve briefly in the British army. Discharged in Halifax, Nova Scotia, Tom eventually made his way back to England, where he was living in poor circumstances when the loyalist claims were submitted. Manson's sisters too had left him to live with "some genteel families in the neighborhood," mainly, according to the Chapmans, to escape their difficult sister-in-law, Manson's wife, Elizabeth. Even Manson himself deserted Elizabeth for a while, the Chapmans wrote Manson's mother in Kirkwall, but "unfortunately took to her again." (In 1780 he left her permanently.) The indentured servants had to be abandoned. Like the Browns' servants, they drifted into independent lives in the backcountry. Even the faithful Dr. Taylor broke away, and returned to England via Philadelphia.[32]

As Quakers, the Mansons themselves were not pressed to take the oath to the new government, and were allowed to pass through the lines into British-held territory without harassment. They moved south in stages as the area of British control dwindled. Gradually abandoning the many parcels of land which Manson had bought for himself and had begun to develop—convinced, he said, that "lands [were] the surest property a man could possess"—he resettled on a plantation just south of Augusta, where he continued in trade. But early in 1779 the American forces drove him back to the British troop base in Savannah, from which he returned temporarily to Augusta, only to be faced with an oath of loyalty to the American cause, which "on account of conscientious scruples" he refused to take. But he remained in that upcountry area long enough to encounter the former Whitby land speculator, the founder of Brownsborough, Lieutenant Colonel Thomas Brown, leading his Rangers on their famous assault on Augusta. Brown took advantage of Manson's good standing in the area to send him with a flag of truce to offer terms of surrender to the rebel militia. Several hundred accepted and became prisoners of war on parole. But Brown and his loyalist guerrillas could not control the area they conquered —could not prevent marauding and indiscriminate destruction, could not keep the prisoners of war from drifting back into the rebel fold, could not maintain British dominance even by multiple executions and the transfer of prisoners to the Indians. Even the devastation of hundreds of farms, houses, barns, and forts throughout the Ceded Lands failed to immobilize

---

[32]Taylor to Mrs. Manson, Philadelphia, Nov. 9, 1777, Balfour Papers, D2/9/15; Manson, "Narrative"; Coldham, *American Loyalist Claims*, p. 330; William and John Chapman to Mrs. Marion Manson, Newcastle, Oct. 26, 1778, Balfour Papers, D2/9/15.

the rebels, and in the end, in 1781, after murders and vengeful depredations on both sides, the British troops—and Manson, who had become their supplier, with them—retreated to Savannah.[33]

Manson had already been banished by the state of Georgia, and in May 1781, with his family, he left Georgia for Charleston. Four months later, with great difficulty, they managed to get passage to England. And so, seven years after his exploration of the Ceded Lands, William Manson, the Orkney ship captain, emigrant recruiter, and settlement leader, left America. He had no hope "of ever again returning to the backparts of the provinces (until peace), where most of my lands and settlements lay," but he did hope that when peace was concluded "the landed interest of the friends to the crown, would be secured."[34]

Resettled in his home town of Kirkwall and saddled with responsibility for the support of his family, he made strenuous efforts to recover his losses. He approached the Chapmans for money—the money he believed they owed him for his services—at least to tide him over "until we saw what could be done." But the Chapmans, who had been refusing the bills he drew on them since 1777, were in financial trouble, and since at that point Manson had no vouchers or title deeds to prove his, or their, claims, they ignored his bills for salary and out-of-pocket expenses and his increasingly shrill demands. "You surely dont imagine me metamorphosed into a camel to live upon air," he wrote his former partners; "had it not been for the disinterested generosity of 2 friends that assisted me with a little cash . . . I might have been in jail for debt and my children starving, for any assistance I could get from you."

He had no choice but to ship out again, this time to Jamaica, to serve as the salaried storekeeper in the navy's victualing office on that island. There he remained for eighteen months, until late in 1783, and there he somehow resumed contact with friends in Georgia who had preserved some of the papers he needed to substantiate his losses. Leaving a trail of debts and recrimination behind him, he quit his job in Jamaica, returned to England, engaged in further shipping operations, and began a protracted effort, first to receive temporary help from the government in repayment for his loyalty and services, and thereafter to recover the actual losses he had suffered. In 1783 he submitted to the loyalist claims commissioners a memorial for temporary relief, testifying that Governor Wright had encouraged him to settle his family and others in the Ceded Lands, that because of his loyalty to the crown he had lost property worth £9,000, and

---

[33]Manson, "Narrative"; Davis, "Last Colonial Enthusiast," pp. 28–34. Manson's role in offering amnesty to the Georgia backcountry people under a flag of truce is elaborately documented in the Balfour Papers, D2/44/18. His enumerated expenses total £80 14s.

[34]*Revolutionary Records of the State of Georgia*, II, 244, 245; Manson, "Narrative"; Coldham, *American Loyalist Claims*, p. 331.

that he was "in great distress, has two children & not where with all to support them." As a Quaker, he said, he could not have taken up arms against the Americans, but he had assisted the British war effort in every other way. And he submitted as documentation a certificate of his loyalty signed by Governor Wright.

The claims commissioners, then attempting to reduce the charges of temporary aid and concerned to reward "extraordinary merit," loyalty, and genuine need, were not impressed. Yes, he had no doubt been loyal, and no doubt he had lost some property (though that was not yet documented). But he had never made any active exertions for Britain, and he lacked "peculiar merit." In fact, they felt that "his being the instrument & cause of transplanting so many good subjects from Scotland into America may be considered as [a] demerit." But since he seemed genuinely in need and had been loyal, they gave him "some little assistance," in the form of a pension of £30 a year.[35]

That was temporary relief only, being handed out as charity to hundreds of loyalists; it was hardly a proper restitution for Manson's real losses, and it was entirely independent of his claim as a member of the Chapmans' company enterprise. In the five years that followed, Manson assembled documents to substantiate his and the company's claims to recompense for lost property. In 1788 he was joined in this effort by the London creditors of the now bankrupt Chapmans. The Chapmans' assignees, or receivers, were better connected and probably shrewder than Manson, and by the middle of 1788, to Manson's extreme chagrin, they had entered a claim with the claims commission for a four-to-one division, favoring themselves, of whatever recompense would be forthcoming for the company's losses. Manson's brother Thomas, in London, got wind of the maneuver, and he and Manson immediately fired off heated letters of protest to the commissioners.

In his "Narrative," crowded with facts and figures, he explained exactly what his relationship with the Chapmans had been and how the payments should be divided. On the basis of a pack of documents retracing the whole history of the Georgia venture, he stated that against the £9,255 17s 6d in assets that the company had lost, the Chapmans could reasonably charge only £2,223 3s 7½d: this was the capital they had invested to transport the settlers and establish the town in the Ceded Lands. On the other hand, he

[35] Manson's letters to the Chapmans, to David Balfour, and to William Bigby, London, February–March, 1782; Memorandum of Agreement with William Ward, Feb. 19, 1782; Manson to Balfour, Kirkwall, Jan. 7, 1790: all in Balfour Papers, D2/60 and D2/8/6; Manson, "Narrative"; Coldham, *American Loyalist Claims*, p. 331; AO 12/100/28. For the policies of the government in handling requests for temporary relief in the form of pensions, see Mary Beth Norton, *The British Americans: The Loyalist Exiles in England, 1774–1789* (Boston, 1972), pp. 54–56, 114–121, 225–229. Manson's pension was withdrawn in June 1789: John Jamieson to Manson, London, June 18, 1789, Balfour Papers, D2/8/6.

claimed—as his personal expenditures on behalf of the company and as his unpaid salary as resident manager from September 1775 to September 1781 —the sum of £2,460 16s 3½ d. These were the primary charges against whatever the government gave to the company to repay its lost assets. Once these bills were paid, the rest of the company's lost assets—£4,571 16s 6½ d —was appreciated value, in effect profit, and by the terms of the contract, Manson was entitled to one-fifth of that sum, or £914 7s 3d. The Chapmans' assignees, he conceded, could claim the rest. In addition to all of this there was his own land in Georgia, which he understood had been sold as confiscated property "for upwards of £13,000 sterling, payable in gold and silver."[36]

Despite all the calculations and all the documentation, Manson's claim, one of thousands filed with the commission, had weaknesses. Not only was some of the crucial evidence missing, and not only was much of his argument based on interpretation of the terms of his partnership with the Chapmans, but his claim was vulnerable on the point the commissioners had made clear to him in 1783. The fact that he had brought out a number of British inhabitants to America, the commissioners had said, was a "demerit"; but Governor Wright himself had solicited settlers, and the land could only be obtained that way. And there were other major, positive features he could point to. He recalled that he had personally, and successfully, carried into the backcountry of Georgia, under a flag of truce, an offer of pardon to any rebels who surrendered their arms. He recalled too that he had repeatedly been forced to flee from his house and family and hide in the woods. And he recalled, finally, that he had been imprisoned by the rebels, then banished, and his property confiscated.[37]

The end came in a blur of legalities. Late in 1788, after bitter wrangling, Manson and the Chapmans' assignees came to a private agreement. The Chapmans accepted Manson's accounting, which specified approximately the same amount of out-of-pocket losses for the two parties—a total of £4,683 19s 10d. Anything up to that total that the government granted would therefore be divided equally; anything above that amount, up to the full claim of £9,255 17s 6d, they would divide according to the terms of the original contract: four-fifths for the Chapmans, one-fifth for Manson. On September 18, 1789, the London bankers Barclay and Tritton wrote Manson

[36] Thomas Manson to William Manson, London, Dec. 10, 1788, same to Claims Commissioners, Dec. 12, 1788, and William Manson to Claims Commissioners, Dec. 18, 1788: all in Balfour Papers, D2/8/6; Coldham, *American Loyalist Claims*, pp. 87, 331; Manson, "Narrative." Manson's itemization of the company's debt to him personally, for salary and out-of-pocket expenses, is in the Balfour Papers, D2/9/4; his specification of the Chapmans' capital investments is in his "Narrative." The actual sales of parcels of Manson's land are documented in *Revolutionary Records of the State of Georgia*, I, 566, 572, 574, 578, 580, 586, 592; and in *Early Records of Georgia*, I, 238, 260, 269, 271; II, 118.
[37] Coldham, *American Loyalist Claims*, p. 331.

in Kirkwall that the government had awarded the claimants a total of £2,663 7s 8d, and that his share, when commissions and legal fees were paid, was £1,323 16s 10d—his salary, in effect, for the thirteen years since the company's founding.[38]

With that Manson had to be content. If he ever returned to Georgia to see what had become of the hundred northcountry people he had transported in the *Georgia Packet,* no record of the trip survives. Friendsborough as a community dissolved in the wartime confusion, its name soon forgotten, and Manson's former servants scattered into settlements throughout the backcountry. By the time Manson died, in 1808, few of them would have recalled the importance of this enterprising Orkney ship captain to the course of their lives, or the importance of a family of Newcastle merchants whose gamble in the Ceded Lands had ended in disaster.

[38]"Memorandum of Agreement," preceded by a flurry of letters from and to Manson, Dec. 1788, D2/8/6, and Barclay and Tritton to William Manson, London, Sept. 18, 1789, Balfour Papers, D2/18/8. The terms of the final agreement differed from Manson's sketch in his "Narrative" in that he then insisted that his charge against the company be paid before any other claim no matter what sum the government granted. The official register of payments to the loyalists has two entries for Manson and the Chapmans' assignees—£516 to Manson personally and £2,100 to the assignees— which together are slightly less than the sum the bankers actually received from the government. The funds granted probably earned interest before they were distributed. Loyalist Transcripts, XI, 212–213, 168–169.

16

New York: Swarming to the North

THE enterprises of James Hogg, of the Browns, and of William Manson are extraordinary, not in their substance, which illustrates in typical ways how ordinary people, in the years immediately preceding the Revolution, were transplanted from Britain to remote places on the inland arc of settlement in North America. What is exceptional about them is the fullness of their documentation. The surviving records in these cases are unusually complete. As do few other records of the time, they allow one to see the precise ways in which small increments to the American population came about. They reveal something of individual motivation, and they allow one to trace complete trajectories of life careers whose central episodes are voyages from Britain to a western wilderness world whose actuality few of these emigrants could imagine. Hogg's personal motivation and plans—his arrangements with Inglis; the swarming to the departing *Bachelor* of hundreds of free, independent, but threatened and worried Scots, diminished in their fortunes but still capable of mobilizing a modicum of capital; Hogg's selection among them; the arrangements made for their transatlantic voyage: all of this was characteristic of innumerable small-scale emigrations taking place throughout the coastal region of northern and western Scotland, and of Yorkshire, Northumberland, Durham, Cumberland, and Lancashire as well. Characteristic too is the Browns' enterprise in the Ceded Lands deep in inland Georgia—their recruitment, in Whitby and the Orkneys, of settlers to open their wilderness plantation on the Broad River, and the scattering of that contingent, at the outbreak of the Revolution, into the surrounding countryside. And similarly revealing, and unique in their detail, are the account books kept by the Browns' former ship captain, William Manson, as he struggled, on behalf of Manson & Chapman, to profit from the craft services as well as the plantation labor of the two shiploads of emigrants he transported from Newcastle to Rocky Creek.

Such detailed records, all of them related to entries in the Register of emigrants, are rare, and, with one dramatic exception, their likes are not to be found among the surviving evidences of settlement in the far *northern* sector of the inland arc, where immigrants from overseas were particularly prominent. During these pre-Revolutionary years three huge swaths of land in the north of the area claimed by the colony of New York were being opened to settlement: the great wedge of over three million acres west of the Hudson River and south of the Mohawk; the broad strip stretching due north from Albany to Lake Champlain on both sides of the Hudson; and, far to the east, the west side of the upper Connecticut River, territory disputed between New York and New Hampshire, which would eventually form part of the state of Vermont.

For the huge sweep of land stretching west two hundred miles from the Connecticut River across Vermont, across the Green Mountains, across the Hudson River, and farther west along the Mohawk to Fort Stanwix, close to Lake Ontario, records of various densities survive from a series of enterprises that account for the presence of British emigrants in these northern regions. These records, of people whose lives are associated in various ways with the Register of emigrants, illustrate especially well the *variety* of processes by which these transfers and relocations of people were accomplished, and something of the range of experiences these voyagers endured.

The prism of this process of scattered relocation was the dock area of the port of New York, the main entrance into the colony's upcountry lands. The protected East River shore, from Manhattan's southern tip north approximately a mile to the present site of the Brooklyn Bridge, bristled with wharves, piers, and docks that provided the loading space and the warehousing for some 700 vessels that arrived in the port annually—schooners and sloops in the coastal, Hudson River, and West Indies trades, larger ships of all kinds in transatlantic commerce. In the spring and early fall the harbor was crowded with these sailing vessels, many of which bore emigrants from all over the Atlantic world, principally from Britain.[1] Precisely how many of the incoming vessels carried voyagers from the home island to the narrow, crowded streets of this port town of 25,000 people cannot be established: an uncountable number of commercial vessels landing goods from Britain brought with them a few passengers in addition to their cargoes. But the main carriers of people can be identified, if not in the departures for New York in the Register of emigrants, then in the New

[1]Carl Abbott, "The Neighborhoods of New York, 1760–1775," *New York History*, 55 (1974), 41–42; Bruce M. Wilkenfeld, "Revolutionary New York, 1776," in *New York: The Centennial Years, 1676–1976*, ed. Milton M. Klein (Port Washington, N.Y., 1976), pp. 49–50, 55.

York newspapers, which reported ship arrivals in the port with fair regularity.

In all, in the years of the Register's effective existence, there is evidence that 42 vessels arrived with emigrants from Britain at the docks of Manhattan, 29 of which had been recorded by the customs officials in the Register. The 29 vessels with registered emigrants—16 from England, 13 from Scotland—bore 1,954 voyagers unequally divided between the two regions. The 13 vessels from Scottish ports, carrying on the average over five times as many passengers as those that left from English ports, account for about 85% of the total number of passengers (1,653). How many emigrants the 13 nonregistered vessels that were known to have carried passengers from British ports may have added to the total can only be estimated: certainly many more than the 1,278 reported casually in the newspapers and personal correspondences.

Thus a minimum of 2,000 newcomers arrived from Britain in the port of New York in the two years before warfare closed New York's harbor to normal traffic, and it is likely that 1,300 more arrived as well—a total that is equivalent to approximately 13% of the city of New York's total population in 1775. These incoming voyagers—a typical mix of artisans and farm workers, with far more families among the Scots, hence many more Scottish than English women and children—were objects of great attention. Their arrivals in the port of New York were reported not only in the New York newspapers and not only by visitors and officials in New York but by newspapers everywhere in the colonies—in New England no less than in the Chesapeake region, in Nova Scotia no less than in South Carolina. Partly this attention to arrivals in New York was the product of the relatively efficient distribution of New York newspapers, which facilitated reprinting elsewhere. Partly too it was the result of the reported numbers of immigrants involved, hence of the importance of New York as a distribution center for immigrants.[2]

[2]The sheer sensationalism of some of the arrival notices in the newspapers also enhanced their popularity. One of the most widely publicized events in the history of Anglo-American migration in these years was the tragic voyage of the *Nancy*, a badly overloaded, ill-equipped, ill-staffed brig from the North Sea port of Sunderland. Its owners and crew, in an arrangement to people Lord Dunmore's 51,000-acre plot in the far northern wilderness of New York, loaded the vessel beyond all capacity with impoverished Gaelic-speaking Scots from Sutherlandshire and Caithness. Disease, undernourishment, the brutality of the crew, and constant gale weather reduced everyone, passengers and crew alike, to panic, then to savagery. When, after 13 weeks at sea, the wrecked vessel appeared in New York, approximately a third of the passengers had died (one account reported 81 dead, another 104), and a number of the survivors—brutalized, half starved, and sick—succumbed soon thereafter. And even their arrival was miserable. Because there was sickness aboard the *Nancy*, the vessel was quarantined for 10 days on Andrews's Island in the harbor, where the passengers were given temporary assistance. At the end of December they finally managed to get into town, "weak and emaciated, thinly clad, some of them sickly, most of them without money, and none knowing where to go, or how to obtain necessaries, or shelter themselves from the inclemency of the weather, which was freezing cold, and the ground covered with snow, their condition appeared

Baron Johnson and the Mohawk Marchlands

All of this was vital economic news, especially important to land speculators and developers, who scrutinized and acted upon these notices week after week. Most deeply interested were the many patentees and claimants of land that lay far out on the huge northern periphery of settlement in upcountry New York.

Most of the early seventeenth-century land patents that lay close in along the Hudson below Albany had long since been settled and had been developed into tenanted estates or divided into individual farms. But as early as the 1730s there had been rivalry among land speculators for control of the rich lands in the river valleys north and west of the Hudson, between the Catskills and the Adirondacks. A few small settlements of Germans and Dutch had long been established along the Mohawk, the central valley of that frontier area, but steady population growth had begun only after the arrival in 1738 of William Johnson. This young Scotch-Irishman was the nephew and land agent of the naval commander and politician Sir Peter Warren, who had received a large land grant near the eastern end of the Mohawk, at its juncture with the Schoharie. Over the next thirty years Johnson (after 1755 Sir William) dominated this wilderness region. His accomplishments were extraordinary. He established peaceful relations with the Six Nations of Indians whose land he and his people were invading, set up trading stores at strategic spots, bought land and arranged for

---

to be truly deplorable." Since few could speak English, they could not easily explain what had happened, but the benevolent resources of the city were soon mobilized. Sermons were preached on their behalf, funds were collected for them in the churches, and notices were placed in the newspapers advertising their need for employment. The emigrants failed in their efforts to bring the owners and the ship captain to trial for their brutality and irresponsibility. Their only recourse was publicity, and of that they had no cause to complain. The most complete account of the voyage appears in a lengthy two-part article in the *New-York Journal; or the General Advertiser,* Jan. 13 and 20, 1774, reprinted in its entirety in the *Nova-Scotia Gazette and the Weekly Chronicle,* Feb. 22, 1774. Partial accounts of the voyage appeared in almost every newspaper in America, including three in Boston, three in Philadelphia (one of them German), two in New York, and two in Virginia. And the story was picked up in the relevant parts of Britain as well—in the West Riding of Yorkshire, where most of the English emigrants to New York came from, in the East Riding, in Northumberland, and in Scotland. Dunmore's involvement in population recruitment, which lies behind the episode, emerges in incidental references in newspaper reports: *New-York Gazette: and the Weekly Mercury,* Dec. 20, 1773; *Virginia Gazette* (Purdie and Dixon), Jan. 6, 1774. Before leaving New York in 1771 after his one-year tenure as governor of the colony, Dunmore had traveled north to inspect the land he had bought east of Crown Point. He made it known that he intended to bring to this remote property people "from his own country" and that despite his departure he had "not yet laid aside that design." Goldsbrow Banyar to Sir William Johnson, New York [City], July 18, 1771, *Papers of Sir William Johnson,* ed. James Sullivan *et al.* (Albany, 1921–1965), VIII, 192. But the New York purchase was a small affair for Dunmore. Later, as governor of Virginia, he laid claim to almost four million acres, mainly in the Ohio Valley.

"Indian Council at Johnson Hall." Painting by E. L. Henry.

others to buy land throughout the region, helped to organize and personally led the British and Indian forces in the northwestern campaigns of the Seven Years War, and established himself in a remarkable biracial manor court, where he lived the uninhibited life of a marchland baron, surrounded by his illegitimate children by two successive common-law wives, one a runaway German indentured servant, the other a Mohawk Indian, and by other, more casual connections. After 1763 his "very comfortable" manor house, Johnson Hall, with its gardens and fields "cleared in an absolute forest" just north of the Mohawk River, was the site of conferences with Indian chiefs; it was there he managed his commercial affairs, and it was there he pursued his great passion, accumulating land and managing the settlement of "industrious people."[3]

From the beginning Johnson brought into the region successive groups of settlers—his Scotch-Irish countrymen first, then New Englanders, then

[3]Edith M. Fox, *Land Speculation in the Mohawk Country* (Ithaca, N.Y., 1949); Ruth L. Higgins, *Expansion in New York: with Especial Reference to the Eighteenth Century* (Columbus, Ohio, 1931), chaps. 1–7; Milton W. Hamilton, *Sir William Johnson: Colonial American, 1715–1763* (Port Washington, N.Y., 1976); (on Johnson's wives, Catherine Weissenburg and Mary Brant, see pp. 33–35, 304–305; on his children, pp. 306–310). The quotations are from Lord Adam Gordon's "Journal of an Officer . . . in 1764 and 1765," in *Travels in the American Colonies,* ed. Newton D. Mereness (New York, 1916), p. 417.

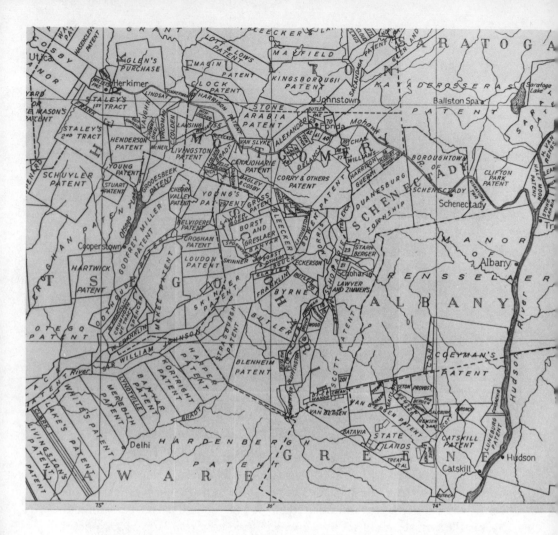

*Modern reconstruction of land claims in the Hudson, Mohawk, Schoharie,
and Susquehanna river valleys.*

English, and in the 1760s, Scots. By the mid-1760s the European settlements
had thickened out north and south of the Mohawk as far west as Fort
Stanwix, ninety-five miles from the Hudson, and had expanded steadily
southward, into the fertile Cherry Valley near Otsego Lake and into the
"Old England District" stretching out to the region's natural western
frontier at the Unadilla River. And everywhere throughout the northwest
region, claims were made to parcels of undistributed land. Physically, by
the mid-1760s, the land was still largely empty, still almost entirely undeveloped, but legally it had become an impenetrable maze of patent titles,
vague claims, abstractly defined tracts, "purchases," and designated but
undeveloped townships. Many of these patents, claims, and designations
had indistinct boundaries; some overlapped others; some were immense in

size; some (226) were so small they are identified only by number, not by name, on the one comprehensive map that has been made of these claims. Most were inert, mere legal assertions, but after 1763 they represented valuable potentialities. Everywhere in those years there was a sense of expectation in the northern borderland, a belief that huge profits were about to be made, that great hopes and soaring speculations would soon be realized.

But while these possibilities were hopeful for Anglo-American speculators, they were threatening to the Indians whose hunting grounds these lands still were. As the white population increased and as land speculation became heated, the Indians, their native territory preempted, felt pressed; conflict seemed inevitable. It was to satisfy the Indians in their justified claims to vital hunting grounds and at the same time to open these lands to further settlement that Johnson negotiated the Fort Stanwix Treaty of 1768. By its terms the Indians retained their property north and west of Stanwix (modern Rome, New York) but the new boundary of the crown's land fell due south from that point along the Unadilla, eighty miles west of the Hudson, thus formally opening for settlement parallel east-west valleys formed by tributaries of the Delaware and Susquehanna rivers.

Even before the terms of the Stanwix treaty were known and long before the treaty was ratified in 1770, speculators, most of them organized initially in small syndicates to avoid the limitations on individual grants, raced into the area to negotiate purchases directly from the Indians, which they hoped the crown would later validate, and took out a range of new land patents with officials in New York City. The most quickly developed of the new patents (most of them dated between 1769 and 1771) were concentrated in the center of the released area and were shaped like vertical slices running north and south through a horizontal east-west strip about ten miles wide, formed by the branches of the Susquehanna and Delaware rivers.

Johnson himself had claim to 100,000 acres in the northern sector of that region. A Scotch-Irishman named John Harper, who had wandered all over New England before settling in Cherry Valley, led a group in purchasing 250,000 acres from the Indians and in patenting 22,000 acres for immediate development. Lawrence Kortright, a New York city merchant, scion of an old Dutch family who had made a fortune in privateering and helped found the city's Chamber of Commerce, took title to another 22,000-acre plot, alongside Harper's, and the colony's deputy secretary and court official, the merchant Goldsbrow Banyar, patented a third such slice, alongside Kortright's. Other parcels filled out the western end of this strip between the branches of the Susquehanna and Delaware rivers. And at the mountainous eastern end two huge patents extended the range of new land claims out to the Schoharie: the Strasburgh Patent, organized by one of Johnson's lieutenants, John Butler, and the Blenheim Patent, taken out by a prosperous west Yorkshireman, John Wetherhead, who had recently arrived from England and had quickly established himself as a merchant of consequence in Manhattan, with close business ties to Johnson on the Mohawk.[4]

But the real value of all these grants, patents, and purchases, the old and the new, depended on the recruitment of people if only because the validity of land titles rested on specific numbers of settlers arriving in designated periods of time: in the case of the Johnson, Harper, Kortright, and Banyar patents, one family for each 1,000 acres within 3 years, and at least 3 out of every 50 acres brought under cultivation in that time. So here, as everywhere throughout the great arc of North American land development, immigrants were sought, in large numbers and small, to settle on the land.[5]

Johnson was perhaps the region's most successful recruiter of settlers. His reach was wide. His fame, his many contacts both in Britain and America, and his skillful entrepreneurship brought settlers to his lands throughout these years. Some simply arrived, unknown and unannounced —a group of Highlanders, for example, who in May 1773 suddenly appeared at Johnson Hall "of their own free choice, & without any endeavor of mine," Johnson wrote. They had already received "sundry proposals from different gentlemen" and Johnson was careful not to seem to be tempting them away from previous commitments. He went out of his way to inform them that Major Skene's terms for land sales or rentals at Skenesborough in the north, just off the south bay of Lake Champlain, were better than anything they would be offered anywhere else. Such caution and scrupulousness were characteristic of Johnson, and necessary; competition for settlers was so intense that patentees often resorted to sharp practices which a magisterial figure like Johnson had carefully to avoid. "I could not think of engaging with persons," he wrote one of the people who had been dealing with these unknown Scots, "who had entered into terms with others, & I presume no gentleman would interfere with any persons who had taken up lands from me, if that circumstance was known." Still, Johnson was a land dealer, and a successful one, and having taken all reasonable precautions against seeming to snatch these land-hungry Scots from other landowners, he pointed out to them that the "neighborhood, market & quality" of the land at his disposal were such that he could rent them out on better terms and faster than was consistent with what he considered to be "good policy." Whereupon several of the Highlanders set out immediately to inspect his land, got surveys made quickly, and began the initial

[4]Hazel C. Mathews, *The Mark of Honour* (Toronto, 1965), chap. 1, p. 36; Eugene R. Fingerhut, "Assimilation of Immigrants on the Frontier of New York, 1764–1776" (Ph.D. diss., Columbia Univ., 1962), p. 201.

[5]Mathews, *Mark of Honour*, p. 10.

AREA OF SETTLEMENT
IN UPCOUNTRY
NEW YORK, 1760–1776

.... Present-day state boundaries — — — County boundaries, 1775

0   50 Miles
0   50 Kilometers

St. Lawrence River

Beekmantown

Lake Champlain

ADIRONDACK MOUNTAINS

Crown Point

CHARLOTTE COUNTY

Lake George

Skenesborough

TRYON COUNTY

Lake Ontario

NEW

YORK

Batten Kill

Oswego

Fort Stanwix
Oriskany

MOUNTAINS

Mohawk River

KINGSBOROUGH PATENT

Johnstown

Fort Johnson
Fort Hunter
Schenectady

Saratoga

Lake Oneida

Seneca R.

Finger Lakes

Unadilla River

Otsego Lake

CHERRY VALLEY

Schoharie Creek

ALBANY

Schoharie

Albany

COUNTY

Towoga River

APPALACHIAN

Chenango River

Susquehanna River

OLD ENGLAND DISTRICT

JOHNSON PATENT

STRASBURG PATENT

HARPER PATENT
KORTRIGHT PATENT
BANYAR PATENT

BLENHEIM PATENT

West Branch Delaware R.

East Branch Delaware R.

KATSKILL MOUNTAINS

Katskill

Kingston

New Paltz

DUTCHESS COUNTY

FORT STANWIX TREATY LINE

emung R.

Susquehanna River

Lackawanna River

WYOMING VALLEY

ULSTER

COUNTY

Hudson River

ORANGE

COUNTY

WESTCHESTER COUNTY

Delaware River

PENNSYLVANIA

NEW JERSEY

New York

16.A

clearings for farms. By the end of June they were reported to be "much pleased with their situations."[6]

More often the immigrants Johnson settled on sections of his immense properties came to him with recommendations or had made previous arrangements with him. So the Reverend Harry Munro of Albany recommended to Johnson the "fair, unblemished character," certified in various "credentials & testimonials," of a group of seventeen Scotch families who were looking for land and had turned to him for advice. They swore they had made no previous commitments to other landlords, and Munro felt they "may in time prove useful & good tenants." Furthermore, "if these will like your proposals, I have reason to think, some hundreds of families will soon follow." When, later, Johnson came to believe that they had in fact originally been subsidized to settle on land owned by Munro himself, he made them sign an affidavit forswearing even "the smalles conection with Mr. Munroe, or . . . an agreement with him, or recd any money from him."[7]

The *Pearl*'s "Genteel People of Considerable Property"

Johnson's most curious, and important, link to an immigrant group in these pre-Revolutionary years emerged in the fall of 1773, a few months after the unknown Highlanders appeared, when he welcomed to the north country some of the most consequential Scots to appear in New York in these years. They had first come together as a group in September, when they had boarded the ship *Pearl* at Fort William in the southern Scottish Highlands. They had gathered from all over eastern, especially southeastern, Scotland —from villages in Morayshire and Inverness-shire in the Highlands, and in Roxburghshire, Wigtownshire, and Kirkcudbrightshire in the Lowlands. But the key cluster aboard the *Pearl*—the organizers and managers —came from close by the exit port. They were the four Macdonells, three brothers and their first cousin, of Glen Garry, near the ruins of their Donald clan's former stronghold, Invergarry Castle, and only fifteen miles from Fort William. The Macdonells were Roman Catholics, once Jacobites and still alienated and discontented, and they had fallen into dangerous economic difficulties. "The hardships and oppressions of different kinds, imposed upon them by the landholders," it was said, simply forced them "to

[6]William Johnson to John Reid, Johnson Hall, [June 6, 1773], *Johnson Papers*, VIII, 816; *South-Carolina Gazette; And Country Journal*, July 20, 1773.
[7]Rev. Harry Munro to William Johnson, Albany, May 21, 1773, *Johnson Papers*, XII, 1023; Statement of Joseph Chew, Johnstown, May 3, 1774, *ibid.*, p. 1087; Duncan Fraser, "Sir John Johnson's Rent Roll of the Kingsborough Patent," *Ontario History*, 52 (1960), 181.

abandon their native country . . . if their farms could but have afforded them bread and water, they would have been satisfied to stay at home."

Under this pressure they had organized a company of like-minded Scots from the neighboring glens—Glen Moriston (where Dr. Johnson and Boswell on their Highland trip that year found little English spoken and first encountered mass emigration), Glen Urquhart, and Strath Glass. They had then arranged for passage, and had announced the ship's departure to attract others to join the venture. All of this was standard procedure, but at some point a special element had entered in. One of the Macdonells' sons, Archibald, had emigrated to New York sometime earlier, had established himself as a merchant in New York City, and had made contact with Johnson. It was probably through Archibald that a kinship relationship between Johnson and the Macdonells was discovered, and it was he who conveyed Johnson's encouragement to the Macdonells to settle on his land when they arrived in New York. On the basis of this, the brothers in Scotland had apparently written to Johnson, and it was with some kind of assurance from him in hand (a published account said an actual "grant of lands in Albany") that they had boarded the *Pearl* at Fort William on August 31. They just missed the severe north Atlantic storms that battered the *Bachelor*. The trip was quick enough—six weeks and six days—though not without tragedy: smallpox swept through the vessel and killed 25 of the children aboard.[8]

Their arrival in New York on October 18, like their departure from Fort William, was well covered by the press. The *New-York Gazette* described the *Pearl*'s "280 souls, all of them, about a single score excepted, of the Clan M'Donald" as "very respectable . . . full of health, and ready money to purchase each man his freehold." The *New-York Journal* called them "genteel people, of considerable property," and the *Nova-Scotia Gazette*, quoting a letter from Scotland, reported them to be "the finest set of fellows in the Highlands, and it is allowed they carry at least £6,000 sterling in ready cash with them." Representatives of this "great acquisition to this province" immediately inquired into the possibility of buying or renting land and were referred to the merchants Banyar and Kortright, with whom they held discussions. Then on October 28, ten days after their arrival, most of them boarded a sloop for Albany, drank toasts to the King's health and the province's prosperity, thanked their hosts for their kindness, and set out on

[8]Mathews, *Mark of Honour*, pp. ix–xi; *New-York Journal; or, the General Advertiser*, Oct. 28, 1773 (extracting a letter from Fort William, Scotland, originally printed in the *York Courant*, Sept. 7 and in *Gentlemen's Magazine*, Sept. 30); *ibid.*, Oct. 21; W. L. Scott, "The Macdonells of Leek, Collachie and Aberchalder," Canadian Catholic Historical Association, *Report* (1934–1935), 29–30. Another key role in establishing the Johnson-Macdonell connection may have been played by Hugh Fraser, one of several Scottish veterans of the Seven Years War who had settled on Johnson's land. Archibald Macdonell's wife was a Fraser, and Hugh's kinsman Simon Fraser came over on the *Pearl*. Fraser, "John Johnson's Rent Roll," pp. 181, 182.

the next leg of their voyage "to the lands which they are going to view, and where they expect to settle."[9]

The bulk of the party remained at Albany while two groups of representatives proceeded to the Mohawk and then separated. One, led by the most prosperous among them, went south from the Mohawk along the Schoharie and then west over hilly countryside to inspect the lands of Kortright and Banyar they had discussed in the city. The other group, led by one of the Macdonells, proceeded to Johnson Hall and discussed terms with Sir William. Four possible sites came under discussion with Johnson, and the Scots set out their terms in clear, if somewhat clumsily Gaelicized, language. They pointed out, first, that they had "a great desire of settling under your wing," and furthermore that they had mutual interests: "you have large estates to make & we some influence over people tho' at a distance that may be of consequence in subsequent years." They would be happy to settle with him "if the situation & quality of the land is attracting."

As for the four sites under discussion, the main one was some part of the huge Kingsborough and the adjoining Mayfield patents north of the Mohawk. Kingsborough, a plot of 66,000 acres that stretched 12 miles along the Mohawk and from 3 to 6 miles north to the Adirondacks, had been patented in 1767, and since 1771 Johnson had been advertising exceedingly generous terms to anyone who would settle there: leases for 3 lives, 5 years rent free, then for 10 years rent at only 50s (New York currency) per 100 acres, thereafter £4—and free mills, schools, and roads. The trouble here, the Scots' agents said, was not the terms but the extent of the property. Settlement on the Kingsborough patent would involve them in such great distances from markets, sawmills, and gristmills that they feared they would run into the same old problem of costly land carriages and customs duties which many of them had emigrated to escape; they did not now "incline to be the first introducers of it by compact in the New World." Of the cheapest land, on a plot adjoining the Schoharie, they knew nothing about the soil or situation. As for the third parcel, next to a patent of Lord Adam Gordon, they wanted to know "what its sett in fee simple [was] or if any advantages of saw or grist mills fish or fowl attend it." And they asked the same questions concerning the fourth plot, on the Susquehanna.

They urged Johnson, rather shrewdly, to be forthcoming in his response since their party was "still in a fluctuating situation but we believe they will adhere to us if Sir William gives the encouragement their sobriety

---

[9] *New-York Gazette: and the Weekly Mercury,* Oct. 25, 1773 (reprinted in *South-Carolina Gazette* on Nov. 22 and in the *Nova-Scotia Gazette* on Nov. 23, 1773), Nov. 1, 1773; *New-York Journal; or, the General Advertiser,* Oct. 21, 28, 1773; *Nova-Scotia Gazette,* Jan. 4, 1774; Mathews, *Mark of Honour,* p. 5.

& industry will merit." And then they stated a set of general demands they hoped Sir William would meet. They wanted, first, an advance of start-up and maintenance costs for the first year; second, looking to the future, some "room or scouth in our vicinity in order that such of our friends & country-men as will incline to follow our fate may sit down in our neighbourhood"; and third, a guarantee from Johnson that he would buy the land back at market price from those among them "calling ourselves gentlemen" if they were "inclined to remove after a few years expence and toil in clearing lands &c."[10]

Johnson's reply is not recorded, but the representatives to the Kortright and Banyar lands reported to their compatriots waiting in Albany such "flattering encouragement" from the owners' agents resident on the land that they returned quickly to New York City to commit the terms to writing and confirm them with the owners. On the basis of these prelimi-nary arrangements and reports, the former passengers on the *Pearl*, only a month after their arrival in America, made their decisions. A few joined an earlier group of Scotch Catholics at a plot known as Johnson's Bush near Johnstown, north of the Mohawk; others settled on the Kingsborough Patent; a few wandered off to join relatives from earlier migrations far to the east of the Hudson, near the present town of Bennington, Vermont. But the great majority settled on the land between the branches of the Delaware and Susquehanna rivers that had been offered to them on such flattering terms. The individual parcels they were given were scattered through the low uplands, the flat rich bottomlands, and the arable sloping hillsides of the property recently patented by Kortright, Banyar, Harper, and also the ubiquitous Johnson.

But though the *Pearl*'s families spread out through this district seeking the most promising farmlands in the hilly countryside, they did not scatter widely. Almost all of them settled within a radius of six miles from the modern village of Kortright Center, which lies in the middle of Lawrence Kortright's original patent of 1770. The *Pearl*'s passengers, who had gath-ered from all over southeastern Scotland but especially from the region of Glen Garry in the south of Inverness-shire, now lived close enough to each other to communicate easily. And they lived, moreover, in a rocky country-side of rolling uplands and sloping hills that was surprisingly similar to their native land. Similar in many ways—yet different too: different above all in the dense hemlock forest cover that gave the hillsides not the soft green

[10]*Ibid.*, pp. 7, 13; Scott, "Macdonells," pp. 29–31; Fingerhut, "Assimilation of Immigrants," pp. 212–213, 219. Johnson apparently did provide the initial maintenance costs they requested. In 1776 his son Sir John wrote that he had been supporting the Macdonells for two years, and that their debt to him approached £2,000. John Johnson to General Schuyler, Johnson Hall, May 18, 1776, in *American Archives*, ed. Peter Force (Washington, D.C., 1837–1853), 4th ser., VI, col. 644.

color they now have and not the bare, open, brown and green appearance of the Scottish countryside, but a "dark blue approaching black" appearance, and that rendered the earth itself dark, shadowy, and silent.[11]

There, on those rich, dark-forested hillsides, the *Pearl*'s Scots made their initial clearings and began their renewed lives as settlers on the far outer periphery of the British-American world. A year later Johnson reported they were doing very well—which gave him great satisfaction, he said, "there being nothing upon earth [that] delights me more than to see the rude woods made cultivable and afford sustenance to the poor & distressed." By then their hopes that their "friends & country men" would join them "in our neighborhood" had been realized, and the "room or scouth" they had reserved for them had been put to good use. In the course of the next two years the British customs officials recorded the departure of four vessels for New York from south Scottish ports, carrying in all 607 passengers. How many of them joined the voyagers of 1773 on properties near the Mohawk and at the head of the Delaware is not fully known. Certainly some of them. One of the Macdonells reported that a total of 260 Highlanders settled on Johnson's estates in 1772, 1773, and 1774. And a number of the 81 passengers aboard the *Jackie of Glasgow*, which left Stranraer for New York in May 1775, can be traced person by person through various vicissitudes at sea, through their arrival, not in New York as planned but in Philadelphia, and through their slow and laborious pilgrimage north to the Kortright and Banyar patents to join their relatives who had crossed on the *Pearl*. But by the time the *Jackie*'s passengers joined their relatives and friends at the head of the Delaware, the Macdonells' plans for the peaceful development of their new American farms had been blasted by the advent of war.[12]

The Revolution had a peculiarly disruptive impact on the lives of the *Pearl*'s Scots and their former neighbors and friends who followed them. This community formed only a minority element in the mixed German, Scotch-Irish, native American, and English population scattered through the greater Mohawk Valley. The majority of the population followed John Harper and other local leaders in support of the American cause. The Scots, consequently, almost all of whom were loyal to the crown, fell into great difficulties as their leaders joined Johnson's loyalist sons in the British army and as their landlords, Kortright and Banyar, remained neutral and were forced into obscurity. Coercive efforts to recruit the Scots for the patriot army led to resistance; there were demonstrations, reprisals, jailings, seizures of property, and physical flight.

[11] Allan Macdonell to William Johnson, [Albany, Nov. 14, 1773], *Johnson Papers*, VIII, 917; Mathews, *Mark of Honour*, pp. 14–15, 29, app. A; Fraser, "John Johnson's Rent Roll," pp. 179, 180, 182.
[12] William Johnson to John Donell, Johnson Hall, June 28, 1774, *Johnson Papers*, XII, 1111; Mathews, *Mark of Honour*, p. 36.

Some of the arrivals of 1773 and those who had followed them in 1774 and 1775 managed to protect themselves as neutrals and remained through the war on their newly opened farms. But many suffered, and in the end many fled. Some moved west, beyond the Finger Lakes, beyond the Iroquois lands, and across the Niagara River to the nearest safe territory in Britain's province of upper Canada. Some moved north to wilderness townships set aside for loyalist war veterans just across the St. Lawrence boundary line, townships that were formed into counties called Glengarry, Stormont, and Dundas, and whose chief settlement was New Johnstown. And still others moved far to the east, to Nova Scotia, where they joined other refugees in the loyalist boom town of Shelburne at the southern end of the peninsula, and from there scattered thinly into nearby Nova Scotian communities and to settlements in New Brunswick, across the Bay of Fundy.[13]

Thus by the early years of the nineteenth century, there were identifiable clusters of the Scottish emigrants of the pre-Revolutionary years scattered through the land. There was a large central group still in the circle around Kortright and Harpersfield, New York; there were offshoots of those settlements 225 miles to the west, just across the Niagara in upper Canada; there were others in Glengarry, upper Canada, 145 miles north of the Mohawk; and almost 500 miles to the east there were still other remnants of those who had shipped on the *Pearl*, the *Jackie*, and other vessels from southern Scotland, scattered along the southern shore of Nova Scotia and on farms in the valley of the St. John River.

The City Merchants: Wetherhead
and the Blenheim Patent

The fulcrum of this obscure but typical diaspora, the prism that had started the scattering of the flow of migrants into the northern New York wilderness and thereafter to east and to west, had been the land-promotion activities of the New York City merchants Lawrence Kortright and Goldsbrow Banyar. Kortright, who seldom if ever visited his choice plot at the head of the Delaware, concentrated on collecting newcomers and negotiating with them as they came across the city's docks into the town seeking ways and means of establishing themselves on the land. Scots traveling in families were especially convenient for his purpose, and none more so than families that had retained some little substance of property and were themselves able to invest in developing the land. When he came to terms with newly arrived

---

[13] *Ibid.*, chap. 3, p. 39; John G. Harkness, *Stormont, Dundas and Glengarry* (p.p., Ontario, 1946), chap. 4. Of the 232 loyalist claimants from Tryon County, N.Y., 142 had been settlers on Johnson's land. Fraser, "John Johnson's Rent Roll," p. 182. On the later fortunes of the Macdonells, see Scott, "Macdonells," p. 31.

families in New York City, he usually leased 150-acre plots to them, and sent them off up the Hudson and west overland to his property. Theoretically they leased their land from Kortright at six shillings an acre, but in order to attract them Kortright deferred the rent for eight years. By the time these rents came due the world had turned upside down, and Kortright, who had made substantial investments to open his patent, in fact never received any income from the leases.[14]

Kortright was not alone in inspecting arrivals at the East River docks and recruiting settlers from among those who, like the passengers on the *Nancy*, debarked "without money, and [not] knowing where to go, or how to obtain necessaries or shelter themselves from the inclemency of the weather." Nor was he the most active. The New York merchant firm most continuously engaged in importing and distributing immigrants, bound and free, was that of Walter and Thomas Buchanan, uncle and nephew, close relatives and commercial correspondents of the Buchanans of Glasgow and London, a kinship syndicate deeply involved in all aspects of North American trade. The New York Buchanans, importers and distributors of goods from Glasgow, London, Liverpool, and Bristol, and also the largest shipowners of the city, repeatedly received consignments of immigrants and arranged for their distribution. Theirs were the most common newspaper advertisements of the arrival of shiploads of immigrants. Their books alone were said to have recorded the arrival in New York of over 2,000 Highland Scots in the first half of 1775. Typically, they were sent, late that year, by the Buchanans of Greenock, a shipment of 251 immigrants from Strath Glass, Inverness—poor Scotch people, only two of whom were said to have "the appearance of gentlemen" but most of whom, though "very poor," were able to pay their passages. They were "determined to go abroad while they had any remains of their subject [i.e., property] to carry them."[15]

But however continuously involved in the business the Buchanans were, they remained passive recipients. Except for occasional orders for people with particular skills, which they sent to their correspondents overseas, their reach was limited to the city of New York and its surroundings. Some merchants had more direct outreach than the Buchanans: they sought to tap the flows of settlers at their sources. John Wetherhead was one of

---

[14]Fingerhut, "Assimilation of Immigrants," pp. 200–206.
[15]Jacob M. Price, "Buchanan & Simson . . . ," *William and Mary Quarterly*, 3d ser., 40 (1983), 5–8; William M. MacBean, *Biographical Register of St. Andrew's Society of the State of New York* (New York, 1922–1925), I, 97; unsigned letter [New York, June, 1775], Dartmouth Papers, Canada, I, 1202–1205: "it appears (I am told) by the books of Messrs Buchanan, merchants in this place, that above two thousand persons have arrived here from Scotland, mostly Highlanders, during the course of the present year"; Customs Collectors, Fort William, to Board of Customs, Edinburgh, Sept. 3, 1775, T47/12/117.

these more active recruiters, with lines to specific pools of migrants in both England and America.

Wetherhead had arrived in New York from the Yorkshire city of Leeds in the early 1760s and had quickly established himself as a dry-goods merchant, dealing especially in west Yorkshire's prime export, textiles. But his interests soon diversified. He was introduced to Sir William Johnson in 1766, and thereafter he became Johnson's commercial agent in the city, his legal representative, his news bureau, his political operative, and his general factotum, forwarding mail, booking ship passages for Johnson's friends, providing him with schoolmasters, laborers, and a Negro cook. And—inevitably—he joined with Johnson, and even more with the hustling young attorney general, John Tabor Kempe, in extremely ambitious land dealings.[16] In 1769 Wetherhead gave up his retail business altogether and concentrated on land speculation and population recruitment.[17] By the Revolution, which he spent with the British in occupied New York City, he had acquired, by all sorts of maneuvers with Kempe, Johnson, and others, 8 houses and lots in the city, worth over £7,500, and 7 parcels of upcountry land, totaling 60,000 acres, worth just under £19,000. When in 1783 he summarized for the loyalist claims commission his total losses in real estate, commercial paper, and uncollected debts, the total he arrived at was £36,119 14s 10d.[18]

Wetherhead's two most valuable pieces of property were his five-eighths and one-half shares respectively in the Blenheim and Strasburgh patents at the head of the Delaware, just east of Harper's and Kortright's patents; he valued these shares at over £12,000. Of the two, Blenheim, the whole of which totaled 40,000 acres, was the more valuable. It had been acquired just after the Stanwix Treaty, in 1769, by means of a maneuver commonly used to avoid the limitations on individual land purchases. The property was first granted to a group of 39 patentees and then by prearranged token sales quickly transferred to Wetherhead and to four of

[16]Wetherhead's introduction to Johnson, by John Tabor Kempe, is in the *Johnson Papers*, V, 218. In the pages that follow in that volume and in volumes VI and VII there are dozens of letters between the two men that document their close affiliation in business and personal matters. From the start (V, 490) Wetherhead was seeking land for profitable speculation, a matter about which he had been consulting with Kempe before he knew Johnson. Wetherhead to Kempe, Dec. 19, 1766, Kempe Papers; Jack H. Christenson, "The Administration of Land Policy in Colonial New York" (Ph.D. diss., State Univ. of New York at Albany, 1976), pp. 166, 172. For Kempe's holdings with Wetherhead: Catherine S. Crary, "The American Dream: John Tabor Kempe's Rise from Poverty to Riches," *William and Mary Quarterly*, 3d ser., 14 (1957), [186], 192–193.

[17]Wetherhead's ad, announcing his intent "to decline business" and to hold a cash close-out sale of hardwares, clothes, and textiles "at his house in Broad-Way, near the Bowling-Green," is in the *New-York Gazette; and the Weekly Mercury*, May 1, 1769.

[18]AO 12/22/74–75.

Kempe's sisters, who registered the attorney general's 15,000 acres in their names. The Blenheim land, now owned by Wetherhead and Kempe, was hilly—the 2,000-foot Blenheim Mountain, part of the Catskill range, lay within its boundaries—but except for the highest parts it was choice property, exceptionally fertile and well watered. It lacked only access to major markets to make it a speculative gold mine, and Wetherhead turned to this problem forthwith. He spent £350 of his own money to build a wagon road east around the hills and then southeast, probably along Catskill Creek, to join the Hudson directly opposite the well-populated Livingston Manor. And though the Schoharie, which ran along the eastern edge of the patent, gave direct access north to the Mohawk, Wetherhead had two additional roads built to link the property to the newly opened patents to the west along the Delaware and Susquehanna branches. Having thus created new access routes east to the Hudson and west to the Delaware and Susquehanna, Wetherhead turned to recruitment.[19]

His first efforts at attracting settlers to Blenheim were directed east to Connecticut and south to Pennsylvania. He placed an advertisement in at least three issues of the *New-London Gazette* in April and May 1769, stating that the Blenheim and Strasburgh lands were available either for sale or rent —lands "which are undoubtedly the most rich and flourishing settlements in the province. . . . The soil is extremely rich, and it is esteemed one of the finest corn countries on the continent." Easy access to the Mohawk and the Hudson was guaranteed; and further, "the settlers upon it will no where be above four or five miles from some of the settlements, which are increasing very fast on all sides of it." Those interested were referred not only to Wetherhead in New York but to associates of his in Connecticut much involved in upcountry New York land; they could be contacted in Windham, New Haven, and New London. A similar notice, apparently with more specific terms, appeared in the Philadelphia newspapers, and there the response was swift. Representatives of a party of Germans waited on Wetherhead, with results so encouraging that he proposed to Kempe that they immediately print up blank "warrantie" forms. The Germans apparently wanted some kind of a written commitment from the owners pledging them to honor the terms stated in the newspapers. Wetherhead urged that they provide this assurance, "not that I think it necessary but because they do, & if I should make any difficulties about it they may perhaps think there is some secret reason & that all things are not as clear as they ought to be." It was a nuisance, Wetherhead said, but what could one do? "There is, you know, no such thing as combating the prejudices of ignorant people." He had reason to believe that settlers could be attracted across the Hudson from

[19] *Ibid.*, pp. 85–86; Crary, "American Dream," pp. 192–193.

the Beekman family's Rhinebeck estate, and the warranty forms might be useful for them too.[20]

How fully these prospects, drawn from Connecticut, Pennsylvania, and nearby New York communities, satisfied Wetherhead's and Kempe's needs for settlers is not known, but by 1775 there had been enough settlement to drive up the value of their Blenheim lands enormously, and they were eager to realize all the gains possible. In June 1774 Wetherhead, in his search for settlers, reached beyond all of the local American constituencies and appealed directly to his native land. Identifying himself as "formerly of the town of Leeds, in Yorkshire," he advertised the Blenheim lands in the *Leeds Intelligencer*. The property, he explained, in terms that readers in far-off Leeds must have found incomprehensible, was a tract of land "between the cities of New York and Albany fronting upon and adjoining to the old settlements of Schoharry and Breckabeens, along Schoharry River." What he was looking for was a whole community of Yorkshire men and their families, a party of "forty or fifty families of his own countrymen on whose industry and honesty he could entirely depend." To such a party of his own people, approximately 200 in all, or if necessary "to a lesser number of good substantial farmers," he proposed to sell farms or lots in fee simple, at the rate of 6s an acre.[21]

Slowly all of these efforts began to show results. Two "settlements" were sold in 1772, and in 1774 ten more, by which time "settlements were pretty thick" on the Blenheim patent. And the sale price had steadily risen. One plot went for 10s an acre, two others for 14s, and nine for 20s—the last at a profit of 2,300%.[22]

Such was the skyrocket of profits Wetherhead had hoped for and was beginning to realize when the Revolution destroyed all of his enterprises. He had been aggressive throughout, reaching out into the sources of migration not only in the surrounding colonies but also in his native west Yorkshire. But though his notices in Connecticut, Philadelphia, and west Yorkshire were more dynamically enterprising than Kortright's efforts, they were nevertheless still impersonal, and to that extent still passive as a form of recruitment. Other promoters of land settlement in upcountry New York were even more active, more enterprising, than Wetherhead, attempting to reach out personally, and not merely through print, into the potential pools of migrants. Some succeeded, others failed. The initial optimism and the ultimate failure of Daniel MacLeod, in collaboration with the old and influential Beekman family of New York, show the vast geographical dis-

[20] *New-London Gazette*, April 21, 28, May 5, 1769; Wetherhead to Kempe, undated ("Monday Morning"), Kempe Papers, box 1.
[21] *Leeds Intelligencer*, Feb. 21, 1775, reprinted in *Publications of the Thoresby Society*, 38 (1937), 137–138.
[22] AO 12/22/86.

tances involved and the acute sensitivity of responses at the far ends of these extended filiations.

Beekmantown

The Beekmans were among the earliest affluent families of New York, and in the fourth generation, active during the Revolution, they were important in trade, politics, and land development. Their speculative efforts were directed to the colony's far northern wilderness—to the upper end of the Champlain Valley, 150 miles north of Albany, 300 miles north of New York City, and only 15 miles from the border of Quebec. For decades a no-man's land between the warring French and British forces during the colonial wars, separated from the Hudson Valley on the south by a difficult portage and from the St. Lawrence on the north by rapids on the connecting Richelieu River, and bordered by mountains on the west, the region was entirely unsettled until after the end of the war in 1763. Soon thereafter a few frontiersmen and particularly adventurous speculators began to move in. Besides individual settlements by a few farmers from Vermont who squatted on or near the eastern shore of the lake and some French Canadians who appeared in the north, three substantial efforts at community building were launched, by army veterans who had fought in the area, a Scotchman, an Irishman, and a German.

The first, Major Philip Skene, founded a town he called Skenesborough (now Whitehall) on a large grant below the southern tip of the lake, and began developing schemes for establishing a separate colony with himself as governor. The Irishman, William Gilliland, was for a time the most successful of the three. Buying up veterans' military rights to land grants, he brought, in 1765, an entire small colony, complete with cattle, servants, and mill equipment, up the Hudson, overland to Lake George, across the portage to Lake Champlain, and up that lake, to establish a bustling community he called Willsborough on the Bouquet River, just off the lakeshore 40 miles north of Ticonderoga. A decade later Willsborough was flourishing, with 28 dwelling houses, 40 farm buildings, 4 mills, numerous roads, orchards, farms, and gardens. The German, Captain Charles Fredenburgh, went even farther north, to open a small corner of a large grant on the site of the modern city of Plattsburgh. It was to land even more remote than Fredenburgh's—beyond all known European habitation—at the far northern end of Lake Champlain opposite Grand Isle, more than 60 miles north of Ticonderoga, that the Beekmans directed their attention.[23]

[23] Philip L. White, *The Beekmans of New York* (New York, 1956); *idem, Beekmantown, New York: Forest Frontier to Farm Community* (Austin, Tex., 1979), prologue; Doris B. Morton, *Philip Skene of Skenesborough* (Granville, N.Y., 1959), pp. 19, 21–37, 63–64; John Pell, "Philip Skene of Skenes-

Collaborating secretly with the province treasurer, Abraham Lott, a merchant and speculator, and as partners in a 30-man association of largely dummy petitioners, four Beekman brothers, sons of the aged Dr. William Beekman, applied in 1768 for a grant of 30,000 acres on the northwest side of the lake, extending out to include Grand Isle. The fate of the petition was precarious. The Beekmans had enemies in the provincial government, and it was not yet clear whether the British government would respect the grants the French government had already made in the region. But all of these problems were resolved favorably, and in July the terrain was inspected for Lott and the Beekmans by John Kelly, an elusive land jobber —a manipulator who lived on payments earned by promoting land grants. Kelly reported that the plot was fertile, richly timbered, and flat. When the Beekmans received this favorable account they ordered Kelly to make the requisite survey, and in March 1769 the patent for Beekmantown was finally issued. The grant contained the usual stipulation that it would be automatically voided unless within three years one family was settled for each 1,000 acres and three acres in every fifty were cleared.[24]

To keep the land, therefore, and to help recoup the fees of £745 paid various officials for processing the grant as well as the £110 paid Kelly for his services, the Beekmans turned quickly to the basic problem of peopling the land. And like so many others in these years attempting to profit by populating wilderness land, they thought first in utopian, or at least highly schematic, terms. They designed a plan to dispose of their property in blocks three miles square with a village in the middle of each block, containing the town lots (50 by 382 yards) of 124 farming families. These families would also have equal shares of working land—pastureland, cropland, and woodland—totaling in each case forty acres and all held in common. Provisions were made for a market, town hall, church, and granary, but in these idealized subsistence communities there were no plans for gristmills, sawmills, or shops of any kind. The scheme envisioned the peopling of a succession of such three-mile-square blocks, one following another as the population increased.

But where were the people to come from to settle these wilderness farmlands? There is no record of the Beekmans' ruminations on this subject,

---

borough," New York State Historical Association, *Quarterly Journal,* 9 (1928), 27–33. For a summary of Skene's own account of his wartime travails, see Peter W. Coldham, *American Loyalist Claims* (Washington, D.C., 1980), I, 448–449. For a well-documented account of Gilliland's adventure, including an enumeration of the workmen and settlers he brought with him, see Winslow C. Watson, *Pioneer History of the Champlain Valley; Being an Account of the Settlement of the Town of Willsborough by William Gilliland* . . . (Albany, 1863), pp. 23–45, 52–55, 92 ff.; on Fredenburgh, *ibid.,* p. 40n.
[24]White, *Beekmantown,* pp. 3–9. John Kelly was well known throughout the period as a highly active "land jobber." E.g., *Calendar of Historical Manuscripts Relating to the War of the Revolution* . . . (Albany, 1868), I, 677.

but their conclusion is abundantly documented. It centers on one Daniel MacLeod, a Scotch mariner from Kilmory, on the Isle of Arran. MacLeod, who may have been brought into the picture by Kelly, was no stranger to these questions. In 1772 or early 1773 MacLeod had been active in Stornoway, on the Outer Hebridean island of Lewis, attempting to gain control of a large group of emigrants. He had promised to "see them settled to their satisfaction if they would agree to go along with him," but when they had agreed, and—as the customs officials put it—"when it came to the push," he had failed to produce the necessary shipping, and the emigrants had turned to other sponsors.[25]

By the fall of 1773 MacLeod was in New York City and in contact with the Beekmans. Their interests clearly complemented each other. The Beekmans needed settlers for their carefully planned farming communities, and MacLeod, familiar with recruitment from his earlier effort, was certain he could produce them from western Scotland and could profit grandly by doing so. They therefore made an elaborate deal, formalized in a notarized contract. Its terms approximated those of a Scottish landlord with his tacksman, a role that MacLeod in effect was assuming. By its provisions the Beekmans leased the entire township to MacLeod, rent free for five years, at ten pence an acre for the next seven years, thereafter for one shilling an acre. In addition, MacLeod would pay the royal quit rent, beginning in March 1774, except on land set aside for public purposes. What rent and fees MacLeod was to charge the actual settlers was not part of the contract: as usual with tacksmen, that was left for him to decide for himself. When MacLeod produced "a proper number of families" the Beekmans would loan him £600 New York currency, at interest, for seven years to help get them located on the land. The owners would also pay half of MacLeod's expenses in visiting and inspecting the land, and they required him to appoint an agent in New York City to receive the settlers he sent from Scotland and to see to it that they were speedily transported to Beekmantown. MacLeod had until September 1, 1774, to comply with the terms of the contract.[26]

He set to work promptly. On November 7, a week after signing the contract, he set out to inspect the township on the western shore of Lake Champlain. By December 24 he was back in the city and received a glowing letter from the Beekmans, which he no doubt requested for his use in recruitment. The letter praised Beekmantown as "the best land in the county of Charlotte"; it stated, with glaring exaggeration, that it had easy communications with Montreal, Quebec, and New York City; and it men-

[25] White, *Beekmantown*, pp. 10–11; Customs Collectors, Stornoway, to Board of Customs, Edinburgh, Feb. 14, 1774, Stornoway Customs Letter Books.
[26] White, *Beekmantown*, p. 11; the text of the agreement is in the Beekman Papers, box 15, New-York Historical Society.

tioned the district's superb timber resources, its abundant fish, and the great variety of animals and fowl that could be found in the area. A month later, all plans completed, MacLeod boarded the *Needham* for Newry, Ireland, where he was to begin fulfilling his contracted obligations.[27]

Trouble started even before he arrived in the British Isles. He had a terrible voyage, but he managed to get to Newry, and then moved on the short distance to Belfast. There he chartered the 400-ton *Charming Sally* of Philadelphia, a vessel, he wrote, that could easily accommodate 400 adult passengers. While the ship was being provisioned and outfitted he sailed off to Stornoway, 275 miles to the north, only to get stranded on the small isle of Raasay, off Skye, 65 miles short of his goal. From there he wrote the Beekmans to update his schedule. He now expected to load the *Charming Sally* both at Stornoway and along the deep indentation of Loch Broom on the adjacent mainland coast, and he hoped to take on all the people he needed between the 20th of April and the 15th of May, when he planned to set sail for New York. But there was trouble brewing, he reported, quite aside from the weather. He was certain a Captain Chevers was maliciously working against MacLeod's and the Beekmans' interests—how, precisely, he did not say. Despite this, however, he still expected to get his "compl[emen]t for this ship and for another."[28]

He finally got to Stornoway and spent the entire month of May there maneuvering in every way he could think of to get up his shipload of 300 emigrants. After feverish solicitation, he was bitterly disappointed to have to settle for agreements with only 24 individuals. The competition that spring, the observant customs officials reported, was too keen for him. What role the mysterious Captain Chevers played is not recorded. But other promoters and organizers of emigration were known to be at work in Stornoway during these weeks, and they were much more successful than MacLeod in signing up the available voyagers, partly because they had better ties to the local population.

The notorious *Friendship* of Philadelphia had sent out its native Hebridean mate, Colin MacLeod, as early as March to scour the countryside for anyone willing to emigrate; it had been MacLeod's success with the youths around the island that had so alarmed Lord Seaforth's agent and had raised cries of kidnapping that reached the inner offices of Whitehall.[29] When the

[27]MacLeod's inspection trip to the Beekman grant and his plan to leave immediately thereafter for Scotland "to emigrate a considerable number of families to settle that place" were widely reported. From an initial story published in New York on Nov. 8 it was picked up by the *Virginia Gazette* (Rind), Nov. 25; by the *South-Carolina Gazette; And Country Journal,* Nov. 23; and by the *Caledonian Mercury,* Feb. 7, 1774, citing a Virginia source. His departure for Scotland via Newry was reported in the *New-York Journal; or, the General Advertiser,* Jan. 27, 1774.

[28]Daniel MacLeod to Messrs. Lott, Beekman, & Co., Raasay, April 5, 1774, Beekman Papers, box 15.

[29]See above, chap. 9, pp. 309–312.

Friendship weighed anchor on May 2 it carried on board 106 passengers, many of them indentured servants; their sale on the dock at Front Street, Philadelphia, along with the rest of the ship's cargo—beef, butter, and oatmeal—was recorded in the city's newspapers. Even more successful was another Hebridean, John Wyllie, who had gone into trade in Belfast but who returned to Stornoway in May on contract to recruit passengers for the *Peace and Plenty* of New York. To the alarm of the customs officials and to Daniel MacLeod's chagrin, he made off with a party of over 400 passengers drawn from precisely the two areas that MacLeod had targeted.[30]

Whether it was the superior salesmanship of the other recruiting teams that defeated MacLeod, or the relative attractiveness of the terms they offered, or the remoteness of the Beekmans' lands is not known. Whatever the reason, as the *Charming Sally* sailed off from Stornoway on May 30 with only 24 emigrants committed to the Beekmans, MacLeod had to confess that his efforts to populate Beekmantown and his plans for the future had failed. But there was worse to come. On the 6th of August, 650 miles off the North American coast, the *Charming Sally* ran into a severe gale. When a Rhode Island whaling ship came on the floundering vessel two days later, the *Charming Sally* was a wreck: Captain Hodge had "lost all his masts, bowsprit, head, and everything off his deck, split one of his pumps, and received other damage." Of the total of 80 people aboard, 6 had been killed and 15 injured. The whaler supplied the *Charming Sally* with a boat and a few other emergency supplies and then sailed off. Later, a naval vessel discovered the wreck and towed it into Philadelphia. How many of the 24 Hebrideans committed to Beekmantown were among the dead and injured is not known. But none of them ever made it to the shores of Lake Champlain. It was the end for the ambitious MacLeod. On November 1, 1774, he is recorded as borrowing £8 16s from the Beekmans. A week later he was in the poorhouse, and is heard of no more.[31]

Later, after the Revolution, the Beekmans by altogether other means began the settlement of their property. But by then conditions had changed fundamentally. Skene's, Gilliland's, and Fredenburgh's paternalistic com-

[30]Customs Collectors, Stornoway, to Board of Customs, Edinburgh, March 24, May 2, 31, Nov. 14, 1774, Stornoway Customs Letter Books; *Pennsylvania Journal; and the Weekly Advertiser,* June 22, 1774. The *Charming Sally,* with its 24 passengers, was not formally entered in the Register but was described verbally by the Stornoway Customs Collectors in the letter of May 31, 1774; the *Friendship* is entered at T 47/12/16–19. There was a limit to what even the shrewdest recruiters could accomplish in so small a place as Lewis or the mainland port of Lochbroom, from which the *Hector* had departed the year before with 179 passengers. See, e.g., the failure of the *Peace and Plenty* in October 1774, after its success the previous spring: above, chap. 9, n.26.

[31]*Pennsylvania Journal; and the Weekly Advertiser,* Aug. 31 and Sept. 21, 1774; notices also in the *New-York Gazette: and the Weekly Mercury,* Aug. 29, 1774, and *Dunlap's Pennsylvania Packet, or, the General Advertiser,* Sept. 19.

munities had all been wiped out by the Revolution. Individual New England farmers were beginning to move into the region in substantial numbers, and the problem for the Beekmans was how to profit from the settlement of these independent local migrants, at least sufficiently to recover their initial investment of £860, which continued to mount as maintenance costs multiplied. After repeatedly failing, in the 1780s, to sell the whole of the patent in order to reinvest in more manageable forms of commerce, they began the cumbersome process of hiring agents to sell or lease individual lots to farming families in such a way as to increase the value of the unsold portions. But competition from neighboring landowners was stiff and it was impossible effectively to exclude squatters or collect from delinquents. It took eighty years for them to dispose of the entire patent in individual lots, and the family's profits, now spread through dozens of children and grandchildren of the original proprietors, were meager.[32]

The Beekmans' enterprise on Lake Champlain never recovered from Daniel MacLeod's personal failure to import, direct from Britain, a large controlled community of farmers over whom he expected to preside as resident tacksman or principal lessee, a failure that had resulted from circumstances on the far-off island of Lewis and in the port of Stornoway in the Outer Hebrides, thousands of miles—a world away—from the wilderness shores of Lake Champlain. MacLeod's failure was not simply the result of the competition he faced from other agents of ambitious American landowners. It was the result too of the autonomy, the self-determination, of some of the migrant groups themselves. For the recruitment patterns of these years, reflected in the New York entries in the emigration Register, were not simply the product of American landowners drawing otherwise inert people from abroad. They were shaped too by the emigrants themselves: people who, determined to leave their homes, were brought together, organized, and in part financed by their own leaders and who either made the transatlantic crossing without any previous arrangements for land, expecting to shop around for favorable sites, or sent agents ahead to scout out the possibilities in advance.

The dramatic ventures of John Cumming, and of two remarkable Scottish emigration companies, encompass the range of variations of this pattern.

The Rise and Fall of Oswald Field

There is no indication that John Cumming knew anything about the situation in New York before he arrived there on July 13, 1774, but he had every

---

[32]White, *Beekmantown*, pp. 13–26, chap. 5.

reason to be confident that once on the scene he could take care of his needs and those of his people. He was a native of Strathspey, the broad valley of the Spey River, southeast of Inverness in the eastern Highlands, which winds its way northeastward out to the North Sea coast between the terraced peat and moorland slopes of the Monadhliath and Cairngorm mountains. Strathspey was Grant country. Castle Grant, home of the clan's chiefs, was at the edge of the strath's main town, Grantown-on-Spey, and a few miles from Ballindalloch Castle, the home of James Grant, the governor of East Florida. And it was Cumming country too. The two clans, closely intermarried, dominated the broad, arable valley floor, the slopes of the surrounding hillsides, and the pine and birch forests near Grantown. But here as elsewhere in the Highlands conditions for ordinary farmers were poor—conversion to sheep pasturage was widespread in the sixties— and threatened to grow worse.[33] Many of the strath's more ambitious men, faced by the social and economic erosion of the time, wandered away to more promising regions, John Cumming among them. Though his was one of the most prominent families of the region (he was the half-brother of Governor Grant, hence closely related to the chief of the clan, the eighth baronet Grant), he too left Strathspey. He joined his brother Alexander, a prosperous watchmaker in London, and after serving his apprenticeship joined him in partnership. Together the two flourished. Then in 1774, for reasons that are not recorded, John "was advised by his friends" to emigrate, and he decided to do so, though it was not common for people of his position and affluence to leave, and he did not do so in the usual way.[34]

Thirty-four years old, a prosperous artisan-merchant married to a woman ten years his junior and with a young and growing family, Cumming made careful preparations for the journey and for resettlement abroad. He took with him, his brother Alexander later testified, £4,000 in cash and negotiable bills, £1,500 of which Alexander had lent him, and he also had an agreement with his brother that if necessary he could draw on him "for any moderate sums." (His drafts on Alexander would eventually total £1,800.) In addition, he probably had the encouragement, guidance, and perhaps financial support of that ubiquitous Scotch entrepreneur and London merchant Richard Oswald, a close collaborator with Sir James Grant and others in developing American lands.[35]

[33] J. B. Whittow, *Geology and Scenery in Scotland* (Harmondsworth, Eng., 1979), pp. 173–180; Francis Thompson, *Portrait of the Spey* (London, 1979), esp. chap. 6; Henry Hamilton, *The Industrial Revolution in Scotland* (London, 1932), pp. 68–70.
[34] MacBean, *St. Andrew's Society*, I, 151–152; testimony of Alexander Cumming, [1784], AO 12/20/59. On Cumming's relation to Gov. Grant, *Calendar of Historical Manuscripts*, I, 673. Emigration from Strathspey was commonly noted in the colonies; e.g., *Dunlap's Maryland Gazette*, Aug. 22, 1775.
[35] Alexander Cumming's testimony, AO 12/20/39. Mrs. Cumming's age is established in the Register entry for the *George of Greenock*. The Grants' connections with Oswald go far beyond their common interest in East Florida lands. In 1770, when Sir James inherited Ballindalloch, he put

Thus secured, a man who would be known in America as "of pretty considerable influence" in England because of his "interest & connections" there, Cumming returned from London to his native Strathspey and gathered a shipload of neighbors and kin who were willing to emigrate and to resettle under his auspices. In mid-April they set out overland for Greenock, 100 miles to the south, where they arrived on April 22. When the vessel Cumming hired, the *George of Greenock*, was fully loaded, it contained, according to the customs Register, 172 passengers. Of this number, 139—four out of five—were from Strathspey proper, of whom no fewer than 82, or close to 60%, bore the clan surnames of Grant or Cumming. They were farming people, organized largely in family groups. While the repetition of clan names makes the identification of specific nuclear families difficult, the identity of at least 11 families traveling with children is clear, and they are remarkably large units. Two of the Grant families included 11 people each—husband, wife, and 9 children; one of the Cumming and one of the Grant families totaled 9; another Grant family totaled 8; there were four families of 7 each; one of 6; and one of 5. Of those from outside Strathspey, 13 came from within 50 miles of the strath, hence about 90% of the passengers aboard the *George* were from the Strathspey region. The remaining 20 were artisans in their twenties, traveling alone, who had migrated to the port of Greenock from a variety of Scottish towns to await suitable transportation or had sought work there and then decided to join the exodus.[36]

It was this shipload—composed principally of families of Strathspey farmers, Cumming's kin, clansmen, and neighbors, probably supplemented by 30 or 40 indentured servants picked up after the *George*'s official departure from Greenock—that Cumming brought with him to New York.[37] His own people among them were to form the tenantry on the estate he planned to establish in the colony. Upon his arrival, he began searching for land. His attention was drawn to the property in the ancient Catskill Patent

---

Oswald and another in charge of the estate until he could return to England. Alastair M. Grant, *General James Grant of Ballindalloch, 1720–1806* . . . (London, [1930]), p. 79.

[36] Richard Varick to Gen. George Clinton, Fredericksburg, Sept. 28, 1778, *Public Papers of George Clinton, First Governor of New York* (Albany, 1900–1911), IV, 119. For the emigrants' overland trip to Greenock, see the notice in the *Leeds Mercury*, May 10, 1774, reprinted *verbatim* in the *South-Carolina Gazette; And Country Journal*, July 26, 1774. The *George of Greenock*, as entered in the Register at T47/12/26, lists 172 passengers; Cumming himself repeatedly said that he imported over 200 people (AO 12/20/37) and the widely circulated newspaper notices blew the number up to 300 (*Rivington's New-York Gazetteer*, July 14, 1774; *New-York Gazette: and the Weekly Mercury*, July 18, 1774; *Virginia Gazette* (Purdie and Dixon), Aug. 4, 1774; *Pennsylvania Journal; and the Weekly Advertiser*, July 20, 1774; *Massachusetts Gazette; and the Boston Weekly News-Letter*, July 21, 1774; *Scots Magazine*, 36 (Aug., 1774), 446.

[37] On July 21, 1774—six weeks after the *George* arrived—*Rivington's New-York Gazetteer* advertised "a number of healthy men, women, and boys and girls that are servants and redemptioners" still aboard the *George*, "to be disposed of by Walter and Thomas Buchanan and Company."

just west of the Hudson, 30 miles south of Albany, near the exit point of the wagon road from the new Kortright and Wetherhead settlements over the hills to the east. He entered into negotiations with one John Gansevent for the purchase of 1,000 acres of a plot known as "Tapugieht" (anglicized: "Tablegate") which he soon renamed Oswald Field. The price was set at £1,000 New York money (about £715 sterling). Cumming paid half down, most of it in gold or silver, then discovered that Gansevent wished to sell only 700 acres; and so it was concluded. When the final papers were signed in 1776 Cumming's property consisted of 600 acres of woods and 100 acres of "low land," of which 60 acres were already under cultivation.

By then he had established 11 families of his Strathspey kin and neighbors on the property (the rest of the *George*'s passengers must have remained in the city or scattered elsewhere in the colony) and had settled down there himself, with his family, furniture, watchmaker's tools, and musical instruments (including two violins he greatly prized), effects he later estimated were worth £450. And he had begun the development of his property. He cleared 200 acres in addition to the 60 already tilled, built a house worth a minimum of £300, and added 10 log cabins "floored and lofted" for his dependents, and various other buildings, at a cost of £412. Then he began buying up other plots of land—6,700 acres in all—for future development. Within a very few years the property of John Cumming "of Oswald Field, Katts Kill, County of Albany, New York"—land, houses, barns, log cabins, cattle, sheep, farm equipment, and stores of produce— was worth an estimated £11,406 10s. About £2,000 had been spent on the settlement of the Strathspey people, whose transportation Cumming had paid for too.[38]

By early June 1776, when the title to Oswald Field passed to Cumming, the immediate prospects for the future of his New York estate seemed excellent. Cumming had established himself on a fertile tract along the Hudson, had brought over a large number of his countrymen to New York, had secured his own Strathspey kin and neighbors on his land as tenants, and had become a highly respected member of the Hudson River gentry. He was known generally in New York to be a man of means, of probity, and of influence in England. But while life was proceeding nicely on his property along the Hudson, the greater world was in chaos. Radicals and conservatives, Whigs and proto-Loyalists, had been struggling for control of the colony. New York City had long been in upheaval, and the struggle had spread into the countryside. While mob actions and frantic political maneuvering kept the city in turmoil, a series of provincial congresses had met in the safety of the Hudson Valley, the last of which, on July 9, 1776 —a month after Cumming had secured title to his estate—had declared

[38] AO 12/20/53–54, 56–59.

itself to be the legitimate legislature of the state. When in September 1776 the British army took over the city of New York, the center of the Revolutionary movement in the state shifted permanently to Albany. In April 1777 a constitutional convention, meeting in Kingston, less than twenty miles south of Oswald Field, adopted and proclaimed the state's first constitution. Elections were held, and George Clinton, personally well disposed to Cumming, became the first governor.

By the time Clinton took office (July 1777) a state military organization had long been in being and the inhabitants of the Hudson Valley had been forced to declare their allegiance. Indeed a commission was then being created "for detecting and defeating conspiracies in the state of New York" —that is, to defeat the efforts of the Loyalists to rally support and organize resistance to the Revolutionary government. Cumming, whose allegiance to Britain was never in doubt, was trapped, and so too were the Strathspey farmers he had settled on his land.

As early as October 1776 Cumming had emerged as a leader of the Loyalists, though temperate and cautious in his approach. At a rally of the doubtful he said "that those who thought the Congress were in the right" should join the Revolutionary militia, "& that those who thought the King was in the right should stay," though he privately advised those who sought his opinion not to fight against the King. As for himself, though at one point he was quoted as saying he did not know which side was right, he adamantly refused to take the oath to the Revolutionary government. Secret intelligence reaching American headquarters identified Cumming as a "principal" of the counter-Revolutionary forces in Albany County; he was said to be in charge of one of the small contingents of Loyalists who sought, unsuccessfully, to rally the countryside in support of the royal cause. Later in 1776, when the British troops he had counted on failed to appear, he advised those of his dependents who could bear arms to escape quickly, before the winter set in. Some did leave, to join the British army in Canada and elsewhere, once they were assured that Cumming himself would remain behind "to support and protect their wives and children." But Cumming was hopelessly isolated, and he was frustrated and endangered by the failure of the British troops to move north as expected. In January 1777, seeking "instructions how to conduct himself in his critical situation," he managed to get through the American lines into the city. There he conferred with the military commanders, among them his half-brother James Grant, received advice from the former mayor of Albany, Abraham Cuyler, on how the upcountry Loyalists should conduct themselves, and was offered a captaincy in the British army. He declined. He could not abandon "his beloved partner and helpless children" to the mercies of the Revolutionary leadership, he said, and furthermore he was advised by friends in the army that "he might be of much more service to the King's cause by his influence and example" at home than by accepting a commission in the army. (To the Americans, later, he said he had been treated decently by them, and "that he would by no means think of engaging in the [British] service.")

So he returned to Oswald Field. But while preparing a memorial to the Provincial Congress requesting permission to leave New York, he was seized in his house, his papers were confiscated, and he was interrogated at length about his trip to the city. He swore he was not engaged in espionage, passed on to the American authorities everything he had heard in New York about the impending British campaign in the north, reported the information he had received concerning British troop concentrations, and happily repeated the current rumor that 25,000 Russian mercenaries were about to arrive, in addition to 15,000 more British regulars. His aim, he insisted to his interrogators, was to maintain his neutrality and to manage an early departure from the state of New York. But that was not to be. He was officially classified as one of the "dangerous persons to the libertys of America" and was committed to the Kingston jail.

Cumming's vicissitudes after this first confinement, in March 1777, were overwhelming. A state prisoner, he was closely guarded, rumored to be selected for execution, evacuated to a floating jail on the Hudson, allowed to visit his pregnant wife, and then quickly brought back into close confinement. In September he managed to escape, hoping to meet Burgoyne's army moving south from Canada, only to flounder in the woods through most of the winter before being retaken and jailed in Albany. Finally, his case was disposed of by a personal decision of Governor Clinton. Since he was known to be well connected and influential, he and his family and their movable property would be exchanged for an equivalent captive of the British. But illness and a seemingly endless series of mishaps and delays— some tragic, some farcical—intervened, and it was May 1780 before Cumming and his family and a few friends he had helped rescue arrived in New York City. Even then his troubles were not over. The ship they took for their passage to England, loaded with all the possessions they had managed to carry off from Oswald Field, sprang a leak three days out at sea and sank. The passengers were rescued, but all of the cargo was lost.

So Cumming arrived in England stripped of everything he owned and deeply in debt to his brother and other creditors. His property in New York, which he had declined to sell when Clinton had given him the opportunity to do so (it would have discouraged the other Loyalists, he said) was confiscated; none of it was recovered. His plea for emergency assistance was turned down. No case, the Treasury said in 1780: he lacked the necessary documentation. When, three years later, he produced the required papers and was able to convince the claims commissioners of his great losses, of the difficulty he faced in supporting his pregnant wife and four children (he was living, he said, on credit), and of his having dispatched fifty-seven of his people in New York to fight for the British government, the board took a more indulgent view. But his record, like that of the Yorkshireman Manson, late of Georgia, they said, had a serious defect. He was, they stated, "certainly . . . no friend to this country in carrying out so many emigrants." But since thereafter he had "behaved well & preserved his allegiance under great temptations & severe trials" they would allow him a pension of £60 a year. The next year, seeking repayment and not simply emergency charity, he submitted an elaborately detailed memorial enumerating all of his investments and all of his property lost in the Revolution: it came to £7,138 5s. Four years later the decision came down: Cumming was given a total of £967, minus £16 10s in view of his pensions, or just over 2½ s on the pound.[39]

However large his financial losses, Cumming's contribution to the populating and cultivating of British North America was permanent. His estate, in other hands, flourished, and most of his people remained on the land. In May 1781, 58 of the Strathspey emigrants Cumming had taken with him in 1774, grouped into 14 families (22 adults and 36 children, 43 of them Grants or Cummings), petitioned Governor Clinton for permission to leave the state and return to their native Scotland. They were, they said, "ignorant of the nature, cause and consequence of the dispute, being poor and strangers," and they had taken no part whatsoever in the war. But despite their strict neutrality, their region, "Tapugieht," had become an exposed borderland between the contending armies, and their neighbors had told them to leave—to cross the Hudson and not to return without the written permission of the governor. It was this warning, and "our being intirely deceived with regard to the ideas we entertain'd of this country before we came to it," that compelled them to seek permission to return to "the place of our nativity."

It was a reasonable request, the military commanders of the district advised Clinton: "they have as foreigners done us as little injury as any other people of their principle." But Clinton was not obliging. He knew of no families behind British lines seeking to be exchanged, he wrote in response, and so he had no idea when he might accept the Scotch settlers' petition—it being understood that an exchange was the only basis for allowing them to leave. Besides, Cumming had failed to send back two or three British prisoners in exchange for the servants Clinton had permitted him to take along when he left, and that matter "must be settled before any indulgence can be granted the petitioners."[40]

So Cumming's Strathspey kinsmen and neighbors, once emigrants on

[39]*Calendar of Historical Manuscripts*, I, 513, 515–516, 523, 673–674; AO 12/20/38–54 and 12/99/66; Loyalist Transcripts, IV, 144–145, XI, 110–111.
[40]*George Clinton Papers*, VI, 856–858.

the *George*, remained where they were, on the farms Cumming had procured for them at "Tapugieht." In time their lives blended into the society of Catskill, New York. The name that Cumming had given his estate, "Oswald Field," disappeared—no mention of it appears in any history of the region—and his former tenants' farms and their families became in time indistinguishable from those of the rest of the population, who once viewed these Strathspey natives as aliens, and threats to their liberty and safety.

Ryegate

Cumming's small contribution to the peopling of America had differed in its origins from those of Johnson, Kortright, Banyar, Wetherhead, and the Beekmans. These resident American land speculators, seeking settlers from abroad to people the land and make it profitable, had recruited immigrants as they arrived in New York or had attempted to reach overseas to stimulate emigration they might direct to their own purposes. Cumming, an emigrant himself, though exceptionally affluent, had organized his own people into an emigrant group and then, once arrived in New York, negotiated a land purchase for himself and for them. But the Register contains traces of even more self-directing, more autonomous migrant groups than Cumming's that were attracted to cheap land in New York and destined to benefit by the activities of land speculators. And these quite independent groups, who also settled on the far fringes of the colony's frontiers, formed an altogether different kind of organization and followed different procedures for acquiring and settling land.

Sometime in the late months of 1771 and in January 1772 a group of leading farmers and artisans in the villages and farms along the banks of the River Clyde in Scotland, a few miles west of Glasgow, gathered to discuss the possibility of organizing themselves "into a society or copartnership for purchasing lands in any of his Majestys dominions in America." They may have known of a recent precedent: two years earlier ten "of the most substantial gentlemen" on the Isle of Skye, tacksmen and lessees, resentful of recent rent rises and even more of their landlords' "haughty behaviour," had met to form a "freindly society . . . to unite their respective stocks into one capital to make a joint purchase of one hundered thousand acres of land on the continent of North America." Nothing had come of these plans, but the later Clyde-side organizers may have learned from that earlier attempt. Their plans went forward rapidly and within a year were formalized. On February 5, 1773, somewhere in the tiny parish of Inchinnan seven miles west of Glasgow, 138 individuals signed an elaborate Bond of Association as partners in what they called the Scots American Company of Farmers. The long, thirteen-section document, which goes into great detail on the society's organization, lists the occupations and home parishes or villages, and in some cases even the individual farms, of the subscribers—data from which a profile of the membership can be sketched and an explanation of their motives and goals derived.[41]

Nine of the group, including a young land surveyor named James Whitelaw, destined to be the leading figure in the settlement that resulted, lived in Glasgow or its immediate suburbs. A few were residents of villages and farms just east of Glasgow, in western Lanarkshire. But the great majority came from the farmlands immediately west of Glasgow, their homes scattered along the River Clyde, out to the exit port of Greenock and beyond: 88 were residents of villages and farms in Renfrewshire, south of the Clyde, and 24 came from Dumbartonshire, just north of the river. But while residences can be found throughout the Clyde River area, the great majority of the subscribers came from an extremely small territory, 8 to 14 miles west of Glasgow. About half of the subscribers (67) came from only 4 adjacent parishes, 2 on either side of the river: Inchinnan and Erskine on the south bank, and directly opposite them on the north bank, East and West Kilpatrick. Together Inchinnan and Erskine measured only 9 miles by 3; side by side the Kilpatricks were only 6 miles long. Inchinnan, the epicenter of the movement, consisted in its entirety of only 2,400 acres; the 29 subscribers from Inchinnan represent fully a third of the entire adult male population of the parish. Erskine Parish was slightly larger, though its principal village in 1782 had only 13 houses; there the subscribers included about 12 percent of the adult males.[42]

The identification of individual farms makes clear how close-knit the

[41]The Bond of Association is printed in full in *Proceedings of the Vermont Historical Society for the Years 1926–1927–1928* ([Montpelier], 1928), 184–203. The earlier scheme is first described in a letter from Alexander MacLeod to his father, Norman MacLeod of MacLeod, Glendale [Isle of Skye], Feb. 18, 1771, MacLeod MSS, box 62; the once-enclosed handwritten "Advertisement" of the scheme is in box 61. In a later letter, March 11, 1771, MacLeod went into greater detail on the "bond of unity & friendship for subscribing for a capital to purchas lands in Ammerica & settle a colonie of their owne, every subscriber having a share in proportion to his subscription money, no subscriber admitted under ye sum of £20 sterg." So grievous were the economic conditions felt to be, MacLeod wrote, that at the first meeting 30 tacksmen on Sir Alexander MacLeod's estate had signed on and created an initial capital of £2,000: "subscribers are still coming in daily . . . , & the smaller tennants are engageing with ye subscribers as fast as they could wish, many from our country have, & many more will. [I] am even affraid of some of our tacksmen. The thing seems so pleasing to all, from high to low, that like a disease ye infection is catched by one person from anothr; where it will stop is hard to know." *Ibid.*, box 62.

[42]Edward Miller and Frederic P. Wells, *History of Ryegate, Vermont* . . . (St. Johnsbury, Vt., 1913), p. 58; Thomas Burns, "Parish of Inchinnan," and Walter Young, "Parish of Erskine," in *The Statistical Account of Scotland* . . . , comp. John Sinclair (Edinburgh, 1791–1799), III, 532–537, IX, 58–76. Details on these parishes in the paragraphs that follow are taken from these exceptionally informative articles in Sinclair's *Statistical Account*.

subscribers' community was. It was a patchwork of neighborhood clusters. The specific location of the houses or farms of ten of the subscribers in Inchinnan, for example, can be located with precision.[43] The average distance of one of these identified residences to the next was less than 800 yards —a few minutes' walk. And while the residences of the subscribers in Erskine and the Kilpatricks were more scattered, they were all within easy walking distance of each other and part of a tight communication network.

Communication among the subscribers was facilitated by the road system that spread through the region. The great turnpike road from Glasgow to Greenock, a major thoroughfare linking the city to its seaport, cut through both Inchinnan and Erskine parishes. Transport and messages flowed easily along the pike, which was crowded in good weather with carriages, wagons, droves of cattle, and pedestrians with handcarts and bundles, moving out to southern Scotland's main seaport or inland to the metropolis. And the farms in Inchinnan and Erskine were linked by lesser roads to the industrial center of Paisley, a few miles to the south, and to other less important textile towns in the suburbs of Glasgow.

The proximity of these Clyde-side farming parishes to the growing conurbation of Glasgow and its suburban manufacturing centers is the key to most of the subscribers' interest in emigration. The growing urban markets and the sophisticated transport system made increasing profits from agriculture possible, and that in turn put an increasing premium on efficiency in farming and led in the end to painful adjustments in the relation of people to the land.

All of Inchinnan was owned by only a few "heritors," of whom Lord Douglas was the most prominent. His holdings, however, had remained largely wasteland until, in the early 1770s, they were rented to a Mr. George Orde, "a thorough bred farmer" from the east. Bringing with him such innovations as "the two-horse plough, with the curved mould board and feathered sock," he put much effort and expense into leveling and draining the land and subdividing and enclosing the property. In the end his land turned into one of the finest farms of the district. But his efforts, a local historian recorded, "offended the country, who were much prejudiced against such plans of improvement." They resisted as much as they could, endeavoring "to render his situation very disagreeable." But Orde persisted, and soon the heritors followed his lead, until the entire parish was enclosed and the value of the land and of the rents was greatly enhanced. But the displacement of the population was severe. Small holdings were combined into large farms, "one man renting as much land now as 3 or 4 did formerly." Some of the displaced farmers and cottagers moved off to the textile

[43] The eighteenth-century place names are preserved in the Inchinnan section of the Six Inch Ordinance Survey map reproduced in Robert McClelland, *The Church and Parish of Inchinnan: A Brief History* (Paisley, 1905). On the scale of this map, 1 inch = 880 feet.

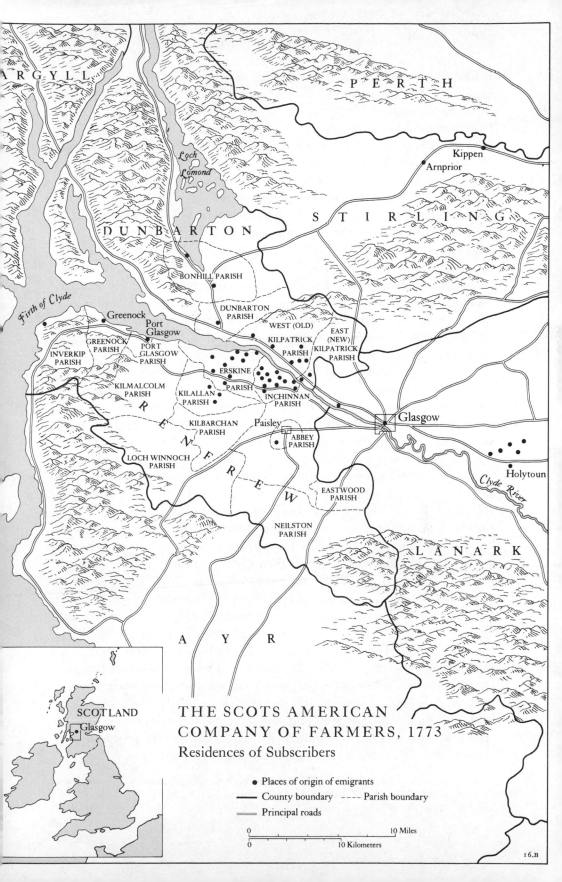

ARGYLL

PERTH

STIRLING

DUNBARTON

Loch Lomond

Kippen
Arnprior

Firth of Clyde

BONHILL PARISH

DUNBARTON PARISH

Greenock

Port Glasgow

WEST (OLD) KILPATRICK PARISH

EAST (NEW) KILPATRICK PARISH

GREENOCK PARISH

INVERKIP PARISH

PORT GLASGOW PARISH

KILMALCOLM PARISH

ERSKINE PARISH

KILALLAN PARISH

INCHINNAN PARISH

Glasgow

KILBARCHAN PARISH

Paisley

ABBEY PARISH

LOCH WINNOCH PARISH

EASTWOOD PARISH

Clyde River

Holytoun

NEILSTON PARISH

LANARK

AYR

SCOTLAND

Glasgow

THE SCOTS AMERICAN COMPANY OF FARMERS, 1773
Residences of Subscribers

- Places of origin of emigrants
—— County boundary ---- Parish boundary
═══ Principal roads

0   10 Miles
0   10 Kilometers

16.B

works in Paisley; some drifted into Glasgow; and many, especially those of some property, began considering emigration.

In Erskine Parish, similarly, agricultural improvements led to social displacements. The main figure was Alexander Lord Blantyre, who had been engaged in scientific farming in East Lothian until he transferred his skills and experimentation to Erskine when he inherited property there in the early 1770s. Again there was resistance to innovation, and so Blantyre resorted to special enticements. He offered his tenants smaller-than-expected rent increases if they would follow strictly a set of precise rules he laid down for the sequence of plantings and the treatment of the land. The strategy worked, and the result was gratifying: a steep rise in productivity and in income, and a steady growth in the value of Blantyre's rent roll. But it also resulted in steady depopulation. The leases on one tract of land, for example, on which twelve families lived in small farms, fell due in 1771. The next year the entire tract was turned into grazing land, and at the same time a few other farms and some cottages "were suppressed"—and so, a local historian wrote, "the population was still farther diminished."

Thus the main impetus behind the forming of an emigration community in the farmlands along the Clyde lay in this process of modernization and its social consequences. Of the 105 subscribers whose occupations were listed and who were not identified by the vague term "residentor," 35, or well over a third, were farmers—not farmworkers, but farmers: that is, yeoman householders, employers of farm laborers. And no doubt some of the "residentors" and some of those of unstated occupations were farmers as well. There is every indication that these were men of some small substance. The rest of the list also suggests people of at least some personal property. Among the 42 artisans who subscribed to the company were bookbinders, brewers, dike builders, and millers, and in addition there was an innkeeper, a land surveyor, a mathematical instrument maker, a schoolmaster, a "writer" (clerk or minor legal functionary), and the overseer of Lord Blantyre's estate. Letters of one of the six "smiths" who subscribed have survived; the writer proves to have been a highly literate small property owner whose income would later be partly derived from rents.[44] The leadership probably lay with six of the subscribers who were merchants from Glasgow, Port Glasgow, and Paisley, and with a few especially affluent individuals like David Bryden, who took out separate subscriptions for his wife, daughter, and servant. Though the list included a laborer, a "workman," a sailor, five quarriers, and ten servants, the membership on the whole was prosperous, by country standards, sufficiently prosperous to support the organization that was so carefully designed.

[44]The two surviving letters of William Russell (identified in the list of subscribers as a smith, from Cornbroe, Old Monkland Parish, Lanarkshire), written to James Whitelaw in 1801 and 1817 (Whitelaw Papers), are discussed below, pp. 630–631.

Each partner entered the society by contributing a sum to the common stock, which entitled him or her (five of the subscribers were women) to a "proportional part of the company's lands." An investment of £2 10s entitled a subscriber to one vote in the company's management; £10 bought one the maximum of two votes. The business of the company, which was to be administered by an annually elected "praeces" and eleven managers (together the Court of Directors) and governed by the full voting membership in biannual general meetings, was to procure land in America and provide for its settlement. For that purpose the Bond of Association provided for the dispatch to America of commissioners to survey all of the available land in the colonies, purchase a sizable plot for the company, have it surveyed, lay out certain lots for the society's common purposes, and mark off the rest of the property in individual parcels that represented multiples of the smallest amount subscribed. They were also to build temporary shelters for those partners who would go to America to claim their allotments, and to begin clearing enough of each of the surveyed plots to provide a year's sustenance for one family. Elaborate plans were also written into the bond for sending back for sale all marketable goods produced in common, for keeping the company's books, for imposing future assessments on partners on both sides of the Atlantic, for confiscating the land of partners who took up their allotments but did not improve them, and for making it possible for partners whose funds were consumed in transportation to receive company loans that would allow them to "rightly settle" their land. The terms for admitting new partners and the possibility of a separate second subscription to increase the common fund were also written into the bond.[45]

Some of the provisions must have seemed visionary even to the authors of the document: the plan, for example, that the partners organize themselves into "clubs" whose officers would serve as intermediaries between the members in these units and the society's general managers. Even more visionary were the assumptions that all the pledged subscriptions would in fact be paid up promptly and that there were idle laborers in the American wilderness who could be hired to clear the subscribers' land, construct housing both individual and common, and prepare the society's institutional property for use. But the main business was realistic enough. A common fund of £1,000 was raised to finance the selection and surveying of a large parcel of land in America, small sections of which the paid-up subscribers could claim as their own entitlement for settlement.[46] And that central effort went forward quickly.

[45]The text of a certificate of new membership is reprinted in Miller and Wells, *Ryegate*, p. 261.
[46]The figure of £1,000 is Whitelaw's, in the brief history of Ryegate he wrote for Zadock Thompson's *Gazetteer of the State of Vermont . . .* (Montpelier, 1824), p. 238. Eugene R. Fingerhut, in his article "From Scots to Americans: Ryegate's Immigrants in the 1770s," *Vermont History*, 35 (1969),

Within sixty days of the signing of the bond two commissioners left Scotland on what would be a four-month, 2,700-mile survey of available American frontier lands. Their inspection tour was the most extensive and closely reported perambulation of the available frontier lands made in pre-Revolutionary America. Covering all of the promising frontier land from far upcountry New York to North Carolina and recorded in day-by-day entries in a journal, it concluded with precisely the kind of land purchase that had been hoped for. And the journal reveals in detail the perceptions and calculations common to all immigrant land purchasers as they pondered the decision of where to buy or rent and where to settle.[47]

The more aggressive of the two commissioners was the land surveyor James Whitelaw, then aged twenty-five, from the Glasgow suburb of Whiteinch. His companion was an older man, a farmer named David Allen, one of the main figures in the core group in Inchinnan, whose farm, Sandieland, lay half a mile south of the Clyde, eight miles from Glasgow. They were provided with letters to a large number of contacts the company had in America, and especially to their countryman, the ubiquitous Reverend John Witherspoon, and to a Philadelphia merchant, William Semple, kinsman of four of the company partners and kinsman also, in all probability, of a leading Renfrewshire landlord, Hugh Lord Semple.

The two commissioners, Whitelaw and Allen, left Greenock on March 25, 1773, and were met on their arrival in Philadelphia, two months later, by Alexander Semple, William's brother, who conducted them to the merchant's house. There by chance they met Dr. Witherspoon, and it was from him, full of good will for their project, that they received their first offer of land. The preacher, they discovered (if they did not already know), was a partner of the Glasgow merchant and customs official John Pagan and his brother, the New York merchant William Pagan (the same Pagans who were collaborating with Witherspoon in Nova Scotia land deals), and a partner too of John Church, resident of Charlestown, New Hampshire. The four together, in a complex tangle of shares, owned a 20,000-acre township called Ryegate, far up on the west bank of the Connecticut River, which had originally been one of the 180 new townships created by Gover-

---

189, 207, finds also expressed in the bond a "dream of a typical Scottish village" with surrounding farmland, a dream he finds ultimately frustrated by the realities of life in America. That the company hoped to re-create a familiar world is natural, but I find no evidence of a distinctive community design written into the bond. The frustrations the company's managers experienced were typical of difficulties faced by hundreds of other settlement organizers, English, New English, Welsh, German, and Scotch-Irish as well as Scotch.

[47] James Whitelaw's Journal is published in full, with a biographical introduction on Whitelaw by Thomas Goodwillie and scattered notes on affairs in Ryegate up to 1794: *Proceedings of the Vermont Historical Society* (1905–1906), 121–155. Unless otherwise indicated, the account that follows of Whitelaw and Allen's inspection tour and their purchase and initial settlement of Ryegate is taken from this document.

John Witherspoon. Painting by Charles Willson Peale. A Presbyterian preacher and president of the College of New Jersey (Princeton), 1768–1794, Witherspoon was himself a Scottish emigrant and became an active promoter of emigration to the American colonies as well as a large-scale land speculator and politician. Repeatedly he sought to settle his countrymen on the lands he had invested in—principally in Nova Scotia and along the upper Connecticut River—but he was as devoted to their interests as he was to his own, and served as a general advisor and guide to various groups settling in the colonies before the Revolution.

nor Benning Wentworth of New Hampshire in the 1760s, but in territory claimed by the province of New York. Witherspoon said he and his colleagues would be happy to sell all or part of Ryegate to the company, but he urged the commissioners "to make every other trial, and not be too hasty in making a bargain."[48]

[48] The provenance of the Ryegate property is exceedingly complicated, and typical of 18th-century land transactions in this disputed northern territory. The main lines are the following. Because of

Other offers came in quickly during their three-day stay in Philadelphia, a city the agents admired and took the occasion to inspect. But while they noted all the possibilities they heard of, they entered into no negotiations, if only because by their instructions they were expected to start their investigations with prearranged meetings in New York. By June 1 they were in that city, having stopped off in Princeton to meet again with Witherspoon and, as it happened, with two prospective settlers in Ryegate, who had just returned from an inspection of the place.

The commissioners' main contact in New York was a Mr. Mason, to whom they delivered their letters of recommendation. Mason was "well pleased with our plan," and immediately brought them together with men in the city who had land to dispose of. In the eight days that followed they gathered all the information they could find about available land and the main landowners in the region and collected new letters of recommendation to residents in the countryside. With the groundwork thus carefully laid, they set out, on June 8, to follow up the leads they had and to inspect the available land.

Their first destination was Albany, which they reached after several stops on the Hudson along the way.[49] In that "handsome little town," a man named Campbell they had been referred to told them of a parcel of land somewhere along the Mohawk which he had heard Sir William Johnson wanted to sell. Equipped with a letter from Campbell to Johnson they journeyed out more than forty miles along the Mohawk, met Sir William at his manor house, and heard his description of the lands he had available for both sale and lease. The next day, accompanied by Johnson's surveyor, they set off to inspect the land Campbell had mentioned to them and which Johnson was indeed eager to sell. It was their first close examination of frontier land for sale and of the terms of sale, and they were disappointed. The land Johnson wanted to *lease*, they discovered, was excellent, though the terms were steep. But the parcel for *sale* was far from excellent, "being about 12 or 14 miles from the Mohawk River and over a high hill, and some

---

doubts over the legal jurisdiction of the area, Church and his associates in effect bought Ryegate twice, once in 1767 from the original New Hampshire grantees, and then again in 1775 (after they had already sold half of it to the Scots Company) from the 19 men, including the land jobber John Kelly, who had been granted the same land by New York in 1772. In 1776 Church sold half of the remaining northern portion to John Pagan, who in 1793 sold out to Witherspoon (in exchange for Nova Scotia lands); and Witherspoon immediately resold the property to a New York merchant, William Neilson. Whitelaw, "Chain of Title," MS 30, folder 6, Whitelaw Papers. For details, see Miller and Wells, *Ryegate*, pp. 9–12, and Whitelaw's enormously complicated history of Neilson's share of the property, Dec. 31, 1798, written in connection with a legal challenge to Neilson's title: WPA typescript (on cards) of Whitelaw's Answer Book, file drawer 1 (1797–1804), Whitelaw Papers.

[49]The Journal from this point on may be supplemented by Whitelaw's letters, all in the Whitelaw Papers. One of the most informative letters—July 13, 1773—is printed in full in Miller and Wells, *Ryegate*, pp. 257–259.

large swamps, also the price we thought high, being a dollar an acre."

So they gave up on the Mohawk lands, returned to Albany, and headed farther north up the Hudson, passing Stillwater and then Saratoga and inspecting lands around both. They then turned east, crossed the Hudson and traveled, on foot and horseback, east along the Battenkill, until, after several stops at houses in small clearings in the woods, they reached their next major contact, Dr. Thomas Clark, one of the most remarkable of the many recent settlers in North America to whom they had been recommended.[50]

Clark lived in the large clearing called New Perth (now Salem, Washington County, New York). A Scotch-Irish preacher, an M.D. from the University of Glasgow, and a veteran of the battle of Culloden (on the King's side), Clark had preached for years in Ballybay, County Monaghan, Ulster, until, in 1764, embroiled in local factional struggles, he had led almost the whole of his Presbyterian parish out of Ballybay, out of Ireland altogether, to New York, where he had planned a new life for them all. A tough and resourceful leader, he had discovered the New Perth plot deep in the woods halfway between the Hudson and the Green Mountains; had leased it from its owners, Oliver DeLancey and his associates; and had brought there some 300 of his parishioners. In the months and years that followed, they had managed to survive the most primitive conditions of settlement and established a stable inland farming community. By the time Whitelaw and Allen arrived there, on June 23, 1773, New Perth, still but a large clearing in the woods, was an oasis for travelers, and Clark had a masterly knowledge of the region's possibilities. He himself had some land for sale, he informed the two commissioners, but not enough for their needs, and he advised them not to bother with lands they had heard about at Crown Point on Lake Champlain. That whole area, he said, was the subject of such jurisdictional contention between New York and New Hampshire that any title they might take out would be legally vulnerable. In fact the whole region was dubious for that reason, and he sent them on their way with new letters of recommendation to his personal acquaintances throughout the colonies.[51]

At that point, just a month after their arrival in America, the commissioners, moving further east toward Witherspoon's land, plunged into the pathless wilderness of the Green Mountains. They followed tree markings, clambered over rocks, wooded hills, "and other difficultys," going for miles without seeing any sign of habitation, until finally, struggling across tree-choked animal trails, they broke through to a clearing, called Chester, just

---

[50]On Clark, see William L. Stone, *Washington County New York, Its History to the Close of the Nineteenth Century* ([New York], 1901), pp. 385–395.

[51]James Whitelaw to William Whitelaw, New York, July 13, 1773, in Miller and Wells, *Ryegate*, p. 258.

east of the mountains. It was close to their immediate destination, Charles-town, New Hampshire, on the opposite side of the Connecticut River. There, on June 26, they found Witherspoon's partner in the Ryegate prop-erty, John Church.

They spent the weekend with Church, undoubtedly reviewing all the possibilities with him and inquiring in detail about the township he owned in part with Witherspoon and the Pagans. Then on June 28 they set off with him on the seventy-two-mile journey from Charlestown north along the Connecticut River to Ryegate. En route, however, they stopped off at Hanover, New Hampshire, not only to visit the "Indian Academy or Colledge" but to quiz the president, Eleazar Wheelock, about "what we had heard concerning his land before we left Scotland." They arrived after dark, and were immediately included in Wheelock's evening prayer meeting, after which they turned to business. His land, Wheelock said, was not extensive—only enough for about thirty families—and he would give it away to anyone, especially Scots, who would come and live there; but the whole region was filling up so rapidly that he expected to have no difficulty disposing of the property.

The next morning they continued on and finally reached Ryegate. They remained there for three days, inspecting every foot of the ground with great care. On the river side, they reported, the land was hilly and quite barren; there were patches of hemlock woods and a few brooks that might serve for mills. But westward there was much better land, thick woods, and a large pond; and in the southern portion, where the forestation was light, the soil was truly excellent, and there were fine pastures and valuable stands of timber. And the towns just to the south of Ryegate—Newbury on the west bank of the river, Haverhill on the east bank—just as Wheelock had said, were being settled so rapidly that there would soon be an excellent extended neighborhood and growing local markets. But despite these hopeful developments Ryegate was still remote from civiliza-tion, with poor access to navigation. Sloops could go north from the sea up the Connecticut River only as far as Hartford, which was two hundred miles south of Ryegate; north of Hartford river traffic was restricted to canoes, and canoes had to be carried over four portages to reach Ryegate. Further, the nearest seaport was Portsmouth, New Hampshire, one hun-dred miles to the southeast over very poor roads. On the other hand the influx of settlers in the new riverbank townships just south of Ryegate was creating a seller's market for farm produce; prices were reaching astronomi-cal levels, at least by Inchinnan standards.

Having satisfied themselves about the land that Witherspoon and his associates had for sale, the commissioners resumed their tour, returning to New York City by the easy route of the Connecticut River and the coast of Long Island Sound. Here, as elsewhere, they took extensive notes on the

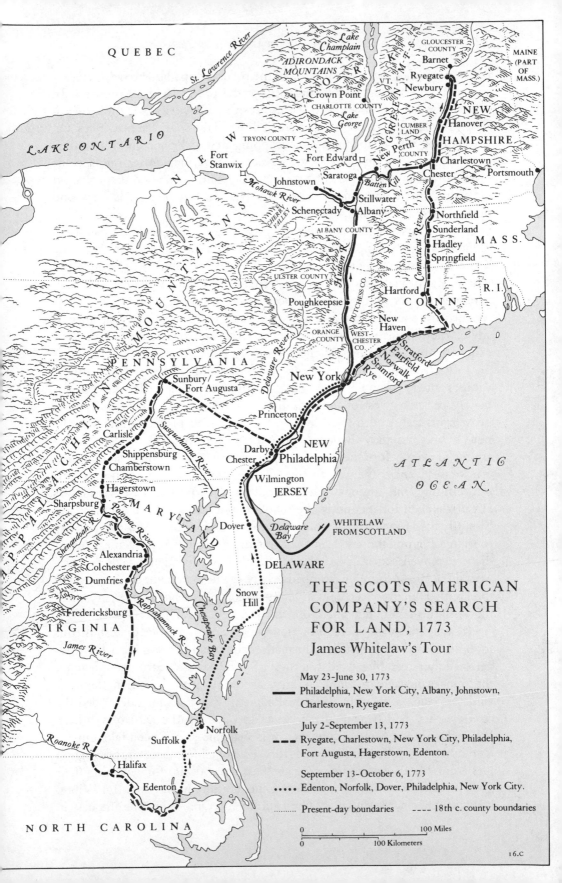

QUEBEC

St. Lawrence River

LAKE ONTARIO

Lake Champlain

ADIRONDACK MOUNTAINS

Crown Point

GLOUCESTER COUNTY
Barnet

Ryegate
Newbury

VT.

Lake George

CHARLOTTE COUNTY

CUMBER LAND

NEW

HANOVER

HAMPSHIRE

TRYON COUNTY

Fort Edward

New Perth

CUMBERLAND COUNTY

Fort Stanwix

Mohawk River

Johnstown

Saratoga

Batten Kill

Charlestown

Chester

Portsmouth

Stillwater

CHERRY VALLEY

Schenectady

Albany

ALBANY COUNTY

Northfield

Sunderland

Hadley

Springfield

MASS.

ULSTER COUNTY

Hudson R.

Connecticut River

DUTCHESS CO.

Poughkeepsie

Hartford

R. I.

CONN.

ORANGE COUNTY

WEST-CHESTER CO.

New Haven

Delaware River

Stratford
Fairfield
Norwalk
Stamford

New York

Rye

Sunbury/
Fort Augusta

PENNSYLVANIA

Susquehanna River

Princeton

ATLANTIC
OCEAN

Carlisle

Shippensburg
Chamberstown

Darby
Chester

NEW

Philadelphia

Hagerstown

Wilmington

JERSEY

Sharpsburg

MARYLAND

Potomac River

Shenandoah R.

Dover

Alexandria
Colchester
Dumfries

Delaware Bay

WHITELAW
FROM SCOTLAND

DELAWARE

Fredericksburg

Rappahannock R.

Snow
Hill

VIRGINIA

James River

Chesapeake Bay

THE SCOTS AMERICAN
COMPANY'S SEARCH
FOR LAND, 1773
James Whitelaw's Tour

Roanoke R.

Suffolk

Norfolk

May 23–June 30, 1773

——— Philadelphia, New York City, Albany, Johnstown,
Charlestown, Ryegate.

Halifax

Edenton

July 2–September 13, 1773

– – – Ryegate, Charlestown, New York City, Philadelphia,
Fort Augusta, Hagerstown, Edenton.

NORTH CAROLINA

September 13–October 6, 1773

· · · · Edenton, Norfolk, Dover, Philadelphia, New York City.

· · · · · · Present-day boundaries   – – – – 18th c. county boundaries

0   100 Miles
0   100 Kilometers

16.C

people they met, the cattle they saw, the roads and paths, the weather, and above all, everything they could learn of the productivity of the land. In New York City, they allowed themselves three days of rest, while beginning to collect information about possibilities in the southern provinces. On July 15 they set out for the south, stopping first at Princeton. There they met Witherspoon again, and the preacher-entrepreneur set out specific terms for selling all or part of Ryegate. But again he advised them that "if we should find a better place for our purpose, to take it, as he is very fond that our scheme should succeed."

They arrived in Philadelphia on July 20, and then packed in six days of intensive study of possibilities in Pennsylvania and the southern colonies. They were assisted by the Semples and four other informants, from all of whom, and from others they were referred to by them, Whitelaw and Allen extracted letters of recommendation to correspondents throughout the western and southern towns and villages, asking for whatever assistance or advice they might be able to provide. Thereupon the two set out on the central and southern legs of their journey.

In Philadelphia much had been said about land on the central Pennsylvania frontier, around Fort Augusta on the Susquehanna River, approximately 120 miles west of the city. It took four days of travel through the prosperous farmland owned by Germans to reach Fort Augusta and the new town, Sunbury, that was springing up nearby, but they were discouraged even before they arrived there. The flat rich countryside of eastern Pennsylvania gave way to rugged, rocky hill country—and even this unpromising land, up to within eight miles of the fort, they discovered, was already spoken for. Scouting the whole region around Fort Augusta and Sunbury they found "no one place large enough for our purpose but plenty too large for our money." So they left the central Pennsylvania frontier district, moved south across the broad, shallow Susquehanna River, traversed the Blue Mountain, stopped briefly at the settlement at Carlisle, and then settled down for ten days in Shippensburg, Pennsylvania, eighty-three miles south of Sunbury and close to the Maryland border.

It was time well spent. For not only were they able to rest in this foothills town and to gather information about land in southern Pennsylvania and western Maryland, but they were able also to learn enough about the trans-Appalachian Ohio country, accessible from southern Pennsylvania, to reach a decision about it. People in Shippensburg described the struggle they had had in former years to open up the land of southern Pennsylvania and how, as soon as it was available, it had been taken up by land-hungry families, to the extent that developed farmland in their region was going for £3 sterling an acre. The best opportunity for repeating their good fortune, they believed, lay across the mountains, in Ohio. But Whitelaw and Allen were dubious. The land on the Ohio might be the best in

America, they reported to the company in Scotland, but "it lies entirely out of the way of all trade, being 300 miles of land carriage from the nearest navigation . . . and the lowest settlements on the Ohio are above 2000 miles from the mouth of the Mississippi . . . so that there is little probability of ever having much trade there." And commodities brought in from the far markets would undoubtedly be sold for extravagant prices.

Their regrets, however, centered not on Ohio but on Pennsylvania. For there was no doubt, they concluded, that Pennsylvania was "the most desirable to live in of any place we have yet seen, but it is mostly settled where it is good, and what is to [be] settle[d] is very dear." The best land was in the hands of the Germans—"a set of people that mind nothing of gayety, but live niggardly and gather together money as fast as they can without having any intercourse with anybody but among themselves." But the land was rich, the people healthy, all sorts of grains, fruits, and vegetables grew in profusion, the air was clean, and even the heat in the summer was not as bad "as people at home are taught to believe."

But good land in Pennsylvania was priced beyond their reach. So they continued south, first to Chambersburg, Pennsylvania; then to Hagerstown and Sharpsburg, Maryland—all "very good land and all settled"; then to northern Virginia (good land, healthy people, but the only available places to buy were 200–300 miles from navigation); then south, across the Rappahannock, across the York, the James, and the Roanoke rivers, until finally, on August 31, five and a half weeks out of Philadelphia, they reached North Carolina, a colony to which so many Scots had emigrated in recent years.

They had contacts everywhere. They stayed first, for a week, with a Mr. Allason just inside the North Carolina border, and saw for the first time that the land was "sandy and much of it covered with pines . . . and a kind of red clay mixed with sand." Allason himself was discouraging: "he does not think that our scheme will suit this place well, as there are no tracts of good land to be had in one place, as the good lands lie mostly in narrow strips along the water sides." Farther on, at a place called Bute, a Renfrewshire emigrant named William Park—one of their own countrymen—referred them to a Mr. Montfort in Halifax, to whom they already had a letter of recommendation from one of their Philadelphia acquaintances. Montfort proved indeed to have land for sale—a 6,000-acre tract, well watered, perfect for raising wheat and tobacco, with streams for mills, and the whole of it only slightly developed; but the price was £7,000 sterling. And he also told them of a 2,400-acre tract near Halifax (£1,000 sterling) and of a 7,000-acre plot in Tryon County ("as rich, fine land as any yet discovered in America": £1,500 sterling "if a purchaser offers soon"; later it would surely go for over £2,000).

Their ultimate destination in North Carolina was Edenton, which they reached on September 13 after three days on the road from Halifax, during which they passed miles of barren sand and lowlands swamped by the rivers' overflow. In Edenton their contact was a Mr. Smith, who told them of the availability of large tracts. "But the price was high and the climate sickly." The whole of North Carolina, the commissioners decided, except for strips of good land here and there, was "sandy and mostly covered with pines and fit for nothing but raising cattle which is the only thing the people in this country depend upon." Indian corn could be raised easily enough, but wheat could be produced only with difficulty; and as for such marginal if lucrative crops as rice and indigo, the culture of them was so unhealthy "that they reason if a negro lives ten years and works among it they have a good bargain of him." And further, the summers were blasting hot, the winters damp and cold, and the people so unhealthy that "we did not enter one single house but we found sick persons, and in some we could not find one whole person to feed our horses." And on top of all of that there was the problem of religion. Officially there was an Episcopal establishment, which was bad enough; but the reality was worse than that. They found "scarce . . . any appearance of religion of any sort anywhere in the colony."

So they quickly left Edenton, their minds settling more and more on the land in the far north, and returned to Philadelphia by way of southern Virginia and the eastern shore of Maryland. After four days in the blessed healthiness of the Quaker city ("where such sicknesses [as fever and ague] seldom or never appear") they went on to Princeton, talked for the third time with Witherspoon, and there, on October 2—four months and three weeks after their arrival in America—they made the purchase they had come for.

As they explained to the company in Scotland, they selected the southern half of the Witherspoon-Pagan-Church township, Ryegate, in far up-country eastern New York (now Vermont) for very substantial reasons. Of the proposals they had received, all of which they submitted to the company at home, Ryegate was the best:

> no place that we have seen is better furnished with grain, flesh, fish, sugar, melons, roots, and other garden stuffs than this . . . here can be had all the necessarys of life and several of the luxuries and we think any that hath joined this plan and comes here and settles and is industrious may have a very genteel and comfortable way of living in a few years.[52]

That much seemed clear. More complicated was why they chose the southern half of the township rather than the northern, or the whole of it. They

[52]Whitelaw to the company, [Feb. 11, 1774], Whitelaw Papers.

had done so for a number of reasons, which Whitelaw enumerated. The southern portion had the best land in the township; it was closer to local supplies and to grist and saw mills; it was well watered by rivers and streams; there was a good docking area for commercial transports at a nearby point on the Connecticut River; and finally, "we are within six miles of a good Presbyterian meeting." Newbury was not only a Presbyterian community, but one that was "very strict about keeping the Sabbath," and it was led by an energetic preacher. Their half of the township included about 10,000 acres "in one contiguous lot," and for this parcel they paid £666 13s 4d sterling (about 16 pence an acre). The sum was to be paid in four equal installments; the first was paid immediately, the rest was due at six-month intervals in 1774 and 1775.[53]

Thus, after their long peregrination and careful study of land along a large portion of the American periphery (May 24–October 2, 1773), Whitelaw and Allen reached their first objective. Immediately thereafter they set out to fulfill the rest of their obligation by preparing the almost completely untouched land in Ryegate for the arrival of the company members. From Princeton they went to New York City, where they joined James Henderson, who had crossed the Atlantic with them, the only other member of the company besides themselves who had so far appeared in America. A carpenter, with precisely the skills most needed to begin house construction, Henderson was an invaluable addition to the small preparatory party. In New York the three purchased tools and other equipment as well as basic provisions, and loaded it all, together with their baggage, onto a rented sloop, which Henderson directed to Hartford for transshipment to Ryegate. Whitelaw and Allen went on ahead and obtained temporary lodging just south of Ryegate with Jacob Bayley, the leading settler in the adjoining town of Newbury. Henderson joined them, and in early November they began the work of opening the wilderness of Ryegate for the company's settlers.

With the concurrence of Church, who came up from Charlestown for the occasion, they drew the official line between north and south Ryegate but then put off surveying the individual lots until they had built temporary shelters on the land. A small parcel, excluded from the company's purchase, was being cleared by an earlier settler, John Hyndman, not a member of the company, whom they had met five months earlier at Witherspoon's in Princeton. He was just beginning to construct a house for himself on his

[53] Miller and Wells, *Ryegate*, p. 40; "Minute of Agreement between David Allen & James Whitelaw . . . and John Witherspoon of Princeton in New Jersey," Oct. 2, 1773, Whitelaw Papers. The formal agreement, Nov. 19, 1773, is also in folder 3. The actual transfer of title—the physical handing over of the deed—was held up until Oct. 31, 1775, by which time New York's jurisdiction over the region had been established and Church and his associates had resold the property to Whitelaw and Allen for £1,186 of New York currency. Miller and Wells, *Ryegate*, pp. 44–46.

lot in the southeast corner of the township, and so the three Scots, in typical frontier fashion, pitched in to help him "both for the conveniency of lodging with him till we built one of our own, and also that he might assist us in building ours." By the end of the year both his and their houses were finished. The two commissioners spent the early spring of 1774 cutting and removing timber while Henderson busied himself making wooden utensils. When the weather cleared Whitelaw went down to Portsmouth and Newburyport and brought back a sleighload of supplies, turned to making maple sugar, and then in mid-April began the task of surveying the lots.

The company's land formed a slanted parallelogram that ran just over three miles along the river and 6½ miles inland—a total acreage over four times the size of Inchinnan Parish. Whitelaw laid off parallel north-south strips one furlong (660 feet) wide, and then began slicing the three-mile-long strips into various-sized lots, ultimately 400 in all, averaging approximately twenty-five acres each. Company members would thus be able to select one or more lots depending on the amount they had invested. Whitelaw himself eventually chose seven sizable lots in two contiguous groups, one adjoining a lot he obtained in northern Newbury that included a site for a gristmill; later he petitioned for five more lots, most of them adjoining his original property. Henderson received six lots and later petitioned for eight more.

The surveying was slow work, and Whitelaw was not eager for the company members to appear in Ryegate before it was completed. In February he estimated that it would be July before he could finish, and he advised prospective emigrants not to arrive before then. What he needed were not land claimants but young laborers equipped with axes, long-handled hoes, and bedding of their own, who would work for the company in clearing the land, erecting temporary shelters, and helping with the surveying. And whoever came first, he wrote the company, should bring with them for general use some excellent beans and potatoes to start up those crops, and a large quantity of cloth, which was very expensive in the colonies.[54]

But the emigrants could not be held off. In May, when Whitelaw was still in the midst of the surveying, the first arrivals, nine single men and one family, appeared on the scene. For the moment all was confusion. The lots were not yet laid off and there were neither sufficient provisions nor adequate shelter for the new arrivals. The family man, Alexander Sim, went to work for Bayley in Newbury and probably housed his family in that adjoining and fairly well-developed township. The others joined Whitelaw in completing the surveying, clearing land, and erecting shelters. Then on July 1, with the surveying done, the newcomers took possession of the property they claimed—twenty-six lots in all; eleven other lots were taken

[54]Whitelaw to the company, [Feb. 11, 1774].

in the names of company members still in Scotland whose emigration was immediately pending and who wanted the land prepared in advance, or who were expecting to remain absentee owners.

Much work remained to be done on the company's joint property and in preparing land for occupancy. With the new arrivals busy on their own land, the commissioners began hiring workers on one-year contracts, some of them company members, some not. Henderson signed on at an annual salary of £17 19s plus food, washing, and lodging. In early October the next two groups arrived, in all five families and five unattached men. They had been en route for over four months, having gone first to Belfast, where they waited five weeks, then spent eight weeks and five days on shipboard crossing the Atlantic. And the next spring, 1775, another family and another unattached man arrived. By then a total of fifteen single men and seven families, members of the company, had made their way from the Clyde ports in Scotland to Newburyport or Portsmouth in New England and had then traveled northeast over the rough New Hampshire roads to the company's property just across the Connecticut River.[55] They were the vanguard. The main body of settlers, sixty in all, set out in April 1775, but fate was against them. As Whitelaw later told the story,

> unfortunately for them, before they arrived, the revolutionary war had commenced, and they were detained in Boston by Gen. Gage, who gave them their choice, either to join the British army, go to Nova Scotia, or Canada, or return to Britain. Some of them settled in Nova Scotia, but they generally returned to Scotland; so that no addition was made to the settlement during the revolution. But they, who had settled previously, maintained their ground.[56]

[55] Henderson's contract, Aug. 1, 1774, Whitelaw Papers; Whitelaw to the company, Ryegate, Oct. 14, 1774.

[56] Whitelaw, "Ryegate" in Thompson's *Gazetteer*, p. 238. The vessel they left on was the *Glasgow Packet*, entered in the Register at T47/12/80. At least 15 of the passengers on that vessel can be traced back to the company's membership list or forward to residence in Ryegate. A number of them are referred to by name in the company's letter to Whitelaw, Renfrew, Aug. 10, 1781, and William Whitelaw to James Whitelaw, Whiteinch, Oct. 23, 1783, Whitelaw Papers.

The *Glasgow Packet* had a tortuous voyage, only the outcome of which appears in Whitelaw's account. It arrived in Boston harbor in mid-June, three or four days before the battle of Bunker Hill (June 17), which much involved naval vessels firing in Boston harbor. Of those who went on to Nova Scotia, at least one family—the 46-year-old Inchinnan farmer John Hall, his wife, and 5 children—eventually made it back from Halifax to Ryegate. Miller and Wells, *Ryegate*, p. 63. Those who returned to Scotland, presumably on the return voyage of the *Glasgow Packet*, arrived in Glasgow on August 1, where their arrival was noted by a rather eloquent Greenock landwaiter, Alexander Campbell. He wrote to a cousin in Argyllshire: "I have often seen and heard of Scots emigrants to America, but never untill now of American emigrants to Scotland. Tempora mutantur. . . . The day on which they sailed [from Boston] they heard a smart and continued firing so that we look out daily for news of a second engagement. The American orator, leader, and demigod, Doctor Warren, was killed in the action. Upon our men coming up to the trenches, one of our officers, seeing the little son of a b——h running off from behind the trenches, poped him

Another, smaller shipment that set off a little later was turned back off the coast of Scotland. But, despite these losses, by mid-1775 a total of 80 lots had been assigned, 64 to company members who had taken up residence, 16 to absentee owners in Scotland. Two years later that same group of residents, supplemented by a few others who had joined them from the New England countryside, chose "home lots in the town spot"—75 in all, 17 of them taken out as reserves for company members still in Scotland.

By then much had happened in the life of the nascent village. To provide temporary shelter for the new arrivals, a two-story frame building capable of housing four families was constructed, and soon thereafter a small log house as well. By December 1774, half a year after the first arrivals had appeared, "all the people had houses built on their lots," Whitelaw reported, "and they were generally well pleased with their situations." The

---

down like a wood-cocky. O! For Hancock, Adams, Putnam & cᵃ sharing the like fate!" And then he added in a PS: "For God sake make the news of the arrival of emigrants from America as publick as possible, to see and prevent our deluded country men from emigrating to a country where nothing but anarchy and confusion reigns." Alexander Campbell to [?], Greenock, Aug. 2, 1775, Barcaldine Muniments, GD 170/1065/1. One of the returnees, a 27-year-old smith and farmer named William Tassie, an original member of the company, made his way to Ryegate twenty years later, only to find the good land taken up. He settled in Groton, a new township just to the west. Waldo F. Glover, "Old Scotland in Vermont," *Vermont History,* new ser., 23 (1955), 96–101. One couple, a Glasgow "coal hewer" named Thomson and his wife, who were emigrating to Ryegate, they said, "for wealth," were still living in Halifax in 1783.

In mid-September the *Glasgow Packet* left Greenock once again for America, this time loaded with equipment for a new regiment, "to be called *The Royal Highland Emigrants.*" *Scots Magazine,* 37 (Dec. 1775), 690. Five weeks later, nine of the passengers signed on for service in the new regiment, pledging themselves to resist the enemy and "to behave ourselves as becomes good soldiers under the pain of military discipline." Papers Relating to the Royal Highland Emigrants (84th Foot) Serving in North America, Lochbuie Muniments, GD 174/2093.

A similar, though more dramatic, fate met the 251 emigrants on the Buchanans' *Glasgow* (T 47/12/117), which left from Fort William on Sept. 4 (*Scots Magazine,* 37 [Dec. 1775], 690). Though the emigrants were confident when they left that New York was not in rebellion "& that they did not think themselves in any danger of being forced to serve either in His Majesty's troops or the Provincials," when they arrived in New York on October 31 the local naval commander, responding to Admiral Graves's orders, sent the vessel on to Boston, then in a state of siege. *Rivington's New-York Gazetteer,* Nov. 2. Graves was adamant: "it surely can never be right," he wrote, "to continue to people a country in absolute rebellion against us. Most of the men will, I believe, enlist in the army"; the rest would be sent to Nova Scotia, where they would be provided for. Vice-Admiral Samuel Graves to Mr. Stevens, Boston, Dec. 4, 1775, CO 5/122. To the extent that the men did enlist in the British army, it was the result—the pro-Revolutionary *Constitutional Gazette* of New York declared (Dec. 30)—of sheer physical compulsion. Those who resisted, the paper reported, were forced to undergo "the greatest tortures, such as their being chained down on their backs to the ring bolts, and fed with bread and water. Several of them suffered this torture for three days before they could be brought to yield and sign the paper of their inlistment. And many of them openly professed their resolution of firing upon their enemies [i.e., the British] in action if reduced to that necessity, and that they could never look on the people of this country, among whom they hoped for an asylum from heavy taxes and oppression, in any other light than friends, and therefore could never think of treating them as enemies." The *Glasgow's* fate was reported widely through the colonies: e.g., *Dunlap's Maryland Gazette,* Nov. 7; *Pennsylvania Journal; and the Weekly Advertiser,* Nov. 8; *South-Carolina Gazette,* Dec. 11.

next year work on a gristmill and a sawmill was begun, and the first death and the first marriages were recorded.

By mid-year 1776, two years after the first clearings had been made, an aerial survey of the town of Ryegate would have revealed approximately two dozen clearings of a few acres each in the southern mid-section of a still patchily forested rectangle of land off the Connecticut River, most of it visually indistinguishable from the rest of the uninhabited New England countryside. Each of the clearings—still overgrown and wild-looking though surrounded by fencing of some sort—had a small crudely built habitation on it, and in a central clearing, which would become the town common, next to a patch of water that would later be called Ticklenaked Pond, stood the only substantial building, the two-story dormitory or barracks that housed the incoming families.

People were at work in all of these scruffy clearings, tearing out bushes, breaking the soil, building fences, and tending a small number of farm animals and cattle. Two clusters of workmen were busy perfecting the gristmills, and in the evenings groups would form to discuss the problems they faced in surviving in this uncultivated land devoid of all the services of civilization, lacking as yet even the comforts of a clergyman and the skills of a physician. They must have compared notes on the quality of the land they had acquired, on the problems of food supply, of sanitation, water, diseases, insects, and community organization. And as they talked, by open bonfires and in small, stuffy, half-dark cabin rooms, attempting to think through the problems they faced, improve their situations, and plan for the future, they edged toward a fundamental shift in the life of their obscure community so remote from the world, a mere scratch in the edge of the northern New England wilderness. The transformation that was taking place can be traced in Whitelaw's surviving correspondence, which is detailed and revealing—a unique set of documents of the time.[57]

The letters Whitelaw received, as he surveyed the land and shared in the work of clearing fields and building cabins, reveal an intense curiosity on the part of everyone involved in the project as to what life in the northern wilderness was really like. When Whitelaw was still touring the colonies in the search for land, his pious parents had written to ask—amid injunctions that James heed the Sabbath, read the Bible, and tell the truth—"how you are taking with that new world of yours whether it be a Canaan or a barren wilderness." All sorts of rumors, they said, were floating about. The company members were as yet in good spirits, "but it might[i]ly depends

[57]All the letters referred to in the paragraphs that follow are in the Whitelaw Papers, principally folder 3.

upon the account that you are to send them." It was all so exotic, so strange. When James "turn rich," the elder Whitelaws mused, he might send "a little compliment of some of your fine skins" to ornament his women friends' cloaks. "A Ethiopian skin" would particularly suit his cousin Ann.[58]

What kind of winters are there, the elder Whitelaw wanted to know; tell us, he wrote in March 1774, "what diet you live upon and how you are lodged or if you love thy cuntray or if you desire any of your friends or aquaintances to come over to you or if you by [i.e., be] coming home yourself." Friends and acquaintances had the same curiosity. A New Yorker who had crossed the ocean with Whitelaw and had urged him to settle in New York wrote to offer his congratulations on the apparent success of Ryegate and to warn him of legal difficulties ahead in confirming title to the land. As for himself, the city of New York, he reported, was full of political and social confusion: people were coming and going in great disarray, business was dull, and "many maids wanting husbands & young men wanting wives," among the latter, himself. What was Whitelaw's situation in Ryegate? "Let me know, my old messmate Whitelaw, whether you have spliced yourself to any Yankey lassie or whether you have ever bundled with them, and how Mr. Henderson comes off with them."[59]

But most of the letters Whitelaw received came from his parents and from the company in Scotland. Tell the news, his parents insisted. Every letter counted. A single message received in Whiteinch praising "the goodnes" of Ryegate and also Allen and Whitelaw's skill as agents "mightily lifted up" some people, but others laughed. And then there were worsening Anglo-American relations and newspaper accounts of Indian wars and scalpings, even in Connecticut. All of that discouraged emigration: "the people here seem not to be so forward of emigrating as sometimes formerly," the elder Whitelaw wrote James late in 1774, "and you had better come home with old David [Allen, then on his way back to Scotland] as stay there to be slaughtered."

When Allen arrived back in Scotland in mid-November 1774, he was able to put most of these rumors to rest, but he brought with him, unwittingly, two letters that proved to be "scuroulous" and damaging to the company's cause. One was from John Wilson, formerly a farmer in Kilmalcolm Parish, Renfrewshire, who had acquired six lots in Ryegate's first division of July 1; the other was from the well-connected Hugh Semple,

[58]William Whitelaw and Marion Hamilton (i.e., Mrs. William Whitelaw) to James Whitelaw, Whiteinch, June 14, 1773, and William Whitelaw to James Whitelaw, Whiteinch, March 25, 1774, Whitelaw Papers.
[59]Same to same, March 12, 1774, and Robert Hyslop to "Dear Shipmates" [i.e., Whitelaw and Allen], New York City, March 28, 1774, Whitelaw Papers. Hyslop and Whitelaw continued to correspond, and must have renewed acquaintances when Whitelaw visited New York. Hyslop to "Old Shipmate" [Whitelaw], Jan. 15, 1798, ibid.

once a "residentor" in Kilbarchan Parish, who had taken four lots in Ryegate. Their letters "much hurt the reputation of Ryegate here." With so little known, with so many uncertainties and so much at stake—and with the Anglo-American crisis reaching a climax—such letters could be deadly for the company.

The company believed these letters, quite by themselves, significantly discouraged further investment in its stock. The sale of odd lots to non-members, which was expected to help the company meet its expenses, fell off, and earlier subscribers continued to stall in paying for their shares and for the additional assessment that had been imposed. And worse might follow. Wilson's letter had fallen into the hands of that ambitious and scientific landlord, Lord Blantyre, and "some of his sycophants." "It gave them such joy that they propose to publish it [to] the world from [the] press. It is very galling to all who are friends to America, and we wish that whoever writes from Ryegate to their friends may be enabled from truth it self to send more comfortable accounts; or at least such as will not give our many enemies such causes to triumph."[60]

But it was Whitelaw's letters that were the company's, and his relatives' and friends', main source of information. And they were discreet, detailed, and, while not always "comfortable," at least optimistic for Ryegate's future. Yet they gradually revealed the slow unraveling of the company's plans and the emergence of a form of independent community life quite different from the overseas establishment the company had designed, a way of life that was consistent with the realities of the New England country-side.

In its essence the company as originally envisaged was to have been a land-owning partnership, some of whose stockholder-partners would live in Scotland, some in Ryegate. The two groups were expected to be jointly and equally responsible for the organization's support through the purchase of shares and through willing responses to whatever special assessments were imposed by the management. The company in its corporate capacity was expected to hire workers, pay its resident manager, Whitelaw, a salary, maintain land and facilities for general use, and have the land cleared in advance of the settlers' arrival and temporary shelters built for them. And it was assumed that the shareholders who remained in Scotland would become absentee landlords and would profit by the rental of their land. By late 1774—barely a year after the first lots were cleared for use—all of these presumptions were being challenged.

The most obvious impetus to change was simply the company's grow-ing insolvency, which was the result of the reluctance of the original

---

[60]William Whitelaw to James Whitelaw, Whiteinch, March 25, 1774, and the company [William Houstoun, Robert Brock, John Paterson, and David Allen] to James Whitelaw, Renfrew, Dec. 27, with a PS by Houstoun alone, Whitelaw Papers.

members to pay for the shares they had reserved and to honor their pledges to respond to assessments levied on them by the management. By the end of 1774 the managers wrote Whitelaw that approximately 60 of the 138 members of the co-partnership had failed to pay for their shares or to respond to the managers' levies, with the result that the company's stock in hand consisted of only £400 to cover the rest of the purchase of the land and the wages and other costs of the workers Whitelaw had hired. As to the grist and saw mills, the company approved their construction, as Whitelaw requested, *provided* the settlers in Ryegate "bear their respective quotas of charges proportional to their shares as well as the members here. . . . This we think most reasonable as such machinerie is more for their convenience then ours." And Whitelaw was instructed to "preremporly require" that the residents fulfill that obligation and also put in the work services they were already pledged to.[61]

Five months later Whitelaw was able to report that the residents had met and had agreed to these terms. But his expenses were far outrunning the company's funds, and so he prepared a radically new business strategy to reduce costs. He now proposed to dismiss all of the company's employees he had hired on an annual wage and to continue the land clearance and building on piecework, per-acre contracts as funds became available. This approach, much cheaper if less continuously operational and less likely to fulfill the company's original goals, would allow him to auction off the organization's cattle and equipment, the sale of which would at least pay for completing the clearance of the thirty acres then being worked on. Moreover, he proposed to discharge himself from his full-time, salaried employment as resident manager, devote himself to developing his own property, and do what he could for the company on a part-time basis, and to do this for an annual payment of £10 plus expenses instead of the £30 a year he had originally agreed to. And he added, significantly, that he intended to go ahead with this plan in a month's time rather than wait for the company to agree, "which may not be for a long time." But he had not determined this alone. "All the people here agree . . . and think it will be of great advantage to the Co."

So in effect in mid-1775 the residents had begun the process of liquidating the company's presence in Ryegate. But Whitelaw's drastic new business strategy did not balance the books. A half-year later the mills were still not paid for, and on February 15, 1776, to cover that expense Whitelaw drew a bill of £100 sterling on the company. Almost two years later, in October 1777, he discovered that not only had the company refused to pay the bill but that even before he had drawn it the managers had declared that he had overdrawn the company's stock and thus had exceeded his commission, and

[61] *Ibid.*

they had instructed him to make no further calls on the company's failing credit. No drafts of his would be honored until he gave a complete accounting of his stewardship. But news of this dire measure had not reached Whitelaw—in fact he had heard nothing from the company for three years after late 1774—and since he failed to acknowledge and comply with the managers' wishes, they discharged him from the company's employ.[62]

All of this became clear in a flurry of letters in mid- and late 1777. Upon discovering what had happened, Whitelaw responded immediately, repeating a financial report he had sent earlier and describing what had developed in the intervening two years. He had received, he explained, a total of £493 9s 6d from the company and expended all but £9 plus the £100 bill the company had refused. The mills, still not fully paid for, were operating, though there were as yet still very few people to use them. All of the company's common land had been cleared and was rented out. The residents were all well, were continuing with the improvement of their property, and were not only providing for their own subsistence but also producing a surplus for sale. What he did not write the company but recorded in his journal was that the tiny community, company members and other residents together, had taken a further step toward autonomy by organizing itself militarily and politically. In May 1776 Ryegate, a village of considerably less than one hundred souls, had convened to choose "military officers": a captain (James Henderson), a "lieutenant captain," and an ensign. And then a week later they selected civil officers: two assessors (one of them Whitelaw), a treasurer, two overseers of highways, two overseers of the poor, a collector, and four constables.[63]

As the town became more autonomous it drew in nonmembers in increasing numbers, and conformed increasingly to the pattern of New England farming communities; less and less did it approximate the arrangement sketched in the co-partnership of the Scots American Company of Farmers. In December 1780 Whitelaw wrote another of his comprehensive letters, this time in effect recommending the complete liquidation of the company's interest in Ryegate. The people here refuse to pay any more of the company's assessments, he explained; they feel they owe the company nothing now that they have settled in America, except perhaps the cost of constructing the mills. "And as for the improvements being all made in general we never heard of it before [and] do not understand it." What they wanted, and said they needed, Whitelaw wrote, was more land and public facilities, especially roads. He listed eleven residents, including himself, who had specific lots they now wanted to buy, property reserved either by the company itself or by absentee stockholders. The company, he sug-

[62]Whitelaw to the company, Ryegate, May 29, 1775 and Feb. 15, 1776, Whitelaw Papers.
[63]Whitelaw to the company, Ryegate, Oct. 28, 1777, *ibid.*; Whitelaw, "Journal," p. 150.

gested, should sell off its common land, though it should require the purchasers to construct a meeting house and other facilities. And it should give up its delusive ideas of making Ryegate a town with a house on every lot. Not a fiftieth of the lots will ever have inhabitants, "and so it would be foolish or even rediculous to build them." And as for a "public farm" owned by the company, the company would never profit from it, any more than individuals living overseas would profit from property *in absentia*. For

> a farm will never be of any advantage here except the owner goes on it and improves it himself and those that thinks to live in Scotland and reap advantage from a farm in this new country will find themselves entirely mistaken and the reason is this, the land is so cheap and so plenty here that there is no person but will rather improve a farm of his own than work for any other person.

The best thing from the settlers' point of view would be "if you would all sell your lands to such as would improve them except such of you that intends to come here soon." In fact, if the company and its absentee shareholders did *not* sell out, the town would be in danger of being deserted. For roads must be built through the reserved property "to accomodate the towns beyond and to do every other public thing." Failure to make these improvements had already caused one-third of the residents to buy land in other towns, and "almost all the rest will leave the town in two or three years from this time unless you either come to settle your lands or sell to those that will." The state was already threatening to confiscate the open land and sell it to finance public works.[64]

Thus the company's liquidation had been set in motion. It could not proceed quickly, however. General meetings were difficult to convene, and their decisions unreliable. A meeting of the membership held on August 3, 1781, voted to sell the mills and to dispose of the common land and the unassigned lots. But the votes were inconclusive since the stockholders' lots could not be sold without their consent, and the group had scattered; some had died. The final liquidation would be a long process in which warnings of forfeitures would have to be issued and acted upon before the lots would be available for sale.[65] And the war disrupted all normal economic activity and made transatlantic communication almost impossible. When the war ended, the process Whitelaw had begun was still incomplete and still complicated; and the complexity was further compounded by a renewal of

[64]Whitelaw to the company, [Ryegate], Dec. 11, 1780, Whitelaw Papers. The quotation from this revealing letter in Miller and Wells, *Ryegate*, p. 47, is full of transcription errors, in effect a loose paraphrase of the original.
[65]Company [William Houstoun and David Allen] to James Whitelaw, Renfrew, Aug. 10, 1781, Whitelaw Papers.

interest in emigration by company members and their acquaintances in postwar Scotland.

In May and June 1783 William Houstoun, *praeces* of the company, wrote to Whitelaw to reestablish ties after the "'state of annihilation" their relationship had suffered during the "long and unprofitable war." Now that, "thank God . . . it is over . . . and peace, that blessing to mankind, is again restored," he was writing to inform Whitelaw that their native country was once again suffering from oppressive government policies, terrible markets, and high prices. The result was that "half the people here would go to America had they the money to go with." Therefore he asked Whitelaw to let them know

> if the lands of Ryegate are answering your expectations in any tolerable degree,—if the people are healthy, and what deaths have happened among our acquaintances—if you were molested or suffered much by the war. And chiefly if a report be true . . . that Vermont, in which it is said Ryegate is included, is declared by Congress to be a free and independent state, and it is also told that you are an Assemblyman of that sovereignty.

Specifically, he asked whether the new laws were "on equitable and liberal principles, such as tend to the security and satisfaction of the people." But the basic questions were "if people from this country will be acceptable among the American states," and "if lands about you are rising in value." And what about specific trades? Is there "any malting or distilling done, or prospect that a demand for it may take place. . . . Are masons in demand among you? brick-makers? carpenters? tanners? We have such who can go, with a little help." And incidentally, Houstoun added, "My oldest son hath bred himself to the stocking trade. Do you think that a stocking frame would be a business of any consequence with you?"[66]

To all of this, expanded in a letter of June 1783 in which Houstoun dealt with the company's tangled financial problems, Whitelaw patiently replied. Yes, he said, all those inclined to emigrate should do so. And those who can should buy up all the forfeited or unwanted lots they can find *before* they come, and acquire at least enough to make up a tract of 100 acres, the minimal size for a workable farm, he said: 200 or 300 acres would be better. If possible lots should be grouped across two or more of the furlong-wide ranges to form a sensible-shaped farming unit. As for the condition of the land, it remained fertile, he wrote. An acre planted with wheat or rye would produce fifteen or more bushels. Meat and agricultural products of all sorts

[66]William Houstoun and David Allen to Whitelaw, May 1, 1783, *ibid.*; William Houstoun to Whitelaw, Renfrew, May 4, 1783, in Miller and Wells, *Ryegate*, pp. 94–95; same to same, June 26, 1783, *ibid.*

were plentiful and the market for them was excellent. Despite all the inconveniences of life in this far province, he wrote—inconveniences such as the absence of money and the necessity to deal in barter—"I think it is much better living here than in Scotland. The people here are all in pretty good circumstances the[re] are none has less than 15 acres clear[ed] and some have near 20 the lowest can raise enough to make a comfortable liv[ing] and the rest in proportion. The country is very healthy and agreeable to British constitutions there having been scarcely any sickness in the town since it was settled." And "the constitution and laws of the state (viz Vermont) [a]re generally allowed to be the best on the continent and the taxes very light though in the other states they are very high."[67]

So Whitelaw continued his advocacy of this still thinly populated New England riverside village. A report of 1787, fourteen years after the town's founding, set the improved land at only 500 acres, all of it in the town's southern division; the northern half was only then being sold off, piecemeal, in intricate transactions by Witherspoon and the Pagans.[68] Company members in Scotland continued to consider the possibility of coming over to claim their now half-forgotten property rights. Houstoun apparently visited the town in 1783 or '84, but then returned home, dithering for years thereafter about the possibilities the town might have for himself and for his eldest son "bred . . . to the stocking trade." In the end Houstoun, a man of substance, gave up his nervous plans and sold the six lots he had so long reserved.[69]

But he was not the only one of the original subscribers who remained in Scotland and brooded over the lost opportunity to break free of the narrow, encrusted world they had known and fling themselves out into the open, unfamiliar, and risky frontier, full of possibilities and full of dangers. William Russell, a prosperous smith from the hamlet of Cornbroe, a few miles east of Glasgow, was a boyhood friend of Whitelaw's, had joined the company at the start, had been with Whitelaw immediately before his departure for America, and had expected to follow him quickly thereafter. Twenty-eight years later, in 1801, he wrote Whitelaw a letter tinged with regret and a sense of loss, and trembling with the uncertain hope that he might yet fulfill his earlier expectation.

Various things had interfered with his plans, he explained: his wife's fear of the sea; the war; and now—was it too late? His first wife was dead, and his second wife "is very fond to be in America," and so too were his two sons and the daughter who lived with him. Of course he was now quite

[67]Whitelaw to the company, Ryegate, Oct. 16, 1783, Whitelaw Papers.
[68]Unsigned letter [probably by Whitelaw], to [?], Dec. 21, 1787, Whitelaw Papers. On the later disposition of the company's land, see above, n.52.
[69]William Houstoun to Whitelaw, Renfrew, June 26, 1783, and David Allen to Whitelaw, May 7, 1787, Whitelaw Papers; Miller and Wells, *Ryegate*, p. 478.

comfortable: he had a bit of property that brought him in some rent, a good garden, and he was surrounded by his family. But, he said, in a strange and moving passage, "thoug I have been so long behind you in Scotland, my heart is in America." What should he do? He was fifty-nine, in good health save for weak eyes, and he already had a son in America, a smith too, who lived in New Jersey. He put it to Whitelaw. "Give me your advice, whether to go to America or stay at home." Whitelaw would surely be the best judge. Russell would do nothing until he heard from him, and he hoped that would be soon so that, if he were to go, he would have time to negotiate the sale of his property to good advantage and "be ready to sail airley in the season." In fact, if Whitelaw favored his coming, perhaps he would have part of Russell's two lots in Ryegate cleared in advance (his son in New Jersey was not farmer enough to do the job); he would be happy, of course, to repay Whitelaw for his expenses. And he ended with greetings from Whitelaw's brother (whose wife's fear of the sea would forever prevent the couple's emigrating) and with a repeated request for advice.

Whitelaw's response is not preserved, but it can be inferred from the next and last letter he received from his old friend. It was written sixteen years later, in 1817, when Russell was seventy-six and Whitelaw sixty-nine. This, Russell wrote, was probably the last letter his old friend would ever receive from him. He had "given over all hopes of being in America or ever seeing you in this present world." He was comfortable in his old age. His land rented well, and he was now the postmaster of Holytoun, two miles from Cornbroe, a position that carried a "cellary." Still, he was full of regrets. He should never have sold his two lots in Ryegate, especially for the £6 he got for them. Conditions were once again terrible in Scotland— taxes sky high, wages low, especially for the weavers. And everyone wanted to emigrate. Two of his former tenants had gone to Virginia and prospered, and his entire family—children, grandchildren, and in-laws—were hoping to emigrate. As for himself, he could only try to fill Whitelaw in on what had happened in his native countryside during his absence, ask for whatever Whitelaw could tell him about all "the particulars in your place," and recall with mingled emotions the opportunity he had had, forty-four years earlier, to follow Whitelaw to the company's land far up on the Connecticut River. They would meet again, he wrote, only in the next world, "that happy place," and thereafter "never pairt."[70]

Some of the original subscribers did join the prewar emigrants in later years, especially in the 1780s, and settled in the town. Several wives and children joined their long-absent husbands and fathers; and a number of young children were sent over to work "in service" in the town until they

[70]William Russell to Whitelaw, Holytoun [near Glasgow], May 2, 1801, and May 15, 1817, Whitelaw Papers.

were old enough to claim as their inheritance the land once reserved and still claimed by their fathers.[71] But these newly arrived company affiliates were few in number. More numerous were the native New Englanders who simply entered Ryegate as they did other towns, and bought parcels of the land that had once been company reserves.

Study of the extant town papers—company records and correspondence, tax lists, town meeting records, and miscellaneous files—covering the twenty-year period after Whitelaw arrived in 1773, reveals a total of seventy-nine names of heads of households, of whom only eighteen—just over one-fifth—had been shareholders in the original company, signatories of the co-partnership drawn up in February 1773. Another sixteen, though not signatories, had bought land through the company or otherwise had been associated with it. The rest—well over half—had come from elsewhere, most of them undoubtedly from the surrounding countryside.[72] In this sense Ryegate was no company town. The company had discovered it, opened it to cultivation, and provided the first settlers. But the company's plans had never fully materialized, and the community had developed into a typical northern New England farming village, somewhat less than half of whose inhabitants were Scotch.

But if the Scots did not dominate the town numerically, they did so in every other way. All of the major landholders and taxpayers, and most of the officeholders, were original members of the company or their close relatives, and the property they accumulated was impressive, certainly by Inchinnan standards. The leading landowner was William Neilson—the name soon became Nelson—a farmer from Erskine Parish who had invested heavily in the company and had arrived with his family in October 1774. In 1790, according to the tax list of that year, he owned 721 acres (over 7% of the company's total purchase), of which 55 were cleared and under cultivation; the assessed value was £140 6s. Ultimately the owner of one of

[71]Whitelaw, "Ryegate" in Thompson's *Gazetteer*, pp. 238–239. Whitelaw's correspondence of 1784 reflects clearly the revived interest in emigration. John Wilson, a company member writing from Partick, just north of the Clyde, May 6, 1784, told Whitelaw that he was sending his 14-year-old son to him to be a servant until the age of 21. Since "he is but young to be sent out of the reach of any frend but you," he begged Whitelaw to take good care of the boy, "keep him in good subjection," instruct him so that he would become "a good man, a good servt, and a good member of society . . . correct with wisdom every vice in its first appearance," and if Ryegate did not yet have regular sabbath worship, keep him from straying on that day and "cause him to read on some good book." "I intend coming out myself in two years," Wilson added, a plan that he repeated to his brother James, already in Ryegate, and that was advanced to the spring of 1785 when he found "there is a great number of people going to America." John Wilson to James Wilson, Nov. 6, 1784. Such letters continue: Allen to Whitelaw, May 7, 1787, and William Whitelaw to James Whitelaw, July 9, 1801, all in Whitelaw Papers.

[72]The company's confused records bear this out. Up to Jan. 1, 1815, the managers in Ryegate sold 121 lots—30% of the 400 original plots—mainly to nonmembers, for a total of $4,045.71. Miller and Wells, *Ryegate*, p. 55.

the town's sawmills, he branched out into the timber trade and river transportation; at his death in 1831, aged eighty-nine, he was the richest man by
far in Ryegate, and probably the richest man in the town's entire history.
The next-largest holdings were those of Andrew Brock, who had arrived,
unmarried, in the first contingent of May 1774, together with his father,
Robert, one of the three original managers who emigrated. The younger
Brock had begun as one of the company's hired laborers, but he quickly
became an independent landowner. In 1790 his property totaled 566 acres,
40 of them under cultivation, assessed at £94 16s. And he had become a
public figure, having served as treasurer (1776), surveyor of highways (1780),
selectman (1782), and assessor (1783). The elder Brock, a landholder too and
in 1786 the owner of mills on nearby streams, had served as the second
military officer ("lieutenant captain"), selectman, and town clerk.[73]

Whitelaw's landholdings were more modest—190 acres, 30 of them
cultivated, assessed at £64 15s—but his prominence is better measured by
his public roles. Town assessor in 1776, he served as both town clerk and
treasurer for 46 years and as postmaster for nearly 30 years. But his officeholding and private business transcended the narrow boundaries of Ryegate. In 1783 he was appointed deputy to Vermont's surveyor-general, and
at that point, after 10 years of service, he gave up his management of the
company's affairs, and turned his duties over to a triumvirate that included
his old companion James Henderson and the affluent William Neilson. In
1787 Whitelaw succeeded to the state's surveyor-generalship, a position he
held for 17 years.

As surveyor-general (he was known thenceforward as "General"
Whitelaw), he took responsibility for surveying much of the middle and
northern sections of the state, adjudicated boundary disputes, consulted on
surveying matters in other states, and drew up detailed maps of Vermont,
the northern United States, and southern Canada. He served also as a
trustee of the county's academy, and in 1798 was appointed by President
Adams to serve as one of the United States commissioners to evaluate
Vermont's property. But by then his private business had become all-
absorbing. In 1796 he had advertised in the newspapers of several states that
he was available to serve as agent for any kind of dealings in Vermont
properties. The response was overwhelming. Every year after 1796 until the
end of his life, twenty-three years later, Whitelaw received between sixty
and one hundred business letters about Vermont real estate, from land
speculators, inheritors of New England properties, and absentee owners.
It seems scarcely possible that any individual—or even a team of land-
conveyance experts—could have handled all of these intricate dealings.

[73] *Ibid.*, pp. 461–462, 261–262.

This business clearly constituted Whitelaw's major work in the final phase of his career.[74]

But he had not forgotten the Scots American Company. As his private business world expanded into a network covering the northeastern United States and the Ohio Valley, the company in Scotland carried on, though in an increasingly desultory way. There were occasional general meetings; but little could be done "because the members are so scattered. Deaths &c have happened." Yet a complete sell-off was risky since there was no way of knowing when paid-up members who had been prevented by the war from settling in America, or their heirs, might appear and claim their property. Gradually, however, the unoccupied lots were sold and the resulting income, plus the rental of some remaining company land, and the profit from the mills (which had not in fact been sold) allowed the company to pay off its debts. Finally, in 1820, Neilson and Henderson, the last resident managers, examined all of the company's books, found the accounts balanced except for some debts difficult to collect, took over these bad debts themselves "for the reward of our services," and closed the books permanently.[75]

So, almost half a century after its creation, the Scots American Company of Farmers came to an end. A number of the first settlers were still alive —Whitelaw was 72, Henderson 71, Neilson 78. Ryegate's population had grown swiftly after the company's reserved land had come more generally on the market and the lots in the northern half had been sold off by Witherspoon and the Pagans. In 1823, when Whitelaw wrote a brief history of the town, he estimated that Ryegate's population had been a mere 187 in 1791, but 406 in 1800, 812 in 1810, and 993 in 1820. There were two Presbyterian churches, he reported, a female charitable society, a library society "with a small but well chosen library. The inhabitants are mostly employed in agriculture, and are industrious and frugal." Dressed, he wrote, largely in homespun clothes, they worked their farms and raised cattle, horses, and poultry. They had the advantage of excellent timber, an "inexhaustible" stone quarry, a river ferry, and two "great roads" that connected them to the neighboring communities. At the center of the town, near Ticklenaked Pond, was a meetinghouse. Eight school districts had their own school-

[74]Goodwillie, Introduction to Whitelaw's Journal, pp. 112–114; Miller and Wells, *Ryegate*, pp. 54, 382. The great mass of Whitelaw's later business dealings—well over 1,500 letters—is carefully preserved and catalogued in the Vermont Historical Society.
[75]David Allen and William Houstoun to the company managers in Ryegate, Renfrew, March 1, 1797, in Miller and Wells, *Ryegate*, pp. 262, 265. On the postwar confusion in the ownership of lots, William Whitelaw to James Whitelaw, Whiteinch, Oct. 23, 1783; Whitelaw to the company, Ryegate, July 1, 1784; company to Whitelaw, Renfrew, Jan. 28, 1784: all in Whitelaw Papers; on the final closing of the books, Miller and Wells, *Ryegate*, pp. 56, 265.

houses, in which 435 students, Whitelaw wrote, were being educated. And the town boasted, besides the two Presbyterian ministers, "one physician, one store, three taverns, seven sawmills, three gristmills, and a hulling mill." The birth and death figures suggest a natural growth rate that was exceptionally high: close to 3% a year. And in addition, Whitelaw wrote, "there is still now and then a family, or young man from Scotland to join the settlement."[76]

Behind all this growth lay the earlier efforts of the Scots American Company of Farmers. In a literal and comprehensive sense it had failed: most of its plans had never materialized, destroyed by the Revolution and its own unrealistic assumptions. But in a specific and narrower sense it had succeeded. Created in the west Lowlands by troubled farmers and artisans of some small substance, the organization had created a refuge for those with the enterprise to risk beginning again in the northern New England wilderness. The financial cost can be measured. During the decade of his management of the company's affairs in America, when the town was founded, Whitelaw expended on the company's behalf a total of £740 14s 5d, in addition to the £666 he had spent to buy the land.[77] But the psychic cost—the balance of deprivation and satisfaction, of fear and security, of isolation and independence—and the cultural transformation, can only be imagined. Dr. Johnson's prediction—that British culture, whose power consisted in its concentration, would disperse and dissipate "in the boundless regions of America"—proved true in these far outer peripheries. The inhabitants of Ryegate, Whitelaw proudly wrote, two-thirds of them of Scottish descent, "still in great measure, follow the habits and subsist upon the diet to which they were accustomed in Scotland." But what he was observing were external and residual traits, quaint vestiges of diminishing importance, transformed in a different environment.

The rich and concentrated culture of Scotland's west Lowlands had faded in the upper Connecticut River valley. The founders' grandchildren, it is true, were no longer physically isolated. Farming villages similar to Ryegate had sprung up on all sides. And one of them, Barnet, just to the north, was populated in part by another Scots emigration society, the "United Company of Farmers for the Shires of Perth and Stirling." This society, formed in villages north of Glasgow, was a smaller, later, and less well-organized imitation of the Ryegate company. It too dispatched agents to scour the American frontier for good land; it too sent emigrants to America on a vessel listed in the Register; it too opened new land along the

[76]Whitelaw, "Ryegate" in Thompson's *Gazetteer*, pp. 239–240. The figures on population growth appear in the manuscript of Whitelaw's article on the town's history (MS 31, folder 14, Whitelaw Papers), but not in the printed version in Thompson's *Gazetteer*.
[77]"Expense Account of General James Whitelaw as Agent for the Scotch Farmers who Purchased the New Town of Ryegate," Whitelaw Papers, MS 32, folder 8.

Connecticut River.[78] But while Barnet, like Newbury to the south, Groton to the west, and Bath across the river to the east, helped relieve the physical isolation of Whitelaw's world, it did not restore the qualities that had been lost. The culture these Yankee villages generated was thinner, shallower, vaguer in their blendings, less rich in complex meanings and subtleties of expression than that of the ancient Renfrewshire and Dunbartonshire communities from which the Ryegate settlers had come.

Whitelaw's Ryegate—like Cumming's "Tapugieht," Hogg's Cross Creek, Dunbar's Manchac, Blinkhorn's Minudie, and Manson's Friends-

[78]The first public notice of the "Arnpyrick Society for Emigrants" is in the *Scots Magazine*, 36 (April 1774), 221, under the dateline "Cardross, near Stirling, April 7"—"A society consisting mostly of farmers is lately established at a village called Arnpyre [i.e., Arnprior] in this country. They have already subscribed 500£ for the purpose of purchasing land in America, to be divided among the subscribers. They have drawn up and printed a system of rules and regulations for their conduct, and are to send out two of their number immediately to America to chuse a proper situation for them." Further notices appeared in *Lloyd's Evening Post*, April 18–20 and 27–29, June 13–15, 1774; in the *Caledonian Mercury*, June 11, 1774, in the *Weekly Magazine, or Edinburgh Amusement*, June 30, 1774 (where the membership is described as West Lothian farmers, "men of substance"), and in the *Scots Magazine*, 37 (Feb., March 1775), 106, 165. The notices were picked up in the usual fashion in the American papers, e.g., *Virginia Gazette* (Purdie and Dixon), Sept. 15, 1774. The society's advance agent was a 27-year-old Stirlingshire farmer, Alexander Harvey, who traveled with a companion to America on the *Matty* (entered in the Register at T47/12 unnumbered folio between 26 and 27) and who, like Whitelaw, kept a journal of his travels in search of land, of his purchase (from the original grantees, the local Stevens family) of 7,000 acres in Barnet, which adjoins Ryegate (at a cost of 14d sterling per acre, or just over £400), and of the distribution of lots, the clearing of the land, and the building of the first dwellings. "Journal of Colonel Alexander Harvey of Scotland and Barnet, Vermont," *Proceedings of the Vermont Historical Society for the Years 1921, 1922, and 1923* (Montpelier, 1924), 201–262. Examination of the main sources—the list of original Barnet landowners, in the Stevens Papers; Barnet Town Meeting Records, and the Rev. David Goodwillie's MS map (1791) of the original lot assignments (in the Proprietors' Book of Records), Town Clerk's Office, Barnet; and Frederic P. Wells, *History of Barnet, Vermont* . . . (Burlington, Vt., 1923)—reveals the identity of 105 householders of the town, 1775–1798. Ten of them, mostly members of the Arnpyrick Society, can be traced back through the Register to villages in Stirlingshire and the countryside just to the east.

Harvey, in his search for land to purchase for the Arnpyrick Society, followed Whitelaw's route of the previous year. He too landed in Philadelphia, called on Witherspoon in Princeton, traveled up the Hudson, then across the Green Mountains to the Connecticut River, up the Connecticut to Ryegate and Barnet, and finally back to the Hudson along a trail south of the Green Mountains, to New York and Philadelphia. But while he then followed Whitelaw's path into west-central Pennsylvania, he gave up at that point and omitted the huge swing south through the western valley system to North Carolina. His journal is less detailed than Whitelaw's, but it too reflects the Scots' shrewd assessment of land deals (including one offered by Wetherhead), their concern for religion, and the network of contacts they had all over seaboard North America. Whitelaw was Harvey's host when he first visited the Barnet area, and in later years the two men had a close business and personal relationship. Harvey died in 1809, a well-established Vermont landowner, a county judge, a militia colonel, and a founder of Peacham Academy. In 1815 his widow, 20 years his junior (she was 14 when they married, and bore 16 children), married Whitelaw, then twice a widower.

Settled in the same migration flow of the pre-Revolutionary years, Ryegate and Barnet, adjoining communities on the far northern periphery of settlement, developed in parallel, and in their later exfoliation intermingled to form part of the distinctive culture of northern provincial New England.

borough—was part of what was commonly called "a poor man's country," though a poor man's country in which some grew rich. It was a risky world where one lived not in a dense and elaborately nuanced human environment that nourished and civilized but also limited one's activities, but in a loose, still-forming society where it was possible to proceed alone, free of encrusted burdens and ancient obligations, and to become, like the emigrant Yorkshireman Luke Harrison, "independant."

ACKNOWLEDGMENTS

Many people, besides those mentioned in the Preface, helped in the preparation of this book, and it is a pleasure now to acknowledge their assistance.

Barbara Nash, computer expert *par excellence,* helped immeasurably in setting up the technical side of the computer project and in overcoming innumerable glitches that arose in the course of that work. She could not have been more knowledgeable or more resourceful over the many months during which the computer project was designed, revised, and finally put into operation.

Lori Mihelich supervised the coding of the information and other preparatory aspects of the computer study, and showed great ingenuity in helping us track down some of the obscure British villages that voyagers came from.

Lee Shai Weissbach, while surveying certain publications and problems for the larger project of which this book is a part, did essential work on the New England town foundings and the resulting decadal settlement maps.

Peggy Burlet gave expert assistance in the initial drafting of the tables. Virginia DeJohn Anderson worked out estimates of the ships and people omitted in the Register, as well as enclosure figures for the relevant districts of Yorkshire, and she drafted a series of maps relating the emigrants' residences to their ports of exit. Susan Faludi assisted in this mapping of residences and internal mobility. And a wonderful group of Harvard students, especially Janet Wollam and Peter Fitzsimmons, pitched in on routine tasks—surveying newspapers, checking citations, etc.—at various times during the book's preparation.

We had assistance on specific matters from many knowledgeable and generous people: Sung Bok Kim, for help on the Cumming material; Arlene Shy, for help with the Shelburne Papers at the Clements Library;

Margaret O'Sullivan, for guidance in the Dartmouth Papers at the Staffordshire County Record Office; Alison Fraser, for assistance with the Manson Papers in the Orkney County Library; John MacLeod of MacLeod, for permission to consult the MacLeod Papers, and Christine Goldesbrough, for assistance in using those papers when they were deposited at the Scottish Record Office in Edinburgh; Claudia Kidwell and her assistants at the Smithsonian Institution, for help in identifying eighteenth-century clothing; Benjamin Labaree, for information on shipping; Mary Beth Norton, for providing material on the Loyalists; Oliver Russell, for access to the MacPherson Grant of Ballindalloch Papers; M. W. Farr for providing a copy of Roger Newdigate's notes on House of Commons debates, in the Warwick County Record Office; Peter Anderson, for access to the National Register of Archives (Scotland) manuscripts; Edwin Newman for information on *The Atlantic Neptune*; Thomas Doerflinger, for references to Thomas Clifford; Edward Papenfuse, for various references, particularly those relating to merchant letterbooks; Jacob Price, that encyclopedia of eighteenth-century commerce and merchants in general and Scots in particular. for answers to many questions; and Wallace MacCaffrey, John Brewer, and David Sacks for providing help on matters concerning early modern Britain, its places, peoples, and processes.

Without the cooperation of the many libraries and repositories cited in the notes, nothing could have been done, but I must mention above all the Widener Library at Harvard University, where I have had the good fortune to have worked for many years. Every scholar who has used that great library knows its riches, but this project tested its capacities in certain areas to the limit, and I was astonished again and again at what it could produce. And what it did not have easily at hand, it could get, with the willing and endlessly resourceful guidance of Nathaniel Bunker, the Charles Warren Bibliographer in American History, and Carolyn Fawcett, specialist in British materials.

I leave for the last the constant companion of this project, Patricia Denault, who, in addition to her duties as Administrative Assistant at the Charles Warren Center for Studies in American History, transcribed sets of documents, edited the annotation, and assisted in innumerable other ways. At times she had excellent help—especially from Christina Dillenbeck, who typed a preliminary version of the entire book; but the burden of turning messy drafts into comprehensible copy, and of reworking the manuscript in an almost endless series of revisions, fell to her. I am deeply grateful to her for her skill, her patience, and her constant good cheer.

INDEX

Abrahams, Joseph, 293
Acadians, 361–2, 415
  confiscated land of, 363, 410
Adams, Samuel and John, 541
Adventure (ship): sale of servants aboard,
    338–9
advertisements
  for immigrants to America, 379, 391,
      547–9, 548–9 *n.*, 560–1, 588, 591,
      605 *n.*
    to St. John Island, 59, 60
  for land
    in Floridas, 432
    in Georgia, 19–20, 547
    in New York, 584, 590
    in Nova Scotia and St. John, 379, 391,
      401–4
  for runaways, 253, 257 *n.*, 350 and *n.*,
      351–2, *illus. following p.* 352
  for workers, *see* labor force, in
      America: recruitment of; servant
      trade: sale and prices of servants:
      advertisements for
ages of emigrants, 127, *table* 128, 129, *table*
    131
  and ages of Connecticut population,
      table 130
  and ages of North American
      population, 129, *table* 130
  distribution patterns of, in America
    by family size and occupation, *table*
      222–3, 224–5

of indentured servants, 225, *table*
    226–7
  by occupation, 218–19, *table* 220–1
flawed reporting of, 81–2
and gender, 130–4, *table* 132–3
and group associations, 135, *table* 136–7,
    illus. 138–9, 141
of indentured servants, 177, *tables* 178–9
of long-distance migrants, 186–7 and
    table
and residences, *table* 132–3
Scottish, 127, *table* 128, 129, 160, 177, *table*
    180–1
see also children
agriculture, *see* enclosure of fields;
    farmers; farmworkers; land, in
    America
Albany, N.Y., 612, 613
  meeting of colonial leaders at (1754),
      357–8
Albion (ship), 413
  passengers on, 413, 419, 422
  voyage of, from Hull to Halifax (1774),
      413, 417
Alexander (ship): voyage of, from
    Highlands to St. John (1772), 399
Alexandria, Va., 338, 345, 346
Allen, David, and Ryegate, 610–20
Allen, Francis, 420–1
almshouses, as source of labor in colonies,
    164 *n.*, 302
Amelia Island, Fla., 438

Bernard Bailyn did his undergraduate work at Williams College and his graduate work at Harvard, where he has taught since 1949 and where, since 1981, he has been Adams University Professor. His previous publications include *The New England Merchants in the Seventeenth Century; The Origins of American Politics; Education in the Forming of American Society; Pamphlets of the American Revolution; The Ideological Origins of the American Revolution,* which received the Pulitzer and Bancroft Prizes in 1968; and *The Ordeal of Thomas Hutchinson,* which won the 1975 National Book Award for History. *The Peopling of British North America,* the introduction to his large-scale work on the transatlantic movement of people to the North American continent, is also available from Vintage Books.